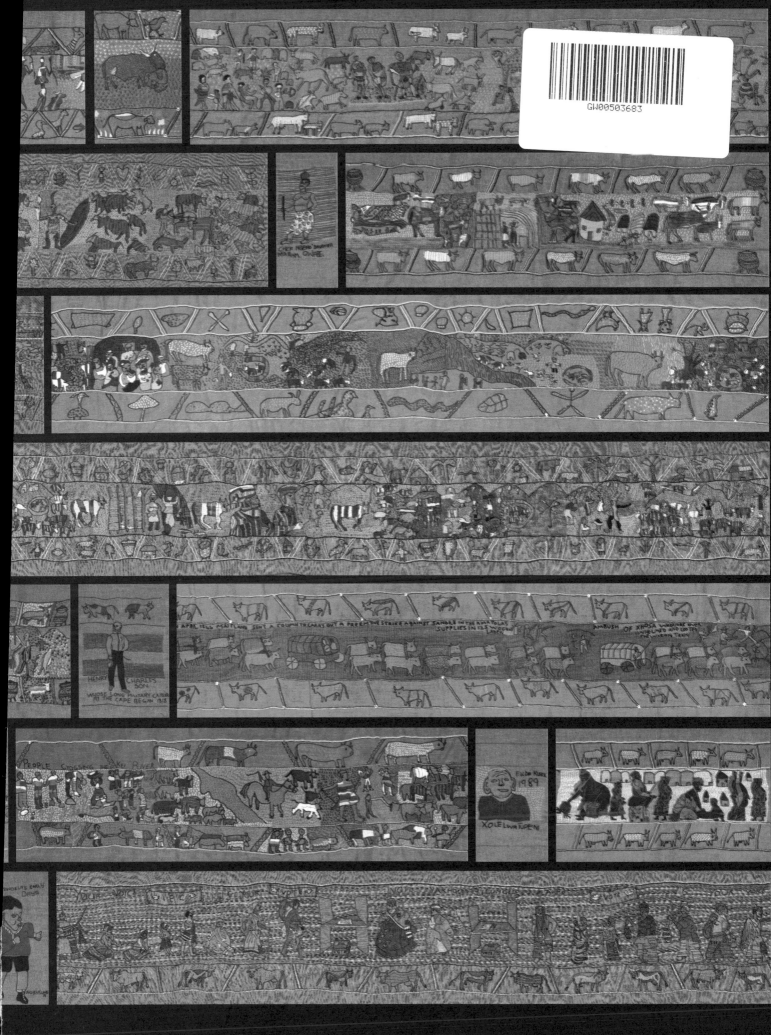

NEW
HISTORY
OF SOUTH AFRICA

Dear daddy

Merry Christmas, hope
this book reminds you
of us when you read
it.

Lots of Love

QW's 1, 2 & 3

X X X
X X
X

December 2008

TAFELBERG

NEW
HISTORY
OF SOUTH AFRICA

Hermann Giliomee

Bernard Mbenga

FRENCH TITLE: *The South African National Coat of Arms draws its central motif from the Linton Rock (on title page), a rock painting on the farm Linton outside Maclear in the Eastern Cape. This complex painting is thought to illustrate the experiences of healers going into a trance. The reclining figure on the left with cloven hoofs and animal form and the snake with the head of an antelope are trance images. A state of trance was said to be like being under water, which could explain the fish and eels surrounding the figure.*

END PAPERS AND COVER BACKGROUND: *Detail from the Keiskamma Tapestry, an embroidered work of art exploring the history of South Africa. The tapestry was created by the Keiskamma Art Project, a group of over a hundred women and a few men from the small town of Hamburg in the Eastern Cape. They combined traditional oral history with written records to embroider their interpretation of the history of South Africa. The work was completed in 2004 and purchased by Standard Bank, which has loaned it to the Parliament of South Africa, where it is on view to the public. It is 102 m long and 50 cm wide. (Photograph by Robert Hofmeyr.)*

COVER: *Cover pictures are of Ngqika, one of the Lydenburg heads, an artist's impression of Shaka, Jan Smuts, Nelson Mandela, and celebrations at the time of the 1994 elections.*

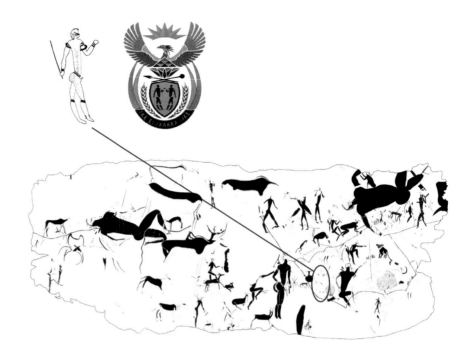

Tafelberg Publishers
a division of NB Publishers
40 Heerengracht, Cape Town, 8000
www.tafelberg.com
© 2007

Picture credits listed on p. 454
Printed and bound by Paarl Print, Oosterland Street, Paarl, South Africa

COVER DESIGN: Abdul Amien
BOOK DESIGN: Nazli Jacobs
COPY EDITOR: Roxanne Reid
PICTURE EDITORS: Anna Erasmus (part one and two) & Elsie Joubert (part three and four)
PROOFREADER: Elizabeth Wilson
INDEXER: Mary Lennox
MAPS: John Hall

First edition, first printing 2007

ISBN 10: 0 624 04359 2

ISBN 13: 978 0 624 04359 1

Contributors

This book has drawn on many contributors. Below is the list of authors and the sub-sections they wrote.
Except where otherwise indicated the respective authors wrote the text of the boxes
in their sub-section. Each author takes responsibility only for his/her own sub-section(s).

PART ONE

❏ Chapter One

Sandra Swart	Early humans
Janette Deacon	The hunter-gatherers of South Africa
Richard Elphick	The Khoikhoi pastoralists
Gavin Whitelaw	The origin of farming in South Africa
Andrew Manson	The Shashe-Limpopo basin and the origin of the Zimbabwe Culture; People of the second millennium

❏ Chapter Two

Richard Elphick	The Khoikhoi and the Dutch
Robert Shell	People of bondage; The Muslim community
Annette Giliomee	The architecture of the colony (drawings by Hannes Meiring)
Andrew Manson	Bastaards
Hermann Giliomee	The company they kept; The baggage in their heads; Across the sandy plain; A colony of settlement; Afrikaners; Resistance to colonial expansion; The Xhosa and the Boers; Changing times; A cauldron of conflict

❏ Chapter Three

Jeff Peires	The British take root; Nxele Makhanda and Ntsikana (box); Hintsa's war (box); Stockenstrom's treaty system (box)
Richard Elphick	The impact of foreign missionaries
Hermann Giliomee	Ending slavery; Religious and cultural states; An unstable frontier; A great trek; A quest for a treaty; A distinctive colony

PART TWO

❏ Chapters Four to Six

Andrew Manson, Bernard Mbenga, and Jeff Peires are jointly responsible for the
text of these chapters, with the exception of the sub-section on the Voortrekkers,
which was written by Hermann Giliomee.

PART THREE

❏ Chapter Seven

Richard Mendelsohn	Kruger's Jew (box)
Kogila Moodley	The battles of Gandhi (box)

Hermann Giliomee wrote the rest of the chapter.

❏ Chapter Eight

Luli Callinicos	The story of gold
Bill Nasson	The war for South Africa
Hermann Giliomee	Johannesburg: an instant city (box); Early prospectors and Randlords (box)
Albert Grundlingh	Piet de Wet (box)

❏ Chapter Nine

	J.P. Brits and Burridge Spies as adapted by Albert Grundlingh

❏ Chapter Ten

	J.P. Brits and Burridge Spies as adapted by Albert Grundlingh

❏ Chapter Eleven

Richard Elphick	A new spiritual force; D.D.T. Jabavu: rallying white and black (box)
Mohamed Adhikari	Coloureds: between white and black
Christopher Saunders	English-speaking whites
Milton Shain and Richard Mendelsohn	The Jewish community
Hermann Giliomee	The first black challenges; The Unity Movement (box); The Indians; English speakers and South Africa's economic advance (box); The Afrikaners

❏ Chapter Twelve

Albert Grundlingh	South Africa at war

Hermann Giliomee wrote the rest of this chapter.

PART FOUR

❏ Chapter Thirteen

Tom Lodge	A resurgent ANC; The ANC turns to the armed struggle
Milton Shain and Richard Mendelsohn	Working class icons (box)
Kogila Moodley	Satyagraha and the Defiance Campaign (box)
Benjamin Pogrund	Robert Sobukwe: a visionary (box)
Howard Barrell	Bram Fischer, an Afrikaner communist (box)

❏ Chapter Fourteen

Khehla Shubane	The Black Consciousness Movement; The Soweto uprising of 1976; A hero in jail and a democratic front; Democratic struggles; Sacrificing schooling (box)
Howard Barrell	The ANC in exile
Annette Seegers	A secret operation; A dirty frontier war

❏ Chapter Fifteen

Tom Lodge	The Mandela factor; The Mandela presidency
Virginia van der Vliet	The HIV-Aids crisis (box); Zackie Achmat and the Treatment Action Campaign (box)
David Welsh	A new constitution
James Myburgh	The ANC's centralisation of power
William Gumede	Pursuing growth and redistribution
Lawrence Schlemmer and Monica Bot	Trying to fashion educational equality
Heribert Adam	South Africa: The foreign view (box)

Hermann Giliomee is responsible for the rest of the material in the three chapters
of Part Four.

Table of Contents

Introduction VIII

Introduction

Until quite recently historians started their accounts of the history of South Africa in the mid-seventeenth century when the Dutch established a refreshment station in what became known as Table Bay. Then the starting point was cautiously extended back to the end of the sixteenth century when the Dutch involvement with the East began and the southern tip of Africa became etched in the European mind as a halfway station.

In 1969 the first volume of the *Oxford History of South Africa*, edited by Monica Wilson and Leonard Thompson, appeared. For the first time extensive coverage was provided of the pre-colonial history of South Africa, with illuminating chapters by an archaeologist and an anthropologist. Over the last two decades two illustrated histories of South Africa have appeared. The first is *An Illustrated History of South Africa*, edited by T. Cameron and S.B. Spies (1986); the second, the *Reader's Digest Illustrated History of South Africa* (1988). In both, experts also cover pre-colonial South African history.

Since the publication of these works there have been dramatic breakthroughs in our understanding of the biological history of human beginnings and of the evolution of all modern people in Africa. Thus this book begins a few million years ago – the earliest period for which we have the relevant data.

Out of Africa all

The fossil record for this era forms an integral part of the 'full' history of the country. The remains of ape-like creatures, the Australopithecine (southern ape man), have been found mainly in South and East Africa, and have been dated to about three million years ago. From the neck up, they were very ape-like; from the neck down, they were much more human-like.

The Australopithecines were uniquely African; they did not live anywhere else outside of Africa. These early creatures, as well as the humans who evolved later, are placed under the hominoid umbrella in the family Hominidae. In South Africa, the remains of the Australopithecines have been found at archaeological sites in what is now called the 'Cradle of Mankind', an area straddling today's Gauteng and North-West provinces.

The first true humans – people capable of making stone tools – populated most of Africa by at least one million years ago. Some of them had moved out of the continent to the Near East, southern Europe, India, Indonesia and parts of Asia. By 200 000 years ago, modern humans who looked very much like us had evolved and replaced their ancestors in eastern Africa.

Migrants all

But the early history of South Africa is not only about the evolution of modern humans between 200 000 and 100 000 years ago; it is also a history of migrations. While everyone now living in the world is 'out of Africa', everyone in South Africa is descended from a migrant. The ability and desire of humans to spread throughout the world and into all kinds of habitats – long before the invention of the wheel, sea-going ships or aircraft – is unparalleled in the animal kingdom.

The first major migrations of modern humans occurred roughly 80 000 years ago. As Nicolas Wade points out in *Before the Dawn: Recovering the Lost History of our Ancestors* (2006), it was also at this point that people began making sophisticated tools out of ivory and bone, and new weapons such as spears that could bring down large animals. At this stage, too, the ancestors of all present human beings, who all lived in Africa, began using true language that could convey complex information.

Emigration out of Africa also occurred at this time, involving a very small number of people, perhaps as few as 150. Initially they carried relatively little genetic variation. They crossed, most likely by boat, at the Gate of Grief at the narrowest point of the Red Sea. Later, the peopling of the present-day Near East, India, Indonesia, Australia, China, Japan and Europe followed. Much later still the first modern humans settled in the Americas, Japan and Oceania.

Around 2 000 years ago, major changes in lifestyle and economy took place when several waves of immigrants moved in the direction of southern Africa. Former hunter-gatherers in Botswana adopted domesticated sheep and cattle from the Iron Age people of West and Central Africa. These new herders, the Khoikhoi, migrated southwards to the western and southern Cape coast about 2 000 years ago.

At roughly the same time, the first Iron Age Bantu-speaking people settled south of the Limpopo and moved rapidly into the eastern half of the country. They were driven by growing numbers and their need for trade and new agricultural land. With them they brought domesticated animals and plants, and knowledge of pottery-making, mining and metal-working. Except in the driest and most inhospitable regions, this farming community gradually replaced the ancient hunting and gathering lifestyle that had persisted for more than a million years.

A millennium and a half later, in 1652, a scattering of the descendants of people who had migrated to Europe 80 000 years earlier migrated to South Africa.

The shaping of South Africa

This book has four parts. The first starts when modern human beings appeared on the scene in Africa and continues through the Stone Age and the Iron Age, up to the founding of a Dutch settlement in Table Bay and the three major migrations during the first four decades of the nineteenth century – the expansion of the Griqua, the Mfecane and the Great Trek. By 1838 a society drawn from three continents had taken shape in the western half of South Africa.

Two institutions played a key role in the first 175 years of the Cape Colony: slavery, which was finally ended in 1838, and the church (or mosque).

The Cape Colony was a slave society, not one in which slave labour was simply one of several forms of labour. All institutions – the labour market, the economy, the legal system, the family and the church – were permeated by slavery. The master-slave model became the model for all other relationships. The abhorrence among whites of all forms of *gelykstelling*, or social levelling, was intimately related to slavery and the masters' control of slaves in a colony where soldiers and policemen were in very short supply outside Cape Town.

As the colonists moved into the interior, they took with them their rejection of social levelling, their exclusion of their slaves and servants from their church and family, and the paternalist ideology to defend these practices. It was also largely the church that kept Afrikaners together as a community, preserved their language and imbued them with a sense of commitment to the country that had become their only home.

Religion also figured prominently in the responses of people other than the colonists. Many slaves turned to Islam in a rejection of the Christian church that was lukewarm about baptising the colonists' slaves or campaigning for more freedom for the slaves. The Xhosa beyond the colonial border considered the Christian religion alien to their belief systems. As Jeff Peires argued in *The House of Phalo*, 'A new religion could appeal only to those whose old world was irrevocably shattered and wanted to build a new one.' For the Xhosa this moment arrived in the 1850s.

From the 1790s Western missionaries were the main actors in the battle for a more equitable society. As Richard Elphick remarks, South Africa was one of the first areas of the world to be inundated by Protestant missionaries. Indigenous Protestantism on a large scale started earlier, and over a wider area, than in most other places in Africa or elsewhere in the world. In no other country did Protestant missionaries play such a big role in politics as in South Africa. The independent Ethiopian and Zionist movements among Africans began earlier than in most other regions.

A mission-educated black elite in the Eastern Cape started newspapers, studied overseas and became lawyers. As late as 1939 more than half of the country's African matriculants came from the British-influenced Eastern Cape mission schools. The African nationalist movement drew from these people. The fact that South Africa today is largely a Christian community with the ruling elite insisting on English as a public language is mostly due to the missionaries.

The book's second part looks at early nineteenth-century changes to the political configuration of the southern African interior, the geographical distribution of its people and its cultures. These changes were once thought to be mostly due to the Mfecane, a term used for the wars initiated by Shaka Zulu, but some recent historians have argued they were actually triggered by interventions from the colonial enclaves of the Cape Colony, Port Natal and Delagoa Bay. These 'great irruptions' remain extremely important in the history of the subcontinent.

Paradoxically, the mother colony based in Cape Town adopted a liberal stance to questions of class and race just when its settler offshoots were plunging ever deeper into the interior. It was the English business class and more particularly manufacturing and commercial interests, sometimes in alliance with missionaries, that promoted this liberalism. It influenced South Africa out of all proportion to the number of people who held liberal views.

White penetration in the deeper interior and African responses shaped the course and nature of future conflict. In the mid-nineteenth century Voortrekkers and Africans shared similar aims of rebuilding fragile communities and seeking security after periods of severe social disruption. This often led to competition for crucial resources, though the stark racial antagonism of recent history in South Africa has masked the extent of their interdependence.

The discovery of gold brought economic growth to the region – with mixed results. It made possible South Africa's transition to industrial economy but also enabled the government to destroy the independent African states, and it set in train the destruction of the rural reserves. Some Africans avoided these pitfalls and temporarily competed in the emergent capitalist economy, either as peasants or as an educated 'middle class'.

The third part discusses the battles in South Africa for political supremacy, mineral wealth and the tapping of the labour resources. This culminated in the South African War of 1899 to 1902. The war shattered the two Boer republics but it also created the conditions for the unification in 1910 of the four colonial states into a state committed to white supremacy. The manufacturing sector steadily expanded but it was only after a sharp rise in the price of gold in 1933 that economic growth took off. At the same time, however, the subsistence crisis in the reserves assumed ominous dimensions.

The final part covers the 60 years after the end of World War II, in which a rapid growth of the manufacturing sector spearheaded the growth of the economy. By 2003 it was the 30th biggest economy in the world. From the 1970s apartheid increasingly constrained growth and triggered mounting international outrage and internal resistance. This period saw the Afrikaner nationalist movement losing its coherence. The combination of rapidly rising black numbers, black urbanisation and mass mobilisation by an ANC-led coalition exerted strong pressure on the government. Though the state was not really under threat, prospects for economic growth seemed bleak. In 1994 power was transferred to a democratically elected government.

A note on historiography

The traditional white historiography that held sway until the 1930s tended to deal more with relations between the British and the Boers than with the so-called 'native question'. Some of the cruder versions referred to the 'hordes' of 'warriors' who tried to usurp a country that the whites were already modernising. Along with this thinking was the claim (now proven myth) of the 'empty land'. According to this the Voortrekkers of the 1830s arrived in empty land depopulated by the Mfecane. On these grounds it was (falsely) claimed that the whites had as much right to the land as the blacks.

A major break with this sort of propagandist historiography came with the publication of the *Oxford History of South Africa* in 1969–1971. This book highlighted the issues of first-millennium food production, cattle-rearing and metallurgy. It also revealed the longevity, complexity and sophistication of the history of the African societies.

From the early 1970s, a new school of 'revisionist' historians began to reveal the diversity and complexity of the processes of transition or transformation among South Africa's rural societies, both black and white. They explained apartheid not in terms of racism, but rather as a direct result of industrialisation. In successive editions of his *South Africa: a Modern History* Rodney Davenport synthesises the work of historians written from a variety of perspectives – revisionist, liberal and nationalist.

From the late 1980s, new trends and paradigms have emerged in South African historiography. Examples of these are the reinterpretation of the causes of the Difaqane (or Mfecane) by Julian Cobbing in 1988, discussed in Part Two. Cheryl Walker explored gender issues in *Women and Gender in Southern Africa* in 1990. In 1994, in *Slavery in South Africa: Captive Labor on the Dutch Frontier*, Fred Morton and Elizabeth Eldredge dealt with the nature and prevalence of African slaves, slavery and Boer slave-raiding on the Cape frontier, the Transvaal and the Orange Free State. In 2002 Carolyn Hamilton *et al.* published a major new work, *Refiguring the Archive*, on the nature and diversity of archives, while in 2003 Nancy Jacobs published *Environment, Power and Injustice*.

The second Anglo-Boer (or South African) War of 1899–1902 is a case where the traditional interpretation – which cast it as a 'white man's war' – has been radically revised. It still is seen as a brutal war. There were the deaths of soldiers on both the Boer and British sides; the deaths of African auxiliaries; the many thousands of Afrikaner women, children and Africans who suffered or died in the desolate concentration camps; and the Boer farms that were put to the torch by British soldiers. Over the last 25 years much more has come to the fore. We now know, for example, about the role of the San, which has hitherto been omitted from practically all of the historiography of the war, as well as the combat roles of blacks, coloureds and Indians in the war. Perhaps the most important work encapsulating the latest thinking on the war, is *Writing a Wider War: Rethinking Gender, Race and Identity in the South African War, 1899–1902*, edited by Greg Cuthbertson, Albert Grundlingh and Mary-Lynn Suttie.

As historians of South African history, we are fully conscious of our apartheid past in which gross racial injustices were committed. We are also aware of some of the distorted historiography of the past. We have set out to redress past distortions and biases. This multi-authored book draws on the perspectives of different 'schools' of historians, while also incorporating the most recent scholarship on South African history. We tried to synthesise the material and to make it accessible to both the academic and the general reader.

Our goal has been to present our history in all its complexity in a fair and balanced manner. We have striven for objectivity. Yet it would be foolhardy to deny the persistence of subjectivity. The British historian Peter Burke put it this way:

> However hard we struggle to avoid the prejudices associated with colour, creed, class or gender, we cannot avoid looking at the past from a particular point of view.

This work is the product of many historians' involvement, as the long list of contributors indicate. As editors, we have attempted to harmonise the various writing styles of the contributors and to keep the language readable. This book rests to a large extent on previous published work by the different contributors. Full references for most of the interpretations that appear here are given in their publications, which are listed in the bibliography at the back.

The book concentrates heavily on the political and to a lesser extent economic history of South Africa. We did not try to cover social and cultural history.

As editors we would like to thank Eloïse Wessels, managing director of NB Publishers, who took a personal interest. Our publisher, Erika Oosthuysen, was a centre of calm, tact and sound judgement holding the project together. Last but by no means least, thanks to our contributors who as true professionals met the tight deadlines and submitted work that was accessible and of a high academic standard.

On behalf of all the contributors we express the wish that this work will help people inside and outside South Africa to come to grips with this complex, difficult, heartbreaking, bewildering, bewitching, beloved land.

HERMANN GILIOMEE
BERNARD MBENGA

Stellenbosch and Mmabatho
March 2007

- For the names of African languages and communities we have followed convention and dropped the prefix, e.g. Pedi rather than Bapedi.
- While we consider all who live in South Africa and identify with the country as Africans, we have followed the current custom of using the terms Africans, blacks and Bantu speakers interchangeably. We have used coloureds for people of mixed race, whites for people of predominantly European background, and Afrikaner for white Afrikaans speakers. We expect that, as with the term African, this term will increasingly come to be used more inclusively.
- Some events may be mentioned more than once because the book follows themes rather than strict chronology.
- Cross-references have been kept to a minimum so as to keep the text simple. The index will reveal all references to an event or theme mentioned in more than one place.

A group photo of miners on the gold fields of the 1890s.
By 1897 about 70 000 black and 10 000 white men were working in the mines
on the Witwatersrand, many of them underground.

1

From the first people to the first settlements

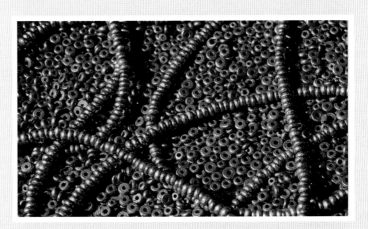

Gold beads found during excavations of royal burials on Mapungubwe hill, the capital of South Africa's earliest civilisation, in Limpopo Province. Some beads were made by pouring droplets of molten gold into water and then flattening them slightly with a small hammer before punching a hole through the centre.

The king at Mapungubwe ruled over a complex society with class distinction and sacred leadership during the 1200s. The wealth of the state derived from agriculture and trade with the east coast. Gold, hides and ivory were taken from Mapungubwe and exchanged for cotton cloth, glass beads, porcelain and other items.

200 000 to 100 000 years ago: Modern humans evolve in Africa, including South Africa.

80 000 years ago: Language emerges in Africa. A small group of Africans leaves East Africa and populates the rest of the world.

2 000 years ago: Hunter-gathererers called San acquire stock in modern Botswana and begin spreading over the western half of South Africa. They call themselves Khoikhoi (or Khoe).

AD

300: Early Iron Age people settle south of the Limpopo.

400: Early Iron Age people settle in KwaZulu-Natal.

600: Early Iron Age people settle in the Eastern Cape.

1220: Middle Iron Age people establish the Kingdom of Mapungubwe in what is now the province of Limpopo.

1450: Late Iron Age people spread over the southern highveld.

1652: The Dutch East India Company establishes a refreshment station at Table Bay.

1657: The Company releases nine of its servants to become full-time farmers.

1658: The first slave ships arrive.

1659–1660: Armed clashes between Europeans and Khoikhoi over land and cattle.

1688: Huguenot refugees arrive and settle mainly in Franschhoek.

1701–1703: Khoisan launch concerted attacks on farmers who have moved into the Land van Waveren (Tulbagh basin).

1713: A smallpox epidemic decimates the southwestern Khoihoi.

1715: Commandos headed and manned by burghers begin to replace government troops on the frontier.

1717: The government issues grazing licences beyond the settled area; this becomes the basis of the loan farm system.

1745: A new drostdy, called Swellendam, is established to administer farmers living between the Breede River and Mossel Bay.

1774: The government authorises the first 'General Commando' not only to recover livestock and punish offenders but wage a general war against the Khoisan along the northern and northeastern border. The northeast remains unsettled for two decades.

1750–1780: The Gqunukhwebe and some other chiefdoms of the Southern Nguni move across the Fish River and into the Zuurveld.

1779–1780: The First Frontier War breaks out after a Boer commando raid some minor Xhosa chiefs west of the Fish River.

1779–1786: The Cape Patriot movement in the Western Cape tries to acquire better representation in government and more free trade.

1780: The government unilaterally proclaims the Fish River as the colony's boundary.

1786: The frontier district of Graaff-Reinet is established.

1792–1793: The Second Frontier War ends inconclusively after an alliance between Ndlambe, son of the Xhosa paramount, and some frontier Boers attacked the Zuurveld Xhosa.

1793–1829: A wave of foreign missionaries begins with the arrival of the Moravians, who re-establish Baviaanskloof, later Genadendal, and the London Missionary Society whose first servants arrive in 1799.

1795: Frontier Boers rebel against the landdrosts of Swellendam and Graaff-Reinet and establish 'republics'.

1795–1803: The British temporarily occupy the Cape on behalf of the Dutch *Stadhouer*.

1798: The first mosque is built.

1799: The Dutch East India Company collapses.

1799–1802: The Third Frontier War leads to a large-scale retreat from the colonists in the east in the face a coalition between Zuurveld Xhosa chiefs and Khoikhoi who rose against the Boers.

1803–1806: The Cape reverts to Dutch control.

1806: Britain reoccupies the Cape.

1807: Britain abolishes the slave trade.

1809: The Hottentot Proclamation introduces contracts for Khoisan servants as a form of protection but also subjects them to pass laws.

1811–1812: The Fourth Frontier War sees a large colonial force of British soldiers, Boer commandos and Khoikhoi serving in the Cape Regiment expel the Xhosa from the Zuurveld.

1812: Grahamstown and Cradock are established.

1818: Ndlambe's forces defeat those of Ngqika, the Xhosa paramount. Colonial forces come to the help of Ngqika.

1819–1820: The Fifth Frontier War starts with an attack by Ndlambe's forces on Grahamstown, which nearly succeeds. The colonial forces drive the Xhosa back and the area between the Kei and Keiskamma rivers is declared a neutral area from which all Xhosa must withdraw.

1820: British settlers arrive.

Early 1820s: Andries Waterboer becomes captain in Griquatown and Adam Kok establishes himself in Philippolis. Trekboers begin to migrate out of the colony.

1828: The Khoisan are freed from all restrictions.

1829: The Kat River settlement for Khoikhoi is founded.

1833: The British government announces the abolition of slavery in 1834 with freed slaves to serve an apprenticeship of four years before finally receiving full freedom in December 1838.

1834: The first frontier farmers, later known as Voortrekkers, start leaving the colony.

1834–1835: The Sixth Frontier War begins with a large-scale invasion of Xhosa initiated by Maqoma and Tyhali to recover lost lands.

1835–1838: The movement later known as the Great Trek becomes widespread.

Introduction

South Africa is one of the few regions of the world where humans have lived continuously for nearly two million years – and where the geology and environmental conditions helped preserve evidence of their presence. In northern Europe and Asia, the story of human dispersal was interrupted for long periods by glaciers; Australia was first inhabited less than 60 000 years ago; and people migrated into the Americas only after about 14 000 years ago.

Modern humans gradually evolved during the Middle Stone Age between 200 000 and 100 000 years ago, also in South Africa. Those who lived in rock shelters left behind layered deposits, showing how hunting and gathering patterns and tool-making traditions changed. Some of the earliest fossils of anatomically modern humans in the world have been found in South Africa at Klasies River (115 000 years ago) and Border Cave.

By 75 000 years ago, people living at Blombos Cave near Still Bay were engraving patterns onto ochre and collecting shells and making holes in them to string together as adornment – some of the earliest dated evidence in the world for such 'modern' behaviour. Rock and cave art in southern Africa dates back as far as any in Europe, although most of the paintings still visible today were probably made within the last 10 000 years.

Southern African rock art shows finer detail than rock art of similar age elsewhere, and is more densely distributed. Over the past 30 years, South African researchers have pioneered the use of ethnographic records to identify psychological and ritual themes in paintings and engravings, strongly influencing rock art research in other parts of the world.

Around 2 000 years ago, major changes in lifestyle took place when several waves of immigrants moved southwards from West and Central Africa, driven by growing numbers and their need for trade and new agricultural land. With them they brought domesticated animals and plants, and knowledge of pottery-making, mining and metalworking.

A little more than 2 000 years ago former hunter-gatherers in Botswana adopted domesticated sheep and cattle from the Iron Age people of West and Central Africa. These new herders, the Khoikhoi, migrated southwards to the Cape coast about 2 000 years ago.

At about the same time, the first Iron Age Bantu-speaking people settled south of the Limpopo and moved rapidly into the eastern half of the country, where summer rainfall fed their millet and sorghum crops. They settled in KwaZulu-Natal by 400 AD and in the eastern Cape by 600 AD.

Iron Age people at Mapungubwe traded with the east coast, acquiring glass beads from India and porcelain from China, as well as cotton cloth. In exchange, they offered gold, ivory and hides. As their wealth accumulated, they established the first southern African kingdom, with its separation of commoners and ritual leaders.

Both Khoikhoi herders and Iron Age farmers interacted with indigenous San hunter-gatherers. San lifestyle, beliefs and rock art gradually changed as they were absorbed into herder and farmer communities in the northern and western part of the country.

When 90 Europeans in the employ of a Dutch company established a refreshment post at the Cape in 1652, some 75 000 Khoikhoi and San lived scattered over what is today the Northern Cape, Western Cape and Eastern Cape. A colony based on slave and Khoikhoi labour left the surplus white population with little choice but to settle deep in the interior. Initially European conquest and colonisation proceeded without much bloodshed, but by 1770 expanding white cattle farmers met strong resistance from the Southern Nguni in the east and the Khoisan in the northeast.

By 1838 the British, who first occupied the Cape in 1795 and then more permanently in 1806, had abolished race discrimination and involuntary labour, including slavery. A mixed population (around 70 000 descended mainly from Europeans and 80 000 mainly from slaves, free blacks and Khoisan) faced the challenge of building a functioning and equitable post-slavery society. At this point some 6 000 Dutch and Afrikaans-speaking farmers and many of their ex-slaves and servants left the colony. This development would profoundly change the history of the interior of South Africa.

The first people

Early humans

All living people are of African descent. It was in Africa that the life of our ancestors who looked like the people of today began hundreds of thousands of years ago. Novelists, film-makers and artists have tried to imagine what their lifestyle must have been like, but we have no modern analogue for such a remote period. What we do know is that some of these people left eastern Africa at least 80 000 years ago and populated the rest of the world.

For this book, we begin the story with a small sample of fossil bones that have been left behind and preserved by chance to give us an idea of what our oldest ancestors looked like. Between about one and three million years ago, a lineage of primates, now known as australopithecines, lived close to present-day Johannesburg. Later, from about 1.8 million years ago, South Africa became home to early humans whose anatomy was closer to ours. They and their descendants have lived here ever since and their history has become part of the landscape.

This chapter traces the evolution of humankind and discusses ways of interpreting our ancient past. It looks at the great migrations, when the first people left the warm African habitats and spread out into Eurasia. It sketches in broad strokes what happened after that.

By 14 000 years ago, hunter-gatherers, ancestors of the people known today as San or Bushmen, were widely dispersed through southern Africa. The switch from stone to iron happened in North Africa 3 000 years ago, and by 2 500 years ago the first sedentary peoples settled in sub-Saharan Africa, bringing with them agriculture, metal-working and pottery. By 2 000 years ago there was a massive revolution in lifestyle in southern Africa. The Khoikhoi in the northern part of what is now called Botswana acquired live-stock from the Bantu-speakers moving into the area, and the Khoikhoi themselves migrated southwards to what was to become South Africa.

Landscapes of history

The landscape has long been seen simply as the canvas on which history is painted, but the environment is integral to the processes of history. History is written on the land. While the big geomorphological changes happen at a pace indiscernible to the human eye, changes in soils, plants and animals reflect changes in the patterns of human history. Processes of settlement remade landscapes and left behind a record on the land itself and beneath its surface.

It is sometimes hard to envision how much environments have transformed over time. 'As solid as rock' is a common simile, but little remains static and the rocks themselves move, break down and re-form – given long enough. The earth itself is about 5 000 million years old. Some 1 000 million years ago, the earth was cool and wet enough for life to begin. Single-cell organisms (bacteria) were the first life on earth and all carried the building blocks of life (DNA), the twenty amino acids that compose the building blocks of proteins in the cells of all living things.

Australopithecines, Homo ergaster *and* Homo sapiens

'We were just another ape,' as Robin Dunbar has remarked. Yet we are different: we are bipedal, have largely naked skin and bigger brains, develop more slowly and live longer.

We split from the chimpanzees, our nearest cousins, about six million years ago, probably in East Africa. Climate changes and earth movements may have fragmented the Miocene forest habitat of the last shared ancestor. Some academics call us the 'Third Chimpanzee' (as distinct from the other two: the common and pygmy chimps). Vicariance divided the ancestral population by ecological barriers presented by the fragmenting habitats.

The evolutionary forces that drove humankind's adaptive survival against vast odds in the African savannah are the key to our story. As Stephen Oppenheimer observes: 'We were not "put" here fully formed,' instead we were 'selected and moulded by a fierce, blind, unthinking environment. Like all evolving species, we had ancestors and cousins who shared some of our abilities but perished in adversity.' Indeed, the australopithecines (meaning 'southern apes') roamed African savannahs from four million years ago to about 1.2 million years ago. The best-known specimen is Lucy, christened by her discoverer, Don Johanson.

What was different about these primates was that they were bipedal (walking upright on two legs). They had longer thighs and shorter arms than other primates. Their hips were less adapted so they probably shambled rather than strode. Certainly bipedalism pre-dated the dramatic increase in brain size and tool use that became the hallmark of modern humans. They remained partially arboreal (tree-dwelling).

True striding bipedalism appeared with the second species of our own genus, *Homo ergaster*, about two million years ago. This meant the development of thighbones that angled inwards so that the knees met. *Homo ergaster*'s angled thighs allowed the feet to be side by side (rather than widely spaced apart), facilitating the ability to walk upright.

This shift to bipedalism corresponded with a time of climate instability. Temperature fluctuation became quite pronounced during the Pliocene Epoch (five million to 1.6 million

  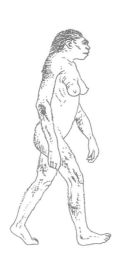 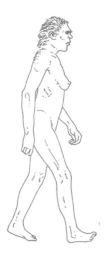 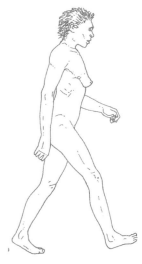

Australopithecus: 'southern ape'. These proto-human hominids walked upright and had longer thighs and shorter arms than other primates. The earliest species were partially tree dwelling. Australopithecines roamed the African savannahs from four to 1.5 million years ago.

Homo habilis: 'handy man'. This species, with an increased brain size, lived from about 2.2 to 1.8 million years ago and was the first member of the genus Homo who made tools.

Homo ergaster: (known as Homo erectus outside Africa) lived 1.8 million to 500 000 years ago. Some individuals left Africa about a million years ago and spread to southern Europe, Russia, the Near East, India, Indonesia and China. They were hunter-gatherers and made stone tools such as hand-axes, cleavers and choppers.

Homo sapiens: 'wise man' (also known as 'archaic Homo sapiens'). They lived about 500 000 to 100 000 years ago throughout Africa, southern Europe and Asia. Their brain size was similar to that of people today, but the shape of the brain suggests they did not think as we do.

Homo sapiens sapiens: the same species as all modern-day humans. Evolved in Africa from archaic Homo sapiens some time between 150 000 and 100 000 years ago. A small group migrated from Africa about 80 000 years ago and replaced the earlier species, including Neanderthals, in Europe and Asia, and eventually populated Australia and the Americas as well.

years ago). During this time, especially around 2.8 million years ago, the world entered a period of intense climate fluctuation, including periods of cooling called ice ages. About two million years ago, this created a cooler, drier climate in Africa, resulting in the expansion of grasslands and loss of forest. This put more pressure on primate populations trying to retreat further and further into the vanishing forests, while some australopithecines moved out into the grasslands. Natural selection driven by these climatic and vegetation changes thus favoured a less arboreal way of life. As John Gribbin notes: 'It was not so much that Lucy and her like left the forests, but that the forests left them.'

Yet the australopithecines' brain size and way of life were not dissimilar to that of their forest-dwelling primate cousins, the chimpanzees. The australopithecines had small brains roughly 380 to 450 cubic centimetres (compared to 300 to 400 cubic centimetres for modern chimpanzees, and 1 350 cubic centimetres for modern humans). The start of the radical brain size increase occurred with the first members of the genus *Homo* about two million years ago. This accelerated with the arrival of *Homo ergaster* and became exponential by the time *Homo sapiens* appeared. Dunbar has argued that the benefit of increased brain size is being able to handle the pressures and enjoy the safety of living in large groups.

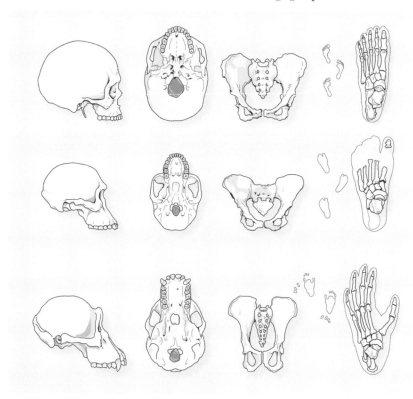

The *Homo* line starts with *Homo habilis* ('handy man'), the first hominid to make tools. They were followed about 1.8 million years ago by *Homo ergaster, also* known as *Homo erectus.* This creature was the first to hunt, probably first to use fire, first to make complex tools, maybe the first to look after the aged and weak. The Turkana boy is a *Homo erectus* who lived 1.6 million years ago in northern Kenya. It is the most complete early human fossil discovered and includes many skeletal elements of *Homo ergaster* not previously known.

Homo ergaster had a skull a third larger than those of most *habilis* specimens, but a brain about three quarters of the size of modern man. Bill Bryson quotes Professor Alan Walker, who notes that if we looked into the eyes of this early human it might appear superficially like us, but cautions: 'You wouldn't connect. You'd be prey.' There are signs, however, that they were becoming a lot closer to modern humans. They were learning to master their environment for the first time, and from about 1.5 million years ago they manufactured relatively sophisticated stone tools.

CLASSIFICATION OF MODERN MAN

Modern man is classified in the following way:

CLASS:	**Mammalia** – warm-blooded, give birth to live young, suckle their young, have hair
ORDER:	**Primates** – part of the monkey and ape family
FAMILY:	**Hominidae**
GENUS:	**Homo** – 'man'
SPECIES:	**sapiens** – 'wise'

The Eve gene

The fossil record is meagre and until recently there were no primate fossil finds from the period four to seven million years ago, when the hominines diverged from the lineage that was to lead to the chimpanzees of today. So other methodologies, such as molecular dating, have been used to fill the missing pieces. While hominid fossils are rare and stumbled upon through luck, the 40 000 genes found within living humans are a vital database on our species' past.

Much evolutionary change is random, especially in the parts of a species' genome that do not influence its survival rate – including a quantity of 'junk DNA' and the DNA contained in the mitochondria of all human cells. Opportunely for the researcher, random processes of this type are subject to statistical laws. As David Christian observes: 'If you take a new deck of cards arranged by suit and number and shuffle it a few times, a statistician can estimate roughly how often it has been shuffled by determining how

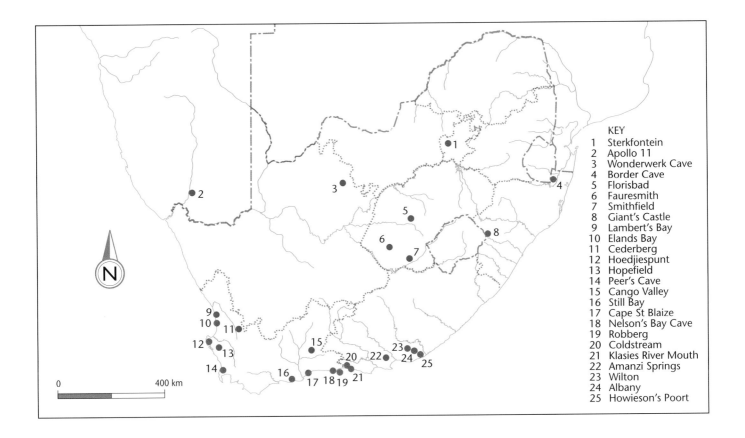

KEY
1 Sterkfontein
2 Apollo 11
3 Wonderwerk Cave
4 Border Cave
5 Florisbad
6 Fauresmith
7 Smithfield
8 Giant's Castle
9 Lambert's Bay
10 Elands Bay
11 Cederberg
12 Hoedjiespunt
13 Hopefield
14 Peer's Cave
15 Cango Valley
16 Still Bay
17 Cape St Blaize
18 Nelson's Bay Cave
19 Robberg
20 Coldstream
21 Klasies River Mouth
22 Amanzi Springs
23 Wilton
24 Albany
25 Howieson's Poort

0   400 km

ABOVE: *Major sites where prehistoric artefacts have been found in South Africa.*

much of the pack differs from its original condition. The larger the number of cards and shuffles, the more precise and reliable such estimates can be.' Researchers have argued that if we take two modern species and determine the variations between their DNA sequences we can ascertain when their two lineages divided from a mutual ancestor.

Mitochondrial DNA (mtDNA) comes from the mother alone and records a pristine family history from one mother to the next. It is particularly useful to researchers (even though it comprises a mere 0.0006% of human nuclear DNA) because it has a high rate of mutation and is easy to obtain for analysis. The only way variation in mtDNA can be introduced is through mutation. The number of mutations separating two mtDNA types

APES AND HOMINIDS: DART'S FIND

The first evidence for the existence of our near ancestors, the australopithecines, and their movement out of the tropical African forest to southern Africa, came from South Africa. In 1924, Raymond Dart, who was born in Australia and in 1922 became professor of Anatomy at the newly established University of the Witwatersrand, learned of a fossil 'baboon' skull that had been found at a limestone quarry near Taung in North West Province. He asked to be sent any more bones or fossils that were found.

It took Dart about a month to remove enough stone surrounding the fossil to reveal the face of a young primate. Dart considered the specimen to be intermediate between apes and humans and quickly wrote a paper for *Nature* that described it and named it *Australopithecus africanus* (southern ape from Africa).

After initial applause, the international scientific establishment rejected the Taung baby as merely an ape. In the 1930s and early 1940s, Robert Broom found many more australopithecine fossils in Gauteng and Limpopo Province and Dart's position was vindicated.

Just like Dart and Broom, Louis Leakey faced scepticism about the idea of an African genesis for humankind when he began to search for human fossils in East Africa in the early 1930s. He and his wife Mary uncovered the first of many hominid fossils at Olduvai Gorge in Tanzania and proved the existence of early hominids in East Africa as well.

Some of the South African fossils can be seen at the Origins Centre at the University of the Witwatersrand and at the interpretative centre for the Cradle of Humankind World Heritage Site at Maropeng near Sterkfontein west of Johannesburg.

is a way of measuring the length of time since they shared a common ancestor. Thus mtDNA provides a genetic clock.

Preliminary studies of human mtDNA divergence led to the 'African Eve' hypothesis that all mtDNA types found in our global human population of today can be tracked back to a single ancestor who lived in Africa about 200 000 to 150 000 years ago.

The idea of one single common ancestor of all humankind sounds a lot more dramatic than it is. Simply put, we all share an ancestor that was not the first or only female alive. She was just a member of a group – but the mtDNA of her contemporaries went extinct because they or their descendants left no progeny at all, or left only male offspring. This 'African Eve' had ancestors, of course, who were also our ancestors but she is simply the most recent common ancestor.

All studies of global human mtDNA divergence have shown that African populations have the biggest mtDNA divergence (followed by Asian and European populations). The fact that Africans have the greatest mtDNA sequence variation proves they have amassed the most mtDNA mutations. This provides compelling evidence for the idea of African origin of humankind because the population with the most diversity is almost certainly the 'ancestral population'. All other population groups seem to be subsets of the diversity found in Africa, which further buttresses the argument for an African origin.

Out of Africa?

By at least a million years ago (and probably closer to two million), early humans were able to expand their range outside Africa. Fossil evidence for this has been found in southern Europe, Russia, the Middle East, Asia and Indonesia, but not in the Americas or in Australia. This dispersal is sometimes called 'Out of Africa I'.

There are two competing theories as to what happened next. The first is the 'multi-regional' hypothesis that modern humans evolved over the past million years from hominid populations already living in Eurasia via gene flow. It postulates that isolated by geography, populations evolved independently, but with occasional interbreeding. The result was separate populations of modern humans, each with distinct physical features. It is characterised by regional continuity of anatomical features and argues for deep genetic divisions between 'races'.

The second is the 'Out of Africa' hypothesis, which argues that modern humans originated in Africa until as recently as 150 000 years ago and then spread out from there. The genetic and fossil evidence for this is more convincing. It contends that the people descended from the first migration out of Africa were replaced by a second, more recent migration of anatomically modern people about 80 000 years ago. Instead of interbreeding with the earlier population, modern humans replaced them, driving them to extinction. The study of mtDNA shows that an unbroken genetic train can be traced back to a common ancestor from Africa. So far there is little evidence of a genetic contribution from non-African populations.

The 'rainbow' species

Hilary and Janette Deacon note: 'All living humans are members of one "rainbow" species, *Homo sapiens*. Not surprisingly, some trivial differences have developed because of our wide geographical distribution.'

The differences, like skin colour, are tiny and superficial. Skin colour, for example, is a perpetual concern in racialised discourse. Our earliest forbears, some six million years ago, probably had lightly pigmented skin covered with dark hair, much like chimpanzees of today. As we evolved, hair was lost and sweat glands developed to help control the body's temperature. By 150 000 years ago we were all probably darkly pigmented. Melanin in darker skins protects against the sun's ultraviolet rays, which cause cancer.

As humans left Africa and moved into less sun-drenched regions, natural selection for lighter skins probably occurred to assist with the synthesis of vitamin D. So skin colour is simply linked to the geographic area of recent origin.

Race has not always been perceived as an 'illusion'. As Saul DuBow has shown, physical anthropologists in the early decades of the twentieth century were shaped by their times:

'[In] charting the paths of evolutionary development they helped confirm – by implicit analogy if not outright comparison – the intrinsic superiority of the white races and the inexorable progress of European civilisation.' However, this was to change over time.

After 1945, there was a new discourse that moved away from thinking in terms of rigidly defined 'races' or 'tribes', and instead adopted ideas like gene 'pools' and 'flows'. This reflects the move away from thinking about classifying people in terms of unchanging 'types' and signalled a fresh emphasis on the dynamic flexibility of human population groups.

The 'herd mentality'?

There has been little biological change in *Homo sapiens* over the past 40 000 years. But the amount of cultural change has been extraordinary, particularly the domestication of plants and animals. The growth of farming and care of herd animals (pastoralism) began one of the most remarkable changes in Earth's ecology. The transition to agriculture, starting around 10 000 years ago, took place in several regions of the world but not initially in Africa. By this time, the cool ice-age landscapes had retreated in the face of warmer, damper environments. People adapted to these changes by making more intensive use of the landscape. At the outset they took advantage of a broad range of plants and animals within each region, but later focused on particular wild plants and animals.

By painstakingly collecting plants and controlling wild herd animals, people could select sought-after characteristics. This process of controlled breeding eventually created new forms of animals and new species of wheat, corn and other plants and useful by-products. Food production started much later in sub-Saharan Africa (as opposed to Eurasia) because of a number of reasons.

Jared Diamond argues that to domesticate wild animals they must be docile, cheap to feed, grow quickly and breed in captivity: 'Eurasia's native cows, sheep, goats, horses and pigs were among the world's few large wild animals to pass all those tests. Their African equivalents – such as the African buffalo, zebra, bush pig, rhino, and hippopotamus – have never been domesticated, not even in modern times.'

Similarly, even though the Sahel and Ethiopia, for example, did produce indigenous crops, there was a much more limited variety of wild 'starting material' suitable for domestication. Diamond further argues that Africa is only about half the size of Eurasia and, moreover, Africa's major axis is north-south, which means widely differing zones of climate, rainfall, day length and plant and animal pathogens (unlike in Eurasia's east-west axis, with the same latitude and similar climates and day lengths). Diamond reasons that this impeded the spread of food production and cultural exchange as 'crops and animals domesticated or acquired in one part of Africa had great difficulty in moving to other parts'. Thus, he concludes, 'The different historical trajectories of Africa and Europe stem ultimately from differences in real estate.'

Massive changes

Africa has also seen massive changes in the last 2 000 years. The southward movement of the Bantu-speaking farmers introduced the Iron Age, with domesticated plants and livestock, pottery, mining and iron-working. The pastoral revolution presented a massive change in lifestyle. There is evidence that sheep were acquired from the north and cattle

Fat-tailed sheep painted on the wall of a rock shelter in the Clanwilliam district. The San and Khoikhoi obtained fat from eland and other wild animals, as well as sheep. They ate it and rubbed it on their skin.

All domesticated cattle introduced to South Africa within the last 2 000 years come from one ancestor, the auroch (extinct wild ox). Two main species were domesticated from the auroch:

1. Bos indicus – the humped, short-horned Zebu was domesticated in the Near East and Indus Valley in about 5000 BC. The species was introduced into eastern Africa through Arab coastal settlements.

2. Bos taurus – these cattle with long horns and no humps were domesticated in North Africa.

Most African cattle stem from Bos taurus, with significant influence from the Zebu type evident in the Afrikander cattle kept by the Khoikhoi herders.

from Bantu-speakers to the east, while goats and dogs were acquired later than sheep and cattle. Sheep were indigenous to the Near East and North Africa, and domesticated in the north about 8 000 years ago. These fat-tailed animals appear to have been in East Africa by 4 000 years ago, and South Africa by 2 000 years ago.

How cattle domestication occurred in Africa has been obscured by ancient migrations and trade. Scientists have long speculated that the domestication of cattle also occurred first in the Near East and that the practice of herding cattle was similarly imported.

But new evidence suggests that Africans independently domesticated cattle. Geneticist Olivier Hanotte notes that there were Near Eastern influences on African herds, but that they were incorporated after local domestication. Archaeological research has shown that the domestication of cattle unfolded differently in Africa than elsewhere in the world. It appears that people living in Central Africa developed cattle domestication on their own, and that the techniques – or the herders themselves – gradually migrated toward the west and the south, spreading domestication across the continent. Most modern African herds represent mixtures of two breeds: Africa's native cattle, called taurines, and a slightly larger Asian breed, known as zebu, which was domesticated before it arrived in Africa.

Long-distance trade across the Indian Ocean brought many domesticated plants and animals to Africa, including the chicken and camel. Presumably trade also brought zebu bulls that farmers interbred with domesticated taurine cows, producing the mixed herds of today.

Pre-history and the future

Our ongoing biological and cultural evolution and adaptation has meant success for our species. We have multiplied from perhaps a few thousand australopithecines three million years ago, to arguably hundreds of thousands of archaic humans by 300 000 years ago, to the six billion people alive today globally. As we trace this trajectory and pursue a variety of disciplines in building up a picture of our past as a species, we should always bear in mind that we are working not with the 'truth', but with 'historical truth'.

History has long been sceptical of absolute truth, but not of partial, contingent and incremental truths. This is a 'working truth' – subject to transformation; it does not deny the reality of the past itself. It still tries to render a depiction – although usually accepts the unlikeliness of actually achieving this depiction – of 'how it actually was', in Ranke's long-derided phrase. In this field – perhaps more so than in any other historical field – there are new breakthroughs every year, new techniques, new discoveries. Everything we believe could change tomorrow.

People 'chastened by the feeling that history happened elsewhere' should remember that Africa was where it all began. As Louis Leakey said: 'Africa's first contribution to human progress' lay in 'the evolution of man himself'.

The hunter-gatherers of South Africa

Hundreds of thousands of generations of Stone Age hunter-gatherers populated the South African landscape for nearly two million years, yet for most of that time we know nothing of their names, language, memories, leaders, beliefs, wars or alliances. Their history cannot be studied by conventional historical methods and has been pieced together by archaeologists who, like detectives, study objects left behind long after the action is over.

This section summarises what is known about the Stone Age, the long period during which humankind evolved. The timescale is vast and hard to comprehend, but it is fortunate that our human ancestors used stone for their tools because it is virtually indestructible. As the process of changes in technology, human evolution, lifestyle and beliefs unfolded, there were major inventions, adaptations to new social and environmental circumstances, migrations to more favourable places and the development of social practices that set the stage with rapidly increasing numbers of people for the faster pace of recent South African history.

History without written records

Because South Africa was part of the geographical area in which the human species evolved, we have an exceptionally complete and detailed archaeological record of the process our ancestors followed to become what we are today. In many northern hemisphere countries, the history of the Stone Age was interrupted by glaciers that covered the landscape for tens of thousands of years.

The same climatic events had a less disruptive effect in southern and eastern Africa. Although some areas were subject to prolonged drought, the continent remained habitable and became the pool from which the rest of the world drew for innovation and inspiration. We talk of the 'global village' and marvel at how easy it is to communicate with people in other parts of the world. The very fact that there are people elsewhere to talk to is the result of human curiosity and our indomitable spirit of adventure more than a million years before trains and aircraft. It encouraged both early and modern humans to move out of Africa and explore the world.

The long history of Stone Age people

The principle of stone tool-making is that suitable rocks can be shaped by striking flakes from a core with a stone hammer. When struck correctly, flakes that come off the core have very sharp edges and make excellent knives, even though they dull very quickly. A good stone knapper can make tools like a hand-axe, cleaver or arrowhead in just a few minutes. Places with good quality rocks like silcrete and hornfels were used by Stone Age people as quarries for raw material for stone tools over many thousands of years. River gravels with conveniently sized cobbles were also popular, especially on terraces along major rivers like the Vaal in the vicinity of Kimberley and along the Eerste River in the vineyards of Stellenbosch.

A classification scheme for Stone Age tools was first published in 1929 by John Goodwin and 'Peter' van Riet Lowe and is still widely used. It is based on observations from all over the subcontinent that show consistent trends in the changing traditions of stone tool-making. Generally speaking, this trend was towards increasingly smaller tools and more efficient use of stone. Hundreds of archaeological excavations since the 1920s, and the advent of radiocarbon dating, have refined the timing and scale of changes in stone tool-making traditions.

There were periods when the trend towards smaller tools was reversed for a few thousand years, and times when sophisticated, well-made tools were followed by equally long periods when the tools were relatively crudely made. It is not clear whether these changes were stylistic or functional, but distinctive styles and techniques often persisted over the whole of southern Africa for tens of thousands of years.

The Earlier Stone Age

The Earlier Stone Age (ESA) was one of the most remarkable technological stages in human history. It is mostly associated with *Homo ergaster*. The oldest stone tools so far identified in South Africa are from Sterkfontein Cave in Gauteng, where they have been found in deposits dated to between 1.7 and two million years ago. They are Oldowan flakes and choppers similar to the tools from the famous Olduvai Gorge in Tanzania. The oldest Acheulian hand-axes are dated to about 1.6 million years ago at Sterkfontein and in East Africa.

For more than a million years the early tool-makers made the same style of Acheulian stone tools as their fathers and mothers before them. They perfected a method of removing flakes from cobbles to create a cutting edge around both sides of an almond-shaped tool known as the hand-axe, which was typically a bit larger than the average hand.

Others were U-shaped with a sharp cutting edge at one end and are known as cleavers. These multipurpose tools were so successful for digging, cutting and skinning that the technique and pattern spread from Africa throughout most of the regions of the world, including southern Europe (where the tool-making stage is known as the Lower Palaeolithic), the Near East, Russia and India. Hand-axes found in India, the Thames

---

CLASSIFICATION OF STONE TOOLS

John Goodwin and 'Peter' van Riet Lowe divided the Stone Age into three main stages in 1929, but the dating of tools only became possible after the 1950s:

- The **Earlier Stone Age** in southern Africa dates from about 1.8 million years ago to about 250 000 years ago.
- The **Middle Stone Age** dates from about 250 000 to about 25 000 years ago.
- The **Later Stone Age** dates from about 25 000 years ago to within the last few hundred years.

Subdivisions are made within the main stages. Some of these are regionally specific and others time-specific. They were often named after the site where they were first described. The Earlier Stone Age includes names like Acheulian (named after St Acheul in France) and Fauresmith in the Free State. The Middle Stone Age has subdivisions such as Mossel Bay, Still Bay and Howieson's Poort. The Later Stone Age includes Oakhurst, Smithfield, Wilton, Albany and Robberg, among others.

Early, Middle and Later Stone Age tools.

Choppers (left) and hand-axes were all-purpose tools made from river cobbles.

Triangular stone points (left and centre) and blades were used as spearheads and knives.

Small tools (microliths) were hafted for cutting (left) and for scraping hides.

The 47 000-hectare Cradle of Humankind is blessed with a greater wealth of early human history than almost any other place on earth. The Cradle contains more than twelve major fossil sites and dozens of minor ones. The Maropeng Visitors Centre at the Cradle of Humankind (near Johannesburg) was opened in 2005. The tumular building is designed to look like an ancient burial mound, though from the rear it looks like a modern structure. Inside, a journey through the evolution of life is presented, and the architecture is symbolic of this journey. Maropeng means 'returning to the place of origin' in Setswana, the local indigenous language. It is a reminder that the ancestors of all humans, wherever they live today, originally came from Africa.

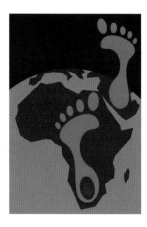

The Maropeng logo shows Africa as the ancestral home of all people, the place where our hominid ancestors stood upright and took the first steps along the path of humanity.

Valley in England and in Stellenbosch in South Africa are almost identical. Contemporary populations in China and Indonesia did not make the same type and quantity of stone tools and seem to have relied more on bamboo and wood. Although Earlier Stone Age people were the first to leave Africa more than 1.5 million years ago, they did not get as far as the Americas or Australia.

The people of the Earlier Stone Age were gatherers and hunters and their mobility made them effective scavengers of the kills of other predators. Although plant remains are almost never preserved in ESA sites, the teeth that have survived show that they were mostly vegetarians. Throughout this period, increases in brain size mostly kept pace with increases in body size – until about 500 000 years ago when the brain developed more rapidly, yet it would have been a time of improving manual and social skills.

ESA tools are not often found associated with fossil bone, but excavations near Hopefield in the Western Cape, dating to perhaps about 500 000 years ago, show well-made hand-axes associated with fauna that includes a range of antelope species and large herbivores like elephant and hippopotamus. This and similar sites indicate that the habitat in which ESA people lived was more diverse and productive than it is today. The distribution of ESA sites in South Africa generally shows that they are clustered in river valleys and around springs and pans. They have been found in fewer than ten cave sites in Africa and southern Europe, suggesting a very different pattern of occupation from Middle Stone Age times.

The Middle Stone Age

The Middle Stone Age (MSA) marks a fundamental change in the techniques of stone tool-making. Hand-axes were replaced with much smaller and thinner flakes that had been carefully shaped before they were struck from the core. The knappers also learned to strike long blades, sometimes as much as 20–30 cm in length, with two sharp sides. Finely controlled flaking created exquisite spearheads, some of which are so rare and well made that they might have been used for ritual purposes. The reduction in size of these tools was certainly a consequence of their being hafted, probably with mastic and twine, onto wooden handles or shafts.

There are too few well-dated sites where MSA tools immediately overlie those dating from the ESA for us to be able to gauge with any accuracy how long it took for the changeover from ESA to MSA to take place in South Africa. It is probably safe to say that the process took tens of thousands of years. Once the change was complete, though, no one ever made hand-axes again.

Initially, MSA tools were made by people not yet fully modern in appearance. They have been classified as archaic *Homo sapiens* and their remains have been found associated with early MSA artifacts at Florisbad in the Free State and Hoedjiespunt near Saldanha Bay. By at least 120 000 years ago, however, it is argued that MSA people had developed a lifestyle and level of human consciousness similar to that of modern people. The implications are that they spoke a relatively sophisticated language, were mentally capable of symbolic and conceptual thought (including art), and therefore had a belief system that influenced their social system. This is supported by three kinds of evidence.

The first is that rare fragments of human bones from Klasies River near Humansdorp in the Eastern Cape and from Border Cave on the border between Swaziland and KwaZulu-Natal are anatomically modern and are classified as *Homo sapiens sapiens*. The remains at both sites date to between about 115 000 and 80 000 years ago and are associated with MSA artifacts. It is misleading to say that this is where modern people evolved and that they moved from South Africa northwards out of Africa. The evidence shows only that South Africa was part of a very large region, including North and East Africa, in which modern humans first evolved and lived.

The second kind of evidence for symbolic thought is in the form of decorative art. Excavations at Blombos Cave on the southern Cape coast near Still Bay have uncovered MSA artifacts, about 75 000 years old, associated with small perforated shells that retain traces of red ochre. This suggests that they had been collected and strung together as a necklace. In the underlying level dated to about 80 000 years ago, two pieces of hard

Sterkfontein Cave near Krugersdorp in Gauteng has produced more pre-human australopithecine fossil specimens (more than 500) than any other single site in the world. The best-known specimen is the almost complete skull of 'Mrs Ples', as it was dubbed by the media at the time of discovery.

The work on early hominid fossils that was started at Sterkfontein by Dr Robert Broom, following on Professor Raymond Dart's discoveries at Taung in 1924, was carried forward in the second half of the twentieth century mainly by Professor Phillip Tobias of the Department of Anatomy at the University of the Witwatersrand and Dr C.K. (Bob) Brain of the Transvaal Museum. Soon after South Africa signed the World Heritage Convention in the late 1990s, a cluster of early hominid sites around Sterkfontein, Swartkrans, Kromdraai and neighbouring properties in Gauteng Province west of Johannes-

burg were nominated and accepted as a World Heritage Site. Since then, the sites at Taung in North West Province and Makapan in Limpopo Province have been added to what is colloquially known as the Cradle of Humankind. Stone tools have been found in the younger layers at some of the same sites, showing that in addition to australopithecines, true humans lived and died there.

All the fossils have been preserved because the bones were deposited between four and one million years ago in lime-rich soils, mostly in erosion cavities in dolomite. Brain's research proved that the australopithecines and many of the other animals whose bones were fossilised in the dolomite were mainly the prey of large carnivores, such as the extinct *Dinofelis*. Burnt bones found at Swartkrans in a layer that includes early human remains suggest that people sheltering in the cavern had learned to use fire at least

a million years ago and this may have helped them to compete with carnivores.

One of the most interesting fossils is the so-called 'Little Foot'. It is older than most of the other australopithecines – about 3.2 million years – and was identified first from its foot bones, which showed it was still partly arboreal. Some careful detective work by Nkwane Molefe and Stephen Motsumi, at the request of Dr Ron Clarke, found the rest of the bones of the skeleton still embedded in the breccia that filled the dolomite cavern at Sterkfontein. The fact that the skeleton is almost complete suggests that this individual was not killed by a carnivore, but possibly fell into a deep cavity and was unable to get out.

These sites create a unique window on the past because of the rare conditions that preserved the bones. Interpretative centres at Sterkfontein and at Maropeng display some of the fossils and explain their significance.

---

ochre were found, engraved with a pattern of lines that form diamond shapes. These are the oldest examples of rock art yet discovered – slightly older than 63 000-year-old fragments of ostrich eggshell decorated with similar patterns of engraved lines from Diepkloof Cave near Elands Bay in the Western Cape.

The oldest dated rock paintings in Africa are also associated with MSA artifacts. Seven small slabs of rock with paintings on them were excavated from the Apollo 11 Cave in southern Namibia and the average of 15 radiocarbon dates on charcoal found at the same level as the painted slabs is 27 500 years. Together these engravings and paintings show that from at least 80 000 years ago, people were capable of making pictorial representations that had symbolic meaning.

The third line of evidence is the lifestyle of MSA people as reflected in the places they chose to live and the food remains they left behind. Whereas ESA sites are mostly in the open, MSA people often lived in caves and rock shelters, returning over and over again to the same place over tens of thousands of years. They were no longer restricted to certain habitats like valleys, but occupied the whole landscape.

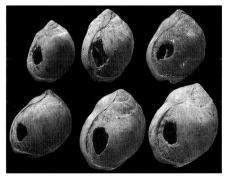

The world's first jewellery: at Blombos near Still Bay, shells were found with drilled holes, suggesting that they had been strung together as a necklace.

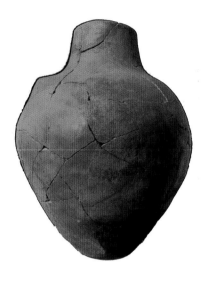

At Blombos, Chris Henshilwood's team found the earliest dated (80 000 BP) rock engravings and personal adornment. The artworks are made on blocks of ochre and the adornment is in the form of small, drilled shell beads.

ABOVE: *A typical Khoikhoi pot, with a neck and pointed base, used to store milk products.*

TOP LEFT: *The world's earliest known artwork: ochre engraved with a geometric pattern.*

TOP RIGHT: *The oldest dated rock paintings in Africa, one of seven small slabs of painted rock from the Apollo 11 Cave in Namibia, dated c.27 500 BP.*

The implications are that they had a much more flexible social structure than their predecessors. Their rock shelters preserve the hearths where people gathered to cook, with rare traces of their plant foods and the bones of a wide variety of animals, mainly antelope. In addition, there is good evidence that MSA people also collected shellfish, marine mammals and fish to add to their diet. This pattern is very similar to that of the Later Stone Age and is fundamentally different from the ESA.

The Later Stone Age

The Later Stone Age (LSA) saw several innovations in the range of artifacts, including items that were still being made by San hunter-gatherers at the time of European contact and up to the twentieth century.

The stone tools were on average smaller than those of the Middle Stone Age and at times included a range of tiny bladelets about 15 mm long that were blunted along the margin opposite to the cutting edge. As components of composite tools, they were firmly embedded in mastic (a plant resin) on wooden and bone hafts. Together with polished bone linkshafts and points, the backed bladelets are very similar to nineteenth-century arrow parts made by the San and are good evidence for the continent-wide diffusion of the bow and arrow. Examples from the Cango Valley in the Western Cape dating to about 18 000 years ago are among the earliest evidence for the bow and arrow.

Other artifacts typical of the San toolkit that are commonly found at LSA sites, especially after about 10 000 years ago, are ostrich eggshell beads, bone and shell pendants and beads, fragments of ostrich eggshell water flasks that were sometimes decorated with incised patterns, tortoiseshell bowls, fragments of digging sticks and their bored stone weights, grindstones and – where conditions for the preservation of organic material are favourable – items such as parts of sewn leather clothing and bags, string, bow staves and matting.

As the San are the best model we have for the hunter-gatherer lifestyle that saw so many generations through the Stone Age, and the LSA toolkit is so similar to that of recent San communities, the temptation is to assume that the history of the LSA is the history of the San. However, this can only be done at a very broad level of generalisation. Even today 'San' does not correlate exactly with language, physical features, material culture and lifestyle any more than does 'European' or 'American'.

- We have no way of knowing what language the San spoke 10 000 or 20 000 years ago, but we can say that in the past 500 years most of the hunter-gatherers in southern Africa spoke a click language, even though linguists do not group all the click languages into the same language family. However, the uniqueness and diversity of the click languages suggest very ancient roots that possibly stretch back into the MSA.
- The physical features of human skeletal remains of LSA people buried mainly within the last 10 000 years were broadly similar to those of the San of the nineteenth and twentieth centuries. The gradual reduction in stature and increasingly gracile features over time indicate a long period of selection that followed similar trends in

hunter-gatherer populations in other parts of the world. People generally have bcome less robust. The DNA of San communities living today confirms their long history in this part of the continent.

- At a gross level, the material culture of LSA people was broadly similar throughout southern Africa over the past 25 000 years, but as population numbers increased, especially in the last 5 000 years, there was greater differentiation in the range and style of stone tools made at about the same time in different places. It is not clear whether these were as a result of differences in style or function, or whether people who spoke a slightly different language made different tools.
- Finally, although we can say without a doubt that the lifestyle of LSA people was that of hunter-gatherers for most of the time, within the last 2 000 years some San who were formerly hunter-gatherers became herders when they acquired sheep, goats and cattle that were introduced from the north by Iron Age Bantu-speaking peoples migrating southwards. The herders have become known as the Khoekhoen, or Khoikhoi. Over the centuries they became more and more distinct from the hunter-gatherers, but retained their LSA toolkit, with the addition of pottery that was used for the storage of dairy products and occasional copper and iron artifacts traded from Iron Age farmers.

The ability of LSA hunter-gatherers to sustain themselves was seriously challenged at least three times in the past 2 000 years – first with the southward migration of the Khoikhoi herders into the western half of the country. Although they appear to have developed a symbiotic relationship with the hunter-gatherers, they attracted individuals to change to herding and weakened hunter-gatherer social cohesion. Second, in the north and east of South Africa, Iron Age farmers settled in the summer rainfall regions within the last 1 800 years to grow crops and tend their stock. They also lived alongside hunter-gatherers, particularly in the Drakensberg region, and developed a working relationship with them, but became more and more powerful in terms of population size and land ownership. Finally, the death knell came with the arrival of European colonists whose commandos with guns and horses decimated the hunter-gatherers within two centuries. Some of this history is reflected in the rock art of the LSA.

Rock art as a record of spiritual beliefs

Rock art by LSA hunter-gatherers can be found in the form of paintings or engravings in almost every district in South Africa. There is no comprehensive list of all sites, and many have not been recorded, but it is estimated that there are at least 20 000 to 30 000 sites and well over a million individual images. Although many are not well preserved, collectively they represent a remarkable record of the beliefs and cultural practices of the people who made them. Most were created by San hunter-gatherers, but Khoikhoi herders and Iron Age farmers added to the collection.

ABOVE: *Rock painting from the Porterville district showing a sailing ship.*

TOP LEFT: *Northern Sotho rock art from Limpopo Province. Made as part of initiation rituals, the white paint was applied with a finger.*

TOP RIGHT: *Rock painting of three medicine men or !gi:ten wearing patterned karosses (cloaks). The central figure has an eland's head, expressing the complex transformation !gi:ten undergo when visiting the spirit world.*

PAINTINGS AND ENGRAVINGS

Rock art includes all paintings and engravings made by people on natural rock. It was made by:

- **painting** images on the rock surface with paint made from natural pigments such as red and yellow ochre, white clay, charcoal or manganese oxide, mixed with binders such as blood, water, plant juices and egg.
- **engraving** images onto rock by removing the weathered outer layer using a single line, or scraping or pecking the surface.

Apart from the engravings and paintings associated with the MSA, most rock paintings and engravings associated with the LSA in South Africa date to within the last 10 000 years. They include small portable slabs with engravings from Wonderwerk Cave near Kuruman in the Northern Cape, painted cobbles from Coldstream and Robberg on the Western Cape's south coast, small pieces of rock with paint on them from KwaZulu-Natal, a large piece of rock with paintings on it that was detached from the wall of a rock shelter near Lambert's Bay on the west coast, and samples of paint with organic matter from the Cederberg and the Drakensberg. The most recent paintings were done during the colonial period and show people in European dress with horses and guns, wagons and even ships.

Rock paintings and engravings are very difficult to date directly. The radiocarbon, or C-14, method needs organic material (from plants or animals). Most of the ingredients in the paints are inorganic (clay, ochre), and although blood, egg and plant juices may have left some organic residue, it is only present in very small quantities. Engravings do not contain organic matter that dates to the act of engraving.

Paintings have also been dated indirectly. Where a painted or engraved stone is found in the floor of a rock shelter, archaeologists have dated charcoal or shell from the same layer with radiocarbon to get an idea of the minimum age of the rock art. At Blombos Cave near Still Bay, optically stimulated luminescence dating was used to date single quartz grains in sand associated with engraved pieces of ochre to about 80 000 years ago.

The hunter-gatherer paintings were generally made with a brush or with a reed 'pen' and have fine lines and delicate details. They were mostly made with red ochre, but yellow, purple, white and black were also used. Most paintings used one colour (monochrome) but some are painted with two (bichrome) or several colours (polychrome). Where the paint is blended from one colour to another, it is referred to as shaded polychrome. Not only did the hunter-gatherers make paint that has lasted thousands of years, they were gifted artists who expressed complex ideas in elegantly simple ways. They were also responsible for the older tradition of rock engravings in the Karoo.

Khoikhoi herders who brought sheep and cattle into this part of South Africa within the last 2 000 years were probably responsible for the most recent phase of painting, in which the paint was applied with a finger instead of a brush. The colours are mostly monochrome and the subject matter is frequently non-representational patterns with symbolic meaning. As the Khoikhoi settled on the land formerly occupied by hunter-gatherers, the San gradually stopped painting as their numbers and cultural activities declined.

Iron Age farmers contributed paintings and engravings in the Eastern Cape, Free State, KwaZulu-Natal, Limpopo, Mpumalanga, Gauteng and North West provinces after they settled there more than 1 000 years ago. Their paintings were also made with a finger or very broad brush and are closely connected to initiation of young men and women.

The meaning of rock art

There is overwhelming evidence that the hunter-gatherer rock paintings and engravings of southern Africa illustrate the metaphors, conventions and practices of a San religion

TOP: *Khoikhoi finger painting from the Carnarvon District, showing patterns used during girls' initiation rites.*

RIGHT: *Recent rock paintings of people in colonial dress, with horses, mules, guns and wagons.*

or belief system that persists to the present day in surviving communities in Namibia and Botswana. It was the glue that bound San families and communities together.

The main source of information on San beliefs in South Africa comes from records made in the 1870s of the customs and beliefs of the /Xam San from the Northern Cape. The records were compiled by Wilhelm Bleek and Lucy Lloyd, who interviewed /Xam men in prison in Cape Town for stock theft and other crimes. Their testimony is very similar to accounts of San interviewed by anthropologists in the twentieth century.

As the ground-breaking research of David Lewis-Williams has shown, animals in rock paintings were important in San beliefs in much the same way as the lamb is a symbol in Christian beliefs and the eagle is important to Native Americans. The eland was believed by the San to give them access to supernatural power for healing sick people, making rain and controlling game animals. Other animals, such as the elephant in the Western Cape and the kudu in Limpopo, had similarly powerful connotations.

Supernatural power was obtained by trained medicine people, or *!gi:ten*, who learned over many years how to control it by entering a trance-like state through dancing and singing. Many of the paintings show processions of people dancing, sometimes wearing karosses (cloaks), sometimes carrying sticks or fly-whisks made from the tails of animals. Women are often shown dancing, too, or clapping their hands. Bags with tassels, shown next to the dancers or processions, were used to carry medicine or herbs such as buchu that helped them to enter a trance and could be used to heal the sick. Mood-altering drugs such as dagga (marijuana) were not generally used.

Paintings and engravings of people with animal heads, or animals with human legs are a multilayered metaphor. They illustrate the sensation experienced by *!gi:ten* in trance, who feel as if they are becoming the animals that give them supernatural power. Death is the metaphor that medicine people use for trance because they feel as if they die and then come alive again.

Ultimately, however, the power of the spirit world was not enough to protect them and rock paintings of soldiers in red coats firing guns at fleeing San as a medicine person lies in trance to one side are a powerful reminder of the events that brought about the end of the Stone Age in South Africa.

The Khoikhoi pastoralists

The Khoikhoi (called 'Hottentots' by early white settlers) were descendants of hunter-gatherers who had acquired livestock centuries earlier, probably in modern Botswana. Supporting a growing population through their pastoral economy they expanded fairly rapidly throughout southern Africa. Those moving into high rainfall areas to the east were probably absorbed over the centuries into Bantu-speaking societies that both kept cattle and cultivated crops; those moving southward and westward tended to retain their purely pastoral economy.

When European settlement began in the mid-seventeenth century, Khoikhoi groups called the Namaqua were settled in modern Namibia and the northeastern Cape; others, including the Korana, along the Orange River; and others, including the Gonaqua, interspersed among the Xhosa in the Eastern Cape. But the largest concentration of Khoikhoi, numbering in the tens of thousands, inhabited the well-watered pasturelands of the southwestern Cape. These 'Cape Khoikhoi' would be the first African population to receive the brunt of white settlement.

The polities of the Khoikhoi
In most areas of southern Africa, including the southwestern Cape, the pastoral Khoikhoi lived near hunter-gatherers who kept neither cattle nor sheep. The hunters were called 'San' by the Khoikhoi, 'Bushmen' by the Dutch. Some Khoikhoi who lost their livestock in times of war or disease fled to the frontier regions and joined San bands, reverting to hunting and gathering, and sometimes attacking the livestock of other Khoikhoi. Many of those whom the colonists called 'Bushmen' were in

BELOW: *Khoikhoi artifacts as drawn by Anders Sparrman in his book* A Voyage to the Cape of Good Hope from the year 1772 to 1776: *woven baskets, leather bangle decorated with beads, dancing rattle worn on the ankle.*

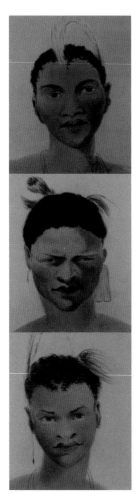

fact former Khoikhoi. For this reason, scholars sometimes find it convenient to refer to hunters and herders together as 'Khoisan'.

Khoisan languages, characterised by implosive consonants or 'clicks', belonged to a totally different language family from those of the Bantu speakers. In contrast to the San, who spoke highly divergent languages, the Khoikhoi spoke closely related dialects of the same language.

From present-day Port Elizabeth to the present Springbok, the Khoikhoi were organised in approximately twelve chiefdoms that the Dutch called 'nations'. Some were ruled by male figures (called 'kings' or 'captains' by the Dutch), but others had no leaders above headmen of small clans.

Though Khoikhoi had no standing armies and no military leaders apart from their chiefs, they seem to have engaged in frequent wars. European observers were deeply impressed by their dexterity in battle and by their skilful use of weapons. Wars were often triggered by cattle theft, murders, and by the abduction of prominent women – provocations that led to vendettas that would smoulder and flare up over the generations. Khoikhoi fought pitched battles, using assegais, bows, stones and darts as offensive weapons; they massed their oxen together as defensive ramparts and drove them forward as flying wedges to gore and trample the enemy.

Such battles, though apparently not very bloody, often resulted in significant transfers of herds and flocks from the vanquished to the victors. In other cases – as, for example, when they faced Dutch soldiers armed with muskets – the Khoikhoi could resort to guerrilla tactics, characterised by swift and overwhelming attack on the enemy's herds.

Before the Dutch arrived, the Cape Khoikhoi herded their cattle and sheep, and also hunted game, in a favoured region of Africa far from cultivating societies that elsewhere would have competed with them for use of well-watered land. Although the Khoikhoi slaughtered cattle only on special occasions, their livestock provided them with milk, their principal source of nutrition, and also skins to make clothing, bags, bottles and other implements. Livestock served, too, as a means of transport and warfare, and the source of prestige and power.

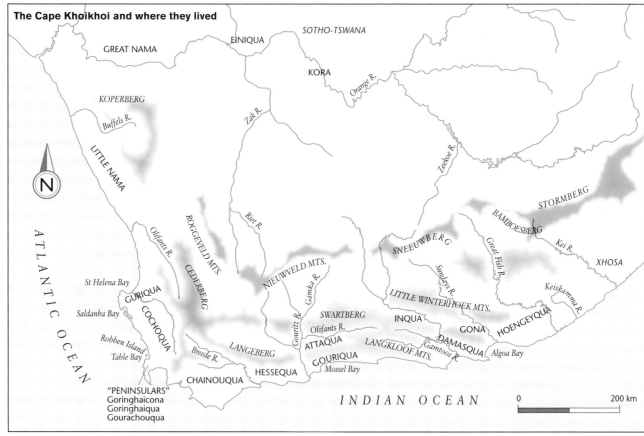

The Cape Khoikhoi and where they lived

The pastoral economy was occasionally a source of abundant wealth for Khoikhoi individuals and communities. But it was also a source of instability. As herders, the Khoikhoi had to move constantly in search of fresh pasture; the basis of their wealth was not land, but the animals themselves. Because livestock was frequently stolen – and also vulnerable to drought, disease, and war – wealth fluctuated dramatically among Khoikhoi as groups and individuals rapidly acquired, and rapidly lost, their herds and flocks.

Khoikhoi society seems to have been rather individualistic, with well-grooved channels of upward and downward mobility. While political power was in theory inherited on the basis of kinship, the rise of rulers was more decisively determined by their ability to amass livestock for themselves and to protect the livestock of their followers.

The Khoikhoi and the San

The instability in Khoikhoi society was further intensified by the nearby presence of San. Some San groups frequently attacked the Khoikhoi, sowing terror by firing off poisoned arrows normally used to hunt great game, and stealing and frequently slaughtering Khoikhoi livestock.

Yet many so-called San also lived peaceably in or on the fringes of Khoikhoi societies, serving Khoikhoi as hunters, guides, or spies and soldiers in time of war. Khoikhoi hired some as herders and took some as wives. In many areas, notably the southwestern Cape, the boundary between Khoikhoi and San became increasingly unclear. Newly impoverished Khoikhoi were often called San, and San who had prospered were absorbed into Khoikhoi lineages and polities.

The coexistence of hunting and herding societies throughout the region created opportunities for upward mobility for enterprising San, and provided the safety net of an alternative lifestyle for newly impoverished pastoralists. But easy passage from herding to hunting would also accelerate the rapid crumbling of Khoikhoi society when it was confronted by Dutch colonialism.

Trading with Europeans

Though Khoikhoi themselves did not apparently smelt metals, the earliest Portuguese visitors attest that they used copper for jewellery and valued iron as tips for their spears; both metals probably reached the Cape through long-distance trade with Bantu-speaking peoples in the interior. Khoikhoi also traded dagga (marijuana). Longstanding demand for these three goods would form the basis of trade with European mariners, particularly the English and the Dutch, who began to call regularly at Table Bay on their way to and from Asia in the 1590s.

At first Khoikhoi were willing to trade large quantities of cattle and sheep desperately needed by hungry European sailors. In return they received small quantities of iron, copper and tobacco (apparently used as a mild dagga substitute). However, they rapidly learned that Europeans valued cattle far more than metal trinkets and tobacco; the price of livestock in Table Bay accordingly rose steadily, prompting some European sailors to resort to outright theft. In the long history of spasmodic trade and conflict at Table Bay, enormous opportunities presented themselves to those Khoikhoi who could master European languages. Two of these – Harry and Doman (see box on page 51) – would play central roles in the politics of the new settlement Jan van Riebeeck founded in 1652.

OPPOSITE: *Three illustrations of Khoikhoi. The Khoikhoi were descendants of hunter-gatherers who had acquired livestock centuries earlier and expanded with their pastoral economy throughout southern Africa. To the east they were probably absorbed into Bantu-speaking societies over the centuries. They also lived near the San and sometimes joined the San when they lost their livestock, reverting to hunting and gathering.*

ABOVE AND LEFT: *The ability of the San to sustain themselves was challenged by the southward migration of Khoikhoi herders into the western part of southern Africa in the past 2 000 years. While some San groups attacked the Khoikhoi, others lived peacefully on the fringes of Khoikhoi societies. The boundary between Khoikhoi and San became increasingly unclear.*

BELOW: *Pot from KwaZulu-Natal in the Kalundu Tradition, dating to the 600–700s. The decoration consists of a band on the rim (much of it broken away), multiple bands in the neck and pendant triangles on the shoulder. It is an example of the most complex decoration of this period. Here the potter gave the triangles special emphasis by scraping away clay so that they stood proud of the surface.*

The origin of farming in South Africa

African farmers first settled in what is now South Africa about 1 700 years ago, bringing a new way of life to the southern reaches of the continent. Farming was originally developed by their ancestors in the vicinity of modern Cameroon and Nigeria, between 2 000 and 4 000 years ago. From there, people spread eastwards and southwards, skirting the tropical forest, which did not provide the right environment for their crops and animals. Their movement was probably driven at least in part by a search for new agricultural lands and iron-ore sources. Farming communities reached what is now northern Angola and East Africa by the early centuries of the first millennium AD. From there people continued to spread southwards into savanna environments with good grazing, arable soils and adequate rainfall for crops such as sorghum, millets, and various legumes and cucurbits.

This section deals with African farmers in South Africa, from their first settlement through to 1800. For space reasons, it excludes discussion of their interaction with hunter-gatherers, although there is much evidence for this. Written reports of African farming life appear only after 1500. For the most part, therefore, their history must be elucidated by archaeological investigation: indeed, there can be no South African history without archaeology.

Pottery of the Kwale Branch style shows that the first farmers in South Africa were descended from people who had lived in East Africa. They settled in the eastern parts of the subcontinent from around 280; sites are recorded in southeast Zimbabwe, near Tzaneen, in the Kruger National Park and in Swaziland and Mozambique. By 400, they had spread south into the coastal parts of KwaZulu-Natal, reaching the middle South Coast.

Other farmers, descended from people who had moved from West Africa into Angola, settled in South Africa from around 550. These people can be identified by Kalundu Tradition pottery. All early Kalundu Tradition sites in South Africa contain evidence, on the pottery, of interaction with Kwale Branch people. Merged styles and borrowed decorative elements occur in varying degrees. This interaction most likely included marriages. We do not yet know the implications of this for the evolution of language.

Four distinct ceramic style clusters evolved out of Kalundu-Kwale interactions. By the late 700s, the makers of these four clusters had spread into bushveld environments to the southernmost limits of the summer rainfall region, near modern East London. The Kalundu pottery style dominates in all four clusters and it is tempting to accept that this signifies a domination of the Kalundu language. The emergence of the four style clusters and their subsequent diverging history suggests a linguistic differentiation that sharpened through time.

As a rule, farmers selected river- or lakeside locations for settlement. Sites can be as much as five to ten hectares in area, frequently with dense concentrations of artifactual remains. Many have evidence of long or multiple occupations. The surrounding bushveld provided wood for industrial and domestic use and offered year-round sweet grazing, while farmers in some areas probably exploited the summer grazing potential of grasslands on the higher ground above the valleys. Crops included bulrush millet, finger millet and sorghum. Evidence from KwaZulu-Natal and elsewhere in southern Africa indicates that pulses (Bambara groundnuts and cow peas) and cucurbits (African melons and gourds) were also cultivated. Wild plants were also exploited for food; carbonised marula seeds, for instance, are common on several sites.

For meat, communities were heavily dependent on domestic cattle, sheep and goats, while chickens probably supplied an occasional meal. Hunting was generally of limited dietary significance; people hunted primates, carnivores, various ungulates, larger mammals such as elephant and hippopotamus, and smaller mammals like pangolin, water mongoose and hare for dietary interest, ritual and social requirements, and simple recreation. Hunting was more important in areas with poor grazing; people living in what is now the Kruger National Park focused on large, herd animals and at only a single first millennium AD site did the contribution of domestic meat equal that of hunted meat. Livestock in this area was most likely retained for social use – in exchange relationships, for instance.

Rivers were exploited only rarely for food, but people within reach of the coast made use of resources in the intertidal and near-shore zone. For example, sites 25 kilometres inland of modern Durban contained marine fish and shellfish remains. Harvesting trips to the coast would most likely have been timed to coincide with spring low tides. On the shore, the opposite end of the harvesting cycle is preserved in middens (refuse heaps) containing shellfish remains, ceramics, hearths and fire-stones. The extent to which inland visitors to the coast actively fished is unknown; perhaps they acquired fish from people in the coastal belt who were practised in the exploitation of marine and estuarine resources. The species identified include those easily trapped in estuaries, and black and white musselcrackers – landed today with some difficulty using lines off rocky promontories.

Settlement organisation and society

For some years now, archaeological research has focused on understanding how these various technical aspects of early farming were integrated into a particular way of life. To do this, archaeologists examined settlement organisation. A relationship between social and settlement organisation exists throughout the world. For African farmers in South Africa there is, firstly, an underlying regularity in the way in which traditional homesteads are organised. Secondly, complex relations exist between the spatial code in the homestead (how it is organised) and other symbolic codes. In other words, traditional settlement patterns reflect and make statements about, for example, the roles of men and women, differential control of resources, kinship relations, social hierarchies, and the relationship with the ancestral world.

Archaeologists have captured the essence of homestead organisation in an idealised model called the Central Cattle Pattern. In this pattern, wives live in houses arranged in ranked order around a central area containing cattle pens and a court. Each wife stores grain from her fields in granaries in the courtyard of her house, but grain controlled by the homestead head is stored in the central area. Ceremonies such as weddings take place in the central area and important people are buried there, usually in or close to the cattle pen. These are generally men related by blood to the homestead head, though this status can be extended to other deceased family members (in the case of political leaders, for example). The central area is a male area, where men gather and do men's work; access by women and their movement within it is controlled. By contrast, the residential zone is associated with women. Men, of course, sleep and act in the residential zone, and houses are typically divided internally on gender lines, but this does not change its association.

Central Cattle Pattern homesteads are built only by Eastern Bantu speakers who are patrilineal (descent is through the father), have hereditary male leadership and a preference for bridewealth in cattle, and hold particular beliefs about the role of ancestors in daily life. Thus, the presence of the pattern today and in the archaeological past indicates the presence of people with these interrelated cultural attributes. Since archaeological research shows that the Central Cattle Pattern existed among both Kwale Branch and Kalundu Tradition people, so must the associated gender, kinship and power relations have existed. To argue for similarity at this deep cultural level between the present and the past does not deny history, as some scholars might think. Instead, it provides a context within which people made history.

The Central Cattle Pattern also provides a context for the interpretation of enigmatic

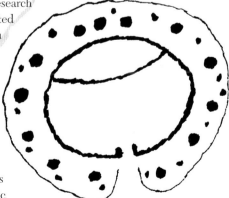

ABOVE: *A pair of partially excavated iron furnaces from the Thukela valley, KwaZulu-Natal, probably dating to the 1700s. The furnaces belonged to ironworkers of a Dlamini clan who traded iron hoes, spears and axes for livestock and food from neighbouring grassland areas, including the Free State highveld.*

LEFT: *A rock engraving near Muden, KwaZulu-Natal, showing a homestead with a Central Cattle Pattern layout. The cattle pen is in the centre, surrounded by houses (the larger dots), granaries (the smaller dots) and a fence.*

remains from the first millennium AD. The 800s site of Ndondondwane in the Thukela valley yielded the remains of at least four hollow ceramic 'heads', with crocodilian 'beaks' or snouts and bulging eyes. Some are large enough to have been worn by a person, and this was possibly their purpose.

The artifacts bring to mind the extraordinary Lydenburg heads, now also shown to date to the 800s rather than 500 as previously believed. Ray Inskeep and Tim Maggs noted that when new, 'with fresh white slip, or paint and glittering specularite, [the Lydenburg heads] must have been dramatic objects to behold'. Details of the sculpted mouths on four of the seven heads link them strongly to rites of passage. These contain evenly spaced peg-like teeth, separated into two groups by a gap in front. The gap probably represents dental mutilation suffered by young people in their teenage years, which served to mark them indelibly as adults. Human skeletal remains show that the lower four and two central upper incisors were extracted, and the upper lateral incisors and neighbouring canines were chipped to create rough points. This representation of the operation, and the context of the Ndondondwane heads, suggests that these remarkable artifacts were part of the initiation paraphernalia used in premarital schools held in the central part of the settlement.

Some sites have yielded broken ceramic figurines of human females, with featureless heads and stubby limbs, prominent navels and protruding buttocks, or a combination of these features. Some have rows of impressions and incised lines possibly representing scarification, other marks seem to represent genitalia. Available data show that the central court midden was a common, but not the only, place of discard. It would seem that the figurines were deliberately broken, which is a practice typically associated with rites of passage – the breakage symbolises an irreversible change in an individual's status. Perhaps the figurines were used as props in lessons where young people learnt proper adult behaviour.

Generally, ceramic figurines are few in number, but this is not the case at the 900s site of Schroda in the Limpopo valley. Here, a single excavation unit yielded over 2 000 fragments. As on other sites, the Schroda figurines occurred in two contexts. A particular stylised female form was widely distributed on the site. These were probably fertility 'dolls' kept by girls and women. Others were concentrated in the central area, close to the cattle pen. These include anthropomorphic figures, non-domestic and fantasy animals (including birds), and phallic shapes, all made of coarse clay, as well as domestic animals and phalli, made of fine clay.

It is worth noting that today it is the responsibility of chiefs to convene communal rites of passage such as premarital schools. Given the evidence for the Central Cattle Pattern and its associated relations of authority, it is probable that this was also the case

in the first millennium AD. This would indicate that the sites of Ndondondwane, Lydenburg and Schroda represent the settlements of chiefs. In the Schroda case, the figurines were probably used in premarital schools for girls.

The Shashe-Limpopo basin and the origin of the Zimbabwe Culture

Around 900, Zhizo farmers living in what is now Zimbabwe moved into the Shashe-Limpopo basin where modern South Africa, Zimbabwe and Botswana meet. By this time Swahili, Arabic, Indian and Indonesian merchants involved in the Indian Ocean trade system had begun to show an interest in the resources of the Sofalan hinterland, that is, the country inland of the Mozambican coast. These resources included ivory, iron and gold.

The Zhizo move was probably driven by a desire to take advantage of the growing trade. At that time the Limpopo valley was too arid for regularly successful agriculture, but it did support herds of elephants. Indeed, most Zhizo sites in the basin are situated on high ground away from the more arable soils where the elephants would have roamed. The Zhizo chief most likely lived at a large site known today as Schroda, which probably housed up to 500 people and contains substantial quantities of ivory. Other remains include glass beads, cowrie shells and the remains of carnivores, possibly hunted to obtain pelts for export. Schroda was most probably a point of export of trade materials to the coast in the vicinity of Vilanculos Bay, and from there to distant lands. In return, Zhizo people received glass beads, cloth and other exotica.

The wide distribution of Zhizo glass beads in southern Africa indicates that Zhizo people used trade goods to acquire both export materials and agricultural produce to supplement their own farming efforts. Intriguingly, Zhizo glass beads do not occur in great numbers in Swahili sites farther north along the east African coast. It seems likely that the key trading partners of the Limpopo Zhizo were Indonesians and Madagascans of Indonesian descent, rather than traders using the monsoonal wind system that facilitated trade between Africa, Arabia and India. Indonesian merchants could have sailed directly from southeast Asia to Madagascar and the Africa coast in about a month using the equatorial trade winds, and a variety of data suggests that they did so.

Schroda's burgeoning wealth attracted the attention of Kalundu people further south, who moved north around 1000 and took control of the region. This movement is archaeologically recognisable from the appearance of Kalundu ceramics throughout the Shashe-Limpopo basin. These people established a capital at a site we call K2, which at its largest housed up to 1 500 people. In the following 200 years, K2 leaders accumulated enormous

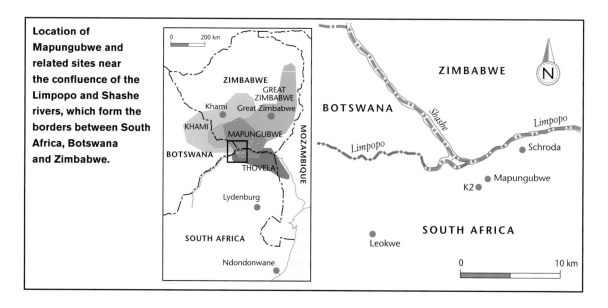

Location of Mapungubwe and related sites near the confluence of the Limpopo and Shashe rivers, which form the borders between South Africa, Botswana and Zimbabwe.

BELOW: *An artist's impression of Mapungubwe in the thirteenth century AD. It shows the central hill, where only the royal family lived, and the homes of commoners on the southern terrace below. The layout of the town is quite different from K2, which was the capital between 1000 and 1200. K2 initially had a central cattle pen and court, with houses surrounding them. From around 1150, cattle were penned elsewhere and the central cattle pen was eventually covered by the growing court midden.*

wealth in the form of trade goods, and changed the way in which wealth was distributed in society. In contrast to the wide dispersal of trade goods in Zhizo times, K2 leaders introduced a tight control on trade goods, so that in their imported form they were largely retained by the elite. Local specialists, for example, melted and recast imported glass beads into larger 'garden rollers' and it is these that were dispersed through trade and social networks in the interior. The extent of their distribution shows that K2 was at the centre of an enormous sphere of interaction.

Control of the trade allowed K2 leaders and their associates to accumulate wealth different from traditional forms such as cattle. However, wealth in trade goods would certainly have been complemented by wealth in cattle, which would have been consistent with their status in society and allowed them to participate in conventional exchange relationships. In time, the leaders probably came to possess virtually all the cattle in the chiefdom. The archaeological evidence shows that around 1150, the central cattle pen at K2 fell into dis-

use and was covered over by the growing court midden. In other words, the organisation of space at K2 was altered so that it no longer conformed to the Central Cattle Pattern. This probably indicates that cattle became the exclusive property of the elite; that ordinary people, commoners, no longer had access to power through the accumulation of cattle. The K2 elite had created a separate, royal category for themselves: class distinction had evolved.

The success of the K2 elite was aided by an improvement in the climate, which permitted an intensification of agricultural production in the basin and provided critical support for a rapidly growing population. Further, a particular combination of riverine and topographical features in the basin allowed for floodplain agriculture, at least in years of high rainfall. In this sense, the Limpopo was the Nile of South Africa. Also, the increased complexity of K2 society was reflected in a more complex management of the land and other resources. Specialists focused on crop production on the lands either side of the river (by now the elephants had been driven away!), or on management of livestock, or on pottery or garden roller bead production. Among these specialists were descendents of the original Zhizo people. While most had been driven westward by the Kalundu takeover, those who stayed behind retained their own identity within the dominant K2 polity. Their distinctiveness was perhaps possible because K2 people regarded them as 'First People', with a special connection to the land. As such the Zhizo descendents seem to have become specialists in crafts, cattle herding and ritual. First People status, however, would have excluded them from political power; rather, it would more likely have been a resource exploited and manipulated by the K2 leadership.

The Mapungubwe period

Around 1220 a new capital was established at Mapungubwe, about a kilometre from K2. It is likely that the move was prompted partly by what must have been an increasingly disturbing contradiction between the spatial code at K2, albeit altered by the removal of cattle from the centre, and the new form of social organisation – a settlement built for a ranked society was not appropriate for one with class distinction.

The king moved his residence to the top of Mapungubwe hill to express spatially his separation from his subjects. Also, this allowed him to associate more directly with the symbolic significance of rainmaking (*see box*).

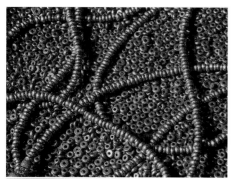

TOP: *Large quantities of gold beads were excavated from three royal burial sites on Mapungubwe hill.*

BOTTOM: *The 'board' game known today as* mankala *or* morabaraba *has been played in Africa for many hundreds of years – as this example found on Mapungubwe hill shows. Small pebbles are placed in the rows of hollows made in the rock; players move them around according to the rules of the game. The game was possibly introduced to Africa from Indonesia. Versions of this game are still played to this day throughout Africa, typically by men.*

While the king and his wives and some attendants lived on the hilltop, the remainder of the population in the new capital lived at the base of Mapungubwe hill, with royal residences on the lower slopes. Some 5 000 people lived there. The front of the capital was demarcated by a long stone wall. Elsewhere, stone walls indicated high status areas. The organisation of buildings, spaces such as the court, passages and walling in the capital show that Mapungubwe was the first of the Zimbabwe Culture centres. After 1300, the Mapungubwe layout was adopted and elaborated by the architects of Great Zimbabwe.

Disaster struck the Mapungubwe kingdom around 1300. Rockfalls from the hill damaged Mapungubwe town and the onset of the Little Ice Age resulted in a drop in agricultural production. The king's subjects possibly concluded that he had lost favour with God. This could have contributed to the break up of the kingdom.

Also, people living to the northeast wrested control of the international trade from Mapungubwe. These people were related to Mapungubwe people and fell within the Mapungubwe sphere of influence, but on ceramic style grounds they spoke another Kalundu dialect. Their leaders claimed royal status and built Great Zimbabwe as their capital. For 150 years, Great Zimbabwe was centre of the most powerful state that had yet existed in southern Africa.

Great Zimbabwe began to lose control of the area it controlled from about 1400, when the importance of gold as an export commodity allowed people living close to gold reserves to challenge the capital's authority. Most important of these was the regional elite based at Khami in southwest Zimbabwe. Ceramic style and wall decoration shows that Khami ancestry led back to Mapungubwe, and it may even be that Khami people felt that their rightful position within the state had been usurped by Great Zimbabwe. Whatever the case, the gold fields they controlled gave them an economic advantage over Great Zimbabwe. By 1450, Khami had become the most important Zimbabwe Culture capital.

We know from pottery style, wall decoration and linguistic data that Great Zimbabwe people spoke Karanga, a Shona dialect. Similarly, we can trace another Shona dialect, Kalanga, back to Khami, Mapungubwe and K2. Given the relationship between ceramic style and language, this indicates that the Kalundu languages were early forms of Shona.

People of the second millennium

In the first few centuries of the second millennium AD, two new pottery styles appear south of the Limpopo River. These represent the ancestors of Nguni and Sotho-Tswana speakers, who today constitute the majority of South Africa's population.

The Nguni

East of the uKhahlamba-Drakensberg, the Kalundu pottery style was replaced around 1030 by a noticeably different style called Blackburn. Since Blackburn gives rise several centuries later to the pottery styles made by Nguni speakers, it must mark the settlement of Nguni speakers in South Africa. Anthropological and linguistic evidence shows that their ancestors lived in the Great Lakes region in East Africa during the first

millennium AD. Their move from East Africa was possibly driven by too dry a climate there during the Medieval Warm Epoch, between 900 and 1290.

The replacement of Kalundu with Blackburn appears abrupt, but relations between the incoming Nguni and the already established Kalundu farming communities are still unresearched. Linguistic data show that modern Zulu contains a residue of the Kalundu language, which appears to have been an ancestral form of Shona. This independent finding is consistent with the Kalundu ceramic evidence associated with the origins of the Zimbabwe Culture.

Nguni sites are different in character from the earlier Kalundu sites, being generally smaller and containing thinner and more sparsely distributed residues. Many represent small homesteads. The earliest are close to the coast. The archaeology shows that people built beehive huts up to 5.5 metres in diameter, kept cattle, gathered mussels and oysters from rocky outcrops on the seashore, and ate fish, which they possibly trapped in estuaries.

From around 1300, Nguni farmers began to move inland into grassland areas, where they built stonewalled homesteads. Grasslands were not ideal environments for African subsistence farmers, though people must already have been familiar with them through earlier use as a summer grazing resource. Settlement there was not simply a case of expanded resource utilisation.

The move coincided with the onset of the Little Ice Age in the late 1200s. Temperatures dropped worldwide: the annual growth rings of a yellowwood tree felled near Howick in 1916 show that growth in the 1300s was slower for longer than at any other time in the rest of the second millennium AD. Agricultural productivity would have dropped too, causing a crisis that very likely provoked violence as farmers competed for diminished resources. That this was so is indicated by the locations of the earliest grassland sites, in defendable positions on steep-sided hilltops or spurs, and often a good distance from water and arable land. Since one of the principal ways of resolving tension was to move away from it, this social stress was most probably the motor that drove Nguni farmers into the grasslands and forced them to build in less-than-ideal places.

Some farmers crossed the escarpment and settled in the 1400s and 1500s on grasslands deep in the interior, north and south of the Vaal River. These were the Fokeng. Although a Sotho-speaking group in historical times, new archaeological research suggests that they were originally Nguni. Distinct from other Sotho-Tswana groups, the Fokeng have their origin site at Ntsuanatsatsi hill in the northeast of today's Free State, and their ceramics are related to the Blackburn style of the Nguni. Fokeng distinctiveness is also suggested by the missionary Ellenberger's claim that the Fokeng dialect, customs and dress were adopted by the Sotho-speaking Kwena, who moved south of the Vaal River perhaps around the mid-1600s.

Kwena oral traditions suggest that they merged with the Fokeng early on at the place of origin, Ntsuanatsatsi, though this is not detectable in the ceramics. These traditions probably represent Kwena efforts to legitimise their occupation of Fokeng lands. By the

TOP LEFT: *Stone walls built between 1300 and 1650 by Nguni speakers in what was once grasslands, KwaZulu-Natal.*

TOP RIGHT: *These stone walls once made up a set of livestock enclosures in the centre of an Nguni homestead near modern Babanango in KwaZulu-Natal. This homestead was part of a Khumalo chiefdom in the late 1700s.*

OPPOSITE: *This gold rhinoceros lay for 700 years in a royal grave on Mapungubwe hill before it was unearthed in 1933. It is the most widely recognised of the gold artifacts found in southern Africa and the only complete animal. (Many fragments of gold-plated figurines were found, but no other complete animal.)*
The rhinoceros is just over fifteen centimetres long. Its body was a wooden core covered by two sheets of gold foil held in place by minute gold nails. The tail is solid gold, the horn gold plate and the eyes are made of rounded nails. It can be seen in the Mapungubwe museum in Pretoria.
South Africa has adopted the gold rhino as the symbol of the Order of Mapungubwe, which the government awards for exceptional achievement. The first recipient was Nelson Mandela.

TOP LEFT: *The remains of the floor of a house built in the 1500–1600s by Western Sotho-Tswana people near modern Thabazimbi, Limpopo. In the middle of the floor is a hollow used as a hearth; right behind it is a raised area for storage.*

MIDDLE: *This is what a cooking enclosure would have looked like between 1700 and 1840. This one has been reconstructed on a Western Sotho-Tswana site at Suikerbosrand in Gauteng.*

RIGHT: *A close-up of a stone wall at Molokwane in North West Province, still standing from the time it was built by people of a Kwena chiefdom (a Western Sotho-Tswana group) in the late 1700s or early 1800s.*

1900s, the Free State Fokeng were 'people of the dew', scattered and apparently without political ambition, but respected as First People.

Archaeological remains in KwaZulu-Natal dating to between 1300 and 1650 include hut floors, granary platforms, grindstones and livestock remains. These remains are consistent with homestead descriptions from Portuguese shipwreck survivors in the 1500s: 'a few houses around a kraal, in which there were about a hundred cows and a hundred and twenty very large sheep . . . Here lived an old man with his sons and grandsons.' Among the foods the Portuguese recorded were sour milk, beer, bread and, along the coast, fish.

In the following centuries, social and environmental adversity prompted a series of uncoordinated northwesterly movements by small groups across the escarpment. The Phetla, Polane and Phuti – offshoots of the Zizi of the Thukela basin – crossed the uKhahlamba-Drakensberg from 1600 onwards, in one instance at least, according to tradition, to resolve tension. Nguni-like settlement layouts in the Caledon valley and near modern Winburg in the Free State may be a consequence of these movements. All spoke a form of Sesotho by the 1800s.

North of the Vaal River, Nguni-speakers intruded into areas occupied by Sotho communities, reaching the Waterberg from the early 1600s onwards. Other Nguni communities reached the Mpumalanga escarpment where they became known as Koni (= Nguni in Sotho). Around 1700, the ancestors of the Northern and Southern Ndebele settled north of the Vaal River. This movement coincided with the peak of the Little Ice Age, which caused harsh climatic conditions on a worldwide scale. Differences in the expression of homestead layout and ancestry claims link Northern and Southern Ndebele respectively to origins in northern KwaZulu-Natal and the Thukela basin. As a consequence of movements and interaction, various Nguni communities became 'Sotho-ised' or heavily influenced by the Venda. Others retained an Nguni identity.

In the 1700s, international trade grew in significance as a social force. Control of trade wealth was a key factor in the development of large, centralised Northern Nguni polities, just as it had been 800 years earlier in the Limpopo valley.

The Sotho-Tswana

The first pottery in South Africa associated with the Sotho-Tswana is called Icon and dates to between 1300 and 1500. As with the Nguni, anthropological and linguistic data suggest an East African origin for Sotho-Tswana speakers, though in this case in what is now Tanzania. The earliest Sotho-Tswana were concentrated in the northern part of South Africa. By 1500 they had expanded to the south and west and separated into three distinct clusters, defined in terms of ceramic style.

There is a close correspondence between these ceramic style clusters and separate branches of the Sotho-Tswana. Thus, the Western Sotho-Tswana cluster, north of the

Waterberg and west to the Limpopo, is associated with the Hurutshe and Kwena branch, while the Southwestern cluster, in the Magaliesberg and south to the Vaal, is linked to the Rolong and Tlhaping branch. A Northwestern cluster occurs in Botswana and northwest South Africa, but its more recent history is currently unknown. The Southern Sotho-Tswana cluster, associated with the Fokeng, has an Nguni origin. Since each Sotho-Tswana branch claims a separate origin, represented by these ceramic clusters, the Icon phase of Sotho-Tswana settlement in South Africa is beyond oral tradition.

Fokeng communities expanded north, west and southwards from the Ntsuanatsatsi area. They reached the edges of the Caledon valley in the 1600s, where the Phetla had already settled. North of the Vaal they made contact with Southwestern and then Western Sotho-Tswana folk. In the Waterberg in the 1600s, conflict over limited resources seems to have provoked discord, in this case between Nguni speakers and mixed groups of Fokeng and Western Sotho-Tswana people. Sometime before 1700, some Western Sotho-Tswana people, including Kwena communities, moved south across the Vaal, into the Fokeng area. As a result of this contact and acculturation, the Fokeng became Sotho and, in the Free State, all but vanished. In turn, Western and Southwestern groups in the 1700s adopted building in stone from the Fokeng. People of each cluster built distinctive stonewalled settlements, which presumably reflected the details of their earlier settlements of wood and thatch. The variously organised settlements, like ceramics, allow archaeologists to trace movement and interaction across the landscape. What is clear is that pulses of settlement shifts and conflict seem to have been at least partly a response to climatic flux during the Little Ice Age. For instance, an improved climate after 1700 made it possible for Southwestern Sotho-Tswana to settle south of the Vaal River, on the western edges of Fokeng-Kwena territory.

From 1750 onwards, intensifying trade and more intrusive colonial expansion increasingly affected Sotho-Tswana societies. Competition and conflict for resources eventually forced some chiefdoms to 'implode' into huge defensive settlements such as Molokwane, Kaditshwene and Dithakong, which in the early 1800s housed 10 000 people or more.

Venda origins

Around 1300, Mapungubwe leaders and their followers established themselves on the northern side of the Soutpansberg range. The mountains are rich in metal ores, good soils and pasture, and at that time would have harboured abundant game, particularly elephant. These resources clearly attracted Mapungubwe people, who remained there after the collapse of the Mapungubwe state. Related Kalundu Tradition people lived to the south of the mountains. There is archaeological evidence of interaction between north and south, but the mountains functioned as a relatively rigid ethnic and economic boundary separating the Mapungubwe elite from communities on the southern slopes. The sharpness of this boundary was maintained after early Sotho-Tswana people settled in the south in about

1350 where they seem to have absorbed the established Kalundu people after a fairly brief period.

Khami-style stonewalled palaces were built in the Soutpansberg from 1450. These sites could represent an expansion southwards of the Khami state, or Khami leaders seeking independence from the main Khami state. Whatever the case, the area fell under the control of Khami dynasties, which replaced the Mapungubwe elite. The Khami leaders re-established links with Indian Ocean traders, exporting ivory, gold and copper. The mountain boundary between Shona and Sotho became more permeable as Sotho speakers participated increasingly in the trade, and Sotho sites were established on the northern side. This interaction must have included marriage between Kalanga and Sotho speakers, and in the 1500s it resulted in a merged Kalanga/Sotho ceramic style called Tavhatshena. This style marks the emergence of the Venda language: linguistically, Venda has a Kalanga-like grammar and phonology and a Sotho-like vocabulary. Interestingly, Venda emerged on 'commoner' Sotho sites, but the distribution of the Venda pottery style shows that it was widely spoken in the Soutpansberg by 1650.

The Khami area in southwest Zimbabwe suffered a civil war in the mid-1600s out of which several smaller scale leaders emerged. The famous Rozwi leader Changamire Dombolakonachingwango conquered and reunited them in about 1680. Following a succession dispute after his death in the 1690s, the Singo split from the Rozwi and invaded and unified Venda polities in the Soutpansberg. They established a capital at Dzata, built of dark blue stone, and became Venda by adopting the language of their conquered subjects.

The Singo maintained the external trade, but changing dynamics within the external trade routes from around 1700 gradually reduced Singo control of the east coast trade. In

THE INDIAN OCEAN TRADING SYSTEM

Exchange relationships were an integral component of life from the first settlement of African farmers. The key exchange was wives for cattle. Exchange for material goods was less vital and, in the first millennium AD, often difficult to detect because the savanna areas in which people lived provided a relatively common set of resources. Nevertheless, it is sometimes clear that material goods (and probably other items, long since perished) were carried across space and social boundaries.

Once people settled in the grasslands, they were confronted by a more uneven distribution of resources. They were forced to build in stone, use dung as fuel and acquire hoes and other metal items from wood- and ore-rich areas. Critical exchange relationships were established, stretched and strengthened over a considerably greater area by this resource unevenness, encouraging interaction across social boundaries but also providing a means of exploitation.

Trade with foreign merchants had the same impact, but added new resources of value (gold, tin, cloth, beads, brass) and altered perceptions of old ones (ivory, cattle,

people). South Africa's first point of integration into foreign trade networks was the Limpopo valley and seems mainly to have been with Indonesians. This suffered a setback after an attack by Indonesian bandits on Sofalan trading stations in 945–46. Swahili, Arabic and Indian traders, important trading partners in K2 and Mapungubwe, seem to have played a key role in its revival. As the distribution of garden roller beads and other trade goods indicates, Schroda, K2 and Mapungubwe were the centres of extensive internal exchange networks. Iron, for instance, was traded into the Limpopo valley from ore-rich areas in modern Botswana.

With the shift in emphasis from Mapungubwe to Great Zimbabwe in about 1300, the impact of foreign trade on people south of the Limpopo diminished considerably. But when Khami succeeded Great Zimbabwe some 150 years later, South Africa was reconnected to the international trade system. Khami leaders in the Soutpansberg actively pursued coastal markets for their ivory, copper and gold. From the Rooiberg area further west, miners and metallurgists produced tin for the Khami state.

Portuguese traders penetrated the Indian Ocean trade system after 1500. Their main focus in southern Africa was on the Shona area, but they also brought international trade to the hinterland of Delagoa Bay. Imports made an early impact. Archaeological and documentary evidence suggests that in the 1590s, Nguni farmers in the Thukela valley, some 400 kilometres south of Delagoa Bay, had both knowledge of and a desire for cloth and imported brass. At this time also, the Portuguese noted variation in the size of political entities south of Delagoa Bay. It seems possible that even the then limited trade at the bay was stimulating growth in chiefdom size. Deep in the interior in the Thabazimbi area, new research shows that Western Sotho-Tswana people were cultivating maize by the 1600s. Maize is an American crop brought to Africa by the Portuguese. Its early cultivation in the Thabazimbi area was most certainly related to the trade in tin. Later, maize was more widely cultivated in the east of South Africa, where its failure in drought years around 1800 contributed to political and social turmoil.

particular, the growing importance of Delagoa Bay and Natal Bay as points of access to the interior allowed other people to control and exploit trade wealth. The result was the fragmentation of the Venda polity.

The origin of black political communities

The population movements that took place in southern Africa over many hundreds of years were usually described in old-style histories as 'Bantu migrations', and were depicted by thick arrows on maps indicating the alleged lines of march. Migration in the sense of deliberately motivated change of location did of course occur, but it cannot be accepted as a suitable description of the process whereby most of southern Africa became populated by people speaking related Bantu languages.

Migration implies rapid movement, whereas archaeological evidence shows that the dispersion of Bantu-speaking peoples within southern Africa occurred over a period of centuries. It also implies nomadism and rootless wandering, which is contrary to the deep attachment felt by Iron Age peoples for their home places. Finally, migration implies exclusive occupation of a single place by a defined group of people, whereas in southern Africa the dispersion of some peoples did not necessarily imply the ejection of others.

Historical perspective reveals two distinct and contradictory processes that shaped the early history of Iron Age southern Africa — segmentation and differentiation.

Segmentation is the name given to the process whereby a group subdivided into two or more groups. It occurred in a domestic unit when the sons of a household grew up and left to establish their own households elsewhere. Scarcity of natural resources led to dispersed settlements, linked by ties of kinship and sentiment to the parent household. Segmentation of this sort was thus a continuous natural process, a consequence of the eternal human cycle of reproduction and maturation.

Differentiation is the name given to the process whereby certain individuals came to secure political, social and economic power over others.

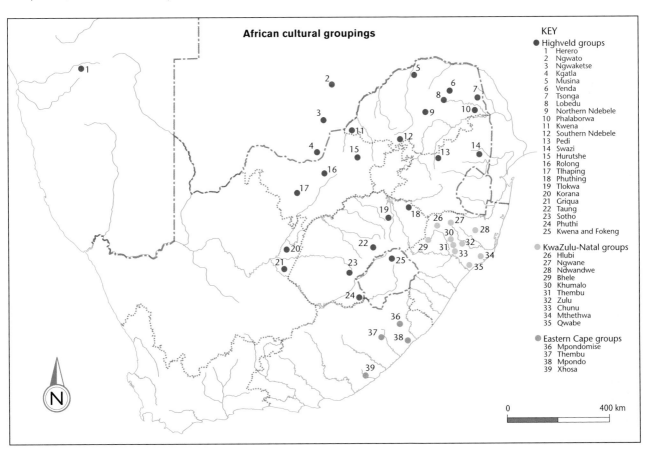

African cultural groupings

KEY

● Highveld groups
1 Herero
2 Ngwato
3 Ngwaketse
4 Kgatla
5 Musina
6 Venda
7 Tsonga
8 Lobedu
9 Northern Ndebele
10 Phalaborwa
11 Kwena
12 Southern Ndebele
13 Pedi
14 Swazi
15 Hurutshe
16 Rolong
17 Tlhaping
18 Phuthing
19 Tlokwa
20 Korana
21 Griqua
22 Taung
23 Sotho
24 Phuthi
25 Kwena and Fokeng

● KwaZulu-Natal groups
26 Hlubi
27 Ngwane
28 Ndwandwe
29 Bhele
30 Khumalo
31 Thembu
32 Zulu
33 Chunu
34 Mthethwa
35 Qwabe

● Eastern Cape groups
36 Mpondomise
37 Thembu
38 Mpondo
39 Xhosa

0   400 km

TOP: *Related homesteads formed a lineage which would later only be recognisable by their common names, common praises or their animal totems. This was the totem of Mujaji (or Modjadji), the Rain Queen of the Lobedu*

BELOW: *Bhaca women sing and dance at the First Fruits ceremony, as depicted by the artist Gerard Bhengu.*

Segmentation

Segmentation implies the separation of groups related by descent from a common ancestor or origin. This breaking away (or fission) might occur due to the following circumstances:

- When the sons of a household established their own households. Often this was effected by several men from the same age-sets (in Nguni languages *amabutho*, in Sotho *swana mephato*) who followed powerful men or younger chiefs to set up new villages.
- When environmental decline and/or overpopulation, often coupled with a scarcity of natural resources, forced people to find new arable land, water resources or pastures.
- When there was a response to trading opportunities and the need to control trading routes.
- When the need for safety provided the impetus for moving away from long-established settlements.

Territorial expansion was more often by means of a slow diffusion of small communities rather than a rapid 'migration' of large numbers of people. Human movement did not always imply movement onto virgin land. Frequently other people occupied such land, or had done so in former times.

Thus segmentation was accompanied by incorporation of weaker groups, formation of alliances, or establishment of relations of patronage between incoming and existing communities. The ability to store wealth in the form of cattle provided an effective means of attracting support – more so than establishing dominance through superior military power. This did not mean, however, that armed conflict did not occur. Raiding for cattle or women was a frequent phenomenon. Cruel or autocratic leaders were often forced out of power.

Differentiation

Differentiation describes the way certain individuals came to exercise political, social and economic control over others. This gave rise to three social categories in pre-colonial societies – chiefs, commoners and clients.

The basic social and economic unit in almost all southern African societies is that of the homestead. Except in a few exceptional cases, such as advanced senility, the head of the homestead was the eldest male. He enjoyed a position of considerable power, including authority in the spheres of religion, economy and social relations. His authority was derived from this genealogical seniority, and the status of the other males in the homestead also depended on their genealogical rank. Like children, women had rights and obligations, but were regarded as perpetual minors and excluded from a formal voice in homestead affairs. They could not inherit or pass on significant material goods. Chiefs replicated the functions of the homestead head on a larger scale.

The economic power and control of the homestead head derived from the fact that he inherited the accumulated wealth of his forebears. The allocation of fields for cultivation and cattle was in his hands. He controlled social relations such as marriage through the possession of bride-wealth cattle.

A number of related homesteads formed a lineage, which would assist and advise each other when circumstances required. After several generations these ties may only have been recognisable by a common set of names, praises or – particularly among the Sotho-Tswana – a totemic animal. These common observances provided for the ties of clanship. The unity of the various clans differed. Among some clans, ties were quite strong – for example, through the recognition of one individual or family as head or chief; among others ties were diluted through the incorporation of newcomers, strangers or refugees. Thus some clans were controlled by powerful and recognised chiefs, whereas in other clans the leading figures exercised only ritualistic or religious control.

Thus when the chief allocated lands, ordered the harvesting of the first fruits, went to war, or offered sacrifices for victory in war, he was acting for a collective of homestead heads. There was, however, no neat correlation between clanship and territorial occupation.

Through the processes of segmentation and incorporation, no part of South Africa was inhabited by a single pure clan or chiefdom. Consequently, chieftainship derived from two imperatives; out of loyalty to the original clan of a locality, and out of the need to take collective action with unrelated groups when necessary, for example in defence, rainmaking and legal arbitration.

The chief's position as sole owner of land, people and property contained within it the seeds of hierarchy and domination. Chiefs were richer than commoners and used their positions of power to secure more wealth. They could squeeze their followers for more tribute or labour obligations. They could strip commoners of hard-earned riches through manipulation of witchcraft accusations and inheritance laws.

Given such authoritarian stature, why were chiefs not cast off as tyrants? They were of course required to adjudicate laws, to protect the community in times of trouble, to provide food in times of famine and to invoke the spirits of the ancestors. Such chiefs needed to be politically astute if not downright cunning. Nevertheless, they were forced to recognise certain boundaries to their actions, but were no more immune than others to the pressures of brotherly rivalry.

All chiefs before the advent of standing armies in 1800 depended on the voluntary compliance of their subjects and needed to keep followers contented. A wise chief rarely acted against the will of his people, and would generally consult with his people and take the advice of the elders. Many cruel or stingy chiefs were simply abandoned or ousted and replaced by followers.

Clients and clientship

Clients were poor men contracted to work for a chief or rich man for payment in kind. Impoverishment could easily occur in pre-colonial South Africa. A man could lose everything through war, disease or natural calamities. He would then approach a more fortunate individual for cattle on loan. He would receive a portion of the milk of the cattle he tended and rebuild his own herd by keeping some of the calves he reared.

Clientship should therefore not be confused with servitude, as clients were in a transitional state back to economic independence and full membership of the society. Types of servitude did exist, though, particularly in Tswana society, when the status of a client became permanent and was passed on to his descendants. This was known as the *Botlhanka* system.

Regional development and settlement

Earlier historians such as G.M. Theal and G.W. Stow were fascinated by the question of the origins of the Bantu-speaking people. They assumed that this migration occurred in

The Pitso, *or public meeting, of the Tlhaping. In his journal from 1828, George Thompson describes such a meeting deciding to declare war. He says that everybody gathered in an open space, encircled by a grass hedge. Soldiers with their shields and spears formed half of the circle, the other half consisting of women, children and elderly men. After half an hour of dancing, the king pointed his spear in the direction of the enemy and the soldiers answered with a loud hissing 'sss'-sound, showing their approval.*

'waves' of immigrants from East and Central Africa, then diverged to give rise to a distinctive demographic pattern that saw Nguni speakers along the southeastern seaboard and the Sotho-Tswana populating the central interior plateau.

In the early 1930s, A.T. Bryant propounded the view that the Nguni speakers lived in stable and constant clans until the rise of the Zulu. This interpretation dominated the thinking of later historians for nearly half a century. As discussed above, this construction falsely assumes that the migration occurred in distinct ethnic groups, instead as part of a process of gradual segmentation and diffusion.

The Sotho-Tswana from an early stage dominated in the land north of the Vaal River. The Transvaal Ndebele moved to this region around 1700 long after the Sotho-Tswana. The adoption or borrowing of cultural aspects among different ethnic groups testifies to the degree of interaction between them. In the light of this ethnic diversity the search for a 'pure' form of Sotho or Nguni 'culture' or origin is rendered meaningless.

The Sotho-Tswana

The Sotho-Tswana chiefdoms of the inland plateau were the products of a complex interaction between intrusive lineages and resident local groups. Oral tradition mentions both negroid and Khoisan stone age people as the earliest residents of the highveld before the arrival of the first Sotho-Tswana lineages dispersing from the greater Magaliesberg area. The Fokeng, who are today Sotho-speaking, were long believed to be the first Sotho speakers on the highveld and have always been respected by oral historians as the most ancient of the Sotho peoples. Recent archaeological research has suggested, however, that the Fokeng were originally Nguni in culture and dispersed from Ntsuanatsatsi near Frankfort in the present Free State.

Of the Sotho-Tswana lineages originating around the Magaliesberg, the Hurutshe, based in what is today the Rustenburg-Marico district, were apparently the first to become pre-eminent. By 1750, they had become accepted as the 'senior tribe of the Bechuana', and given ritual respect in ceremonies. A rift among the Hurutshe had given rise to the Kwena lineage, which subdivided later to form the Ngwaketse and Ngwato lineages and the Kgatla. A third lineage cluster, the Rolong, emerged. They settled in the Madikwe River region, but were displaced by the Hurutshe in about 1600, and moved south of the Molopo River. Their near relations and occasional subordinates, the Tlhaping, settled slightly to the south, in the region of modern-day Kudumane (Kuruman).

After 1750, attempts were made by a range of subordinate chiefdoms to unshackle themselves from Hurutshe hegemony. Oral records point to increasing conflict among nearly all the chiefdoms in the central/western highveld towards the end of the century, nearly all led by 'warrior' chiefs. The Fokeng under Sekete and Thethe fought first with the Tlokwa and later with the Kgatla ba Kgafela. The Kwena ba Magopa under More were also locked in conflict with the Kgatla. Meanwhile, from their stronghold in the Leolu mountains, the Pedi under Thulare intervened decisively in the affairs of the central highveld, establishing a stronghold. This conflict was the consequence – or

ABOVE: *Ngwato (a Tswana group) bone ornaments as drawn by Andrew Smith.*

OPPOSITE: *Abundant evidence shows that trade spanned southern Africa in precolonial times. One of the earliest trade items was dagga, being smoked here in a group.*

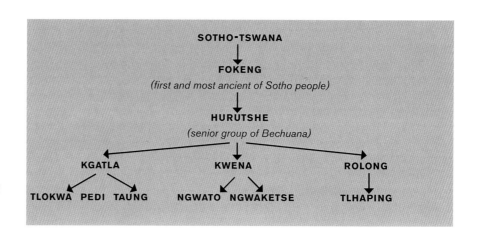

SOTHO-TSWANA

↓

FOKENG
(first and most ancient of Sotho people)

↓

HURUTSHE
(senior group of Bechuana)

KGATLA   **KWENA**   **ROLONG**

TLOKWA PEDI TAUNG   **NGWATO NGWAKETSE**   **TLHAPING**

EARLY TRADE

Reference to Africans as subsistence farmers creates the impression that they had few commercial interests beyond the mealie patch and the cattle kraal. Yet there is abundant evidence of pre-colonial trade routes spanning the subcontinent. The driving forces were the unequal distribution of minerals in southern Africa and the desire for cattle among the metal-working peoples. A demand among the non-agricultural Khoisan for tobacco and dagga also led to a vigorous exchange of goods.

The Hurutshe and Kwena of the Rustenburg-Marico district mined iron and copper, which passed via the 'Briqua' or 'goat-people' (the Tlhaping and Fokeng of the southern highveld) to the Khoi of the Orange River and Great Karoo, and thence to the metal-hungry Xhosa and Thembu of the Eastern Cape. From the northeast the iron and copper mines of Musina (Messina), Venda and Phalaborwa served the eastern Transvaal and trans-Limpopo region. The principal carriers of this trade were the Lemba and Tsonga of Delagoa Bay.

Along the Orange River, the exchange rates were as follows: a heifer was worth eight spears, an axe, an awl, a small bag of tobacco and a small bag of dagga, whereas an ox or a bull was worth only five spears, 'plus all the other things as for a heifer'.

possibly the cause – of an increasing frequency of cattle raids, the seizure of women and captives and competition over trade. The extent of this trade is well documented in the archaeological and historical record. The main trade routes were from Maputo in the east, northwest into the Okavango and central Namibia, and south along the Orange River.

A number of features particular to the Sotho-Tswana stand out. They lived in large towns built largely of stone, some containing up to 15 000 people. The towns were divided into 'wards' with ward heads who exercised autonomous control over local affairs. Cattle were kept at outposts, where they were tended by young men. Women and girls supplied the inhabitants with agricultural products. They were tied into a relentless cycle of labour and were likened by the first missionaries to 'beasts of burden'.

Compared with the Nguni speakers, there was a greater degree of dependence by the Sotho-Tswana chiefs on the ward heads, who acted as a kind of intermediary between chief and subjects. This may account for the important role played by the *Pitso*, or public meeting of household heads, which ratified major decisions.

The Nguni

The earliest Nguni speakers probably lived in numerous small-scale autonomous communities. The coastal belt they occupied had better natural resources than the interior and provided for mixed pastoralism and agriculture. This allowed people to live in more scattered communities where the homestead head reigned supreme. As already noted, though, there were ties through marriage (to outside kinship groups) and through chiefly allegiances to a wider community.

How then did the Nguni speakers become the separate kingdoms of the Zulu, Swazi, Mpondo, Thembu and Xhosa of today? The first thing to understand is that the clearcut

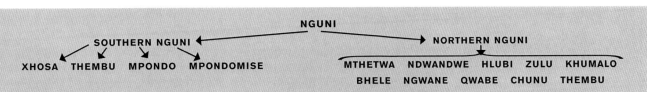

Before 1600 southern Nguni clans began to expand, incorporating neighbouring clans. The Thembu, Mpondo and Mpondomise and Xhosa kingdoms formed and were well established in the 1660s. The majority of southerners never became part of a centralised kingdom, intermarried Khoikhoi and retained circumcision.

These kingdoms established themselves later than the southern Nguni in the 1810s. Most northerners became part of the Zulu kingdom between the Phongolo and Thukela rivers and abolished circumcision. Africans from the Cape Colony were labelled Xhosa even though they were Mpondo or Thembu and people from Natal labelled Zulu even if they were Hlubi or Bhele.

A Rolong man

A Xhosa woman

The Pondo, Somi

A Zulu man

distinction made today between the Xhosa and the Zulu has no basis in culture or history, but arises out of the colonial distinction between the Cape and Natal colonies. Both speak essentially the same language and share essentially the same customs, but the historical experiences at the northern end of the Nguni culture area differed considerably from the historical experiences at the southern end. The majority of northerners became part of the Zulu kingdom, which abolished circumcision. The majority of southerners never became part of any strongly centralised kingdom, intermarried with Khoikhoi and retained circumcision. Later, Africans from the Cape Colony working in Johannesburg were labelled as Xhosa even though they were actually Mpondo or Thembu; Africans from Natal working in Johannesburg were labelled as Zulu, even if they were actually Hlubi or Bhele and their forefathers fought valiantly against Shaka.

The political transformations associated with the name of Shaka, who ruled from 1818 to 1828, eventually saw the Zulu kingdom controlling the territory between the Phongolo and Thukela rivers. The different chiefdoms of that region and beyond were incorporated into the Zulu kingdom. However, developments among the southern Nguni took a different course. For unknown reasons, certain southern Nguni clans began to expand their power some time before 1600, subjecting and incorporating neighbouring clans. Tshawe founded the Xhosa kingdom by defeating the Cirha and Jwarha clans. His descendants expanded the kingdom by settling in new territory and bringing people living there under the control of the amaTshawe.

This process of expansion was still in progress when the Xhosa ran up against the Cape colonists in the 1770s. East of the Kei River, the Hala, Nyawuza and Majole clans carved out the Tyhembu, Mpondo and Mpondomise kingdoms respectively. These kingdoms may pre-date the Xhosa. Certainly all the southern Nguni kingdoms were in place 150 years before the rise of the Mthethwa or Ndwandwe in the 1810s, in present-day KwaZulu-Natal. But though extensive, they were weak. The heirs of the founders were not able to discipline junior chiefs or check rivalries within the royal lineage. Commoners could resist chiefly demands by easily changing allegiances.

The Venda

Until recently, it was thought that the Venda kingdom was Shona in origin and crossed the Limpopo River into South Africa in about 1700 with the migration of the Singo clan (a division of the Changamire Rozwi of Zimbabwe). Recent research shows that a distinctive Venda group with respect to religion, culture, language and social organisation pre-existed the Singo. These early proto-Venda were organised in the state of Thovela, comprising various ethnic groups including the Ngona, the Mbedzi and some pre-Singo Shona groups. They built in stone, mined gold, copper and tin and hunted for ivory, which they traded with the Lemba.

The Singo came to dominate the Venda state through their warrior chief Dimbanyika. His son Popi, attempted to recreate the main features of the Changamire kingdom. He adopted the name Thoho-ya-Ndou (Head of the Elephant) and became the most powerful of Venda rulers. Brotherly rivalries led to the division of the Venda after his death into the house of Ramabulana and that of Tshivase.

The Lobedu and Tsonga

The Lobedu are based north of today's Tzaneen. Dzugudini, the daughter of a Shona chief, is said to have founded the kingdom, but it is possible that a proto-Lobedu community existed before her arrival. There was a period of civil conflict during the reign of King Mugodo some time before 1800, and he was replaced by his daughter Mujaji. After this, the Lobedu were ruled by queens, whose power was based on the role they played in the Lobedu rain cult, and on 'wife exchanges' whereby she allocated wives to different district heads, thus binding them into a complex system of subordination.

The earliest traditions of Tsonga traders place them in the hinterland of Delagoa Bay, and suggest they derived from diverse origins, including Shona and Sotho influences. They are associated with the traditions of the Kwena-Pedi who settled around the bay as early as the seventeenth century. The Portuguese recorded the presence of the large

Tembe kingdom along the coastline and stretching 500 kilometres into the interior. They traded a long distance up the Limpopo and Nkomati rivers, for gold, iron, copper, ivory, horns, cloth and furs.

Their trading partners included the Venda, Sotho and Portuguese. The Maputo lineage had established power at Delagoa Bay by about 1750. By the 1780s, six or seven boat-loads were arriving in Delagoa Bay annually from down the Nkomati and Maputo rivers. Early in the nineteenth century Tsonga traders were reported to be trading as far west as the Hurutshe capital, near modern Zeerust.

The power of the chiefs increases

From about the middle of the eighteenth century, events in southern Africa developed in such a way as to strengthen the hand of the chiefs. Overpopulation made prime eco-logical locations harder to find. Competition for resources became sharper, and com-moners were more willing to subject themselves to those chiefs best able to guarantee their subsistence. Furthermore, the new products traded at Delagoa Bay after 1750 fur-nished the chiefs with new means of patronage and incentives to expand their territory.

These pressures were particularly acute in what is today northern KwaZulu-Natal, leading ultimately to the rise of the Zulu kingdom under Shaka and a period of disper-sion known as the Difaqane or Mfecane (see page 124).

ABOVE: *Mujaji IV, seated on her throne. Since the first Mujaji succeeded her father, King Mugodo, the Lobedu have been ruled by queens.*

OPPOSITE: *Four photographs by German anthropologist Gustav Fritsch, who travelled through South Africa from 1863 to 1866. He wrote about the indigenous people of South Africa and took many detailed portrait photographs of the people he met.*

THE COPPER MINERS OF MUSINA

The following Sotho text by M.F. Mamedi was collected by N. J. Warmelo in the 1930s. It relates the story of how a Tsonga group came to mine copper at Musina.

The Musina people appeared from the east and came to Phalaborwa . . . Then they said: 'Young men, scatter and seek for a place where copper may be found . . .' Then Nkopetsekwa's people found it at Great Musina; they went on and made another mine at Mpedi, after that they made another mine at Small Mpedi, another hill.

The Musina people brought with them hammers and crowbars and bellows. The crowbar was for digging, and was made of a piece of iron inserted into the end of a heavy stick. The bellows were made of a cow hide or the skin of an antelope. They also plaited very long cords of leather which would not break. Then they made a big basket, tied the cords to it, and, getting into it, the sons of Musina went down the shaft. There they mined the copper, by the light of candles made from the leaves of the mokxote tree . . . At that time there was neither girl nor youth nor man nor woman that stayed at home. The girls gathered the leaves of the mephane trees to make the fires . . .

When they were mining the copper, they brought the ore to the surface in the skins of impala, buffalo or gnu. They brought the copper out in the form of stones or dust. The stones they then broke up with ham-mers and put into winnowing baskets. They winnowed this and eliminated the dust, so that only the copper remained, which they put into crucibles and heated up . . .

After the division had been made, each might sell his share . . . but the cattle they did not keep, they slaughtered the animals for the young men who did the hard work and ate meat every day.

CHAPTER TWO

A new society drawn from three continents

The company they kept

By the 1650s the Dutch were the world's leading trading nation and the mighty *Vereenigde Oostindische Compagnie* (VOC) the world's largest trading enterprise. Amsterdam, its home base, was a huge entrepôt for pepper and spices, sugar, tobacco, timber and manufactured articles from across the globe. VOC policies and laws would set in train processes that would profoundly shape the colonial society established at the Cape.

It was predominantly black pepper, supplemented by cloves, nutmeg, cinnamon and mace, which lured the Dutch at the end of the sixteenth century over the dangerous seas to the Far East. These products were found only in a handful of countries, including present-day India, Malaysia and Indonesia. Pepper was used to preserve food at a time when the use of ice had not yet been realised. It was worth more than gold in weight. By the end of the seventeenth century the VOC was importing more than four million pounds of pepper annually, far outstripping other products. In the eighteenth century sugar and coffee from Java would become increasingly important imports.

The first journeys

The discovery of the compass by the end of the thirteenth century made possible long voyages out of sight of land. The adventurous spirit and questing mind of the Renaissance drove the Portuguese to embark on voyages to new worlds in the late fifteenth century. They also sought new riches and unknown profits. The ships sent out by Prince Henry the Navigator in Lisbon reached Guinea on the coast of Africa, and then in 1486 Bartholomew Diaz rounded the Cape.

In July 1497 Vasco da Gama boldly sailed across the Atlantic to avoid the doldrums, then used the west wind to get to the Cape. In St Helena Bay Da Gama's crew traded with some Khoikhoi before sailing round the Cape and landing in Mossel Bay, where they again traded with Khoikhoi. On Christmas day 1497 Da Gama named the coast near the Kei River *Terro do Natal*. In May 1498, Malabar on the west coast of India was reached. Da Gama returned to Portugal with a small cargo of pepper and cinnamon.

Dutch trading houses acted as middlemen for the Portuguese, distributing the merchandise in the North European market. By the end of the sixteenth century this trading system disintegrated. The Portuguese had no answer to English privateers in the southern Atlantic Ocean. The northern provinces of the Netherlands had fought themselves free of the control of Philip of Spain, who also was king of Portugal. In 1585 Philip confiscated all foreign ships in Lisbon, but the Dutch had become a major sea power, able to harass Portuguese and Spanish ships.

As a result of the uncertainty of supply and a rapidly rising demand, the price of pepper shot up. In 1584 Jan Huygen van Linschoten embarked on a voyage to India, publishing a description of the route and a merchant's guide on his return. In 1595 nine Dutch merchants sent Cornelis and Frederik de Houtman on a voyage to the East. They returned in 1597. The Dutch involvement with the East had begun. Soon the need arose for a halfway station where sailors, desperately ill from scurvy, could get fresh fruit and vegetables.

TOP: 'De peper is onder de speseryen een van de grootsten handel in Oost-indien en brengt de Maatschappy groot voordeel toe.' *(Of all the spices, pepper is one of the most important trade goods in East India and is very profitable to the Company too.) From* Nieuhofs Gedenkwaerdige Zee en Lantreize door de voornaemste Landschappen van West en Oost Indien, *published in 1682. The picture shows how pepper grows on a tree.*

OPPOSITE TOP: *It was common practice in European colonies in the Far East, and also at the Cape, for women of high rank, such as this Portuguese lady and her daughters, to be carried in a chair by slaves to the church and social occasions.*

The first multinational corporation

By 1600 several small states in the Indonesian Archipelago were geared towards foreign trade with merchants from China, India and other Asian countries, and also from Europe. To capture this trade, Dutch merchants in 1602 established the *Vereenigde Oostindische Compagnie* (VOC) in Amsterdam as a chartered company. Two years earlier the English East India Company had been founded in London.

When the journal *The Economist* published a 'Millennium Edition' 400 years later, it observed that in their impact on the world, both good and bad, perhaps only the companies of Henry Ford and Bill Gates matched the two East India Companies. The VOC could be called the world's first multinational corporation. During the first decade of the Cape station (1652–1662), 205 ships with 40 200 people on board sailed to the East, while 103 ships with some 13 000 people returned to the Netherlands.

The VOC established itself by following more or less in the footsteps of the Portuguese but aiming to eliminate them as rivals. Although the VOC proclaimed free trade, it practised a monopoly wherever it could. It evicted most of its European rivals from the East, compelling local rulers to grant it exclusive trading rights. Soon it had seized Bantam, the Moluccas, Java and Amboyna.

In 1619 it introduced a regular government under a governor general, presiding over a Council of India, in Jakarta, which it renamed Batavia. The city became the capital of the VOC's Eastern empire. The Company, a sovereign power in its own right according to its 1602 charter, could recruit soldiers, wage war, enter into treaties with other powers and maintain order in the settlements it had founded. Dutchmen in its employ swore fealty both to the Company and the States General in the Netherlands. All Europeans in its settlements were subject both to the laws of the Netherlands and to the regulations framed by the Company.

The VOC paid most of the officials in its empire a measly salary. To compensate for their low pay, many of its staff stole from their employer, embezzling or trading for their own account. Jan van Riebeeck, the man the VOC chose to oversee the establishment of the Cape station, had earlier been fined for private trading and recalled from a post in Japan.

A 'rendezvous' at the Cape

Apart from its strategic value, the settlement at the tip of Africa did not offer much. It had no great staple products, such as rice, sugar, tobacco, wool or timber, which could integrate the colony into the world's trade systems. Beyond its coastal mountains the climate was harsh and the soil mostly poor. Apart from livestock, the prospects for trade with the indigenous Khoikhoi and the San who populated a large part of the subcontinent, were limited. They were much less developed culturally and technologically than the peoples the Dutch had encountered in the East.

Vasco da Gama, captain of the first fleet to travel from Europe around the Cape to the East.

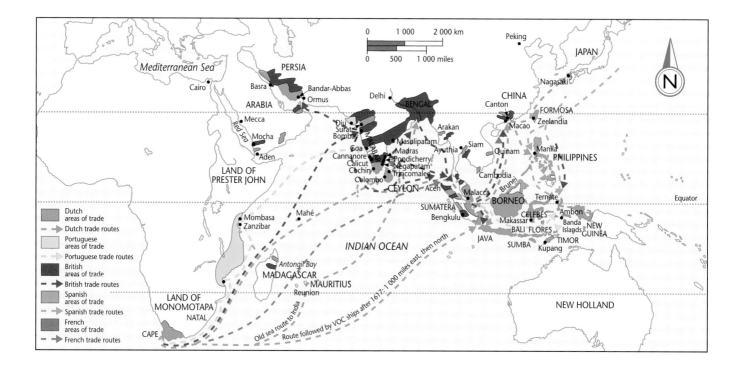

ABOVE: *Areas of trade in the seventeenth century.*

But the Company was never very interested in the hinterland. What counted was that Table Bay, named by Joris van Spilbergen in 1601, and Saldanha Bay were ideal halfway stations to the main destinations of the VOC: the spice archipelago of Java and Sumatra.

In 1650 the VOC's directors, called the *Heren XVII* (Lords Seventeen), decided to establish a 'rendezvous and stronghold' at the Cape. Their objectives were modest. It was to be a refreshment station to victual passing ships with fruit and vegetables from a modest garden and with meat bartered from the Khoisan. It was to exist for the Company's benefit and the interest of the mother country. Its territory was to be kept as confined as possible to save expenses.

In terms of the VOC's instructions the officials would associate amiably with people belonging to the 'wild nations' for the sake of the cattle trade, but otherwise would keep to themselves and their task of making the outpost self-sufficient. The settlement in Table Bay became known as the Cape. The name Cape Town became common only in the next century. It would be largely people from Europe who would settle at the Cape as colonists.

The baggage in their heads

The intellectual baggage in the heads of the first European immigrants was much more important than their clothes and other belongings. Of the external influences that shaped Cape society the most fundamental were the Roman-Dutch law, the Reformed religion, early capitalism, and the laws and practices the VOC had developed in running its colonies in the East.

Two quite different influences had an impact on the Cape. One was the egalitarian tendencies of the Netherlands, the other the 'aristocratic' or hierarchical tendencies emanating from the Dutch possessions in the Far East. When the VOC founded the Cape in 1652 it placed it under the authority of both the directors of the Company in Amsterdam, called the Lords Seventeen, and the Council of India in Batavia. Until 1731, the Cape was effectively governed from Batavia. It was also profoundly influenced by the regulations, practices and attitudes that were imported by officials who spent time there before being stationed at the Cape.

Influences from Europe: an egalitarian tendency

Compared to the rest of Europe, the social structure of the Netherlands was fluid, unique in the mobility people enjoyed and in the absence of sharp class cleavages. In the province of Holland, Roman-Dutch law, the established form of justice, conferred no special privileges on the nobility, but in the words of the great jurist Voetius, it 'preserves equality and binds the citizens equally'. It was this law with its egalitarian thrust that would be applied at the Cape.

The Dutch displayed no great deference to religious or secular authorities. There was no strong central state, only a loose confederation of provinces with the Prince of Orange as the symbolic head. The Reformed church, which was the official denomination, was based on Calvinist dogma. Laymen could seek God's grace and the community of the holy without using anyone as intermediary. The church and its institutions were open to criticism. More than one minister contrasted the lack of respect of Dutch laymen for their ministers with the humble deference displayed by Spanish and Portuguese Roman Catholics towards their priests.

More than elsewhere capitalism had permeated Dutch society, where the aristocracy and landed gentry were much less dominant. People in the Netherlands enjoyed the most individual mobility and the greatest advances in Europe towards the idea of equality before the law. Below the fairly small strata of the aristocracy and the 'high bourgeoisie' was a wide stratum of the 'broad citizenry' and 'middle estate', consisting of skilled artisans, shopkeepers and suppliers of goods. A poor man could aspire to rise up from the proletariat to enter the *middestand*, the middle class. Citizens in the Netherlands had more liberty to pursue their own interests than elsewhere in Europe.

Most of the immigrants who became free burghers at the Cape were poor, humble and ignorant, but the term 'burgher' was the same as that used for those at the centre of the seventeenth-century Dutch world: the prosperous, self-confident burghers of the Dutch cities portrayed in the work of Rembrandt, Steen, Vermeer, Hals and other painters. The Dutch burgher was not a bourgeois defined by economic function and power but 'a citizen first and *homo economicus* second'. The Company servants released at the Cape aspired to the same status as the Dutch burghers, although the high Company officials scoffed at this pretence.

BELOW: *An engraving made by J.W. Heydt in 1744 shows the meeting hall of the Council of India in Batavia – the room from which the Cape was governed. Note the ostentatious display of wealth with carved furniture, doors and screen, black-and-white marble floors, works of art and a huge umbrella lamp. The governor general had the largest chair.*

OPPOSITE BOTTOM: *The well-known portraits of Jan and Maria van Riebeeck are in fact not the Van Riebeecks at all, but the Vermuyden-Kettinghs. The face on the previous South African note, too, was not Van Riebeeck's but Vermuyden's. This authentic painting of Van Riebeeck is from* De Stichter *by E.C. Godée Molsbergen. No image of Maria van Riebeeck exists. 'Her' statue in Cape Town in fact shows the wife of the chairman of the Dutch committee that helped to organise the 1952 Van Riebeeck festival in Cape Town.*

In the early seventeenth century the Dutch officials and traders in the East did not display the same degree of cultural chauvinism and racial arrogance that would later be so characteristic of Europeans in the colonies. Europe had not yet undergone its economic and technological revolution. There was little that gave it an edge over the complex societies of the East. Fire power helped, but in the dense populations of the East it was of limited use. Some eastern products, such as textiles, were distinctly better than those the Europeans brought to the market.

In terms of cuisine the East had much to offer the Dutch colonists in the East. Dishes such as bobotie, kebabs, chutney and samosas, together with rice and spices like cinnamon, pepper, cloves, ginger, turmeric and saffron, became part and parcel of the food culture at the Cape.

Hierarchical tendencies: influences from the Far East

A complex society, drawing from a medley of cultures, developed in the Dutch possessions in the East. Europeans borrowed slavery and the ostentatious display of wealth of the Asian elite; some Asians acquired the dress, manners and religion of the Dutch. With a big imbalance in the sexes, Dutch men commonly formed relationships with Asian or Eurasian women. (The Afrikaans word *naai* or *nai* for sexual intercourse derives from the Malay-Indonesian word for the Eastern or Eurasian mistress of a Dutch burgher.) If married, an Eastern woman acquired the national status of her husband. Simon van der Stel, who became Commander of the Cape in 1679, was himself the product of such an intermixture. His mother, Maria Lievens, was born in Batavia, the daughter of a Dutch sea captain and Monica da Costa, an indigenous woman from the East.

RIGHT: *Baron van Rheede van Oudtshoorn's funeral, showing the ostentatious display of power and status in the case of burial of a high-ranking official. The Cape took such practices over from the VOC possessions in the East.*

As would also happen in Cape Town, the top Company officials and wealthiest burghers clung tenaciously to their rank and right of precedence. Rank determined seats in church and at public functions, and places in funeral processions The wealthy were ready to display their status ostentatiously, as in a grand mansion, a retinue of servants, a parasol carried by a servant, and festive house parties with dancing on the veranda to music supplied by a slave orchestra. Almost everyone with some pretensions to status keenly aspired to the role of a slave-owner who abstained from manual labour. As in Indonesia, European children at the Cape were left almost entirely to the care of female slaves.

The Reformed Church was the dominant church in the Netherlands and the only church the Company permitted in its overseas possessions. In the Netherlands it was supportive of the state, but retained a fair degree of independence with respect to faith and its internal organisation and the 'calling' of ministers.

In the East and at the Cape the government completely dominated the church. The clergy were salaried employees of the state and were expected to be obedient and respectful towards government. Congregations could not issue a call for their own minister, although this was a coveted prerogative of the Protestant churches in Europe. Until the end of its rule at the Cape, it prevented the establishment of a synod of the different congregations. The official church policy decreed that baptised slaves should be set free; the Company, however, had the last say. It set very tough conditions under which slaves could be freed, and as a result very few were freed in its possessions.

The official categories the Company created, taken from Batavia, profoundly shaped the administration of the colony. There was firstly the distinction between Company servants and free burghers, which came into effect when nine Company servants were released at the Cape in 1657 to become full-time farmers. The other main legal distinction was between these two groups – both free – and the slaves. Finally, there was the distinction between these three groups and the indigenous Khoisan, who, initially at least, were deemed to be outside the Company's laws.

Thus there were four status groups – Company servants, free burghers, slaves and 'aliens' or 'natives'. The statutory group, rather than one's race or colour or religion, determined whether and how someone would get on in life. As used by officials and the courts it determined domicile, right of movement, military service and land ownership.

More than 300 years later a system called apartheid was introduced, which was also squarely based on groups defined by the law, each with different rights and obligations. Like the VOC's system, apartheid functioned in a society with a surprisingly small police force. The system vitally depended on the groups accepting and internalising their official status group, keeping to and policing themselves and not attempting to bring about *gelykstelling*, or social levelling, of the different status groups.

ABOVE: *Anna de Koning and her husband, the explorer and captain Oloff Bergh. Anna was the daughter of the slave Angela, who came from Bengal on the northeast coast of India, and the slave Domingo de Koning. Bergh bought the farm Constantia; after his death, Anna farmed there on her own for ten years.*

LEFT: *The Reformed Church was the only church the VOC permitted. Church services were initially held on the ship* Drommedaris *and then in the Fort and in the Castle. The 'Mother Church' was consecrated in 1707. In 1843 a new building erected (shown here) on the same site, the 'Groote Kerk', was consecrated. A newer version of the church still stands in Adderley Street.*

A complex settlement

At the Cape two traditions clashed. The European heritage of freedom, mobility and the questioning of secular and religious authority came up against the Eastern influence of slavery, hierarchy, status consciousness and – among the poorer Europeans – a phobia about *gelyk-stelling*, or social levelling, with slaves. Poor Europeans and defenceless slaves found themselves thrown together in a settlement whose natural beauty belied the tough and often cruel circumstances in which people had to survive.

On 6 April 1652, three Dutch ships arrived in Table Bay and some 90 Europeans disembarked. Living in huts and tents, they built a fort called Good Hope on the site of the present Parade. A year later they moved in, but in the following year Fort Good Hope's mud walls started collapsing. A tiny settlement called De Kaap slowly began to extend its frontiers. Not far from the fort lay the Company Gardens and further south, at Rondebosch, the Company's own farm and orchard. A big barn called Groote Schuur was built here. The first free burghers received farms on either side of the Liesbeek River.

In 1666, work started on a structure called The Castle to replace the Fort Good Hope, but it was more than eleven years before most of it was completed. Initially church services, which were compulsory for Company employees, were held in the fort and subsequently in The Castle. It was only in 1704 that construction of a church was completed and services could be held there.

A first school, which took in slaves without age restrictions, was started in 1658. The pupils received 'a tot of brandy and tobacco' as incentive. The first public school, whose pupils were mainly children of Company servants, opened in 1663. Outside Cape Town the first public school was established in Stellenbosch in 1683.

For the first three decades most of the immigrants were single Dutch males. In 1688 a large party of French Huguenots, composed mostly of families, arrived. They now formed almost a fifth of the total European population. From the mid-1680s to 1729 a total of 289 Huguenots arrived. Apart from the French women, the female European immigrants were Dutch. Some of them were girls sent from orphanages in the Netherlands. In the eighteenth century most of the male immigrants were single Germans.

Free and unfree immigrants

Europeans who entered service on the lower VOC rungs faced an unpromising career. The Company enlisted its recruits for five years. Few inhabitants of the free Netherlands would sign up as sailors or soldiers except out of necessity. A sailor or a soldier's daily wage was five times less than that received by a polder boy or a peat-cutter in the

OPPOSITE: *The slave ship, the* Leijdsman, *sailing near Madagascar. Two thirds of the total number of slaves imported to the VOC Lodge had been acquired in Madagascar. Such voyages usually originated at the Cape. The Dutch acquired their slaves through trading rather than raiding. Slaves were traded primarily for firearms and powder, brandy, beads and Spanish reals of eight. In cash terms the prices ranged from 20 to 30 rixdollars (a rixdollar was equal to four British shillings).*

BOTTOM: *An orphanage in Amsterdam. In the early years many orphaned girls came out to the Cape and probably formed the majority of the 55 European women in a free population of 259 at the Cape. Many became stammoeders of Afrikaner families.*

A QUESTION OF BURGHER RIGHTS

The Company authorities disputed the comparison that the free burghers made with their counterparts in the Netherlands, since the Company that granted privileges could also withdraw them. It had the power to free burghers from its service, but also to force those who had misbehaved to return to the Company's service, or to deport them.

The officials were technically correct, but they had to concede that the burghers were no mere serfs. The burghers enjoyed no special rights that elevated them over others, but they nevertheless claimed special privileges. Burgher rights got entangled with the rights of baptised people. In the seventeenth and eighteenth centuries the sacrament of baptism was the key to civil status, including the right to inherit, marry in the church, be buried in a Christian cemetery and give testimony in court.

The burghers at the Cape had responsibilities rather than rights. They were the only people in the countryside who had the duty of performing commando service and paying taxes. They believed this gave them the right to hold the office of *heemraad*, or field-cornet, and that it gave them the strongest claim to land. Later they would call coloured people who wished to be called burghers *knapsakburgers*, or back-pocket burghers, because they paid no taxes and were not called upon to do commando duty.

Netherlands. They had to endure bad food, ferocious discipline and disease. Death was frequent on the ships. Some 15–20% of those who set sail perished on the Company's outward voyages every year. A career in the Company was truly for those who could think of no other solution to their problems.

Yet those who enlisted in the Company's service were enterprising enough to take the risk of working in a distant country for the required term of five years. Some of the Germans who came to the Cape were tradesmen whose lives (or whose parents' lives) had been disrupted by the Thirty Years' War, which ended in 1648. It was they who fared best in their new homeland at the tip of Africa. Most of the single males who immigrated to the Cape were illiterate or semi-literate peasants or labourers employed by the Company as sailors or soldiers.

In 1658 the first slave ships arrived. The *Amersfoort* had captured a Portuguese slaver en route to Brazil. Many died on the way to Cape Town but 75 were landed. The *Hasselt* landed 228 slaves from Angola, described as attractive, sturdily built and cheerful. In total 65 000 slaves were imported during the Company period.

Although the high officials lorded it over the Cape, these two groups of immigrants, the one free and the other unfree, determined the character of the settlement. By 1690 there was a free burgher population of 788 and a slave population of 381. A century later the burgher total stood at roughly 20 000 and the slave population at nearly 26 000. But, while the numbers of the burghers swelled as a result of an astounding birth rate, the slave population, due to physical and psychological hardship, did not reproduce itself. Their numbers had to be supplemented through continual immigration.

From the start the Cape was a slave society and not one in which slave labour was simply one of several forms of labour. A slave society is one in which all institutions – the labour market, the economy, the legal system, the family and the church – are permeated by slavery. The master-slave model served as the model for all other relationships.

The first free burghers

The first free burghers' instructions were simple: a vegetable and fruit garden had to be laid out, a fort and a hospital had to be built and cattle had to be acquired from the native people through barter. Colonisation was in no one's mind. But it did not escape Van Riebeeck's attention that the land on the eastern side of Table Mountain, 'traversed by the loveliest fresh rivers one could desire', was eminently suitable for agriculture. In 1657 he released nine Company servants to become full-time farmers on their plots of 13,3 morgen (about 11,4 hectares).

RIGHT: *Willem Berg's canteen in Dorp Street, Cape Town. Cape Town was a multi-racial and multi-lingual city with numerous canteens and boarding houses catering for visitors from the passing ships and the interior. A licence to keep a canteen was prized. Many of them were open on Sundays.*

BELOW: *A slave or Khoikhoi servant transporting wine to Cape Town. The VOC leased the wine trade to contractors, who had to supply wine to the Company at low prices. The VOC kept a monopoly on selling wine to taverns, which meant that farmers could not sell their wine in private trade.*

The Company did not release its European employees in order to implement some grandiose scheme. Some of the VOC's top officials would have preferred Chinese or free blacks to European farmers, and in their letters they frequently expressed contempt for the abilities of the free burghers. Company officials never ceased to be outraged by what they regarded as the ordinary burghers' preposterous demands. Van Riebeeck obviously thought that the burghers ought to be grateful for the freedom they had received and should therefore subordinate their own interests to those of the Company.

Van Riebeeck, almost without reflection, believed that the intensive cultivation of land in a rotation system was the best for producing food. It would bring about a neat, compact settlement that would not extend much beyond the shadow of the coastal fort. But such a system of intensive agriculture required an injection of capital, which the burghers did not have, and strenuous labour, for which they had little enthusiasm. Officials in colonies across the world discovered that if slaves or indigenous labour could be found, European immigrants refused to do manual work. Only farmers with labour and capital, and who were farming for themselves, could do the job at the Cape.

The farmers living near the Cape market had to operate in a buyers' market that was heavily tilted in favour of the Company. Wheat had to be offered first to the Company at prices it fixed. The Company also had first claim on vegetables and fruit. It leased the wine trade to contractors, who had to supply wine to the Company at low prices. They had a monopoly to sell wine to the numerous taverns in the port city, which meant that farmers could not retail their own. The sale of meat was leased in a similar way.

With burghers instructed to sell their produce to the ships only three days after they had docked in Table Bay, large-scale smuggling of all kinds of products was the order of the day. The prospects for export were not bright. In 1659 Van Riebeeck wrote that 'to the honour of God the first wine from Cape grapes was produced'. However, the wine was too poor to export in large volumes. The Company rejected appeals from the burghers to export their own produce in its own ships.

A struggle to survive

In the first two decades the farmers struggled to survive because the prices the Company fixed for their produce were far too low. Van Riebeeck conceded in a letter in 1661 that the free burghers could scarcely subsist on what they were paid for cultivating their wheat. Three years later, the government decided to distribute Sunday church collections and some petty fines to poor burghers burdened with 'naked children, and [who] from simple poverty must sleep each night beside the livestock in the stable on a little straw and the naked earth'.

Although the government intermittently banned the cattle trade, its reach was not nearly far enough to stamp it out. It also could do little if burghers grazed their cattle beyond the limits of their plots. Van Riebeeck left the Cape in 1662 understanding that his original idea of an intensive settlement had failed. A large area he once thought could provide subsistence for thousands of families was considered fully occupied after a mere fifteen farms had been parcelled out.

The burghers in the town in Table Bay had better opportunities than the farmers working as carpenters, bricklayers, smiths and keepers of taverns. Most kept boarding houses, and they frequently circumvented the restrictions on selling Cape merchandise to passing sailors and on buying European goods. More than one Company official expressed the desire to rid the Cape of the 'scum' and called taverns the 'mother of all scandalous practices'.

The farming burgher became a special kind of burgher who, unlike his counterpart in the town, worked for something more than his immediate interests. These men had, in their own words, become 'defenders of the land' against internal enemies, along with being the indispensable producers of food.

Burghers in government

Although the officials always tried to downplay the political rights of the burghers, they had representatives on some of the most important governing bodies. This enhanced their claim that they were not simply agents of the Company. It was true that they were not represented in the Council of Policy, made up of the highest Company officials. However, when the highest court, the Court Justice sat, three burghers were on the bench whenever the court heard cases involving a burgher. These burgher councillors were entitled to present burgher grievances to visiting commissioners. Thus from an early stage they could speak on behalf of the body of freemen.

Two burghers sat with the same number of officials on two other important boards. One was the Matrimonial Court, before which couples intending to get married had to appear, and the other was the Orphan Chamber. No widower or widow might remarry before satisfying the board that the rights of their children had been safeguarded. In the eighteenth century all wills and inventories of estates had to be registered with it. Since money often had to be deposited, it also served as a loan bank in a settlement that would have no regular commercial bank until deep into the nineteenth century.

LEFT: *A seventeenth-century engraving in Thomas Herbert's* Zee en Lant Reijse *shows the Khoikhoi and Dutch bartering sheep and cattle for copper and tobacco.*

ABOVE: *An illustration found in the 1777 travel diary of explorer and VOC officer R.J. Gordon. It shows chief Coba wearing the Grenadier helmet of the elite VOC troops. The helmet was given to Coba by Gordon as a peace offer.*

OPPOSITE: *The foreground of this illustration from Bogaarts's* Historische Reizen *from 1711 depicts the traditional way of life that Autshumato (Harry), Krotoa (Eva) and Doman left behind when they became interpreters for the Dutch. The background shows the Dutch way of life beginning to take root.*

The Khoikhoi and the Dutch

With the coming of the Dutch settlement, the Khoikhoi faced a much stronger demand for their cattle. They were now called on not only to feed VOC ships, which arrived in larger numbers than formerly, but also to support the garrison and hospital. Soon the Company would settle free burghers in the vicinity of the fort and further inland. The free burghers would put even greater pressure on Khoikhoi herds, while also encroaching on their pastures and hunting grounds.

While the Company strove to be the sole buyer and to keep prices low, the Khoikhoi tried to protect the viability of their herds by selling only sheep or sickly cattle. Deeply frustrated about the reluctance of the Khoikhoi to trade, Commander Van Riebeeck contemplated enslaving the Khoikhoi near his fort and seizing their herds and flocks. But the Company was anxious to avoid deep entanglements in southern Africa; it had declared the Khoikhoi a free people who could be neither conquered nor enslaved. Somewhat grudgingly, Van Riebeeck abided by this policy, devoting much of his ten-year command to intricate diplomatic manoeuvres designed to win the goodwill of at least some Khoikhoi.

Disputes and war

Trade disputes and charges of theft caused great tension between colonists and the Khoikhoi who, for their part, feared that the settlement of free burghers in 1657 would eventually deprive them of their valuable pastures and watering places. In 1659 Khoikhoi led by the interpreter Doman mounted a series of rapid and successful raids on free burghers' herds.

The ensuing First Khoikhoi-Dutch War, which lasted almost a year, resulted in only a few deaths. Initiative lay chiefly with the Khoikhoi, who attacked, often in groups of several hundred, and usually on rainy days to thwart the function of the Dutch matchlocks. Instructed by Doman, who had witnessed Dutch military tactics in Java, they darted about erratically to frustrate Dutch marksmen. Commander Van Riebeeck responded with defensive tactics, withdrawing the free burghers to the fort, temporarily arming the slaves (an extraordinarily risky measure), and building a strong kraal to protect the colony's remaining livestock.

Lacking firearms and unwilling to storm the central fort, the Khoikhoi eventually signalled their willingness to parley. A peace was negotiated that implicitly recognised that the war had ended in stalemate. The Khoikhoi returned no livestock seized in the war and paid no reparations. Yet they did accept the continued European occupation of the Cape peninsula, an ominous threat to their perseverance as an independent people.

After the First Khoikhoi-Dutch War, the Cape commanders, anxious to find more willing Khoikhoi sellers, sent buying expeditions deeper and deeper into the interior, where they made contact with new Khoikhoi communities. The actions of Company soldiers and traders, rather than white settlers, were largely responsible for eroding the independence of the Cape Khoikhoi.

By the late 1660s a number of defensive measures (watch houses, mounted patrols, and an almond hedge to control access routes to the colony) had made the colony secure; Company directors in the Netherlands progressively lost interest in Khoikhoi affairs and Cape commanders acquired more leeway for aggressive policies.

Resistance by Gonnema and Dorha

In 1673 the Company went to war with the Cochoqua, an inland group whose leader Gonnema they accused, often on shaky grounds, of numerous assaults on Europeans. The Second Khoikhoi-Dutch War consisted chiefly of punitive Dutch expeditions directed against Gonnema and other peoples only tenuously associated with his alleged offences. These gave the Company a fine yield of livestock and prompted numerous Khoikhoi groups to offer their services to the Dutch. In 1677 Gonnema concluded peace with the colony, promising to bring it an annual 'tribute' of 30 head of cattle. Though the Company

The new Dutch colony presented opportunities to talented Khoikhoi, particularly those with linguistic abilities. Three translators, none apparently born of high birth or wealth, rose to become, for a while, eminent and prosperous intermediaries between Europeans and Khoikhoi.

Autshumato ('Harry') was a cattleless Strandloper (beachcomber) who, while living on Robben Island, ran a 'post office' for the English and sailors of other nationalities, who left letters for countrymen passing by in coming months.

In the early years of the settlement, Harry established himself as Commander Van Riebeeck's only interpreter, providing advice on Khoikhoi politics and bringing Khoikhoi cattle traders to the fort. By 1658 Harry had amassed large herds and flocks and emerged as a leader of herders who had once despised him as a scavenger. In the First Khoikhoi-Dutch War, Van Riebeeck, again suspicious of Harry's shifting allegiances, imprisoned him on Robben Island, from which he escaped in a leaky boat. He then became a spokesman for one Khoikhoi group after another. He died, without livestock but with his prestige somewhat restored, in 1663 – the year after Van Riebeeck's departure from the Cape.

A contrast to Harry in every way was his young relative Krotoa or 'Eva', who took service in the Van Riebeeck household, where she mastered Dutch and Portuguese and responded eagerly to Christian instruction given her by Maria van Riebeeck, the commander's wife. Eva established herself as a staunch friend of the Dutch, negotiating a co-operative relationship between the fort and the followers of her rich relative Oedasoa. She was later instrumental in working out terms for ending the First Dutch-Khoikhoi War.

In the 1650s Eva was the only figure possessing an intimate knowledge of both Khoikhoi and Dutch culture; as she passed back and forth between one society and the other, she exchanged her Dutch clothing for Khoikhoi skins, and vice versa. She was baptised in 1662 and married in 1664 in a church ceremony to the explorer Pieter van Meerhoff. The Company, which favoured total cultural assimilation for Khoikhoi, gave her a generous dowry. Eva bore Van Meerhoff three children, and accompanied him during his command at Robben Island. Later, on an expedition to Madagascar, Van Meerhoff was killed in a skirmish.

For a while Eva remained a respectable member of European society, but soon started to drink heavily and turned to prostitution. She spent much of the last five years of her life on Robben Island, imprisoned for immoral behaviour. At her death the Dutch saw her tragic life as proof that Khoikhoi were unable to absorb the best of European culture; 'With the dogs she returned to her own vomit,' the official diarist recorded, 'a clear illustration that nature, no matter how tightly muzzled by imprinted moral principles . . . reverts to its inborn qualities.'

Little is known of the origins of Doman, the third of the great interpreters, but he was clearly not of chiefly rank. In 1657–58 the Dutch, judging him a good potential translator, took him to Batavia (Jakarta), their capital in the East Indies. Here he witnessed both the potential power of Dutch colonialism and the climax of anti-colonial resistance on the north shore of the island. Doman declared his allegiance to the Dutch and claimed to be attracted to Christianity. This was a purely tactical profession, for on his return to the Cape he became an outspoken opponent of Van Riebeeck's policies and a loud critic of Eva, ridiculing her Christianity and shouting, 'There comes the advocate of the Dutch; she will tell her people some stories and lies and will finally betray them all.'

With the support of some younger Khoikhoi leaders, he attacked the free burghers, thus triggering the First Khoikhoi-Dutch War. After initial successes, Doman was seriously injured in a skirmish; his Khoikhoi followers retreated into the interior, quarrelled among themselves, and abused Doman for their defeats. He died less than four years later, apparently unlamented.

Of the three strategies chosen by the interpreters – Harry to use the Dutch in pursuit of his personal agendas, Eva to win their affection through loyal service, Doman to resist their colonial expansion – all proved starkly unsuccessful. All three died in poverty, having forfeited the high status they had once gained from their command of language.

did not always insist on strict payment of the tribute, Gonnema remained overtly submissive to his conquerors until his death in 1685 or 1686.

With the Company's hegemony over the Cape Khoikhoi now secure, a new tactic emerged among Khoikhoi leaders – best exemplified by Dorha, a Chainouqua captain the Dutch called 'Klaas'. An ally of the Dutch in the war against Gonnema, Dorha persuaded the Company to entrust him with increasing quantities of trade goods, which he exchanged inland for livestock on its behalf, keeping a percentage for himself. In time he amassed considerable wealth and a numerous following, concluding alliances with chiefs with a lineage status higher than his own.

The Company found Dorha to be a cheaper source of livestock than their own barter expeditions. In addition, he became their trusted informant and advisor on Khoikhoi affairs. Notwithstanding his usefulness and loyalty, Governor Van der Stel, acting in 1693 on allegations that convinced few contemporary observers, terminated the twenty-year alliance, arrested Dorha and seized all his livestock.

The Company now fell back upon its own trading expeditions, extorting tribute in

A THREAT TO A WAY OF LIFE

The switch to extensive agriculture and the increasing involvement of burghers in cattle trading and cattle farming threatened the way of life of the approximately 100 000 Khoikhoi living in the area of the present Western Cape.

Those living in the Cape Peninsula and vicinity were called the Kaapmans, or Peninsulars. Realising that the Europeans had come to stay, they became hostile and acutely concerned when the burghers ploughed their fields for the first time. They attacked farms and sought to prevent occupation of their grazing lands near the Cape. In 1659 the Peninsulars attacked under Doman, the first indigenous leader who chose to resist colonial expansion.

In April 1660 Van Riebeeck reported that peace had been concluded with the Peninsulars, although they had insisted that the Dutch had been appropriating 'more and more of their land, which had been theirs all these centuries'. When Van Riebeeck remarked that there was not enough grazing land for all, the Peninsulars asked: 'Have we then no reason to prevent you from getting cattle, since if you have a large number, you will take up all our grazing grounds for them?' They continued: 'As for your claim that the land is not big enough for both of us, who should rather in justice give way, the rightful owner or the foreign intruder?' Van Riebeeck did not enter into an argument.

cattle from Khoikhoi chiefs in return for assurances that they would not be attacked. Free burghers, too, began to send raiding parties deep into the interior. By 1700 evidence was mounting that many Khoikhoi had been divested of their livestock and were living in penury throughout the southwestern Cape.

The free burghers spread inland more slowly than the Company's influence had done; they typically settled in areas where the social cohesion and prosperity of Khoikhoi had already been damaged by earlier contacts. In the new settlements of Stellenbosch (founded in 1679) and Drakenstein (1687), the ratio of slaves to freemen was at first much lower than near Cape Town. Settlers accordingly sought to hire Khoikhoi, first to tend flocks and herds, for which they already had abundant skills, and later to acquire the agricultural techniques needed to cultivate and reap grains, prune vines and drive wagons.

The switch to extensive agriculture and the increasing involvement of burghers in cattle trading and cattle farming threatened the way of life of the approximately 100 000 Khoikhoi living in the area of the present Western Cape.

Since it had long been the custom for impoverished Khoikhoi to take service with wealthier Khoikhoi, their employment with Europeans required no novel response. However, on white farms the Khoikhoi usually worked for only tobacco, food and drink; though some white employers allowed them to acquire and keep a few calves or lambs, most Khoikhoi found little chance to restart their herds and flocks.

As Khoikhoi were losing their economic independence, they increasingly found themselves subject to Dutch jurisdiction whenever they got into disputes with whites or slaves. The Dutch courts treated Khoikhoi reasonably fairly in the seventeenth century; Khoikhoi charges against whites were heard by the courts, and their testimonies taken seriously. But the dispensing of sentences was highly unequal: a white convicted of murdering a Khoikhoi paid a fine or was banished from the colony, while a Khoikhoi convicted of murdering a white was executed.

After 1700 the decline of Khoikhoi as independent people accelerated rapidly. Many suffered losses in warfare triggered by the northward expansion of settlement into the Tulbagh basin. Barter expeditions by settlers often deteriorated into cattle raids. And

Khoikhoi herdsmen and women who went to work on Dutch farms slowly lost their economic independence, culture and traditional way of dress. The two paintings on the right are of people in an advanced stage of acculturation. They were probably exceptions among the Khoikhoi until the second half of the nineteenth century.

then in 1713 a smallpox epidemic hit the colony, killing hundreds of Europeans and slaves, but proving much more lethal among Khoikhoi on white farms and in independent clans. One contemporary estimated that scarcely one in ten Khoikhoi in the Cape region survived. Even if that number is an exaggeration, independent Khoikhoi social structure had virtually disappeared from the southwestern Cape.

People of bondage

Almost from the start the Cape was a slave society. Bereft of freedom and status, slaves defined the liberties and status of others. They formed the labour force of the colony. In Cape Town the men worked in the market gardens and provided the artisan skills; on the farms they worked in the fields and vineyards. The women served as cooks, nannies and wet-nurses in the house. The children were the playmates of their masters' children. The incorporation of the domestic slaves in the colonists' 'family' laid the foundation for the kind of society that developed in the colony.

ABOVE: *Slaves were sold almost every week at auctions under a large tree in Church Square, next to the Slave Lodge. Today a commemorative stone marks this spot.*

Most slaves were to be found in the urban and periurban areas, and the probability of slaves being sold was always highest in Cape Town, where slaves were sold almost every week in the popular auctions in Church Square. These were held under a large tree, next to the Company's Slave Lodge and facing the rear of the Dutch Reformed Church.

Between 1652 and 1808, when the slave trade stopped, approximately 63 000 slaves were imported. In all, 26.4% of the colony's slaves were from Africa, 25.1% from Madagascar, and 25.9% were brought from India and 22.7% from Indonesia.

Officials and burghers perceived each group of slaves differently, attributing skills and character to the country of origin and engaging in crude racial and geographical stereotypes. Slaves from Bengal or the Coast of Coromandel, Surat and Macassar, had a reputation as skilful needlewomen and were used in this capacity. Slaves from Mozambique were deemed to be mild and patient but Malays viewed as treacherous and inclined to run amuck. Highly sought-after slaves were Cape-born mulattoes – the offspring of liaisons between Europeans and slaves – who were called Afrikanders by the British. A commentator noted: 'The Afrikander women are the favourite slaves of the mistress, arranging and keeping everything in order, and are entrusted with all that is valuable – more like companions than slaves; but the mistress rarely and the slave never, forget their relative situations, and however familiar in private, in the presence of another, due form prevails.'

There were four groups of slaves: those in the employ of the Company, those owned by the Company's officials, and those owned by the colony's burghers – representing the overwhelming majority of slaves – while a fourth and very minor group of slaves was owned by the free blacks. For more than a century Cape slavery was predominantly urban. As late as 1767, more than 40% of all the colony's slaves lived in Cape Town.

The Slave Lodge

The most prominent group of slaves was those who belonged to the Company. Almost all were housed in the Slave Lodge. The Company used hundreds of slaves for various tasks, such as running the Company's market garden plantation, working in the hospital, building the port's considerable fortifications and performing the town's unattractive chores, such as removing slurry to the beach. Slaves called 'Caffers' (*see box on page 54*) acted as a police force, dispensing rough justice. After a century the Company's slave force had grown to 1 000.

The Lodge, usually called the *Loots* or *Logie*, was a large, windowless building. It was located at the top of the main thoroughfare, next to the Company's nine-acre vegetable garden, and across the street from the large Company hospital. The Lodge was virtually a fortress run by Company officials on a military system.

Few Europeans entered the Lodge by choice, except during one hour each night when it became an active brothel for the local garrison. There were almost as many slave women as men in the Lodge, sometimes more. A couple from the Slave Lodge could get permission to be placed on the 'marriage list', but the Dutch Reformed Church never

BELOW: *A slave 'Afrikaner', known as Jonker Afrikaner. The offspring of European and slave liaisons born at the Cape were the most sought after as slaves. The British (but not the burghers) called these people the Afrikanders, or Afrikaners.*

sanctioned or even recorded such slave marriages. Slaves owned by the colonists were not permitted to marry until 1823.

Mortality for the slaves of the Lodge was high. Throughout the period of slavery there was a clear excess of deaths and runaways over births among the Lodge slaves. It was nothing short of a demographic sinkhole.

Some of the slaves in private hands qualified as artisans. The three leading trades were those of mason, blacksmith and carpenter. Most of the owners lived in Table Valley and owned small businesses there.

Life was particularly tough for slaves who worked on the farms near Cape Town that were intensively cultivated, with wine, wheat, rye and barley being the predominant crops. Hard work throughout the year was the slaves' lot. So indispensable was slave labour to these farms that it was generally thought the economy would collapse if slavery were abolished.

Slaves lived out their lives on wine and wheat farms, separated from each other and rarely visiting the few towns and villages of the interior. Katie Jacobs, a slave born in the Malmesbury district in the nineteenth century, was separated from her Malagasy-speaking mother by sale to an owner in the next valley and neither saw nor heard from her again. There were also a few slaves to be found on extensive sheep and cattle farms that the

A DIFFERENT KIND OF POLICE FORCE

A force of slaves called 'Caffers' acted as the executive arm of the Fiscal, or state prosecutor. In his work on Cape slavery, *Children of Bondage*, Robert Shell explains the word's curious etymology. Originally it was an Arabic noun meaning 'ungrateful'; by association, those who did not believe in Allah were ungrateful. All non-Jews, non-Christians, and non-Muslims – people 'not of the book' – were thus considered 'Caffers'.

It was from the Dutch possessions in the Indonesian Archipelago that the word was re-exported to Cape Town. In most documents of 1682 through 1786, 'Caffers of the Justice Department', as they were actually called, were Asian full-breed men. In the nineteenth century, the British – probably picking up the word (and the original derivation) from the Arabs on the east coast of Africa – reintroduced the term, this time applying it to all Africans on the Eastern frontier.

Although the Caffers occupied a despised echelon of the slave hierarchy, the Company issued them superior clothing – special police uniforms with waistcoats. They were the only slaves allowed to bear arms. According to an account, they 'are armed with a sword with iron hilt, carry . . . a

palang or heavy club, wear a grey uniform consisting of a short coat with blue lapels, a waistcoat and trousers, and receive some petty perquisites as well'.

Unlike other slaves, Company and privately owned, who were subject to various curfews, the Caffers were permitted – actually required – to roam around the Cape day and night, enforcing the curfews. This they did, executing rough justice on all – also Europeans who were guilty of the smallest infringement of Cape law.

It fell to the Caffers to carry out the ghoulish sentences the Court of Justice concocted. In February 1724, the court sentenced a slave for murder and arson, and ordered the Caffers to 'cut off his right

hand' (the murder weapon), after which he was to be 'half-strangled and killed on a slow fire' (the punishment for starting a fire). For even minor crimes – such as smoking a pipe in the street – the Caffers were instructed to inflict severe floggings. Because of the fire hazard in Cape Town, any person, 'without distinction', found smoking a pipe in the street was to be 'soundly' beaten by the Caffers. A high proportion of the sentences handed down by the Court of Justice ended with the words 'to be handed over to the executioner and be beaten by the Caffers'.

When the British took over from the Dutch they entrenched the use of the term and extended it to apply to all Africans (and not just to those of the Eastern frontier). In the minds of its users, it took on new connotations of all kinds of inferiority, primitiveness and backwardness. Thus what had started as a descriptive and 'innocent' term gradually became a derogatory and insulting one in the minds of both Europeans and Africans. It is this latter meaning of the term 'Kaffir' that has stuck in the minds of all, black and white, to this day. In present-day South Africa the word remains the gravest slur. (In this book 'Caffer' is used only to refer to slaves from Indonesia who served as a police force in the Company period.)

colonists carved out in the eighteenth century. Typically on such a farm, an overseer or the son of the owner supervised a few Khoikhoi herdsmen, or a few older slaves who had been 'farmed out' would be there on their own. Here they lived out their lives in great isolation.

Nannies and wet-nurses

Almost all female slaves lived in the house and were part of the household. Their role was that of servant, cook, nanny, surrogate mother and sometimes wet-nurse as well. Slave women also busied themselves with crocheting, embroidering, sewing, knitting and laundering. In Cape Town the female slaves in the ubiquitous boarding houses ministered to all the needs of the revitalised sailors and officers.

A single slave woman often performed the roles of midwife, wet-nurse and nanny. The slave nurse-nanny was there to assist at the birth; she suckled the child; she carried the settler's infant to be baptised; and she was the child's companion when it was time to go to school. 'Such a slave is very well treated,' Otto Mentzel, an astute observer, noted. 'In addition to good food, she gets many presents with the prospect of manumission for good service in the bringing up of several children.'

In this way slave women were not only brought into the bosom of the family, so to speak, but also actually became in a literal sense the bosom of the burgher family. Wet-nursing was frowned on in metropolitan Holland at this time, but settler women had slaves to employ to feed their infants. Cape settler women clearly perceived that there was some sort of link between lactation and ovulation. The Cape wet-nurse, by lactating for the biological mother, ensured that the biological mother would be ovulating again sooner than if she were breast-feeding. Therefore the birth intervals between her children would be shorter.

The seventeenth-century Batavian slur that such household slave women were *naai mandjes* (*naai* means to sew or to have intercourse; *mandje* is a basket or basin) also recalls that such activities could serve a dual purpose. So important was the wet-nurse to the slave society that two other terms entered the colonial creole language: *minnemoer* or *mina* (love-mother) and *aiya* (old nursemaid). These words have survived, as has the nanny herself.

Punishment and paternalism

Slaves convicted of serious offences – and this included lifting a hand against a master, setting a house on fire or making advances to a European woman – were commonly punished harshly: impaled, branded and quartered. The extreme penalty was death

TOP: *This detail from a drawing by W.E. Sherwill shows slave artisans working on a rooftop. Almost all masons and carpenters were slaves. The best were hired out by their masters at high rates.*

ABOVE: *An overdressed Cape farmer or Company official supervising a slave.*

OPPOSITE TOP: *The two-storey Slave Lodge in Cape Town housed most of the slaves the Company owned. It was located at the top of today's Adderley Street, close to the Company Gardens and the hospital.*

OPPOSITE MIDDLE: *The Cape hangman, as drawn by Lady Anne Barnard. He was one of the 'Caffers' drawn from the ranks of the slaves, issued with special police uniforms and the only slaves allowed to bear arms.*

OPPOSITE BOTTOM: *A police officer ('Caffer') with a rod leading a slave, part of a painting of Greenmarket Square by Johannes Rach in c.1761.*

OPPOSITE TOP: *The caption to this illustration in the first edition of John Barrow's* Travels into the Interior of Southern Africa *(1802) reads: 'The Dutch mode of punishing the [Khoikhoi] slaves by flogging them until he has smoked as many pipes of tobacco as he might judge the magnitude of the crime to deserve.' The practice of using pipes as timing devices during floggings was recorded in the Dutch Indonesian possessions. In this case the owner (on the left) had decided the crime warranted a 'four pipe' punishment.*

OPPOSITE MIDDLE: *Two 'prize slaves' painted by Thomas Baines. Prize slaves were slaves 'liberated' by the British ships, and who served as indentured labourers at the Cape.*

OPPOSITE BOTTOM: *Free Blacks were excluded from most occupations and many turned to fishing.*

BELOW: *Hendrik Cloete, the builder of Groot Constantia wine estate, smoking at the card table while his slave holds his pipe. In similar vein, in about 1775 Johannes Rach painted a lady in Batavia with a slave holding her binoculars.*

preceded by torture. Convicted slaves were broken alive on the wheel, their flesh was pulled off with red-hot tongs; slaves were mutilated, impaled or slowly strangled. The bodies of the executed were left hanging on gibbets or exposed after mutilation in Cape Town or on farmsteads. By 1727 there were so many disfigured and mutilated living slaves that the government decided to brand escaped slaves on the back in order to spare the feelings of the colonists, particularly pregnant women.

But while these gruesome punishments acted as a kind of deterrent, this does not mean that the masters' control of slaves depended in the first place on whips and chains. Physical coercion alone can never explain why slavery as a system worked in South Africa. This is particularly true of the isolated farms, far removed from police and military force stationed in Cape Town.

The authorities limited punishment of privately owned slaves to 'domestic correction', the same type of punishment a husband and father could apply to his wife and children. Chains and whips were forbidden. The wording of the relevant statute is clear: 'The owner is allowed, in the case of a slave making a mistake, to correct such a slave with domestic punishment, it is not permitted to set a slave in irons, or worse, to torture or otherwise maltreat the slave.'

A 'sort of child of the family'

The main method private owners used to control their slaves, especially the slaves in the household, was by incorporating them into their extended families in a system the historians of slavery call paternalism. The household, or the 'family', provided the only 'home' there was for slaves who had been uprooted from their own culture and kin. The slave remained an outsider in all civic and legal matters, but the slave owner always insisted

---

THE COMPLEXITIES OF SLAVERY

The following two documents demonstrate the different types of control the masters tried to impose and the third captures the tortured soul of a slave who, apart from having lost his freedom, bitterly resented the alien culture imposed on him, and also the lack of a wife.

The case of Gottlieb Opperman and his slave Dam

An extreme example of the patriarch was Gottlieb Christiaan Opperman, a German immigrant and *stamvader* of the Opperman family. When his slave boy, Dam, was caught after running away for a third time, he had him beaten on the bare buttocks by two of his slaves 'for the length of time it takes to smoke a pipe'. Four colonists remonstrated with Opperman to no avail. He told them 'no one in Africa understood politics as he did', and forced Dam to tread acorns in a bucket for three hours, claiming that was typical punishment for children in Germany. Dam was much weakened by this torture and died. Opperman did not receive the death penalty, but the government reissued the proclamation against 'barbaric treatment and the striking of slaves'.

The report of Lady Anne Barnard

Examples of genuine emotional ties between owner and slave exist in the historical record as well. Lady Anne Barnard, an English socialite, came across it in 1797 near present day Paarl: 'The room [was] filled with slaves – a dozen at least – here they were particularly clean and neat, Myfrow [my woman, the mistress] sat like Charity tormented by a Legion of devils, with a black babie in her arms, one on each knee and three or four larger ones around her, smiling benign on the little mortals who seemed very sweet creatures and develish [sic] only in their hue . . .'

The anguish of Cupido of Malabar

In 1743 the slave Cupido belonging to Jan van Straaten entered the house while his master was away, carrying a knife, musket and a box of gunpowder. He threatened to kill his mistress, who was alone at home with her child, but also tried to kill himself. She fled with her child and Cupido was caught before he could commit suicide. He was brought to trial and sentenced to die a cruel death. According to the court report, he asked his mistress: 'What do you want now, that I should murder you, or myself?' then put the back of the knife against his throat, asking if she wanted to see him slit his throat. She inquired why he wanted to do this, and whether something was wrong with him, to which he replied: 'So much.'

The court report added: 'And, after the prisoner took off his jacket and shirt and threw them down on the ground, he said, pointing to his leather trousers: "I am not used to wearing trousers like these, I have already worked two or three years here, and I do not see the baas buying more jongens or nonje buying a meijd for me, baas and nonje may talk and laugh very well".'

that the slave was part of the larger 'family', which was presented to the slave as a poor but tangible consolation.

Travellers to the Cape in the eighteenth and nineteenth centuries increasingly referred to this phenomenon. In the final years of the eighteenth century Lady Anne Barnard, a newly arrived English socialite, wrote that she was unsure whether she should give a necklace to a slave woman who belonged to her hosts *before* handing out gifts to the natural members of their family. When she asked, they both laughed and cried aloud: 'Not to think anything of that – that she [the slave woman] had been born in the house, and was a sort of child of the family – and that if I had the beads, to give her them.'

The phrase 'born in the same house' invariably referred to a slave's special status in the slave-owning family. Cape slave owners went to considerable lengths to keep slaves, especially female slaves, as 'part of the family'. To sell such slaves to outsiders would have perverted the paternalism. The slaves of deceased slave owners tended to go to relatives, not strangers.

Paternalism never entailed equality with other members of the household. Even the young daughters were allowed to punish adult household slaves. At some point in every slave's life, usually at the young master's or mistress's maturity, there arose a simultaneous realisation that while the master or mistress was bound for adulthood, the slave – in the settlers' eyes – was scheduled for perpetual childhood and dependence, and the demeaning obscurity that went with that fate. No matter what their age – or status – all Cape slaves remained 'boys' or 'girls'.

Naming a slave

All Cape slaves were known in the community by their first names. The slave trader or the new owner gave slaves new names, and the legal transfer of ownership was the place to rename a slave. The daily, community-wide, repetitive use of the first name and no other was an important part of the process of socialising slaves into their status of unending childhood.

The names could be facetious (Clever or *Slim*, Sweet Potato or *Patat*), or were taken from calendar months (April or September) or the Old Testament (Solomon or Moses). Classical names (Cupido or Titus) and indigenous names were also given. Only rarely was the name that of the owner or his children.

The dispute over baptism

The question whether and when slaves should be baptised kept the church and the colonists occupied until well in the nineteenth century. As we have seen, baptism was an important ritual acting as a condition for the exercise of many rights (*see box on page 47*).

At the Synod of Dordt held in 1618–1619 the Reformed Church in the Netherlands agreed that all heathen children in a household, whether slave or free, should enjoy the right of Christian instruction. But it was the head of that household, not the Church and not the parents of the child, who had the primary responsibility for deciding about baptising slaves and heathens.

It was also decided that baptised slaves 'should enjoy equal rights with other Christians'. Baptised slaves could not be sold to heathens, but could be passed to other Christians by inheritance or gift. There was no clear agreement on the proper age at which a slave should be baptised and no mention of how these precepts were to be enforced. All these matters were left to the head of the household.

By about 1725, it had become clear that some owners were denying their infant slaves the right to baptism. Otto Mentzel, writing of the 1740s, noted, 'It is a matter for regret that the children born in slavery are neither baptised nor given any religious instruction. There is a common and well-grounded belief that Christians must not be held in bondage; hence only such children as are intended for emancipation are baptised.' The Church records show a clear trend toward fewer baptisms over the century.

Most slave owners did not bother with their slaves' baptism at all. By the late eighteenth century, pews specially built for slaves in the Mother Church (*Moederkerk*) of Cape Town were empty Sunday after Sunday. While no slave owner, no matter how

cynical, would dare claim that slaves had *no* right to baptism, the owner could justify a delay in baptism by arguing that slaves should be instructed before they were baptised. Then the slave owner could, through endless domestic ruses, postpone bringing the slaves into the Christian community and thereby avoid any risk of reducing the marketability of his slaves. Put in purely materialistic terms: slaves were safer investments if they were *not* Christian, a conviction that continued until emancipation.

Of the 2 543 slave baptisms from 1652 to 1795, 1 715 were of slave children belonging to the Dutch East India Company – an average of one per month. These Lodge slaves were considered part of the 'household' of the Company, and all slaves born into the household of the Lodge were baptised. This meant that private owners baptised a total of 828 slaves– an average of less than nine a year. Of the few slave owners who did baptise their infant slaves, most were wealthy individuals.

The quest for freedom

All slaves yearned for freedom but few managed to escape. They could run away to places where fugitive slaves hid. There were such maroon societies at Faure, Hangklip, and on Table Mountain itself. Several small, stable maroon societies in the colony offered succour to runaway slaves, and these havens survived throughout the period. The 60-slave Hangklip community that lived in a cave lasted for a century, virtually undisturbed until slavery ended in 1834.

The other route to freedom was through manumission and becoming a free black. Freedom was not a right conferred by the state, but a favour granted within the household. Manumitted people were termed *vrijzwarten,* free blacks, even if descended from a European parent. The manumission regulations were framed more in cultural than legal terms. The ability to understand, speak and write Dutch headed the established list of manumission requirements.

From 1715 to 1791 the Council of Policy received a total of 1 075 manumission requests, of which only 81 involved Company slaves. The manumission rate in the colony was low, indeed extremely low. The average per year was only 0.165% of the slave force. The figure for Brazil and Peru was six times higher than that at the Cape. The fact that the proportion of the free population at the Cape remained very small in the 1820s and 1830s, except in Cape Town, had momentous consequences for future race relations. Virtually all people who were desperately poor and had no status were black; all the richer people were white. An association between whiteness and success arose.

POPULATION OF THE CAPE COLONY			
Year	European free burghers	Burghers' slaves	Free blacks
1670	125	52	13
1690	788	381	48
1730	2 540	4 037	221
1770	7 736	8 200	352
1798	c.20 000	25 754	c.1 700

OPPOSITE TOP: *The walled execution grounds outside the Castle, drawn by Lady Anne Barnard in about 1798. The harshest penalty was death preceded by torture. Convicted slaves were broken on the wheel, their flesh pulled off with red-hot tongs, they were impaled on the impaling spike or slowly strangled and left hanging on the gibbet.*

OPPOSITE BOTTOM: *The wheel and gibbet can be seen to the left of the ship. The wheel was used to break the backs of condemned people before they were executed and the gibbet was a form of gallows from which the bodies of the executed were hung.*

Freed male slaves at the Cape began their freedom with a combination of formidable disadvantages. Among these were prejudice, poverty, the inability to obtain credit, and also the extreme difficulty of obtaining gainful employment. Free blacks were excluded from most occupations as early as 1727. Burgher councillors even forbade free blacks to sell such pathetic sundries as 'toast and cakes' on the streets. Many were forced to turn to the precarious occupation of fishing the most dangerous waters of the South Atlantic. Although some freed slaves had to be helped by the poor fund of the Church, most found succour among the sympathetic free black Muslim community, many of whom owned slaves themselves and were regular manumitters.

Mixed liaisons

During the early years, the situation was fluid enough for some children born outside wedlock from unions of non-European parents to be accepted into the European community. The slave Armosyn Claasz gave birth to the children of four different fathers in the Company's Slave Lodge, some described as *halfslag* (half-caste), which means that the father was white. Many of these children and their descendants were absorbed into what became prominent Afrikaner families.

During his 1685 visit to the Cape, High Commissioner H.A. van Reede prohibited marriages between Europeans and *heelslag*, or full-blooded slave women (that is, of pure Asian or African origin). He did, however, permit marriages with *halfslag* women, with the intention of assimilating such half-castes into the European population. Fathers generally would not own up to their liaisons with slaves, and therefore they did not help their children by slave mothers to gain their freedom – a fact of Cape life that Van Reede's regulations were meant to address.

In the period of Company rule, just over 1 000 ex-slave and native women married free burghers of European descent (and only two male ex-slaves married free women of European descent). When one considers that 65 000 slaves were imported into the Cape and almost an equal number were born into slavery, it is clear that the chances of a slave's entering the ranks of colonial society were small and highly gendered, and, moreover, that they declined with time as the price of slaves rose. No one could marry a slave: she first had to be manumitted. At the end of the eighteenth century Willem Klomphaan tried to manumit his slave mistress and his two children but died before he could pay the full sum.

Across the sandy plain

For seventeen years after Van Riebeeck's departure, the settlement did not extend beyond the sandy plains skirting the peninsula, principally because of continued Khoikhoi resistance. When the resistance crumbled by the end of the 1670s, the Company decided to extend the settlement across the sandy plain. There were now 142 adult free burghers, half of them farmers. Simon van der Stel, who arrived in 1679 as commander of the Cape settlement, was entrusted with the task of supervising the expansion.

In 1679 Simon van der Stel founded the settlement of Stellenbosch some 50 km away from the fort in Table Bay. Shortly afterwards the government built a drostdy, the seat of local government, and appointed an official as landdrost, and four burghers as *heemraden*, or councillors.

TOP: *Permission for the building of a Lutheran church was not granted until 1780, by which time the principle of one language and one church for the European community had become well established.*

BOTTOM: *Simon van der Stel's grandmother was an indigenous woman from Batavia called Mai Monica da Costa – a 'coloured' woman in today's parlance. There is a possibility that both Simon and his son, Willem Adriaan, did not look European, as suggested by this painting.*

The government set no legal limits for the size of the farms in the Stellenbosch settlement. With the market far away and the road tough to travel on, land suitable for arable agriculture was mostly used for grazing. Very much the same pattern unfolded in Drakenstein (later called Paarl), French Hoek, Tygerberg, Wagenmakersvallei (Wellington), Swartland (Malmesbury) and the Land van Waveren (Tulbagh), all settled by the end of the first decade of the eighteenth century.

The arrival of the Huguenots

In 1688 a party of some 180 French Huguenots arrived, fleeing religious persecution in France and Belgium. Simon van der Stel settled most of them in Franschhoek and Drakenstein (today's town of Paarl) and gave instructions that the French be interspersed with the other burghers 'so that they could learn our language and morals, and be integrated with the Dutch nation'.

The authorities in Amsterdam took a more lenient line, however, and permitted them to form a congregation. In 1691 Drakenstein became the third congregation after the Cape and Stellenbosch. But the policy of forced cultural assimilation remained in force; by 1750 no one under the age of 40 could still speak French.

The Huguenots did much to stabilise the free burgher population. Without a fatherland to return to, they had to take root or disappear. Religious persecution had made them more determined and more prepared to overcome obstacles. Descendants of the Huguenots were to establish positions of leadership in Afrikaner society out of all proportion to their numbers. Some 40 Huguenot surnames still survive.

The Huguenots made a difference in another important respect. Previously, the shortage of European women prompted many men to take half-caste slaves as brides or mistresses. The Huguenots were generally already married, young as well as fecund. As the girls in these large families grew up, men's stable liaisons with non-European women declined and a clearer pattern of endogamy became established.

German immigrants

During the eighteenth century Germans were the major source of recruitment from Europe to the burgher community. Almost all arrived as sailors or soldiers, who entered the Cape as single men. They often were in a parlous financial situation. Some managed to find a European wife but many lived outside wedlock with someone not of European origin. The children from the latter liaisons tended to become part of the slave or Khoikhoi community. The VOC made no effort to accommodate the religious sensibilities of the Germans. Permission for a Lutheran Church was not granted until 1780, and by then the principle of one language and one church for the European community had become well established.

Three momentous decisions

Between 1707 and 1717 three momentous decisions were taken that would affect the colony's character and pave the way for white supremacy. The first was not a new decision but an endorsement of an earlier one to leave agricultural production in the hands of free burghers, who were all of European stock. The second was to prefer slaves over whites as labourers. The third was the acceptance of the loan farm system and unsystematic colonisation.

The last of these made rapid European expansion over a large territory possible. Hand in hand with this went the administrative system of the vast interior in which burghers played a key role. At the centre stood the College of Landdrost and *Heemraden*, assisted by field-cornets in the different wards, who inspected land claims and called up burghers for commando duty. Except for the landdrost, all were burghers.

By 1700 there was nothing to indicate that the settlement between the sea and the mountain ranges would burst its seams and become a sizeable colony. The settlement had become self-sufficient in wheat, wine and meat. In the Land van Waveren (later Tulbagh) San offered stout resistance to further expansion. The officials still exerted firm control. Simon van der Stel and his son, Willem Adriaan, who succeeded him, opposed any expansion beyond the coastal plain. The former predicted that if no obstacles were put in place to extensive cattle farming 'all of Africa would not be big enough to satisfy this type of people'. The settlement was small enough for officials to act swiftly against recalcitrant burghers.

Endorsing food production by burghers

In 1657, when the first free burghers began farming, the Company issued firm instructions that officials were not to supply the market with food since the burghers, who depended on food production, would otherwise be unable to survive. However, Simon van der Stel received the farm Constantia (later Groot Constantia) from the Lords Seventeen. A few years later, his son Willem Adriaan van der Stel received another farm, called Vergelegen, at the foot of the Hottentots-Holland mountains.

Other land was granted to several high officials and the governor's brother, a free burgher. By 1705 land covering a third of the farming area of the colony was in the hands of twenty Company officials. They had set in motion a plan to give them a monopoly in the sale of wine, meat, fish and wheat.

The wealthier farmers felt the most threatened. Adam Tas sent a petition accusing the Cape officials of misconduct to the authorities in Batavia, who forwarded it to Amsterdam. The Lords Seventeen demanded that the Cape officials explain their conduct. Outraged, the officials locked up Tas and some ringleaders in the 'Dark Hole' in the Castle (the seat of government).

By now, the colony was in turmoil, while in Amsterdam some leading Cape burghers lobbied against the Cape officials. Early in 1707 the Cape received the dramatic news that the Lords Seventeen in Amsterdam were recalling Van der Stel and certain officials, including Johannes Starrenburg, landdrost of Stellenbosch. They forbade all officials to own land or trade on the Cape market and they had to dispose of all their land-holdings.

It was a resounding burgher victory. A coalition of burghers had defeated the officials and entrenched their role as the sole suppliers of food. It was in these circumstances that the young Hendrik Biebouw and his friends, who lived on the periphery of burgher society, staged a celebration in the hamlet of Stellenbosch. It would have gone unnoticed by history but for Biebouw's identification of himself as an Afrikaner, at least 80 years before the burghers began to use the term widely for themselves.

ABOVE: *Travelling by ox-wagon was slow, uncomfortable and demanding. This illustration is from* Travels in the Interior of Southern Africa *by W.J. Burchell.*

BELOW RIGHT: *When Governor Willem Adriaan van der Stel entered the produce market in competition with the free burghers, they complained to the Directorate in Holland. As documentary proof of the gains reaped by the governor, they forwarded this drawing of the farm Vergelegen with their complaint.*

BELOW LEFT: *The accused Van der Stel sent an extensive defence, accompanied by another drawing. This drawing shows the house from the opposite side. Van der Stel had deliberately hidden the huge octagonal garden in front of his house.*

Perpetuating slave labour

Not until 1716 did serious discussion take place on the question of slave labour. In this year a letter by the Lords Seventeen posed the question whether the Cape should continue to import slaves or whether it should turn to the assisted immigration of free, European labourers, who could go on to become overseers and artisans, and ultimately even farmers. Most members of the council had no stomach for a class of free European labourers who, in the words of the secretary, would 'have little respect for their master and [would] lay down the law for him'. Predicting that more immigrants would simply increase the number of poor burghers, the Council recommended the importation of slaves as the cheapest and most desirable option.

The die was cast. The colony would not be able to grow out of its economic straitjacket by enlarging the market. This it could have done if there was a steady increase of cash-earning wage labourers. Instead, the colony stuck to slaves. The burghers also saw little need for European immigrants to supplement their numbers and assist them in building a European colony. Slaves satisfied most of the labour needs of the Western Cape. The burghers were defining their survival not in terms of a large self-sufficient European society, but in their ability to ensure that the land and other opportunities were reserved for them and their children.

Opting for unsystematic colonisation

In 1714 another fateful decision was taken. Considering the area west of the mountain ranges fully settled, the government allowed the loan farm system to develop beyond the mountains through the issuing of grazing licences. This gave a farmer the use of a minimum of 6 000 acres of land for a small annual fee of 24 rixdollars, which was equal to the value of two cows. The *opstal*, though not the land, could be purchased.

Many farmers stayed on their farms but instructed their sons to take out farms for themselves. A special class of colonists came into existence, called the trekboers. They combined hunting with the seasonal migration of their livestock.

In a country in which 'free land' initially seemed unlimited and game abounded, the pioneer could penetrate the interior without concerns about food. When a trekboer in 1834 was asked how far he intended to penetrate into the interior, he lifted his hand to indicate a spot far away and remarked: 'To beyond the other side.'

The system of loan farms provided the foundation for the unsystematic colonisation of the interior. It saw a thin layer of colonists spreading themselves over a vast area. As a result roads, towns, markets and a more stratified society with a division of labour were very slow to develop. The government did not like it, but unwittingly it had created an important safety valve for the poorer burghers, whose opportunities in the west of the

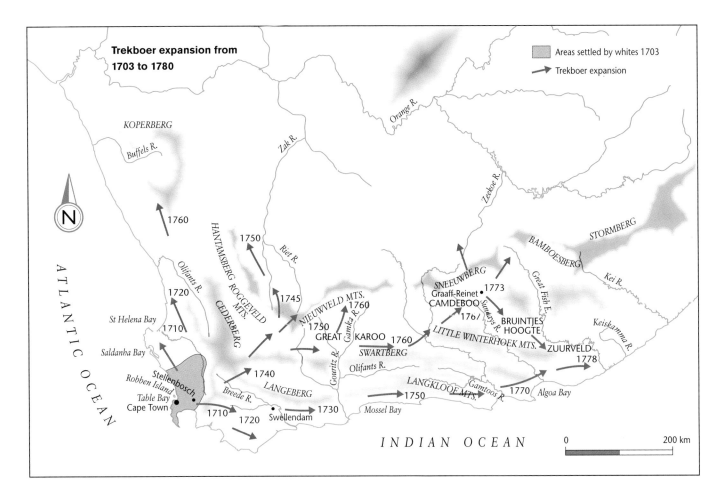

MY NAME IS VAN DER MERWE

colony were rapidly declining. Life as a trekboer could be lonely but it beat that of a labourer on a wine or wheat farm.

The administrative system of the interior districts rested on a local board called the *collegie*, or college. It consisted of a landdrost, who was a government official, and *heemraden*, who were prominent burghers. A College of Landdrost and *Heemraden* was introduced in Swellendam in 1743 and in Graaff-Reinet in 1786. The college dealt monthly with conflicts over land and applications for land and water rights. It mediated in civil disputes and settled minor criminal cases, such as assault, though it could also impose severe punishment, like lashes, on insubordinate slaves. In serious criminal cases, as when a slave died at the hands of the master, the college collected evidence for the Court of Justice to hear the case.

The system relied heavily on burghers filling the office of *veldwachtmeester* (later field-cornet), one for each *wyk* (ward or division) of the district, doing their duty. They had to inform the burghers of government proclamations, report on crimes, hold post-mortems into unnatural deaths, inspect land claims, and call the burghers out on commando.

From the start the burghers played a key role in the defence of the district. All male burghers had to perform military service and take part in annual training. In each division the burghers elected their officers and each district had a *Krygsraad*, or Council of War, of senior officers, who supervised the militia under the overall control of the land-drost. Soon it was apparent that an unofficial division of labour was taking place. After 1715 the Company largely turned the defence of the interior over to the burghers, who now indeed had become the 'defenders of the land'. *(See page 49.)*

A colony of settlement

Economically and socially the colony could be divided into three distinct areas: those living in De Kaap (later called Cape Town), the wine and wheat farming community of the rural Western Cape, and the stock farmers of the frontier beyond the first mountain ranges.

MY NAME IS VAN DER MERWE
Driving this expansion was a fast-growing burgher population. The burghers married early and families tended to be large. The *stamvader*, or progenitor, of the best-known and largest Afrikaner family of today, Van der Merwe, was Willem Schalkszoon, who became a burgher in 1661. He and his wife, Elsje Cloete, had thirteen children. Two of their four sons died early and the third had eight children, but this family line became extinct in the fourth generation. The fourth son, Schalk Willemszoon, and Anna Prevot had seventeen children, ten of whom were sons. They, in turn, fathered 90 children carrying the family name. With the 45 children of the seven daughters, Schalk and Anna van der Merwe had an astounding 135 grandchildren.

OPPOSITE: *'The house of a cattle farmer', showing a tan pit and soap manufacturing. (Drawing by R.H. Dingley, 1819.)*

THE ARCHITECTURE OF THE COLONY

A traveller who arrived in the Cape Colony in the first or second decade of the nineteenth century would have been able to identify several distinctive styles of architecture. First there were the *matjieshuise* of the Khoikhoi, who built dome-like structures of reeds, branches, grass and sometimes skins. Some of them can still be seen today in the Port Nolloth area. Towards the east, the rondavel-type huts of the Xhosa dotted the hills and plains of the land across the Fish River.

In the southwestern Cape, particularly on the wine farms, the Cape Dutch architecture could be found. By the end of the nineteenth century it was described by Sir Herbert Baker, architect of the Union Buildings, as 'surely the most beautiful residential architecture in the world'. Unlike the indigenous *matjieshuise* and Xhosa huts, Cape Dutch architecture was a blend of ingredients from Europe, Africa and the Dutch Indies. It was at its most attractive when the house was built on a wine farm in a spacious yard amidst gardens, oak trees and vineyards, with a mountain as backdrop.

A typical house or hartebeest hut of a trekboer as drawn by C. Bell (TOP LEFT), a Khoikhoi matjieshuis (BOTTOM LEFT), a rondawel-type hut built by the Xhosa in the nineteenth century (TOP MIDDLE) and the mansion at Morgenster, near Somerset West, a typical example of Cape Dutch architecture – all drawn by Hannes Meiring.

Many of these houses were built by artisans who came from the East as slaves. In the absence of hard brick, the houses had to be built with inferior walling material (rubble, clay and unburnt brick) and were nearly always covered with lime plaster. The building materials determined the form and structure. They provided for walls with vertical but little lateral strength and forced on the builder a roof span limited to six metres. Two or three rooms of that width were strung in a row on the model of the longhouse tradition of northwestern Europe (several rooms parallel to the street front). Wings were added on later and led to letters-of-the-alphabet plans (H-plan and T-plan). In contrast to the gables in the Netherlands that covered the entire narrow front of a house, the Cape Dutch gable was in the middle of the front wall with a long thatched roof covering it. The single most distinctive feature of the architecture, the gable, not only kept the front door drip free, but also allowed light into the attic through the dormer window. Decorations were in malleable plaster.

The curvilinear Baroque/Rococo gable of the second half of the eighteenth century was replaced by a rectilinear Neoclassicism with plastered pediments and pilasters.

The oldest existing Cape Dutch gable is to be found on Joostenburg, near Paarl (1756). The most outstanding examples of Cape Dutch architecture include Morgenster near Somerset West (1786), La Provence near Franschhoek (1800) and Schoongezicht near Stellenbosch (1814).

TRAVELS INTO THE INTERIOR

Travelling by ox wagon was slow, uncomfortable and frequently physically demanding of both driver and passengers. Travellers averaged only six hours a day because of the difficulties of crossing rivers, the rough roads, and the frequent stops necessitated by damaged wagons or thirsty and tired oxen or horses. A trip between Cape Town and Swellendam took at least 60 hours or close to two weeks. In 1803 the daughter of an official commented on the strange spectacle of frontier families travelling to Cape Town to get married or baptised: 'Many take the whole household, wives, children and animals, all go along. The journey takes as long as month and is quite patriarchal.'

There were three routes linking the Cape and the interior: Hottentot Holland's Kloof was the route between Cape Town and the eastern parts of the colony along the coast; Roodezand Kloof skirted the present day Tulbagh and Ceres and went on to Graaff-Reinet, and Eland's Kloof opened up the communication with Namaqualand.

All the passes were exceptionally difficult to use. Roodezand was steep, rocky, and filled with potholes and soft sand. As a result, it could do considerable damage to wagons, the wheels of which either broke against the rocks, or sunk into the sand. The narrowness of the pass was worsened by the dense and lush vegetation. On many occasions, travellers would have to unpack and dismantle their wagons, and then carry their goods and provisions through the kloof.

The roads were deeply cut sand-tracks. These simple tracks were frequently in bad repair. It took six hours to travel from Cape Town over the sandy Cape Flats to Stellenbosch, with a line of poles indicating the route to follow.

Travellers had to rely for sustenance on their own food stores, and on the hospitality of the farmers residing along the routes they would travel. They often remarked upon the kindness of the farmers along the routes. In his journal, James Ewart notes: 'The best trait in the character of the Boer is his acknowledged hospitality, a virtue which may have developed from necessity, for when traversing the almost trackless region over which they are dispersed, they must depend entirely upon each other.'

Cape Town was a multiracial and multilingual city. A quarter to a third of all the burghers lived in Cape Town, engaging in commerce and petty trade. Life revolved around the Castle, which housed the Company's headquarters and garrison, numerous taverns, and boarding houses that provided hospitality for visitors. The city was considered to be the centre of cultural and intellectual life, but in fact it was a backwater. Until the end of the Company period there was no high school, no theatre, no public hall of entertainment, no bookshop, and no newspaper. Most people did not read and public amusements were few. Dances in the wealthiest private houses, with slaves providing the music, were very popular.

While Cape Town's natural beauty was widely hailed, not everyone was pleased with the town. In 1710 Johanna Maria van Riebeeck, a granddaughter of the founder and wife of the governor-general of Dutch India, was dismissive in her comments. 'The governor's house looks like a maze and the other houses resemble prisons. The [Khoikhoi] are ugly, stinking people, the Dutch keep their houses in a slovenly way . . . and the way of life is peculiar. The governor is a man with a certain courtly elegance, but everything is done in the [Khoikhoi] style. Nevertheless the food is better than in Batavia and so is the climate.'

Life on the platteland

On the coastal plain, production expanded steadily. Between 1720 and 1790 the number of vines increased more than fourfold, the wheat crop trebled, and the average net value of cultivators' estates grew by nearly three times.

By the 1730s a landed 'gentry' had emerged. Measured by land holdings, vines planted, by wheat crops and livestock, the gentry made up 10–20% of the rural burgher population. They tended to pass their wealth down from one generation to the next. The names of these families are still common Afrikaner names today: Cloete, De Villiers, De Vos, Du Plessis, Du Preez, Du Toit, Joubert, Le Roux, Malan, Marais, Minnaar, Morkel, Myburgh, Retief, Roux, Theron, Van Brackel and Van der Byl. It is striking that more than half were descendants of Huguenots.

By the second half of the eighteenth century, the Western Cape gentry had amassed sufficient wealth to engage in some conspicuous consumption. Mansions built in the Cape Dutch style were a splendid example. A visitor wrote in 1783 that on several farms he had observed 'nothing except signs of affluence and prosperity, to the extent that, in addition to splendours and magnificence in clothes and carriages, the houses are filled with elegant furniture and the tables decked with silverware and served by tidily clothed slaves'.

Slaveholding was widespread in Cape Town and the rural Western Cape. Baron Van Imhoff remarked in 1743 that having 'imported slaves every common or ordinary European becomes a gentleman and prefers to be served rather than to serve'. In Cape Town, two-thirds of the burghers held slaves by the end of the century and 70% of the farmers in Stellenbosch and Drakenstein owned at least one slave. A visitor to Cape Town observed that there seemed to be twenty blacks for every white on the street.

In the stock-farming interior there was little building (the town of Swellendam had only four houses 40 years after it was founded), no mining, no industry, no shops, and no professional military establishment. Almost all the burghers in the interior farmed or lived on farms. By 1770 stock farmers formed two-thirds of all farmers in the colony.

The burghers' interaction with the Khoisan led to large-scale cultural borrowing. In some aspects the trekboers resembled Africans rather than their kinsmen in the west. Like the Khoikhoi, they stored milk in skin sacks, dried strips of game (later called biltong), wore *veldschoenen* (sandals made from cowhide) and sometimes animal skins. Both Afrikaners and Basters (*see page 68*) were forced to develop a pragmatic lifestyle that made survival possible in the African interior.

Subsistence farming predominated, but all the farmers remained tied to the market. They needed, at a minimum, to purchase a gun, ammunition and a wagon, and most required axes, spades, hammers, crowbars, bolts, lanterns, clothes and essential groceries. To buy such goods stock farmers sold stock to the market, and tried to supplement their income by marketing soap, tallow, butter, wax, dried fruit, hides, skins, horns and seed.

Farmers kept large herds, often too large for their farms. It was the only way they could accumulate wealth since land was not bought and sold for profit, and the Company, at certain times, prohibited the selling of loan farms. Farmers with an acceptable farm tended to stay there and, once the frontier had closed, several generations would live on the same farm.

The more affluent gradually improved their condition of rough comfort. They built better houses and bought cloth to turn into European-style clothes. By the end of the eighteenth century the wealthier Graaff-Reinet burghers were acquiring mirrors, curtains, table linen, porcelain, copper candlesticks, even four-poster beds. An increasing division of wealth steadily became evident in the frontier districts.

The area of European occupation grew almost tenfold between 1703 and 1780. In 1798 the government fixed the boundaries of an area covering 286 000 square kilometres, running from the Buffels (or Koussie) River in the west to the Nuweveld mountains in the northeast, and from there down to the sea along the Tarka, Baviaans and Fish rivers.

LEFT: *Captain Hendrik Storm with his son and daughter, each attended by a personal slave waiting in the background. The location is a house in central Cape Town.*

MIDDLE: *The burghers' interaction with the Khoisan led to a large-scale cultural borrowing. Like the Khoikhoi they stored milk in skin sacks, dried strips of game, and wore shoes made from animal skins. This picture by R.H. Dingley shows the 'Interior of my room at the Van der Marvels,' Great Fish River, 1816.*

RIGHT: *The Muller family at Graaff-Reinet. C.T. Muller arrived at the Cape from Germany in 1790. He married R.C. Boshoff and they settled in Swellendam before moving to Graaff-Reinet in 1812, where he set up a trading business. He is surrounded by his wife and four daughters, engaged in needlework, reading, writing and playing musical instruments.*

The rise of the new communities

In the course of the eighteenth century new communities – defined by race, religion and culture, and differential access to land and power – began to emerge. In the almost complete absence of the written word, they lacked the prophets or scribes who could 'imagine' a new community and exhort followers to pursue a particular mission. They were tied together as a community through the spoken word.

Among the communities in the colony who began to crystallise in the eighteenth century were the 'Bastaards', Muslims and Afrikaners. Along the northern and eastern frontier, people of mixed origins lived alongside and sometimes among the frontier burghers. They were commonly called 'Baster' or by the Dutch word 'Bastaard', which referred to the offspring of liaisons between Europeans, slaves and Khoikhoi, but also to subordinate blacks who could speak Dutch and ride and shoot.

Bastaards

On white-owned farms Bastaards, or Basters, did more skilled jobs than hired or domestic labour – working, for instance, as craftsmen and transport riders – and they took these skills with them later into the interior. They originally referred to themselves as 'Bastaards', not to denote illegitimacy, but their status as a people with a greater 'civilisation' and an attachment to Christianity than the Khoikhoi or slaves. They could speak Afrikaans.

In the second half of the eighteenth century small Baster communities had been formed in the fringe areas of the northwest – Namaqualand, Cederberg, Bokkeveld, Hantam and the Roggeveld – and on the eastern frontier. In the 1798 census of Graaff-Reinet district, some 5–10% of the district's farming population were listed separately as 'baptised Bastaards'. They had European names and their children were baptised in the church (although increasingly, apparently, in separate ceremonies). They were called upon to do commando service.

Basters were, nevertheless, increasingly squeezed out from the land they held. On contested claims, burghers invariably had the stronger claim and better access to the field-cornets who reported on any such claims. Heinrich Lichtenstein, a German traveller who traversed the colony in the first years of the nineteenth century, commented: '[The] white children of the colonists did not hesitate to make use of the right of the strongest to drive their half yellow relations out of the places where they had fixed abodes. These bastard [Khoikhoi] were then obliged to seek an asylum in more remote parts . . .' Basters and other people of mixed racial origin moved first to the outer limits of the colony and then beyond its borders.

Adam Kok, a freed slave who managed to obtain burgher rights and a farm near the present Piketberg, founded the most vigorous mixed community. According to one tradition he married the daughter of the chief of a Khoikhoi clan, the Chariguriqua (the root of the name 'Griqua'), during the 1750s. Kok attracted a following as he moved up from Piketberg to Little Namaqualand. By the 1790s a son of Adam Kok, Cornelis Kok, moved out of the colony to the Orange River and then eastwards along the bank to what is now known as Griqualand West. He had gathered with him a large number of Basters, some Khoikhoi, and escaped slaves.

On the urging of the missionary John Campbell, they came up with the name Griqua. They established a rudimentary system of government based on leaders called *kaptyns* and magistrates drawn from individuals within the leading families. Prominent among them were the Kok and Barends families, and the Waterboer family complex.

These families assumed stability by eschewing a life of pure raiding and establishing trade links with their neighbours. Andries Waterboer allegedly had no white parentage and was a dependant of Adam Kok. However, he later allied himself to the church, acting as an interpreter, and rose to influence after 1820 when he was appointed *kaptyn*. In an attempt to achieve a greater measure of political autonomy the Griqua invited the missionaries to join them.

In 1804–05 they founded a settlement called Klaarwater, later Griquatown. Chronic internal divisions and environmental uncertainty bedevilled the different Griqua communities. The essential tension was between wanting to be within the colonial fold, with the security and economic opportunities it presented, and yet to be independent from it.

The missionaries had their own aims in Christianising the Griqua, which basically were to transform them into a settled agricultural and pastoral group. In 1813 Campbell drew up a constitution for them, which effectively stripped the *kaptyns* of much of their power. This created tension, but the missionaries did offer some protection and accord the Griqua a degree of respectability.

Relations between Waterboer and the Kok/Barends family complex were poor. Adam Kok II and Barend Barends moved away from Griquatown with their followers to Campbell and Danielskuil, respectively. Later Kok moved to Philippolis, and Barends to Boetsap. This strengthened the hand of Andries Waterboer, who became the dominant figure in Griquatown itself, and the protégé of the missionaries.

The Griqua were the first people from the Cape who settled beyond the Orange River – an area known as Transorangia. Some Griqua raided the Tlhaping, a Setswana-speaking African community; others obtained cattle from them, which they then traded with the Cape Colony for firearms, horses and wagons. They also acted as middlemen in a lucrative ivory trade between the Batswana and the Colony, while some engaged in hunting for ivory themselves.

The Muslim community

Muslims arrived as exiles, convicts and slaves. The exiles were mostly political leaders whom the Company had dethroned in their Eastern possessions and arrived at the Cape accompanied by a following of co-religionists. Among the early political exiles was Sheikh Yussuf, widely regarded as an Islamic saint, who arrived at the Cape in 1694 with a party of 49 followers. His home near the Macassar Downs became a gathering spot for Muslims and runaway slaves until his death in May 1699.

The core of the Cape's *imam* community was drawn from the nearly 3 000 convicts (*bandietten*) who arrived at the Cape from the East to work in gangs on the fortification and harbour works of Cape Town.

The majority of the Cape's Muslim population was drawn from the slaves imported by the VOC from the East. The Muslim sympathies of this group were first noticed in the 1770s by George Forster, an English explorer who mentioned that a few slaves 'weekly meet in a private house belonging to a free Mohammedan, in order to read, or rather chaunt, several prayers and chapters of the Koran'.

THE JUDGEMENT OF AN IMAM

As early as 1725 the *imams* made their moral presence felt at the Cape, in the following case outside the Slave Lodge, the notorious Company brothel. Apparently an elderly Muslim pointed at the sailors swaying in line waiting for the whores, and said: 'You Dutch Christians preach to us of your superior religion. The Calvinists are, to hear them, the salt of the earth with God-given morals . . . Look at how you really are. You behave like swine, like drunken, whoring pigs. I would never allow my daughter to marry a Dutchman. I would break her neck first. Now you have the better ships, the bigger guns, and you make us your slaves. But one day Allah will be revenged.'

ABOVE: *An imam, a Muslim spiritual leader, who later also joined slave couples in matrimony.*

LEFT: *A Malay funeral in Cape Town, as depicted by 'E.K.' in 1858.*

OPPOSITE TOP: *Along the northern and eastern frontier people of mixed origin lived alongside and sometimes among the frontier burghers. They referred to themselves as Bastaards, not to denote illegitimacy, but to point to their status as 'more civilised' people, more attached to Christianity than the Khoikhoi or slaves. This picture shows 'Le Bastaard' in T. Arbousset and F. Doumas's* Relation d'un Voyage d' Exploration, *Paris 1842.*

OPPOSITE MIDDLE: *This painting by S. Daniell shows a Bastaard boy from the Fish River area.*

OPPOSITE BOTTOM: *Adam Kok, a freed slave, founded the Griqua community. According to tradition, he married the daughter of the chief of the Chariguriqua (which provided the root of the name Griqua).*

The private slave owners at the Cape had very few slaves baptised or manumitted. Many of the several hundred slave men at the Cape who bought their freedom or received it as a gift from their owners did not turn to Christianity or its missionaries, whom they saw as having rejected them, but to Islam and the Cape *imams*.

The Muslim free blacks used their relative prosperity to free their own slaves and set a dramatic example by manumitting others, including Christian slaves. The Christian missionary, John Philip, noticed in 1831 that the Muslims 'seldom retain in slavery those that embrace their religion, & to the honour of the Malays it must be stated many instances have occurred in which, at public sales, they have purchased aged & wretched creatures, irrespective of their religion, to make them free'.

Islam's authentic universalism had a powerful appeal. Even a convicted felon or a humble slave could be a leader in the Cape Muslim religious community. In this sort of status inversion, the entire Muslim community could in a sense, if not ignore, then bypass the demeaning European-imposed slave status. Achmat of Bengal, a slave in the eyes of the settlers, for example, was appointed chief *imam* of the Dorp Street mosque in 1807.

The Cape *ulama* became a closed, hereditary class in which, increasingly, sons followed fathers as *imams*. They were the first Cape Muslims to go on *hajj*; they were the first to write religious and other manuscripts – including *Azimats* – in the new Arabic-Afrikaans; they established *madrasahs*; manumitted slaves; ran congregations; conducted marriages; performed funerals; and, for the most part, successfully interlocuted with the colonial authorities.

Afrikaners

By the end of the eighteenth century a new sense of community had crystallised in the Western Cape. There was no single fatherland with which all could identify. A recent study calculated the composition of the Afrikaners by 1807 as follows: Dutch 34%, German 29%, French 25%, and non-European 5%. There was a sense of being a distinct community, called Afrikaners (and sometimes also Christians) rather than Dutch or French or German. Admiral J.S. Stavorinus wrote in 1770: 'Although the first colonists here were composed of various nations, they are, by the operation of time, now so thoroughly blended together, that they are not to be distinguished from each other; even most of such as have been born in Europe, and who have resided here for some years, changed their national character, for that of this country.'

The rise of Afrikaans

In 1822 William Burchell observed that all those born in the Cape Colony who were not of English but of German, Dutch or French descent, and who spoke Dutch, called themselves 'Africaanders'. Another observer wrote: '[They] all speak a very bad sort of Dutch language . . . and style themselves as an original nation, Africanes [*sic*].'

The 'bad sort of Dutch language' referred to would come to be known as Afrikaans. Earlier, in 1685, a senior official considered it necessary to warn against a corruption of Dutch. But the government's ability to impose the official form of Dutch was limited. Schools offered a rudimentary education and were poorly attended. The government was even less able to compel slaves and Khoikhoi servants to adhere to the formal rules of official Dutch.

Afrikaans was, in its essence, a dialect of Dutch that had over time undergone a limited measure of creolisation, or deviation from the basic Dutch structure. In the Western Cape, especially in its rural towns and farms, the main variety of Afrikaans took root as the shared cultural creation, in countless small-scale localities, of Europeans and non-Europeans, whites and blacks, masters and slaves. Dutch was simplified and a considerable amount of Malayo-Portuguese, as spoken among the slaves, was injected (The expression *baie dankie* – 'thank you' – reflects both the derivation from Dutch and the borrowing of the Malay *banja*.) By the end of the seventeenth century Cape Dutch had largely become what is now Afrikaans.

There were limits to the extent of creolisation. There were few big plantations where large groups of slaves or servants could develop a fully fledged Creole language among themselves. By the end of the eighteenth century half the speakers of Afrikaans were of European descent and continued to be influenced by Dutch as both the written and the main public language. By the end of the eighteenth century the Dutch *Staten* Bible was widely read by burghers. The church itself tried strenuously to preserve Dutch until the third decade of the twentieth century. In all these ways Dutch both supported and stemmed the development of Afrikaans. Without the continued use of Dutch, particularly in the church and as written medium, Afrikaans would in all probability have been swept aside by English in the nineteenth century. (*See also 'The Muslims' on page 101*.)

Patriots and a founding myth

A much-enhanced sense of political consciousness amongst the burghers was in evidence in the struggle of the Cape Patriots between 1778 and 1787, which in turn drew inspiration from the Patriot movement in the Netherlands which challenged the self-appointed regents who thwarted the aspirations of the burghers. But although the Cape burghers quoted from or circulated documents by Enlightenment thinkers, they were preoccupied with local concerns. Despite the 1706 ban on private economic activities by officials (*see page 61*), conflict over economic opportunities persisted between burghers and Company servants at the Cape. By the 1770s VOC officials had become much shrewder in disguising their trading activities.

The Cape Patriots' political demands were ambitious. They asked for seven seats for burghers on the Council of Policy when matters affecting burghers were discussed, and for half the seats on the Court of Justice. They sought a clearer definition of burgher rights, the codification of laws, and the prohibition of the banishment of burghers except by permission of the burgher councillors.

The Patriots' other concern was economic. They complained about the trading activities of officials and the lack of free trade, asked for better prices for products, leave to export cargoes annually to the Netherlands, for free trade with the East Indies and a reduction in farm rents. Of greater significance were the social tensions reflected in the Patriots' documents. They asked, for example, that white men not be arrested by Caffers (slaves who served as policemen, *see box on page 54*), and that burghers be allowed to punish their own slaves.

All the petitions and deputations to the Netherlands achieved little. The VOC rejected the key demand, namely burgher representation on the Council of Policy, but it permitted

ABOVE: *Arabic Afrikaans. Muslims were the first to use Afrikaans in printed form. They used Arabic script for religious and other manuscripts.*

OPPOSITE TOP: *The tomb of Sheikh Yussuf, a member of the royal family on the island of Macassar. He was banished by the Company authorities in the East and travelled to the Cape with 49 members of his retinue. Their small settlement on the mouth of the Eerste River attracted many Muslim visitors from across the Peninsula.*

OPPOSITE MIDDLE: *Islam, as an egalitarian religion, appealed to many freed slaves. This picture shows a Cape Muslim couple.*

OPPOSITE BOTTOM LEFT: *Johanna Margaretha Duminy was a fourth generation South African of Huguenot stock. Her father, B. Noth-ling, born in Germany, arrived at the Cape in 1746 as a soldier for the VOC. In 1792 she and her husband Francois Renier Duminy moved to their newly built house, Le Jardin, in Tafel Valley where she wrote her diary.*

OPPOSITE BOTTOM RIGHT: *J.J.L. Wernich and his family in his Cape Town house. It is not clear whether the adjoining room with its large stock of wine casks was a wine cellar or a trading store. Officially Wernich was a gardener and a painter. (Pastel and water-colour by P.W. Regnault, 1754.)*

six rather than three burghers on the Council of Justice. Burghers would no longer be re-enlisted in the Company's service. They were not allowed to trade in their own ships, although the directors did permit free trade with foreign ships – but only after the Company's needs had been met. In the Western Cape the activities of the Patriots fizzled out as the burghers waited to see what the momentous developments in Europe held in store for them.

In 1787 the Patriot movement in the Netherlands was crushed after the *Stadholder* called in Prussian troops. Large numbers of Patriots emigrated to other countries, particularly to the newly independent United States of America. The Cape movement also disintegrated.

Resistance to colonial expansion

For the Khoikhoi the eighteenth century was a time of trouble and trauma as one catastrophe after the other hit them. It was estimated that only one in ten survived the smallpox epidemic of 1713 in the southwestern Cape. Epidemics also struck in the 1750s and the 1780s, wiping out half the Gona, one of the largest polities in the east. Scab and other diseases decimated their herds. From the 1750s the Xhosa, moving in clans, started pushing in from the east on the Gona, while individual trekboer families had moved over the Breede River and were taking up land ever further east.

By the beginning of the eighteenth century the Hessequa, Gouriqua and the Attaqua were living undisturbed on the broad coastal plain beyond the Hottentots Holland mountains. The Gona and the Hoengeiqua lay further to the east, in the land between the Fish and the Gamtoos rivers.

The relative lack of Khoikhoi political cohesion made it very difficult for them to withstand San raids. In 1752 a Dutch observer wrote about the Gona in the east: '[All] these [Khoikhoi], who formerly were rich in cattle, are now, through the thefts of the Bushmen, entirely destitute of them. Some have been killed and some are scattered through wars with each other and with the [Xhosa]. Those who are still around here and there consist of various groups, which have united together. They live like Bushmen from stealing, hunting and eating anything capable which they find in the field or along the shore.'

Migrations in the eastern Cape

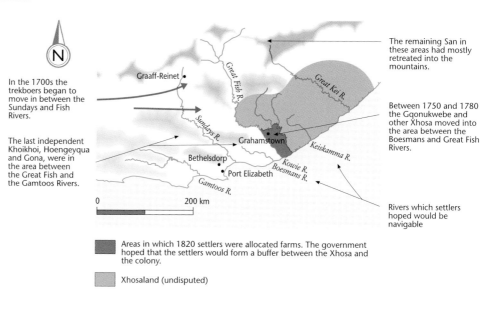

In the 1700s the trekboers began to move in between the Sundays and Fish Rivers.

The last independent Khoikhoi, Hoengeyqua and Gona, were in the area between the Great Fish and the Gamtoos Rivers.

The remaining San in these areas had mostly retreated into the mountains.

Between 1750 and 1780 the Gqonukwebe and other Xhosa moved into the area between the Boesmans and Great Fish Rivers.

Rivers which settlers hoped would be navigable

Areas in which 1820 settlers were allocated farms. The government hoped that the settlers would form a buffer between the Xhosa and the colony.

Xhosaland (undisputed)

Those people described as living 'like Bushmen' were in some cases aborigines, who spoke non-Khoikhoi languages and whose ancestors had lived in the area as hunters long before the arrival of the Khoikhoi or Xhosa. They did not breed cattle but had learnt how to deal with them by working for the Khoikhoi or by theft. But there were also among them Khoikhoi who had lost their cattle and now tried to regroup by hunting and raiding. San raiders often consisted of both categories of people, prompting contemporaries to call them Bushmen-Hottentots and historians to call them Khoisan.

The resistance of the San

From the 1770s the San on the colony's northeastern frontier offered fierce resistance when the trekboers encroached on their hunting fields. They were distressed also by the large numbers of game killed by the farmers, often simply for sport. Koerikei, the famous chief of the 'Chinese' San, asked a farmer: 'What are you doing in my land? . . . You have taken all the places where the eland and the other game live. Why did you not stay where the sun goes down, where you first came from?'

The battles of 1770 to 1810 between burghers and San were as merciless as those fought between pastoralists and herders on any frontier. San killed and maimed the burghers' cattle and sheep at random, murdered herders and mutilated their corpses. Once a farmer woke up in the morning to find his herders slain and 40 cattle and 200 sheep – all his stock – dead. During the last quarter of the eighteenth century the San refused to be deterred by the commandos and began to attack houses as well as livestock. By 1774 the government gave orders to a burgher, Commandant Rudolph Opperman, to head up a commando on the northern frontier. It first had to try to resolve the crisis peacefully, but if that failed, to wage war. The marauders, if necessary, were to be *verdelgen*, or 'eradicated' – that is, killed or expelled – to help the colonists to return to their abandoned farms. The commando, consisting of 100 'Christians' and 150 Khoikhoi, returned at the end of 1774, having killed 503 San and captured 241 across the width of the northern frontier.

Opperman's commando failed in its principal mission to establish peace. The relentless battle between burghers and San continued. According to official figures, commandos killed 2 480 San and captured 654 between 1786 and 1795, when San captured 19 161 cattle and 84 094 sheep and killed 276 herdsmen, making much of the northeastern frontier uninhabitable for the burghers. British officials considered Sneeuwberg, the large division north of the town of Graaff-Reinet, to be in a state of perpetual warfare in the final years of the century.

An aspect of the Opperman commando that deserves to be emphasised is the capturing of San women and children. The government approved of the practice, intending to save lives, particularly during massacres where every member of a San band was shot on the spot. The commandos captured women and children left at the scene of the battle, giving some of the women to the Khoikhoi who had fought with the commando. The children were indentured on the farms until the age of eighteen or 25, with the government's permission.

Soon, capturing women and children became an end in itself for some burghers. In 1780 Dirk Koetse wrote to a militia officer who had called out a commando against some San: 'I have desired my [Khoikhoi] to catch a little one for me, and I beg of you that if he gets one, he may be allowed to keep it.' By 1795 there were an estimated 1 000 war captives in the district of Graaff-Reinet, and

'CONCILIATION RATHER THAN TERROR'
There was a case where a burgher leader radically reconsidered the options in the struggle between burghers and San in the late eighteenth century. He was Field Commandant J.P. van der Walt, who headed up several commandos that rode out in the northeastern frontier in the 1770s and 1780s. In 1793 he settled in a division largely abandoned after Bushman attacks. He received a free hand from the government to set himself up and, as the government's letter phrased it, 'with the help of his family to eradicate and extirpate the robbers'. There is no evidence that at this time he questioned the commando campaigns or the capturing of San children.

Five years later, however, he had changed his views. After repeated commandos had been unable to prevent the San from staging attacks along a broad swathe on the northern frontier, many burghers abandoned their farms. Van der Walt asked the landdrost to refuse requests for commandos to attack the San and capture children since 'the burghers would also give their all if they were robbed of their children'.

Under his leadership the burghers donated 283 sheep and supplies of tobacco and beads to the Bushman clans to induce them to live peacefully on farms of their own. The veldwachtmeesters of Mid-Roggeveld and of Hantam also began to collect sheep and other gifts to hand over to the Khoikhoi to persuade them to stop stealing. Although attacks by the San on some parts of the northern frontier continued until the beginning of the second decade of the next century, Colonel Collins wrote in 1809 how satisfactory it was 'to observe the anxiety evinced by the farmers of the northeastern districts to preserve peace with that people rather by conciliation than by terror'. During the 1820s Landdrost Andries Stockenstrom and the missionary James Clarke made similar statements. In other districts, however, the capture of women and children continued.

LEFT: *Commandos often captured Khoisan women and children left at the scene of a battle. (Painting by F. Steeb.)*

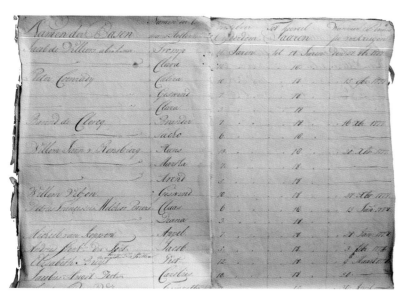

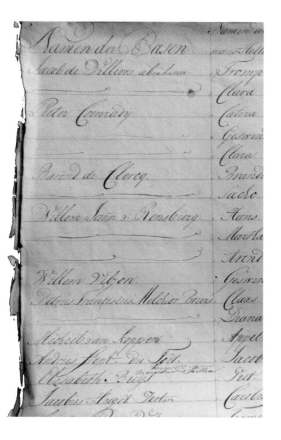

Khoisan children were indentured on farms up to the age of 18, or 25 years with the government's permission. These are lists of the names of such inboekselingen.

some burghers asked that those who did commando duty be allowed to sell their captives. In 1817, Andries Stockenstrom, a widely respected landdrost in the district, reported a continuing widespread traffic in San children.

The Khoikhoi squeezed

The independence of the Khoikhoi disintegrated as the trekboers swept across the coastal plain, while the Xhosa to their east absorbed them. Large numbers of Khoikhoi were incorporated by Xhosa chiefdoms, particularly the Gqunukhwebe and the Ntinde. They did not enter as equals. This was because they were poor, not because they were deemed racially inferior. Since biological mixing with the Xhosa occurred freely they did not form a separate caste; their descendants became Xhosa. At the same time Khoikhoi submission was not entirely voluntary. Some resisted the Xhosa and sought the service of the Boers instead of the Xhosa.

Initially many farmers did not treat a Khoikhoi as mere labourers but allowed them to retain their stock and links with their kinsmen. This was possible in the early stages when land was still plentiful.

The demands the colonists imposed on the Khoikhoi were most exacting. They provided invaluable knowledge about maintaining pastoral production in an arid environment, but they had to yield their land and sometimes their cattle as well. As herdsmen they were targets for the raiders. As members of the commando they fought at the front.

Some frontiersmen forced the Khoikhoi to work for them, they beat them and threatened to shoot them, and mercilessly whipped those who had fled and were recaptured. Such Khoikhoi were little more than serfs or slaves.

But force could be counterproductive. The allegiance of the Khoikhoi sent out on commandos could not be won by beatings. Many burghers worked out a more stable relationship; one that historians have called 'clientship'. In the clientship tradition a poor and insecure Khoikhoi would seek the protection of a burgher as patron, and work for him. In exchange the patron helped him build up his livestock on a frontier. It was when the farm no longer could carry all the people and cattle that conflict erupted.

Many masters told their clients to reduce their stock and, instead of offering incentives, compelled them to work. Masters also prevented the Khoikhoi from leaving under the pretence that their children were still 'indentured' or they claimed 'damages' because of the worker's negligence.

Many Khoikhoi were becoming part of a captive labour force. Not only the Khoikhoi 'serfs', who had been bludgeoned into submission, but also many Khoikhoi clients, began to find their situation intolerable. When they resisted, their masters resorted to violent punishment. The clientship relationship had broken down.

To prevent their labourers from leaving, some farmers introduced mechanisms developed in the slave society of the Western Cape, particularly passes and indentureship. In the final decades of the eighteenth century the district authorities in Graaff-Reinet and Swellendam introduced pass regulations, with masters issuing passes. If a labourer left a farm without a pass, a commando would hunt him down.

Along with passes, indentureship was imported from Western Cape farms, where liaisons between slave men and Khoikhoi women were common. Farmers indentured the children of such liaisons until the age of eighteen or 21 or 25. This custom was formally introduced in 1775, but there is good reason to believe that it had been practised earlier. On farms in the interior the system started in the same way, but it was soon expanded to cases where both parents were Khoikhoi.

Masters used this device to prevent labourers from leaving, justifying it with the same paternalistic ideology as they justified slavery. In 1809 a balanced report by a British officer,

Colonel Richard Collins, noted: 'A [Khoikhoi] can now seldom get away at the expiration of his term. If he should happen to be in debt to his master . . . he is not allowed to take his children, or he is detained under some frivolous pretence, such as that of cattle having died through his neglect, and he is not permitted to satisfy any demands of this nature otherwise than by personal service.'

There are indications that, in the final two decades of the century, some Graaff-Reinet farms were the scenes of acts of great cruelty. Honoratus Maynier, secretary of the district from 1789 and landdrost from 1792, encouraged the Khoikhoi to file complaints against masters who maltreated them. The resulting reports contain evidence of severe punishments, and of masters' refusal to let their servants go. There were increasing reports of Khoikhoi seeking refuge among the Xhosa, taking with them both guns and horses, which had given the frontier burghers such a great advantage over their own adversaries. Fugitive Khoikhoi captured or destroyed stock, burned crops and razed homes.

The Xhosa and the Boers

The Xhosa and the advancing farmers encountered each other during the 1770s west of the Fish River. On a visit to the frontier in 1778, the governor of the colony, Joachim van Plettenberg, asked some Gwali chiefs to respect the Fish and Bushman river mountains as the border between the colony and the land of the Xhosa. The Gwali chief had no right to enter into an agreement that bound other Xhosa chiefdoms – and colonial officials failed to understand this. To compound matters, the government in 1780 proclaimed the Fish river along its entire length as the boundary between the colony and the land of the Xhosa. Unable to live with or without the other, the two communities were drawn into a tangled web from which it was impossible to extricate themselves.

In the early stages of the settlement of the Zuurveld, the Xhosa and the burghers lived peaceably together most of the time, or at least that was how the Xhosa later remembered it. In 1819 a Xhosa councillor reminisced about the early days of white-black contact: 'When our fathers and the fathers of the amabulu [Boers] first settled in the Zuurveld they dwelt together in peace. Their flocks grazed the same hills, and their herdsmen smoked together out of the same pipes.' The councillor attributed the conflicts that broke out to cattle raiding on the part of the Boers, but obviously conflicts over pasture were almost inevitable once an area became more fully settled.

LEFT: *A cartoon denouncing the indenture system. See the notices on the wall. It is not clear why the farmer and his accomplice are shown as Romans – perhaps to refer to Roman slavery.*

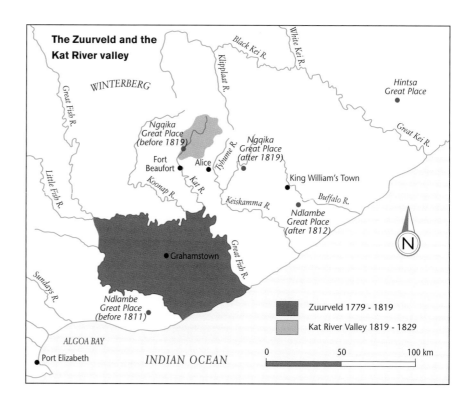

The Zuurveld and the Kat River valley

WINTERBERG

Hintsa Great Place

Ngqika Great Place (before 1819)

Fort Beaufort

Alice

Ngqika Great Place (after 1819)

King William's Town

Ndlambe Great Place (after 1812)

Grahamstown

Ndlambe Great Place (before 1811)

ALGOA BAY

Port Elizabeth

INDIAN OCEAN

Great Fish R.
Little Fish R.
Sundays R.
Koonap R.
Kat R.
Tyhume R.
Keiskamma R.
Buffalo R.
Great Fish R.
Klipplaat R.
Black Kei R.
White Kei R.
Great Kei R.

Zuurveld 1779 - 1819
Kat River Valley 1819 - 1829

0   50   100 km

Ties that chafed and bound

Both the Xhosa and the Boers were cattle-farming societies competing for finite land and pasture resources on the frontier. At the same time, they traded with each other, and growing numbers of Xhosa worked as cattle herders on farms. The Company banned all trade with the Xhosa, but the burghers nonetheless enthusiastically sought to trade because they could acquire cattle cheaply in exchange for tobacco, copper, iron and beads.

Unlike the Khoikhoi, the Xhosa could retaliate if duped or dispossessed of their cattle. Colonel Collins wrote that the Xhosa, at first, 'gave their cattle and labour without knowing its value, but a little experience having opened their eyes on these points, altercations

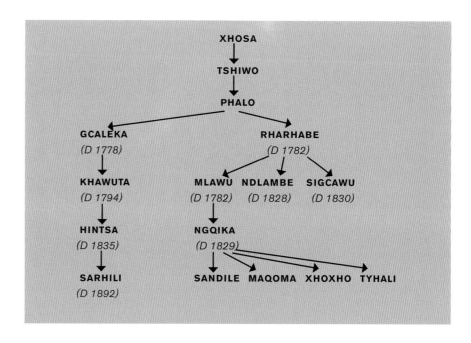

XHOSA

TSHIWO

PHALO

GCALEKA (D 1778)

RHARHABE (D 1782)

KHAWUTA (D 1794)

MLAWU (D 1782)   NDLAMBE (D 1828)   SIGCAWU (D 1830)

HINTSA (D 1835)

NGQIKA (D 1829)

SARHILI (D 1892)

SANDILE   MAQOMA   XHOXHO   TYHALI

between them and the farmers were the necessary consequence. These contentions grew into enmities.'

The tie of labour also bound and chafed. Many Xhosa began to work on farms – sometimes for food and other times for beads, buttons and trinkets, or a heifer or two. Some burghers beat and humiliated their Xhosa workers as they did the Khoikhoi, but with the Xhosa chiefdoms intact, maltreated workers could draw on their chiefs to avenge themselves. Many years later an old coloured man said of the pioneer frontier: 'The [Xhosa], when not regularly paid or [when they were] flogged, informed their chief and came and stole cattle from the farmers by way of repaying themselves for the injuries they had sustained.'

Despite this, the frontier farmers continued to employ Xhosa servants. At the same time, however, they remained anxious about the large numbers of Xhosa in their vicinity, especially those who wandered in parties through the district. They became increasingly irritated by frequent requests from Xhosas who stopped at their houses and begged for 'presents'.

The points on which the Boers felt superior – the Christian religion, monogamous marriage, dress and artifacts of western civilisation – had little meaning for the Xhosa. For their part, the Xhosa attempted to enmesh the farmers in their networks and eventually integrate them into their society along the pattern of the Xhosa absorption of Khoikhoi clans. Trading and military alliances all formed part of the Xhosa's initial interaction with another society, followed by marriage and other forms of social incorporation. All hinged on outsiders accepting African leadership and on payment of tribute to a chief, according to Xhosa custom.

The first frontier war

In 1779 Willem Prinsloo, a farmer living in the vicinity of Bosberg, near the present Somerset East, shot a Xhosa dead. Soon the incident escalated into a war, with raids and counter raids. The district authority in Stellenbosch called out a commando under Adriaan van Jaarsveld. They seized back some 5 000 head of cattle and drove the Xhosa over the central sector of the eastern border.

He and his men also perpetrated a massacre. Encountering a group of Dange in the field, Van Jaarsveld tossed out some pieces of tobacco to them and gave the order to fire while they were scrambling to pick them up. This massacre was remembered for many generations among the Xhosa, who gave Van Jaarsveld the nickname of the 'Red Captain'.

The focal point of the interaction between the frontier farmers and Xhosa now shifted to the Zuurveld. It was narrowly defined as the area between the Fish and the Bushman rivers, but more broadly as extending to the Sundays River and Algoa Bay.

In 1786 the government carved out a new district with a drostdy in Graaff-Reinet. Moritz Hermann Otto Woeke was appointed as landdrost for the new district. He soon grasped the impossibility of attempting to impose laws in the district with only three or four messengers-cum-policemen as his staff. In despair, he reported that unless he was supported by 50 or 60 soldiers 'the rot will continue . . . and if not suppressed will increase to such an extent that everyone will act arbitrarily and do everything at his sweet will'.

A new frontier district

Many Xhosa worked peacefully on farms, but in the Zuurveld there was a persistent note of low-level conflict. The instability was aggravated by intra-white and intra-black conflicts. The Rharhabe chief, wanting to bring the Zuurveld Xhosa to accept his authority, turned to the farmers for support. When Rharhabe died in 1780, the regent, Ndlambe, continued the efforts to subordinate the Zuurveld Xhosa chiefs with the help of the frontier colonists.

In 1792 Ndlambe found an ally in Barend Lindeque, a field-cornet. Without any authority he called out a commando that briefly joined forces with Ndlambe's men and attempted to expel the Zuurveld Xhosa. It ended in disaster when they counter-attacked. Ndlambe and his men retreated, leaving the Zuurveld farmers to face the wrath of the Zuurveld Xhosa, who no longer feared their guns.

FRONTIER WARS

VOC Frontier Wars

First War	1779 – 1780
Second War	1792 – 1793
Third War	1799 – 1802

British Frontier Wars

Fourth War	1811 – 1812
Fifth War	1819 – 1820
Sixth War	1834 – 1835
Seventh War	1846 – 1847
Eighth War	1850–1851

THE ZUURVELD: A CONTESTED ZONE

For several decades after 1775 the Zuurveld, a coastal stretch of approximately 150 kilometres between the Fish and Sundays rivers, was a zone of fierce contests. The pastures are suitable for both sheep and cattle farming. The river valleys, with their dense, semi-succulent, thorny thickets and sweetveld, provide good grazing throughout the year. Thus the early pastoral occupants concentrated themselves in the valleys, using the plains mainly as summer pastures.

As the Zuurveld became more densely settled, one of the biggest problems was to achieve the desired rotation of livestock between sourveld in the summer and sweetveld in the winter. Such transhumance led to territorial disputes between different communities. Farmers complained that the Xhosa overgrazed and ruined the land by burning. For their part, the Xhosa never ceased to be puzzled about how much land a single farmer could claim for his exclusive use. It was difficult for the farmers to resolve the issue by force. The advantages elsewhere provided by their guns and horses were neutralised by the opportunities the Xhosa had for concealment in the Zuurveld's dense bush. At a meeting of burgher officers in 1794, Commandant Adriaan van Jaarsveld proposed that 'for the sake of lasting peace with the Xhosa the Zuurveld, which had been their land, should be given back to them'.

By the beginning of the nineteenth century the Dutch colonists had largely moved away from the Zuurveld. However, in 1820 many of the British settlers were put there as a human barrier against attacks.

It was in the Zuurveld that the farmers developed the technique of the laager as a way of defending themselves against a large enemy force. As Commandant Adriaan van Jaarsveld observed, this was really a military camp, with 50 or more heavy wagons in a circle, and thorn trees thrust between the openings. In the middle were four wagons in a square, roofed over with planks and raw hides to serve as protection for women, the elderly and children. Here the farmers could defend themselves until reinforcements arrived or the enemy decided to retreat.

Faced by a large enemy force, farmers developed the technique of a laager for defence.

As the Zuurveld Xhosa burned houses, raided cattle and killed herdsmen, penetrating even the Swellendam district, the colonists evacuated the southeastern part of the colony in headlong flight. Of the 120 Zuurveld homesteads, only four were not burned down. Some 300 families lost all their possessions. It was the greatest disaster the farmers had ever experienced – and worse was to follow.

In 1793 a large commando of Graaff-Reinet and Swellendam burghers recaptured some cattle, but large numbers remained in Xhosa possession and the Zuurveld Xhosa remained where they were. For many of the Zuurveld burghers the appointment in 1793 of Honoratus Maynier as landdrost of Graaff-Reinet compounded the crisis. He has been depicted as a negrophile, but he was rather a typical Company servant, whose first concern was to avoid trouble with the Xhosa because war was risky and expensive.

Frontier 'republics'

In 1795 a burgher rebellion broke out. At the centre of it was a clash between the sheep farmers from the Sneeuwberg – who insisted that the energies of the district be spent on fighting the San – and cattle farmers of the eastern and southeastern divisions (Bruintjes Hoogte and Zuurveld) – who wanted the Xhosa driven over the border and their stolen cattle recaptured. Maynier had the backing of all the *heemraden* and burgher officers in deciding not to send a commando against the Xhosa at a time when the danger from the San was worse than ever. In February 1795 a party of armed burghers from the southeast appeared at the drostdy and ordered Maynier to leave the town. Claiming to be acting on behalf of the *volkstem*, the voice of the people, some of the *heemraden* and militia officers took over the administration. Wearing the tricolour cockade of the French revolution, they labelled the district government a 'National Convention', and refused to pay taxes to the Company or obey its laws.

In Swellendam, too, in June 1795, a group of 60 burghers terming themselves 'Nationals' deposed the landdrost who, along with Maynier, had led the unsuccessful 1793 commando. The rebels appointed their own 'National' landdrost and a new governing body, also called the 'National Convention', protested against the taxes and inflation, and asked for the indentureship system to be extended to Khoikhoi children, and for the right to hold San captives as property, which meant that they could buy and sell them like slaves. The Swellendam rebellion soon fizzled out, however.

The constitutional ideas of the rebels were murky. They did not proclaim republics, as is often assumed, but rather expressed the desire for their districts to fall directly under the new republic in the Netherlands. But cut off as they were from the Netherlands, no one could think of a mechanism to establish direct contact with the republican government in The Hague. All this, however, became immaterial in September 1795, when Britain took occupation of the Cape.

The rebels enjoyed only the shadow of power. After the 1795 uprising, the Cape government cut off the ammunition supply to the Graaff-Reinet burghers, leaving them exposed to attacks by the indigenous people. At a meeting in August 1796 the northern and western divisions decided to accept British authority. Early in 1797 the rebels on the eastern frontier capitulated.

The Dutch East India Company finally collapsed under a burden of debt in 1798. The Batavian Republic transferred the task of ruling its territories to the Council for Asiatic Possessions. Shortly after the Peace of Amiens was concluded in 1802 the council sent out two top officials, J.W. Janssens and J.A. de Mist, to assume control of the administration of the Cape. The Cape was now under direct control of the Dutch government. But war soon resumed in Europe and in 1806 the Cape once again was conquered by Britain. It was to remain a British colony for more than a century.

Changing times

Soon after the British government had taken over the Cape in 1795, the first proper census found that there were approximately 20 000 colonists, 25 754 slaves and approximately 1 700 free blacks. The Khoikhoi and Bastaards were first enumerated in 1820, when they totalled 25 975. The total number of people in the colonial boundaries – apart from the Xhosa and San in some of the frontier districts – was probably between 60 000 and 70 000 by the end of the eighteenth century. In the interior, Stellenbosch – the only town of significance – still had fewer than 50 houses. There were no newspapers, no theatre, no publishers and no organised sport in the colony.

When the VOC rule over the Cape collapsed in 1795 it signalled the demise of the old world of status groups, each with its own set of rights, privileges and obligations, or disabilities and lack of rights. Everyone was now a British subject, a word that carried a quite different connotation to burgher – especially in placing everyone in a position of equality before the law. In effect, however, only the white colonists were equal before the law in the first two decades of the second British occupation. The Dutch-speaking white colonists nevertheless continued to reject any form of *gelykstelling*, or status levelling, as when a slave or a descendant of slaves claimed rights and privileges.

The British were firmer than the VOC in insisting that the Khoikhoi had recourse to the courts and the right to own land, but in practice these rights amounted to little since most Khoikhoi were not Christians and so could not swear an oath. Without an oath their evidence counted for less. So, too, almost no Khoikhoi owned land. Lord Charles

Somerset, the third governor of the second British occupation, said that the Khoikhoi could become owners of farms, but he could mention only small grants made to three Khoikhoi and three Bastaard-Khoikhoi.

Even after 1828, when the Khoisan were 'freed' by Ordinance 50, the British granted land only to applicants with sufficient capital, which the Khoikhoi invariably lacked. There was only one successful Khoikhoi applicant for a farm in the eastern districts. For such reasons, the burghers continued to think of themselves as a superior kind of subject with special rights and privileges.

'A necessary evil'

The coming of the British provided an injection to both the Cape economy and the institution of slavery. Britain was the leading trading nation of the world and was rapidly on its way to becoming the world's industrial powerhouse. As a colony of Britain, the Cape was much better integrated with the world's trading networks. The local market expanded strongly, resulting in a voracious demand for slave labour to produce wheat and wine.

With slaves one of the most important forms of property in the Cape Colony, any attack on the institution would severely damage their owners' financial prospects. On the arable farms slaves represented 13–17% of the total value. They were the principal mortgageable assets in the colony. Although slavery did not ordinarily adapt well to cities, Cape Town was an exception where hiring out slave artisans yielded a return of 18% in the 1820s.

BELOW: *The picture shows slaves being sold by auction. Although Britain banned the slave trade, close to 40% of Stellenbosch and Drakenstein farmers used only slave labour in 1806. Slave labour enabled production of wheat and wine in the Cape Colony to treble between the 1790s and 1820s.*

Pressure for the abolition of the slave trade had built up sufficiently in Britain for the new British government at the Cape to seek an opinion on ending the importation of slaves into the colony. In 1797 it turned to Willem Stephanus van Ryneveld, a progressive thinker, and asked him a simple question: could the colony survive without further importing slaves?

Van Ryneveld recognised that slavery had made the burghers 'lazy, haughty and brutal', but argued that it had become 'a necessary evil', which could not be removed without sacrificing 'the Colony and perhaps the poor slaves that are in it'. Ending slavery would ultimately be the work 'not of years, but as it were of centuries'. 'Slavery,' he concluded, 'is hard of itself, but it has become a necessary evil in the colony.'

In 1808 Britain banned the slave trade. Despite this, the production of both wheat and wine in the Cape Colony trebled between the mid-1790s and the mid-1820s, with close to 40% of Stellenbosch and Drakenstein farmers using only slave labour in 1806. Slaves now became much more expensive and had to work much harder.

A slave insurrection

In 1808 the colony was shaken by an event that was in some ways more a demonstration by slaves than an uprising. The main instigators were two passing Irish sailors, James Hooper and Michael Kelly, and two slaves, Abraham and Louis. They assembled slaves from the farms for a march to Cape Town. They planned to gather town slaves and establish a new government that would decree emancipation. About 300 slaves and some Khoikhoi servants from Koeberg and Tygerberg farms defied the authority of their masters and joined the march to Cape Town. As Abraham told a slave woman: 'Tomorrow the troop [sic] will hoist a red flag and fight itself free, and then the slave women will all be able to say "Jij" ["you" instead of "thou"] to their mistresses.'

The judge in the court case that followed called this form of address so 'disrespectful in the Dutch language' that Abraham, in his view, could use it only in a context of resistance and revolt. The revolt was swiftly quashed and the government sent most of the slaves back to their masters. James Hooper, Abraham and three other slaves were executed.

A cauldron of conflict

The British had hoped not to become embroiled in a frontier conflict but they soon were drawn in. From 1799 to 1836 three so-called frontier wars between the Xhosa and the frontier Boers erupted. As was the case before 1795, the conflicts were always over cattle and land and there was never any declaration of war. The hostilities could be seen more as an intensification of raids than wars with clear-cut objectives. The wars intensified rather than settled the conflict.

Invariably the conflicts were triggered by internal power struggles within Xhosa and Boer society respectively. In the early years of British rule there was still a distinct power vacuum. Consequently, leaders pursuing narrow objectives could easily upset the precarious power balance and fragile stability by reckless acts. But soon another disruptive force appeared on the scene: governors and senior military officers who did not understand the complexities of the frontier conflict and rushed in to impose what seemed to them to be solutions.

A turbulent frontier

By 1795 Ndlambe, regent of the Rharhabe chiefdom, stood out as the most powerful Xhosa chief in the western flank of Xhosa society. However, he was toppled at around that time by Ngqika, who was then only sixteen or seventeen years old. He fled west of the Fish where he sought to subordinate the Zuurveld chiefs to his authority.

In the early years of the century Ngqika looked like a major new political force. Intelligent and determined, he had a burning ambition and a ruthless disposition. He concentrated power by deposing councillors and bringing their people directly under him and seizing the entire estate of deceased commoners. Early in the next century he had come to see himself as the supreme chief of all the Xhosa and was recognised as such by the government in Cape Town.

BELOW: *Ngqika (1780–1829), grandson of Rharhabe and the senior chief in western Xhosaland.*

But the seeds of his downfall had already been sown. He never recovered from the clash with Ndlambe, who remained a formidable enemy. Ngqika turned out to be a petulant, avaricious and short-sighted leader who betrayed his people for personal gain. His alliance with the frontier colonists helped him little. His hunger for power and wealth alienated many followers. Many moved into the Zuurveld to escape his clutches.

On the colonial side there were still farmers harbouring a grievance about cattle losses in previous wars. Some of the disaffected frontiersmen set free Adriaan van Jaarsveld, a burgher commandant with some popular support, after he was arrested early in 1799 on a charge of fraud. The ideas of the rebels were vague, but they hoped that Coenraad de Buys (*see box*) would enlist Ngqika's help to assist them in overcoming the Zuurveld Xhosa and in defeating any British attempt to subjugate them.

The new British rulers lost little time in setting out to crush the rebellion. The arrival on the frontier of a British force that included some 50 Khoikhoi soldiers and the arrest of the rebel leaders made a powerful impression on the frontier Khoikhoi. A crowd of some 500 Khoikhoi servants under Klaas Stuurman rebelled against their masters and made off with guns and clothes and then flocked to the military force. They asked the commander to restore Khoikhoi independence before departing. A court declared later that the Khoikhoi had either been incited or had acted from 'a notion they also have conceived of liberty and equality'.

A headlong flight

The British force attempted to obey the instruction to 'gently hush' the Zuurveld Xhosa over the Fish River, but it had to beat a hasty retreat to its ship in Algoa Bay. Sensing that they were being left in the lurch and afraid of returning to their masters, many of the Khoikhoi joined the Zuurveld Xhosa and began raiding farms over a broad swathe. In their ranks were many who had fought in burgher commandos and knew all their strengths and weaknesses. They had both horses and guns and were backed up by large numbers of Xhosa fighters on foot. Suffering from an acute shortage of ammunition, with the government having cut supplies, the colonists embarked in headlong flight. The insurgents raided far and wide, burning farms and carrying away stock. By mid-1799 virtually all the Zuurveld farmers had fled.

The situation was destabilised further by the arrival in Graaff-Reinet of the Rev. Johannes van der Kemp, a Dutch missionary employed by the London Missionary Society (LMS). In the town he encountered James Read, another LMS missionary, and decided to join him. With nearly 1 000 Khoikhoi converging on the town of Graaff-Reinet to seek security and food, Landrost Maynier provided supplies and allowed the missionaries to use the colonists' church for religious instruction. The Boers planned to attack the town but held off. Just before the British left they gave the two missionaries an abandoned farm near Algoa Bay to establish a mission station. They called it Bethelsdorp.

Xhosa raids continued. By early 1803 observers put the number of farms 'burnt, plundered and abandoned' at 470, a figure equal to almost half of the farms registered in Graaff-Reinet and Swellendam. Stock losses were estimated at 50 000 cattle and 50 000 sheep. A wealthy Western Cape farmer believed the losses so enormous that the Graaff-Reinet district would not return to prosperity for fifteen years.

The representatives of the Batavian Republic who administered the Cape from 1803–1806, like the British before them, deplored the brutality with which some frontiersmen treated their servants. But the farms needed labour and the Batavians saw no alternative but for the Khoikhoi to return to the farms. When some chiefs accepted land offered to them by the government, their resistance disintegrated. To improve control over the interior, the government established two new districts, Tulbagh in the west and Uitenhage, with a drostdy of the same name, near Algoa Bay.

In 1806 Britain took possession of the Cape again. Stability on the frontier steadily deteriorated, with no single pocket of power able to assert its authority. In 1807 Ngqika was badly beaten in a battle by his rival, Ndlambe, and fled with his followers to the Amatola mountains, where, it is said, even his own children starved. Ndlambe and Chungwa were now in control of the Zuurveld.

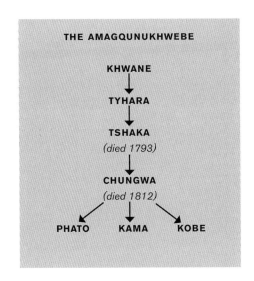

THE AMAGQUNUKHWEBE

KHWANE
↓
TYHARA
↓
TSHAKA
(died 1793)
↓
CHUNGWA
(died 1812)
↓
PHATO   KAMA   KOBE

'A proper degree of terror'

Over the previous 40 years the Xhosa, in the eyes of the Boers, had been many things – foes, certainly, but also trading partners, labourers and potential military allies. Instead of concentrating on dislodging the Xhosa and making it impossible for a return, the commandos focused on capturing cattle.

It was the British military that would try a radical solution: total expulsion by an overwhelming force. To Colonel John Graham, the officer who would conduct the expulsion, the Xhosa were simply 'horrid savages'. He ordered the pursuit of plundering parties of Xhosa to their settlements where 'every man Kaffer' who could be found was to be slain. If possible the chief had to be 'destroyed'. All was designed to inspire the Xhosa with 'a proper degree of terror and respect' to prevent their return.

In the final months of 1811 a large force was assembled of 440 British troops, 431 Khoikhoi soldiers and 450 burghers on commando. In the first three months of 1812 this force expelled some 8 000 Xhosa from the Zuurveld and destroyed their crops. A series of forts was built along the border. Two new frontier villages, Grahamstown and Cradock, were marked out.

For the Xhosa, the expulsion of 1811–1812 and the follow-up operation were new and shattering experiences, nothing less than total war. The number of lives lost, the killing of the chief Chungwa in his bed by soldiers and the destruction of Xhosa chiefdoms in the Zuurveld were incomprehensible to them. They discovered that the colony could draw on more military and other resources than they could ever imagine. Nor did the conquerors deign to incorporate the defeated into their society. They were pushed away as if they were not fit to live with. The military expedition etched out the 'otherness' of Africans and Europeans in the starkest possible way.

'Strict and equal justice'

To extend firmer control over the frontier zone, the British administration did two things. The one step was a failure, the other a success.

In an attempt to regulate the employment and movement of the Khoikhoi, the Hottentot Proclamation of 1809 was issued. It decreed that written work contracts had to be drawn up, and instructed all Khoikhoi to a 'fixed place of abode' without which they could not travel without a pass. It meant that a worker who left an unjust master before his time expired was in violation of the law. Intended to protect the Khoikhoi, the proclamation placed them at the mercy of the powerful.

A more successful reform was the introduction of an annual circuit court, with judges from Cape Town touring the interior to hear cases. The 1812 circuit became known as the Black Circuit, because of the many charges of maltreatment of Khoikhoi labourers raised by the missionaries Van der Kemp and Read from their mission station in

TOP: *Colonel John Graham established Grahamstown in the immediate aftermath of the Fourth Frontier War (1811–1812), when he used a large force to drive many of the Zuurveld Xhosa across the Fish River.*

OPPOSITE: *Bethelsdorp, the mission station that the two missionaries Johannes van der Kemp and James Read established on an abandoned farm in 1803.*

ANDRIES STOCKENSTROM

From an early age the young Andries Stock-enstrom believed that justice fairly dispensed was the key to stability on the frontier. In 1811, the missionaries Johannes van der Kemp and James Read accused Landrost Cuyler of Uitenhage of blatantly favouring burghers over the Khoikhoi and demanded complete equality between colonists and the Khoikhoi. Although this stand ran into tough opposition from the burghers, Stockenstrom, who was then just eighteen and had grown up in the hierarchical social order of the Company, took a similar line to the missionaries on equality before the law – a view he would hold for the rest of his life. 'Strict and equal justice at all costs is the only safe course,' he maintained, later also extending this principle to the relationship between burghers and Xhosa.

Stockenstrom was a slave-owner himself and to some extent shared the paternalistic world-view of the Dutch-speaking colonists. But with his strong commitment to the rule of law and justice, he supported the need for sweeping reforms. He was an articulate exponent of the view that colonists had to be won over to the cause of reform rather than have reforms imposed from outside. Unlike most well-educated people born at the Cape during the reign of the Company, he identified himself as an Afrikaner and a Boer. A brave, honest and fiercely independent man with no illusions about human nature, he shrank from the hypocrisy on all sides of the frontier conflict. In 1816 he observed that 'the greatest majority of the Boer population is not opposed to equal justice to black and white'. The core problem, he believed, was the inadequacy of the legal system. Despite the establishment of some new districts, most farms were still a considerable distance from the towns, making it difficult for masters to lay complaints before the magistrate.

Bethelsdorp. The effect of the Black Circuit was great, and for the first time frontier burghers appeared before a high court in their districts to answer charges brought against them by their servants.

The government also stationed Khoikhoi troops at the border posts to assist the landdrosts. It did away with the loan farm system, which it considered to be a cause of frontier lawlessness. The new system of perpetual quitrent title required that farms be surveyed and that beacons mark their borders. The government's inability to process the new system created insecurity, which fed into the inclination of the more lawless frontiersmen to challenge government.

The Slagtersnek Rebellion

In 1813 Andries Stockenstrom, a 20-year-old deputy landdrost stationed at the newly founded town of Cradock, faced a major test. Early in that year a Khoikhoi labourer named Booy lodged a complaint about his master. The master was Freek Bezuidenhout, a notorious frontier ruffian who lived with a Baster woman and whose Baster son called him 'baas'. Booy claimed that his master had withheld his wages and had severely assaulted him.

Bezuidenhout was one of a number of disaffected, relatively poor colonists in the remote area of Bosberg, Bruintjeshoogte and Tarka. A shortage of land was a major source of discontent, and another was the presence on the frontier of Khoikhoi and other 'coloured' troops under white officers. As Stockenstrom would later remark, 'the people were talking that the "black nation was protected and not the Christians"'.

Stockenstrom would have a remarkable career as frontier administrator, spanning 25 years. He was an honest, brave and fiercely independent man who shrank from the hypocrisy so abundant in the frontier conflict. He was committed to the principles of the strict preservation of order, and equal and impartial justice to all. From the start, Stockenstrom saw the issue as involving a clear choice between order and civilisation on the one hand, and anarchy on the other.

When Bezuidenhout ignored the summons, a company of two British officers and twelve Khoikhoi troops arrived at Bezuidenhout's house. A brief battle ensued and Bezuidenhout was killed. At the funeral a plot was hatched to embark on rebellion.

The rebels' plans were far-fetched. One proposed to make a deal with Ngqika. He could take possession of the Zuurveld in exchange for driving away the Cape Regiment, expelling all officials on the frontier and allowing the rebels to occupy the fertile Kat River Valley in the land of the Xhosa. Burghers who refused to join were threatened with death and having their families and property given over to the Xhosa.

Stockenstrom persuaded the influential burghers not to back the rebellion. In the end, there were only 60 rebels, who surrendered without a shot being fired. After being sentenced, five of the leaders were hanged. Most of the colonists now accepted British rule. In 1816 Stockenstrom observed that 'the greatest majority of the Boer population was not opposed to equal justice to black and white'. The core problem, he believed, was the inadequacy of the legal and administrative system. Despite the establishment of some new districts, most farms were still a long distance from the towns, making it very difficult for masters to lay complaints before the magistrate.

A proper British colony

The British take root

Britain temporarily occupied the Cape between 1795 and 1803 and although it was determined not to cede it again after reoccupation in 1806 the Cape's status as a proper British colony was only formalised in 1814. In this year, the main European powers accepted a peace treaty to conclude the wars that started soon after a revolution broke out in France in 1789. In the peace treaty Britain restored to the Netherlands the rich East Indies and all other colonies taken by her during the Napoleonic wars – except the Cape and what had become British Guiana. The Cape would remain a proper British colony until 1910 when it entered into the Union of South Africa.

For much of the period between 1795 and 1814 governing the Cape was a frustrating affair. In London the European war overshadowed all other matters. Governors had to wait six months for a reply to issues they raised. There was no clarity about the respective powers of the civilian governor and the chief military officer. Financially the Cape was in a mess.

The former Company officials who advised the governors urged caution. It took almost fifteen years before English was imposed as the sole official language and even then English managed to establish a firm foothold only in Cape Town (*see page 96*).

Lord Charles Henry Somerset, governor of the Cape Colony from 1814–1826, favoured autocratic rule, press censorship and the anglicisation of the Cape.

When Lord Charles Somerset assumed the governorship of the Cape in 1814, there was no reason to expect that any major transformation of Cape Society was in prospect. The royal commission issued for his guidance stated that the 'administration of Justice and the Peace of the Settlement should, as nearly as circumstances will permit, be exercised by you in conformity to the laws and institutions which subsisted under the Ancient [i.e. Dutch] Government'. The British ruled the Cape but there was not initially very much that was British about it.

Such instructions were very congenial to Lord Charles Somerset, one of the most aristocratic of aristocrats, but it was his misfortune to govern at a time when the new social forces generated in a rapidly industrialising Great Britain engulfed the colony, sweeping aside not only Somerset himself but the social and economic order that had emerged out of more than a century of Dutch rule. The double explosion of the 1820 settlers at the periphery of the Colony and the 'revolution in government' at its centre reverberated far beyond the borders of the Colony and set the parameters within which the history of the next 50 years was played out.

Lord Charles and the settlers

The origins of the 1820 settler experiment are to be found in Great Britain and not at the Cape itself. Theories of 'overpopulation' were gaining ground in Britain as a convenient explanation for the mass unemployment and political riots that racked the country in the aftermath of the Napoleonic wars. The Chancellor of the Exchequer approved a grant of £50 000 to assist 'persons disposed to emigrate' to move to the Cape. Over 80 000 hopeful emigrants applied and, between April and June 1820, some 4 000 English-speaking people arrived to settle the eastern districts of the Colony, precisely those districts adjacent to the Xhosa border.

In its origins, the 1820 settlement was nothing but a political stunt by a Tory government desperate to demonstrate public concern for the unemployed. But the Colonial

ABOVE: *'Settlers camping near the Fish River, 1837' by F.T. I'Ons. Note the gloomy and wild background overshadowing the tiny tent and wagon, the only shelter in an inhospitable landscape.*

Office was quite aware of the real difficulties the settlers would face and it was not prepared to turn the Cape Colony into a dumping ground for paupers. The vast majority of settlers were neither proprietors nor paupers; they were respectable individuals possessed of some financial means but lacking the large capital necessary to support a whole party of employees. They were not rural people. Fully 50% of them were urban artisans, and they had no intention of staying on the rural smallholdings where they were initially located. Unwilling rather than unable to make a living off the land, they turned with enthusiasm to the more profitable avenues of trade and manufacture.

Above all, they were people habituated to the use of money in commercial transactions. They bartered cheap but attractive goods such as cloth and iron utensils with Afrikaners and Xhosa alike, in exchange for valuable commodities such as cattle-hides and ivory, which fetched high cash prices on the English market. The quest for these commodities soon drew the settlers deep into the African interior and unleashed a new dynamic of colonial expansionism hitherto unknown to the colonial Afrikaners, who sought land for subsistence purposes only.

The British settlers were mostly of a class that enjoyed limited democratic rights in Britain and, naturally, expected equivalent rights in any colony governed by the British Crown. The naked power patronage openly exhibited by Lord Charles and his clique of intimates gave rise to a stream of complaints and celebrated cases. Notable among the complainants was one Bishop Burnett, a gentleman farmer bankrupted by his attempts to break into the monopoly of military contracts enjoyed by the government farm at Somerset East.

Burnett's attempts to gain legal redress eventually exposed the arbitrary nature of the Cape judicial system and of Roman-Dutch law itself. The accused had no right to summons his own witnesses or cross-examine the witnesses of the prosecution. The Fiscal, or Prosecutor, was also one of the judges and there was no trial by jury. None of the top judicial officials could even speak English with any comfort. Bishop Burnett proclaimed that he was an Englishman in an English colony, and that Roman-Dutch law was no more relevant to his case than 'the laws of the Danes or the Calmuc Tartars'. Other sensational cases followed, not least one suggesting that Lord Charles had compromised himself sexually with the strangely effeminate military surgeon, Dr James Barry.

What made all this especially unbearable for Somerset was that detailed reports of these trials were printed in George Greig's *The South African Commercial Advertiser*, the first independent newspaper ever published at the Cape (1824). Prior to this, the weekly

All among the Hottentots! or the Blessings of Emigration to the Cape of Forlorn Hope to be half roasted by the Sun & devoured by the Natives!! _ recommended to the Serious consideration of all those who are about to Emigrate !!
Copied from one by me I. Cruikshank

LEFT: *Cartoonist George Cruikshank's alarmist drawing shows what, according to him, awaits the 1820 British settlers in South Africa – cannibalism, burning houses, wild animals.*

Government Gazette had been the only permitted news medium and the authorities had underlined their opposition to a free flow of information by seizing a printing press found on board an 1820 settler ship.

Greig's own attempts to start a newspaper were stalled for six months until, having discovered that there was no actual law in place to stop publication, Greig went ahead regardless. At the same time Thomas Pringle and John Fairbairn, who edited a small literary journal, were threatened with prosecution. Through their unyielding refusal to accept any concession less than full press freedom, Greig and Fairbairn eventually carried their point.

Suspended for a second time for continued attacks on Somerset, the *Advertiser* was reinstated in October 1828 and this time there was no turning back. By Ordinance 60 of 1829, the Cape press was finally freed from the executive control of government and allowed to print whatever it liked. John Fairbairn took over as editor of the *Advertiser* and, over the next twenty years played a key role in the battle for greater democracy and a more liberal Cape. (*See box on page 97.*)

The revolution in government

The Dutch East India Company was an archetypal phenomenon of the mercantilist age that was characterised by the close identification of government and commercial enterprise. Such a relationship often resulted in confusion between public and private enterprises, between the revenue of the state and the income of its officials. Cape officials habitually augmented their salaries by holding a number of incompatible offices simultaneously. They collected the greater part of their salaries directly from fees paid for services rendered. Many ran private businesses on the side, and did not scruple to grant themselves substantial loans, contracts and monopolies, known as *pachts*.

The Cape elite was tiny, and officials, merchants and landowners were linked together by ties of blood and marriage to form a closed network. One example is that of the Burgher Senate, a self-perpetuating body of four members, which administered the affairs of Cape Town. It controlled the collection of taxes, which it assessed to its members' own advantage and that of their friends, and also disposed of various other privileges, such as the licensing of butchers and bakers.

The networks of patronage and influence that dominated Cape Town were replicated on a smaller scale in the country districts. The landrosts, district secretaries and Boards of *Heemraden* had considerable administrative powers in respect of finance, taxation and

OX-WAGGONS: KEEP LEFT

Concern about the frequent traffic accidents in Cape Town and traffic noise dates back two centuries. The Earl of Caledon, the first civil governor in the second British occupation issued the following proclamation on 23 June 1809:

Whereas it has been represented to me that accidents frequently happen, and that great danger is incurred, especially in the night time, from the negligence or misconduct of the Drivers of Carriages, and particularly of Bullock Waggons passing backwards and forwards from and to the Country and the Cape Town . . . I do hereby order and command, that the following Regulations shall be strictly observed.

All persons [shall] . . . give in to the Fiscal, or the Landdrosts of their respective Districts their names, and likewise how many Carts or Waggons they possess, in order that the same may be registered, and that they may receive a certificate upon a Stamp of Six Stivers for each Waggon.

And in order that the utmost regularity may be observed by the Drivers of all such Carts and Waggons, and likewise by those of all sorts of Carriages whatsoever, I do hereby command and direct that henceforth all Carriages of every denomination, whether drawn by Horses or Oxen, shall keep on the left hand side of the Road or Street, giving always the right hand to the Carriages they meet; and should any damage be done to either Carriage, Cart, or Waggon, whilst on its proper side of the road, by another out of its place, then and in that case the owner of such Carriage, Cart, or Waggon shall not only repair and make good the injury sustained, but likewise in case of refusal be obliged to pay a fine of 20 Rixdollars for having offended against the Law . . .

Besides an administrative revolution, the colonial government after 1806 introduced British ideas about architecture, urban planning, dress, emblems, etiquette and many other aspects of the social order. At Greenmarket Square, the thatched Cape Dutch building next to the Town House, as drawn by C. D'Oyly (top), lost both its gable and thatch, as can be seen in the bottom painting by Thomas Bowler.

allocation of land and labour. These powers were selectively applied, and the Boards were often guilty of 'a sacrifice of the public revenue, either in subservience to their own views, or to the interests of their neighbours'. Since revenue was unable to keep pace with expenditure, the early governors resorted to massive injections of paper money. 'As to our finances, we are perfect bankrupts, and it is needless to conceal it,' the Cape Colonial Secretary reported in 1825, 'we have not enough to pay our own salaries.'

The Cape was not the only newly acquired colony in these desperate straits. Similar conditions also obtained in Mauritius and Sri Lanka, and in 1822 the British Government appointed a Commission of Eastern Inquiry. The commissioners were J. T. Bigge and W. Colebrooke. Few South Africans have ever heard of them, or of Lieutenant-Governor Richard Bourke under whom they worked. Nevertheless, it was these faceless bureaucrats who carried out a veritable 'revolution in government' which finally 'cast off the old skin' of the VOC era and remodelled the Cape in the British image as best they could.

The first task of the commissioners was to create an independent legal system that could guard against both arbitrary misuse of power and corruption within the ranks of the administration. A new Supreme Court was therefore instituted, headed by a chief justice and attorney-general sent out from Britain. All future judges had to be chosen from the British bar, and all Cape lawyers were required to take their degrees in Britain. The language of the courts was changed to English and the jury system was introduced.

Associated with the introduction of an impartial judicial system was the introduction of a more efficient and honest civil service capable of withstanding the temptations of government patronage. Public officials were no longer allowed to hold more than one office, and they were forbidden to collect their salaries in the form of cash fees for services rendered. Strongholds of the old Cape elite, such as the Burgher Senate and the Orphan Chamber, were reformed or closed down. Resident magistrates took over judicial duties from the landdrosts of the country districts, and civil commissioners took over the collection of taxes, the keeping of accounts and the allocation of land. Ordinance 33 of 1827 did away with the old Boards of *Heemraden* altogether.

As representatives of a home government committed to principles of free trade, the commissioners reviewed with distaste the piecemeal system of rents, tithes and taxes from which government revenue was derived, as well as the motley array of licences, concessions and monopolies that had fed the government patronage network. Out went the monopolies of butchers, bakers, wine traders and auctioneers. Local taxes and tithes were abolished, and new roads and the introduction of a postal service facilitated trade. The Land Board was revamped and steps were taken to improve the speed and accuracy of surveying.

The attitude of the commissioners towards the social structure of the colony was similarly shaped by their commitment to a free and efficient economy. The poor administrative record of the old system led the commissioners to believe that local bias and racial prejudice disqualified Cape Afrikaners from holding official positions. Conversely, they believed that the servile condition of the Khoikhoi and the free blacks inhibited productivity. The efficiency of Khoikhoi artisans when fairly remunerated and the success of a Khoikhoi farmer at Clanwilliam encouraged the commissioners to believe that, once granted personal liberty and security of property, the Khoikhoi and other people of colour would become 'industrious farmers and respectable members of the community'.

This economic imperative was equally responsible – with missionary pressure and liberal humanitarianism – in bringing about the famous Ordinance 50 of 1828, one of the foundation stones of what came to be called 'Cape liberalism'. Ordinance 50 repealed existing oppressive laws, outlawed dubious varieties of labour contracts, and specifically reaffirmed the right of Khoikhoi and free people of colour to buy and own land and property on the same basis as white people.

Most important of all was the second clause. It stated that 'no [Khoikhoi] or other free person of colour, lawfully residing in this Colony, shall be subject to any compulsory service to which other of His Majesty's subjects therein are not liable, nor to any hindrance, molestation, fine, imprisonment, or punishment of any kind whatsoever . . . unless after trial in due course of law'.

The intention of Ordinance 50 may well have been to free up labour on Afrikaner farms for the use of British settlers in the Eastern Cape, but it did at least free the Khoikhoi from the threat of legally endorsed coerced labour under the pretence of anti-vagrancy laws. What Ordinance 50 did not do was to alleviate the economic plight of the coloured person. It distributed labour more fairly between English and Afrikaans and it protected the rights of the labourer to a certain extent, but the population nevertheless remained 'free men who depend on employment for food' rather than independent producers. The result was that the Western Cape especially retained the same basic class and racial structure as in the days of slavery, though the distinction was no longer between free and unfree but between rich and poor.

Ending slavery

While the frontier conflict occupied the government's mind for long periods, another social issue loomed large. This was amelioration of slavery as a prelude to their emancipation. This happened in three stages: first the banning of the slave trade in 1808, then the amelioration measures and finally the act of abolition. This process did not trigger a revolt, not because the government handled it so well, but because the mightiest empire in the world ruled a colony with relatively small numbers of slaves and colonists.

After the British ended the slave trade in 1808, slave prices at the Cape increased four-fold until 1824. At the same time the government moved to make slavery more tolerable. It abolished the ban on selling Christian slaves but granted baptised and confirmed slaves some privileges, such as the right to legal marriage, the right to have their children legalised, and the liberty to attend church services at certain times.

For most owners, Christianity for slaves still represented too grave a risk, both in terms of the money invested in slaves and a possible loss of control over them. The manumission level dropped to levels as low as that in the US slave South, the slave society with

TOP: *A Khoikhoi family. Ordinance 50 of 1828 repealed oppressive laws, but the Khoikhoi remained 'free men who depend on employment for food' rather than independent producers.*

the lowest recorded manumission rate in the Americas. In the Cape Colony between 1808 and 1824, only 86 slaves, or an average of six per year, out of a total of more than 35 000 slaves were baptised.

Slaves and their religion

By 1825 many slaves had come to see Christianity as the religion of slave-owners, and, with the door to the Christian church virtually closed to them, growing numbers turned to Islam (*see also page 101*). In 1825, the first year in which records were kept, there were 846 male and 422 female Muslims. Some observers believed that, by the mid-1830s, most Cape Town slaves were Muslims. The authorities were becoming concerned about the rapid spread of Islam.

Slave-owners slowly began to devote themselves with greater energy to win slaves for Christianity. They had come to believe that Christianity could help rather than hinder the owners in controlling their slaves. Landdrost Stockenstrom and the Graaff-Reinet *heemraden* wrote in a 1826 letter: '[The] more they [the slaves] made religious principles their own, the better they would be as servants and the greater the benefits to their owners.' But the Dutch Reformed Church (DRC) left this field largely to the *Zuid-Afri-kaansche Zending Genootschap* and other missionary societies, and to the English churches. Until Emancipation Day the rate of slave baptism and confirmation in the DRC remained very low.

Slave emancipation

As late as 1825 all signs pointed to slavery's remaining a permanent feature of Cape society. In the preceding decade wine farmers had experienced a boom with the reduction of the British tariff on Cape wine, and owners had large amounts of capital locked up in slaves, whose price remained high. Then everything changed rapidly and radically. In 1825 Britain lowered the tariffs on continental wines, making it very difficult for Cape wines to compete. Not only the wine industry but the entire Cape economy sank into a deep depression.

With the value of Western Cape slaves dropping sharply, investment in slaves was suddenly much less profitable. Owners who had bought slaves on credit or had put them up as surety for loans faced economic ruin. Their only hope was that the government would bail them out by paying adequate compensation when it set the slaves free.

Many slave-owners believed that their old paternalist world was on the brink of collapse. They were upset by reform measures, such as one ordinance that permitted the courts to accept the evidence of slaves without corroboration from a colonist. An 1826 memorandum from Stellenbosch complained that this practice placed the slave-owner, who had to pay taxes and help defend the colony, in an inferior position to his slave.

De Zuid-Afrikaan, the Dutch-language newspaper that first appeared in 1830, articulated the temper of the Afrikaner slave-owners. It was incensed when the government issued regulations limiting corporal punishment of slaves and banned protest meetings against the measure. In 1831 a new measure gave slave-protectors the right to inspect slave quarters and compelled farmers to hand in their punishment record books twice a year. This caused a near-riot in Stellenbosch. *De Zuid-Afrikaan* spoke openly of resistance, warning of 'the rights of Dutch burghers and the length of Boer rifles'.

The imperial government did not seriously consider the burghers' proposals to free the slaves. It was – with some justification – suspicious of their intentions. It knew also that the anti-slavery agitation in London could not be denied its prize of prompt abolition. It decided on rapid abolition in all its colonies, with monetary compensation to owners. Slaves would be emancipated on 1 December 1834, but they would have to serve their masters a further four years as apprentices before receiving their freedom on 1 December 1838.

Sidelined, slave-owners accepted the inevitable, but were outraged over the inadequacy of the compensation. (The government paid £34 per slave, far less than the £73 computed by the committee appointed to evaluate the financial value of the colony's slaves.) Another grievance was over the fact that compensation was to be paid out only in London, which few farmers could arrange to reach on their own. Claims therefore had to be handed to agents, who took a hefty slice.

ABOVE: *A slave rejoices at his freedom, as drawn by F.T. I'Ons.*

BELOW: *Emancipation Day, 1 December 1838. Ex-slaves celebrate their freedom in a march.*

The surprise of Emancipation Day

Masters and slaves approached Emancipation Day with starkly different expectations. The slaves had fervently prayed for the day, but had no idea what their new status would bring. The masters dreaded a scenario of slaves embarking on an orgy of revenge leading to a total collapse of the social order.

Emancipation Day, 1 December 1838, surprised everyone. Instead of the skies falling, they opened: three days of heavy rain, flooded rivers and snow on the mountaintops compelled all believers to try to fathom the heavenly meaning. For some slaves it symbolised the tears of slaves who had died before liberation, but for slave-owners it signalled some kind of divine intervention to save the colony from all kinds of disasters.

The Tulbagh correspondent of *De Zuid-Afrikaan* reported that the ex-apprentices were 'quiet, proper and peaceful', adding: 'We look upon the weather as providentially

happening . . . [For] a great part [it] occasioned the avoidance of idle assemblages, and its [sic] consequences; and also prevented improper rejoicing and drunkenness from which nothing but evil must have arisen.' Reports from other parts of the country indicated that the vast majority of the ex-apprentices were sober and orderly and that many went to church. In Stellenbosch they filled the church of the Rhenish Missionary Society on the Braak (the town square), to overflowing for each of the three worship services.

THE LIFE OF KATIE JACOBS, A SLAVE WET-NURSE

Only one full interview with a Cape slave has been recorded. It was conducted with Katie Jacobs in 1910 when she was 96 years old and living in appalling circumstances in District Six, Cape Town. She was born six years after the slave trade had been stopped. Slave owners were entirely dependent on the domestic slave trade for obtaining legal slaves. The separation of slave families, as Katie's story illustrates, was commonplace during this period, as was the incorporation of the slave into the slave owner's intimate family life.

Katie was a wet-nurse, housemaid, farmhand and shepherd to the Mostert family, descendants of the first free burghers, who had migrated to the Swartland. Apart from being forced to wear a man's clothes, her experience was entirely typical of slave women at the Cape.

'I was born on Mr M[ostert]'s farm, near Kalabas Kraal,' she recalled. 'I don't know the exact day, but I was between nineteen and twenty years when we were freed. My father was a Malagasy, and my mother a Cape woman. I began to work when still very young. When my *baas*, through old age, was unable to continue farming, he distributed most of his chattels among his

sons, whom he had set up as farmers in the neighbourhood. I and some cattle and horses were given to *baas* Kootje; my mother and some more cattle were presented to another son in Frenchhoek. From that day I never saw my mother, nor do I know what became of her. Though I did not know how long it would take to perform the journey to Frenchhoek, I often desired to see my mother. The *baas*, however, always refused my request. I think he was afraid that I would not return.'

She continued: 'I had a husband though we were not legally married. My first child died in infancy. I was a healthy woman, and

as my *missus* was in rather delicate health, I became foster mother to her first-born son and heir. During this time I was well looked after, and became one of the family; that is, I was made to sleep on the floor of the dining-room near the bedroom door to be at hand when the young *baas* wanted another drink [of milk]. One evening we were ordered to appear next morning in our best clothes and await further instructions. During the day we were marched into the dining-room, and without any previous warning we were told by a magistrate that in four years we would be free.

'My master offered to take Jacob [Katie's husband] and me into his service at £1 10s. and 10s. a month respectively, and food and house. Jacob at first appeared determined to leave the district where he had suffered so much. My *missus* wept at the idea of my leaving her. "No; you must stay!" she cried. "Think of my son, whom you have suckled and nursed, and who has now grown so fond of you. What will become of him? No; you must stay; you cannot go!"

'Finally, my husband gave way, and we remained at the farm for three or four years.'

TOP: *The slave Katie Jacobs, photographed with two of her great-great-grandchildren.*

Emancipation's aftermath

The colonists feared a massive labour shortage but, as a levelheaded observer, H. Calderwood, remarked in December 1838, '[I]t is ridiculous to talk of them [the freed slaves] refusing to work when they know very well they must either work or starve.' Many stayed with their masters but as many left them for a day or permanently. Perhaps a thousand or two built makeshift homes on government land on the outskirts of towns and villages, and another thousand may have gone to live at missionary stations. Since the government made no land available for small-scale farmers, the majority had little option but to remain lowly labourers.

Emancipation did produce some subtle changes in labour relations on the farms. The days of complete submission had gone. A.J. Louw, a wealthy farmer from Koeberg, complained in December 1838: 'They come to the field after the sun has risen and if we look sour about it, they go away and abandon work.' Workers tended to shun long-term contracts. A correspondent explained to *De Zuid-Afrikaan*: '[They] have been in many cases so accustomed to harsh treatment, and have seen their race suffer so much from bad masters, that they are unwilling to extend their services, until they ascertain the character of their masters.' The correspondent added that masters had been 'too familiar with the whip, the cat and the samboc'.

Masters had to employ day labourers, a practice they disliked, but cash wages remained very low and workers were paid mostly in food, wine (perpetuating the 'tot' system of slavery in which abundant liquor was supplied), clothes, housing and stock. While under slavery some had received land for garden plots and pasturage for their cattle, and in the aftermath of emancipation this developed into a system of labour tenancy. Masters continued to clamour for a vagrancy law to secure a cheap and docile labour force, but the government refused.

The fears about economic ruin for the agricultural sector did not materialise. Between 1834 and 1842 wheat and barley production dropped by a third, but then went up to earlier levels. Wine production was little affected. By the mid-1840s arable production was back at its pre-emancipation levels.

Religious and cultural states

The Christian church played no major role in ending slavery at the Cape. From the 1820s, however, leading colonists stressed the role the church had to play in facilitating the transition from slave to free labour. Slowly the idea died that a Christian slave would be difficult to discipline due to a presumed equality of spiritual status. Among slaves there was a rapid extension of Christianity and the Muslim faith in the first half of the nineteenth century. Both Christian missionaries and Muslim *imams* cared for more than the spiritual well-being of their followers. They helped slaves and Khoisan labourers to adapt to a harsh and cruel world and, in some cases, to use the legal system to seek redress. Both Christianity and Islam stressed literacy not as a goal in itself but to understand a holy message. Religion and education remained closely tied until the end of the nineteenth century.

Many Europeans in the colonies did not take church attendance very seriously, but for most religion explained their world. Acting on the underlying assumption that a single orthodox truth revealed the mysteries of creation and life, the colonial state did its best

ABOVE: *Jacob and Lotje, slaves on the farm Langverwacht between Stellenbosch and Kuilsrivier. They were owned by the De Waal family.*

BELOW LEFT: *Both Christianity and Islam stressed literacy. Religion and education therefore remained closely tied. The picture shows the old school in Noordhoek.*

BELOW: *In 1799 the colonists founded the first local missionary society, the Zuid-Afrikaansche Zending Genootschap (S.A. Missionary Society). This ZAZG church still stands in central Cape Town.*

BOTTOM: *Burghers on the remote frontier were prepared to travel far to have their children baptised and confirmed. Here they are gathering at Colesberg for the* nachtmaal *(communion), as depicted in Andrew Smith's journal.*

OPPOSITE: *Farmers tended to leave education in the hands of an itinerant teacher, or* knecht, *shown here smoking his pipe.*

to impose religious uniformity and if possible a single church denomination. The Christian religion also determined the European colonists' secular standing. To be called a Christian during the seventeenth and eighteenth centuries in the European colonies meant much more than a religious designation. As Winthrop Jordan, a historian of the American colonies wrote, the concept embedded in the term Christian seems to have conveyed much of the idea and feeling of 'us against them: to be Christian was to be civilized rather than barbarous, English rather than African, white rather than black'.

Perhaps because no single European nationality colonised the Cape the colonists were even more inclined to use their Christian faith as a political and social identity. It was a widespread practice for burghers to refer to themselves as Christians, and others, too, called them by that name. A frontiersman, seeing two members of his community in the company of a Khoikhoi and an Englishman, remarked: 'Here come two Christians, a [Khoikhoi] and an Englishman.'

Spreading the Word and literacy

During the first century of the settlement the burghers did not initially appear to be particularly religious or close to the church. After touring the colony the Dutch official G. W. van Imhoff wrote in 1743 that 'indifference and ignorance in the frontier districts is such that it has the appearance more of an assembly of blind heathen than a colony of European Christians'.

Much of this appearance was due to neglect by the Company, which established the first congregation at the Cape immediately after founding the settlement, but waited more than 30 years to form the next congregations at Stellenbosch in 1686 and Drakenstein, later called Paarl, in 1691. Some 50 years later, and only after Van Imhoff's report, two more were established, Roodezand (now Tulbagh) in 1743 and Swartland (now Malmesbury) in 1745. Another 50 years passed before two more were added: Graaff-Reinet in 1792 and Swellendam in 1798.

From the 1790s something of a religious awakening swept over the colony, and the proportion of confirmed members of the church in the burgher population rose steadily. In the 1830s one traveller stated: 'There are certainly no people in the world who are so truly God-fearing as the Afrikaner.' Another described the burghers as 'a serious and religious people . . . with strong sentiments of genuine piety . . . [They] are consistent members of the Christian church.' Burghers on the remote frontier were prepared to travel as far as 800 kilometres to have their children baptised and confirmed at Roode-

zand. Parents tended to make consent for marriage contingent on both partners being confirmed. Confirmation came to be seen as the threshold that had to be passed for full incorporation into burgher society.

A general missionary fervour was lacking on the part of either the Company or the burghers. There was no independent religious order that was committed to missionary work, such as the Jesuits, who spearheaded the expansion of Catholicism in the colonial world. As paid Company servants, the few ministers in the colony had neither the resources nor the inclination to extend their task beyond attending to the spiritual needs of the burghers and others of European descent. They saw no material gain in converting slaves or the Khoisan, and conversion happened only for those who worked for a pious employer.

Acting at the behest of the Rev. Michiel Christiaan Vos, a Cape-born minister, and Dr Johannes van der Kemp, a Dutch-born missionary, the colonists in 1799 founded the first local missionary society, the *Zuid-Afrikaansche Zending Genootschap*. In Cape Town and across the western part of the colony, the society erected chapels, called *gestichten*, where coloured Christians worshipped. Foreign missionary societies also took an active interest in the Cape.

At the Cape, slaveholding and Christianity became closely associated with each other. But it was also Christian churches and associations in Britain that from the 1780s led the struggle against slavery. In 1824 the Chief Justice, Johannes Andreas Truter, drew attention to this in an address to the South African Missionary Society, which local colonists founded in 1799. He also told his audience that the Cape church had to play an important role in smoothing the transition to a new labour system. The task of all Christian associations was to work towards a future order in which the ex-slave would serve the master 'out of love for his duty', while the master treated the slave with Christian tolerance 'as someone of the same nature as himself'.

Despite the devotion to the Word, the colonists were remarkably lax about education for their children. In 1812 the judges of the Circuit Court remarked on the 'miserable state of instruction and civilisation of the youth, which we have met almost everywhere'. Pupils did not acquire much more than basic literacy and knowledge of the bare essentials of the Calvinist doctrine. Many did not attend schools at all. In 1812 the judges found that children of many affluent families could not write or read. Early in the nineteenth century, only 100 out of 3 000 white children in the district Graaff-Reinet received formal education.

In the few other *kerkplekke*, or 'church towns', the *koster* (verger) usually doubled as teacher, imparting a smattering of education. Farmers tended to leave the task to a lowly itinerant teacher, or *knecht*. In 1804 John Barrow wrote: 'At one place that we passed the poor schoolmaster was drawing the plough, while a [Khoikhoi] had the more honourable post of holding and directing it.' But even in Cape Town the colonists' demand for education was weak. In 1809 there were six Dutch schools with a total of 515 pupils against two slave schools with a total of 1 162 pupils.

Different faiths, different tongues

Religious pluralism ultimately ensured language pluralism. Hand in hand the VOC and the Dutch Reformed Church promoted the Reformed faith and the Dutch language. Only in 1778 did the government allow the Lutherans to worship in public. After the British took over the Cape in 1795 the British government kept the Dutch Reformed Church as an established church, along with the Anglican Church. It paid over to both a large amount in subsidies to defray salaries and part of the expenses for erecting new church buildings, but retained the right to station, transfer and depose ministers.

It also permitted the Malay community the right of public worship. In 1804 the Batavians offered 'the protection of the law on equal terms' of religious associations that 'respected a Supreme Being'. Roman Catholics and Jews now also settled at the Cape.

The spectacular advance of Britain as a world power bred a conviction among its

subjects that their way of doing things was superior. In 1822 the colonial secretary, W.W. Bird, who was married to a Dutch-speaking woman, wrote of the Englishman's conviction that 'nothing can be right or proper that is not English, and to which he is unaccustomed'. An English nationalism became the dominant ideology in urban life across much of South Africa, expressed in the English language and reinforced by its symbols of dress, emblems, architecture, food and polite conventions. Robert Ross made the valid point that an English nationalism was the 'prime nationalism to which both Afrikaner and African nationalism reacted'.

The Dutch-speaking colonists found the idea of English cultural supremacy difficult to refute. By 1806 the colony could boast of no great economic advances or cultural achievements, apart from the Cape Dutch homesteads (*see box on pages 64 and 65*). There were no books, paintings or innovations on which Afrikaners could pride themselves. They were a rural, isolated, relatively backward people, with only a few receiving more than a rudimentary education.

English commentators deplored the social distortions and lack of cultural achievements they found at the Cape. A general theme was that the Dutch East India Company was unfit for governing such a place. It had neglected education, stifled trade and enterprise, supported slavery and its pernicious social influences, failed to check trekboer expansion, and allowed the oppression of the indigenous Khoisan.

After formally acquiring the Cape in 1814, Britain resolved to develop it, extend it and 'civilise' it. The first big step was a new language policy. In 1821 Henry Ellis, the deputy colonial secretary, argued that the proclamation of English as the language of government had become essential.

The changes in the judicial system made a serious dent in the self-esteem of the Afrikaner colonists. From 1828 English was formally the only language of the courts; evidence given in Dutch had to be translated. The British jury system was introduced to decide on matters of fact, with proficiency in English the principal criterion for selection. After 1834 jurors who failed the language test could be challenged. For English to become the sole public language, it had to prevail in the schools, and above all the press.

It failed. The government established free public schools giving instruction in English in the main towns, but the initial enthusiasm among the colonists dwindled because the syllabus was often irrelevant to people in the veld. Very few learnt English. In 1863 the chief official for education stated that only one-tenth of children in the colony could read English 'with tolerable accuracy and intelligibly'.

In higher education English prevailed. The leadership of the Dutch Reformed Church did not mind that most of the staff of the Athenaeum (later the South African College and yet later the University of Cape Town), which it helped to found in 1829, was English or Scottish, but became upset when the college wanted to offer religious instruction. It feared that students would end up as members of an English church.

Dutch also held its own in the press under British rule. No Dutch newspaper or magazine in the modern sense of the word had appeared during the period of rule by the Dutch East India Company, nor for more than two decades of British rule. In 1824, the same year in which *The South African Commercial Advertiser* was published for the first time, a Dutch magazine appeared – *Het Nederduitsch Zuid-Afrikaansch Tijdschrift* (*NZAT*), edited by Abraham Faure, minister of the Dutch Reformed parish in Cape Town. Faure joined George Greig, John Fairbairn and Thomas Pringle in fighting an effort by the governor, Lord Charles Somerset, to clamp down on a free press.

The Dutch colonists groped for a new definition of themselves as a community. Faure's *NZAT* proposed a dual identity. The burghers had to be loyal British subjects, but also identify with their particular history and cultural distinctiveness. In its first editorial, published on 9 April 1830, the first Dutch newspaper, *De Zuid-Afrikaan*, declared that it 'wanted to hoist a banner which will serve as a rallying point for all colonists, old and new'. It gave the name 'Afrikaner' to these old and new colonists: 'All who inhabit this land and derive nourishment from its bosom are Africans [*sic*].' In the Dutch text the name 'Afrikaner' was used.

Two men worked closely together to fight for the freedom of the press. They were John Fairbairn, editor of *The Commercial Advertiser*, and Christoffel Brand, who took a leading hand in founding *De Zuid-Afrikaan* and was its main editorial influence. Both papers represented quite different interests. The English newspaper favoured the interests of the merchants who wanted to rid the colony immediately of slave labour; the Dutch paper voiced the interests of slave-owners, who wanted self-government first in order to control the process of emancipation.

When Fairbairn approached Brand about a joint approach to the issues of representation and abolition, all the latter did was to give vague assurances that under a system of representative government the 'owners of slaves [would] pay attention to the interests of themselves, as well as the interests of the slaves'.

Faced with Brand's prevarication, Fairbairn began to question the idea that representative institutions should precede emancipation. He feared that a legislative assembly dominated by Afrikaner slave-owners would not abolish slavery. His suspicion was fed by the outrage of slave-owners, and of *De Zuid-Afrikaan* in particular, over amelioration, especially the regulations limiting the corporal punishment of slaves.

Fairbairn openly began to question the commitment of *De Zuid-Afrikaan* to the reform and abolition of slavery. The shift in his position corresponded with his move into the circles of John Philip. Fairbairn's report of his visit with Philip to the frontier increased the distance between him and Brand, for he set excessive store by the contacts made with the inhabitants of the mission stations. He even expressed the peculiar belief that he and Philip had enough influence to ensure that unprovoked attacks by Khoikhoi or Xhosa on farms would not occur. In the meantime Philip's *Researches in South Africa* had appeared with few good words for the Afrikaner colonists.

De Zuid-Afrikaan was outraged by what it

believed to be a haughty and arrogant attitude. What also rankled was its perception that Fairbairn considered the free press his own personal property and the *Commercial Advertiser* as the only truly independent newspaper. *De Zuid-Afrikaan* declared that, in future, it would focus on four important 'humbugs': 'FREE PRESS humbug, INDEPENDENT NEWSPAPER humbug, MISSIONARY humbug and the most extreme form of all humbugs PHILIPISH humbug.'

The gloves were off. *De Zuid-Afrikaan* and the *Commercial Advertiser* turned their political conflicts into a struggle between Afrikaner and English colonists for the higher moral ground. The Dutch paper denounced 'English hypocrisy', charging abolitionists with constantly singling out the inhumanity of slave-owners, but overlooking the huge profits their own forebears had made from the slave trade.

At a meeting of slave-holders Brand hit out at people who 'accuse us Afrikaners of being vicious oafs'. In an angry response, Fairbairn wrote that a legislative assembly for the Cape dominated by Afrikaner slave-

owners would be 'a ridiculous insult to the common sense of mankind'. While he disliked the autocratic rule at the Cape, the despotism of 50 Koeberg Boers was 'fifty thousand times worse'. Fairbairn nevertheless found a reason to be optimistic: 'JOHN BULL has been awakened from his dream of confidence in the Afrikander.' Because of this 'all danger of Dutch domination' was at an end.

The Imperial government took the controversy seriously enough to delay granting self-government for more than two decades, not only because it thought it would leave slaves and Khoisan at the mercy of the colonists, but also because it feared a confrontation between Dutch and English-speaking colonists.

Yet all this thunder and lightning subsided. There was more that kept the two white groups together than set them apart. They were, after all, a small minority in a colony with a large slave population and an insecure frontier in the east.

ABOVE: *Georg Schmidt, the first full-time missionary in South Africa, ministered from 1737 to 1744 among the Khoisan on the fringes of the colony.*

BELOW RIGHT: *In 1792, the Moravians re-established Genadendal (earlier Baviaans-kloof) in 1792 after government interference had forced the first missionary to close it down in 1744. With more than 1 000 inhabitants it was for a time the second biggest settlement, after Cape Town. Its knife-works was the colony's first substantial workshop. Genadendal aimed to become a self-sufficient agricultural settlement, but did not quite attain that ideal.*

But the crucial test was the church. Aware of the Dutch Reformed Church's importance, Lord Charles Somerset, who served as governor between 1814 and 1826, first sought Dutch ministers to fill vacancies in the Dutch church. When that failed, he recruited Scottish ministers, who had to become proficient in Dutch. (By 1834, of the 22 Dutch Reformed ministers, twelve would be Scots.) Somerset began urging the Cape clergy to use English in the church, pointing out that proficiency in English would benefit colonial youth who desired employment in government.

Chief Justice J.A. Truter urged the government to exercise caution. Only when everyone was proficient in English could the step be undertaken 'without any humiliating feeling'. The Dutch Reformed synod that year refused a request by the Scottish ministers to offer some of their services in English. *De Zuid-Afrikaan* warned that English church services would have unintended consequences. In 1834 it wrote: 'Members of the Synod consult ancient history to persuade yourselves that to change the language of your religion you would be taking the first step to betray your belief and religion.'

The battle for a colonial parliament that started in all seriousness in the 1830s once again drew the white colonists nearer to each other. Spokesmen for the two white communities downplayed cultural differences to avoid the impression of any rift between them. In 1837 Brand remarked: 'England has taken from the old colonists of the Cape everything that was dear to them: their country, their laws, their customs, their slaves, yes, even their mother tongue.' The Afrikaner colonists had done everything to prove they were British, but 'their conquerors had continually worked to remind them that they were Hollanders'.

For Brand the goal was the amalgamation of the two white sections. In 1841 he wrote: '[We] are two who must become one and by doing so raise the banner of unanimity in public affairs.' English commentators left little doubt that this 'unanimity' would increasingly be expressed in English cultural terms.

The impact of foreign missionaries

Georg Schmidt, the first full-time missionary in South Africa, ministered from 1737 to 1744 among a small, impoverished population of Khoisan on the fringe of the colony. A man of little education but fervent faith, Schmidt preached that all people, white and black, must be assured 'in their heart of the forgiveness of sins through Jesus's blood' if they wished to escape damnation.

This message repelled many whites who regarded their Christianity as a mark of their identity and privilege as Europeans, but it slowly attracted a few Khoisan, moved by the

implicit affirmation that whites and blacks were equal in the eyes of God. Schmidt baptised five Khoisan and, in defiance of colonial custom, now routinely addressed them as his brothers and sisters. In 1744, lonely and embroiled in a dispute with the authorities, Schmidt left for his Moravian community in Europe and never returned.

Different kinds of mission

In 1792, three Moravian missionaries arrived at the place where Schmidt had preached. There they met Magdalena, one of Schmidt's converts. Now elderly and blind, Magdalena had kept her Christian faith alive for half a century, without apparent outside help; a younger woman read to her regularly from the Bible Schmidt had given her. The Moravians resolved to found a Christian community on that spot. Later named Genadendal, it was the first of hundreds of mission stations in South Africa. Genadendal was a tightly disciplined and industrious community under the firm, paternal control of German missionaries and enjoyed the favour of many in the colonial elite.

A second kind of mission, less congenial to the authorities, was founded by Johannes Theodorus van der Kemp, an energetic Dutch member of the London Missionary Society (LMS). A brilliant scholar and army officer, Van der Kemp had been dramatically converted to evangelical Christianity after the death of his wife and child in a freak boating accident. Bethelsdorp, the mission station he founded in 1802 near the future Port Elizabeth, would become a powerful symbol in South African history (*see page 82*).

Many Khoikhoi saw the Bethelsdorp mission station as a refuge from the labour demands of white farmers, who in turn regarded it as a hotbed of Khoisan absconding from their contracted obligations. Nor did the ascetic and scholarly Van der Kemp – indifferent to his clothing, his comfort, and his dignity as a white man in Africa – endear himself to South African whites. He married a fourteen-year old Malagasy slave girl, and campaigned outspokenly against the labour practices of the Boers. By his death in 1811 he had baptised more than 100 Khoisan, but had also established a pattern of tension between the LMS and white settlers that would last for a century.

Van der Kemp's political radicalism, though not his unconventional lifestyle, was perpetuated by Dr John Philip, superintendent of the LMS, who dominated the racial politics of southern Africa from the 1820s to the 1840s. Philip contended for the equal legal rights of Khoisan and whites within the Cape Colony, and advocated strengthening African chiefdoms against the advance of white settlement. With this he earned the century long enmity of white settlers, including some who desired to trek from the Cape Colony to a place 'where the domination of Doctor Philip is not acknowledged'. A Scottish mill-worker with a doctorate purchased from Princeton University, Philip was the clearest missionary voice for racial equality, the initiator of a moderate Christian liberalism that would inspire white and black opponents of white domination until the 1950s.

The spread of missions

Numerous Protestant mission societies entered South Africa in the early nineteenth century, so that by 1884 fifteen missions (British, American, German, Scandinavian, Swiss and French) ran at least 380 mission stations. Catholic work among Africans began at mid-century but for many decades was limited to a few regions, such as Lesotho and Natal, and remained vastly overshadowed by the Protestants.

Many missionaries disapproved of mission stations, which they saw fostering artificial, isolated Christian communities and splitting African societies between Christian and non-Christian parties. Still, in the turbulent politics of nineteenth-century southern Africa, the mission station – often located on land granted by an African ruler who sought missionaries' technical expertise and advice – provided a reasonably secure, semi-autonomous location for missionaries to build up their churches. In most regions conversions were discouragingly slow, and mission communities often appeared to nearby Africans as a hotbed of refugees, outcasts, rebels and persons accused of witchcraft and other crimes. On mission stations almost everywhere women outnumbered men.

Among Khoisan, whose independence had been lost early, conversions were numerous and quick, and in communities such as Lesotho, where Moshoeshoe befriended the

missionaries and took an interest in their beliefs, significant conversions took place in the ruling class. But, as a rule, the most striking achievement of nineteenth-century missionaries was not the conversion of individual Africans but the introduction of agricultural techniques such as irrigation and ploughing, the inculcation of literacy, and the dispensing of rudimentary Western medicines.

The most successful evangelists were African Christians themselves. After minimum contact with white missionaries, Ntsikana (c.1780–1821), Xhosa evangelist, prophet and hymnodist, preached the Christian gospel in a purely Xhosa setting with Xhosa language, imagery, literary and musical forms. Charles Pamla, a former shepherd who became a lay preacher, translated for the California evangelist William Taylor as the pair ignited American-style revivals all over southeastern Africa in 1866, with thousands of Africans declaring their faith in Christ.

ABOVE: *Ntsikana (c.1780–1821), Xhosa evangelist and prophet, preached the gospel in Xhosa, using traditional imagery and music.*

RIGHT: *Ntsikana's version of the Christian church praise song as recorded by J.W. Bokwe in* Ibali Lika Ntsikana *in 1914.*

"DALIBOM" KA-NTSIKANA.
LIFE CREATOR.

NOTE.—*Ntsikana after his "Bell" would settle the assembly down with chanting "Dalibom"—Life Creator, or "Ingoma Enqukuva"—Round Hymn, also reproduced below.*

KEY A♭.

s :—:s	m :—:m	l₁ :r :—	s₁ :—:—	l₁ :r : .r	s₁ :—:s₁
1. He !	Nanko - k' u	Da - li - bom		Wa-se - s'kolwe - ni.	
2. He !	Nanko - k' u	Da - li - bom		Os'bize - sihle - li.	
3. He !	Nanko - k' u	Da - li - bom		Wasinga pezu - lu.	

Translated these lines are
1. See ! there stands the Life-Creator ; He of the School.
2. See ! there stands the Life-Creator ; Who calls us to rise,
3. See ! there stands the Life-Creator ; He has ascended.

Only a minority of missionaries followed Van der Kemp and Philip into active political advocacy. Some, like the French missionaries in Moshoeshoe's Lesotho, wrote favourable accounts of their host kingdoms and publicly resisted colonial encroachment on their territory. Others, like many Wesleyans and German Lutherans, cultivated close ties with settler communities, their children frequently marrying into settler families and becoming white South Africans.

In the late nineteenth century, as British imperialism spread throughout much of Africa, English-speaking missionaries tended to be pro-Empire, but not necessarily pro-white settler, while many continental missionaries manifested suspicion of British motives. But the vast majority of missionaries attempted to minimise the political aspects of their work, seeking a neutral middle ground between black and white, and devoting themselves to the upkeep of their stations and the growth of their churches.

The Dutch Reformed Church, too, became intensely mission minded. The spiritual home of most Dutch settlers, it faced a dilemma when black converts of its missions sought to use formerly all-white sanctuaries for worship, prayer or confirmations.

To enlist white settlers' support for missions, the Dutch Reformed synod declared, in 1857, that where racial prejudice made it necessary, 'the congregations raised up, or to be raised up, from the Heathen, shall enjoy their Christian rights in a separate building or institution'. Late in the nineteenth century the Dutch Reformed Church strengthened its role as a *volkskerk* (church of the Afrikaner people). Its ecclesiastical segregation enabled it to participate actively in white nationalist endeavors while retaining a fervent commitment to missionary work.

By the turn of the twentieth century, conversions of Africans to Christianity came more rapidly. By then, most had lost or were losing their political independence, while they were experiencing drastic social change initiated by contact with the colonial economy. Deprived of the security of a stable society and its associated belief systems, many were open to a new message.

The Christian gospel was now being preached in many areas by African converts using the scriptures in vernacular translation. Migrant labourers converted to Christianity on the Witwatersrand gold mines headed back to the countryside, witnessing to their new faith. And African parents, formerly sceptical of mission-run schools, increasingly encouraged their children to attend, in the hope that literacy and skill in English or Dutch would help them prosper in the new colonial order. By 1911, almost a third of a million Africans, Indians and Coloureds were communicants (not just adherents) of Christian churches, while about 176 000 pupils of colour were studying in mission schools. Missionaries spread English among the African elite.

The Muslims

Even more so than with Christianity, education and religion were closely tied up in the Muslim schools. The first *madrasah* was established in 1793 in Dorp Street, Cape Town. The Muslims were sufficiently impressed by the greater religious tolerance of the new British rulers to ask permission in 1800 for building a mosque.

Madrasahs taught more pupils of colour than all the other educational institutions in town. A school conducted by the *imam* taught more than 370 slaves in the 1820s. Two years later an even larger *madrasah* instructed 425 free blacks and slaves. Many schools were run by elderly retired *imams*. In the 1850s it was reported that the two large schools taught pupils to read the Koran in Arabic.

The language of the Cape Muslims was Afrikaans. In their schools pupils were taught to read and write Afrikaans in the Arabic script. During the 1840s an observer wrote: 'All the Malays in Cape Town speak Dutch but the better class understand and write Arabic and Malay.' But the Dutch was, actually, Afrikaans (or a creolised Dutch). The first Afrikaans book, printed around 1856, used Arabic script. By the end of the century at least eleven Arabic-Afrikaans works had been produced.

Thus it was not the Afrikaner community or the Christian church that used Afrikaans first as a written medium but the Muslim community in Cape Town. When Arnold Pannevis, in the early 1870s, considered translating the Bible into Afrikaans because of the large numbers of illiterate people, both white and coloured, Afrikaans was already an established medium of religious instruction in the Cape Muslim community. English was becoming the language of the Afrikaner elite in Cape Town and many rural villages. J.H.H. de Waal, one of the main protagonists of Afrikaans, later wrote that by the 1890s only the Muslim community had remained loyal to Afrikaans.

ABOVE: *The prophet and war doctor Nxele Makhanda led the Xhosa forces at the battle of Grahamstown (1819) and drowned while attempting to escape from Robben Island.*

OPPOSITE: *Maqoma, son of Ngqika, bitterly resented the expulsion of his community from the Kat River valley and played a leading role in the Xhosa invasion of the colony in the Sixth Frontier War (1834–1835).*

An unstable frontier

An unstable peace is one that embitters 'the losers without depriving them of the capacity for seeking revenge and without establishing a system able to restrain them – and then taking the trouble to make it work'. So wrote an historian of the Punic Wars between Rome and Carthage. Such a peace also characterised the frontier between the colonists and the Xhosa between 1812 and 1835. Hampered by financial constraints and bewildered by the complexities of the problem, the British governors struggled to formulate a fixed frontier policy. This inconsistency was exacerbated by the Imperial government's interventions. In all, the policy amounted in the words of Andries Stockenstrom to a 'vacillating and contradictory doctrine'.

Together with the lack of land, a sense of pervasive insecurity gave rise to large numbers of farmers trekking out of the colony in a movement that would become known as the Great Trek (*see page 108*).

In the early months of 1812, a colonial force drove the Xhosa over the Fish, but they were by no means conquered. The military force stationed on the Fish River was much too small to deter the Xhosa from engaging in cross-border raids. The colonists remained fearful. In 1817 it was found that 90 of the 145 burgher families in the southeastern region of the colony had abandoned their dwellings, while the rest were ready to flee.

Lord Charles Somerset, who became governor in 1814, was a brash and wilful man with no grasp of the complexities of the frontier problem. He wanted the Xhosa chiefs to assume collective responsibility for thefts under a 'spoor' or reprisal system. It was supposed to work as follows: a farmer would report losses to a military post, and a patrol would follow the tracks to the first kraal, which would hand over the stolen cattle or pay compensation. A chief innocent of the theft could recoup the loss by demanding the equivalent number of cattle from the real thieves. From the start it was a disastrous policy. The man on whom part of the burden of making it work fell was Andries Stockenstrom, who became landdrost of Graaff-Reinet in 1815 at the age of 22. His leverage was reduced when the districts of Albany and Somerset were established in 1820, but he remained influential for a considerable length of time.

A Xhosa chief's dilemma

Instead of ending cattle raids, the expulsion of the Xhosa from the Zuurveld had exacerbated the problem. In 1817 Somerset arrived on the frontier intending to impose his conception of a solution. He summoned Ngqika and told him that the theft of cattle and horses had to stop and that it was Ngqika's responsibility to make sure that it did. For Ngqika the task was impossible. He had, he said, no real power over other chiefs, and if he were to act against the thieves among his own followers they would join other chiefs (*see box*). Aware of Ngqika'a weakness, Somerset promised active military assistance.

In 1818 Ndlambe inflicted a shattering defeat on Ngqika, who appealed to the British government for help, whereupon a force of soldiers, burghers and Khoikhoi troops rode out and defeated Ndlambe's force. British soldiers backed by burgher commandos blasted the wooded valleys causing few casualties, but enabling the capture of 23 000 cattle, almost the entire subsistence of Ndlambe's followers.

In 1819 a Xhosa force struck back. The 'war doctor' Nxele (or Makhanda), who had the chief Ndlambe as his patron, attacked the small garrison town of Grahamstown with 6 000 men. Assisted by Khoikhoi marksmen, the garrison narrowly averted defeat and possibly also the collapse of the settlement on the southeastern frontier. When another large force of soldiers, Khoikhoi troops and burgher commandos went out, the Xhosa fled towards the Kei River, Nxele gave himself up and the war was ended.

Somerset now hit on the idea of an unpopulated zone beyond the boundary. He promptly designated the area between the Fish and the Keiskamma rivers as a neutral belt that everyone living there had to evacuate. Even Ngqika, the government's chief ally, was told to leave his land, estimated at 10 000 square kilometres between the Kat and Keiskamma rivers – 'as fine a portion of ground as to be found in any part of the world', Somerset called it. In addition, he had to continue to act against cattle thieves.

He reportedly remarked that 'although indebted to the English for his existence as chief, yet when he looked upon the fine country taken from him, he could not but think his benefactors oppressive'. He was now completely discredited. His sons, Maqoma and Tyhali, bitterly resented leaving their home in the Kat River Valley in the ceded territory. They despised their father as a craven, vacillating, drunken coward.

Soon it became clear that the ban on settlement applied only to the Xhosa. The 'neutral territory' became the Ceded or Conquered Territory. Effectively nearly 7 800 square kilometres had been added to a colony already hard to defend. The government gave out farms to burghers and settlers in the northern part of the neutral belt.

The Ceded Territory was a turning point in frontier relations. With the further loss of land as a result of having to give up the neutral belt, the Xhosa found the land deprivation acute; the western Xhosa who were driven eastward impinged on other peoples already hard-pressed for pastoral land. For many Xhosa survival had become a desperate struggle and the loss of both the Zuurveld and the Ceded Territory a grievous injustice.

Soon other injustices were piled upon this. Patrols and commandos headed by British officers and consisting of British soldiers, as well as mixed units of burghers and soldiers, performed the task of recovering stolen cattle and increasingly harassed kraals in their efforts to recover stolen cattle and stamp out theft. The reprisal system failed and was open to all kinds of abuse. Since farms were not fenced, stock losses were frequent. When stock went missing farmers went to the nearest military post and applied for a search party, with no effort having been made to check whether the stock had actually been stolen.

Kraals were seldom given the opportunity to prove their innocence. The patrols often plundered innocent kraals and consequently they simply invited Xhosa counter-raids. The Xhosa told Stockenstrom: 'We do not care how many Xhosa you shoot if they come into your country, and you catch them stealing, but for every cow you take from our country you make a thief.'

The loss of land in the Ceded Territory remained a burning grievance among the Xhosa, particularly for Maqoma, the son of Ngqika. He was allowed to return to the Kat River Valley, one of the few well-watered spots in a period of severe droughts, but was expelled again. Stockenstrom used the land to establish the Kat River settlement for the Khoikhoi to serve as a defensive barrier against invaders.

The insecurity of the farmers

It was not only the Xhosa who suffered from lack of security, but the frontier farmers as well. After the war of 1819 the government created Grahamstown and Somerset as new districts, but it did not station a strong police or military force on the frontier. Several large regions, for instance Tarka, were virtually without any defence. The government nevertheless steadily increased the restrictions on the burghers acting against raiders.

Ordinance 9 of 1825 curtailed the right of colonists to fire on persons suspected of being vagrants, deserters or escaped convicts. Commandos were only allowed to pursue and recover stolen cattle if they were still in sight. In 1828 Attorney-General A. Oliphant wrote: 'In no case should deadly weapons be used until all other means have proved abortive . . . Patience and forbearance . . . surely ought always to be exercised when the life of a fellow creature is at stake.'

Stockenstrom believed that military force should be used sparingly and only when absolutely necessary. At the same time he felt it was of overriding importance to leave the Xhosa in no doubt about the government's resolve to defend the colony and to punish

NXELE MAKHANDA AND NTSIKANA

Indigenous African religion recognises a High God who created the earth and everything on it. The living are connected to the dead by the spirits of the deceased, who appear to them in dreams and help them to negotiate the dangers of the visible world. The white invaders who came out of the sea could not be accommodated within the confines of this cosmology, and the Xhosa had to seek explanations and solutions from among the religious ideas of the invaders themselves. From this intellectual ferment, two contradictory alternatives emerged.

The first explanation came from the renowned war doctor Nxele Makhanda (often spelt Makana). He maintained that the whites had killed Tayi, the son of God, for which great crime they had been thrown into the sea. The second explanation came from Ntsikana, a simple homestead-head who one day had the vision of a strange ray of light shining off his favourite ox. He became inspired, he heard voices, and he composed a famous hymn in which God is compared to a 'great cloak' (ingub'enkhulu) that protects and comforts the true believers.

Politics as well as ideology divided Nxele from Ntsikana. Nxele was the war doctor of Ndlambe, the principal chief in arms against the colonists. Ntsikana remained loyal to Ngqika, Ndlambe's nephew who was in alliance with the colony. Nxele promised to raise the dead at Cove Rock near East London, but Ntsikana knew better. 'You only go to wash yourselves with salt water,' he mocked.

Militarily, however, Nxele had the edge. Ndlambe's army defeated Ngqika at the great battle of Amalinde (October 1818), thus precipitating the Fifth Frontier War (1819–1820). Nxele staked all on the capture of Grahamstown, the defences of which he had carefully studied while seemingly engaged in theological discussions with the colonial military chaplain. But the charms of Nxele were no match for the cannons of the British. Nxele surrendered and eventually drowned in 1820 attempting to escape from Robben Island. Ntsikana died the following year, entrusting his followers to the missionaries and preaching peace and submission to the last.

ABOVE: *The frontier conflict was not only a struggle between white and black farmers over land, labour and cattle. There was a third party: British military officers, merchants and speculators out to make money. This painting of the Grahamstown market shows traders buying and selling hides and horns.*

BELOW: *The British force that arrived at the frontier included some 50 Khoikhoi soldiers, making a huge impression on the frontier Khoikhoi. This picture is of a private in the Cape Corps, sketched by Lady Anne Barnard.*

stock theft. By the end of the 1820s he expressed concern that government policy had swung from great severity to 'sacrificing the safety of [His Majesty's] subjects' and 'paralysing their efforts to defend their lives and property'.

'Most clamorous against the [Xhosa] nation'

The frontier conflict was not simply a struggle between white and black farmers over land, labour and cattle. There was a third party: British military officers and, aligned to them, British merchants and speculators based mainly in Grahamstown. Their mouthpiece, the *Grahamstown Journal*, propagated colonial expansion into Xhosa territory and the complete subordination of the Xhosa with a large military presence, as well as increased military expenditure. To merchants, this held out the prospect of much greater profits in a lucrative trade in the smuggling of arms and in land speculation. The expansionist lobby constantly exaggerated the aggressive nature of the Xhosa and their culpability in the frontier unrest. In 1837, Governor Napier referred to the *Grahamstown Journal* and the merchant lobby in the town as those 'most clamorous against the [Xhosa] nation'.

The principal figure among the British military on the frontier was the tempestuous and aggressive Colonel Henry Somerset, the governor's son. In 1823 he became officer in charge of the Khoikhoi-manned Cape Regiment stationed on the frontier. He headed many of the frequent patrols and commandos against the Xhosa who had seeped back into the Ceded Territory. He also attacked Xhosa chiefdoms far away from the frontier. These expeditions carried off large numbers of cattle, and distributed them to colonists who had suffered losses.

By the early 1830s Stockenstrom had lost all faith in the patrols and commandos that kept the Xhosa in a constant state of alarm, marching at night and attacking at dawn, and firing at random. Sometimes patrols and commandos went out every week. At a homestead they burned the huts, seized cattle and drove off the inhabitants. Most Xhosa living there, innocent or guilty, fled. Tyhali once asked: 'Shall I never have peace in my own country? Am I to be treated in this way, day after day?'

The role of soldiers and military

Stockenstrom began to suspect that the frequent patrols were part of a sinister agenda to drive the Xhosa on the border to a desperate incursion into the colony, which could

A QUESTION OF SURVIVAL: STOCKENSTROM'S OPTIONS

The question of survival on the frontier came up in a week-long informal discussion in 1825 at Graaff-Reinet, where Stockenstrom played host to two missionaries, Dr John Philip and Dr William Wright of the London Missionary Society (LMS), and a British settler, Thomas Pringle, with a strongly liberal reputation.

Philip and his friends considered the Xhosa peace loving, dependable, honest and credible, whereas the colonists were deemed full of 'insatiable avarice and rapacity'. In the larger scheme of things Philip wanted slaves, free blacks and Khoisan people living among the burghers to be fully integrated in society. Stockenstrom thought he downplayed Xhosa and Khoisan responsibility for cattle raids.

The options for the frontier farmers were simple: '[We] must either run away, sit still and have our throats cut or defend what we have.' Running away was not an option; the burghers should not withdraw from the frontier region. (Ten years later Stockenstrom would condemn the outward movement that became known as the Great Trek.) He dismissed with contempt the notion that the burghers did not have the right to defend themselves. To 'defend what we have', and to identify the principles on which that defence should rest, preoccupied Stockenstrom throughout his career.

He suggested two principles by which to live: truth and justice. As a government man, he saw it as his duty to seek the truth impartially and dispassionately. To deny the blood shed and cruelty of colonial conquest was 'ridiculous' and 'dishonest', but he also insisted that the atrocities were something of the past, and that every burgher 'with the slightest decency and respectability' accepted these facts and lamented them. As he wrote elsewhere, leading burghers had spoken to him 'a thousand times' about the injustice of taking the property of the border chiefdoms.

But if there was little dispute between Stockenstrom and his guests about the past, there was no agreement about the present. He wrote: '[They] certainly tried my temper by the virulence with which they persisted to denounce the present generation of the colonists and refused to make any allowance for their actual position, which rendered self-defence absolutely necessary for the preservation of both parties.' Deadlocked in their argument, the guests tried to silence Stockenstrom by remarking: 'You [the colonists] have no business here at all.' To this the landdrost replied that no people violated this principle more than the British.

On another occasion Stockenstrom said: 'But I am not called upon to please either party [white colonists or blacks]. I have the cause of truth to serve. I am to call "murder murder" and "plunder plunder", whatever the colour of the perpetrator's skin . . .' Philip and his other guests found 'some reason' in this argument, but were sceptical whether the soil existed in which 'justice and moderation could be cultivated'.

XHOSA CHIEFS AND COMMON BOERS

A particularly strong grievance among the Xhosa was the indignities and maltreatment chiefs had to suffer as a result of rude and provocative behaviour on the part of farmers and soldiers. No commoner could approach the Great Place without his head covered, or lift his hand against a chief. Part of the shock of the devastating Xhosa defeat in the Fourth Frontier War (1811–1812) was the death of Chungwa, who was shot in his hut while ill. (It was later discovered that this was to avenge the massacre of the party of Anders Stockenstrom, the father of Andries.)

The Xhosa chiefs insisted that they be treated with proper respect. Ngqika once broke off negotiations with Boers because they asked him to return some cattle. He told Landdrost Alberti that he was not prepared to be messed on by dogs – that is, people he did not consider his equals. The Boers and British soldiers considered themselves superior to all Xhosa, including chiefs. At Fort Willshire visiting chiefs were subjected to humiliating treatment.

As the frontier crisis intensified, the chiefs feared for their lives. Ndlambe declared that he was hunted like a springbok. His brother Sigcawu was shot in 1830. The wounding of Xhoxho, one of Ngqika's younger sons, was said to have precipitated the Sixth Frontier War (1834–1835). The Xhosa reportedly said, 'It is better that we die than be treated thus . . . Life is no use to us if they shoot our chiefs.'

The most shocking act was the killing by British soldiers of Hintsa, the Xhosa paramount and Gcaleka chief, in the final stages of this war (see box on page 106).

ABOVE: 'Hoped-for downfall of Stockenstrom': a few army officers, who had lost property as a result of Stockenstrom's frontier policy, commissioned a series of caricatures. The bitterness of the eastern settlers is evident in the caricatures, drawn by F. I'Ons and printed in the Grahamstown Journal in 1838.

BELOW: A watercolour of Xhoxho by F. I'Ons. The wounding of Xhoxho, one of Ngqika's sons, was said to have precipitated the Sixth Frontier War of 1834–1835.

The Sixth Frontier War of 1834–1835 is known to the Xhosa as Hintsa's War. It was not started by King Hintsa but by the Maqoma and Tyhali, Xhosa chiefs on the immediate colonial border who were infuriated by the loss of their lands and the ongoing raids of the colonial commandos. But the death of Hintsa during this war has overshadowed all else in the collective memory of the Xhosa.

Hintsa was not active in the actual military operation, although he had sanctioned the war and allowed the fighting chiefs to hide their cattle in his country. When the British forces crossed the Kei River, Hintsa entered the British camp at Butterworth to negotiate with Governor Sir Benjamin D'Urban and General Harry Smith. He had been assured of his personal safety, but found himself held hostage against the payment of 25 000 cattle

Sarhili

Xhosa – and the source of future wars. 'Where is my father?' asked Hintsa's son Sarhili on the eve of the War of the Axe. 'He is dead. He died at the hands of these people. He was killed in his own house. He died without fighting . . . Today, we all fight.'

The same Hintsa War also saw another potent cause of future battles in the form of the Mfengu revolt. Mfengu is actually a somewhat derogatory term meaning 'homeless people in search of work'. It was used at the time as shorthand for Hlubi, Bhele and Zizi

people who had left Natal during the time of Shaka Zulu. Most of them had been soldiers in the army of Matiwane, chief of the Ngwane, who had confronted the three kings of the Eastern Cape – Xhosa, Thembu and Mpondo – at the Battle of Mbholompo near Mthatha (August 1828), the biggest battle ever fought on Eastern Cape soil. Matiwane's army was scattered and his followers dispersed. Many of them found work in Hintsa's country but they were not regarded as equals of the Xhosa. Discontented, they found a

'Mfengu' woman

listening ear in Rev. John Ayliff, the missionary at Butterworth. When the British forces crossed the Kei in 1835, the Mfengu revolted and joined the British army, taking their employers' cattle with them.

Under a milkwood tree in Peddie district where they settled, the Mfengu swore a great oath to accept Christianity, educate their children and obey the government. They fought alongside the colonial forces in the wars that followed, not as subordinates but as allies in the cause of Christian civilisation. They were an integral part of the Cape liberal experiment, the hollowness of which they only discovered when it was already too late.

Hintsa

and 500 horses. 'What have the cattle done that you want them?' he asked. 'Why must I see my subjects deprived of them?'

At the Nqabarha River, Hintsa made a dash for freedom. He was pulled off his horse, shot through the back and through the leg. A colonial volunteer named George Southey, coming up fast behind him, blew away the top of his head. After that, his ears were cut off and his body otherwise mutilated, an act that shocked the British government in London and eventually led to the repudiation of Governor D'Urban. Hintsa's death was ever after a cause of intense anger among the

'Mfengu' man

then be used as a pretext for a further colonial land grab contemplated by British soldiers in alliance with British merchants and land speculators. He wrote of people 'desiring a chain of sanguinary wars' that would cost vast amounts of money but 'would popularise themselves by bringing enormous fortunes to some dozens of speculators and overwhelm headquarters with patronage'. He appealed to government to bring to an end the patrols attempting to drive the Xhosa and other Bantu-speakers out of the neutral territory altogether.

Considering Stockenstrom a colonial who did not know his proper place, Colonel Somerset, appealed over Stockenstrom's head to the governor and continued his patrols. In 1833 Stockenstrom travelled to London to seek more power for his post, and resigned when it was denied. He decided to leave the Cape permanently for Sweden, the country of his father's birth. After his departure the government's frontier policy lost the little credibility it still had in the eyes of both the burghers and the Xhosa.

The Sixth Frontier War (1834–1835) was a profound shock to all the frontier colonists. Twenty whites and 80 Khoikhoi were killed, 455 homesteads were burned down and thousands of horses, cattle and sheep were carried off. They had believed a Xhosa invasion impossible. Their hope that the colony's counterattack would bring stability was soon dashed. An English-speaker wrote in April 1836 from the Lower Fish River that the Afrikaner farmers had little hope for the future, adding: 'One said that in his father's lifetime and his own they had been five times clean swept out by the [Xhosa].'

A large colonial force counterattacked and drove the Xhosa far eastwards. Subsequently the governor, Sir Benjamin D'Urban, extended the eastern border of the colony to the Kei River and the source of the Wit Kei in the Stormberg, with the newly acquired territory designated as the Province of Queen Adelaide. This raised strong hopes among the burghers that a large new region would become available for farms. However, a select parliamentary committee in London was hearing evidence on the treatment of indigenous peoples. The missionary John Philip had become one of the main sources of information to the Imperial government, cutting much of the ground from underneath D'Urban's feet.

A key witness was Stockenstrom, who had travelled from Sweden to London to testify. He blamed much of the violence on the reprisal system and the patrols and commandos. Many of these actions, he said, were based on fraudulent claims about theft and on a desire to grab more land from the Xhosa.

On 26 December 1835 the colonial secretary in the Imperial government, Lord Glenelg, reversed D'Urban's decisions. The colonists had expected the Xhosa to be forced to pay for instituting another war, but Glenelg declared that the Xhosa had been driven 'by a long series of acts of injustice and spoliation' and had 'ample justification' for invading the colony.

He now announced that the Province of Queen Adelaide was to be abandoned and the colonial boundary moved back from the Kei to the Keiskamma, Tyhume and Gaga rivers, with colonial control over the area between the Fish and the Keiskamma (the neutral territory). The chiefs had to abandon all claims to this land, but the government was prepared to 'lend' this region to chiefs and their subjects on condition of good behaviour. Glenelg appointed Stockenstrom to return to the Cape as lieutenant-governor and implement his ideas for a stable system on the frontier (*see box on page 117*). For many of the frontier farmers the retrocession of the Province of Queen Adelaide and the general tenor of Glenelg's dispatch was a final blow that prompted them to join the trek that had begun before the war.

Stockenstrom assumed office in Grahamstown on 3 September 1836. His priority was to give people on both sides of the frontier a sense of security and stability. The Xhosa had to be left in peace and the reprisals and commandos had to cease. The colonists had to be allowed to protect their property and life against plunderers and, if necessary, shoot the assailants. A line of military posts manned by a strong force was necessary. He recommended additional resident magistrates in Cradock, Colesberg and a place further east.

A great trek

Two streams of Afrikaner migrants left the colony in the second quarter of the nineteenth century. The first was an emigration of people called trekboers, who moved across the border as individual families in search of better pasture; the others moved in trek parties and emphasised political issues. They would later be called Voortrekkers.

Their trek was a bold and dramatic response to a political crisis that had engulfed the eastern and northeastern districts of the Cape Colony from the mid-1820s to the end of the 1830s. It was fairly orderly mass rebellion against a breakdown of security that the participants considered intolerable. Many also moved because all the land in the frontier districts had been taken. Thus the trek was also a solution to a material problem.

Why they left

Two documents highlight the causes of the Great Trek. Frequently cited is the manifesto the Voortrekker leader Piet Retief published in the *Grahamstown Journal* on the eve of the departure of his trek in 1837. It is a combination of burning grievances and good intentions. It has a ring of eloquence but lacks frankness and authenticity. It sounds like the work of a scriptwriter and the author was probably Louis Meurant, a young newspaper editor.

Another source often cited is a statement of Anna Steenkamp, Retief's niece, whose principal objection was that slaves had been 'placed on an equal footing with Christians, contrary to the laws of God, and the natural distinction of race and religion . . . wherefore we rather withdraw in order to preserve our doctrines in purity'.

Steenkamp's main grievance probably related to the tough stand the government took against any racial discrimination in the Dutch Reformed Church, which for all practical purposes was a state church. Khoikhoi now got married in church and received the sacraments here. All this upset the trekkers greatly, but they always had the option of establishing another church.

It cannot be assumed on the basis of Steenkamp's words alone that the Voortrekkers left mainly because of the introduction of equality before the law after Ordinance 50 of 1828 had lifted all legal restrictions on the Khoikhoi or because of the emancipation of the slaves in 1834.

There is also another revealing source, but it has seldom been cited in connection with the trek. The author was Olive Schreiner, an early feminist writer with strong liberal convictions. As a governess in the frontier districts of Colesberg and Cradock between 1874 and 1881, she knew the people, and the stories they told, well.

Referring to the losses the people suffered in successive wars, the arrogant way in which officials dealt with the frontier farmers, even those who had fought in the frontier wars, and government bungling with respect to the payment of compensation for slave owners, she wrote: 'But that which most embittered the hearts of the colonists was the cold indifference with which they were treated, and the consciousness that they were regarded as a subject and inferior race … [The] feeling of bitterness became so intense that about the year 1836 large numbers of individuals determined to leave forever the Colony and the homes which they had created.'

The causes of the trek were complex but can be summarised in a single sentence. The trekkers left because of a lack of land, labour and security, which they felt unable to address due to a lack of representation, giving rise to a profound sense of marginalisation.

Lack of land

A shortage of land had long been acute on the frontier, and the situation had steadily worsened between 1812 and the mid-1830s. During the eighteenth century the farmers, or their sons or sons-in-law, moved on to new land after pastures had been exhausted. But that depended on 'free' land – that is, land that could be taken without any cost and converted into a loan farm.

TOP: *The Great Trek was partly an orderly mass rebellion against a breakdown of security that the participants considered intolerable. W.H. Coetzer drew this trekker family.*

ABOVE: *As governess in the frontier districts, author Olive Schreiner knew well many of the stories told about the Voortrekkers. She remarked: 'But that which most embittered the hearts of the colonists was the cold indifference with which they were treated, and the consciousness that they were regarded as a subject and inferior race.'*

Early in the nineteenth century this way of life came to an end. In 1813 the British abolished the familiar loan farm system, and introduced a system of perpetual quitrent tenure. There was a long delay in the issue of title deeds, farms were wrongly surveyed and in some cases corrupt surveyors pocketed the money.

From the early 1830s the government returned land applications with a note that it could no longer issue land. The market price of established farms rose sharply. People left the colony because they wished to obtain new land to practise subsistence farming along traditional lines.

There seemed to be abundant free land beyond the colonial borders. By the mid-1820s migrant farmers, called trekboers in the north and northeast, were already expanding beyond the border, and severe droughts spurred them on. Initially they made humble requests to cross the border only as a temporary relief measure. But, by the end of the 1820s, these trekboers were no longer asking permission, and simply informing the authorities in Graaff-Reinet that they were crossing the boundary. Many trekboers sold their farms and moved to the other side of the border.

Lack of labour

Labour had long been a critical issue. The farms were large and homesteads were six or seven kilometres apart, with no fences to keep cattle in. Particularly after Ordinance 50 there was a severe shortage of cattle herders. Farmers did not pay their servants well. Dr Philip believed that the farmers would attract labour if they offered good cash wages, but Afrikaner colonists were much slower than their British counterparts to switch to commercial farming and cash wages. Those farmers with sufficient land hoped to retain labourers by displaying a benign paternalism, particularly by allowing servants to keep some stock. However, the growing pressure on the land meant that few farmers could provide the Khoikhoi with enough land for their own stock.

Ordinance 50 of 1828 freed the Khoikhoi from all curbs on their movement, and they began moving away in large numbers from the farms. An observer who described the scene on the frontier, wrote: 'I have myself known farms which had been completely abandoned by the last remaining [Khoikhoi] having given up service or retired to the missionary schools, taking with them the flocks or herds which they have earned in their employer's service and rejecting every offer or bribe to continue any longer in such service.'

The Khoisan who left settled either on missionary stations, or squatted on crown land or on the outskirts of towns. In 1842 a senior British officer commented: 'It is idle to say why do the farmers not properly guard their cattle, the thing I say is impossible in this country where servants are not to be had.'

Ordinance 50 of 1828 freed the Khoikhoi from all curbs on their movement. Large numbers moved to the mission stations. These Khoikhoi huts were scattered around the Kamiesberg mission.

A photograph of an unknown Voortrekker.

Sir Benjamin D'Urban, governor of the Cape Colony from 1834–1838. His annexation of the territory between the Keiskamma and the Kei after the Sixth Frontier War and his depiction of the Xhosa as 'irreclaimable savages' caused an uproar in philanthropic circles in London. His extension of the colonial territory was overruled by the imperial government.

Some Voortrekker leaders were slave-holders but they could not have rallied support for the trek simply by denouncing emancipation. Louis Tregardt, a leader, owned ten slaves but the other 29 families in his trek had only five slaves among them. Only one-fifth of the colony's slaves were in the districts from which the greatest number of Voortrekkers came.

Still, the loss of patriarchal authority over slaves or servants was an important reason why many trekkers left. Ordinance 50 proscribed the punishment of Khoisan labourers by masters. On 1 December 1834 the right to punish slaves, now called apprentices, was also abolished. Labourers, particularly slave apprentices after 1834, felt free to take their masters or mistresses to court. Several Voortrekker leaders had had brushes with the law about punishing their slaves or servants.

Lack of security

Another central reason for the trek was the grave insecurity on the frontier. In Tarka and other parts of the northeastern border, Bushmen bands had been stealing cattle; by 1832 large numbers of Mantatees, fleeing from enemies beyond the border, entered the frontier zone. Wandering parties moved across the frontier, stealing or begging for food.

Government agents could issue passes for short periods; those who wished to stay longer to work had to negotiate a contract. In reality the government was unable to control the influx. Most frontier burghers did not know how to cope with vagrancy and constant cattle theft; many had experienced heavy losses of flocks and herds, and some were afraid for their lives.

The lack of government authority was worst in the large Tarka area, covering an area of more than 44 200 square kilometres. A justice of the peace stationed at the town of Cradock, assisted by a single constable, had to maintain order. After 1825, with the increase of complaints against masters, the inadequate administrative structure also became a major issue. Most people had to travel two or three days to the drostdy to lay a complaint, appear before a court to give evidence, or answer a summons.

The greatest discontent was aroused when burghers were compelled to appear in court after they had taken action against black vagrants or thieves. 'There are no rights for burghers any more, but only for blacks,' a distressed field-cornet exclaimed. He had been summoned to court after he had acted against 'insolent' Khoikhoi who had refused to leave a farm. A burgher remarked: 'The protection of the Law is known only by name,' and Governor D'Urban declared bluntly that the magistracy of Somerset was 'little better than a dead letter'.

Political marginalisation

Lack of land, labour and security were serious sources of discontent. Yet by themselves they are not enough to explain why not only landless people left the colony but also fairly wealthy farmers, who sold their farms cheaply. To understand this, their grievances about a lack of representation must be taken into account.

This was keenly felt because labouring classes were now on an equal footing with them. These feelings were rooted in the status distinctions of the VOC that were not formally racial. There was no developed theory of racism among the frontier farmers, or among Afrikaners in general, during the nineteenth century. Stockenstrom remarked: 'The theory which makes the blacks irreclaimable savages, fit only to be exterminated, like the wolves, was not of Boer origin.' He had no doubt that such racism was of British origins. Indeed Sir Benjamin D'Urban, the governor of the Cape Colony, had coined the very term 'irreclaimable savages' for the Xhosa.

A lack of representative bodies where they could voice their complaints was one of the important reasons why so many believed it was impossible to remain in the colony.

The abolition of the colleges of landdrost and *heemraden* in 1828 was part of the progressive overhaul of the system of administration. While this reform was an important stage in the modernisation of the government, its defect was that it removed all those institutions that the frontier burghers trusted at a time that they had to come to grips with a major political and social transformation. In effect they had been left with virtually

no form of representation. Historian Eric Walker wrote that the effect of the reforms was to give the colony a greater efficiency at the price of almost all proper sharing in the functioning of government.

Stockenstrom supported the reforms in principle as part of thoroughgoing modernisation. Still, he considered it of the greatest importance to win broad acceptance for the far-reaching reforms among the burghers. He would later call it a great mistake to abolish the colleges of landdrost and *heemraden*, the means through which government could influence the whole community. From this point on, he wrote: '[All] confidence between the Government and the masses ceased, and many of the evils which have retarded our advancement and disturbed our peace may be traced to misunderstandings which the executive had not the means nor the channels of clearing up.'

Responding to Stockenstrom's remark that they intended to leave the colony in order to lead a lawless existence, some of the prospective Voortrekkers in the northeastern divisions replied: 'It is the contrary, we leave the Colony because we know of neither Government nor Law – of the Government we know nothing except when we have money to pay and the law never reaches us except to fine or otherwise punish, often for acts we did not know to be wrong. Our Field Cornets can give us no assistance, as they are as much in the darkness as ourselves. We are like lost sheep.'

The burghers felt that they had been marginalised and disempowered where they lived. An official tried to give words to their feelings: 'Now we have a Civil Commissioner to receive our money for Government and for Land Surveyors, a Magistrate to punish us, a clerk of Peace to prosecute us and get us in the *Tronk* [prison], but no *Heemraad* to tell us whether things are right or wrong.'

ABOVE: *An artist's imagining of Voortrekker leader Piet Retief.*

'A strange and moving spectacle'

'History had seldom witnessed a stranger and more moving spectacle than that of well-to-do farmers, some in their first flush of youth and others already bending under the weight of years, forsaking their farms and homesteads, packing their families with all their household goods into the unwieldy ox-wagon, driving their flocks and herds before them, and trekking away to the distant, unknown interior.' This was a description of what became known as the Great Trek that appeared in a biography of Andrew Murray, ordained in 1849 in Bloemfontein as the first Dutch Reformed minister in a parish beyond the Orange River.

Between 1835 and 1845, parties of burgher families, later called Voortrekkers, and their servants, moved out of the Cape Colony in considerable numbers. They mingled with the trekboers who had left the colony earlier and were sojourning in the trans-Orange area before many of them moved on into Natal or the Transvaal. In the first wave of the emigration of the Voortrekkers, which ended in 1840, some 6 000 people trekked (20% of the whites in the eastern districts and 10% of the colony's whites). By 1845 some 2 300 families, or 15 000 burghers and their families – accompanied by an estimated 5 000 servants – had left the colony.

Officials and church leaders realised immediately that this was an event of major significance and almost unanimously condemned the trek; some were concerned about the impact on indigenous populations, some about the fate of the trekkers. Prominent frontier colonist Gideon Joubert expected the trekkers to be destroyed speedily and the survivors forced to return or degenerate into a state 'worse than that of the heathen'. The synod of the Dutch Reformed Church in 1837 expressed its concern over the 'departure into the desert, without a Moses or Aaron' by people looking for a 'Canaan' without having been given a 'promise or direction'. *De Zuid-Afrikaan*, the only Dutch newspaper, was dismayed that the Voortrekkers had removed themselves from British authority.

At the time when the trekkers began to leave the colony in the 1830s, there was intensive contact between Europeans and Africans along a line of approximately 200 kilometres near the Fish River. Beyond that were only a few places where Europeans were in contact with people who were not European. In the vicinity of Port Natal (the present Durban) a few English traders and hunters were living among a large indigenous population.

Among the principal groupings living in the areas to which the emigrants were moving was Mzilikazi's Ndebele kingdom, which had established itself in the Marico Valley, in what would become known as the western Transvaal. Using tactics based on the Zulu style of fighting, the Ndebele army had laid waste large parts of what would become known as the Transvaal and northern Free State. Another chief, Moshoeshoe, who had built the Basotho nation out of refugees, occupied land east and west of the Caledon River. In Natal the Mfecane (*see page 124*) involved the consolidation of the Zulu kingdom. Here Dingane had become king of the Zulu nation after assassinating Shaka.

Into the interior

Migrating frontier farmers, called trekboers, had for two decades partly settled on the highveld, grazing cattle north and south of the Orange according to season. Unlike with the Voortrekkers, political considerations were not foremost in the trekboers' migrations.

Various Voortrekker parties set out from different localities at different times, each of them organised by a prominent local personality, such as Hendrik Potgieter of Tarka, Gerrit Maritz of Graaff-Reinet and Piet Uys of Uitenhage. Most parties numbered more than 100. Given the nature of the mobilisation, personality clashes were inevitable and the Voortrekkers struggled to agree on a common strategy and a common government. Louis Tregardt, the first important leader, travelled no further across the frontier than the White Kei River, where he was given land by the Xhosa king Hintsa in 1834.

Later the same year, the Sixth Frontier War broke out and Tregardt was accused of gun-running. He and Janse Van Rensburg, the other early trek leader, headed for the Portuguese seaport of Delagoa Bay. But when Tregardt and most of his party died of fever and the Tsonga wiped out the Van Rensburg party, the other Voortrekkers decided to look for safer pastures.

Hendrik Potgieter's trek moved out of the Tarka area across the colonial boundary in late 1835 or early 1836. Gerrit Maritz and his trek left Graaff-Reinet in September 1836, with more than 700 people, some 100 of them white male adults. Maritz took along legal works, including a study by Grotius, and a cannon – a great legal book and an instrument of violence, the two main means of asserting white supremacy. By the spring of 1837 there were five or six large camps between the Orange and Vaal rivers and a total of 2 000 trekkers.

The emigrants were well aware that their adversaries suspected they intended to embark on a campaign of African dispossession. They saw blacks as people with whom they had to reach a working relationship. They coveted them as labourers and wanted them as allies against other blacks. Their commandos always included blacks, usually as *agterryers*, people entrusted with tending the horses and preparing the food. The first large

ABOVE: *The trekboers, including the family of Paul Kruger, were migrating frontier farmers. Unlike the Voortrekkers, politics were not a major consideration in their migrations. They grazed their cattle north and south of the Orange River according to the season. These interior and exterior views are of a trekboer house in the Transvaal.*

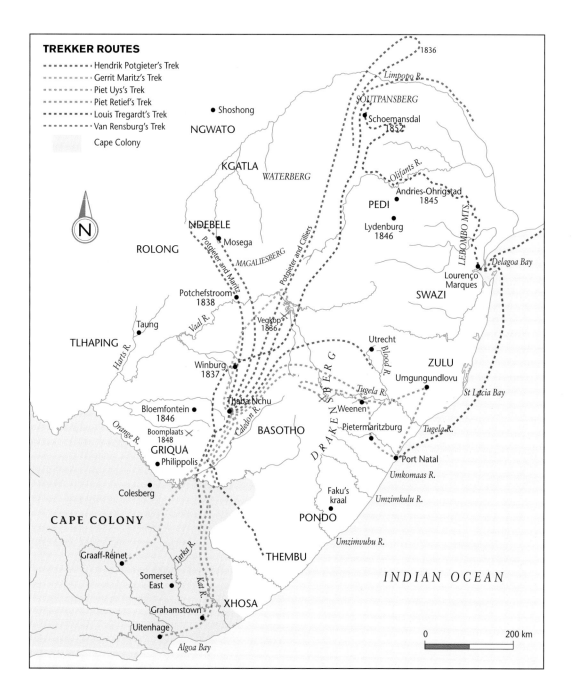

TREKKER ROUTES

- - - - - - Hendrik Potgieter's Trek
- - - - - - Gerrit Maritz's Trek
- - - - - - Piet Uys's Trek
- - - - - - Piet Retief's Trek
- - - - - - Louis Tregardt's Trek
- - - - - - Van Rensburg's Trek

Cape Colony

ABOVE: The routes followed by the various trekker parties in what later came to be known as the Great Trek.

commando of armed burghers on horseback, headed by Potgieter and Maritz, had 103 trekkers and 40 coloured men, with 60 blacks to assist them.

Among the intellectual baggage of the Voortrekkers were policies like the reprisal system, practices such as the capturing and indenturing of indigenous children, fighting techniques like the commando (*see box on page 72*) and the laager (*see box on page 78*), and the treaty as a model of 'international' relations. Verbal agreements or formal treaties with chiefs were part and parcel of the eastern frontier scene. While the trekkers were leaving, Andries Stockenstrom, on behalf of the colony, signed treaties with various chiefs as partners in maintaining peace and good order.

Potgieter's trek began with only 33 arms-bearing men, along with women and children, and increased to 200 after the parties of Sarel Cilliers and Casper Kruger joined them. Potgieter, an energetic, active man with a taciturn temperament, concluded agreements with African chiefs to live in peace, but in August 1836 an Ndebele patrol attacked the Liebenberg family, part of Potgieter's trek, and killed six men, two women and six children. The Ndebele's primary aim was probably to plunder the large herds of cattle the trekkers had brought with them.

Then on 20 October 1836 an Ndebele army of 4 000 to 6 000 men attacked Potgieter's laager; in the Battle of Vegkop, 35 trekkers beat off the massive Ndebele attack with the loss of only two lives. The Ndebele did succeed in carrying off almost all the trekkers' cattle, and in January commandos went out to punish Mzilikazi. The first, headed by Potgieter and Maritz, killed 400, sacked Mzilikazi's village at Mosega and took 7 000 cattle. In November another commando, headed by Potgieter and Piet Uys, forced Mzilikazi to flee to the present Zimbabwe. There were no serious rivals now to the emigrants on the plateau of the highveld.

Trouble within

African enemies were not the only challenge. Divisions, schisms and squabbles among themselves nearly destroyed the trek. Trekker leaders were wealthy men but lacked the economic controls ordinarily available to enforce loyalty and discipline. The trek had a levelling effect on the class hierarchy. In the end the leadership had to rely on the established patriarchal family structure and on military reputation to maintain their control.

But even the leaders did not agree on their ultimate destination, apart from wanting to settle near an outlet to the sea. Retief was intent on Natal, Potgieter on the highveld of the Transvaal. Potgieter sought an agreement with the Portuguese in Mozambique over access to the port of Delagoa Bay (now Maputo) – as far away as possible from British authority – so that he could establish *de facto* independence. Retief, on the other hand, preferred to negotiate with Britain for independence.

Ecclesiastical and political disputes, too, threatened the treks. In the absence of a Dutch Reformed Church minister, Erasmus Smit – brother-in-law of Maritz and a former missionary in the service of the London Missionary Society – tried to step into the breach, but he was old, sickly, not ordained, and rumoured to be an alcoholic. Many trekkers found him unacceptable. Arguments over the form of political organisation also ruptured the trekker community. Potgieter, a patriarchal figure, concentrated on the welfare of his own trek party, which developed into an autocracy under the Potgieter clan. Maritz, by contrast, viewed the trek as a common enterprise – a *vereenigde maatschappij* (united community) or a *volk* – and called for the leaders' submission to an elected council.

There were brief moments of unity. In December 1836, while the treks of Potgieter and Maritz were at Thaba Nchu, the trekkers elected a *Burgerraad* (Burgher Council) of seven burghers with Maritz as civilian president and Potgieter as military commander. The *Burgerraad* supervised the making and enforcement of laws. But Maritz and Potgieter soon fell out and the *Burgerraad* was split.

When Retief arrived in Thaba Nchu the next April, he was unanimously elected 'governor' of the trekkers and took over the post of military commander from Potgieter. Maritz became 'judge president of the Council of Policy' and 'deputy governor.' Potgieter's exclusion was confirmed two months later when a meeting at Winburg adopted nine articles, setting up the 'Free Province of New Holland in South East Africa' with Retief as 'overseer' of the *Maatschappij*, as the collective Voortrekker society was called.

TOP: *In 1836 the Ndebele army attacked Potgieter's laager at the Battle of Vegkop.*

ABOVE: *Erasmus Smit (1778–1863), brother-in-law of Gerrit Maritz and former missionary in the service of the London Missionary Society, was supposed to be the Voortrekkers' minister but many found him unacceptable. He was old, sickly and probably an alcoholic.*

A quest for a treaty

As Edgar Brookes and Colin Webb remark in their history of Natal, in the immediate aftermath of the Mfecane the region must have looked like Paradise. Daniël Bezuidenhout, a trekker, noted that the lush area lay 'waste and unoccupied'.

Piet Retief thought that the Boers and the Zulu could live side by side, but Francis Owen, a missionary who lived near Dingane and had some first-hand experience of him, told him that the king would never grant land to the trekkers. Retief responded that it was imperative that the Zulu learn to trust the Boers. He was by nature a risk-taker and was now prepared to take the greatest gamble of his life. Owen warned him not to go near

Dingane with a commando, but he summarily dismissed the advice. 'It takes a Dutchman,' he reportedly replied, 'not an Englishman' to understand a black person.

When Retief accompanied by a few men approached Dingane in October 1837 to sign a treaty, the king indicated that he would consider granting the extensive area between the Mzimvubu and Thukela (Tugela) rivers, on condition that Retief recovered cattle stolen from him by Sekonyela, the Tlokwa chief.

As the negotiations proceeded, Retief made mistakes that lengthened the odds against him. He told Dingane of the severe punishment the trekkers had inflicted on Mzilikazi, and Dingane's councillors who accompanied Retief and his men to Sekonyela noticed how disrespectfully they treated the chief. 'Would Dingane be treated the same way?' they asked. The answer was: 'We shall treat Dingane in the same way should we find him to be a rogue.'

All this helped to heighten Dingane's sense of grave insecurity. In the early 1830s Jacob Hlambamanzi, an interpreter with some knowledge of the Eastern Cape, told Dingane of the sequence of events he could expect: 'At first the white people came and took a part of the land; they then increased and drove them further back, and have repeatedly taken more land as well as cattle.' There was a long-standing Zulu oral tradition that when Shaka was killed, he said to Dingane: 'You kill me thinking you will rule, but the swallows will do that', meaning the white people because they built houses with mud.

Dingane was afraid of trekkers armed with guns, who were approaching his kingdom after destroying the Ndebele. His efforts to acquire more guns had failed. Retief had refused his pleas to hand him Sekonyela's guns and horse. The small number of English hunters and traders in Port Natal did not represent a threat, but 1 000 Voortrekker wagons that had spread out in the Upper Thukela valley by the end of 1837 did. Retief displayed an extraordinary faith in the possibility of a treaty with Dingane that could somehow resolve matters to the mutual satisfaction of both sides.

Stockenstrom told Piet Retief that he could not understand how the Voortrekkers could survive as whites in Africa except by remaining under the British government and its system of law and order, however temporarily defective. He expressed his astonishment that the trekkers seemed to prefer the protection of Dingane and Mzilikazi – the two major chiefs in the deep interior – to that of the British government.

After the ruinous Sixth Frontier War Stockenstrom proposed a treaty system (*see box*) to settle conflicts in place of the old military solutions. For him treaties could only work if a key principle was observed: the acknowledgement of the right to the territory of its then actual possessors. Hand in hand with this had to go the recognition of the power and status of the indigenous chief and a commitment to the preservation of the polity he

As lieutenant-governor of the Eastern Cape, Stockenstrom had a full mandate from the Colonial Office to implement an entirely new frontier policy based on treaties and mutual respect rather than reprisals and mutual hatred. The colonial government stationed diplomatic agents in the Ceded Territory and the Xhosa chiefs stationed reliable councillors to watch the drifts (river-crossings) for stolen cattle. The key to the cattle-theft problem, Stockenstrom believed, was to force the farmers to take proper care of their own cattle. Colonial cattle, actually stolen and promptly reported, were reclaimable under the treaties and the chiefs were responsible for returning them to the farmers. Archival records show that when the treaty system was implemented by enlightened officials like C.L. Stretch, the diplomatic agent at Block Drift (later the town of Alice), the Xhosa chiefs did honour their treaty obligations and stolen cattle were indeed returned.

But although Stockenstrom was lieutenant-governor, D'Urban was still governor, and most of the frontier officials were D'Urban men. The settlers had a redoubtable and articulate spokesman in the editor of the *Grahamstown Journal*, Robert Godlonton, who weekly fulminated against the treaty system, asserting that its regulations were unworkable and that it enabled the Xhosa to steal colonial cattle with impunity. Stockenstrom was vilified as an unscrupulous

Robert Godlonton

careerist who had sold out the settlers for his private benefit.

Enlightened colonial officials were in short supply on the Eastern frontier and, in any case, the question of stolen cattle was merely a cover for the real question – land. The settlers had passed through Xhosaland during the campaign of 1834–1835, and had liked what they had seen. 'The appearance of the country is very fine,' wrote one settler, 'it will make excellent sheep farms.' Two years later, Queen Victoria ascended to the throne. The Imperial era was about to begin in earnest. American Indians and South Sea islanders were dying like flies of European diseases,

as the Khoikhoi had done before them. Science itself seemed to proclaim the inevitable victory of the white race, as did settler leader J.M. Bowker in his notorious 'springbok speech':

> The day was when our plains were covered with tens of thousands of springboks; they are gone now, and who regrets it? Their place is occupied with tens of thousands of merino . . . I begin to think that he too [the Xhosa] must give place, and why not? Is it just that a few thousands of ruthless worthless savages are to sit like a nightmare upon a land that would support millions of civilised men happily?

Stockenstrom could do little about the *Grahamstown Journal* but he could not tolerate disloyalty in his senior officials. He sued the Civil Commissioner of Albany for libel, but lost and subsequently resigned. Napier, the new governor, was unable to maintain Stockenstrom's system and the next governor, Maitland, unilaterally imposed entirely new treaties on reluctant chiefs. Tension rose and when a Xhosa named Tsili stole an axe from a trader in Fort Beaufort in March 1846, he unwittingly set off a train events that commenced with the War of the Axe and ended some twelve years later with the complete and final destruction of the Xhosa nation.

controlled. The system could work, provided the British government was prepared to put major resources behind it and stand up against the lobby of English merchants, speculators and soldiers intent on dispossessing the Xhosa.

The final years of the 1830s had brought the Cape Colony to the end of an epoch. In 1836 Stockenstrom had formulated the fundamental choice before the European colonists: 'We must have either extermination [meaning the dispossession and breaking up of African chiefdoms] or conciliation and justice: a middle course is ruin.'

The developments between the end of 1834 and the end of 1838 represented the middle course that Stockenstrom wanted to avoid. There was the descent into large-scale killing and massacre – the Sixth Frontier War, the battles of the Voortrekkers and Ndebeles, the massacre of Retief and some seventy men in Dingane's place and 500 more of his followers at Weenen, and the death of 3 000 Zulus at the hands of Andries Pretorius and his men at the Ncome River, later called Blood River.

The latter events are described in Part Two because they can only be understood within the context of the conditions created by the Mfecane, which was also characterised by the 'crushing' of adversaries and large-scale dislocation of people. When the

ABOVE: *English-speaking settlers found a spokesman in Robert Godlonton, editor of the* Grahamstown Journal, *who became rich from judicious investments and speculation. He opposed Stockenstrom's treaty system and advocated seizing more land from the Xhosa.*

Voortrekkers arrived in the deep interior the rebuilding of African polities had just begun.

White and black would discover that they had to co-exist because neither had the means to overwhelm the other.

A distinctive colony

The settlement at the Cape was easily established because the Khoikhoi were small in numbers and technologically not well advanced. The fact that the food plants and animals of South Africa were unsuitable for domestication was one reason why the Khoikhoi living in the vicinity of the Cape were not more developed. After 60 years of European settlement they were decimated by smallpox. By the 1840s the Kat River settlement and a few missionary stations were the only places where they enjoyed some freedom and autonomy.

The Bantu-speaking peoples who lived on both sides of the Fish River suffered no similar demographic disaster as a result of the diseases the colonists brought with them. As cultivators and pastoralists they formed societies far more capable of resisting European expansion. But after British leadership and other military resources had been injected into the frontier conflict the remorseless dispossession of the Xhosa began. They would not be displaced completely but were left without a viable territory. Their incorporation into colonial society and the breaking up of traditional society proceeded apace.

Economically the Cape had been transformed from the mercantilist policies of the VOC to a society that was fully integrated in the British economic system, with capitalist enterprise and materialist progress at its centre. The colonists had long believed that it was impossible to maintain the production of wheat and wine without slavery. They were wrong in both respects. By the mid 1840s slavery was gone but production levels quickly recovered. Wool had begun its march to become the main export article.

Culturally the colony had acquired a character that was neither European, nor African nor Asian. The form of government and the administration was now English, and so was the dominant fashion in dress, manners and public etiquette in Cape Town. In the city the Dutch kept the boarding houses. A small 'gentry' lived in the fine Cape Dutch houses in the towns and on the wine farms of the western Cape. The people who built the mansions and worked in the gardens, vineyards and the wheat fields were of African and Asian origin. Most of what was distinctive in the cuisine was imported from the East.

English was the language of instruction in most of the schools in the rudimentary system of education, but the Muslims used Arabic and Afrikaans in instructing the faithful. Ministers of the Reformed Church persisted with Dutch although most of their congregation understood Afrikaans better. On the eastern frontier the missionaries spread not only the Word but also the message that command of the English language and English dress was a prerequisite of 'civilisation'. The weakening of Xhosa resistance also meant a major surge of Christian and British influence.

The legislation distinguishing between the free and unfree had all been removed by 1838. Slavery was ended without any upheaval, but the institution cast a long shadow, most notably the practice of indentured labour and the ideology of paternalism. There was no racial legislation, but because slavery and freedom so closely correlated with race for more than nearly two centuries, the informal racial distinctions survived. The fact that no land was made available to ex-slaves meant that they were compelled to work for a master if they wanted to live. In 1841 the government passed the Masters and Servants Act, which suited the employers well because it made a breach of contract a criminal offence.

The Cape Colony was one of the few places in the world where in the absence of a legislative assembly a sizeable number of slave-owners had no say in the process of ending slavery. Consequently the issues of slavery and freedom were never properly debated. It was in their common demand for a colonial assembly that the two white communities

drew together. Since the Imperial government recognised no colour distinction the demand for a colonial assembly had to be made in non-racial terms.

By the time representative rule was introduced in 1853 the total population had passed a quarter million and there were about 50 towns in the colony. The economy had begun to diversify. By the early 1860s a start had been made with a modern education system for the children of the colonists. Some well-known schools had been established, including Diocesan College (Bishops) in 1849, St Andrews (Grahamstown) in 1855 and Grey Institute in Port Elizabeth (1856) and Stellenbosch Gymnasium (1866). There also were numerous mission schools providing education to coloured and black children, often taking in white children as well. A lively press flourished, publishing newspapers both in English and Dutch.

As the next section will show, it was this colony – one that after 1795 legally became increasingly non-racial, liberal and egalitarian – that would spew forth the Griquas, colonists and settlers who would embark on the processes of military conquest, dispossession and subjugation beyond the colony's borders.

By the 1840s the dominant fashion in dress, manners and public etiquette in Cape Town was English. This painting, called 'A stroll in the Company Gardens on a Sunday afternoon' clearly shows the English dress adopted.

From the great irruptions to African nationalism

A famous painting by Frederick I'Ons, usually known as the 'Sandile group'. Sandile (1820–1878), standing at the centre, is addressing the Ngqika Xhosa chiefs just before the outbreak of the War of the Axe (1846). The Grahamstown Journal *said, 'The redoubtable chief is . . . delivering an address with the gesticulations and energy he knew so well to exercise.' Here is an example of Sandile's style of oratory from the run-up to the later 1850 war: 'The whole of Xhosaland is dotted over with the habitations of the white man, and with the surveyors' flags . . . he [Sandile himself] might die, but it should never be said that he died in peaceable time – for it should be universally known that he died in the ranks fighting for the land of Rharhabe.'*

1800: Portuguese strengthen control over Delagoa Bay to gain access to ivory and slaves.

1800–1820: Conflict among Tswana chiefdoms on western highveld.

1818: Zwide of the Ndwandwe captures and kills Dingiswayo of the Mthethwa; Shaka takes control of the Mthethwa.

1819: The Ndwandwe fall apart; Shoshangane and Zwangendaba move to Delagoa Bay; Zwide takes his followers to modern Swaziland.

1820–1822: The Chunu and Thembu leave Zululand and cross the Mzimkhulu River.

1822–1826: Refugees from the Caledon valley attack the southern Tswana.

1822–1840: Moshoeshoe consolidates and expands his Sotho kingdom.

1823: Mpangazitha's Hlubi flee across the Drakensberg; the Thlaping are attacked at Dithakong, saved by the intervention of missionaries and Griqua.

1824: Port Natal founded as a trading post; Zwide dies and Shaka attacks his son.

1824–1825: Zwangendaba and Nxaba move into modern Zimbabwe.

1825: The Khumalo (later Ndebele) under Mzilikazi settle along the Vaal River, having left Zululand some years before.

1826: Mzilikazi moves west to the Madikwe (Marico) River and subjugates the Tswana.

1828–1837: Sekwati takes control of the Pedi in today's Mpumalanga and strengthens Pedi paramountcy.

1829: Jan Bloem's Griqua and Tswana allies raid Mzilikazi's Ndebele.

1830–1834: Sekonyela's Tlokwa gain dominance in the Caledon valley.

1836: Combined Voortrekker/Griqua/Tswana attack on Mzilikazi at Mosega; Ndebele begin to trek to Zimbabwe (Matebeleland).

1837: Adam Kok III assumes power over the Griqua at Philippolis.

1838: Retief's party is killed at Dingane's capital, Mgungundlhlovu; Voortrekkers under Pretorius defeat the Zulu at Ncome (Blood) River.

1839: Republic of Natalia founded.

1843: Napier Treaty with Griqua and Moshoeshoe's Sotho; Boer-Sotho conflict looms in Transorangia.

1844: Natal annexed to the Cape.

1845: British Resident appointed in Transorangia; Potgieter's Voortrekkers settle at Ohrigstad in the eastern Transvaal and negotiate an agreement with Sekwati (Pedi).

1846: Swazi paramount, Mswati, signs a treaty with Potgieter ceding land in the eastern Transvaal.

1847: Sir Harry Smith appointed Cape governor; he expands the Cape to the Orange River, prompting widespread opposition.

1848: Battle of Boomplaats (Boers and British).

1849: Anti-Convict Association formed to oppose convicts being sent to the Cape; Warden Line is declared and Sotho cede territory north of the Caledon River; Orange River Sovereignty is declared; Ohrigstad is abandoned and Trekkers move to Schoemansdal and Lydenburg.

1850: Andries Stockenstrom's 'Popular Party' wins elections for the Legislative Council; the bid for representative government for the Cape gains pace; Kat River 'rebels' side with the Xhosa at the battle of Mlanjeni during the Eighth Frontier War.

1852: Sand River Convention leads to the formation of the ZAR.

1853: Theophilus Shepstone appointed Secretary for Native Affairs in Natal; a new Cape constitution gives coloured males the franchise in elections for the legislature.

1854: Bloemfontein Convention is signed and Orange Free State (OFS) formed.

1857: Xhosa kill infected cattle following Nongqawuse's prophecy.

1858: Treaty of Aliwal North; Sotho cede further land.

1860: Indentured Indian labourers arrive in Natal; Griqua under Adam Kok trek from the OFS to Matatiele (Griqualand East).

1866: Treaty of Thaba Bosiu; Sotho lose more territory.

1867: Diamonds discovered at Hopetown, south of Orange River; Trekkers abandon Schoemansdal.

1868: Basutoland annexed as a British protectorate.

1871: The Keate Award; Crown Colony of Griqualand West is declared.

1874: Langalibalele 'Affair' in Natal; impetus for confederation in South Africa grows.

1874–1875: Carnarvon's Confederation Plan adopted.

1875: Black Flag rebellion: white diggers refuse to disarm.

1876: Pedi kingdom invaded by ZAR.

1877: Britain annexes ZAR.

1878: Griqua Rebellion in Griqualand West; British and Swazi forces attack the Pedi, defeating them in 1879.

1879: British troops invade Zululand and are defeated at Isandlwana.

1880: 'Gun War' in Basutoland; Cape's Sprigg ministry falls; Rhodes forms De Beers Mining Company; Zulu are defeated at Ulundi and Cetshwayo is captured; Anglo-Boer War in the Transvaal.

1881: Sir Garnet Wolesley divides Zululand and civil strife ensues; Transvaal-based mercenaries attack the Rolong; Transvaal wins back independence by the Treaty of Pretoria; gold discovered at Barberton.

1882: Republics of Goshen and Stellaland formed in the land of the southern Tswana; convict labour used at the diamond fields.

1883: Cetshwayo reinstated but civil strife continues.

1885: Warren Expedition to Bechuanaland and declaration of Crown Colony of British Bechuanaland.

1887: Zululand annexed to the Crown, opposed by uSuthu loyalists.

1888: Rhodes gains full control of De Beers.

1889: In Zululand Dinuzulu surrenders, is found guilty of high treason and sent to St Helena.

1894: Britain annexes Pondoland.

1894: ZAR forces defeat Venda in the Zoutpansberg.

1895: British Bechuanaland annexed to the Cape Colony.

1895–1896: Jameson Raid into the Transvaal.

1896: Langeberg Rebellion in British Bechuanaland.

1896–1897: Rinderpest epidemic.

1899: South African War breaks out.

Introduction

The early nineteenth century saw major changes to the political configuration of the southern African interior, the geographical distribution of its people and its cultures. These changes were once thought to be mostly due to the Mfecane, a term used to denote the wars initiated by Shaka Zulu, but some recent historians have argued that Shaka's role had been exaggerated, and that the events of the Mfecane were actually triggered by interventions from the colonial enclaves of the Cape Colony, Port Natal and Delagoa Bay. These 'great irruptions' remain very important in the history of the subcontinent as far north as today's Zambia, Malawi and southern Tanzania.

Paradoxically, the mother colony based in Cape Town adopted a liberal stance to questions of class and race just when its settler offshoots were plunging ever deeper into the interior. White penetration and African response shaped the course and nature of future conflict. In the mid-nineteenth century Voortrekkers and Africans shared similar aims of rebuilding fragile communities and seeking security after periods of severe social disruption. This often led to competition for crucial resources, though the stark racial antagonism that characterised recent historical epochs in South Africa has masked the extent of their interdependence.

The discovery of diamonds and gold in the late nineteenth century set South Africa on the road to mining success which was for many years the prime motor for economic growth. This reverberated across southern and central Africa as men were drawn into the mines. Griqualand West was claimed by the British Empire in the name of the Griqua nation, but black people generally benefited little. The dynamics of the mining process led inexorably to the economic monopoly of De Beers Consolidated and the closed compound system for black workers.

Imperial intervention in the diamond fields marked a decisive shift in the balance of power between British colonies, trekker republics and independent African kingdoms. Imperial involvement in the interior became less hesitant, and resources of land and labour were harnessed more efficiently for capitalist transformation in the latter decades of the nineteenth and the twentieth century. It also raised levels of direct military conflict to an unprecedented level, caused the destruction of independent African states and set Boers and British on a collision course.

The early twentieth century was the beginning of rapid economic and social transformation. Among whites there was the growth of a wealthy industrial capitalist class and large landowners; among Africans the emergence of predominantly wage and migrant labourers, increasingly detached from their communities. Women's roles became more diversified and important in the rural milieu, as they increasingly took control over homestead production. This period also signaled the onset of rural poverty in the reserves and elsewhere, as new demands and pressures drove the traditional rural economy to the point of collapse. Some Africans avoided these pitfalls and temporarily competed in the emergent capitalist economy, either as peasants or as an educated 'middle class' finding succour from the liberal constitution of the Cape Colony and filling a small niche in white society.

The destruction of African kingdoms and the subordination of African economies, exemplified in the migrant labour system, created new classes and new aspirations among the black majority. This was most pronounced in the Eastern Cape, scene of 100 years of frontier war. The fall of the independent Xhosa nation was preceded by the great Nongqawuse cattle-killing movement of 1856–1857, which effectively discredited traditionalist responses to the colonial intrusion. African optimism born out of a prosperous peasant economy turned to disillusion as Cape liberalism began to show its limitations. The 1890s saw the emergence of recognisable black nationalism on a national rather than an ethnic basis, and the emergence of early black political leaders.

CHAPTER FOUR

A time of trouble and rapid transformation

ABOVE: *Before the 1970s historians thought that the Mfecane, or upheaval, occurred at the end of the eighteenth century and derived from the growth of the Zulu kingdom under Shaka. The Zulu impact has now been questioned, the beginning extended back to the 1750s, the geographic focus widened to include the interior of the country, and European trade seen as one of the possible causes. This painting by C.D. Bell depicts Ndebele warriors during the time of the Mfecane. Bell accompanied Rev. Andrew Smith on his journey through South Africa during 1834–1835.*

The Mfecane

For most African societies in South Africa the hallmarks of the nineteenth century were difficulty, conflict, dislocation, reorganisation, and finally subjugation. The appearance of the Griqua north of the Orange River heralded the imminent arrival of European styles of life, war and government. Before the full impact of this was experienced, however, most communities were subjected to the vagaries and hardships of the Mfecane.

Literal translations of this term show up assumptions about the Mfecane 'concept'. In older historical works it was a time of 'convulsions', of 'crushing' and of 'wandering hordes', initiated almost solely by Shaka and the Zulu. But new interpretations have identified new suspects: Europeans at the Cape and Delagoa Bay; European surrogates like the Griqua on the highveld. Historians are divided as to the causes, but the events constituting the term Mfecane reshaped the political landscape of southern Africa.

During the last half of the eighteenth century and the first quarter of the nineteenth, dramatic developments transformed the nature of African societies, and altered the demographic shape of South Africa. These have been referred to as the Mfecane (for Nguni speakers) and Difaqane (for Sotho-Tswana speakers) on the highveld. Before the 1970s, scholars generally thought that these changes derived from the growth of the Zulu kingdom under Shaka in southeast Africa, and that the changes had begun to occur at the end of the eighteenth century. Since the early 1990s such views have been modified. It is now accepted that the Zulu were by no means the only ones responsible for the warfare that spread throughout the southeast African coastal areas and the inland regions.

Now it is generally recognised that other African chiefdoms responded just as vigorously and innovatively to the changing conditions of the late eighteenth century. The geographic focus of the process has been expanded to include the interior of South Africa, and the beginning of the Mfecane has been extended backwards from about the 1790s to the mid-eighteenth century. Geographically, the sphere of the Mfecane has now been broadened to include communities of the entire western highveld.

Nor was the conflict exclusively one between Africans. It has been argued that increasing European penetration into South Africa from the Cape and Mozambique destabilised the African communities along the coast and into the interior. Historians are more divided, however, over the degree to which whites are responsible for the commotions of the Mfecane.

How did the Mfecane begin?

To understand this transformation it is necessary to pose three straightforward questions, which to some extent belie their complexity. How did the Mfecane begin? Why did it occur? And what were its consequences?

The discussion begins by tracing developments in the present area of KwaZulu-Natal on the southeastern seaboard. From 1780, in the territory from Delagoa Bay to the Thukela

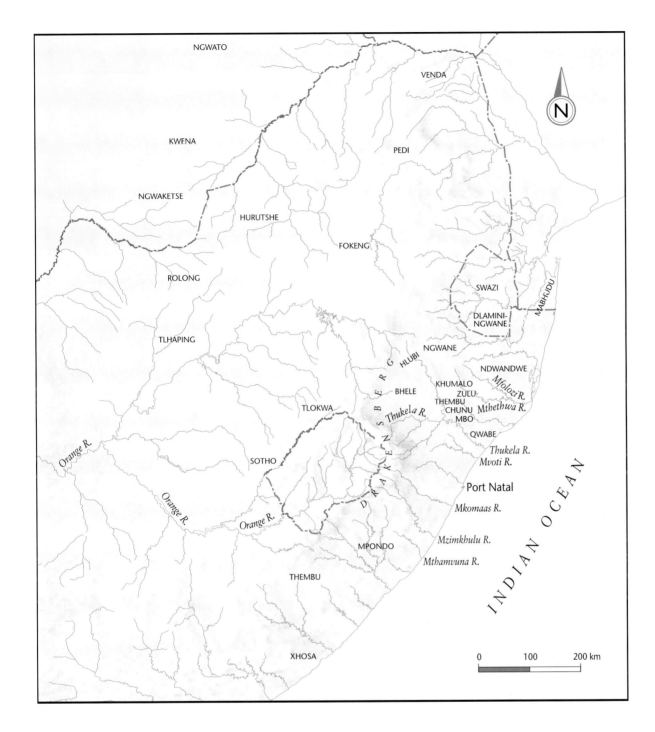

MAP: *African groupings at the time of the Mfecane.*

(Tugela) River, a number of African chiefdoms began to expand in size and grow in power. These included the Mabhudu and Tembe, under Makhasane, near the coast. Weaker communities were dominated or expelled from the region. Even the nascent Pedi kingdom some 300 kilometres away in the interior felt the effects of this.

Further south, a similar pattern emerged, with the Ndwandwe and Mthethwa chiefdoms increasing their numbers and competing for allies. This led groups some distance away from these expanding chiefdoms to strengthen their military capabilities – including the Hlubi in the Drakensberg foothills, and the Qwabe below the Thukela River.

Some chiefdoms caught up in the conflict between these competing power blocs chose to flee. The Ngwane under Matiwane's leadership moved westwards, attacking the Hlubi and killing their chief, Mthimkhulu. The Hlubi split apart; some abandoned their homeland and others merged with the Ngwane. Chief Matiwane settled in the region of

Thought to be Shaka's nephew, as depicted by G.F. Angas.

Mzilikazi, chief of the Khumalo (later known as the Ndebele).

A sketch by A.G. Bain of the son of Chief Faku of the Mpondo. Faku strengthened his kingdom during the Mfecane by absorbing refugees. He survived Zulu invasions in 1824 and 1828, losing many cattle, but emerging politically stronger.

modern Bergville, incorporating smaller groups such as the Zizi and Bhele. He was now the dominant figure in the upper Thukela.

After 1810 Dingiswayo of the Mthethwa surrounded himself with allies and forced those who refused to join him into tributary status. One of these confederates was the Zulu. When their chief Senzangakhona died, Dingiswayo intervened and appointed Shaka as leader.

By 1818 the rivalry for power in the region between the Mthethwa and the Ndwandwe under Zwide was reaching a climax. The Ndwandwe resided in present-day northern Zulu-land and, like Dingiswayo, Zwide commanded the loyalty of a number of smaller chiefdoms. A difference between them was that the Mthethwa built loyalties around common trade interests in cattle and ivory, while the Ndwandwe seemed to rely on the support of related communities.

In 1818 Dingiswayo was captured by Zwide and killed. This allowed Shaka to step into the power vacuum and take control of the Mthethwa. Zwide then turned his attention to the Zulu, seeing them as the only ones capable of thwarting his control over the former Mthethwa confederacy. But Shaka had managed to weld his neighbours into an alliance against the Ndwandwe. These included the powerful Qwabe chiefdom, which previously had rivalled the Zulu for dominance between the White Mfolozi and Thukela rivers.

Zwide's first attack against the Zulu was inconclusive, but in another raid his troops overstretched themselves, driving far into the Thukela River region. Shaka's army forced the Ndwandwe into headlong flight. The Ndwandwe, in all likelihood already experiencing internal stress, disintegrated. Soshangane and Zwangendaba of the Jele and Gaza chiefdoms, who were principal allies of Zwide, moved first to the Delagoa Bay region and then later trekked north. Zwide himself attempted to regroup north of the Phongolo River.

The Zulu then took steps to secure their position in the region across the White Mfolozi and southwards along the lower Thukela and Mzinyathi rivers. This represented a consolidation of existing territorial gains. Contrary to popular historical conceptions, the Zulu kingdom did not have the capacity to extend its sway to the Delagoa Bay (near present-day Maputo) region. Nor was it immediately secure to its south. Shaka had to manoeuvre client chiefs into positions of power to ensure security along his southern border. These included Magaye of the Cele chiefdom – which had been long dominant along the lower Mvoti – and Zihandlo of the Mkhize chiefdom.

The turmoil spreads

To the north, Soshangane eventually established himself along the Nkomati River. He gathered his followers and migrated into southern Mozambique to form the Gaza kingdom. Zwangendaba and Nxaba, leaders of other factions of the Ndwandwe, moved across the Zambezi into what is today eastern Zimbabwe, and from here to present-day eastern and western Zambia, central Malawi and southern Tanzania. Zwide, seeking greater security, moved into what is today central Swaziland, where he managed to attract more followers from weaker chiefdoms. He died in about 1824 and two years later Shaka launched a massive attack on Zwide's son. At a battle north of the Phongolo River the Ndwandwe were heavily defeated. They splintered; some joined Soshangane, others were absorbed into the Zulu kingdom and others joined the other rising power in the region – the Ndebele.

The Ndebele, led by Mzilikazi, were from the Khumalo clan, situated between the Zulu and Ndwandwe. To avoid involvement in this growing competition between his neighbours, Mzilikazi chose to move away. The date of this migration is uncertain: by 1825 he was settled along the Vaal River and then moved north to the Apies River. Some accounts suggest he attacked the Pedi, a very powerful polity. A few years later the Ndebele were to destabilise – and then control – a huge region on the western highveld.

To the southwest, the conflict spread south and across the Drakensberg onto the southern highveld. Mpangazitha's Hlubi crossed the Drakensberg and attacked the Tlokwa under Manthatisi, causing her and other communities to raid in the vicinity of the Vaal and Sand rivers. Both groups settled in the Caledon valley, where the Ngwane under Matiwane joined them. Tensions between these three chiefdoms simmered on until in 1825 the Hlubi were soundly defeated by the Tlokwa and were either incorporated into their ranks or fled into Xhosaland to join Matiwane's army or to become part of the so-called

Mfengu (the hungry ones) – refugees who later were called the Fingo and settled in the Butterworth district of the Eastern Cape.

From 1822 refugees from the Caledon valley – the Phuting, the Taung, the Fokeng and the Hlakwana, who had been caught up in this conflict – moved west, severely disrupting the southern Tswana. The Rolong and Tlhaping were subjected to constant raids between 1823 and 1826. The Fokeng under Sebetwane were to survive the turmoil and establish the Kololo kingdom in what is today western Zambia.

Directly south of the Zulu, beyond the Mzimkhulu River, a similar pattern emerged. A number of chiefdoms displaced by the upheavals from about 1815 chose to cross the Mzimkhulu to avoid being caught up in the turmoil. The Chunu and Thembu were the first to arrive in the early 1820s, followed by smaller groups. This brought them into the sphere of influence of the Mpondo under Faku and precipitated a degree of tension and political instability. The Chunu and Thembu could either accept Mpondo hegemony, or try to retain a degree of independence on the margin of Mpondo territory. As it turned out, the Thembu under Ngoza were attacked by Faku and fell apart, and the Chunu were attacked and destroyed by the Zulu, who wanted to maintain some security on their southern border.

The Difaqane on the highveld

Only recently have historians and archaeologists noticed that a similar pattern of conflict and competition engulfed the Sotho-Tswana-speaking chiefdoms stretching from the eastern fringes of the Kalahari desert to the Limpopo valley and right down to the Free State/Lesotho region. From about 1750 internecine and civil wars struck the Hurutshe, Kwena, Kgatla, Fokeng and Rolong in the former western Transvaal. A similar, though less pronounced pattern emerged among the Pedi/Venda along the Limpopo valley and Fokeng/Kgatla/Kwena lineages in the southern highveld.

This created an ongoing process whereby chiefdoms broke apart, migrated and then frequently merged with other more powerful groups. Once-powerful dynasties found themselves assailed by stronger alliances, which over time broke down their unity, leading to fragmentation. This pattern intensified in the later eighteenth century. Early in the nineteenth century, the Ngwaketse broke the dominance of the Hurutshe in the Madikwe River region, the Tlhaping seized control from the Rolong south of the Molopo and the Kgatla-Pedi rose to power on the Lydenburg plateau.

These Sotho-Tswana-speaking chiefdoms were perhaps not based on the same kind of militarism and chiefly autocracy as many of the Nguni, and were unable to withstand the scale and intensity of the raiders who entered their territories from 1822.

Why did the Mfecane occur?

Before the 1960s much historical writing on the period focused on the 'wars of Tshaka', which then set off a chain reaction of warfare and migration. This was seized upon by apologists for the apartheid system to create what has been called the 'myth of the empty land' – the idea that the Zulu were responsible for the depopulation of the interior, and that the homelands merely conformed to the pattern of African settlement as the whites encountered it in the 1830s.

By the 1960s historians wanted to show that Africans acted rationally to new challenges and developments on the continent. The Mfecane was now portrayed in a positive light as ushering in a period of state building, of innovative rulers in South Africa and states strong enough to challenge white expansion in the interior.

Further research into pre-colonial southern African history threw up new ideas. Some historians argued that overpopulation due to the availability of secure food resources (particularly maize), or the effect of climatic changes caused by drought and long-term environmental degradation may have caused competition for grazing land.

By the 1970s different propositions were put forward. Possibly the entry of new trade goods into southern Africa may have created competition and the need to wield sufficient power to control access to this trade. European demands for ivory and gold may have been the reason for the sudden militarisation of Nguni states and the reorganisation

THE MYTH OF THE EMPTY LAND
An early writer, W.C. Holden, first floated the myth of the 'empty land' in *The Past and Future of the Kaffir Races* (1866). In order to legitimise white settlement, he suggested that whites and Africans entered southern Africa at roughly the same time. In 1901 the idea was taken up and reinforced by George McCall Theal when he claimed that Africans migrating southwards, and the Dutch migrating northwards at the same time, met on the Fish River in the eighteenth century. Theal in fact rejected any assertion that Africans had lived in the Zuurveld for many generations before the arrival of whites. Therefore, he argued, neither the whites nor the blacks had any more right to the land than the other. The influence of Theal was so long-lasting that as late as 1975 the then leading Afrikaner historian, F.A. van Jaarsveld, not only acknowledged Theal's influence but also reiterated his original claim that in South Africa, 'White and Bantu met one another along the east coast as a result of independent movements in opposite directions . . .'.

The first scholar to refute the 'empty land' myth was anthropologist Monica Wilson. In 1959, she rejected an assertion by Eric Louw, then South Africa's Minister of Foreign Affairs, that whites and blacks had arrived in the country simultaneously. Drawing on the reports of shipwrecked European sailors, she demonstrated that Africans had lived in the Ciskei and Transkei long before whites arrived there. Later scholars, notably archaeologists, have clearly demonstrated both the antiquity and continuity of the occupation of large regions in the interior of South Africa by the ancestors of the present-day African communities such as the Tswana and many others. Archaeologist Revil Mason, who worked at Broederstroom in the Magalies valley west of Pretoria, concluded that 'iron and copper producing Negroid pastoralists' began inhabiting the area from about 350 AD to 600 AD. Subsequently, several other archaeologists have reiterated the same point about the antiquity of the African occupation of South African land, which clearly laid to rest the 'myth of the empty land'.

of their economies. Historians examined the possible impact on African societies of the growing trade in gold, ivory and slaves at Delagoa Bay from the mid-eighteenth century, and attempted to quantify the scale of the trade in slaves.

As far as the highveld is concerned, slightly different reasons have been advanced to explain the upheavals. The focus here is on cattle accumulation and the impact of trade. Chiefs who had large herds and sufficient pastureland could attract followers and distribute cattle to supporters or destitute individuals. The *bogadi*, or bridewealth system, placed an even greater premium on cattle, which in turn allowed men access to wives and independent homesteads.

As archaeologists particularly have noted, the Sotho-Tswana were 'cattle-centred' societies. Environmental decline placed a strain on grazing, leading to competition. Storage of wealth in the form of cattle made such societies vulnerable to diseases and cattle raids.

In addition, evidence suggests that the Tswana particularly were on the convergence of trade routes into the interior. Emanating from the west (present-day Angola), the east (Mozambique) and the Cape, these mercantile contacts had a long history. The trade was steady but not spectacular. The usual trade items were beads, copper, iron and cloth in return for ivory, skins (karosses) and cattle. Towards the end of the eighteenth century, however, there was a sudden increased demand for trade items from the Tswana.

This came from two quarters – from the advance of the Cape frontier and settlement of Griqua and Kora communities along the lower and middle Orange River, and from Delagoa Bay, where the demand for ivory intensified. As ivory became a more and more desired item, it led to competition for hunting grounds and control over trade routes, and the necessity for well-organised hunting parties. Among Africans, this created rivalry on the one hand, and on the other the need for larger and more centralised communities.

All of these explanations imply some sort of rational internal response by Africans to these developments, which might account for the Mfecane. However, these explanations for the Mfecane were strongly challenged by Julian Cobbing in the late 1980s (*see box*).

From small lineages to proto-states

How did societies that previously had lived in fairly small family-based communities, transform themselves into larger, more militarised, more centralised 'states'?

Historians have tried to explain this by reference to the *amabutho*. These were originally work parties organised according to age, which rendered service to the chief. But by the late eighteenth century the need for Nguni-speaking communities to obtain more ivory for trade, and more land for cultivation, led to a reorganisation of the *amabutho*.

THE 'COBBING THESIS'

Historian Julian Cobbing's argument against conventional versions of the Mfecane rests on one central point: that the 'time of troubles' was caused by expeditions and raiding parties whose object was to seize labour and slaves from African communities. The individuals responsible for this were whites living in the Cape Colony or in Portuguese Mozambique. The Griqua and Kora, who were alleged to have indulged in similar activities, were seen as surrogates of the colonists. European colonists, representative of capitalist interests both in South Africa and abroad, were now to blame for the upheavals, and the Zulu relegated to a lesser role.

In order to prove his hypothesis Cobbing argued that:

- the seizure of slaves close to Delagoa Bay instigated conflict and violence among people in the vicinity
- missionaries such as Robert Moffat and John Melvill were slave raiders and traders in disguise, and were deliberately pressing the African people of the northern frontier into labour at the Cape (the battles at Dithakong in 1823 and Mbholompo in 1828, Cobbing argued, were examples of such slave raids)
- the Griqua and Kora were allies of the colonists and were furthering their aims by conducting an illicit slave trade among the communities along the northeast frontier.

Cobbing and other scholars who espoused his argument refuted the view that the Zulu were warmongers, intent on military domination of vast tracts of land. The Zulu under Shaka were portrayed as a defensive, rather than offensive state, and not very different from a host of other 'states' that emerged in southern Africa shortly before. They did not initiate the *amabutho*, or age-set regiments, but expanded them and used them for non-military purposes as well. It was argued that the number of deaths due to military conflict was overstated, and incidents of cannibalism so frequently associated with these years were exaggerated.

Both white commentators who ventured into what became the Colony of Natal around this time, and local African traditions, for different reasons, distorted the picture by presenting Shaka as the 'Grim Reaper' of South Africa. Some historians, following Cobbing, have gone so far as to suggest that the term Mfecane should be relinquished.

Several historians found Cobbing's argument, though thought-provoking, to be factually flawed. It inserted one argument in sharp contrast to previous ones, and placed whites as the central players, underplaying the role and interests of African communities. Some argued that it was just as speculative as the arguments he had rejected. But few would now suggest there was no influence deriving from the Cape or overseas markets in the time of troubles that struck southern African during these decades. Historians generally still remain divided over the importance that should be accorded to the Zulu in this period of important transformation. Chiefdoms other than the Zulu were equally, if not more responsible, for the onset of the Mfecane.

Their size and range of duties were increased. The young men found themselves undertaking jobs such as hunting and herding on behalf of the chief and senior men.

Later, towards the beginning of the nineteenth century, the *amabutho* seem to have taken on increased military duties. They were also brought much more closely under the control of their respective leaders. In the case of the Zulu the *amabutho* became a permanent feature of the kingdom centred at the royal household, and were recruited in age-sets, rather than in regional communities, to offset local loyalties. Young women were similarly brought under chiefly control.

The female age-sets, or *izigodlo*, could be made to perform duties for the chief or could be given in marriage to powerful men in the chiefdom, thus ensuring their continued loyalty. These expanded powers allowed the ruling families to cement their control, and to offer economic security and protection which in turn attracted smaller or more threatened communities of individuals. In this way there was a centralisation of power and a growth in their size and administrative complexity.

ABOVE: *According to historian Julian Cobbing, the upheaval caused by European-led expeditions and raiding parties seizing labour and slaves from African communities largely precipitated the Mfecane. (Painting by C.D. Bell.)*

The Difaqane impacted on the Griqua, who were drawn into the battle of Dithakong in June 1823. Interpretations on the reasons for this event and its consequences differ among historians, but Robert Moffat of the London Missionary Society asked the Griqua to assist in repelling an attack on the town of Dithakong – the residence of the Tlhaping under Mothibi – by a militant group of Fokeng, Phuting and Hlakwana. Adam Kok, Barend Barends and Andries Waterboer responded to Moffat's appeal and 100 armed and mounted Griqua successfully routed the attackers.

From 1826 the Ndebele under Mzilikazi established themselves on the western highveld, forcing most Tswana chiefdoms into tributary status. These developments disrupted trading relations between the Griqua and their northern partners, and posed a threat to hunting operations north of the Molopo River. In 1829 the Griqua under Jan Bloem entered into a military alliance with some Tswana groups and sent a commando against Mzilikazi.

The raid was initially successful, but the Ndebele launched a counter-offensive and more than 50 of Bloem's men were killed. Barends then took up cudgels to try to force the Ndebele out of the region. Seeing it as a visionary mission, in 1830 he gathered around him groups united in enmity to Mzilikazi. In June 1831 a combined Griqua/Rolong/Tlhaping commando marched on Mzilikazi. Nearly half of the 1 000-strong force was Griqua. This commando seized as many as 6 000 Ndebele cattle but the Ndebele again fol-

lowed up this raid with a counter-offensive, surprising Barends' camp at night and killing possibly as many as 400 Griqua.

The balance of power over the next few years lay with Mzilikazi, who established military outposts to the south. When the Voortrekkers arrived in the region in 1836, however, the Griqua quickly saw their potential as allies and in 1836 they participated in a combined Voortrekker/Rolong/Griqua attack on the Ndebele at Mosega. Thus Mzilikazi's decision to trek away from the Marico district in 1837 was in part due to pressure exerted by Griqua communities.

Cobbing and some others have portrayed the role of the Griqua in the history of Transorangia (the Free State of today) as being disruptive, painting them as marauders ruthlessly seizing men and cattle, which were often sent southwards to the Cape. Dithakong has been cited as just such an example. A similar assertion has been made regarding their role at the battle of Mbholompo against Matiwane's Ngwane in 1828.

These assertions are largely without foundation. The Griqua *kaptyns* often responded differently to the various problems they faced, according to particular circumstance and the strategy of particular leaders. This included dynastic marriages with African groups, such as the Tlhaping, and trading alliances with other communities in Transorangia. No doubt, as conditions in Transorangia later became more competitive, the level of raids and reprisals became intensified and all communities reacted accordingly.

TOP: *Griquas riding oxen, from Andrew Smith's journal.*

ABOVE: *A parade of warriors before Mzilikazi. In 1829 the Griquas entered into a military alliance with Tswana groups and sent a commando against Mzilikazi.*

The aftermath of the Mfecane

What were the Mfecane's consequences? Ironically, perhaps, the conflict and adversity also gave rise to the emergence of a new crop of leaders that gathered together, reorganised and rebuilt their shattered communities. Notable among such leaders and their societies on the highveld were Moletsane of the Taung, Moshoeshoe of the Sotho, Mzilikazi of the Ndebele, Sekwati of the Pedi, Manthatisi and her son Sekonyela of the Tlokwa, and Montshiwa of the Rolong.

Manthatisi and Sekonyela of the Tlokwa

Manthatisi became a regent queen of the Tlokwa when her husband died soon after 1815, acting on behalf of her son Sekonyela, then still a minor. Although portrayed as an evil woman by some contemporary Europeans, such as Dr Andrew Smith, she was a strong, capable and popular leader, both in war and peace. Her followers called her 'Mosayane'

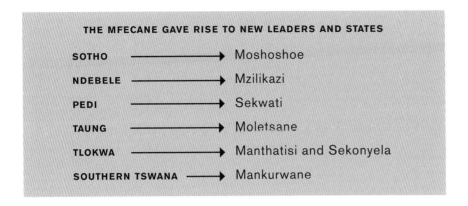

THE MFECANE GAVE RISE TO NEW LEADERS AND STATES

SOTHO ⟶	Moshoshoe
NDEBELE ⟶	Mzilikazi
PEDI ⟶	Sekwati
TAUNG ⟶	Moletsane
TLOKWA ⟶	Manthatisi and Sekonyela
SOUTHERN TSWANA ⟶	Mankurwane

(the little one) because of her small stature. Her popularity is clearly indicated by the fact that instead of her people being known as Tlokwa, they became known as 'Manthatisi'. Unlike other chiefs who fell victim to the Difaqane wars, she successfully kept her people together in the midst of frequent raids by Nguni groups to the south.

With no fixed abode after having been routed by the Hlubi, Manthatisi and her bands wandered from place to place in search of security. They moved in complete family units with the few cattle and possessions they could protect from other marauders. Under these circumstances of fear and insecurity, the very young, the sick and the very old were often simply abandoned and left to die or they became victims of other marauders.

Fear and insecurity also resulted in the abandoning of agriculture and the slaughtering of livestock throughout the southern Sotho region. If they attempted to farm or rear livestock and they were successful, they became the targets of other plundering bands. Thus hunting and gathering wild foods became the major means of sustenance. Smith also reported cases of cannibalism, which subsequent writers exaggerated to give the impression that the practice was widespread.

The Tlokwa did not flee from their country but chose to retreat to more defensible positions. Like many other communities affected by the violence of the Difaqane, the Tlokwa adopted new tactics of fighting and defence, some of which they had learnt from the Nguni. As the conflict was subsiding, the Tlokwa settled at Khoro-e-Betlwa on the north bank of the Caledon River. Their new home, near modern Fickburg, was a flat-topped mountain retreat, or *qhobosheane* in Sesotho, and thus a natural fortress.

Numbering some 24 000 by 1833, Sekonyela's cosmopolitan community consisted of a mixture of the Tlokwa themselves, some Sotho, as well as Hlubi and Ngwane refugees. Seeking refuge on hilltops was not necessarily the practice of only weak communities. Mokuoane, chief of the Phuting, and Moshoeshoe are other examples. People were attracted to Sekonyela's community for two reasons. The first was the safety they offered due to their position and the military skills of Sekonyela, for which he was famous. The second was the possibility of gaining a share of plundered cattle.

From Khoro-e-Betlwa, Sekonyela's lands extended roughly 50 kilometres to the north and eastwards to the source of the Caledon River. Headmen ruling over villages reported to Sekonyela. On the edges of his lands, Sekonyela placed satellite communities specifically to report to him about the approach of his enemies.

Although Sekonyela was a successful and strong military leader, he had certain weaknesses. During times of peace, for example, he would simply usurp his own followers' cattle. As a way of making peace with the Tlokwa's neighbours, Manthatisi arranged marriage alliances for her son with some of Moshoeshoe's daughters. In May 1852, through his raids on Moshoeshoe's kingdom, Sekonyela finally provoked conflict with Moshoeshoe, who retaliated so decisively that the Tlokwa eventually lost their independence.

Moletsane of the Taung

Another leader of a plundering band of followers in the southern Sotho area was Moletsane, whose people were the Taung. He succeeded in rallying together his people and bringing about a degree of order and normality among them. Probably tired of the

TOP: *Manthatisi became regent queen of the Tlokwa in about 1815, acting on behalf of her son Sekonyela. With no fixed abode after having been routed by Hlubi, her bands roamed from place to place and finally settled on a hilltop on the north bank of the Caledon River. English missionaries knew her people as the 'Mantatees', but all warring bands that wandered across the plains of the interior were 'Mantatees' to the white settlers. This watercolour by 'J.W.' is titled 'Bechuana warrior Mantatees'.*

MIDDLE: *Sekonyela, chief of the Tlokwa, in 1834.*

BOTTOM: *Moletsane, chief of the Taung who obtained refuge under the Griqua leader Adam Kok at Philippolis during the Mfecane.*

violence of the Difaqane, he obtained refuge with the Griqua leader Adam Kok at Philippolis. French missionaries convinced him to leave Philippolis in 1836 with a small following of only 150 people, and settle at Beerseba under the Rev. Samuel Rolland. Two years later, when the Taung and their missionary tried to return to their original homeland on the Sand River, they found it already occupied by the Voortrekkers.

Moshoeshoe came to their rescue when he permitted them to settle at Mekwatleng on the edge of what he considered to be his territory. Other wandering bands joined Moletsane at Mekwatleng, where he was allowed considerable autonomy over his own area, but under the overall suzerainty of Moshoeshoe. Moletsane later proved to be a very useful ally to Moshoeshoe in times of conflict over land between the Sotho and the Rolong-bo-Seleka at Thaba Nchu on the one hand, and the Boers on the other.

Moshoeshoe and the Sotho

The Sotho 'nation' managed to survive in one form or another from the 1820s to the present, a remarkable achievement given the difficult conditions that prevailed in the region throughout the nineteenth century. Unlike Sekonyela or Moletsane, Moshoeshoe neither participated directly in a Difaqane raiding community nor left his home base between the Maluti mountains and the Caledon River. He was attacked intermittently by practically all of the main Difaqane marauders, but still was able to build his paramountcy over the Sotho.

RIGHT: *Sotho war dances as illustrated by C.D. Bell in Andrew Smith's journal 1834–1836. Sotho military tactics and innovations were primarily for defence, using the Sotho knobkerrie, long spear, battle-axe and cow-hide shield. The Sotho did not use the short stabbing spear invented by Shaka. From the 1820s to the early 1830s, their formidable army repeatedly and successfully defended the fledgling Sotho 'nation' against external invaders, notably the Tlokwa of Chief Sekonyela, the Ngwane of Matiwane and the Ndebele of Mzilikazi. Sotho territorial chiefs commanded their own military formations and King Moshoeshoe had his own royal regiment, commanded by Makoanyane, but the Sotho did not have professional full-time regiments.*

When the wars began, Moshoshoe used a combination of force and diplomacy to build his power and following. In order to avoid confrontation, he sent tribute to Matiwane of the Ngwane, to the Tlokwa, and later to Shaka of the Zulu. This was the strategy of diplomacy for which Moshoeshoe later became famous. In 1822, apparently anticipating Tlokwa invasion, he had moved his people to Butha-Buthe, a flat-topped mountain, for better defence. When they were attacked, the Sotho rolled boulders down the steep slopes of the mountain and onto the invaders. Simultaneously, Moshoeshoe bargained with the invaders not to seize or destroy his accumulated seed grain. Finally, he managed to convince an Nguni marauder, Sepeka, to come to his aid by attacking Sekonyela.

During the fighting, Moshoeshoe escaped to the safety of another flat-topped mountain, Thaba Bosiu. While Moshoeshoe continued to be a rival to Sekonyela, he established alliances with other chiefs to the north, such as Sekwati of the Pedi. To the south, the dominant chief was Mokuoane of the Phuting. In order to pre-empt any plans by Mokuoane to attack Moshoeshoe, Moshoeshoe sent his brother Mohale to negotiate. The two sides struck a deal and remained faithful but independent allies who would sometimes conduct joint cattle raids in the south.

On Thaba Bosiu, Moshoeshoe subjugated its local ruler while maintaining his alliance with Matiwane. This continued until Matiwane's followers, jealous of Moshoeshoe's influence and believing that he was conspiring with Shaka, incited their chief to attack Moshoeshoe in his mountain stronghold. Matiwane was defeated and crossed the Drakensberg in an epic march to the Eastern Cape. Moshoeshoe was now the undisputed ruler of vast lands stretching from the Caledon River and westwards to Thaba Nchu. Thus his emerging kingdom included many hitherto independent chiefdoms, such as the Ramokhele chiefdom of Moseme.

Remnants of broken communities also joined Moshoeshoe for the security and economic stability he could offer. He retained his herds and increased them through frequent raids. Moshoeshoe also increased his popularity and influence through the *mafisa* system in which he loaned cattle to impoverished newcomers. Despite this dependence upon him, Moshoeshoe allowed the satellite chiefs – usually settled on the periphery of the kingdom – to live in their own villages as they wished, following their own traditions.

At the same time Moshoshoe also expected them to contribute to the stability and protection of his emerging kingdom, particularly as buffers against external invaders. Moshoshoe was thus continually expanding the geographical extent of his kingdom as well as its population into a loose but distinct community. Identification with Moshoeshoe's polity was built not around language or culture, but through recognition of allegiance to him.

Despite this relative security the Sotho still continued to face raids from the Kora. Furthermore, from the late 1820s new influences began to filter into the kingdom. Apart from the threats from external African enemies, Moshoeshoe began to hear from returning refugees about the superior technology of the whites.

But perhaps the most important outside contact Moshoshoe made was with the French missionaries Thomas Arbousset, Eugène Casalis and Constant Cosselin. They belonged to the Paris Evangelical Mission Society (PEMS). Invited by Moshoeshoe to his kingdom, they settled at Morija from 1833. Moshoeshoe also settled two of his sons with the

BELOW: *Evening prayer at Morija. The most important outside contact Moshoeshoe made was with the French missionaries. He invited the Paris Evangelical Mission Society (PEMS) to his kingdom, where they were settled from 1833, with Morija as their headquarters.*

LEFT TO RIGHT:

C.D. Bell's illustration of Mzilikazi receiving Robert Moffat and Andrew Smith at Mosega.

Mzilikazi and his warriors dancing.

Of all the Tswana societies the Rolong were among the worst affected by violence of the Difaqane, as unleashed by the Ndebele. Here medicine men are administering the charm to Rolong warriors when going to battle (left) and blowing a counter charm towards the enemy (right).

missionaries at Morija, partly in order to understand their work and motives in greater depth. But once he had gained their confidence, Moshoshoe brought Casalis to live permanently at Thaba Bosiu to be his adviser and diplomatic agent in his dealings with white people.

Thus, as will be shown later, this 'missionary factor' gave Moshoeshoe strength and confidence in his interaction with whites. Many of the early Christians were to form the core of an educated elite, which articulated nationalist sentiments in the following years. The PEMS mission stations were dotted along the southwestern border of the kingdom where they became a buffer against Kora and Boer raids.

The Ndebele state in the western Transvaal

Under their leader Mzilikazi, originally of the Khumalo clan, the people who came to be called the Ndebele moved from present-day KwaZulu-Natal in order to expand their zone of power westwards – not, as usually has been thought, as a result of Zulu aggression. They headed northwards, eventually settling in and controlling approximately the same area as what later became the Transvaal. From the mid-1820s, they embarked on a process of state-building.

Small in number at first, the Ndebele expanded by incorporating conquered peoples into their ranks. Indeed, during the whole of its brief ten-year period of militaristic existence, the Ndebele state was one of raiding and conquering local communities. These were incorporated into Ndebele society as servants, soldiers or client communities located on the periphery of Ndebele settlements. This was partly a defensive tactic, to protect the Ndebele from possible Griqua and Kora raids, and from the Zulu, who coveted Mzilikazi's increasing cattle herds.

Ndebele towns and military outposts were located mainly in the Mosega Basin on the upper Madikwe River. In the east, cattle posts extended from the upper Odi River to the Pilanesberg mountains. The average population of an Ndebele town was about 700 people. Apart from military preoccupations in every Ndebele settlement, food production by women was also a major undertaking.

After the Griqua/ Ndebele confrontations of 1829 and 1831, a scientific explorer from the Cape, Dr Andrew Smith, linked up with the London Missionary Society's Robert Moffat at Kuruman, and travelled together to Mosega where Mzilikazi expressed his wish to have white missionaries and traders in his kingdom. Mzilikazi also established diplomatic relations with the Cape authorities.

In 1833 he moved northwest, settling between the Marico (Madikwe) and Crocodile rivers. During their occupation of the Madikwe valley, the Ndebele were preoccupied with defence against external aggressors and establishing 'proper' political relations with their subject communities. Mzilikazi was extremely sensitive to armed parties entering his kingdom, especially from the south, from where he thought danger was most likely to come.

When the Ndebele were eventually displaced from the highveld by the Voortrekkers in 1837, they trekked over the Limpopo River to present-day Zimbabwe.

Tswana societies

All Tswana groups, just like the Sotho, were affected by the violence of the Difaqane. The Tswana were not so adept at nation building as the Sotho. Two factors contributed to this. First, Tswana chiefdoms were numerous, autonomous and disunited before, during and even after the Difaqane. Second, many other Tswana societies, such as the Kgatla-ba-Kgafela and the Fokeng, had internal power struggles of their own. Both these factors weakened them. The Tswana tended to regroup along former lines after the Difaqane rather than build new societies.

The Tswana faced the depredations of the early Difaqane raiders as well as the later power of the Ndebele. Between 1823 and 1826, the Rolong were attacked by the Phuting, the Hlakwana, the Taung and the Fokeng, who had fled their homelands in the east. Driven by hunger, these people raided for cattle and attempted successfully to drive the Rolong out of their best lands. The Rolong were forced to move from one settlement to another to escape attack. Communities fell apart and the Rolong chiefs Sefunyela, Tawana and Gontle struggled to retain adherents. People tended to huddle in smaller groups around what arable and grazing lands remained.

From 1826 to 1836 the Ndebele introduced a period of ambiguous peace. Although the former raiders were displaced, the Ndebele brought the Tswana under tighter and more centralised control. Most of the Tswana groups were forced to flee their homes following Ndebele attacks upon them. Examples are the Tlokwa-baga-Sedumedi, Kwena-ba-Modimosana, Phalane and Kgatla of the Pilanesberg, the Hurutshe near the modern-day town of Zeerust and the Pedi of today's Mpumalanga Province. They were able to return only after the expulsion of the Ndebele by the Voortrekkers from the western Transvaal in January 1837.

Yet other communities did not flee from their homes. An example is the Ramokhele branch of the Taung who lived a precarious existence under Chief Moseme at Thaba Nchu, close to the Modder River. To the northeast there was a similar situation in which Tswana groups were barely surviving by hunting and stealing, under constant fear of attack from the Ndebele.

Of all the Tswana societies, perhaps the worst affected by the violence of the Difaqane unleashed by the Ndebele were the western Rolong. Between 1826 and 1832 the presence of the Ndebele brought them some security against attack from other groups fleeing the Difaqane. But in 1832 two Ndebele representatives sent by Mzilikazi to oversee the Rolong capital, Khunwana (just west of the present-day town of Mafikeng), were put to death by the Rolong, who distrusted Ndebele motives.

This incident provoked a devastating reprisal. In 1833 an Ndebele army surrounded Khunwana at night and launched a surprise pre-dawn attack. Indiscriminate slaughter of men, women and children followed. Consequently, large numbers of homeless refugees were forced to wander the lands between the Vaal River and Philippolis. The Rolong themselves fled south. At the same time, another Ndebele force attacked a branch of the Kwena under Khama who lived near the Madikwe-Odi confluence. The Kwena were

Kwena with supplies for Mzilikazi. As subjects of the Ndebele, the Kwena were obliged to offer Mzilikazi tribute.

Robert Moffat of the London Missionary Society. He worked among the Tlhaping at their capital Dithakong from 1816 and obtained the help of the Griqua for them at the Battle of Dithakong in 1820.

A Tlhaping chief and his wife, as observed by John Campbell at Kuruman in the 1820s, before life was disrupted by the Difaqane.

RIGHT: *Thaba Mosega, the hill at the heart of Sekwati's Pedi capital. Sekwati became chief in about 1828 and had established full control over the area by 1837.*

defeated and their population scattered or captured. The Hurutshe of Chief Mokgatlha, although not attacked (because they were Mzilikazi's acknowledged vassals), nevertheless panicked and also fled south when they heard of the Rolong's fate. The uprooting of so many communities led to general starvation.

But in the Madikwe valley, not all of the Tswana communities fled their homes. Some remained and accepted Ndebele rule. Others worked for the Ndebele either in agriculture or tending livestock, all the while being checked on by the Ndebele for loyalty. The subject chiefs regularly paid tribute to Mzilikazi in various forms, such as tobacco, karosses, iron tools and weapons. As long as they paid tribute, the subject peoples were left in peace by the Ndebele rulers.

Some Tswana reconstructed their broken societies only with the aid of European missionaries who had settled among them just before the Difaqane. To the extreme southwest, the Tlhaping and their close neighbours, the Tlharo and Kgalagadi, were spared the ravages of the Difaqane due to the role and presence of the London Missionary Society's Robert Moffat at the Tlhaping capital, Dithakong. Moffat had worked among the Tlhaping from 1816 and offered them protection at the battle of Dithakong in 1820, and afterwards. Moroka's Rolong-bo-Seleka of the present-day Thaba Nchu area survived due to the critical and timely role of missionaries, whose presence deterred potential enemies from attacking them – such as the Taung, and Moshoeshoe, who claimed they occupied Sotho territory.

In 1833 they were resettled by missionary James Archbell at a flat-topped hill to the west called Thaba Nchu. From the four mission stations they founded in the area, the missionaries provided both practical and spiritual assistance to the Seleka, the Griqua and the Korana. Moroka himself never became a Christian but depended on missionary help in his struggle with Moshoeshoe over the latter's land claims in an area inhabited by Moroka's people. Moroka remained at Thaba Nchu and never returned to his original homeland of Khunwana even after the expulsion of the Ndebele.

The Pedi

During the Difaqane, the Pedi leader in what is today Mpumalanga used similar strategies to the Sotho societies to the south. Around 1828 Sekwati took over the paramountcy by force and established full control over the region by 1837. Like Moshoeshoe to the south, Sekwati built his power and chiefdom partly through diplomacy, by establishing alliances with neighbouring chiefdoms to increase his military and productive capacity. The practice also enabled Sekwati to create a network of relationships of patronage and clientage, which boosted his position as ruler. At the same time, he kept a close eye over local rivals.

Refugees fleeing from warfare in southern Mozambique, and from Swazi raids on communities of the lowveld and escarpment, all headed for the relative security of Sekwati's Pedi kingdom. Stripped of their economic and social support, such as cattle and networks of kinship alliance, these refugees entered into relations of close dependence with the Pedi paramount chief through loans of cattle.

The establishment of a lasting security for Sekwati proved arduous, largely because of the expanding sphere of raids by the Swazi. In about 1838 a Swazi army sent by the regent, Somcuba, attacked the Pedi stronghold at Phiring, but was repulsed with limited loss of life and stock. But perhaps the worst victims of Swazi raids were groups located between the Swazi kingdom and the Pedi, such as the Koni, the Pai, the Pulana and the Kutswe.

Later the Pedi faced an even more formidable external enemy. In 1851 a Zulu army sent by King Mpande made two attempts to storm the Pedi stronghold – to no avail, thanks to the use of guns they had recently begun to acquire. Pre-empting a further Zulu attack, Sekwati sent gifts of ostrich feathers to Mphande and perhaps continued to pay him tribute regularly.

The Swazi

The Swazi nation, just like those of the Sotho, the Pedi and others, was forged during the turmoil of the Difaqane. During the rule of Zwide over the Ndwandwe, Sobhuza was forced to flee north. Here, in the general area of what was later to be called Swaziland, Sobhuza rallied together diverse communities of the Sotho, Tsonga and Nguni into a restructured Ngwane (or proto-Swazi) state. However, Zwide frequently raided the fledgling kingdom.

The invasions made Sobhuza a homeless refugee, forced to abandon his capital, Shiselweni, and change capitals many times. He eventually sought refuge with a Sotho chief, Magoboyi, around the Dlomodlomo mountains to the northwest. Fortunately for Sobhuza, Zwide became preoccupied with his conflicts with the Mthethwa and the Zulu. Sobhuza used this opportunity to reorganise his forces, although still under Magoboyi's authority. He attacked and defeated neighbouring chiefdoms and within one year had grown quite powerful, to the extent that it began to worry even his host, Magoboyi. But more worrying to Sobhuza himself were challenges to his authority by close relatives, all of which failed. In 1819, after Shaka routed Zwide's armies in the Mhlatuze valley, near modern Eshowe, Sobhuza finally felt secure enough to return to Shiselweni.

ABOVE: *Sobhuza rallied together diverse communities of the Sotho, Tsonga and Nguni and embarked on the conquest of what was to become Swaziland in about 1820. This picture of the Royal Kraal of the Great Place, Swaziland, is from J.A. Ingram's* Land of Gold, Diamonds and Ivory, *1889.*

The relative security of Shiselweni attracted many refugees to augment Sobhuza's power. As a precaution against attack from Shaka, Sobhuza began to look to the north of Shiselweni for natural fortresses he could use in the event of attack. He therefore embarked upon the conquest of what was to become central Swaziland in about 1820. This area included the fertile and well-watered Ezulwini valley. To the west was the Mdimba mountain range, where cave fortresses were ideal for cover during battle.

Sobhuza used a careful strategy of both conquest and diplomacy against recalcitrant groups. First, he attacked and defeated the weakest groups, such as the Magagula, the Ngwenya, the Dlhadlha and the Mavimbela. Many others simply subordinated themselves to Sobhuza. The more formidable Maseko, however, kept their autonomy, despite Sobhuza having married one of his daughters, laMbombotsi, to their king Mgazi, as a strategy of eventually subordinating the group.

In the long run, however, the Maseko were defeated when their soldiers were lured into a 'joint hunt' for wild animals. They were attacked unawares, defeated and scattered into different parts of the region. The Ngwane were clearly on the ascendancy. To further consolidate his power, Sobhuza allocated each of his sons a chiefdom to rule. But the conquered areas still remained unsettled and insecure, with security generally prevailing only in the military towns.

BELOW: *In 1826 Shaka made himself king of the land north of the Thukela River. This is thought to be a portrayal by Lieutenant James King, a Port Natal trader, reproduced in* Travels and Adventures *by Nathaniel Isaacs, 1836. Henry Francis Fynn describes Shaka in his 1824 diary: 'Round his forehead he wore a turban of otter skin with a crane feather and the ring on his head was decorated with red feathers of the Loorie, tied to thorns which were stuck in his hair. Earrings of sugarcane, carved round the edge, were in his earlobes, which had been cut to admit them. From shoulder to shoulder he wore bunches of skins of monkey and genet, twisted and hanging half down his body. Round his legs and arms were white ox-tails, cut in the middle to allow the hair to hang down. He also wore a petticoat of monkey and genet skins, twisted with tassels and a white shield with a single black spot and assegai.'*

The greatest threat to Ngwane security and Sobhuza's rule came from the south, but Shaka ruled for just twelve years during which his military priorities lay elsewhere, mainly in defensive strategies. Sobhuza also resorted to diplomacy to help his state survive.

For example, he made rain for the Zulu and married two of his daughters to the Zulu king. Despite these overtures of peace, Shaka sent an army to attack the Swazi in 1827 – but the Swazi's use of their defensive strongholds in the Mdimba mountains ensured that the Zulu attack was a failure. Simultaneous Zulu attacks on the Mpondo and the Shangane kingdom to the north overstretched Zulu resources, which also facilitated Swazi resistance.

The death of Shaka on 22 September 1828 and the succession of Dingane brought a welcome respite for the Swazi. Taking advantage of this opportunity, Sobhuza consolidated his position as king and expanded his boundaries as far as the Sabie River to the north and the Steenkampsberg to the west. Stability and prosperity reigned once more. In 1839 a Swazi army was able to rout Dingane's troops in open battle. Sobhuza died at about this time.

SHAKA ZULU

Shaka was born around 1790, the son but not the Great Son of Senzangakhona, chief of the Zulu. It appears that he was an illegitimate child and he and his mother lived in different places while he was growing up. Eventually, Shaka was taken in by Dingiswayo, chief of the Mthethwa, who was building up his army to challenge other chiefs for domination of the area north of the Thukela River. When Senzangakhona died, Dingiswayo helped Shaka to claim the Zulu throne. Later, when Zwide, chief of the Ndwandwe, killed Dingiswayo, Shaka assumed generalship of the Mthethwa forces. Zwide was defeated in 1819 and, in a series of campaigns that lasted until 1826, Shaka made himself king over all the lands north of the Thukela.

Shaka was reputed by his enemies to have performed acts of great cruelty – killing people to fill a donga, or cutting open a pregnant woman to see how the baby lay in the womb – but he finally overreached himself by sending his regiments to fight in distant places far beyond their logistical range. No sooner had they returned from an unsuccessful campaign in Mpondoland than Shaka sent them off to Bhalule in southern Mozambique. Mbopa, Shaka's personal servant, incited the king's brothers to kill the 'madman,' and he was stabbed to death in September 1828.

Don't you know it is the sons of [Senzangakhona] who have killed [Shaka] for his base and barbarous conduct, and to preserve the nation of the [Zulu], the sons of our fathers, that you may live in peace and enjoy your homes and your families.

Dingane then assumed the Zulu throne with the praise name Malumele (the intervener), because it was he who had intervened to save the Zulu from the madness of Shaka.

Shaka's name is forever associated with the Zulu kingdom he brought to maturity, even if he did not initiate it. The kingdom was characterised above all by the institution of named age-regiments, or *amabutho*, who lived in military camps and supported themselves on the cattle of the king. The warriors were forbidden to marry or establish their own homesteads until the ceremony of putting on their headrings, which replaced circumcision as the rite of passage marking the transition to manhood. In this way, the king was able to maintain a standing army subject entirely to his will and his direction.

This historical view of Shaka and the Zulu kingdom has been challenged by the Cobbing school of historians (*see box on page 129*). These historians claim that the Zulu kingdom was not as new, as blood-

thirsty or as effective as usually depicted. They argue that white and oral sources have, though for very different reasons, colluded in the portrayal of 'Shaka-the-monster', whether to justify colonial conquest or the fratricide of Dingane, or simply to glorify an imaginary past for political or propagandist reasons. Some may certainly be inclined to agree with Dan Wylie, the latest proponent of the Cobbing school, in his book *Myth of Iron* (2006), where he writes that 'the material for a trustworthy biography of Shaka simply does not exist'. Others, however, may feel that we have more than enough material to identify, if not Shaka personally, then at least the Shakan state as a major motor of South African history.

CHAPTER FIVE

Consolidation and expansion of the colonial presence

The making of the liberal Cape

Looked at from the vantage point of a democratic non-racial South Africa, the nineteenth-century may seem like one long bloody history of dispossession, the details of which are of little interest today. The Cape Colony of that time was not, however, a monolithic machine but a two-headed monster; although it was very powerful when the two heads faced in the same direction, it was wracked by internal contradictions which had concrete outcomes that can still be felt today. Most notably, with regard to the different characteristics giving birth to different provinces, and with regard to the origins of modern African nationalism, especially in the Eastern Cape.

Past historians have tended to personalise colonial history around historical figures, heroes or villains, courageous colonists versus interfering missionaries, or high-minded missionaries versus brutal colonists. Everything depended on whether the historian in question was a conservative or a liberal. Yet other white historians theorised about something they called 'the imperial factor', meaning that imperialists in London thought very differently from settlers in South Africa itself. Black historians, for their part, have seen little to differentiate between the various blends of imperialism, racism and colonialism.

Yet there were differences, and these were significant. They stemmed not from personalities or ideology or class differences between aristocrats and traders. They stemmed from the fact that South Africa was not a settler colony like Australia or Canada, nor was it a trading colony such as the Gold Coast or Singapore. Rather, it was a little bit of both. Settler farmers wished to appropriate the land and labour of indigenous societies, but settler merchants and missionaries wished to enhance their productive and purchasing power. From this difference arose much else.

One of the great paradoxes of South African history is that the old Cape Colony, which spewed forth the forces of dispossession and subjugation, remained itself a bastion of egalitarianism, embodied in the nominally non-racial Cape Constitution of 1853 and normally referred to in history books as the liberal Cape. This paradox is even more surprising when one considers that the genesis of the liberal constitution occurred while the Cape was governed by the violently pro-settler Sir Harry Smith, engaged in two desperate frontier wars and politically dominated by land-hungry Eastern Cape settlers led by the newspaper editor, Robert Godlonton. To understand how this came to be requires looking more closely at two iconic events of the mid-nineteenth century: the anti-convict agitation of 1849 and the Kat River Rebellion of 1850.

The anti-convict agitation – South Africa's first mass movement

Sir Harry Smith, the British soldier indirectly responsible for the murder of the Xhosa king Hintsa in 1835 (*see box on page 106*), was appointed Governor of the Cape, primarily to defeat the Xhosa armies in the long drawn out War of the Axe (1846–1847). By the time he arrived in December, the war was already over but Sir Harry was not to be

Within three weeks of his arrival, Sir Harry Smith doubled the size of the Cape Colony by extending the border to the Orange River. Within three months he added the whole of the Free State.

denied his glory. He immediately set about extending the boundaries of Great Britain's South African empire to a quite unprecedented extent. Within three weeks of his arrival, he literally doubled the size of the colony by extending its border all the way to the Orange River, and within three months he had added the whole of what is now the Free State under the name 'Orange River Sovereignty'.

All of this was for the benefit of a small clique of Eastern Cape settlers who had been Sir Harry's friends since the Hintsa War. Neither the Afrikaner Boers nor the British government was consulted, let alone the overwhelming mass of black Africans who suddenly found themselves proclaimed subjects of the white Queen.

Smith's aggressive imperialism soon provoked a counter-reaction among significant elements of the Cape's privileged classes. The first element was the Cape Town merchant elite, who had become restive under the iron hand of John Montagu, Smith's top civilian administrator, and who thought that the time had come for those who paid the taxes to run the government. They found their spokesperson in John Fairbairn, the veteran campaigner for the freedom of the press (*see box on page* 97).

The second element was the Afrikaans-speaking community of the Cape Midlands and the Eastern Cape who were unable to express their views in English, and who relied entirely on the voice of their hero, Sir Andries Stockenstrom. The white Afrikaners, those who remained behind after the trek, followed Stockenstrom because he was one of them. The coloured Afrikaners followed Stockenstrom because he was father of Ordinance 50 in 1828, which made people of all colours equal before the law, and the founder in 1829 of the Kat River Settlement, the one small part of the Cape Colony where people defined as 'coloured' were free to enjoy the same human rights as other people in the Cape Colony.

These disparate elements were fused into a single 'popular party' by an event in 1849. Smith's unilateral expansion of the Cape boundaries had not been appreciated in London, which was worried about the financial implications of fighting white Afrikaners as well as black Africans. Smith's aggression had already led to one clash with the Voortrekkers between the Orange and the Vaal (the Battle of Boomplaats in 1848), and London was not too stupid to see new conflicts looming with the Xhosa and the Sotho. Smith himself was uncomfortably aware that he was losing credibility at the Colonial Office, and he tried to placate it by accepting 300 British and Irish convicts sent to the Cape aboard a ship called the *Neptune*.

The Anti-Convict Association was South Africa's first mass movement. It mobilised in Cape Town, multiplied demonstrations and petitions, and proclaimed a boycott against any merchant supplying provisions to the convict ship. The popular members resigned from the governor's Legislative Council and left Smith politically dependent on the

BELOW: *The huge anti-convict meeting outside the Commercial Exchange Building in Cape Town on 4 July 1849. The anti-convict campaign directed against the convict ship* Neptune *was the first genuinely popular and democratic movement in South Africa. It provided a common focus for disparate forces opposed to the reactionary autocracy of Governor Sir Harry Smith, and introduced mass demonstrations and boycotts to the streets of Cape Town. It was indirectly responsible for the relatively liberal and colour-blind Cape Constitution of 1854.*

extreme Eastern Cape settlers headed by Godlonton. The struggle lasted five months, until the *Neptune* and its convicts departed in February 1850.

New elections were held for the Legislative Council and, despite the indirect method of election cooked up by Smith, the popular party swept the polls with Stockenstrom coming in first and Robert Godlonton, the leading settler, no higher than eleventh. The battle for a representative government now began in earnest, with Stockenstrom and Fairbairn travelling to London to put the case of the popular party directly to the Imperial government.

But what kind of representative government was it to be? More especially what implications did representative government have for the majority of the population, who were not classified as white? Representative government is not the same as democratic government. Voting at the Cape, like all of Britain's other colonies, was for men only, and only for men who were also landowners. Moreover, at this time the borders of the Colony did not extend beyond the Keiskamma River. Very few Xhosa-speakers resided within the Colony itself, and there was no expectation that this was about to change.

Since race was not an acceptable legal category at the Cape since Ordinance 50 of 1828, there could be no overt discrimination in terms of race. The discriminatory component of the franchise legislation was therefore expressed in terms of the value of the property that a man was required to possess in order to qualify for a vote. The debate between liberals and conservatives was fought over the question of whether the property qualification should stand at £25, which would allow most adult males outside the rural areas to vote, or whether it should stand at £50, a qualification which effectively placed the vote beyond the reach of anybody except males of European descent. This debate had been going on ever since the idea of representative government for the Cape was first proposed in 1848. But it was only to be concluded after the outbreak of the Kat River rebellion.

RIGHT: *The Cape Legislative Council of 1850, drawn by A. Hayes, as published in the* Cape Argus *of 26 March 1924. The elections to the Legislative Council, although held on a very conservative and indirect franchise, returned five out of five members of the 'popular' democratic party: Brand, Stockenstrom (standing), Reitz, Fairbairn and Wicht. When Governor Smith invoked his authority to replace Wicht with Robert Godlonton, an ultra-reactionary from the Eastern Cape who had only finished eleventh in the poll, the other members resigned in protest.*

LEFT: *The anti-convict association attempted on 10 July 1849 to persuade the pro-Smith nominated members to resign. This drawing by A. Hayes was used to illustrate an article in the* Cape Argus *entitled 'Mobbing the Legislative Council'.*

The Kat River rebellion

Andries Stockenstrom, who was then commissioner-general of the Eastern districts, established the Kat River Settlement in 1829. His ulterior motive was to create a buffer zone between white farms – his own included – and independent Xhosaland. The earliest settlers were drawn from the overcrowded mission lands at Bethelsdorp and elsewhere in the Colony. Their exposed military position, coupled with the fact that they were settlers on lands seized from the Xhosa chief Maqoma, condemned them to fight on the colonial side for a cause that was not theirs. Officially, however, the purpose of the settlement was a lofty one indeed – 'to collect the remnants of the [Khoikhoi] race, to save them from extirpation, to civilise and Christianise them'.

The Kat River Settlement was the only part of the Cape Colony where people not defined as white could own land in peace. As one group of petitioners put it in 1849, 'in the land of our fathers, an area of country larger than England, we have scarcely an inch of land on which to set our feet, the Kat River and the sterile spots of the Missionary Institutions excepted'. The Kat River Settlement was much more than a district, it was a symbol of freedom, it was the promise of a better life, and it continued to draw coloured labourers from settler farms, thereby raising the ire of precisely those settlers on whom Sir Harry Smith had most come to depend.

Smith appointed his cronies T.J. Biddulph, followed by T.H. Bowker, as magistrates in Kat River. They tried to requisition Kat River people as wagon drivers and skilled labourers but were refused. 'A concourse of rebellious idle paupers,' declared the magistrates and proceeded to impose onerous taxes on the cutting of timber, and excessive rentals equivalent to more than ten times those paid by white settlers.

The Kat River people saw themselves more and more as second-class citizens and became increasingly apprehensive about threatened vagrancy laws designed to force them into employment on white farms. When the Xhosa rose against the whites for the eighth time (War of Mlanjeni, 1850), the majority of the Kat River people rose with them. In previous wars, they had fought with the colonial forces as fellow Christians. Now the Khoi

BELOW: *Philipton in the Kat River Settlement. The Kat River Settlement, established in 1829, was a symbol of freedom since people not defined as 'white' could own land there.*

garrison at Fort Armstrong in the Kat River valley mutinied against their white officers. 'The missionaries have for years written,' they said, 'and their writings won't help. We are now going to stand up for our own affairs. We shall show the settlers that we too are men.'

Many Kat River rebels were trained marksmen and they joined the Xhosa chief Maqoma in his epic defence of the natural stronghold of the Waterkloof (Mtontsi). But the military aspect of the Kat River uprising was probably not its most important aspect. As Governor Smith remarked with singular perspicacity, 'I regard this almost general disaffection of the Coloured classes within the Colony as of far greater moment than the outbreak of the [Xhosa].' For the grievances of the Kat River were indeed also the grievances of the whole of the dispossessed and landless coloured classes throughout the Cape. They were expressed in universal and apocalyptic terms by Willem Uithaalder, the Kat River leader, who spoke of 'the oppression and complete ruin of the coloured and poor of this land, a land which we, as natives, may just claim as our motherland . . . Rise manfully and unanimously as a nation, and children of one house.'

It was a message that was not lost on the coloured levies of Caledon and Swellendam, Genadendal and Riversdale, soldiers who arrived in the Eastern Cape only to find their sympathies engaged on the side of the people they had come to fight against. The colonial military noted with disappointment that their hitherto tractable foot soldiers had 'imbibed a feeling that the [Khoikhoi] and [Xhosa] are fighting for the land formerly theirs, and are right in so doing'. Smith could only get them going by threatening them with 'decimation on the Spanish principle' (that is, shooting one in every ten), and even that did not work for very long.

The Khoikhoi on Shiloh and Theopolis mission stations rose in solidarity with the Kat River rebels, and the colonial authorities hastily shipped their reluctant soldiers back to the Western Cape – by sea so as not to 'infect' the coloured communities along their route of march.

The Cape Colony had thus very narrowly escaped an all-out war of the classes and races, and the lesson was not lost on the more farsighted of the colonial officials, more especially William Porter, the attorney-general. Porter saw very clearly that the small white minority could only survive in South Africa with the support of the coloured classes, and that support could be secured only by meaningful political rights. As he put it, Porter said that he 'would rather meet the Hottentot at the hustings voting for his representative than meet him in the wilds with his gun upon his shoulder'.

And so the lower, more liberal franchise was pushed through the relevant legislative processes until it became part of the new constitution confirmed by an Imperial Order-in-Council in March 1853. By this constitution, all adult male British subjects, regardless of colour, were entitled to the franchise and to seek election to the legislature. Thus was born the liberal Cape. It lasted less than 50 years, if the tampering with the franchise in the late 1880s is taken as the start of its demise.

TOP: *Many Kat River rebels were trained marksmen.*

BOTTOM: *This painting by C.D. Bell shows Maqoma, the Xhosa chief. The Kat River rebels joined Maqoma in his defence of Waterkloof.*

Colonial expansion into the South African interior

By contrast with the setbacks they experienced in the Cape Colony, the British settler element gained huge ground in the Free State and Natal. The history of South Africa at this time indeed proves that the pen is mightier than the sword as an instrument of territorial acquisition. There was a limit to the amount of land that a farmer could farm, but there was seemingly no limit to the extent of land that an Imperial power could distribute to its well-connected friends. Frustrated by the obdurate resistance of the Xhosa to their immediate east, the settlers turned their attention to the seemingly easier pickings further afield.

Southern Transorangia (Free State)

Southern Transorangia (as the Free State was then called) was in 1840 politically dominated by the Griqua captaincy of Adam Kok III at Philippolis. He had come to power in 1837. By 1838 a *raad*, or council, had produced a code of laws with field-cornets in each division acting as officials of the *raad*.

Relations between the Griqua captaincies at Philippolis, Campbell and Griquatown had been strained due to the interference of Dr John Philip, a superintendent of the London Missionary Society and the Griquas' missionary patron. Philip favoured Andries Waterboer as supreme head of the Griqua, based in Griquatown, lying 200 kilometres to the northwest on the other side of the Orange River. However, in 1837 Waterboer and Adam Kok signed a treaty of mutual protection and collaboration between their respective councils. The Griqua enjoyed a period of relative peace and prosperity.

Fearing that the Boers in the area would destroy the independence of the Griqua captaincies and of the Sotho under Moshoeshoe, Philip persuaded the Governor Sir George Napier to sign treaties in 1843 with Waterboer and Kok and the Sotho chief, Moshoeshoe, in which they agreed to help preserve peace and security. But treaties could not protect Griqua autonomy or prevent the Griqua captains from alienating more and more land to whites.

Neither the trekboers nor the Voortrekkers immediately challenged the formal Griqua or Sotho authority over them that the treaties implied. They did not object to asking Moshoeshoe's permission to settle on his land, nor to his overall authority. They were willing, at first, to deal with Kok and Waterboer on a basis of equality. In 1844 Hendrik Potgieter – the Voortrekker leader who as 'head commandant' claimed control of the Voortrekkers between Potchefstroom and Winburg – offered a treaty to Kok. 'We are emigrants,' Potgieter wrote, '[who] . . . together with you dwell in the same strange land and we desire to be regarded as neither more nor less than your fellow-emigrants, inhabiting the country, enjoying the same privileges with you. It is by no means the intention of the Head Commandant and his Council to bring any native chief under their laws and authority but to leave each one to exercise his own authority.'

But both trekboers and Voortrekkers protested when the Griqua authority arrested whites, and they had far more firepower than Kok and Waterboer, whose support in Cape Town was dwindling. The Cape government had lost faith in the treaties and Philip's political influence was on the wane. The Griqua were determined to remain on good terms with both the British and their missionaries, and as far as possible with the Boers. This was an untenable situation. For example, Adam Kok III handed over a group of Boers wanted by the British authorities for murder in 1845, prompting conflict with the Boers. The Griqua also complained of cattle theft by the Boers.

In 1845 Governor of the Cape Sir Peregrine Maitland appointed a British Resident in Transorangia. The Boers could now rent land from the Griqua under strict conditions. This and the emigration of a number of disgruntled Boers temporarily eased the tension.

But British policy was not constant. Sir Harry Smith, who became governor of the Cape in December 1847, was of a quite different temperament from his predecessors, Sir George Napier and Sir Peregrine Maitland. Not content with doubling the size of the Cape within two months after his arrival, he set his sights on Transorangia as well. He intervened with Adam Kok in the name of the Afrikaners settled in Griqua territory, as the following remarkable scene described by Kok himself demonstrates:

Sir George Napier

Sir Peregrine Maitland

TOP: *Philippolis in the Transorangia (the present day Free State province). The old Griqua* kaptyn *Adam Kok II abandoned his original capital at Griquatown in about 1819 because he could not abide missionary discipline. Kok's people led a wandering life for several years until they reconciled with the missionaries in 1827 and established another capital at Philippolis, named after the missionary superintendent, Dr John Philip.*

> Adam Kok: I am satisfied with the treaty of Sir Peregrine Maitland which has been approved by Her Majesty the Queen.
> Upon this His Excellency exclaimed in a passion, Treaty is nonsense – Damn the treaty. And taking off his glasses he dashed them on the table.
> Southey, His Excellency cried, tell him I am Governor General. I shall hang the black fellow on this beam. Tell him, Southey, to leave the room immediately.

The Afrikaners were not much better treated. Smith promised them that Great Britain would not annexe their territory unless 80% of them were in favour. They were not, but Smith went ahead and annexed it anyway. Andries Pretorius approached Moshoeshoe to form a common front against British imperialism but Moshoeshoe was hesitant. Pretorius's reputed words to Moshoeshoe have a prophetic ring: 'You don't know the English. They are an odd people. Remember my word. You will repent for having joined them.'

Smith made short work of the Afrikaners at Boomplaats (1848) and in 1849 Moshoeshoe was bullied into accepting an unfavourable boundary known as the Warden Line. Smith was now the master of 2.5 million acres of Transorangia land, which he gave away to no more than 139 English friends – only 40 of whom actually lived on their properties. This speculator's paradise was known as the Orange River Sovereignty. It lasted only six years. The British government became disillusioned with Sir Harry and – after the Sotho defeated the British at Berea in 1852 – frightened of Moshoeshoe. The few British settlers were expendable and, by the Bloemfontein Convention of 1854, the Imperial government ceded Transorangia to the Afrikaners under the name of the Orange Free State.

Natal

Natal had been regarded as part of the British sphere of influence since the establishment of the first trading post in Port Natal in 1824, but the early English traders and hunters found themselves unable to secure a stable relationship with Dingane after the assassination of Shaka.

Numerous attempts were made by interested merchants in Cape Town and the Eastern Cape to pressurise the Imperial government into taking a more active role but nothing was done until 1837 when, in the shadow of the Great Trek, London appointed independent

BELOW: *An advertisement for merino sheep in the Graaff Reinet* Herald *of 28 February 1853.*

EXPANSION OF WOOL FARMING

'The appearance of the country is very fine. It will make excellent sheep farms.' Thus mused one of the British settlers on active service in Xhosaland during the 1834–1835 Frontier War. These words proved prophetic. Sheep are indigenous to South Africa, but the indigenous fat-tailed sheep, though good for eating, produced wool too greasy to feed the dark textile mills of Victorian Britain.

Wool production within Britain itself could not keep pace with the expansion of Britain's textile industry and from the 1840s it went into decline. By 1850 Britain was importing 49% of all its raw wool requirements, a figure that rose to 80% by 1900. Australia was the main source of Britain's wool supply but it was soon discovered, notably by 1820 settler Richard Daniell of Sidbury, that Australia's merino sheep flourished just as well at the Cape.

Wool soon became South Africa's leading export, overtaking wine in the 1840s and increasing nearly tenfold between 1839 (266 tons) and 1851 (2 472 tons). This was facilitated by merchants such as the Mosenthal brothers, who established a store in Port Elizabeth in 1842. Mosenthal's stores not only provided a ready market for

the farmer, but also served as a source of easy finance, even issuing its own banknotes. Wealthy wool farmers and local dignitaries, such as J.C. Molteno of Beaufort West, opened their own local banks and ran the local Divisional Councils, which had extensive powers of land allocation.

Wool farming, more than most other branches of agriculture, required extensive tracts of cheap land. British settlers soon snapped up the abandoned farms of departing Voortrekkers, following which they swal-

lowed most of the Northern Cape in the wake of Sir Harry Smith's unilateral extension of the Cape boundary to the Orange River in 1847. Once merino had been introduced, land values escalated fourfold or higher even in relatively unpromising districts such as Colesberg. The prospect of such windfall profits fuelled the speculative mania, giving rise to an acute thirst for the lands of the Free State by merchants and financiers who never had the slightest intention of actually going to live there.

missionary Allen Gardiner as Justice of the Peace. Gardiner had no funds, no military resources and no clear mandate, and the tiny English community, numbering no more than 40 males, threw their weight behind the Voortrekker leader Piet Retief when he reached Natal in October 1837.

With the wisdom of hindsight, it seems that Retief was incredibly naive in his dealings with Dingane. In his defence, it needs to be said that he was seeking no more from Dingane than Louis Tregardt had formerly received from the Xhosa king Hintsa, and that Dingane himself had made some sort of similar agreement with Gardiner in June 1835.

But Dingane had experienced more than enough trouble from the handful of whites at Port Natal and had no intention of allowing more than 1 000 tough and heavily armed farmers to settle permanently in his immediate neighbourhood. On Dingane's instructions Piet Retief and his 67 men were overpowered and killed at Mgungundhlovu Great Place in February 1838. Dingane's armies massacred some 500 more of Retief's followers at Weenen, two-thirds of them women and children, half of them black. The trekker leader Piet Uys fell with his men in battle a month later while Hendrik Potgieter beat an ignominious retreat back to the highveld. Port Natal was razed to the ground, the surviving missionaries and traders escaping by ship.

It was at this point that Andries Pretorius arrived from Graaff-Reinet, reorganised the trekker army and invaded KwaZulu. Supported by 500 men and armed with cannon, Pretorius took up a strong position at the Ncome River and waited for the Zulu charge. Again and again, the warriors rushed the laager; again and again trekker firepower drove them back. Some 3 000 Zulu died that 16 December 1838, and the Zulu kingdom never really recovered. Dingane's half-brother Mpande allied with Pretorius to defeat Dingane, who was eventually killed by the Swazi as he tried to regroup further north. Europeans now increasingly began to dictate the nature of Zulu politics.

In March 1839 the Voortrekkers declared the republic of Natalia at Pietermaritzburg, and Pretorius established his farm on the site of the future Edenvale. But the Afrikaner population of Natalia never numbered more than 6 000, including women and children, and its economy fell into the same speculative trap as its British counterparts, none proving more energetic in this respect than Commandant Gert Rudolph who claimed 40 farms totalling 250 000 acres.

Raiding not farming was Natalia's forte, and in 1840 the Natalians raided the Bhaca chief Ncaphayi, seizing 3 000 cattle and abducting seventeen children for distribution as apprentices among the farmers. But Bhacaland was deep in the heart of the British sphere of influence, the missionaries complained, and Cape Governor Napier sent a force of 250 men to Port Natal to make good Britain's historical claims to Natal. In the initial skirmish the British suffered serious losses.

But once reinforcements arrived, the Voortrekkers put up little further resistance. Natal was annexed to the Cape in May 1844, and elevated to the status of a Crown Colony in December 1845.

TOP TO BOTTOM: *Dingane is shown 'in his ordinary and dancing dress' in Gardiner's* Narrative of a Journey to the Zoolu Country in South Africa, *1836.*

RIGHT: *Mgungundhlovu, Great Place of Dingane, where Retief and 67 companions perished in 1838.*

The British force under Captain T.C. Smith, sent out in 1842 to annex Natal, included Henry Cloete, an anglicised Cape Afrikaner, who was appointed as a special commissioner for land claims. In July that year, after the British force had prevailed militarily, the Volksraad invited Cloete to Pietermaritzburg and, while a hostile crowd of Voortrekkers gathered outside the building, deliberated with him, eventually deciding to submit to British authority.

Cloete's arrival exposed the class and gender divisions in trekker society. The poor and illiterate were more vociferous in rejecting British authority than the more prosperous, and the men more inclined to submit than the women. Afrikaner women were a driving force behind the trek. A British settler on the frontier wrote while the trek was getting underway: 'They fancy they are under a divine impulse ... the women seem more bent on it than the men.'

The trekker women had not left the colony as mere adjuncts of their husbands; they had helped to make decisions and had enforced discipline over servants. This authority over servants was greatly undermined in the decade before the trek when servants and apprentice slaves began to take their masters and mistresses to court.

Trekker women had made their presence felt as early as 1838 when a British force briefly annexed Port Natal. The commander reported that opposition to British rule was particularly strong among Afrikaner women. They had experienced great want and insecurity, but 'they all rejected with scorn the idea of returning to the Colony'. He added: 'If any of the men began to droop or lose courage, they urged them on to fresh exertions and kept alive the spirit of resistance within them.'

At the meeting in Pietermaritzburg, Afrikaner women gave Cloete a baptism of fire, with the redoubtable Susanna Smit playing a leading role. She was the sister of Gerrit Maritz and the wife of Erasmus Smit, a missionary-cum-teacher.

Henry Cloete

Smit headed the delegation of Afrikaner women who confronted Cloete. He reported that they expressed 'their fixed determination never to yield to British authority ... but [that] they would walk out by the Draaksberg [Drakensberg] barefooted, to die in freedom, as death was dearer to them than the loss of liberty'. They told Cloete that as a result of the battles they had fought alongside the men, the men had promised them 'a voice in all matters concerning the state of this country'. Yet the all-male Volksraad was now submitting to the British despite the women's protests. The women's fury dismayed Cloete; he considered it 'a disgrace on their husbands to allow them such a state of freedom'.

Their protests were in vain, and by 1843 it had become clear that Britain would impose equality before the law. Susanna Smit, despite announcing her willingness to walk barefoot over the Drakensberg to escape British control, continued to live under British rule in Natal for more than two decades.

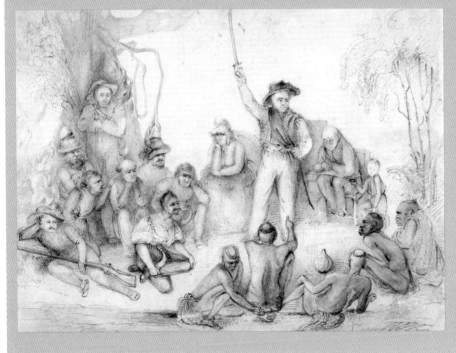

TOP: *Advocate Henry Cloete was appointed special commissioner for land claims in Natal in 1842. His task was to assure the Voortrekkers in Natal that the British would honour legitimate land claims.*

ABOVE: *Andries Pretorius speaking to delegates sent by Dingane to Port Natal (Durban) in 1839. To the left of Pretorius is one of the few depictions of a trekker woman that we have. This sketch was made by J.A. Harding of the 72nd Highlanders.*

BELOW: *Sir Theophilus Shepstone, the*
originator of the location system. Shepstone's
model, based on European understanding
(or distortion) of African traditional political
organisation, was utilised extensively in
southern and central Africa by later colonial
administrations.

The following years were marked by the gradual withdrawal of the Afrikaner population and the demarcation of thirteen 'native reserves' by the newly appointed head of Native Affairs, Theophilus Shepstone.

When Sir Harry Smith assumed the governorship in December 1847, two million acres of fertile Natal land were available to white speculators, and Sir Henry generously gave away this huge territory to no more than 360 claimants. Thirteen commercial firms, mostly based in Cape Town, owned 230 000 acres for which they had paid a miserly two pennies per acre.

In April 1859, Bergtheil and Coqui, the biggest landowners, founded the Natal Land and Colonisation Company which owned 250 000 acres altogether. Their profits arose not out of production but out of the sale of their shares on the London Stock Exchange. Two pennies an acre translated into Company shares at eleven shillings and sixpence an acre, a profit of 1000%.

Thus was Natal colonised on paper before it was colonised on the ground. But it was a period when settlers were not too difficult to find. This was the age of colonial theorists such as Edward Gibbon Wakefield, and of the Irish potato famine. Between 1847 and 1851 some 250 000 settlers a year departed Britain and Ireland, of whom a mere 5 000 came to Natal. The main brain behind this scheme was Joseph Byrne who in all probability never actually set foot in Natal himself. The emigrants were promised twenty acres each but most of them were never able to take possession. Byrne went bust and in 1851 Britain halted all state-aided emigration to Natal.

THE SHEPSTONE SYSTEM: THE FIRST 'LOCATIONS'

Sir Theophilus Shepstone was appointed diplomatic agent to the 'Native Tribes' in 1846, a post that was upgraded in 1853 to Secretary for Native Affairs. He played a crucial role in Natal's early history, and was responsible for the general administration of Natal's black population.

Confronting a large African population in the years after the Mfecane, Shepstone did not believe they could be reconstituted purely along former traditional lines as before. He did believe, however, that features of pre-colonial life should be maintained,

and would intervene in African affairs if necessary to ensure its preservation, particularly if chiefs or indunas were uncooperative. This was illustrated in the way he deposed the Hlubi chief Langalibalele.

Fundamental to his system of governance was the belief that Africans should occupy locations or reserves, designated around areas of dense population. White magistrates were to administer the ten recommended locations with the assistance of a black police force. Missionaries were encouraged to settle Africans on land, to convert them to Christianity and get them to assume 'industrious habits'. The designated chiefs had the authority to settle issues relating to 'Native Law'. If individuals objected to such decisions, they could appeal to the magistrate. Magistrates in turn presided over issues relating to English law, though cases were resolved through a judicious combination of both systems.

Shepstone ensured that the black population paid for its own administrative costs. He did this by forcing chiefs to collect taxes, the most common being the hut tax, imposed on every male homestead. Africans also had to pay an indirect tax on imported goods such as woollen clothes and blankets. In 1872, taxes collected from Africans

accounted for £142 000 – approximately 75% of administrative costs in respect of Africans. Thus a portion of the homestead's production was diverted to the Colony in the form of tax, rent or labour.

Shepstone's system was remarkably successful in retaining peace and security in Natal, and simultaneously provided a steady flow of workers onto white farms and elsewhere – though he was constantly faced with demands from settlers for more labour. But it had flaws. For example, many Africans had no hereditary allegiances, and as they moved away from the locations, they shed what allegiances they might have had. Chiefs tended to lose authority in such cases. Similarly, African converts, or *Kholwa*, distanced themselves from traditional rulers or structures.

An important aspect of the Shepstone system was its use elsewhere, in other districts and states in South Africa, especially Zululand, Griqualand West and the Transvaal, and in British Bechuanaland (now the Far Northern Cape). It was the Shepstone model more than any other that paved the way for the segregationist regimes of the twentieth century, more especially the Native Administration Act of 1927 and the homeland ventures thereafter.

Indians arrived in South Africa to resolve a labour shortage blamed on Shepstone's 'native' system, which was seen as bottling up African labour in the reserves. Fortuitously, the British authorities in India had decided in 1860 to include Natal in the indenture system, which in part gave rise to the Indian diaspora. They came to Natal mainly in two groups – indentured labourers and passenger Indians, the latter paying for their own passages. Some smaller categories also arrived, such as 'special servants' (employed in clubs and hotels) and Mauritian Indians contracted to the Natal Railways Company.

Altogether some 150 000 indentured Indians arrived over a 50-year period. They were divided almost equally into Tamil speakers from south India, and people from the Hindi-speaking regions of north India. Though of different languages and castes, they shared a common background of poverty in India.

Passenger Indians came mainly from west India (Gujerat) and arrived a decade after the indentured Indians. They shared more common origins and language. They possessed some capital and came initially to serve the trading needs of the inden-

tured, but spread into the growing towns of the interior of South Africa.

A third category of Indian emerged in time. These were free Indians – those who were issued with a free discharge certificate on completion of their indentures. In theory, they could do any jobs and could live where they chose in South Africa. Many free Indians entered into market gardening or became fishermen, traders or hawkers.

Theoretically, working conditions for the indentured Indians appeared reasonable. Their contracts laid down the conditions of work in respect to hours, wages and rations, and so forth. In practice, they worked long hours, twelve to fifteen a day, were poorly housed and seldom received rations. They were flogged or imprisoned for desertion. Local white magistrates rarely sympathised with indentured labourers or took up their complaints in the face of the powerful Natal sugar faming interests. Thus cases were infrequently heard and justice even less often meted out.

In a strange country, unable to speak local languages, the indentured Indians were also deprived of basic family life. Many left wives behind in India who never joined them. Only a quarter of them were

women (the white farmers objected to female labourers because they could not be used for manual work in the fields) and this imbalance led to social disruption and prostitution. In any event, no law existed for the recognition of Indian marriages by the Natal government. In addition to these hardships, little attempt was made to provide for their medical and educational needs.

This left Natal as a colony in search of a reason for its existence. Cotton was tried, notably by Bergtheil, but proved unsustainable. White settlers tried but failed to compete with African farmers in the production of indigenous crops such as maize. But back in 1842, the commander of Port Natal reported that sugar cane, a non-indigenous crop dependent on plantation labour, thrived in the soil and climate of Natal.

The first pioneer was the British settler Edmund Morewood, who experimented with sugar at his farm Compensation Flats on the Natal north coast. Assisted by better plants from Mauritius and tariff protection from the Natal government, sugar flourished and the acreage of land under sugar cane expanded from 538 acres in 1854 to 12 781 acres in 1866. The number of sugar mills increased from six to 64 over the same period.

If Natal sugar was to compete with Britain's other sugar colonies in Mauritius and the Caribbean, however, it had to access labour that was equally cheap. African labour was not voluntarily forthcoming, as Africans were still able to rent land cheaply from the big land companies. Nor were the settlers, few and militarily weak, in a position to force Africans into slave-like plantation labour. Some plantations brought in Tsonga labour from the Mozambique borderlands, but the most important social consequence of the Natal sugar economy was its dependence on unskilled labour from the Indian subcontinent.

Between 1860 and 1911, more than 150 000 indentured labourers were shipped out of Calcutta and Madras to Natal. The Natal government paid the travel costs of the indentured labourers who, on arrival in Natal, were assigned to an employer identified by

ABOVE: *One of the 150 000 indentured Indians who came to Natal between 1800 and 1911. Once freed from their indentures, many found work as market gardeners in the coastal districts of Natal.*

government on conditions of service also identified by government. No wonder that Hugh Tinker, the world authority on Indian indentured labour in this period, has labelled it 'a new system of slavery'.

The indentured labourers were entitled to a free passage home after ten years or – at least until 1890 – a free plot of land. Due to poor economic prospects in India, about 52% of the indentured labourers remained in Natal after their contracts had expired.

About fifteen years later, Natal had become established as a place where Indian people lived and began to attract voluntary immigrants known as 'passengers' because they paid their own travel costs. Although all Indian immigrants landed in Natal, many of the passengers made their way inland, thereby adding a significant new element to South Africa's diversity.

White settlement on the highveld and African reaction

From the time of the arrival of whites in the Transvaal in the late 1830s until the late 1860s, the political situation was fluid. Neither the trekkers nor African communities gained complete political ascendance. There was 'an absence of clear-cut definition before the colonial state takes over'. Representatives of the white community – whether traders, hunters, missionaries or local leaders – began to play a more pronounced role in internal or intra-African affairs. On both sides the chances for opportunistic or individualist action became greater.

The trekkers

By the beginning of the 1840s Hendrik Potgieter had established his personal authority over the trekkers in the Potchestroom-Winburg area that straddled the Vaal River. In 1845 he moved to Ohrigstad in the bushveld of the northeastern Transvaal. Potchefstroom was to remain an 'adjunct' settlement. The community here was plagued by tsetse fly and, as more and more livestock perished, the trekkers turned to elephant hunting and the ivory trade. Potgieter's followers maintained a tenuous existence in this region for the next fifteen years. The Potgieter family (Hendrik died in 1852) ran the settlement virtually as a personal fiefdom.

In Ohrigstad itself there was growing tension between Potgieter and a Natal faction of trekkers wedded to the ideal of democratic government in the form of a Volksraad. In addition, the Natal faction saw the best means of survival as being in orderly cattle-farming rather than nomadic hunting, which might endanger relations with African chiefdoms. The Volksraad faction entered into a treaty with the Swazi, essentially to counter an earlier agreement made by Potgieter with the Pedi paramount, Sekwati. In return the Boer trekkers were expected to protect the Swazi from Zulu attacks, which on one occasion they did.

RIGHT: *When livestock perished, the trekkers increasingly turned to elephant hunting and traded ivory. C.D. Bell depicts a hunter using the carcass of an elephant as shelter on a rainy afternoon.*

The shifting nature of political alliances between and within African and trekker society is a particular feature of this period in the Transvaal. Despite superior weaponry, the trekker settlements were obliged to enter into treaties with their African neighbours. This ambivalence laid the foundation for an uncertain relationship between the trekkers and African communities.

Potgieter was given to reckless and vicious attacks on powerful African neighbours, which antagonised the Volksraad party and a considerable number of his own followers. After one such engagement the community split, Potgieter taking his followers to the Soutpansberg and the rest moving to Lydenburg. Ohrigstad was abandoned. Three separate trekker communities now existed north of the Vaal – Potchestroom, Lydenburg, and Potgieter's people in the Soutpansberg.

Trekker unity remained a chimera. None of the independent statelets wished to concede political control to another, and various unity talks and agreements were worth little more than the paper they were signed on. Stephanus Schoeman, who took over the Soutpansbergers, was particularly aloof from the others. Only in 1860, largely due to the efforts of Marthinus Pretorius, did the three groups reach consensus.

After his defeat in 1848 at Boomplaats at the hands of Harry Smith, Andries Pretorius fled, and soon built up a new following near the modern Pretoria. Because of rivalry with Potgieter, he organised trekkers outside Potgieter's own sphere of influence, and in 1849 established a Volksraad for the entire Transvaal region. The Volksraad gave Pretorius a mandate to negotiate a political settlement with Britain for trekkers living north of the Vaal River.

By 1850 Britain had begun to turn its back on the highveld. It had little enthusiasm for supporting expansionist and militaristic English merchants and speculators clamouring for Moshoeshoe's land. Instead, it looked to the trekkers to settle border disputes with African chiefdoms, subjugate Africans into a labour force, and establish commercial relations with the British colonies. Therefore, at the Sand River Convention of 1852, Britain gave Transvaal Afrikaners the right to govern themselves and to purchase ammunition from the British colonies; promised to disclaim all prior alliances with the 'coloured nations' north of the Vaal, and to prohibit the arms trade with Africans. Britain's main demand was that no slavery be permitted in the republic.

Britain had, in effect, abandoned its treaties with non-European chiefs, and had given the trekkers political power and access to ammunition. Without much preparation and with no fanfare, the Zuid-Afrikaansche Republiek (ZAR) was established in 1852, and two years later the Republic of the Orange Free State (OFS). There were now some 20 000 burghers in the ZAR north of the Vaal and 15 000 in the OFS between the Vaal and the Orange. Some OFS burghers kept alive the idea of the incorporation of their state into the Cape Colony until the late 1860s, but the majority of burghers became staunch republicans. Since it controlled the ports and the supply of ammunition, Britain had little to fear from the financially strapped republics.

The economy of the ZAR was too weak to weld Boer society together and to underpin an efficient state. Burghers were hard-pressed and reluctant to pay taxes, and ignored call-ups for commando. The state was almost solely dependent on subsistence farming and markets and towns were slow to develop. State officials were often paid in kind, particularly in land, for their services. Under such circumstances, land accumulation through the holding of public office became a time-honoured practice in the ZAR and competition for the key posts of veldcornet, commandant and landdrost was almost an all-absorbing feature of local trekker politics.

Black and white societies shared similar aims of gaining and retaining access to productive resources of land, labour and game in the region. Thus the trekkers tried to coerce labour and/or tribute from African chiefdoms on the basis that they were owners and masters of the land. As already noted, African societies in the late 1830s and 1840s had been remarkably successful in reconstituting themselves. Often the trekkers resorted to random violence to obtain their aims. This is best illustrated in the seizure of young African captives who were euphemistically 'apprenticed' to trekker families. These captives were supposedly orphans but this was rarely the case. Rev. Freeman of

Marthinus Wessel Pretorius, son of Andries, was elected the first president of the ZAR in 1857. When he was sworn in at Potchefstroom the national flag, the Vierkleur, was raised for the first time. Preoccupied with uniting the ZAR with the Republic of the Orange Free State (OFS), Pretorius got himself elected president of the OFS as well. The ensuing confusion nearly led to civil war in the Transvaal. Pretorius resigned as president of the OFS and in 1864 was once again elected president of the ZAR. His efforts to establish control over African chiefdoms to the north and to acquire a port on the east coast were unsuccessful. His inept handling of ZAR claims to the diamond fields ended in disaster when – without consulting the Volksraad – he declared the Republic willing to submit to the finding of the arbitrators, who turned out to be interested parties. In 1871 he was forced to resign and Thomas Francois Burgers succeeded him in 1872.

THE VOORTREKKERS: A CHOSEN PEOPLE?

A key issue in accounts of the shaping of the Afrikaner community is whether the Afrikaners from an early stage considered themselves – in a similar way to the Ancient Hebrews – as a people with a covenant with God, specially chosen to fulfil a divine plan.

It has been argued that the Afrikaners only started viewing themselves as a chosen people with a divine mission when Kruger started to expound this idea in the 1880s. It is also maintained that only after the South African War (1899–1902) did a group of Dopper (Gereformeerde church) intellectuals

in Potchefstroom turn the idea of a chosen people into a motivating ideology.

But there is indeed evidence that some Voortrekkers, specifically the Doppers, saw themselves as chosen. As a DRC minister in Bloemfontein between 1849 and 1860, Andrew Murray noted the tendency among the trekkers (he appeared to have the Doppers in mind), 'not to distinguish clearly between the relations of Israel and their own to the savages with whom they saw themselves surrounded . . . They thought that in going forth to conquer them they were extending Christianity.'

W.W. Collins, who had lived in the Orange Free State since the early days of the republic, emphasised the commitment of a divine mission even more clearly. His reminiscences of 1858 referred to the Doppers as a 'peculiar sect', evidently obsessed with 'Jehova's wonderful manifestation to his ancient people in . . . the Old Testament'. '[The Doppers] seem to be possessed with the idea that they too are a Divinely favoured people in the same sense that Israel was, and have been signally endowed by the Almighty with sufficient intuitive knowledge and understanding to undertake any mental or other duties.'

There was no single sense of mission among the Voortrekkers; even among the Doppers there were differences about the

nature of their mission – to conquer the land, do missionary work, or live by an almost literal understanding of the Bible? The most famous Dopper, Paul Kruger, often spoke of the Transvaal burghers as 'God's people like in the ancient Covenant' but he did not subscribe to the heresy that all black people were inferior and eternally doomed. Apart from Calvinism, Kruger's guiding principle was a fierce determination to preserve the ZAR's republican freedom – convinced he would be accursed if he did not.

The 'chosen people' theology was by no means a mainstream doctrine or a source of common inspiration. Church schisms racked the Transvaal burgher community, and the three Reformed churches watched each other with suspicion. The Hervormde Kerk, while relatively liberal in its theological views, firmly opposed all missionary work. The Dopper majority accepted missionary work as long as it avoided the 'abomination' of common worship. They preferred German missionaries, most of whom expected their converts to respect the existing social hierarchy. The pro-British DRC ministers were more liberal in their attitudes towards blacks but, while in principle in favour of missionary work, did very little in practice.

ABOVE: *In the 1880s, Paul Kruger started expounding the idea that the Afrikaners must see themselves as a chosen group with a divine mission.*

the London Missionary Society provides a typical account of how these apprentices, or *inboekselinge*, were obtained.

> A party of Boers came and demanded orphans who might be there. After much altercation and the steady refusal of the [Hurutshe] chief to give up the orphans, the Boers demanded the children of the people. The Boers began to seize them and put them into wagons; the men interfered; the Boers fired and in the result most of the men were killed defending their families and the wagons were loaded with children and driven off as booty.

The captives often became permanent workers, and adopted the language and social norms of trekker society. Brought up on Boer farms, these people became skilled and served in a variety of roles essential to the Boer economy, like wagon-repairing, hunting, gun-maintenance and ploughing. Veldcornets and other local officials pressured chiefs into providing labour. If they did not, they could be punished – for example, by flogging.

The Sotho under Moshoeshoe

A number of Voortrekkers joined those trekboers already in Transorangia and began to make new homes in the rich Caledon valley, around mission stations where Sotho and Tswana communities had already settled. As the Boers built permanent homes, they began to claim land ownership.

The increasing Boer presence alarmed Moshoeshoe. In 1843 he requested the British authorities at the Cape to stop the Boers from building on land he considered to be his. The outcome of this request was the Napier Treaty signed between Moshoeshoe and Adam Kok, advised and assisted by the missionaries Eugène Casalis and John Philip on the one hand, and the Cape governor Sir George Napier on the other. This treaty recognised the jurisdiction of Moshoeshoe over his lands between the Orange and the Caledon rivers and also a strip of land west of the Caledon.

The treaty was immediately opposed by the Wesleyan missionaries and the chiefs whose communities they worked among, on the grounds that it took away some of their lands. In 1849 the British Resident in the recently proclaimed Orange River Sovereignty, between the Orange and Vaal rivers, established boundaries between areas claimed by the various communities. This resulted in Moshoeshoe losing some of his kingdom's land.

The period 1848–1854 marked the second phase of missionary activity in the kingdom, characterised by conflict between the Paris Evangelical Mission Society missionaries and the Sotho. In this conflict, Sotho traditionalists insisted on a return to traditional religion and practices and the expulsion of all whites, including the missionaries, from the kingdom.

Although the missionaries defended Sotho land rights, and Casalis was Moshoeshoe's diplomatic agent, the Sotho were nevertheless upset by the missionary preaching against revenge and the theft of cattle. Leading the call for the return to tradition, Moshoeshoe kept his people away from the missionaries and led the revival of rituals of war and other tradional practices. In defiance against Christianity, he married even more wives.

Although Moshoeshoe had remained loyal to all British governments at the Cape, the relationship deteriorated after the British persuaded Moshoeshoe to relinquish lands north of the Caledon occupied by the Tlokwa. He refused and after a cattle raid against the Tlokwa the British decided to enforce compliance from him. British forces invaded his kingdom in 1851 and then again in 1852, but the Sotho defeated the invaders and forced them to retreat.

In true diplomatic style, Moshoeshoe sued for peace even though effectively he had the upper hand. Two years later, the British and the Boers signed the Bloemfontein Convention, which gave the Boers sovereignty over what was now known as the Orange Free State. Consequently Moshoeshoe was to fend for himself.

Most problematic was the boundary dispute between the Boers and the Sotho in the Caledon River valley, and conflicting land claims of Chief Moroka and Korana chiefs. To settle these claims, bring peace into the area and identify future aggressors, the Warden Line was promulgated in 1849. This boundary was constantly revised but neither side was ever satisfied with it, and Lesotho continues to claim parts of the Free State right up to the present day. Moshoeshoe defeated the Free State quite comprehensively in 1858 (Senekal's War) but was persuaded by his missionaries to allow Governor Sir George Grey to mediate. By the boundary determination of Aliwal North in 1858, Grey deprived the Sotho of the fruits of their victory without satisfying the Free Staters.

LEFT: *King Moshoeshoe of the Sotho, a sculpture by Samuel Makoayane.*

This peace simply sowed the seeds of the next war. The Free State, now led by President Jan Brand, was far better prepared for the second round (Seqiti War of 1865) and the military balance of power shifted dramatically. The Free State was aided by Moroka's Rolong and by the people of the Wittebergen reserve (later Herschel) in the Cape Colony, because they believed the Free Staters would help them gain access to more land.

The Sotho stood alone, barred by colonial laws from obtaining weapons. By the end of the following year, they were defeated by Boer numerical and military strength. Letsie, heir apparent to the aging Moshoeshoe, sued for peace. According to the Treaty of Thaba Bosiu signed on 26 March 1866, the size of the kingdom was greatly reduced, to what is today Lesotho. Two-thirds of Sotho arable land was lost through this treaty, while thousands of Sotho cattle and sheep were lost to the Boers following the defeat. After his people had harvested their crops, Letsie resumed the war, but again the Sotho were defeated. Again Moshoeshoe was forced to seek British protection. This time, on 26 March 1868, High Commissioner Sir Philip Wodehouse proclaimed the annexation of the land of the Sotho, named Basutoland, as a British protectorate.

In 1871 Basutoland was annexed to the Cape Colony. The Cape adopted a policy of making Basutoland pay for its own administration through taxation, and weakening the power of the chiefs. Development of the territory was of less importance to the authorities than the firm imposition of law and order. From their side the Sotho objected to the unilateral imposition of colonial policies, and to ways in which their taxes were being used. They requested some form of representation in the council of government, but the request was rejected. The escalating discontent of the Sotho was to spill over into the so-called Gun War of 1880–1881.

The acceptance of colonialism by the Sotho represented a compromise: British protection in return for a limited territorial integrity. It was a more desirable option than incorporation into the Orange Free State. That the kingdom survived in the face of white expansion, taxation, labour demands, and internal stress caused by tension between chiefs and commoners is an extraordinary achievement.

The southern Tswana

The fortunes of the southern Tswana (principally the Tlhaping and Tlharo) rose after the Difaqane. As in many other societies discussed in this section, this was due to the acquisition of firearms and missionary support. Firearms presented increased hunting opportunities and of course greater defensive capacity; missionaries brought economic innovation, such as in irrigation and ploughing. The main beneficiaries of this economic revolution were the traditional elites. This situation came to an end in the late 1860s with the discovery of diamonds. The southern Tswana were among the very first to experience the pressure of colonial advance, after the discovery of diamonds in 1867. In 1876–1878 some Tlhaping and Tlharo chiefdoms mounted resistance to colonial occupation. This mis-termed Griqua Rebellion was crushed, and the African population subjected to the demands of the colonial authorities in the form of increased taxation and a locations policy that confined them to areas with large concentrations of Africans, usually under the control of approved traditional leadership.

The Rolong to the north faced a different set of difficulties. In 1841 Moroko's son Tawana had trekked from Thaba Nchu back to their homeland near the Molopo River. However, the Boers in the Transvaal prevented their settlement. They wanted to expand their border westwards into irrigable lands near present-day Mafikeng. Their ambitions were strengthened by internal rivalry between the Tshidi under chief Montshiwa on the one hand and, on the other, Rapulana and Ratlou factions of the Rolong. The 'freebooters', or mercenaries, who wanted Montshiwa's land, enlisted the support of his African rivals to advance their claim. Montshiwa, who succeeded Tawana, had to seek sanctuary among the Ngwaketse in present-day Botswana until 1851. Low-intensity conflict continued over the next three decades, depending on the ebb and flow of political events in South Africa.

LEFT: *Montshiwa, chief of the Tshidi Rolong, with his favourite wife, Gaeshele Motshegare, in 1890.*

OPPOSITE PAGE TOP: *Sir George Grey. During Senekal's War in 1858, Moshoeshoe defeated the Free State but the boundary determination by Sir George Grey deprived Lesotho of the fruits of its victory.*

OPPOSITE PAGE MIDDLE: *A Tlhaping warrior and woman. The fortunes of the Tlhaping rose after the Difaqane because they had both firearms and missionary support. But in the 1860s, with the discovery of diamonds, the Tlhaping faced new problems.*

OPPOSITE PAGE BOTTOM: *Mahuto, wife of the Tlhaping chief Mahura at Taung, as depicted by Reverend Campbell.*

The Pedi

The establishment of Potgieter's trekker community at Ohrigstad, east of the Steelpoort River, in 1845 introduced a new dimension to the balance of power in the eastern Transvaal. Some African communities – such as the Pedi, the Kopa under Boleu and the Ndzundza under Mabhogo – cautiously welcomed these trekkers, who were the followers of Andries Hendrik Potgieter and J.J. Burger. They hoped that the trekker presence, because of their possession of guns, would discourage any attacks by the Swazi, the Zulu and the Gaza Nguni against the peoples of the region.

From the start the trekker settlement was riddled with dissension and disunity due to power and economic struggles between the Potgieter and Burger factions. To legitimise his claims to power and authority over the trekker community, Potgieter negotiated with Sekwati in 1845. Although the contents of that 'agreement' are not known, it was claimed by the trekkers that all rights to the land had been alienated to them through that 'treaty'.

The 'agreement', however, did not specify the precise extent of the land alleged to have been alienated to the trekkers. It seems likely that while the trekkers considered the 'treaty' valid, the Pedi viewed it differently. As other African chiefs in the region did, Sekwati probably allocated the trekkers land for their settlement and use, but considered such land as belonging to him and his people.

As Sekwati refused to part with any of his land, the trekkers considered other alternatives to gain rights to land. In July 1846 they concluded a treaty with the Swazi king, Mswati, who claimed sovereignty over much of the northeastern Transvaal. In that treaty, parts of the Pedi, Ndzundza-Ndebele, Kopa and Koni chiefdoms – which were in fact beyond the Swazi sovereignty – were ceded to the trekkers. The Pedi and other chiefdoms in the area held the belief that they had merely ceded to the trekkers rights of occupation and use of the land, but not perpetual ownership or ultimate control over it, as the trekkers maintained. These contradictory perceptions would inevitably lead to conflict.

Other sources of conflict emanated from trekker raids on African societies, and demands for their agricultural labour and other forms of tribute on the basis of their claim to land ownership. For a while, the trekkers had some success at growing wheat, maize and beans, but they faced problems of diseases such as malaria and tsetse fly, and the long distance from markets. These problems forced them to abandon Ohrigstad. In 1848 and 1849 some of the trekkers went north and founded the town of Schoemansdal, while others founded Lydenburg to the south. Unwilling to use family labour, the trekkers

ABOVE: *Sekhukhune, eldest son of Sekwati, succeeded his father in 1861. His accession to power heralded a shift in Pedi attitude to the Boers and they agreed on peaceful co-existence and military co-operation.*

RIGHT: *Lydenburg in the 1860s. The trekker community at Ohrigstad divided in 1856: Andries Potgieter moved to Schoemansdal in the Soutpansberg and the remainder moved southwards to Lydenburg.*

resorted to forcing Africans into, especially, agricultural labour service for them, under the *inboekseling* ('apprentice') system.

African resistance to trekker demands for labour and tribute was enhanced by their possession of guns. Also, by the early 1850s many trekker families had moved away from Ohrigstad, leaving those smaller and scattered groups that remained more vulnerable to African attacks. The trekkers were thus unable to enforce their demands for labour and tribute because both the contract labourers and even the *inboekselinge* deserted their masters. These deserters were able to take refuge in some of the African chiefdoms in the region that were still independent and relatively powerful. Taking advantage of the vulnerability of the Boers, African groups such as the Koni stole Boer cattle. The Boers blamed Sekwati and Mabhogo, leaders of two of the strongest kingdoms in the region, for their misfortunes.

In 1852, alarmed that the balance of power now seemed to have tilted against them, the Boers launched an unsuccessful attack on the Pedi stronghold, Phiring. There followed a stalemate in which the Boers continued to complain about lack of labour. In 1857, a treaty between Sekwati and the Boers stated that the Steelpoort River was the boundary between the Pedi kingdom to the north and the Lydenburg Republic to the south. This agreement seemed to be an admission by the Lydenburg authorities that they had no jurisdiction over the Pedi kingdom. Communities to the south, on the other hand, such as the Kopa and Ndzundza-Ndebele, were considered to be under Boer authority.

Sekwati died in September 1861 and was succeeded by his eldest son, Sekhukhune. His accession to power heralded a temporary shift in Pedi attitude to the Boers. Sekhukhune was from a relatively junior house and his position was insecure due to internal rivalry from his brothers, Mampuru and Mojaledi. In the early 1860s his brothers sought refuge among the Ndzundza-Ndebele, also competitors for power in the region.

Moreover, the long-standing threat of Swazi interference and attacks on the Pedi had not subsided. Sekhukhune feared that the disaffected Mampuru might link up with the Swazi army to attack the Pedi kingdom in order to overthrow him. In response to these threats, Sekhukhune agreed to peaceful co-existence and co-operation with the trekkers, including military co-operation. Thus, on 3 November 1863, Sekhukhune sent the Pedi army to assist Boer commandos in attempting to dislodge the Ndzundza-Ndebele from their fortified stronghold. But the Pedi gave up when they realised that the Boers made them do all the fighting, while the Boers only provided covering fire.

In the late 1860s, ZAR authority over much of the north and northeastern Transvaal was at its lowest; it was resisted not only by the Pedi but also by other groups, such as the Venda. That is why in 1867 the Boers abandoned Schoemansdal and much of the area between the Olifants and the Limpopo rivers. Meanwhile, those few whites who remained had to pay tribute to the local African chiefs. The balance of power was later to tilt again in favour of the Boers. In the meantime, however, the Pedi had another factor to deal with: the missionaries.

Like many post-Difaqane societies, the Pedi accepted missionaries – in this case Alexander Merensky and Albert Nachtigal of the Berlin Mission Society (BMS) from Germany. Their first mission station was opened in 1860 at the capital, Thaba Mosega. Four years later, three more stations were opened at Khalatlou, Phatametsane and GaRatau.

Sekhukhune himself never became a Christian. He disliked the missionaries' attitudes to traditional rituals and the support given by Christians to his rival Mampuru. Nonetheless he continued to protect the Christians from the more extreme traditionalists who called for more drastic action than just tolerance. Like the Paris Evangelical Mission Society (PEMS) missionaries among the Sotho to the south, the BMS missionaries provided the Pedi king with political and diplomatic guidance and advice.

But, unlike the PEMS missionaries who openly and consistently supported Moshoeshoe, the BMS missionaries formally undertook to support the ZAR government interests and even to 'maintain law and order' among the Pedi. The BMS missionaries were well aware that the ZAR claim to authority over the Pedi was in fact dubious. At the same time, they recognised that their long-term interests lay with the Boer authorities. Indeed, in 1863, the ZAR government officially appointed Merensky as its representative among the Pedi.

Following an attempt by Sekhukhune to enforce compliance from the Christian elements, relations deteriorated. The Christians were ordered to leave Thaba Mosega. Pleas to the king to reverse his decision were ignored and Merensky left with his followers in 1865 to found a new mission station, aptly named Botshabelo, or place of refuge.

Another important consequence of white settlement and economic activity in the Transvaal and elsewhere was the onset of migrant labour among the Pedi, which dated back to the 1840s. By the early 1860s, as in other African chiefdoms, hundreds of Pedi men each year travelled to the Cape Colony. From 1869, when diamond mining at Kimberley opened up a new market for labour, the Pedi and Tsonga were the major sources of labour. On their return home, the migrants purchased guns, with which they were able to defend themselves against the Swazi, the Zulu and the trekkers, and to hunt for skins, horns and ivory. By 1862 thousands of guns were brought into the northeastern Transvaal. On arrival at home, they also bought cattle.

Initially, it was mainly refugees and rootless individuals impoverished by the ravages of the Difaqane that became migrant labourers. But by the 1870s, most young men went into

ABOVE: *Alexander Merensky (top) and Albert Nachtigal of the Berlin Mission Society were accepted by the Pedi and they started their first mission at the Pedi capital, Thaba Mosega, in 1860.*

LEFT: *Fort Wilhelm and Botshabelo in 1867. When Sekhukune ordered the Christians to leave in 1865, Merensky and his followers founded a new station called Botshabelo – place of refuge.*

migrant labour simply for economic reasons, irrespective of social status. The Pedi king received as tribute £1 from the earnings of every returning migrant, a common practice among other African royals, such as Mokgatle of the Fokeng and Moshoeshoe of the Sotho.

By the late 1860s the Pedi had emerged as a relatively powerful kingdom, and could keep the ambitions of the Boers in the Transvaal at bay. They were to face a more determined challenge to this independence in the next decade.

The Swazi

After initial disputes about his legitimacy as Sobhuza's successor, Mswati succeeded his father. A rebellion against Mswati by his brothers followed shortly after he came to power, but he survived it. The disputes died down somewhat but simmered for the rest of Mswati's reign. This threat was countered in a number of ways, both to consolidate Mswati's position and to forestall future threats. A series of reforms was instituted by the Queen Mother, the king's paternal uncle Malunge, and his eldest brother Malambule, who acted as regent until 1845 when the young king underwent circumcision.

The threat to Mswati's position was far from over. The 1840s saw rebellion against him by two of his brothers, Fokoti and Malambule. In 1846 Mswati sought and obtained the support of a faction of the Boer community at Ohrigstad in the eastern Transvaal, led by Hendrik Potgieter, to whom he ceded an area of land as part of an 'agreement'. He did this to strengthen his position against internal threats and Zulu aggression. Between 1856 and 1865, Mswati embarked on a campaign of expanding his territory to the southwest and northeast. By the time of Mswati's death in 1865, the Swazi state was firmly established and its government fully in the hands of the royal family.

Mswati did not leave an acknowledged successor but there were two contenders, Mbilini and Ludvonga. The latter, though still a minor, succeeded Mswati at the end of 1865. Mbilini tried unsuccessfully to get the support of the Lydenburg Boers. A pressing problem of the 1860s was Boer pressure upon Swazi-claimed land. The white population in the eastern Transvaal was growing and they were occupying more and more land. Consequently, in 1866 the Boers and the Swazi came to a tentative agreement in which a boundary between the Transvaal and Swazi territory was recognised. The boundaries of Swaziland were formally defined and recognised only in 1880.

RIGHT: *Labotsibeni (standing, centre) came to power as Regent Queen of Swaziland when King Ngwane V died in December 1899, three months into the South African War. She acted as regent on behalf of Nkhotfotjeni, four-month-old son and heir of the late king. Also popularly known as Gwamile, Labotsibeni was greatly respected by her people, who referred to her as the Ndlovukazi, or 'she-elephant'. Under her leadership, Swaziland remained neutral in the South African War. In 1900, unwilling to fall under possible Boer rule, she sought British protection for her kingdom. This was granted in December 1906, when the kingdom was placed under the British High Commissioner for South Africa. She relinquished the regency in December 1921 when Nkhotfotjeni, now of age, ascended the Swazi throne as king, assuming the name Sobhuza II.*

Diamonds and after

The first indication of the vast mineral wealth of South Africa was the diamond picked up in 1867 by the Jacobs children south of the Orange River, close to where Hopetown stands today. The word soon spread and by 1870 more than 10 000 diggers of all colours and nations were busily engaged along the banks of the Vaal River searching for the precious little stones. But the wealth in the river was as nothing compared to the treasure underground. The diamonds found on the farm of the brothers De Beer proved to be the tip of a diamond iceberg that eventually became the Kimberley 'Big Hole'.

To whom did these diamonds belong? The answer at first seemed obvious. The De Beers were Free Staters and the diamond fields, a mere 160 kilometres from Bloemfontein, lay between the rivers that formed the natural boundaries of the Free State. Great Britain and its Cape Colony had no presence and no claim in their own right. British interests therefore concealed themselves behind the somewhat dubious claims of Nicolaas Waterboer, the chief of Griquatown many kilometres away. The charade was fronted by a clever lawyer named David Arnot, himself almost a Griqua, but the real decisions were taken behind the scenes, and when the lieutenant-governor of Natal was appointed as mediator, the result was a foregone conclusion. The Keate Award of 1871 confirmed the claims of Waterboer.

ABOVE: *David Arnot, legal representative of Griqua chief Nicolaas Waterboer, successfully claimed the diamond fields on behalf of the Griqua. It later transpired that the Griquas were merely the pawns of British interests since the British had no legitimate claims of their own. Arnot himself was said to be of Griqua descent.*

LEFT: *The mine at Kimberley in 1876, painted by H.C.S. Wright.*

The creation of Griqualand West

In October 1871, almost immediately after the Keate Award, Governor Sir Henry Barkly annexed the diamond fields under the name of the Crown Colony of Griqualand West, but the Griquas themselves derived no benefit from the steps taken in their name. They had served their purpose as cat's paws of imperialism, enabling the Imperial authorities to acquire control over mineral-rich lands. In November 1876 Lieutenant-Governor Lanyon embarked on a surveying process with the intention of confining indigenous black people to strategically placed rural locations comprising no more than 10% of the original Griqualand. And between 1875 and 1878 a dodgy legal mechanism called the Griqualand West Land Court stripped the remaining Griquas of the little they had left.

Chief Waterboer, in whose name the diamond fields had been annexed, was arrested and imprisoned in 1876 when he tried to free some of his followers from a prison work gang. In 1878, numbers of Griqua, Korana and Tswana who had lost their land rose in rebellion and attacked white traders and land surveyors. Defeat was inevitable, and hundreds of prisoners were marched off to Kimberley and forced to work as labourers on the mines that had been stolen from them.

Old-style historians used to see the diamond fields dispute mainly as an event leading up to the South African War of 1899–1902. But just as the historical significance of that war has been reconsidered in the light of later events, so too has new significance been detected in the story of Kimberley and the diamond field discoveries. The development of the diamond fields was accompanied by the development of two new institutions – monopoly capitalism and migrant labour. Both shaped the future of South Africa for the next 100 years or more, so that when even greater mineral discoveries were made on the Witwatersrand fifteen years later, the institutional arrangements they adopted had already been put in place.

The diamond monopoly

In 1871 more than 2 000 diggers, several of them black, owned the diamond fields. Within seventeen years, 2 000 had been reduced to just one, De Beers Consolidated Mines. The early period is known as the 'Diggers Democracy'; the later period is still with us in South Africa today. How did this change come about?

During the Diggers Democracy, regulations limited each digger to a maximum of two claims, each claim measuring 30 x 30 Cape feet (about 9.5 metres). The maximum number of claims per digger was later increased to ten, but claims could also be subdivided into halves, quarters and even sixteenths. Each registered claim was separated from its neighbours by a roadway 2.25 metres wide, which was not supposed to be worked, but the deeper down the diggers went the greater the temptation to burrow sideways into the diamondiferous earth that was supporting the roadway. Long before the diggers penetrated the maximum depth of about 365 metres, roadways were collapsing, mines were flooding, rocks were falling, and it became clear that more sophisticated methods and machines were required.

The costs of mining rose while the price of diamonds fell due to the increase in supply. The poor got poorer and were forced to sell their claims to the rich, who were becoming even richer. By 1881 the number of claim owners had been reduced to 71, but there were only twelve who really counted; by March 1888, the twelve had been reduced to one man – Cecil John Rhodes.

Legend has it that Rhodes clinched his victory over rival capitalist Barney Barnato by offering him membership of the Kimberley Club to which Barnato, as a Jew, had been

A VAAL RIVER "BULL'S" DREAM.

denied access. The reality was inevitably more complex. Rhodes won in the end because he was an Englishman in a British colony, an English politician strongly allied with the Afrikaner Bond, a Parliamentarian who sat on government commissions in an industry that depended on government support.

But more than that Rhodes was a financier who genuinely engaged with problems of production whereas Barnato was little more than a lucky speculator. Rhodes had a precocious understanding of the importance of mechanisation ['the application of machinery to diamonds will lick depreciation in prices', he wrote at the tender age of 23 years]. Whereas others speculated in land and shares, Rhodes invested heavily in pumps, crushing machines and haulage equipment, and he was prepared to accept shares rather than cash in payment for services rendered.

By 1885 Rhodes had gained control of three of Kimberley's four mines, with only the Kimberley Central mine remaining outside his grasp. But Kimberley Central was by far the richest of the mines, and Rhodes knew that he would be finished if ever the various owners at Central got their act together. Having secured the financial muscle of the Rothschild Banking group, Rhodes launched a pre-emptive strike, and in March 1888 De Beers Consolidated Mines Limited was born. The Trust Deed of the new company permitted it to engage in any business enterprise, to annexe land anywhere in Africa, to govern foreign territory, even to maintain a standing army if it so desired. In his opening address, Rhodes promised the shareholders to make De Beers 'the richest, the greatest, and the most powerful Company the world has ever seen'.

But the more money De Beers made in Kimberley, the worse off Kimberley became. De Beers was a monopoly, and the logic of the diamond monopoly was to downsize, to cut costs, to cut production, to cut small entrepreneurs out of retail. Among the first steps taken by Rhodes after he gained control was to reduce output by a half and lay off 1 000 workers. A procession of unemployed mineworkers, white and black, marched to Kimberley and burned Rhodes in effigy, with the following words: 'We will now commit to the flames . . . a traitor to his adopted country, a panderer to the selfish greed of a few purse-proud speculators, and a public pest. May the Lord perish him. Amen.'

Close to 75% of De Beers' disbursements were paid outside South Africa. Three months after the inception of the new company, a disastrous fire broke out at De Beers and 202 men died, mainly because the mine never wasted money on emergency exits and insisted on continuing operations for eight hours after the fire had actually started. Deprived of its small diggers and its small shopkeepers, its remaining residents locked up in closed compounds or working for De Beers, Kimberley declined from a glittering 'city of diamonds' to, in the words of Sarah Gertrude Millin, 'a small, stagnant town' servicing a big hole.

OPPOSITE PAGE TOP: *Migrant workers on their way to the mines. In the wake of the discovery of diamonds, two new systems that would greatly influence South Africa followed. These were migrant labour and monopoly capitalism.*

OPPOSITE PAGE MIDDLE: *Cecil John Rhodes (1853-1902) arrived in South Africa at the age of seventeen. His unique combination of engineering and financial skills, coupled with his imperial connections, made him master of the diamond fields, prime minister of the Cape and, through his British South Africa Company, owner of most of Zimbabwe and Zambia.*

OPPOSITE PAGE BOTTOM: *A cartoon of the diamond diggings at Kimberley. According to the author Sarah Gertrude Millin, Kimberley was not a 'glittering city of diamonds', but 'a small stagnant town' servicing a big hole. Everything revolved around the diamonds.*

BELOW: *The diamond diggers at their midday meal.*

The foundation of De Beers Consolidated did not yet mean that Rhodes was out of the woods. Rhodes was above all a producer, but his partners in De Beers were merchants, financiers and speculators. Rhodes soon clashed with a cartel of four leading diamond merchants known as The Syndicate, who banded together in 1892 to control the price of diamonds. Rhodes doubled production and stockpiled diamonds at great personal cost, so as to break The Syndicate's stranglehold. It was clear that the dynamics of the diamond industry necessitated vertical as well as horizontal integration, control of marketing as well as control of production. In April 1892 Rhodes and The Syndicate reached an agreement and created a reserve fund to support the diamond price. The agreement finally mutated into the Diamond Corporation (founded 1930), for many years the only institution through which diamonds could be sold on the international market.

Rhodes did not live to enjoy the fruits of his monopoly, dying in 1902 at the age of 49. The luck of the great Barnato finally ran out in 1897 when Barnato either jumped overboard or was pushed by his nephew, motivated less perhaps by greed than by his uncle's endless chattering, while travelling to England by ship.

Among the capitalist titans who organised themselves as The Syndicate to do battle with Cecil Rhodes in 1892 – including Barnato himself, Randlords Julius Wernher and Alfred Beit, and the Mosenthal brothers, masters of the wool trade and a great commercial empire stretching from Port Elizabeth to present-day Botswana – one might easily have missed the obscure figure of immigrant diamond dealer, Anton Dunkelsbuhler. But Dunkelsbuhler did well out of being a member of The Syndicate. So well in fact that in 1896 he called his nephew from Germany to assist in the family business. In 1917 the nephew, whose name was Ernest Oppenheimer, founded the Anglo American Corporation which, within a few years, was to absorb De Beers Consolidated and thus consummate the marriage of diamonds and gold.

Origins of the migrant labour system

Along with the concentration of ownership by monopoly interests, and interconnected with it, came the origins of the migrant labour system that reached its mature form after the opening of the gold mines and dominated the South African economy over 100 years of segregation and apartheid. Not that contract labour and exploitative conditions were new to the Africans of South Africa, but institutionalised forms of labour control such as the compound system now emerged, and in the industrial environment exploitative relations now assumed the same racial form as that which already existed in the rural areas.

It is striking that the Diggers Democracy phase of diamond mining was not necessarily racially exclusive and that it mobilised black labour on the basis of incentives rather than coercion. Richard Southey, the lieutenant-governor of Griqualand West, understood the need to attract black labour to the diamond mines, and he insisted that blacks as well as whites had a right to own claims. The last of the black claimholders, Rev. Gwayi Tyamzashe, was still holding on at Dutoitspan as late as 1883.

Southey further allowed black migrants who lacked any capital to buy a claim the right to sort through the 'debris' or mine dumps and to keep whatever overlooked diamonds they happened to find. The wages paid to black workers on the diamond fields were reputedly the highest paid anywhere in South Africa.

BELOW: *The first diamonds were found in the river diggings near the present Barkly West. But the real wealth was located in the 'dry diggings' on the farms, starting with Jagersfontein in August 1870. Dutoitspan, below, was the second of the dry diggings. The farmer Adriaan van Wyk had innocently used the diamondiferous ground while building his house, and diamonds were first noticed cemented into his walls. Rhodes's career began at Dutoitspan, described as follows by an early visitor: 'One afternoon in the distance we caught sight of the diamond fields. People gazed with the same interest and excitement as those who see the outline of an unknown land. Many a heart beat faster as the Diamond City of the Plains became less and less indistinct, and those whose everything depended on the success of their expedition watched this ghost-like series of tents grow whiter and whiter as they outlined clearer.' (Painting by H.C.S. Wright.)*

Most important of all, Southey recognised the one incentive guaranteed to attract black workers to the diamond fields – the right to buy and own guns. By the 1870s, far-sighted black rulers could foresee the time that they would have to fight for their independence and they began to arm their people accordingly. Foremost among these was King Sekhukhune of the Pedi who sent whole regiments (travelling 200 men at a time on account of the dangers of the journey) to work in Kimberley. The average labour term varied between four and eight months – corresponding, as historian Peter Delius has sardonically observed, 'broadly with the time required to purchase a gun'. Another who accumulated firearms on the diamond fields was the Hlubi chief Langalibalele, and it was the demand of the magistrate that he surrender his guns that sparked Langalibalele's rebellion in 1873.

The same pressures that resulted in the concentration of capital – rising costs and falling diamond prices – likewise impacted on the relatively favourable position of the black workers. Not for the last time in the history of South Africa, the white underclasses attempted to preserve a privileged position at the expense of others. The white leaders of the so-called Black Flag rebellion of 1875 accused black workers of undermining the price of diamonds by flooding the market with stolen diamonds and diamonds from the 'debris' mine dumps. Lieutenant-Governor Southey called troops from Cape Town to put down the rebellion but found to his surprise that he himself was to be removed.

The fall of Southey, a former comrade-in-arms of Sir Harry Smith and brother to the man who shot King Hintsa, shows just how fast the mineral revolution was rendering Cape liberalism obsolete. The very elementary liberal principle, upheld in this case by Southey, that all men had an equal right to the pursuit of property became intolerable to colonial administrators and mining magnates as soon as the property in question was firearms or diamondiferous land and the men were black. Colonel Owen William Lanyon, Southey's successor, immediately removed all restrictions on the ownership of diamond claims, and this victory was soon followed by various measures intended to discipline the black labour force.

When these disciplinary measures threatened their labour supply – 30 000 Africans left the diamond fields in 1882 – the mining companies looked to convict labour. In 1884 De Beers built its own convict station with 25 security guards housing some 400 convicts. Between 1873 and 1887, some 67 000 convicts passed through Kimberley's prisons. The mines found prison labour cheap and tractable, and soon – in the name of anti-theft security – hit on the idea of housing their workers in entirely self-sufficient closed compounds. Workers shopped at the company store and were treated at the company clinic. Escorted by guards armed with clubs, the workers marched from the compound straight to work along walkways covered to prevent any communication with outsiders.

Different ethnic groups were deliberately kept apart from each other to make it 'difficult for the natives to form riotous combinations'. Black workers deemed 'troublesome or turbulent' were expelled, but only after first taking photographs which were pasted into a blacklist kept at the compound entrance. When these measures fell short, the compound managers could always call on government, as they did at Wesselton mine in March 1894 when three miners were shot dead by the Kimberley Mounted Police and compound guards.

Meanwhile, the continuing mechanisation of the mines made it necessary to import skilled labourers from Europe. These foreign immigrants lived freely in their own homes and received higher wages than the indigenous Africans emerging from their closed compounds to perform heavy labour for a minimal wage, a

ABOVE: *Richard Southey, lieutenant-governor of Griqualand West, understood the need to attract black labour to the diamond mines, even if the only way to do it was to sell them guns. He supported the rights of small claim owners, both black and white, but was removed by the Imperial authorities after the Black Flag rebellion of 1875.*

BELOW: *Workers' compounds at the diamond fields. When new disciplinary measures led to 30 000 Africans leaving the diamond fields in 1882, the mining companies turned to convict labour. Finding convict labour cheap and easily disciplined, the mines developed the system of closed compounds for all labourers, whether convicts or not.*

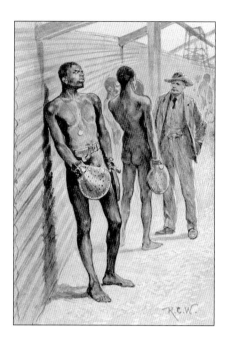

TOP: *Workers in compounds wearing mittens to prevent them from stealing diamonds.*

ABOVE: *British Colonial Secretary Lord Carnarvon, also known as 'Twitters', promoted confederation in South Africa after the discovery of its mineral wealth.*

situation that Europeans in Europe would rightly have rejected. This racial division of the workforce into white skilled and black unskilled labour was Kimberley's last legacy to the political economy of the emerging South Africa.

From diamonds to confederation

The political impact on southern Africa of the diamond discoveries was reflected in its effect on the southern African economy. Before the revelation of South Africa's mineral wealth, Great Britain's interest in the subcontinent was limited to the strategic importance of the coastline, control of which was essential to the defence of her Indian Empire. The South African interior was another story. Economically, it was marginal at best. At worst, it was a black hole of quarrelsome and greedy settlers dragging a reluctant Imperial government into costly and avoidable 'native wars'.

The diamond discoveries changed the picture, more especially because the near-coincidental discovery of gold in what are today Zimbabwe and Botswana gave hints of the riches yet to come. Britain started to take note that it was no longer the only role player in the region. The Portuguese were taking steps to firm up their claims to Delagoa Bay, and President M.W. Pretorius of the ZAR contemplated the annexation of great swathes of Africa from Lake Ngami in the west to the Indian Ocean.

Most important, the relatively small problem of Griqualand West had sensitised the British government that the economic viability of the mineral discoveries was threatened by the chaotic and expensive methods whereby black labour was recruited for the mines. It was not that black people were unwilling to work, as the 1 000-kilometre trek of the Pedi to Kimberley conclusively proved. It was that the price of this labour was far too high. Payment in guns threatened white military superiority. Payment in money threatened not only low-wage white agriculture but the building of railroads on which access to the mineral wealth itself depended.

Britain viewed independent Afrikaner republics and independent African kingdoms as political anachronisms retarding economic development. The ZAR, for example, introduced pass laws to keep workers on the farms and did not stop short of kidnapping migrants en route to the mines. Its hut taxes and land grabbing provoked war with the Pedi kingdom, and that was even worse.

The Zulu kingdom, on the other hand, trained its young men up as warriors rather than labourers. As Theophilus Shepstone put it, 'Had Cetshwayo's thirty thousand warriors been in time changed to labourers working for wages, Zululand would have been a peaceful prosperous country instead of what it now is, a source of perpetual danger to itself and its neighbours.'

Come the hour, come the man. In 1874 the man was the British colonial secretary, Lord Carnarvon, known to his colleagues as 'Twitters'. Carnarvon had united the British colonies in Canada in 1867, and was anxious to repeat the trick in South Africa. Even when it became clear that the white settler governments wanted nothing to do with confederation, Carnarvon persisted. He saw the weakness of the ZAR as a definite opportunity, and a false report that Sekhukhune's Pedi army had routed the Afrikaner forces gave him an idea. He informed his subordinates that they should 'let slip no opportunity of justly acquiring the Transvaal', and he appointed two dedicated imperialists to important positions. Sir Bartle Frere, who had succeeded in promoting unity in India, was appointed high commissioner and Theophilus Shepstone as special commissioner with powers to annexe the ZAR (known to the British as the Transvaal). Shepstone was told to persuade the Afrikaners to agree but, if not, to press on regardless, 'for we cannot please everyone'.

Shepstone's annexation of the ZAR in April 1877 set off a chain reaction that eventually led to the great South African War of 1899–1902 and its result, the consolidation of a single powerful South African state, politically dominated by white people and economically dependent on the controlled supply of cheap black labour. The Zulu kingdom of Cetshwayo was the first casualty of this process.

CHAPTER SIX

From the fall of kingdoms to the rise of nationalism

African kingdoms: conquest and survival

In the 1870s settler and colonial determination to bring blacks more firmly under political control undermined the hard-won security that many African societies had achieved. This was due to changed economic conditions in South Africa's hinterland and the consequent need to secure sufficient political authority over Africans, to ensure security and access to labour. This section examines this process and the attempt by these societies to resist the extension of colonial control over them.

The destruction of the Zulu kingdom 1879–1896

Sir Bartle Frere was appointed high commissioner to South Africa in 1879 to realise the policy of confederation. Shepstone provided him with the arguments and motivation he required. The Zulu, Shepstone averred, had revived their military power under Cetshwayo. The kingdom was a threat to peace and prosperity in South Africa. Moreover, Cetshwayo's leaders had personally insulted him. On 11 December 1878, under the flimsy pretext of a few minor border incursions into Natal by Cetshwayo's followers, the Zulu were given an impossible ultimatum that they should disarm and Cetshwayo should forsake his sovereignty.

The inevitable invasion of Zululand began after the ultimatum had expired in January 1879. Instead of fragmenting the Zulu as Shepstone predicted, this made the Zulu rally to their king's cause. Under the overall command of Lord Chelmsford, the Imperial forces – many of them colonials or members of the Natal Native Contingent – converged on Cetshwayo's royal capital at oNdini. Chelmsford's column split in two; one force, in a state of total unpreparedness, was repulsed by the Zulu at Isandlwana on 22 January (*see box on page 166*).

A day later, a depot at Rorke's Drift was attacked against the orders of Cetshwayo, who favoured a defensive strategy. The Zulu force suffered 500 casualties in this fruitless engagement. Chelmsford hurried back to Natal. The might of the British army had suffered a severe repulse and any thoughts of a quick British victory put to rest, but the Zulu themselves suffered terrible casualties, and worse was to follow.

After the defeat at Isandlwana British pride had to be restored, and reinforcements were sent for. Chelmsford's army advanced again into Zululand, inflicting heavy defeats on the Zulu at Gingindlovu and Khambula in April. The Zulu were now on the back foot. In July Chelmsford moved in on oNdini, and in a final onslaught known as the battle of Ulundi, secured an overwhelming military success. More than 1 000 Zulu were killed, and Cetshwayo was forced to flee for safety. He was captured in the Ngome forest in August and exiled to the Cape. The Zulu were instructed to return to their homesteads and resume productive activities. The British were at pains to explain that the war was against the Zulu royal house.

The war itself had not destroyed the kingdom, but subsequent events served to divide the Zulu and undermine their economic and social

The Battle of Rorke's Drift is depicted in this painting in the Library of Parliament. The day after the battle at Isandlwana, against the wishes of Cetshwayo, a Zulu reserve that had not fought at Isandlwana and was led by Prince Dabulamanzi, attacked a hastily erected fort at Rorke's Drift. Some 500 Zulu were killed in the engagement. Rorke's Drift presented Britain with 'much needed propaganda to counter the Zulu success at Isandlwana'.

British forces advanced into Zululand in three columns; one from the Transvaal, one from the south through Eshowe and the other in the centre, through Rorke's Drift and the Mzinyathi River. The centre column, led by Lord Chelmsford, crossed into Zululand on 11 January 1879. The Zulu army, ritually sprinkled for war, left kwaNodwengu on 17 January under the command of chiefs Ntshingwayo kaMahole Khoza and Mavumengwana kaNdlela Ntuli. Cetshwayo had promised his men that the British would be defeated in a 'single day'.

On 20 January Chelmsford encamped at Isandlwana hill. He encountered some local resistance and – mistakenly assuming it to be the main Zulu force – divided his column, taking half to support an engagement some fifteen kilometres away. Colonel Henry Pulleine was left in charge of the remaining forces, but did not laager his camp, as the wagons would be needed shortly to transport supplies. Colonel A.W. Durnford arrived the next day with a detachment to reinforce the camp and take over command.

Durnford, described as being 'as plucky as a lion but as imprudent as a child', impetuously pursued a Zulu foraging party. Coming over the ridge of the Mabaso heights, to his horror he encountered the Zulu army, 20 000 strong, massed below. The Zulu had not intended to attack then as it was a new moon and it was considered unwise to fight on a 'dark day'. Once discovered, however, they had no choice but to go on the offensive. Pulleine was forced to spread his

fire-power over a long distance instead of concentrating his men in a tight formation.

The Zulu steadily advanced in the horn formation, their centre, or chest, pitted against Pulleine's left flank. They suffered huge losses as the British concentrated fire on the chest, and the attack temporarily stalled. But the Zulu left horn outflanked Durnford's infantry and descended on the British camp from behind. Realising he was surrounded, Pulleine tried to retreat in order to save the endangered camp. This allowed the Zulu centre to advance again. Raising the national cry of 'uSuthu' the Zulu

impi interposed themselves between the retreating British and their camp. Hand to hand combat ensued and the Zulu carried the day. A detachment of British troops tried to mount a final stand at a stream two miles away, but most retreated to Rorke's Drift or fled down the Mzinyathi River with the Zulu in pursuit.

The British lost 52 officers, 727 white soldiers and 471 black men of the Native Contingent – a third of Chelmsford's men. The Zulu, 'as was their custom, took no prisoners at Isandlwana, and spared no lives, despite pleas for mercy'. Virtually everything in the camp was carried off as booty.

ABOVE: *The monument commemorating the Battle of Isandlwana. Its main feature is a bronze necklace. Only warriors of exceptional bravery were permitted to wear a stylised necklace differing from the traditional one in its use of ornate beads, thornlike spikes and lion's claws. The necklace is placed on a circular base, reminiscent of Zulu kraals and huts and symbolising unity. Four large headrests are set into the wall of the base; this represents the four Zulu regiments taking part in the battle and honours the ancestors.*

cohesion. Taking a leaf out of Shepstone's 'native policy', Sir Garnet Wolseley, the new British commander in Natal, divided the kingdom into thirteen territories under appointed chiefs. They were meant to represent the chiefly lineages of pre-Shakan times, a shaky argument, especially as one of them was John Dunn, who had joined the British when hostilities began. Others had either been outrightly opposed to Cetshwayo or had shown little loyalty to him during the war. Their allegiance was to those who had appointed them, and Britain effectively began to administer indirect rule over Zululand. Melmoth Osborn, who enthusiastically supported Shepstone's views, was appointed as British Resident in Zululand.

Unsurprisingly Zululand suffered civil strife as a result of this arrangement. Those who continued to espouse the old Zulu order were known as the uSuthu, and were led by Ndabuko kaMpande, Cetshwayo's brother. They were to come into conflict with the appointed chiefs and by 1887 had 'fought themselves to a standstill'.

In addition, a hut tax was imposed, not only on each hut but on every wife regardless

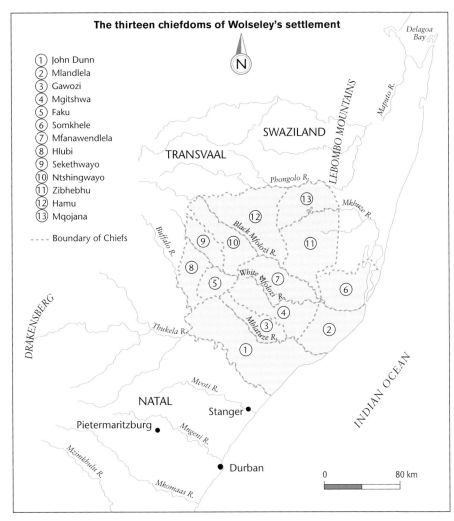

The thirteen chiefdoms of Wolseley's settlement

1. John Dunn
2. Mlandlela
3. Gawozi
4. Mgitshwa
5. Faku
6. Somkhele
7. Mfanawendlela
8. Hlubi
9. Sekethwayo
10. Ntshingwayo
11. Zibhebhu
12. Hamu
13. Mqojana

- - - - Boundary of Chiefs

LEFT: *The thirteen chiefdoms of Wolseley's settlement. When he became the new British commander in Natal, Sir Garnet Wolseley set about dividing the area into the thirteen territories shown here under chiefs appointed by himself. It was said that they represented the chiefly lineages of pre-Shakan times, an unconvincing claim, especially since the white trader and gun dealer John Dunn was one of them. Britain effectively began to administer indirect rule over Zululand, giving rise to growing civil strife and unrest.*

of whether she occupied a hut. Wolseley's infamous settlement of Zululand had not destroyed the Zulu homestead, the basic productive unit in the kingdom's economy, nor had the Zulu been deprived of their land. The hut tax, however, served to divert some of the surplus accruing to an individual homestead head to the British government. Over 70% of the annual cost of administering Zululand was derived from this tax.

As the civil war intensified, the British realised that the settlement was simply not workable. Cetshwayo, encouraged by Bishop Colenso and his daughter Harriette who both visited him in Cape Town, petitioned the British government and was granted permission to visit England to put forward his case for the restoration of the Zulu monarchy. In Zululand similar petitions were presented to the British Resident by the uSuthu.

Early in 1883 Cetshwayo was reinstalled as king, but his powers had been severely reduced. He was confined to a smaller area, surrounded by his enemies, and his every move was watched by a Resident. Those who wished to show their loyalty to Cetshwayo were obliged to move into his central district of the kingdom. Zibhebhu, an arch opponent of Cetshwayo, whose allegiance was more to the colonial order than the royal house, and who occupied a large tract of territory to Cetshwayo's north, forced uSuthu loyalists resident in his portion to return to Cetshwayo's area.

A pre-emptive strike by the uSuthu against Zibhebhu failed. Later Zibhebhu and Hamu, another of the appointed chiefs, invaded the uSuthu. Cetshwayo was soundly defeated at his newly built capital at oNdini in 1883. The level of bloodshed exceeded anything the Zulu had experienced during Cetshwayo's reign. Matters worsened for the uSuthu when Cetshwayo died in late 1883. The balance of power in Zululand had now shifted decisively to the Imperial administration and its supporters in Zululand.

BELOW: *Cetshwayo and Bishop Colenso's daughter Harriette, who visited him in exile in Cape Town.*

TOP: *King Dinuzulu, son of Cetshwayo and leader of the uSuthu (loyalist) faction of the kingdom. In 1889 he was found guilty of treason and imprisoned on St Helena.*

BOTTOM: *President Thomas Francois Burgers of the Zuid-Afrikaansche Republiek (ZAR). Educated at Utrecht in Holland, Burgers became president of the ZAR in 1872. Though he was a man of energy and ideas, the ZAR was economically and politically fragile, and was easily annexed by Britain in 1877.*

In a last-ditch measure to regain power, Cetshwayo's son, Dinuzulu, entered into a treaty with the Transvaal. In military terms, the alliance proved successful and Zibhebhu's army was forced out of the loyalists' territory. But it came at a huge cost. In return for their assistance, the Boers were promised vast tracts of territory on Zululand's western margin, which they called The New Republic, with its 'capital' at Vryheid.

When the Transvaalers tried to claim even more land than what was agreed upon, the uSuthu refused. Sensing complete chaos in Zululand, the British intervened. Dinuzulu was allowed to retain control of his portion of central Zululand, but the Boers were also acknowledged as owners of the New Republic, and a Reserve area was set aside for those opposed to the loyalists. In Natal, pressure mounted for the annexation of Zululand, and almost inevitably it was annexed to the Crown in 1887. The promulgation of a Code of Laws placed Zululand under a similar 'Native Policy' to that existing in Natal.

Once more the uSuthu mounted resistance to the annexation. Again Zibhebhu's services were called upon. The revolt was spectacularly successful for a short period. Making good use of the mountainous terrain, the uSuthu under Dinuzulu repulsed a police contingent sent to arrest their leaders, and Zibhebhu's followers were attacked by Dinuzulu and forced to flee hastily from the Ndwandwe district. Finally reinforcements arrived, the uSuthu were driven from their hideouts, and Dinuzulu surrendered. In 1889, he and his leading adherents were tried for treason, found guilty and sentenced to prison terms on St Helena.

In 1894 Dinuzulu was pardoned and allowed to return to Zululand, but as a mere induna with no chiefly powers or privileges. To appease colonial interests, his return was coupled to the annexation of Zululand by Natal in 1897.

After eighteen years, settler interests had prevailed in the land of the Zulu, and the plans Shepstone initially envisaged for the kingdom could be put in place. White settlers and traders entered Zululand in increasing numbers. Zululand was thus 'reconstructed'. The territory was divided among compliant chiefs who ruled with limited authority. The governor of Natal became the supreme chief over Zululand. The situation was worsened by the outbreak of a number of natural disasters between 1894 and 1897. Locusts, drought and the devastating rinderpest epidemic of 1897 led to a massive decline in homestead production.

Already under stress from the imposition of the hut tax, many more Zulu men were forced onto the Witwatersrand labour market to make ends meet and pay taxes. The gradual emergence of a permanent labouring class alongside a traditional economy based on homestead production and cattle-keeping led in time to new social divisions in Zulu society.

The destruction of the Pedi kingdom

The same forces that imperilled the Zulu Kingdom threatened other powerful African kingdoms almost simultaneously. As already noted, relations between the Pedi and the Zuid-Afrikaansche Republiek (ZAR) deteriorated after the opening up of the diamond fields. This was to culminate in an attack on the Pedi instigated by President Thomas Francois Burgers.

In July 1876, on the orders of President Burgers, the ZAR army, supported by the Swazi army and other Africans from the eastern Transvaal, invaded the Pedi chiefdom. Pedi resistance was so successful that by early August the invaders had abandoned the exercise. The Boer-led attack failed for a number of reasons, such as poor morale among the Boers and poor leadership by Burgers, an ex-minister of the Dutch Reformed Church. Clearly, by now the Pedi kingdom had become an alternative focus of power to that of the ZAR.

The invasion was precipitated by a complex combination of factors. By the early 1870s, the kingdom's population and military power had grown considerably due to the accumulation of firearms, resulting in a number of Pedi military victories against the Swazi. This served to undermine ZAR authority. There were also struggles over labour following the migration of Pedi men to the diamond fields. Sekhukhune rejected ZAR claims to land in the Pedi heartland, while Boer-Pedi disputes continued. The Boers attacked

After the South African War (1899–1902), the Joint Imperial and Colonial Commission in 1904 handed over to Natal some of the most agriculturally productive land in Zululand. To force the Zulu into closer labour relations with South Africa's modernising post-war economy, a poll tax of £1 per annum was imposed on every adult male, save those already paying the hut tax. The news was greeted with dismay and anger by a people already facing extreme economic pressure and social dislocation. Acts of resistance broke out around Pietermaritzburg and a few white farmers and a policeman were killed. Martial law was proclaimed and the killers executed.

In the Mpanza valley in the Umvoti district, a minor chief of the Zondi, Bhambatha, flatly refused to collect the poll tax and threatened white authorities with death if they attempted to do so in his district. Attempts to enforce his compliance failed and he was deposed and another chief appointed in his place.

Bhambatha fled to Zululand and met with Dinuzulu, who had returned from exile in 1898. It is not certain whether the Zulu king offered tangible support, but Bhambatha's wife did remain at Dinuzulu's royal homestead. Bhambatha returned to Natal to continue his campaign of resistance. In April 1906 he ambushed a police force near Greytown and killed four policemen, one of whose body was mutilated. He fled to the home of chief Sigananda Shezi of the Cube chiefdom, near the Nkandla forest. By now, general lawlessness had broken out in many districts of northern Natal and Zululand.

For the Natal authorities this was untenable. Under the command of Colonel Duncan Mckenzie, a large militia was raised from Natal, Johannesburg and the Cape. On 9 June, Mckenzie's troops encountered the 'rebels' along the Mome stream near the Nkandla forest. In a half-hour's engagement, Bhambatha's followers were massacred, and nearly 600 lives were shed. Bhambatha's body was decapitated. Several influential chiefs continued resistance in the Lower Thukela River area until July, but the rebellion was effectively crushed. Over the next six months 5 000 dissidents were arrested, tried and some eventually served life sentences.

The Natal colonists sought a scapegoat for a rebellion that had been of their own making, and lighted upon the person of Dinuzulu. Nothing in his actions indicated active support for the rebellion, though the Zulu regarded him as a figurehead for it. But, as the son of Cetshwayo, he embodied the Zulu threat to white security in Natal and Zululand, so he was deemed to have supported Bhambatha, and tried in 1907 for high treason, rebellion and murder. He was sentenced to four years imprisonment but released before his death in 1913. He stated at his trial: 'My sole crime is that I am the son of Cetshwayo. My trouble is like that of no one else. It beset me when I was a child and my father was taken by the white people from me and it is still besetting me . . . . All our family die of harassing . . . and now of all our house I am left alone.'

A Native Affairs Commission appointed to investigate the rebellion identified overpopulation, land pressure and poverty as the underlying causes. Certain reforms were introduced but were insufficient to address the roots of Zulu disaffection. Had they been more radical, they undoubtedly would have threatened white interests in Zululand and would almost certainly not have been adopted.

The Bhambatha rebellion has rightly been seen as the last episode of African military resistance to colonial domination in South Africa.

Pedi labour migrants, passing through Boer-occupied land on their return from a labour term at the diamond fields in Kimberley, and took the guns with which they had been paid away from them.

Meanwhile, large numbers of armed returning Pedi migrants led to growing Boer rumours and fears of Pedi preparations for war. Boer-Pedi hostilities continued for two years, following the abortive Boer invasion of the Pedi kingdom. Unbeknown to the Pedi, however, the British authorities were planning to annex the Transvaal, preparatory to an invasion of their kingdom. This was in fact part of the plan of Secretary of State for the Colonies Lord Carnarvon, to bring together the two British colonies of the Cape and Natal and the two Boer republics into a confederation of states.

A number of factors prompted the British authorities to intervene in the Transvaal. The threats to the free flow of Pedi migrant labour to the diamond fields posed by Boer attacks upon the migrants threatened the stability of diamond mining. The ongoing struggles over land and labour in the Transvaal underpinned the fear of African resistance and even possible revolt, as indicated by the outcome of the abortive Boer invasion of the Pedi in 1876. Independent African states, argued Theophilus Shepstone in Natal, might sooner or later combine and act together against the burgeoning British rule.

Shepstone further argued that imperial expansion into the Transvaal would, as was already happening in Natal, pay for itself through the use of African chiefs, African taxes and African police. Lastly, the ZAR had no resource capacity to enforce labour service by Africans or collect taxes. Such arguments by Shepstone convinced Lord Carnarvon about the need for imperial intervention in the Transvaal. It was annexed in 1877.

Sekhukhune was advised by the British authorities that he should submit to their authority, and a fine of 2 000 cattle was imposed upon him, supposedly for suffering incurred by the Boers in the 1876 campaign. Sekhukhune could hardly meet such a demand; the Pedi had after all, suffered from the conflict with the ZAR and had been hard hit by a drought. Secretary for Native Affairs, Sir Theophilus Shepstone, annexed the Transvaal in January 1877 and began to push more strongly for imperial intervention. Some minor incidents were used as an excuse to attack the Pedi and war broke out in 1878. But British attention was diverted temporarily to Natal and the war with the Zulu.

After the defeat of the Zulu, Shepstone and Sir Garnet Wolseley hoped that Sekhukhune would see the futility of resisting British hegemony. Consequently, another set of demands was presented to Sekhukhune. The Pedi prevaricated and Wolseley decided to subjugate them; an act that would not only destroy one of the strongest independent African kingdoms in the Transvaal, but also restore the military prestige of the British in the eyes of the Transvaal burghers.

The Pedi defended their capital quite successfully but the British, assisted by Swazi regiments and other African auxiliaries from within the Transvaal, were able to surround them. The Pedi were defeated and Sekhukhune was captured and taken to Pretoria to be imprisoned. Pedi losses were considerable; at least a quarter of Sekhukhune's 4 000 men lost their lives. The British abandoned the Transvaal some three years later and the Pedi were subject once again to the vagaries of rule by the ZAR.

RIGHT: *In 1878 the British defeated the Pedi and Sekhukhune was captured and taken to Pretoria to be imprisoned. This picture shows Sekhukhune and his wives on the wagon.*

The Sotho

The defeat of the British at Isandlwana (*see box on page 166*) led to a general outcry in the Cape Colony for the disarming of Africans, and Prime Minister John Sprigg introduced legislation to this effect. The Sotho objected vehemently, seeing it as an indication of a lack of trust in them by the British. Moreover, guns had been hard earned at the Kimberley mines and on white farms, and no compensation was offered for them.

Moshoeshoe's successor, Letsie, accepted Sprigg's decision, but his brother Masupha and Letsie's son, Lerotholi, did not. A minor civil conflict broke out between those who handed in guns, and those who did not. In these general circumstances of chaos, Sprigg travelled personally to Basutoland and offered to revise his edict regarding guns. He failed totally and whites were placed under siege in Basutoland. In support, the Mpondomise in the northeastern Cape came out in revolt and a handful of whites was killed near Qumbu.

British troops were now sent to Basutoland to quell the revolt, and eventually a cease-fire was declared. Sprigg's ministry fell as a consequence of his failure to disarm the Sotho, and the enormous expense that this so-called Gun War incurred. A peace treaty was signed, which stipulated that the Sotho should register their guns rather than hand them in.

Though this represented a backtracking on the part of the Cape, Masupha still did

not accept it. Again total confusion reigned between those considered loyal to the Cape government, and those who wanted no compromise. More out of despair than general policy, the Cape government requested the Crown to take over rule in Basutoland, which it did in 1884. Ultimately, British control ensured that Basutoland remained independent from the political developments in South Africa. Its future was therefore to be significantly different from that of most other African groups discussed in this section.

The Swazi

Although the Boers and the Swazi had reached apparent agreement over recognition of a boundary in 1866 this did not signal the end of Boer pressure upon Swazi land. In 1868 the ZAR proclaimed its annexation of Swaziland but failed to put the annexation into practice. Seven years later the ZAR persuaded the Swazi to sign a treaty agreeing to become its subject colony.

Between 1875 and 1877 the Zulu under Cetshwayo were threatening to invade Swaziland. If these threats had materialised, they might have crippled the Swazi state because of its own internal crises. Towards the end of Ludvonga's minority (he had succeeded his father Mswati), just when he was being prepared to take over the kingship, he fell ill and died unexpectedly. Uncertainty and squabbles over the succession followed briefly until Mbandzeni succeeded as king. Timid and ineffectual at first, Mbandzeni began to assert himself from the late 1870s.

The 1870s were also an important period for Swazi history because of the issue of white intrusion into the kingdom. White encroachment into the kingdom occurred in two ways. The first was through an influx of concessionaires and the second through formal colonial annexation. From 1873 when gold was discovered in the eastern Transvaal, white concession hunters came to Swaziland hoping to find gold and make a fortune. Very many other whites were granted grazing, hunting and woodcutting concessions. In 1876, for example, Mbandzeni gave away a grazing concession of 36 000 acres to Joachim Ferreira and Ignatius Maritz.

During the mid-1880s, fortune-seekers flocked into the country. Overwhelmed by their numbers, Mbandzeni sought the assistance of 'Offy' Shepstone (son of Sir Theophilus Shepstone of Natal) whom he appointed as advisor to the Swazi kingdom. The appointment, however, had no official standing with either the British authorities or the Transvaal government.

For a while Shepstone was able to control the activities of the concession hunters – for which he was disliked by the Boer graziers in the kingdom who

wished to acquire the land for freehold tenure. In the late 1880s the granting of concessions continued unabated as Mbandzeni, whose health was then failing, unsuccessfully attempted to restrict Shepstone's mandate.

White intrusion into the kingdom also slowly eroded its independence and the extent of its territory. This was achieved through boundary delimitations. In 1880 a British-appointed commission demarcated a new Swazi-Transvaal boundary by which the Swazi lost some lands in the northwest and northeast parts of the kingdom. While Swazi independence was recognised by the Pretoria Convention of 1881, the Boers were still continually attempting to incorporate the kingdom. In 1885, for example, Vice-President Piet Joubert and J.C. Krogh unsuccessfully tried to make Swaziland a protectorate of the Transvaal. Formerly landdrost at Wakkerstroom, Krogh later became the Transvaal's 'special commissioner' for Swaziland during the Boer occupation of the kingdom from February 1895 to June 1903.

While the late 1880s saw serious threats to Swazi independence, it was also a period of serious internal power squabbles, accompanied by numerous killings and the execution of some leading councillors accused of plotting to overthrow the ailing Mbandzeni. He died in 1889 and was succeeded by Ngwane V, aged only 14.

At his young age Ngwane was unable to exercise authority. Between 1890 and 1894 a number of conventions was held between leaders of the ZAR and the British authorities to decide the future of Swaziland. The major contentions of these conventions were about whether control over Swaziland was to come under the ZAR or the British. The ZAR pushed for the right to rule the kingdom, while the Swazi themselves strongly preferred British rule and protection. In 1895 the British allowed Swaziland to become a protectorate under the ZAR, much to the dislike of the Swazi. However, this was only a temporary state of affairs, which was ended by the South African War of 1899–1902. Following the Boer defeat by the British, the Transvaal relinquished control of Swaziland and both territories became British colonies, though the governor of the Transvaal was given power to govern Swaziland of behalf of the British Crown. He did so through a series of proclamations that, though they recognised Swazi law and custom, were not issued in consultation with the Swazi people.

The Hlubi under Langalibalele

The 1870s also saw the destruction of the Hlubi chiefdom in Natal. Langalibalele, a hereditary chief of the Hlubi, living near modern Estcourt in the Drakensberg foothills, was summonsed to Pietermaritzburg for failure to register his firearms. He refused and a force was sent against him. Langalibalele fled the colony, but three of the colonial troops were killed in a skirmish on the Bushman's River Pass.

The Hlubi were deemed to be in rebellion. The chief was subsequently captured and sent to Pietermaritzburg, where he was subjected to a trial by a kangaroo court filled with substantive and procedural irregularities. The punishment meted out to the Hlubi by Lieutenant-Governor Sir Benjamin Pine far exceeded his powers. It included the breaking up of their location and confiscation of their cattle, and Langalibalele's imprisonment on Robben Island.

The handling of the Langalibalele affair in 1873–1874 indicated to the British authorities that Natal could not be trusted to deal with its own affairs. Such irresponsibility convinced the Imperial authorities that Natal was not ready for responsible government, and should be brought under the umbrella of South African confederation.

The Tlhaping and Rolong

For the southern Tswana too this was a time of conflict. The Tlhaping and Rolong occupied territory north of Griqualand West, between the Vaal and Molopo rivers. After the annexation of the ZAR by the British in 1877, Montshiwa of the Rolong felt safer from ZAR aggression. But after the republic regained its independence in 1881, full-scale war broke out between the mercenaries on one side – mostly Boers from the Transvaal and a number of adventurers from Britain and other European countries – and the Tshidi-Rolong on the other. Montshiwa himself recruited British mercenaries to assist him. One of these men, Christopher Bethell, was an aristocrat with strong political connections

Chief Langalibalele was known as 'Long Belly' by Sir Garnet Wolesley, who could 'never spell his infernal barbarian cognomen'. Langalibalele's rebellion caused a crisis in Natal. It was described as 'the most wonderful case of blunders for men past infancy to have made' and strengthened Carnarvon's case for confederation.

back in England. Bethell, who took a Tswana wife, was killed in an engagement with the freebooters shortly before peace was brokered.

In 1882 Montshiwa, facing starvation, was forced to surrender to the authorities of the ZAR. He was presented with an impossible list of demands by Commandant J.P. Snyman of Marico – the cession of all Rolong land south of the Molopo and payment of £16 000 in compensation. The short-lived Republic of Goshen was established in Montshiwa's territory in 1882. Like Goshen, Stellaland comprised mainly white former mercenaries, united under a rudimentary form of government.

To the south, the Tlhaping chief Mankurwane antagonised the Transvaalers by attacking a Kora settlement at Mamusa in 1881. The Kora enlisted the support of Transvaal 'volunteers', who were themselves interested in gaining a foothold on Tlhaping land, and seized the chance to come to the aid of the Kora. Expected British intervention never came and Mankurwane was forced to give up many of his farms to the Stellaland Republic in 1883. Spurred on by the humanitarian urgings of John Mackenzie of the London Missionary Society, by a growing momentum for imperial intervention in Britain in the face of Boer intervention in Griqualand West, and by German expansion from southwest Africa, the British sent an expeditionary force of 4 000 men under General Charles Warren to remove the Republics of Goshen and Stellaland.

British Bechuanaland – an area that included these two republics – was annexed to Britain in 1885. As elsewhere, however, protection came at a cost. Only 8% of the Colony's land was reserved for African occupation. Most of the Stellalanders' land claims were recognised. By 1885 the Crown Colony was in debt, the 'native reserves' were seen as bottling up much needed labour for the Cape, and Cecil Rhodes agitated for the transference of Bechuanaland into the hands of his British South Africa Company. The Colonial Office in London approved annexation directly to the Cape Colony in 1895, provided 'native interests' were guaranteed. Both Mankurwane and Montshiwa expressed reservations about annexation to the Cape, realising they would be subject to a far harsher Cape 'native policy'.

The distinction was made almost immediately apparent. Taxes were more effectively gathered, further land was expropriated, cattle that strayed from the locations were impounded and more game was exterminated. The southern Tswana, in the face of

ABOVE: *A Kora warrior, mounted and armed. Mankurwane, the Tlhaping chief, attacked the Kora in 1881.*

BELOW: *The scene after a big hunt. As land was expropriated and taxes increased, more people, both black and white, turned to hunting. Game was exterminated in large numbers.*

BELOW: *A Griqua family at home as recorded by C.D. Bell in 1834. This way of life came to an end after the Orange Free State was proclaimed in 1854 and the Griqua trekked across the Drakensberg to Natal in the1860s.*

growing impoverishment, turned to their traditional leaders. Several of them began to vent anger against local storekeepers and tear down beacons marking their reserves. Rumour and fear filled Bechuanaland.

Then in 1886 the authorities ordered the shooting of cattle to prevent the spread of rinderpest. Full-scale rebellion broke out. The eight-month Langeberg campaign was launched to wipe out any African opposition to the colonial regime. The chiefs who led the rebellion – Toto, Luka Jantjie and Galeshewe – were captured. Luka was beheaded and the others imprisoned. To the north, Montshiwa stayed out of the hostilities, but his followers were confined to smaller reserves and to the demands of the Cape government. The last remnants of southern Tswana independence effectively had been removed.

THE END OF GRIQUA INDEPENDENCE

In the 1840s and 1850s many Griqua continued to thrive economically. To the south, the advance of the merino wool belt allowed many to trade in horses with the farmers, and later to engage successfully in merino sheep farming. In the northern interior some took advantage of the thriving trade in ivory. Between 1850 and 1860 many were drawn into the mainstream of the country's economic development, while some disposed of their land to the Boers.

In 1854 the Boer republic of the Orange Free State (OFS) was proclaimed between the Vaal and the Orange rivers. The Griqua under Adam Kok III grew uneasy, believing there was no future for them in the OFS. They had two choices – to cease as a community or to trek. They chose the latter. Reports filtered through from residents of a former 'coloured' community at Kat River in the Eastern Cape that there was unoccupied land across the Drakensberg, between the Mzimkhulu and Mzimvubu rivers, known as Nomansland – later Griqualand East. Kok's followers sold off their land and began their epic trek in 1860, arriving in Griqualand East via Matatiele and Mount Currie.

They were moderately successful in setting up home there. The church maintained its unity, local African chiefdoms were driven out of Griqualand or brought under control, Griqua government was restored and a capital established at Kokstad. After some initial difficulty, their animals adapted to the new environment.

Several factors contributed to the disintegration of the East Griqualand community over the next decade. Firstly, though their occupation of the territory was supported by governors at the Cape, it antagonised the Natal government and its white colonists, who coveted the good farmland within its borders. Secondly, Adam Kok had no designated heir, and the disintegrative tendencies so common in Griqua society were to come to the fore after his death. The British began a slow takeover of East Griqualand from 1872, starting by imposing magisterial control. In 1874 J.M. Orpen, an avowed opponent of Griqua autonomy, was appointed as British Resident. There was no consultation, though Kok was appointed an official of the new dispensation. The Griquas' view of themselves as a proud and independent people was dealt a severe blow.

In 1875 Kok died as a result of an accident in his cart. The British allowed the Griqua to sell off land to outsiders, and the ban Kok had imposed on selling alcohol was lifted. Many Griqua began to sell off their land and succumb to the temptations of drink. A new magistrate, William Blythe, was appointed whom the Griqua particularly resented.

In 1875 Lodewyk Kok was arrested for an alleged altercation with a white trader, and a group of Griqua left Griqualand, returning later with some Mpondo recruits and former 'Kat River Rebels' under Smith Pommer. Their intention was probably to discuss the arrest, but Blythe took it as a threat and attacked this party of about 500 men. About 33 Griqua were killed and Pommer was executed. Prisoners were taken. The 'rebellion' was over.

In 1878 East Griqualand was annexed – the Griqua had lost their independence. At the funeral of Adam Kok III his cousin Adam 'Eta' Kok captured the disintegration in these words:

> He is the last of his race. After him there will be no coloured king or chief in Colonial South Africa . . . Take a good look into that grave . . . Do you realise that our nationality lies there? There lie the remains of one South African chief who never fired at a British soldier though sometimes provoked beyond human endurance.

The Venda

After the abandonment of Schoemansdal by the Boers in 1867, the Venda *swart skuts* (*see box*), together with the Tsonga, took control of the ivory trade in this region. By the 1880s, however, the Boers were in much firmer control of the Transvaal following the Pretoria Convention signed between British and Boer leaders in 1881. This recognised the Transvaal as an independent state and gave the Boers the confidence to deal with recalcitrant African communities more decisively. In 1884 the London Convention lent further muscle to the Boer state by giving it control over native policy. Thus the Transvaal could bring unwilling African communities under its jurisdiction and control.

As the Boers began to reoccupy the Zoutpansberg area in the 1880s, they carried out military campaigns against the Venda in order to bring them under Boer government control. In the mid-1890s, Makhado's successor, Mphephu, defended Venda independence and refused to submit to Boer rule. But in 1898 a Boer force of some 4 000 men invaded and defeated the Venda. Chief Mphephu and many thousands of his followers fled across the Limpopo River into Shona country in present-day Zimbabwe. Thus ended the freedom of the last independent African chiefdom in South Africa.

The cattle have gone

The colonial irruption was a catastrophe for traditional African societies that obviously lacked the material resources to withstand the onslaught from *phesheya* (out there). Beings from beyond the sea must have appeared to eighteenth-century Africans much as beings from outer space would appear to us today. But outgunned and out-resourced though they were, African societies were possessed of a resilience based on intricate and coherent social, economic and cultural structures. They resisted for many years but continual defeats on the battlefield necessarily led to adaptation, accommodation and ultimately absorption into the emerging global society and culture.

This section will concentrate on the Xhosa experience because the Xhosa faced the Europeans for longer, and their experiences are well documented. However, it needs to be remembered that variations on the Xhosa experience occurred in every other part of South Africa.

The catastrophe of Nongqawuse

The first missionary to appear among the Xhosa was the Rev. J.T. van der Kemp, a religious zealot with little attachment to European cultural values. He stayed little more than a year at the Mgqakhwebe River, near modern King William's Town in the Eastern Cape, but he left some very potent ideas behind. Van der Kemp's Xhosa name was uNyengane ('the one who comes to give secretly'), and the Xhosa regarded him as a benefactor who had disclosed to them secrets hitherto unknown.

LEFT: *Porters with ivory on the beach. The ivory trade was lucrative; after the abandonment of Schoemansdal by the Boers in 1867, the Venda and Tsonga took over trade in ivory.*

On a certain day in April 1856 at the Gxarha River in the present-day Centane district of the Eastern Cape, two young girls went down to the fields to scare the birds away from the standing corn. Nongqawuse, the older of the two, was an orphan girl staying with her uncle Mhlakaza. Suddenly, Nongqawuse heard her name called and she saw two strangers standing in a bush adjoining the garden. They entrusted her with the following important message:

Tell that the whole community will rise from the dead; and that all cattle now living must be slaughtered, for they have been reared by contaminated hands because there are people about who deal in witchcraft.

There shall be no cultivation but great new grainpits must be dug, new houses must be built; and great strong cattle-enclosures must be erected. Cut out new milksacks and weave many doors from buka roots. So says the Chief Napakade, the descendent of Sifuba-Sibanzi.

Historians believed for many years that the cattle-killing prophecies signified the victory of superstition and a relapse into traditional beliefs. It has now been discovered, however, that Nongqawuse's uncle Mhlakaza had been a Christian convert and evangelist, and that many of the ideas of the cattle-killing are derived from Christian doctrines such as the Resurrection.

ABOVE: *Nongqawuse (right), prophetess of the cattle killing, and Nonkosi (left), an eleven-year-old prophetess. They were held captive in King William's Town, where this photograph was taken, after the failure of the prophecies.*

New images of God, Satan, the death of the Son of God, the Apocalypse and the Resurrection were embraced by visionaries such as Ntsikana and Nxele Makanda (*see box on page 103*). Ntsikana preached peace and submission, and his great hymn inspired growing numbers of indigenous converts, or *amagqobhoka* (people pierced by holes through which Christianity had entered). Nxele, on the other hand, preached apocalypse and practised war. Defeated at Grahamstown in 1819, he was eventually drowned trying to escape from Robben Island.

But it was always said that Nxele would come back, and in 1850 he seemed to have returned in the form of Mlanjeni ('the riverman'), a sickly youth of eighteen who lived in the river and had the power to cast out witchcraft and foretell the future. Mlanjeni, like Nxele before him, was *ithola*, a war doctor, and the Eighth Frontier War (1850–1853) bears his name among the Xhosa even to this day. The Xhosa were not broken by the Mlanjeni War but they were not victorious either, and they lost yet more land. War doctors did not succeed against whites, but quite suddenly a brand new vision appeared, a vision that promised to solve all problems and bring about a 'happy time for all' – the vision of Nongqawuse (*see box*).

> She told the people, she told them all
> That the dead will arise from the graves
> Bringing joy and bringing wealth
> But she was telling a lie.

The impact of Nongqawuse's prophecies was largely due to the spread of lungsickness, an exotic cattle disease that arrived from Europe in 1854. The most sinister characteristic of lungsickness is that it was spread by 'lungers', cattle perfectly healthy in their outward appearance, but highly contagious in terms of infecting other cattle. The Xhosa quarantined their cattle but were helpless against the 'lungers'. This unstoppable disease lent credence to Nongqawuse's contention that the Xhosa had done evil and everything belonging to them was consequently rotten. Only by completely removing the contaminated animals from the earth could space be made for the pure new cattle offered by the messianic figure she called Sifuba-Sibanzi ('the Broad-Chested One').

The Xhosa did not immediately accept the prophecies, but they gained a critical convert in the person of Sarhili, the Xhosa king. The existence of a small minority of unbelievers only served to provide Nongqawuse with an excuse for repeated postponements of the promised day. The situation was made even worse by the repeated interventions of Sir George Grey, the ruthless and paranoid governor of the Cape.

After eighteen months, it was all over: 400 000 cattle had been slaughtered and as many as 40 000 Xhosa were dead of starvation. A similar number entered the Cape Colony in search of labour opportunities, and while they were absent from their homesteads Sir George Grey stole their land and imprisoned their chiefs on Robben Island. The stubborn resistance of the Xhosa, which had held up colonial expansion for more than 80 years, was over.

The peasant moment

The more the Xhosa traditional leaders joined the ranks of the slaughterers, the more the fate of the traditional social and economic order became tied up with the fate of Nongqawuse's prophecies. When they failed, the entire traditional order fell with them, never to rise again except as an empty shell.

But not all the Xhosa followed Nongqawuse. A minority, maybe 10 or 20%, refused to kill their cattle. The doomed believers referred to these men as *amagogotya*, stingy, hard people who stand aside when you need help, who put their selfish interests ahead of the interests of the nation. After the catastrophe was over, the *amagogotya* formed one component of the new class, which – following the convention established by the historian Colin Bundy – can be called 'peasants'.

The other components of this peasantry were convinced adherents of mission Christianity. What united the *amagogotya* and the Mfengu peasants, the population of displaced persons from the Mfecane, was their common and positive response to the new economic and political opportunities on offer from the liberal Cape.

What were these new opportunities?

- The right to own and accumulate private property, land and capital goods such as ploughs and wagons, free of collective obligations imposed by the chiefs in the name of the community.
- Access to national markets on equal footing with the white settlers.
- Access to education, information and technical knowledge.
- Political rights, including the right to a government protective of one's interests and chosen by oneself.

BELOW: *Sir George Grey (Governor of the Cape, 1854-1861) took advantage of Nongqawuse's prophecies to appoint headmen and policemen. He stockpiled food, but he only distributed it to the starving Xhosa after they had committed themselves to labour contracts. He imprisoned the Xhosa chiefs on Robben Island, and seized their lands for white settlement. Many Xhosa believe that he directly instigated the Nongqawuse prophecies himself but this cannot be proven.*

Time would tell that the 'peasant moment' was built on an illusion – the illusion that the colonial situation could accommodate black people on an equal footing with white people. The 'peasant moment' is nevertheless historically important because it demonstrates the capacity and the potential of the black farmer and the black entrepreneur, a capacity and potential that were shut down in the course of South Africa's transition from an agrarian to an industrial society.

The peasants obtained their land foothold in the Cape due to the expedient decision of the Cape authorities to allocate strategically located territories to black farmers for the sake of creating buffer zones between white farmers and black traditionalists. That the peasants seized their opportunities is shown by the following quotations from Colin Bundy's seminal book, *The Rise and Fall of the South African Peasantry*.

> All these people are in the strictest sense agriculturalists . . . They are the largest producers of grain in the division; without them the trade of Queenstown would not be anything like what it is at present. It is an indisputable fact that comparing them with Europeans, taking man for man and acre for acre, the native produces from a smaller extent of ground, and with more primitive appliances, more than the Europeans.
> (Queenstown, 1881)

> Many cattle are fattened here for the markets . . . Dealers and purchasers procure large quantities of slaughter animals from this district. The wheat and other cereals rendered excellent crops . . . The peasants were yearly becoming richer, and there is an increasing desire to obtain land . . . Taking everything into consideration, the native district of Peddie surpasses the European district of Albany in its productive powers.
> (Peddie, 1870–1875)

> Wherever I went I found substantial huts and brick or stone tenements. In many cases, substantial brick houses had been erected and fruit trees had been planted; wherever a stream of water could be made available it had been led out and the soil cultivated as far as it could be irrigated; the slopes of the hills and even the summits of the mountains were cultivated wherever a plough could be introduced.
> (Hewu, 1876)

Peasant production in Natal and in the two Boer republics differed from the Cape less in terms of economic practice than in terms of political profile. Or, to put it another way, the peasants were there but they were politically invisible due to constraints at the political level.

Under the conditions of poorly capitalised, labour-intensive agriculture that existed in the three northern territories, African peasants were able to produce more at a lower cost than white farmers, particularly with regard to familiar staple crops such as maize. Essentially, land was worth little without labour to work it. White farmers, with an abundance of land and a shortage of labour, inclined to stock farming, while Africans concentrated on agricultural production for the urban market. Africans in Natal exported maize all the way to Cape Town in the 1850s, even earlier than they produced maize for the diamond fields in the 1870s.

For most of the nineteenth century, access to land was not as severe a problem for Africans as it later became. Loss of land was a political problem, a spiritual problem, but from a narrowly economic point of view, land was still available in the nineteenth century to enterprising people who were prepared to take available opportunities. In Natal, for example, five out of six million theoretically white acres in 1870 were in fact owned by big land companies who were quite willing to rent it out to Africans while waiting for the value of land to rise.

Land companies also rented out extensive lands to Africans in the Voortrekker republics; the proprietor known to Sotho speakers as Mmangolwana was in fact the Vereeniging Estate Land Company. Sharecropping or 'farming on the halves' – personified by 'Oom Kas' Maine in Charles van Onselen's famous biography *The Seed is Mine* – was

also prevalent and so popular among the poorer class of Afrikaner farmers, especially in the Free State, that it took the Native Lands Act of 1913 to stamp it out.

Politically, however, the peasant outside the Cape Colony was almost voiceless. The main exceptions were the *amakholwa* (believers) communities of Natal, roughly equivalent to the mission peasants of the Eastern Cape. Most notable among these was the Edendale community near Pietermaritzburg, which expanded out of its home base and replicated itself in different parts of Natal, and the 47 African planters of Mvoti (Groutville) who cultivated 300 acres of sugar cane and milled 140 tons of sugar by 1871.

Natal also had one advantage over the Eastern Cape in that it was serviced by the American Board Missions, through which early Natal African leaders such as John L. Dube and Pixley Seme were exposed to black American models of economic upliftment. Political representation for blacks was, however, a no-go area in Natal. The advent in Natal of responsible government in 1893 represented a setback, not a platform, for African political aspirations.

'Friends of the natives' and the origins of African nationalism

The economic hub of the Eastern Cape peasantry was King William's Town, the fourth biggest centre of the old Cape Colony, much bigger then than the port of East London and dependent for its prosperity almost entirely on peasant production. King William's Town was also a centre of mission activity, and many of the prominent white merchants and professionals were closely connected to the Scottish missionaries of nearby Alice. Their intellectual, spiritual and economic sympathies aligned with the emerging black peasant class and they were clearly distinguishable from the white farming community, as was demonstrated in the famous case of

THE CATTLE HAVE GONE

Zimkile! Mfo wehlanga,
Phuthuma, phuthuma;
Yishiy' imfakadolo.
Phuthuma ngosiba;
Thabath' iphepha neinki;
Likhaka lakho eli.
Ayemk' amalungelo.
Qubula usiba;
Ngxasha, ngxasha ngeinki.
Hlala esitulweni,
Ungangeni kwaHoho;
Dubula ngosiba.   *I.W.W. Citashe (1882)*

The cattle have gone! Man of my nation,
Pursue them, pursue them,
Lay aside your Snyder rifle,
Pursue them with a pen;
Take up paper and ink.
It is your shield.
Our rights are going,
Grab a pen;
Load, load, with ink,
Sit on that chair,
Do not enter the Hoho forest;
Fire with the pen.

ABOVE: *Dr W.B. Rubusana (1858–1936), Congregationalist minister, newspaper editor, and the only African elected to any of the Parliamentary structures of the old dispensation (he was Member of the Provincial Council for Thembuland, 1910–1914). Rubusana played a leading role in the foundation of the ANC but his influence was undermined by his political rivalry with J.T. Jabavu.*

OPPOSITE PAGE: *Tiyo Soga (1829–1871) and his Scottish wife Janet (born Burnside). He was the first black minister ordained into a European church, and son of one of the Great Councillors of the Xhosa chief Ngqika. Tiyo Soga's great hymn 'Lizalis' idinga lakho' (Fulfil your promise) is still very popular today.* The Inheritance of My Children, *a personal document he wrote shortly before his premature death, is one of earliest expressions of black consciousness in South African history.*

Rev. John Davidson Don, a Presbyterian minister prosecuted by the Cape authorities for protesting against the murder of a black labourer in 1885.

The liberal element made common cause with the emerging black elite to support 'friends of the natives' in elections to the Cape Colonial Parliament. Due to the colour-blind franchise, black voters constituted more than 40% of the electorate in six Eastern Cape seats, and more than 20% of the electorate in 22 seats altogether. Cape politicians employed black political agents to mobilise black voters. In 1884 King William's Town businessmen Richard Rose-Innes and James Weir sponsored a young black intellectual named John Tengo Jabavu who, frustrated by missionary censorship at Lovedale, resolved to start his own newspaper. This was *Imvo Zabantsundu*, the first black-owned and edited newspaper in any South African African language *(see box on page 287)*.

Jabavu was not South Africa's first black political leader – that honour belongs to Rev. Simon Sihlali of Cala who was elected president of South Africa's first black political party, *Imbumba yaManyama* (founded Port Elizabeth 1882) – but he provided the rising black elite with an articulate voice, a platform and a role model. Organisations by the name of Iliso Lomzi ('the Eye of the Nation') sprang up in many of the smaller Eastern Cape towns, and in 1887 these convened a 'Union of Native Vigilance Associations' (*Imbumba Yeliliso Lomzi Ontsundu*), a direct forerunner of the African National Congress.

The number of black voters in the six key Eastern Cape seats increased sixfold between 1882 and 1886, and it seemed only a matter of time before black people utilised their voting strength to bypass the 'friends of the natives' and represent themselves directly in the colonial legislature.

But direct African representation in the legislature was not something that the framers of the liberal Cape constitution had ever envisaged. Their intention had been to incorporate black and coloured people into the system, not to create avenues whereby the system itself would be challenged.

White farmers began to mobilise on their own account, and in 1880 South Africa's first formal political party, the Afrikaner Bond, was founded to protect white interests. It soon took aim at the liberal franchise. Voting qualifications were raised by the Parliamentary Voters Registration Act (1887) and the Franchise and Ballot Act (1892), so that the more rapidly black people qualified to vote, the more rapidly the colonial Parliament moved the goalposts.

The black vote itself split as the different white political factions – one headed by Cecil Rhodes and the other by the old-style 'friends of the natives' – exploited ethnic tensions to factionalise the black elite from within, one faction looking to Jabavu and the other to Dr W.B. Rubusana, a Congregational minister turned newspaper editor. Black politicians became overly absorbed in their own disputes. They failed to present a united front, thus allowing successive white administrations to roll back the gains of Cape liberalism. They also proved unable to come up with a coherent ideology at the political level, continuing to look to the Queen to save black South Africans from settler oppression. It was only after the Imperial government blessed the unification of South Africa under a racist constitution in 1910 that the stage was set for a new organisation and a new approach.

The painful paradoxes associated with being a black man in a white-dominated world are exemplified in the life of Tiyo Soga, the first black minister ordained into a church in Europe.

Tiyo Soga was born in 1829, the son of one of the Great Councillors of the Xhosa chief Ngqika. He came under the influence of the Scottish missionaries and was educated at Lovedale. The missionaries took him to Scotland during the War of the Axe, so he was never circumcised and therefore never qualified as a fully adult man according to Xhosa custom. In 1856, he married a Scotswoman, Janet Burnside, an extremely happy marriage that produced children who were also educated in Scotland. He was steeped in British culture and translated classics such as *The Pilgrim's Progress* into Xhosa, as well as composing some notable Xhosa hymns that are still very popular today.

Despite this seemingly complete immersion in European culture, Tiyo Soga was often forcibly reminded of his inferior status as a black person. The very day he returned to South Africa after his long exile, he was walking the streets of Port Elizabeth with his new wife when a voice called out, 'Shame on Scotland.' Lower-class whites mocked him with impunity for his European attire. White intellectuals, influenced by Social Darwinism, engaged him in debate concerning the inevitable extinction of the black 'race' by their white superiors.

Tiyo responded with an unequivocal assertion of the primacy of black rights in Africa, the black continent. 'Africa was of God given to the race of Ham,' he argued. And it was only a matter of time before Africa was Christianised, according to the Biblical prophecy: 'Ethiopia shall soon stretch her hands to God.' On a more personal note, dying young of tuberculosis, Tiyo Soga left this letter to his sons under the title of 'The Inheritance of My Children':

> If you wish to gain credit for yourselves – if you do not wish to feel the taunt of men, which you may sometimes well feel – take your place in the world as coloured, not as white men; as [Xhosas], not as Englishmen . . . for your own sakes never appear ashamed that your father was a [Xhosa], and that you inherited some African blood. It is every bit as good as that which flows in the veins of my fairer brethren.

Janet and Tiyo Soga

Black ministers of the next generation were even more forceful in their rejection of white hegemony. They found themselves, in the words of Bishop Dwane, members of 'a church that practised discrimination in salaries, in its denial of equal opportunities, and its show of paternalism and overt racism'.

The first 'Ethiopian' to break away was Nehemiah Tile, a Methodist minister close to King Ngangelizwe of the Thembu. Tile undermined the authority of the white magistrates, saying that Ngangelizwe should come directly under the Queen, not under the white settlers of the Cape, and that the Thembu should have their own state church, similar to the Church of England. He further aroused the wrath of the Methodist missionaries by donating an ox at the circumcision of Ngangelizwe's son, Dalindyebo, thereby proclaiming that African ceremonies were compatible with Christian belief. Expelled from the church, Tile founded the Thembu Church of South Africa in about 1890. Although the church did not long survive his death, Tile's example was followed by many prominent African churchmen, such as Mangena Mokone (linked up with the black American AME Church), P.J. Mzimba (founder of the Presbyterian Church in Africa) and J.M. Dwane (founder of the Order of Ethiopia within the Anglican Church).

FRIENDS OF THE NATIVES' AND THE ORIGINS OF AFRICAN NATIONALISM

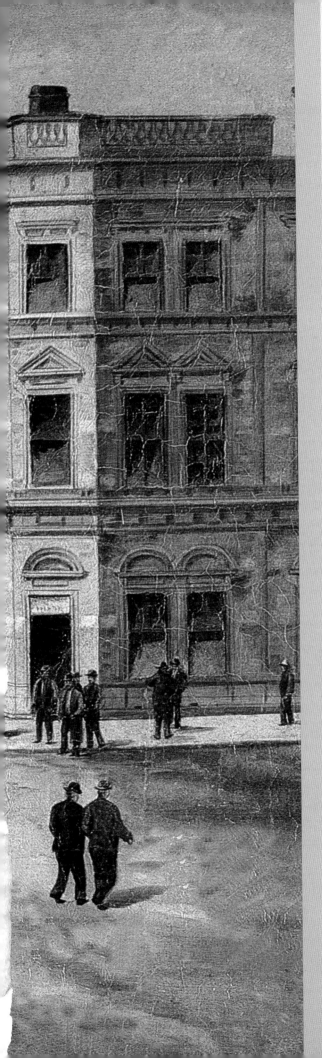

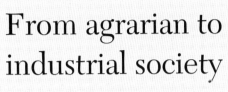

From agrarian to industrial society

(1850–1945)

The business centre of Johannesburg. The tented mining camp of the first few years quickly gave way to a mining town whose business district with shops, banks, saloons and offices grew up around the market square. It developed along an east-west axis, with most of the white workers living in Fordsburg and Vrededorp in the east and the black migrant labourers in compounds close to the mines. In the early years Afrikaners, along with a few 'Cape coloured' people and immigrants, offered a cab service using Cape carts. The town drew avaricious moneymen, schemers and criminals along with miners, white and black. There was a virtual explosion of industrial enterprise. At the top of Johannesburg's social pyramid were the mining house magnates, the so-called Randlords, and at the bottom, the flotsam and jetsam. By the mid-1890s the streets teemed with diggers, prostitutes, gamblers, saloonkeepers, washerwomen and domestic servants.

The painting, by an unknown artist, is described as follows: 'From the Stock Exchange corner (Simmonds Street) looking east. On the left is Corner House and on the south side of Commissioner Street the Commercial Buildings (also called Robinson's Buildings), Green's Chambers, Barnato Building, the Fountain Bar and the Rand Club.'

1877: Theophilus Shepstone annexes the Zuid-Afrikaansche Republiek (ZAR) to the British crown.

1880: S.J. du Toit founds the Afrikaner Bond.

1880–1881: Transvaal Afrikaners revolt against British rule, defeat a British force at Majuba and receive qualified independence.

1883: Paul Kruger becomes ZAR president; J.T. Jabavu founds his own newspaper *Imvo Zabantsundu* ('Native Opinion').

1886: Gold is discovered on the Witwatersrand.

1890: Cecil John Rhodes becomes prime minister of the Cape Colony.

1895: M.T. Steyn becomes president of the Republic of the Orange Free State.

1895–1896: The Jameson Raid into the Transvaal fails to bring about an Uitlander uprising.

1895: Enoch Sontonga composes Nkosi Sikelel' iAfrika.

1899-1902: South African War.

1902: Coloured leaders in Cape Town found the African Political Organisation; Abdullah Abdurahman becomes leader two years later.

1905: The Lagden Commission proposes a ban on black land-ownership in 'white' areas; and the reservation of land for Africans in part of the rural areas.

1906: The first issue of *Sunday Times* appears.

1907: A strike of English-speaking white workers on the gold mines leads to large-scale Afrikaner recruitment.

1908–1914: Mohandas Gandhi leads a passive resistance campaign to protest about discrimination against Indians.

1909: A delegation of African and coloured representatives led by William Schreiner protests in London against black and coloured exclusion in the draft South African Act.

1910: Unification of South Africa; Louis Botha becomes the first prime minister; the Labour Party and the Unionist Party are formed as the main vehicles for English-speaking voters.

1911: The South African Party (SAP) under the leadership of Botha is formed; blacks are barred from skilled jobs on mines and railways.

1912: South African Native National Congress (SANNC, later African National Congress) is formed.

1913: The Natives Land Act sets aside 10.5 million morgen of land (about 7% of the country's land area) for Africans but prohibits purchases and sharecropping in the rest of the country. Sol Plaatje, secretary of the SANNC, reports on the suffering caused by the Act.

1913: Some 9 000 African workers strike.

1913–1914: White mine workers strike.

1914: J.B.M. Hertzog founds the National Party (NP); South Africa enters the war in Europe; an armed Boer rebellion breaks out in the north.

1915: The first copy of *De Burger* appears.

1918: The Afrikaner Broederbond is established in Johannesburg.

1920: The Industrial and Commercial Workers' Union of Africa (ICU), the first African trade union, is founded.

1921: The SAP absorbs Unionists; government forces shoot down 163 members of a black religious sect near Queenstown.

1922: The Stallard report recommends allowing 'natives' in the urban areas only 'as long as their presence is demanded by the wants of the white population'; government forces kill 100 of the Bondelswarts in South West Africa, who had been resisting paying taxes.

1922: Major white strike and urban uprising on the Witwatersrand.

1923: Native Urban Areas Act devolves the function of implementing pass laws and administering African townships onto white municipalities; property rights are not allowed in the 'locations'.

1924: The NP under Hertzog forms a Pact government with the Labour Party and implements 'civilised labour' policy.

1925: Afrikaans is declared an official language.

1928: A South African national flag (orange-white-blue) is used for the first time alongside the Union Jack; the Communist Party decides to work towards 'an independent native republic' as a stage towards a workers' and peasants' revolution.

1929–1932: Great Depression and prolonged drought.

1933–1934: Coalition government between the NP and SAP.

1934: The United Party is formed with Hertzog as leader and prime minister and Smuts as deputy leader. They agree to disagree on South Africa's right to remain neutral if Britain declares war. D.F. Malan's Gesuiwerde National Party is formed and becomes the official opposition. The Status Act affirms the status of South Africa as a 'sovereign independent state'. Member states of the British Commonwealth now enjoy something approaching co-equal status.

1935: 400 delegates establish the All-African Convention (AAC) to coordinate the struggles of all Africans.

1938: Celebration of the centenary of the Great Trek triggers mass Afrikaner enthusiasm.

1939: South Africa enters the war in Europe on the side of Britain, causing the UP to split and Smuts to become prime minister.

1940: Alfred Xuma is elected ANC president and begins to rejuvenate the organisation; he gives the go-ahead for the formation of the Congress Youth League.

1943: The NP under Malan makes gains in the election.

Introduction

In the 1850s South Africa was a thinly populated region based on subsistence agriculture whose population was more than 90% rural. Within a hundred years, it had turned into a rapidly urbanising industrial economy. In 1865 Cape Town, the largest city with a population of 38 000, was rivalled only by Port Elizabeth as a trading and financial centre. By 1950 Johannesburg was by far the largest city and Durban the major port. The contribution of mining and manufacturing was twice that of agriculture, and the two sectors employed a million people, fewer than a third of them white.

The transformation of the political systems was equally dramatic. In the 1850s the four colonial states each received a form of representative government – the Cape Colony a parliament, Natal a legislative council and the two republics each a Volksraad and a president. But power lay elsewhere. Britain controlled the republics through their indebtedness to British merchants and ports, while British-appointed officials still imposed their will on the legislature in the Cape and Natal.

It was only when gold promised to make the Zuid-Afrikaansche Republiek (ZAR) the richest state in South Africa, that Britain found it necessary to wage war to reassert its dominance. The unexpectedly high human and material costs of the conflict sapped the will of the imperial power and scared away British immigration.

After 1902 the politicians of the colonial states grasped the initiative to build their own, white-controlled union. By 1934 the Union of South Africa was for all practical purposes an independent state. But although called a union, the society was a motley and mutually antagonistic collection of communities. No South Africanism had developed in the face of an advancing Afrikaner nationalism and retreating British imperialism. Apart from their economic interdependence there was little else that bound the South Africans together.

The glitter of gold and the symbolism of white power hid the fact that the population until 1933 was predominantly poor and black. The politician John X. Merriman realised as early as the 1880s that South Africa could never be considered a white man's country. He pointed out that white power could only be justified if whites became established as a 'healthy core group' committed to the task of rehabilitating the poor and disadvantaged majority population.

To establish that healthy core group was difficult and the government's efforts continued well into the second half of the twentieth century. The poor white question dominated white politics during the first four decades of the twentieth century. There were several reasons for the poverty. The frontier had begun to close in the 1870s and 1880s, leaving a large poorly educated rural population without any skills for the urban labour market. For the first time church and political leaders recognised the problem and focused all their attention on white poverty. The devastation of the South African War of 1899–1902 compounded the crisis.

At the same time approximately 400 000 white immigrants entered South Africa between 1870 and 1900, which represented a larger number than the entire 1870 white population of 340 000. They filled most of the available openings in the upper ranks of the labour market.

By 1900 only 10 000 Afrikaners did not live on farms; by 1936 half of the community had urbanised and many were struggling to cope in the cities. In the violent strikes of the first twelve years of Union Afrikaner workers formed a proto-revolutionary, disaffected mass. A quarter of the Afrikaners were considered to be destitute by 1930.

The fact was that the poverty of coloured people, Indians and blacks was even worse. By 1930 the reserves could no longer feed their population, which was beginning to stream to the cities.

A VISION OF RACE AND EMPIRE

Cecil John Rhodes was born in England in 1853 and arrived in South Africa in 1870 at the age of seventeen. By 1880 he had made a great diamond fortune in Kimberley. In late 1881 he moved to Cape Town and into politics. He became a towering figure. Close friends spoke of the 'sheer natural power of his mind', his magnetic powers of persuasion, and his love of nature and art.

Rhodes was a man of the boldest vision. He believed the world needed the leadership of the Teutonic races – the people of Britain and the whites in her colonies, and the American and German nations. His dream was to expand the British Empire in Africa from the Cape up to the East African highlands. There it had to meet up with a southward British thrust from Cairo and the Nile Valley. To promote his vision he set up Rhodes scholarships at Oxford for young men from the British Empire, Germany and the United States.

But there was a dark side, captured by the jibe that he was a man with a first-rate mind and second-rate principles. Devious in pursuit of his grand visions, he believed that every man had his price and could be squared.

Rhodes set out to woo J.H. (Onze Jan) Hofmeyr and the Afrikaner Bond. While affluent Cape Englishmen constructed houses in British styles, Rhodes commissioned the design for a Cape Dutch house to which he gave a Dutch name, Groote Schuur. By the mid-1890s Rhodes had become so desperate to realise his vision of a white-ruled united South Africa under the British flag that he took the gamble of what became known as the Jameson Raid. He was forced to resign as Cape prime minister but soon plotted revenge and entered the election of 1898 under the banner of the 'Party of Progress'. He died in 1902 murmuring 'so little done, so much to do'.

CHAPTER SEVEN

From territorial expression to sovereign state

The roots of segregation

During the 1850s, 'South Africa' was a mere territorial expression devoid of real unity. Towards the eastern and the northern parts of the region whites controlled large parts only precariously. Some white politicians argued against further expansion. The society that took shape between 1850 and 1910 was unique in the world of European colonisation. It was neither a self-sufficient, essentially white society like Australia, nor was it an India, where Europeans played a limited role as rulers, traders and missionaries. South Africa was something in between: whites steadily achieved dominance but remained dependent on blacks as labourers or sharecroppers.

South Africa was unique in another way as well. It was one of the very few European colonial settlements where the dominant racial minority was ethnically divided. The division was between the Dutch and English 'races', as the communities were called at the time. They were prepared to suspend their political rivalry only where it jeopardised white supremacy itself. This was particularly the case in the Cape Colony, where Afrikaners had a majority of almost three to one over the English.

The incorporation of large groups of blacks took place in a piecemeal way. In the Zuid-Afrikaansche Republiek (ZAR) the burghers had effective control over only the southern half until the 1880s. In Natal the settlers formed a small minority among the great majority of blacks. White control over all of Natal was only established towards the end of the nineteenth century. It incorporated Zululand in 1897.

The Cape Colony incorporated British Kaffraria (the future Ciskei) in 1865 and in 1879 annexed Fingoland and Griqualand East, which formed approximately two-thirds of the territory between the Cape and Natal. It incorporated Gcalekaland and Thembuland in 1885 and Mpondoland in 1894. The 181 000 white population of 1865 had doubled to 376 000 by 1891, while blacks within the colonial boundaries had increased fivefold from 314 000 to 1 480 000.

In the making of the policy later known as segregation, the reserves carved out by Theophilus Shepstone in Natal were influential. So were the precedents established in the mining town of Kimberley that sprung up in the late 1860s. The Cape abandoned the idea of Sir George Grey during the 1850s of assimilating the blacks into European culture and institutions. The conviction grew that subject peoples had to be ruled through their own customs rather than be assimilated into Western culture. In 1887 and 1892 the liberal constitution was dealt a major blow by legislation that excluded traditional Africans from the vote and raised the property qualification.

Cecil John Rhodes, who became prime minister in 1890, dreamed of a South African state under the British flag (*see box*). Since blacks might then outnumber whites by six to one or even more he looked for a racial policy that would ensure whites could stay the dominant race. After consultation with J.H. Hofmeyr, leader of the Afrikaner Bond, he worked for what he would later call a 'Natives' Bill for Africa', with principles that could be applied throughout South Africa and the rest of the subcontinent. This was the background to the Glen Grey Act of 1894 (*see box*).

THE GLEN GREY EXPERIMENT

The laboratory for the ideas of Cecil Rhodes and Jan Hofmeyr was the African reserve next to Queenstown, originally called the Tambookie Location but later renamed Glen Grey. The reserve had been created in 1853 to accommodate the black population displaced by white commercial farms in the Queenstown district.

Many of the Glen Grey people had become successful peasant farmers but others had no interest in farming and supported themselves by occasional wage labour. Some of the colonial officials blamed these non-productive residents for the overcrowding of the reserves, and thus was born the idea of dividing the black population between serious and respectable peasant farmers, voting for their own councils in their own areas, and wage labourers with limited land rights destined to earn their living by migrant labour on the mines and commercial farms.

The Glen Grey Act of 1894 entrenched white supremacy through creating a special title that allowed prosperous blacks to hold land, but gave them political representation in their own local councils rather than in the government of the Cape itself. The law provided for farms of four morgen, each granted on the basis of ownership or freehold. The eldest son would inherit the plot. The intention was that other sons would be forced to learn 'the dignity of labour' and to seek work in the colony. A tax of ten shillings a head was imposed to press all the younger sons to find work to pay the tax. These men were expected to return to the reserve after they had stopped working in the colony, with communal grazing rights meant to meet their needs. Ownership of the new plots would not qualify blacks for the vote.

It was hoped that the Act would deflect black political attention away from Parliament to new institutions in the reserves. There were Location Boards, elected by registered plot holders, and District Councils, for which the Location Boards elected six members, while the government appointed another six to advise on local issues such as the allocation of local levies for public works, schools and clinics. The Glen Grey plan was meant to provide for productive black peasants to influence politics where they lived, but it did not work out this way. The labour tax and the imposition of individual land tenure were fiercely resisted and never actually implemented. The most lasting significance of the Act was its displacement of the political rights of Africans living in communal areas, away from the seat of power in Parliament and into Local Councils which, by their nature, were precluded from dealing with national issues. In this respect, the Glen Grey Act was indeed most successful, and the District Councils established in consequence later became the basis of the independent homeland parliaments.

By the end of the century a much greater number of black migrants began to move between the reserves, but there were also growing numbers living on a permanent basis on the edges of towns and cities. In 1899 W.P. Schreiner, prime minister of the Cape, said that it would be best to get such clusters of blacks 'compounded'. At the end of their period of service they had to 'go back to the place whence they came – to the native territories, where they should really make their home'. Officials seized on an outbreak of bubonic plague in the largest cities as an excuse to house blacks some distance away in locations. The idea of sealing off the white city from the black locations had begun to take root. Between 1902 and 1904 cities across South Africa passed legislation compelling blacks to live in such segregated locations.

The Cape's liberal tradition, though weakened, still retained the right of all people regardless of colour to own property. The vote was essentially reserved for westernised people. During the 1890s the number of coloured voters on the electoral roll went up from approximately 5 000 to 13 900. Parties competed actively for their vote. Coloured people took the opportunities offered to them for education and industrial training and by the end of the century dominated at least half of the trades in Cape Town and the major western Cape towns.

ABOVE: *A postage stamp depicting the Bunga. The most substantial of the District Councils created by the Glen Grey Act was the United Transkeian Territories General Council, popularly known as the Bunga. It incorporated 27 magisterial districts, though ironically enough Glen Grey itself remained in the Ciskei. From 1976 to 1994 this dignified and spacious building housed the Legislative Assembly of the separate development Republic of Transkei. It is now home to the Nelson Mandela Museum.*

Yet as prominent liberal Cape politician J.W. Sauer remarked, 'political equality is by no means social equality'. Even in Cape Town – racially the most fluid of all South African towns and cities – integration was, as Vivian Bickford-Smith observed, a lower-class phenomenon. Even if socially respectable coloured people could pass for white, 'whiteness was inextricably linked with social and political supremacy'.

The Dutch Reformed, Methodist and Wesleyan churches and non-denominational government schools were de facto segregated. First-class railway carriages, bathing houses, hotel tables and reserved seats in theatres were effectively kept for whites alone. Sport was largely segregated. A reporter from the Scottish *Dundee Advertiser* wrote in 1894 that although coloureds were equal in the eyes of the law there was a 'line' between them and whites that was 'almost as rigidly drawn as if they were a lower range of beings'.

The English colony of Natal claimed it had a non-racial franchise, but the Legislative Council in 1864 and 1865 effectively removed the black vote. In 1904 only two blacks out of a population of a million blacks qualified for the vote. In Pietermaritzburg the most heated speeches were made in denunciation of Shepstone's location system. The voters wanted legislation that, as Alan Hattersley phrased it, aimed to 'raise its barbarous subjects from idle, insolent and uncontrollable savage habits to those of a steady, industrious, humble and moral demeanour'.

In the two Boer republics, the franchise for any people who were not white was ruled out from the outset. Within the Orange Free State's borders the republic carved out three tiny, isolated reserves for blacks, a total of 74 000 morgen, less than 1% of the land. It made no allowance for African customs and refused to recognise African tribal law or traditional marriages. All civil and criminal disputes were under the jurisdiction of Roman-Dutch law, whatever the race or status of the litigants themselves. But the Free State authorities also introduced black 'block men' to help administer the Waaihoek township of Bloemfontein. John Tengo Jabavu wrote approvingly of the system, noting that Waaihoek had its own 'town hall and a council of its own composed of Natives, which is presided over by a Mayor'. In 1896 black residents petitioned the Bloemfontein municipality to apply the pass laws less stringently and complained about overbearing police attitudes.

The ZAR appointed the president as paramount chief over all the native communities. He was to uphold African traditional law in all the African areas but appoint white officials as Native Commissioners in each. The London Convention of 1884 required the ZAR to introduce a 'Locations Commission' to demarcate reserves for each ethnic group. But little additional land for locations was set aside and for some groups no provision was made at all.

Rank and file ZAR burghers strongly opposed reserves, or locations as they were called there, but Paul Kruger argued in 1893 that small African groups especially needed some land to be set aside for them so that they did not feel oppressed. He asked: 'Is it fair or Christian to drive them off the land?' Against this stood the insatiable demand for land among his voters. By 1900 it was estimated that between a fifth and a quarter of blacks in the ZAR lived in locations in the rural areas. Blacks could buy land elsewhere but only through third parties, such as missionaries, who registered the land for them in a trust that they administered.

A black South Africa

The numbers officials gave for blacks were mainly guesswork. Some appeared in a book of 1878 by the famous British author Anthony Trollope and are reproduced here *(see box)*. Trollope called South Africa a black man's country, in which the number of all who were not white was put at nearly two million against fewer than 350 000 whites. Using modern methods, demographer Jan Sadie in 2002 projected the 1878 figure for blacks (excluding coloured people, Indians and whites) at 2.2 million.

POPULATION IN SOUTH AFRICAN TERRITORIES, 1878			
	Whites	Blacks and Coloureds	Total
Cape	235 000	485 000	720 000
Ciskei		335 000	335 000
Transkei		501 000	501 000
Diamond Fields	15 000	30 000	45 000
Natal	20 000	320 000	340 000
OFS	30 000	15 000	45 000
ZAR	40 000	250 000	290 000
Total	340 000	1 936 000	2 276 000

Economic opportunities

British immigrants seized most of the new opportunities that became available in South Africa. In the towns and cities they became the tradesmen and artisans. Along with Jews from Europe, they took over trading with farmers in the interior and with Xhosa peasant farmers on the frontier. It was the British who first engaged in large-scale land speculation. During the 1830s they were prominent among those who started wool farming in the eastern part of the Cape Colony, and they founded export-import firms in Port Elizabeth and Cape Town. In the rural towns across South Africa English speakers occupied all the prominent positions. They were engineers of the roads, bridges and railways and deep-level mining shafts, and they were the entrepreneurs who founded sophisticated industrial and financial companies.

Jewish South Africans were prominent in expanding trade across South Africa. Adolph Mosenthal arrived in 1846 from Germany and founded a family trading firm that became one of the largest investors in the diamond industry. In the ZAR Sammy Marks established a special relationship with Kruger's government (*see box*).

Agriculture provided a livelihood for the overwhelming majority of Afrikaners. Since the final decades of the nineteenth century there had been a steady increase in the demand for wheat and dairy products in the western Cape, with fruit exports becoming a promising option. Wine farming, hit hard by phylloxera disease in the 1880s and stagnating until 1910, started to pick up in the first two decades after Union. In the eastern Cape and Karoo midlands the more successful Afrikaner and English wool farmers shared in the steady expansion of wool exports, up from £4 million in 1904 to £20 million in 1919.

But less than a fifth of South Africa consists of arable land fit to plant crops. Large parts are semi-desert with frequent droughts, and other parts get enough rain but have extremely rugged terrain. Stock farming developed as a way of life and means of subsistence and only in the twentieth century as a commercial enterprise.

A wasteful exploitation of agricultural resources contributed to a crisis in pastoral farming. Overstocking, together with grass burning, destroyed the natural vegetation, and thunderstorms swept the topsoil away. Farmers had been accustomed to move on to new grass and fresh land when pastures were exhausted, but by the 1880s the frontier of expansion had closed.

As cultivators, black peasant farmers, using family as a labour force, were well ahead of the republican burghers, who were mostly stock farmers. In 1904 a well-informed observer wrote that in the eastern half of the country, blacks were 'the best all-round cultivators of South Africa so far'.

BELOW: *Black sharecroppers plough their fields. Peasant farmers depending on their families for labour dominated production in the eastern half of South Africa in the second half of the nineteenth century. In 1904 a well-informed observer wrote that the traditional African 'is the best all-round cultivator of South Africa'. Blacks in Basutoland (now Lesotho) and the Free State keenly responded to the large market for wheat, maize and vegetables that had sprung up on the Diamond Fields. Blacks were in a position to move around to explore the best offers from farmers. They were rarely attracted to poorer farmers who lacked land and offered poor terms. During the 1890s a group of farmers from the eastern Free State demanded that the Volksraad prohibit large-scale growing of grain by blacks, because white farmers could not compete. Farmers struck up an arrangement with black sharecroppers, who bore half the risk with them. Land shortage was not yet a problem, with only a small part of the large farms in the republics under cultivation. Replies given to the Transvaal Labour Commission of 1903 revealed that it was rare for more than 100 acres (approximately 40 ha) to be cultivated by a single owner.*

Shortly before the South African War of 1899–1902 President Paul Kruger of the ZAR granted the extraordinary privilege of private use of the state mint to one of his burghers, Sammy Marks, a Lithuanian-born Jew. Arriving in South Africa in 1868 at the age of 24, Marks had worked initially as a peddler and then moved to Kimberley, where he dealt in diamonds and claims. In 1881 he visited Pretoria and met Kruger, discussing the possibility of investment in the infant republic.

Sammy Marks

Kruger promised Marks government support for his ventures. The first of these was a distillery outside Pretoria, the first factory in the ZAR. It was christened De Volkshoop (the People's Hope) by Kruger at its opening, but was more popularly known as Hatherley or Eerste Fabrieken. Marks later established glass and canning factories, as well as a brick and tile works.

After the discovery of gold, Hatherley flourished as its cheap gin and brandy, made with produce supplied by Boer farmers, slaked the thirsts of black and white mine workers. Nearly all of Marks's businesses depended on government favour. To ensure this he wooed the Boer leaders assiduously, with 'soft' loans and gifts large and small. Most importantly, he helped to secure a property deal that made the president a wealthy man. He also gave Pretoria a large sum for the erection of a statue of Kruger.

Marks was a frequent and welcome visitor to the president's home. Kruger clearly enjoyed Marks's company – the lively argument, sometimes bordering on the insolent; the cross-fire of argument-clinching illustrations from their favourite text, the Bible; and

the banter about Marks's supposed religious wrong-headedness.

Marks regarded the coming of the South African War as an unmitigated disaster. During the conflict he successfully performed a balancing act between Boer and Brit. Before the occupation of Pretoria he did his duty as a loyal burgher. Once the British arrived he took the oath of neutrality and served them just as faithfully. When the Boer generals negotiated peace in 1902, they sent for Marks and discussed with him their course of action. The peace conference at Vereeniging was held on Marks's property, where he played a vital role in strengthening the hands of those making peace.

After the war Marks was a strong supporter of Milnerism – the systemic attempt to entrench British cultural values and the English language in the two former republics. Yet with the resurgence of Afrikanerdom he shifted his support to Louis Botha's party. His reward was appointment as a senator in the first Union Parliament and state support in establishing South Africa's first steel works. Marks died in 1920 at the age of 76.

OPPOSITE TOP: *Three types of school. During the 1840s Cape officials James Rose Innes and Langham Dale, and Governor Sir George Grey laid the foundation of a modern, secular, English-medium system of education in the Cape Colony. St Andrew's College (left) represented the pinnacle of the system where children received advanced instruction. Zonnebloem College in Cape Town (second from left) was attended mostly by black and coloured students, but Grey also brought 40 sons of chiefs on the eastern frontier to be educated here. The school on the right, at Elim, was a missionary institution. Almost all coloured and black children and many of the poorer white children received their instruction from such mission schools.*

English cultural dominance

English economic dominance led to English cultural dominance among the white, coloured and black elite. In 1865 the government of the Cape Colony decided that all future instruction in government schools had to be given in English. The few top schools attended by the children of the white elite became bastions of the English cultural influence, among them the Diocesan College (1849) in Cape Town, St Andrew's in Grahamstown (1855) and the Stellenbosch Gymnasium (1866). In the Republic of the Orange Free State the Grey Institute was founded in Bloemfontein in 1856. In Natal the Pietermaritzburg High School (later Maritzburg College) opened its doors in 1863 and Durban High School in 1866.

But overall the level of white education was very poor. In 1875 it was found that three-quarters of white children in the Cape Colony were illiterate. In the republics and Natal it was worse.

Almost all education for coloureds and blacks was in the hands of churches and missionary institutions. Almost without exception they made the teaching of English a high priority. In 1891 a third of the white children in schools in the Cape Colony attended mission schools in which there was no colour bar. Zonnebloem College in Cape Town, started by the Anglican Church, began with white, coloured and black pupils, and later became predominantly a coloured school.

In Xhosa country there were several mission stations spreading English culture, the gospel of work and individual respectability. During the 1850s the Cape governor, Sir George Grey, provided funding for African schools at Healdtown, St Matthews, St Mark's, Salem, Peelton, Mount Coke and in Grahamstown. Lovedale had started earlier, in 1841,

with eleven blacks and nine whites and remained a mixed school until 1878. In 1878 James Stewart wrote: 'All colours, white and black and brown and yellow are to be found among the pupils. They represent nearly all the tribes of South Africa. There are [Xhosas], Fingoes, Hottentots, Pondos, Bechuanas, Basutos, Zulus, English and Dutch.'

By 1887 more than 2 000 blacks had received a missionary education in Lovedale alone. They became teachers, law agents, magistrate's clerks, interpreters, telegraph operators, printers and clerks. In Natal the Adams Mission Station (later Adams College) began teaching blacks in 1853. Its reputation for quality education quickly spread.

A growing political consciousness

In 1853 the Cape Colony received representative government, but the governor, appointed in Britain, still called the shots. Parliament was dominated by the concerns of the English or anglicised section of the community in small towns and in Cape Town and Port Elizabeth. The main issue under discussion was the devolution of power to the eastern districts and the prospects of secession, of interest mainly to English merchants and speculators.

In 1872, the Cape received an advanced form of colonial self-rule with a prime minister heading a cabinet that was accountable to Parliament. Voters had become increasingly worried about excessive government expenditure on military expeditions that had landed the colony in heavy debt. In the absence of political parties, increasing strains developed in the 1870s between the executive and legislature.

These tensions came to a head when Gordon Sprigg formed a cabinet of politicians from the eastern Cape and Cape midlands, with not a single Afrikaner nor western Cape politician. To cover the cost of new railways and colonial intervention in the war between two Xhosa factions, the Sprigg cabinet imposed a tax on brandy producers. On the day the excise law was published, some wine farmers met with Jan Hofmeyr (Onze Jan), editor of *De Zuid-Afrikaan*. He formed a farmers' party, the Zuid-Afrikaansche Boeren Beschermings Vereeniging (BBV), in October 1878. In the 1879 parliamentary election, the BBV won nearly half of the upper-house seats and a third of those in the lower house. But enthusiasm soon dwindled and the BBV failed to extend itself much beyond the western Cape.

Seizing the initiative in June 1879, S.J. du Toit, an Afrikaans *predikant* in Paarl, proposed the formation of an Afrikaner Bond with the slogan of 'Afrika voor de Afrikaners' and with branches across South Africa. On 14 August 1875, Du Toit and seven other Afrikaners had founded the Genootskap van Regte Afrikaners (GRA, the Society of True Afrikaners) in Paarl. They decided that there was an urgent need to persuade the Dutch and Afrikaans-speaking white people to see themselves as a distinct community, calling themselves Afrikaners. The GRA's prime target was the large section of Afrikaners who were not particularly affluent and had received limited education.

To spell out its message, the GRA launched its own newspaper, *Die Afrikaanse Patriot*, its first issue appearing on 15 January 1876. Its style was clear, crisp and concise, with

ABOVE: *A tax imposed on brandy in 1878 led to the establishment in the same year of the Zuid-Afrikaansche Boeren Beschermings Vereeniging (South African Farmers' Protection Society) by Jan Hofmeyr (top) and of the Afrikaner Bond by S.J. du Toit (below) in 1880.*

ABOVE: Die Afrikaanse Patriot, *published in Paarl, was the first Afrikaans newspaper. Its circulation rose to more than 3 000 after the Dutch Reformed Church condemned it as anti-government and too critical.*

BELOW: *Jan Brand, president of the Free State from 1864 to 1888, established the basis for a modern state by introducing proper financial management, a state bank, a sound legal system and a more modern educational system.*

OPPOSITE: *The town of Kimberley had a population of more than 30 000 by 1875.*

simple sentences and very short words. A team effort with Du Toit as its main author produced a nationalist history entitled *Die Geskiedenis van ons Land in die Taal van ons Volk* (The History of our Land in the Language of our People). The *Patriot* played on the Afrikaners' common resentment of free trade in goods and money, and of the wealth of merchants, bankers and other agents of British capitalism. A prime target was the Standard Bank, depicted as a 'gigantic devil fish' that fleeced the colonists and sent a large part of its dividends to its London head office.

The Afrikaner Bond benefited from the upsurge of nationalist emotion when the Transvaal burghers rose against British annexation (1880–1881). Numerous Afrikaner Bond branches were formed across South Africa. Hofmeyr became a member of the Bond and soon began to plot to moderate its aims. In 1883 a congress at Richmond approved the amalgamation of the Bond and the BBV. Hofmeyr became leader of the new Afrikaner Bond. His political skills were formidable, and Cecil John Rhodes considered him the most capable politician in South Africa.

The first black political association was the semi-political Native Educational Association, founded in 1879 in the eastern Cape to promote the 'general welfare of the natives'. In 1882 the Imbumbe Yama Nyama was founded in Port Elizabeth to join blacks together in fighting for national rights.

The colony of Natal

A charter dated 15 July 1856 created the colony of Natal. It was given a legislative council of sixteen members, twelve elected and four officials. As was the case in the Cape Colony, there was no colour bar in the constitution, but it was for all practical purposes impossible for a person who was not white to become a voter. The colony struggled to find its feet, with the value of imports in 1859 almost double that of exports. Between 1857 and 1861 ivory accounted for most of the value of the exports and sugar and molasses for just over one-fifth. After the labour shortage had been solved through the importation of Indians, sugar began its rise as the staple product of the economy.

By 1871 the white population had reached only 18 000 but inspired by the grant of responsible government to the Cape in 1872, the legislative council asked for the same. London had different ideas and sent Sir Garnet Wolseley out as a special commissioner with extensive powers to change the constitution and the native administration. In Pietermaritzburg he entertained the white leadership, 'drowning their liberties in sherry and champagne', in the words of his biographers. On his insistence the representation of the officials on the legislative council and the power of the lieutenant-governor was increased. Natal finally received a parliament in 1893. Zululand was incorporated into Natal in 1897.

It was estimated that by 1872 there were some 17 500 whites, 300 000 blacks and 5 800 Indians. By the end of the decade there were 22 000 whites and 12 800 Indians. The latter helped to push up the production of sugar from 1 173 tons in 1859 to 10 172 tons in 1874. They suffered extensive discrimination, which was highlighted when a young Indian, Mohandas Gandhi, arrived twenty years later *(see box)*.

Fragile republics

The Great Trek produced two states. The Zuid-Afrikaansche Republiek (ZAR), also referred to as the Transvaal, was established in 1852, and the Republic of the Orange Free State (OFS) in 1854. For 20 to 30 years the economies of the two republics were much too weak to weld Boer society together and to underpin an efficient state. Without marketable commodities, currency was soon exhausted and both the state and its burghers became indebted to foreign merchants and banks. Burghers were reluctant to pay taxes, and many ignored the call-ups for commando.

The state squandered its major resource of land by liberally distributing it. In the ZAR absentee landowners and companies accumulated approximately half the land, and half of the burgher population was landless by the end of the century.

In 1871 Britain annexed the rich diamond fields at what would become known as Kimberley despite strong Free State claims. Jan Brand, president from 1864 to 1888,

THE BATTLES OF GANDHI

Deeply intertwined in the lives of Indian South Africans is the impact of Mohandas Karamchand Gandhi, who from 1893–1914 waged many battles to challenge the discrimination they faced. He used the strategy of non-violent resistance, known as satyagraha, or the power of truth.

Gandhi arrived in South Africa in 1893 at the age of 24. The following year he established the Natal Indian Congress as an instrument of protest against racial discrimination and unfair taxes. As a diffident young English-trained lawyer, he was attracted by an offer of employment from an Indian businessman to wage a lawsuit against a relative. The successful resolution of this case through compromise brought Gandhi great recognition, resulting in a lucrative legal practice.

In 1902 he returned to India, with the promise to come back if needed. The growing restrictions on Indian residential and trading rights provided such a need, and Gandhi returned to address the conflict between the Indian community in the Zuid-Afrikaansche Republiek (ZAR), or Transvaal, and the colonial government.

In 1906 he launched the Transvaal Indian passive resistance protest against the Asiatic Law Amendment Ordinance, a new law requiring Indians to be fingerprinted and carry passes. Some 3 000 protesters gathered to oppose the indignity of this. Gandhi, with leaders of other communities in South Africa, went to London to oppose other planned discriminatory legislation. He also served as a link with nationalist leaders in India, drawing attention to measures such as a contract labour tax in Natal which applied only to Indians, and restrictions on land ownership and freedom of movement within the country.

In 1908 a pass-burning demonstration led to his arrest. This form of civil disobedience later resonated with black women, who followed similar methods of protest. In 1913 Indian coal miners and indentured labourers in Natal went on strike, resulting in the arrest of thousands of the resisters.

When Gandhi returned to India in 1914, he had accomplished small gains, but these were quickly reversed through more sophisticated legislation aimed at curtailing the political and economic power of Indians. However, Gandhi's presence in South Africa left an indelible mark on the wider political culture and forms of resistance.

Mohandas Gandhi

ABOVE: *Lord Carnarvon, the British Colonial Secretary in the 1870s, who doggedly kept pushing for a federation joining the two British colonies and the two Boer republics under British sovereignty.*

succeeded in getting Britain to pay the sum of £90 000 as compensation. Brand was a gifted leader and instilled new political confidence. By the early 1880s, he had established the basic framework of a stable state. He put special emphasis on establishing a sound legal and banking system in order to attract trade and other forms of business. He stamped out corruption.

A new British thrust

Britain's acquisition of Basutoland in 1868 and incorporation of the Diamond Fields in 1871 signalled a new imperial thrust from Britain into the South African interior. What lay behind this was the realisation of the economic potential of the region. Britain wanted to benefit from its growth in trade and mining and improved transport and infrastructure. That required the securing of larger supplies of migrant labour for the mines, plantations, farms, and public works of the near interior. Yet, beyond checking any external encroachments by the Boer states, Britain continued to avoid any major political confrontation with republican leadership.

Britain was, however, becoming increasingly frustrated by being saddled with a country divided between settler colonies, Boer republics and subjugated black societies under British authority. Still, London was banking on favourable circumstances in which to draw white territories into a voluntary federation under imperial direction. A more integrated central state would be able to pursue common policies in such matters as trade, defence, and the administration of black people and control of their labour. All that would be required to bring the republican Boers under Britain's colonial wing was firm diplomacy and 'peaceful pressure'.

In the mid-1870s British Colonial Secretary Lord Carnarvon began to push vigorously for a federation of colonies and republics under British sovereignty. It turned out to be hard going. The Boer states had no inclination to negotiate away their free identities, and even the Cape and Natal's response to the idea of a settler confederation was lukewarm. But, like a dog with a bone, Carnarvon would not let go of his bold plan. Following its annexation of the Griqualand West diamond fields in 1871, Britain initiated a confederation policy for its South African territories. With the ZAR wallowing in financial crisis and its southeastern border menaced by powerful Zulu opponents, the time looked ripe for a decisive move.

The shaky ZAR is annexed

The ZAR took long to stabilise. During the 1850s and early 1860s, three or four regions, each with their own personal leaders, constantly vied for power. In the northern part of the republic, the dispersed trekker settlements collapsed in the face of Venda hostility and the trekkers had to abandon entire districts. When Kruger called the burghers out for commandos half of them failed to appear. In the early 1870s a Pedi challenge to the white settlement in the eastern part of the republic forced the ZAR to turn to the Swazi under Mswati for help. By the mid-1870s the Pedi under Sekhukhune were raiding farms in the eastern part of ZAR with impunity.

Thomas François Burgers, a liberal minister who had been suspended by the Reformed Church in the Cape for heresy, became president of the ZAR in 1872. An idealist with grand visions, he lacked the patience to win the trust of an ultra-conservative community. His plans to introduce secular education nearly prompted Paul Kruger to join a trek, later called the Dorsland Trek, through the desert to southern Angola in order to preserve their religious and political belief. More than half of those who left perished or turned back.

Burgers borrowed money on a large scale for grand projects to modernise the republic. He planned a railway line to Delagoa Bay, to secure an outlet free from British control. On a visit to Europe he raised only £90 000 and the venture ended in an enormous loss. Paul Kruger made the cruel but apt comment about his ambitious schemes: 'Burgers wanted to fly, but his wings were clipped in time. Now he has to crawl along with us.'

By early 1877 the state was so deeply in debt that the civil servants could not be paid. Hopelessly divided, the ZAR burghers offered no resistance when Theophilus Shepstone, backed by 25 men, went to Pretoria to annex the state as a British colony.

The rise of Paul Kruger

When Shepstone arrived in Pretoria in January 1877, he wooed the ZAR burghers to secure their consent for annexing the republic as part of a plan to engineer a South African federation. He wrote later that of the 3 000 people he had canvassed before annexing the republic on 12 April 1877, only Paul Kruger was unequivocal in his rejection of such a move. '[He] positively declined to enter into the discussion if that might involve the independence of the state as a republic.'

Kruger took the lead in organising resistance. With the burghers seemingly paralysed by apathy and indifference, Kruger twice went to London as a member of a three-man delegation to persuade the Secretary of State for the Colonies to permit a referendum on Shepstone's claim that the majority of the ZAR burghers favoured annexation.

Slowly Boer resistance mounted. Early in December 1880 mass meetings were held at Paardekraal in the ZAR, attended by thousands of burghers. A meeting on 11 December proclaimed the restoration of the republic. It was the beginning of an armed rebellion. The British were confident the rebels would quickly disperse after the first skirmish. But the burghers were armed with Westley Richard rifles that could kill from 550 metres and, as the enemy soon discovered, they were excellent shots. They destroyed a British column at Bronkhorstspruit, laid siege to the rest of the garrison in Pretoria and Potchefstroom, and attacked the column of Sir George Pomeroy Colley, who had arrived with reinforcements from Natal. On 27 February 1881 this force was routed at Majuba.

Able to draw on only 3 500 troops in all South Africa, the new ministry in London under William Gladstone was in no mood to hang on to the ZAR for the sake of Lord

ABOVE: *The Dorsland Trek. During the 1870s three separate groups of farmers left the Transvaal to settle in the present Namibia and subsequently in Angola. Participants were driven by what was called the* trekgees – *a practice that had begun in the refreshment station of the Cape in the 1690s. It saw stockfarmers, called* trekboers, *roaming about with their livestock beyond the settlement's boundaries. But the Dorsland trekkers were also driven off by the secular reforms of the liberal president of the ZAR, Thomas François Burgers. He wanted to ban religious instruction during school hours. This greatly shocked the more conservative burghers, especially members of the Reformed (Dopper) church like Paul Kruger. Kruger feared for 'the fall of Christendom' and was sorely tempted to join the first trek, but decided to stay to build up a 'pure' church in the Transvaal. The trek went on without him. It was close to an utter disaster. Some 500 to 600 people left from Pretoria and Rustenburg between 1874 and 1880, travelling across the Kalahari desert to South West Africa and the south of present-day Angola on the Dorsland Trek (Thirstland Trek). Between 250 and 300 people perished or turned back.*

Paul Kruger

Carnarvon's discredited federation scheme. Far from helping to achieve South African federation, annexation would stir up vociferous anti-imperial sentiment in Boer communities throughout South Africa. It was also condemned by more moderate English colonial opinion. To meet the ZAR's demands and yet salvage some honour, Britain seized upon the formula of a 'suzerainty', under which Britain would retain an important say in the ZAR's foreign and 'native' affairs.

The ZAR re-emerged in a much better state. The British administrators had reformed its chaotic finances and defective administrative machinery. A separate Department of Native Affairs gave centralised direction to local officials on how to collect taxes and labour service from blacks.

Paul Kruger was elected president in 1883. He believed that only a committed republicanism could act as a counter to British imperialism and Cape Afrikaners' embrace of a colonial nationalism which readily incorporated imperial elements. In developing his republican ideology he stressed the historic links between the heroic acts of the Voortrekkers and the triumphant rebellion and between the burghers' religious and political identity. The commemoration of these events, with the main festival at Paardekraal, became a grand political and religious occasion.

Although increasingly respected as a leader after he became president, Kruger struggled to build up the state in his first three years. He failed to persuade the Cape Colony to reduce custom duties on ZAR goods. This set the scene for a prolonged conflict between him and the two leading Cape politicians, Cecil John Rhodes – who harboured grand designs for extending British influence throughout Africa and uniting South Africa under the British flag (*see box*) – and J.H. (Onze Jan) Hofmeyr, who attached prime importance to the promotion of the interests of the Cape and his constituency. Travelling through the republic, Kruger encouraged the burghers. Help, he said, would surely come, and so it did in 1886 when the rich and abundant goldfields of the Witwatersrand were discovered.

In a few deft strokes historian C.W. de Kiewiet depicts the impact of gold on the republic's revenue: 'In 1884 the Transvaal was barely solvent; three years later, in 1887, its revenue of £638 000 approached that of Natal; two years later again its revenue of £1 500 000 was in hot pursuit of that of the Cape. For every reluctant pound which the ZAR had to spend in 1883 it had twenty-five pounds.'

Kruger's reforms and their critics

Few states, particularly a predominantly rural and backward one like the ZAR, would have coped easily with the mushrooming of a city like Johannesburg and the great influx of immigrants. Yet the ZAR succeeded remarkably well in devising a proper local administration for Johannesburg and other towns, appointing mostly competent officials to run them. It allowed foreign capital into the colony without restrictions, imposed a low tax of only 5% on declared profits, and enacted an efficient mining code. With revenue from the mining industry the ZAR built railways linking Johannesburg to ports, and improved the road system. Enough food reached Johannesburg to feed the rapidly expanding population. After 1895 Kruger made impressive progress with administrative reform.

Kruger's critics hammered the state on two issues: its protectionist economic policies and the franchise. Even before gold was discovered Kruger had accepted a plan for industrialisation that would increase the state's economic independence. It handed to individuals or companies the exclusive right to produce articles such as liquor, soap, bricks, leather and dynamite, all buttressed by heavy protective tariffs. His policy made good sense in a predominantly agrarian society developing its own manufacturing sector, but not in a rapidly expanding gold economy.

The mining industry, intent on holding down costs, complained vociferously about the high railway rates, the price of dynamite, corruption, and the scarcity of black labour, all of which were estimated to cost the mining industry more than £2 million a year. Kruger's proclivity for giving concessions and posts to incompetent family, friends and supporters made matters worse.

From soon after the discovery of gold, thousands of foreign fortune-seekers flooded the ZAR. To prevent these 'Uitlanders' from winning power through the ballot box, Kruger's

RHODES, HOFMEYR AND KRUGER

From the early 1880s Cecil Rhodes began to woo the Afrikaner Bond as the largest bloc in Parliament. He backed Hofmeyr on curtailing the black franchise, blocking certain imports from England and recognising equal rights for Dutch, calling it a 'great disability' to know only one language. The two leaders also agreed on working for a united South Africa under the British flag, with the Cape Colony as the dominant power.

By contrast, Paul Kruger fought for a state under a republican flag and free from British interference. He wanted his state to expand westward but Rhodes was among those who blocked him in 1885 by carving out Bechuanaland. After Kruger had met Rhodes he said: 'The race-horse is swifter than the ox, but the ox can draw the greater load. We shall see.'

Kruger acquiesced in Bechuanaland, hoping that he would be allowed to expand eastward to the sea. When Hofmeyr travelled to Pretoria three years later to inform Kruger that he could not claim Swaziland before he had entered into a customs union determining trade tariffs, Kruger thundered at him in public: 'You are a traitor, a traitor to the Africander cause.'

The opening up of the rich gold fields of Johannesburg gave Kruger the upper hand. The Cape was now very eager to form a customs union that would join the republics and colonies in a common market. Kruger rejected a customs union and imposed heavy duties on Cape goods. He was determined to block the further extension of railway lines from the colonies into the ZAR until a ZAR line to Delagoa Bay had first been completed.

Hofmeyr and Rhodes realised that the Kruger policy would defer the unification of South Africa under the British flag indefinitely. Rhodes determined to remove Kruger, but he had a tacit understanding with the Bond that he would not act on issues that deeply concerned the Afrikaners without consulting Hofmeyr.

In 1889 Rhodes founded the British South African Company (BSA) as the vehicle for founding Rhodesia (now Zimbabwe). In 1890 Rhodes became prime minister of the Cape Colony with the help of the Bond, and was well positioned to advance his aims. Succumbing to Rhodes's blandishments that expansion was an Afrikaner as well as a British imperial project, *De Zuid-Afrikaan* wrote in 1890: 'Under the British flag and with the help of British capital we are marching to the north.' By the end of 1890 a BSA force occupied Mashonaland, and by the end of 1893 the conquest of Matabeleland was all but completed.

The Bond also supported Rhodes in his drive to retain the diamond monopoly of De Beers Consolidated, and allowed him to serve as both prime minister and chairman of the BSA. Bond leadership soon became embroiled in allegations of corruption: It could hardly be coincidental that Bond leaders had just then acquired considerable numbers of shares in De Beers and BSA. John X. Merriman, a leading liberal, expressed horror at what appeared to him to be an abandonment of all principles.

The Cape Afrikaners became what a twentieth-century imperial historian has called the 'ideal prefabricated collaborators'. But Rhodes betrayed them in plotting the downfall of Kruger and the ZAR. Hofmeyr considered this a personal betrayal by a man he had profoundly trusted.

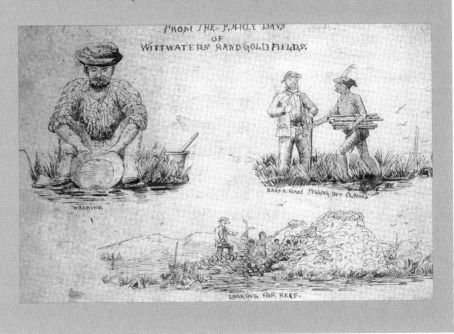

government in 1890 extended the period necessary to qualify for the vote from one year to fourteen years. They also created a second Volksraad to represent Uitlander interests. This became the focus of all the wrath of the immigrant population.

Kruger's principal Afrikaner opposition was a faction called the Progressives, who urged the rapid modernisation of the republic. They operated under the leadership of Commandant-General Piet Joubert, and during the 1890s included bright, enterprising men like Louis Botha, J.H. (Koos) de la Rey, Carl Jeppe, Ewald Esselen and Schalk Burger. They attacked maladministration, corruption, the conservative educational system and the parochial ways of Kruger's government. The Progressives commanded the support of about a third of the elected representatives in both houses of the legislature. In the 1893 presidential election Kruger only narrowly defeated Joubert.

ABOVE: *An illustration 'From The Early Days of the Witwatersrand Gold Fields'.*

THE CONCESSIONS POLICY OF THE KRUGER GOVERNMENT

In 1881 the government of the ZAR under President Paul Kruger introduced a policy of concessions or monopolies. This meant that only one private individual or company was granted the right to supply certain services or goods. Concessions were intended to promote economic development through individuals' capital, technical and managerial skills, which the ZAR state lacked. For instance, prominent burghers were granted concessions to supply water, gas or electricity in the cities.

With the start of gold mining on the Rand from 1886, accusations of overcharging, inefficiency and corruption were frequently levelled against the private monopolies that ran these public amenities. Economically the most important of these concessions were probably those over alcohol, dynamite and railways. The strongest and most persistent criticism, which came from the mine owners, was against these three concessions.

In 1881 the liquor concession was given to Alois Nellmapius, a friend of Paul Kruger, in return for a payment of £1 000 annually. With the establishment of a huge mining labour force on the Rand, to whom large quantities of liquor were sold, Nellmapius made huge profits. In 1892, however, the liquor concession passed on to the partnership of Sammy Marks and Isaac Lewis, who also continued to make huge profits.

The dynamite concession was granted to Edward Lippert in 1887. It specified that he would import the raw materials from Europe, but manufacture the dynamite locally. Although he contravened the agreement by importing the finished product from Europe, the government did not act against him. The mine owners complained that the dynamite was of poor quality and was responsible for a spate of mining accidents. Again, the government would not act. Instead, it pronounced the dynamite 'safe' and continued to support Lippert's concession. British government complaints did not help either.

Lippert continued to import dynamite and the number of mining accidents escalated. Finally the government relented and revoked Lippert's contract in August 1892, but delays in awarding a new concession led to a severe shortage of dynamite, which in turn added to the mining companies' resentment of the government.

In 1894 the Anglo-German Nobel Trust obtained a monopoly over the manufacture of dynamite, gunpowder, ammunition and explosives. The mine owners continued to complain that they were paying much more for dynamite than they would in a free market. Moreover, most of the profits from the sale of dynamite to the mines were going to Europe instead of to the ZAR government. Repeated requests by the Chamber of Mines and the British government for the ZAR to abolish the concessions were ignored. Instead, the dynamite concession was to be renewed for a further fifteen years. The government was reluctant to abolish the concession policy, partly because certain individuals gained financially from shares and bribes. Also, the dynamite company was a major source of government revenue.

Another equally important concession was that granted for the construction of railways. In 1886, when gold was discovered, what was soon to be the Rand had no railways. All transportation was by ox-wagon. Clearly a railway network was urgently needed for the development of the mining industry. In 1887 the Netherlands South African Railway Company (NZASM) was awarded the concession to build railways in the ZAR. NZASM was to build a railway line from Delagoa Bay to the Rand first, before lines from the southern coastal ports could reach the Rand, Kruger insisted. But progress was hampered by delays and financial difficulties. Instead, therefore, the Cape government financed railway construction from the Cape. By 1890 railway lines from the coastal towns were beginning to reach the ZAR and the Orange Free State.

This long-standing conflict between the mine magnates and the Kruger government over monopolies, especially the dynamite concession, was one of the reasons the British administration put forward for the war against the ZAR in October 1899.

OPPOSITE TOP: *Limpopo's Thulamela was a flourishing citadel 600 years ago. This picture shows the walls and the grave of the queen, whose remains were adorned with gold jewellery.*

OPPOSITE MIDDLE: *The mountain at Mapungubwe, with its spectacular view, is now a World Heritage Site in Limpopo. Mapungubwe was the centre of the largest kingdom in the subcontinent, with a population of 5 000, trading in ivory, copper and gold. Following an abrupt climate change in the fourteenth century, the people of Mapungubwe migrated to the superior rainfall area of Zimbabwe, where they may have founded the Shona civilisation.*

The Progressives also demanded a substantial lowering of the franchise qualifications, convinced that the Uitlander demand for the franchise was only a bluff and that they would not sacrifice their British citizenship for the vote. But, prepared as Kruger was to modernise the state, he drew the line at franchise reform. By now there were some 44 000 white foreigners in the ZAR, 28 000 from outside South Africa. These Uitlander males, according to some estimates, outnumbered the burghers eligible to vote.

Kruger himself believed that there were 60 000 to 70 000 Uitlanders and about 30 000 burghers. Perception was what counted. Bold reform of both the severe franchise qualification and a concession on the price of dynamite would have eased much of the agitation against the ZAR. But Kruger obstinately refused to change his position until it was too late. Jan Smuts noted at Kruger's death that 'he typified the Boer character both in its brighter and darker aspects'.

Kruger's reluctance to reform the franchise became the pretext for British aggression, led by Joseph Chamberlain and Alfred Milner. They wanted war not so much because Kruger was obstinate and blocked rapid development, but because he was flexible and pragmatic on most issues and because he appointed bright new men – of whom Smuts was one – to modernise his administration. Left to itself, the ZAR would soon dominate South Africa. This was a prospect that Milner had to prevent, even if it meant war.

CHAPTER EIGHT

Gold and war

The story of gold

The gold reef, a part of which George Harrison discovered on the farm Langlaagte on the Witwatersrand, changed South Africa forever. The discovery of diamonds and gold launched the mining industry and an industrial revolution. Diamonds, coal, gold – all were of great economic interest to the world power, Great Britain. In South Africa new socio-economic classes were formed in the 50 years following the establishment of the gold mines. The period saw the making of magnates and migrants, of millionaires and bankrupts, shopkeepers and entrepreneurs. It also saw the emergence of a new working class – one that was deeply divided along both colour and social lines. Only in the workplace would black and white workers meet, in predefined, strictly hierarchical relationships.

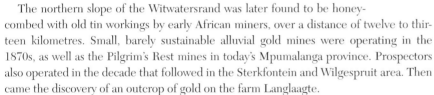

Gold had been mined in South Africa for centuries before colonisation. The finely wrought gold in Mapungubwe and Thulamela and other ancient sites in Limpopo four or five centuries ago provides ample evidence of this. There had also been discoveries by prospectors from 1834 onwards. White prospectors found traces of gold in 1852 and 1853 in the west, and then again in 1870, when Henry Lewis identified a gold-bearing reef on a farm called Blaauwbank. Later prospectors came across circular shafts on the farm Rietfontein (in today's Ekhuruleni).

The northern slope of the Witwatersrand was later found to be honeycombed with old tin workings by early African miners, over a distance of twelve to thirteen kilometres. Small, barely sustainable alluvial gold mines were operating in the 1870s, as well as the Pilgrim's Rest mines in today's Mpumalanga province. Prospectors also operated in the decade that followed in the Sterkfontein and Wilgespruit area. Then came the discovery of an outcrop of gold on the farm Langlaagte.

So promising was this find that public diggings were declared in April 1886. Soon after the Main Reef was discovered in 1886 it was found to extend nearly 50 kilometres to the east and the west through Langlaagte. The tent town of eager (whites only) prospectors from far and wide grew quickly. The town was named after Johann Rissik, acting surveyor-general, and Johannes Pieter Meyer, field-cornet of the ward. It almost instantly grew into a city *(see box)*.

The enthusiasm waned somewhat in the next few years as the growing prospecting population, numbering thousands over that time, realised that plentiful as the deposits of gold ore might be, it was spread thinly in the ground, and that the thread of gold dipped unevenly, going deep down underground. As with Pilgrim's Rest, this began to look like another short-term windfall.

The rise of mining corporations

At this point the finance capital of the world, London, stepped in. The international currency had been fixed to a gold standard, and new technology involving a cyanide amalgamation process to refine the extracted ore ensured that deep-level mining in South Africa

ABOVE: *The woven golden bracelet found on the forearm of a woman of Thulamela, believed to be the king's sister. Altogether, 291 golden beads were found in her grave, the remnants of a multiple stringed bracelet or necklace.*

JOHANNESBURG: AN INSTANT CITY

Gold was discovered on the Witwatersrand in 1886. Never before in world history had a mineral discovery so suddenly and dramatically, and so utterly, transformed an obscure rural backwater and shaped a new country. Gold became the foundation of the monetary system of the industrialised nation and was to dominate the South African economy and its politics for many decades.

Almost overnight Johannesburg turned from a mining camp into one of the most dynamic and volatile cities in the world. There was a virtual explosion of industrial enterprise. Backed by large-scale investment, particularly from Britain, 44 mines were in operation in 1888, with a nominal capital of nearly £7 million and an output worth more than £1 million. By the end of the century the Witwatersrand mines were producing a quarter of the world's gold.

In the early 1890s the industry was employing more than 100 000 men. Johannesburg had a white population of 50 000, only 6 000 of them Afrikaners. The great majority of the rest were British. The gold mines drew avaricious moneymen, schemers and criminals along with miners, white and black. They played host to the mining house magnates, the so-called Randlords, and at the bottom, the flotsam and jetsam.

In the city there were nearly 300 bars, many with back premises that catered to commercial sex. The streets teemed with diggers, prostitutes, gamblers, saloonkeepers, washerwomen and domestic servants. The Afrikaner poor were migrating in a steady stream to the cities to take up jobs as brick makers, cabdrivers and transport riders. Kruger set aside Vrededorp as a suburb for them.

Marching into Johannesburg in 1900 with Lord Roberts' forces, Winston Churchill wrote: 'The whole crest of the Rand ridge was fringed with factory chimneys . . . Before us sprang the evidence of wealth, manufacture and bustling civilisation.' The ZAR had been transformed, along with the rural areas. By the end of the century between a third and a half of the land in the ZAR had come into the hands of foreign individuals or companies, who preferred blacks to burghers as tenants on their land.

would be feasible – but at a cost. Individual prospectors were soon wiped out, for deep-level mining, started in 1895, required massive international capital and resources, justified by the certainty of cheap black labour within southern Africa and a plentiful supply of customers in the international market place. The hour of the mining corporations had arrived. The men who ran them would become immensely wealthy and would soon be called the Randlords (see box).

The gold standard meant that the fixed price of gold could not be dictated by supply and demand; the mining companies had to find a way of cutting costs. This was not an easy undertaking. Aside from expensive, imported high-tech machinery entailing vast sums of capital, administrative and technical skills were crucial. Artisans were in short supply in South Africa and had to be recruited from the coal and gold mines of Britain and Australia. They brought with them a militant craft union experience, and could – and did – demand relatively high wages.

In addition, hundreds of thousands of labourers were needed to dig shafts, hammer (and later drill) holes into the rock. The process was labour intensive; after the rock had been blasted, labourers were required to 'lash and tram' the ore and haul it to the surface so that it could be refined into gold. The mining industry thus found itself, as Jonny Steinberg remarked, in 'an unenviable position of classifying itself as both capital and labour intensive'.

The mining corporations set about creating a labour supply of lowly paid semi-skilled labourers that would balance the high costs of the high-tech machinery and skilled artisans. Several factors assisted them. Struggles for land during the nineteenth century left a largely vulnerable black population. They had experienced an era of warfare involving the defence of their land and cattle against Mzilikazi's warriors, trekkers, British troops, colonial and Boer annexations.

Against this background, the mines were able to extract labour with ease. They were also able to benefit from the experience of diamond mining. For one thing, the diamond mines had established a pattern of migrant labour, and their closed compound system was adapted to the gold mines on a greatly enlarged scale.

Recruiting migrant workers

In the early years the mining companies were guided by Cecil John Rhodes, mining magnate, ardent imperialist and for a time prime minister of the Cape Colony. He facilitated the labour supply through his Glen Grey Act of 1894, a policy designed to force black

Within a few years of the discovery of gold in 1886 the gold mines of the Witwatersrand brought riches undreamed of to the government and to the Randlords, a relatively small group of financiers and magnates at the apex of the mining industry. Gold made some so rich that the London newspapers referred to the top 20 or 30 as the Randlords. They had not become wealthy through luck but were people with remarkable financial and administrative talents. Several had cut their teeth at the diamond mines of Kimberley where they applied the latest techniques and scientific knowledge in overcoming difficulties. They discovered the value of setting up a 'group system' – five or six main 'groups' or 'finance houses' that exercised control of several mining companies by way of the shares they held.

These groups had everything to gain by cooperating in some areas. There was no competition between corporations for markets, and companies could sell all the gold they produced. The profits they made were to a decisive extent determined by their ability to cut costs, particularly labour costs. Hence they formed the Chamber of Mines in 1887 to eliminate competition among them for labour. They also shared technological advances that brought down labour costs.

The mining groups were not united politically. Some were well disposed towards the ZAR, if not necessarily to Paul Kruger personally then to the progressive grouping in the

Volksraad, keen to reform the state. The most prominent were J.B. Robinson, who formed the Robinson Group of companies that did well on the West Rand; Adolf Goertz, a representative of Deutsche Bank, who founded the company that later became Union Corporation; Barney Barnato, who controlled Johannesburg Consolidated Investment; and George Albu, who founded General Mining and Finance Corporation, and whose house 'Northward' was designed by Herbert Baker.

Those Randlords opposing Kruger were all involved in deep-level mining, and felt hamstrung by the government's concessions policy and other inefficient practices. The major mining house was set up by the partnership of Alfred Beit and Julius Wernher. They controlled the London-based company Wernher, Beit & Co. and the Johannesburg-

based H. Eckstein & Co, commonly referred to as Corner House. The two most prominent publicists of the anti-Kruger Randlords were both attached to Corner House – Percy FitzPatrick, author of *Jock of the Bushvold* (1907), and Lionel Phillips. Also opposing Kruger was Abe Bailey, a speculator and stockbroker.

Cecil Rhodes formed Goldfields South Africa as early as 1887 but was seldom seen in Johannesburg. The Anglo-American Corporation was only formed in 1917. Sir Ernest Oppenheimer became the greatest mining magnate of the century and a noted philanthropist. He took the lead in moving the headquarters of his company from London to Johannesburg, positioning it as a genuinely South African company.

The 'South African millionaire' became a stock figure in London musicals. The mining magnates were lampooned and demonised. They successfully resisted trade unions on the mines until the 1920s, which made them hated figures in the eyes of both workers and nationalist politicians. D.C. Boonzaier, a cartoonist on *De Burger*, created the character Hoggenheimer to capture that sentiment. Geoffrey Wheatcroft wrote in his book on the Randlords: 'Hoggenheimer was the archetypal Randlord, the rich and greedy exploiter of government who manipulated government for his own ends. Ernest Oppenheimer was generally assumed to be the target of the Hoggenheimer cartoons.'

THE MAGNATE'S FEAR.

OPPOSITE: *Langlaagte, Johannesburg, was the scene of early surface diggings. The landscape was to change dramatically when British capital invested heavily in deep-level high technology mining.*

ABOVE: *The Randlords' astonishing success brought undreamed of wealth to the Transvaal government, but it came at a price because the Randlords threatened to become more powerful than the state itself. Here a Transvaal government magistrate hears competing claims by small prospectors, while a Randlord, the real winner, looks on.*

LEFT: *D.C. Boonzaier's cartoon character Hoggenheimer. This cartoon shows two competing groups of workers – white and Chinese – played off against each other for the benefit of the mine magnates. It appeared in the* South African News *in 1904, with the caption: 'Keep him down, or he will ask for the vote.'*

RIGHT: *An early recruiting station in a rural area. Financial success depended on minimising labour costs. The Chamber of Mines developed a system of recruiting black labour throughout southern Africa.*

BELOW: *Early gold mining in Johannesburg, showing offices and mine shafts (top), crushed ore being unloaded at the surface (centre) and the pouring of smelted and purified gold (below).*

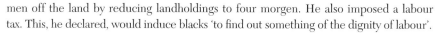

men off the land by reducing landholdings to four morgen. He also imposed a labour tax. This, he declared, would induce blacks 'to find out something of the dignity of labour'.

The migrant system in the diamond fields had proved to be the cheapest form of labour supply. Unattached workers justified lower wages. By supplying the minimum standards of accommodation and a very basic food supply, companies could drive wages and costs down further. The pass laws, introduced in the eighteenth century to control the movements of slaves, were now used to prevent black workers from absconding or moving around to find the best price for their labour.

The Chamber of Mines was directly involved in the recruitment drive. Touts were employed to visit the villages to recruit labourers. Working on commission, the recruiters, personifying a dazzling image of wealth and modernity in their three-piece suits, developed the dexterity of con artists. To disillusioned miners, they became known as *digalajane* (the deceivers) who promised high wages and good working conditions. 'The cows have udders. Come and milk them,' they urged their audiences.

In these ways, an oscillating work force was created. It was not permitted to be permanent, nor was it able or allowed to acquire formal skills, which might lead to higher wages for black miners. They were also prohibited from forming trade unions. New recruits to the mines were given the bare minimum of information and training, including the scarcely basic rudiments of communication in an artificial lingua franca. Fanakalo ('do it like this'), which consisted of instructions and commands, became the hybrid language of black labour on the mines. The most common method of instruction was the officially sanctioned use of the sjambok (leather whip).

Black miners were never given an understanding of the industry as a whole, much less a sense of ownership in the challenges and opportunities in mining. They were told just enough to enable them to function underground. The mining industry therefore bequeathed a short-sighted, inefficient, unskilled and easily replaced black labour force, rather than a skilled and more productive one.

The white labour force

For whites who entered the mines without skills there were hardships. They mostly settled in the poorer, multiracial pockets of the underclass. Afrikaners from the countryside could not find work easily as they did not have industrial skills or the language of the economy, English. Nevertheless the more resourceful turned their rural skills into saleable commodities – brick makers identified clay soil in Newtown, others transported agricultural produce to feed the townspeople. In later years, as Afrikaners recovered politically and gained ascendancy after the 1924 general elections, many found employment in the police force and on the railways. Administrative and corporate work was mainly assigned to the English-speaking.

It was to white miners that the skilled work was assigned. Artisans – engineers, plumbers, carpenters, builders, drillers and supervisors – mostly English-speaking immigrants, held the top jobs, demanding what mine owner Sir George Albu complained were 'exorbitant rates'. 'Why not make the native the real miner?' he asked, 'and thus save much of the money paid to white men for work they never perform?'

In 1907 skilled miners downed tools when the mining companies required them, in a cost-cutting exercise, to increase their tasks from supervising two black drillers to supervising three – work that had once been accepted as skilled work but was now defined as unskilled, and given to workers who earned one tenth of the wage of the skilled white worker. The skilled miners lost that strike. Supervisors did not require much training, and mine managers were quick to turn to Boer refugees from the devastation and land loss of the South African War of 1899–1902.

Although the Afrikaners did not have industrial skills, they had experience of supervising black labour tenants or sharecroppers. They were recruited to break the strike. The outcome was that the artisans pragmatically recruited these new supervisors into their unions, forming the first industrial union (as opposed to the craft unions that had existed before). They chose to combine as a racially defined category of workers to protect their rights against the super-exploited black migrant workers.

With the additional weapon of the vote, they voted into Parliament several Labour Party seats and in 1911 the Mines and Works Act set aside 32 certificated jobs such as engine drivers, carpenters, blasters and other skilled positions for whites, excluding not only blacks but also coloureds, who had formerly been allowed some concessions in the pecking order.

The background to this long period of crude capital accumulation was the racism that pervaded South African white society – from the new industrialists and the ruling class, to the increasing number of traders, clerks and administrators, right down to the artisans and semi-skilled white workers and those supervising black workers underground.

White workers felt their jobs were threatened by the low wages of black workers. They suffered from what Frederick Johnstone termed 'structural insecurity' – those without adequate skills faced the possibility that they could be fired and replaced by experienced, lowly paid black workers. It was this fear that propelled the new industrial unions to push for job reservation and regulations that allowed for training and apprenticeship for whites only.

LEFT: *Early white mine labourers, displaced from the land soon after the South African War, lashing and tramming underground. Note the absence of protective head- and footgear or torches. It was only when the craft union, the Transvaal Miners' Association, opened its membership in 1907 to unskilled white workers (replacing the criterion of skill with race) that working conditions underground began to improve. In 1911 four out of every 1 000 miners were killed in accidents in the gold mines. After the miners' strike in 1913, employers introduced an accident monitoring scheme and the death rate dropped to two and a half per 1 000. In the 1980s, an average of 600 mineworkers died every year on the gold mines.*

BELOW: *The impact of missionary education and industrialisation on an early twentieth-century family spans three worlds – the traditional, the transitional and the modern. Here miners are visiting their rural family.*

OPPOSITE BOTTOM: *Leisure time in a De Beers mine compound in the early 1900s. During the short periods of respite from labour, migrants often resorted to familiar, indigenous and comforting pastimes such as games like* bawu *or* mankala *and craftwork – an affirmation of home and identity.*

The price miners paid

Mining companies paid little attention to health and safety measures – on average, more than 700 miners would be killed in rock bursts every year. According to Gay Seidman's calculation 69 000 miners died from accidents in the mines from 1900 to 1993, with over a million dying from lung and infectious diseases. These ranged from tuberculosis and mesothelioma (commonly known as 'miners' phthisis' acquired from breathing the sharp dust particles of silica released from drilling the rocks) to pneumonia and infections from under-nourishment. The migrant labour system had little interest in the health conditions of black miners once they were home.

White miners, too, paid a heavy price. As full-time workers year after year, they did not receive the respite of even a month between contracts. The narrative of the white working class in the first half of the last century reveals the trauma of siblings, wives and children who lost their loved ones, miners who coughed their lives out in agony. In the early years of the twentieth century, it was found that the white rock driller could hope to live for five years – the average age of mortality was 37 years.

While white workers were given accommodation in family houses and cottages on mine property, migrants were corralled into hostel barracks or 'compounds', whose sleeping quarters consisted of 20 to 60 concrete bunks in each dormitory. The food supply was minimal – a bowl of *mieliepap* (stiff maize porridge) would be supplemented by meat and gravy only if the underground worker had hammered or drilled the obligatory 29 inches of rock per shift.

The work and families of migrants

The compound was designed to maximise control, with the compound manager's office placed in the centre of the courtyard to give him a panoptic view of the entire premises. The lock-up room, the three-metre-high fence and the one entrance and exit to the compound ensured forceful discipline.

At first, migrants who were sent by their traditional leaders in age cohorts were young and unmarried. Indeed, there was an element of pride in undertaking dangerous and difficult work, braving the deep bowels of the earth. For many Sotho, for example, going to the mines became a rite of passage, a test of their manhood prior to marriage. But as the cash economy became entrenched in the rural homesteads, more and more married men came to work to shore up the integrity of the homestead.

The reserves had become reservoirs of labour. Deborah James studied the songs of migrant women and found that they increasingly bore the responsibility of managing the homestead economy, raising the children and caring for the old, the sick and the unemployed. Women became de facto heads of household and in effect their unpaid labour subsidised the cheap labour of migrant workers.

As social coherence and the subsistence economy declined in the rural areas, the

How did migrant labour affect rural life? Migrant workers moved between two economies – the subsistence production of the rural homestead, and working for cash wages in the mines. Migrants used their wages tactically to buttress their rural families and protect them from dissolution and proletarianism. There are two words for work in Xhosa – *ukwakha*, work that builds up the family and homestead in the countryside, and *pangela*, meaning snatching short-term jobs by working for whites.

Remittances from migrant labour were crucial to the well-being of the rural homestead family. In the Tambo homestead in Pondoland, for example, the fortunes of the family declined in the early 1930s with the death of two able-bodied men as a result of a mining accident in Natal. Eventually the

homestead head, Oliver Tambo's father, Manchu, was obliged to sell his ox-cart and then his horses. He struggled to educate his children, for his other brother, who had contracted tuberculosis in the sugar plantations of Natal, had subsidised the education of his brightest two nephews. Yet, as head of the household, Manchu was able to maintain family coherence until his death in 1936.

By the 1950s, many married men were spending almost their entire working lives in the mines and cities. Alfred Qabula, trade unionist and poet, grew up in Flagstaff in the eastern Cape. He reminisced: 'I cannot remember my father well. I only have a faded picture of him in my mind. He stayed on the mines for long periods. We never saw him much. All the cattle, sheep and goats he

had, he bought with the money he earned down in the mines in Johannesburg, where the walls were singing.'

But migrant labour also brought cultural enrichment and cross-cultural expressions. Qabula recalled the excitement of the village at Christmas time, 'the only time people could afford to be together, because of the migrant labour system'. Everyone would return with 'something new'.

> I remember one year, the miners came back with a new dancing style learnt from the Bhaca people. In no time it was taken up by most of the youngsters in our area and it soon became a local way of dancing. We learnt the lesson that when you go somewhere you should come back with something new and progressive for the community. Even if you go to school you should come back with some knowledge to give to the people.

Often the women bore the brunt of the simmering rage of the men, who felt a deep sense of deprivation of their rightful traditional status. Qabula commented:

> That is how they used to be. [My father] used to explode on us and hold us responsible for his harsh life, of which we knew nothing. He and my mother would never stop quarrelling but my father never beat her.

authority of the traditional leader, the chief, was also undermined. Increasingly, their stipends held them hostage, making them accountable to the government, thus contradicting the saying that 'a chief is a chief by the people'. And so the bifurcation of the rural and urban was entrenched. It was the start of the widening gap between the 'two economies', identified as a continuing challenge by President Thabo Mbeki exactly a century later.

Aside from the reserves' supply of migrant labour, black refugees from the farms or displacees of the 1913 Land Act also came to the city to find work. They found humble work in the service sector – as domestic workers, laundrymen (the *amawasha* from Natal), delivery 'boys' for the trading stores, milkmen, cleaners for the shops and factories, and so on. They lived in the poorer areas, but in time segregated residential areas, known as 'locations', were set aside for blacks.

BELOW: *An eastern Cape newspaper announces the outbreak of war.*

BOTTOM: *Britain's colonial secretary, Joseph Chamberlain, who 'forced war on the ZAR'.*

A template for the country

The cost imperatives of the mining industry had initiated far-reaching change. Capitalising on a colonial and racially discriminating foundation, it set a socio-economic template for South Africa's secondary industries and urban life – hostels, cheap black labour, social control of black men and women in the city and the notion that even urban black workers were 'temporary sojourners' in the city. All these established the pattern of South Africa's political economy for the twentieth century and perpetuated racial consciousness and discrimination.

The war for South Africa

The South African War (Anglo-Boer War) of 1899–1902 remains the most terrible and destructive modern armed conflict South Africa has experienced. Its shock waves continued to be felt long after the conclusion of peace in May 1902, and it remains a powerful event in shaping the history of twentieth-century South Africa. One way to understand its significance is to view it, as some historians have done, as a conflict that was as important in the making of modern South Africa as the American Civil War was in the history of the United States. Provoked by imperial aggression, it marked the end of the long process of British conquest of South African societies, black and white.

The march to war

From the early 1890s politics in South Africa became increasingly polarised. This trend was accentuated when the Salisbury government gained power in 1895 and Joseph Chamberlain became colonial secretary. But the roots of war went far deeper. In many ways its origins lay in the discovery of diamonds and the rapid expansion of Kimberley in the late 1860s. The Kimberley diamond fields and the Witwatersrand gold fields and the industrial mining economy acted as magnets to British investment.

Britain, however, continued to steer clear of any major political confrontation with the republican leadership of Paul Kruger. All that Britain needed was to avoid being impetuous and to await the right conditions for the balance of strength and reason to shift in its favour. Movement towards an acceptance of imperial federation would give European Africa its own admirable version of the 1867 Dominion of Canada.

Gold and Anglo-Boer crisis

Things did not go exactly the way Britain anticipated. The discovery of gold in the ZAR in 1886 dramatically transformed the position and future prospects not just of the ZAR, but of South Africa as a whole. Within just a few years, the Witwatersrand mines had become the world's largest single source of gold, and the economic hub of the country shifted from land under the British Crown – the Cape Colony – to an independent republic on the highveld. Kruger was determined to use the revenue and taxes from surging industrial wealth to make the republic not only more modern, but also more self-sufficient and free to pursue its own destiny. From the outset this development looked ominous for Britain – it had no wish to see an independent republic become top dog in South Africa.

Externally, the ZAR lost little time in translating its new economic power into independent action. In 1894, it completed an eastward rail link from the Witwatersrand to Delagoa Bay, giving it access to the coast beyond the British sphere of influence and threatening the trade revenue of their colonial ports. In addition, the republicans imposed heavy duties on goods trains entering from the south, and erected other obstacles to frustrate free commercial traffic from British territory.

As if this were not enough, Pretoria also began to extend political and commercial relations with Germany, one of Britain's great power rivals. One symbol of the increasingly close ties between Pretoria and Berlin was the role of German capital in assisting the formation in 1894 of a ZAR National Bank. For politicians and imperial officials in Whitehall such moves were profoundly disturbing to an existing order of exclusive British power in the region.

Although historians continue to differ over which factors are to be considered most crucial in causing the conflict in 1899, the mining wealth of the Witwatersrand cannot be anywhere other than in the centre of the picture.

By 1898 South Africa produced more than a quarter of all the world's gold, making it a more vital market for British investment and trade than any other country under imperial influence, such as Australia or Canada. To sustain the riches of London as the financial capital of world trade, Britain needed a secure, efficient and prosperous gold-mining industry that could be counted on to send its supplies of ore to the Bank of England and not to the Berlin or Paris vaults of its imperial competitors.

The Kruger government recognised that it was the tax revenue of the mines that was enabling the ZAR to become prosperous. Accordingly, it did what it could to provide profitable industrial conditions, while remaining attentive to the cries of rural Boer land-owners that mining should not be allowed too great a share of the spoils, particularly cheap black labour. Yet, its measures in support of industry were not enough to appease the increasingly discontented, British-dominated mining industry.

Fearful of being swamped politically by an urban swarm of European immigrants who had little in common with Boer society, the ZAR authorities stood firm on excluding them from easily obtaining citizenship rights and political power. This infuriated Johannesburg Uitlander interests and the imperialist press in Britain, which began to campaign against what was depicted as ill-treatment of and discrimination against the Uitlanders. This movement was presented as a unified British imperial cause, although not all Uitlanders were British, and they included anti-capitalist radical miners and artisans who despised the British Empire even more than Boer republicanism.

The Jameson Raid

As anti-republic imperial attitudes hardened by the mid-1890s, restless and perpetually scheming figures decided that the time had come to force a showdown with their Boer opponents. In 1895 the obtrusive Cecil Rhodes, by now premier of the Cape, cooked up a secret armed plot to topple the Kruger government and tip the ZAR into Britain's lap. Rhodes's shadowy sponsorship of an armed expedition amounted to a high-level imperial conspiracy, suggesting at the very least some common purpose between imperial and capitalist interests.

The plotting of a raid on the ZAR implicated Colonial Secretary Joseph Chamberlain and his South African high commissioner, as well as a group of mine owners and Randlords who wanted to replace the Boer government with one that could be influenced more easily by the British business order on the Witwatersrand.

The plan was to stage an Uitlander rebellion as a pretext for a small colonial force to rush into Boer territory in order to protect victimised British nationals against republican reprisal. Such a crisis would give Britain an excuse to intervene directly and assert its authority over the republicans. It was led by one of Rhodes's more militarily incompetent associates, Leander Starr Jameson, and was a complete fiasco. The Uitlanders failed to rise in time as arranged, and Boer commandos easily rounded up Jameson's stranded raiders. Not for nothing has the Jameson Raid been described as one of the great 'cockups' of modern history.

The consequences of the Raid were dismal for the British. Disgraced, Rhodes had to resign as prime minister and never really recovered his power. Britain was condemned internationally for getting itself implicated in a grubby conspiracy

BELOW: *The hopeless military plotter, Dr Leander Starr Jameson, later became prime minister of the Cape Colony.*

BOTTOM: *British imperial adventurism ended in disaster when the Boers squashed the Jameson Raid.*

against an independent, European Christian state. For the empire's domestic critics, the scandalous Jameson invasion proved that Britain had no credible claim upon political morality or principled conduct. In South Africa, far from toppling Paul Kruger, Jameson's bungled intervention merely strengthened his position, boosting his previously fragile electoral popularity. Amidst steadily deepening republican suspicions of imperial intentions, the ZAR now beefed up its standing defensive alliance with the Orange Free State.

In both republics, as well as elsewhere in the region, the failed Raid intensified anti-British imperialist, republican and nationalist feelings within Boer populations. There was even some black support for Boer rights to independence. For Cape journalist John Tengo Jabavu, British plotting to bring down the Boers was just as unsavoury and illegitimate as earlier actions to crush the independence of black people (*see box*).

Most important of all, though, the Jameson Raid taught republican leaders a practical lesson – to prepare for a war that looked as if it might well be just around the corner. In 1897, the ZAR concluded a new military treaty with its Orange Free State ally, pledging mutual support against any external threat to republican independence. At the same time, it embarked on a costly defence programme, stocking up on war supplies and re-arming its forces with modern weaponry, imported mostly from Germany.

Meanwhile, in dealing with the simmering discontent of its Uitlanders, the ZAR was shrewd enough to use both carrot and stick. After 1896, its ruling elite began to do substantially more to accommodate mining needs. At the same time, while the Boers were merciful in their treatment of offending Uitlander rebels and conspirators, immigrant

JOHN TENGO JABAVU'S DISSENTING VOICE

Although the educated black elite supported the British cause, there were dissenting voices. The most prominent of these was John Tengo Jabavu, the influential Mfengu owner and editor of the eastern Cape newspaper, *Imvo Zabantsundu*, founded in King William's Town in 1883. By instinct a humanitarian and a pacifist, Jabavu remained highly

John Tengo Jabavu

critical of British war policy throughout the conflict. In lengthy polemical editorials he argued that the British government had fallen under the influence of irresponsible war factions. The war that had been deliberately provoked was, he declared in disgust, nasty, brutal and wasteful. For the *Imvo* editor, crushing the Boer states solely for the purpose of enforcing British supremacy throughout southern Africa was morally illegitimate.

Jabavu was equally scornful of imperial propaganda claims that war against the republics was intended to bring about political and social reforms to ease the position of their black inhabitants. These claims were, he declared, fraudulent. In a justly famous and perceptive comment in December 1899, *Imvo* stressed that while blacks in the ZAR did not have the vote, the war that was being waged was certainly 'not intended to give them the vote'. In Jabavu's words, African interests were 'outside and distinct from the conflict', and the best that could be hoped for was that due account should be taken of black rights in any final peace settlement.

Appealing to notions of educated commonsense and enlightened rationality, he called repeatedly for peaceful negotiation and arbitration of the Anglo-Boer crisis. This was the position of many liberals, and

naturally his paper featured the anti-war speeches of British Radical Liberals like Lloyd George and Henry Campbell-Bannerman.

At the same time, Jabavu's rejection of war was shaped not only by his deep pacifism. His contempt for Rhodes and strong political association with leading Cape liberals like John X. Merriman and J.W. Sauer who were critics of imperial intervention placed him squarely in the camp of Anglo-Boer conciliation. Indeed, shortly before the outbreak of war he had even been toying with the concept of an African electoral alliance with the Afrikaner Bond.

Inevitably, in a hardening war climate this stubbornly independent and nonconformist position soon got Jabavu into trouble. Black opponents condemned him as unpatriotic and alleged that he was being bribed by the ZAR Volksraad. *Imvo* was burned in the streets by hostile readers and confiscated by military press censors. Losing the financial support of wealthy white patrons, its days as a pro-peace African paper were numbered. With martial law extended to King William's Town, military authority halted publication in August 1901. Jabavu was only able to resume publication in October of the following year, his fortunes much weakened.

political agitation was curbed. The republic steeled itself further against any meaningful constitutional reform that might jeopardise Boer political command.

For another two years or so, there was a stalemate, with no realistic sign of any resolution of the emerging crisis. Although neither side risked the kind of ultimatum or threat to start a war, the Raid had been a watershed moment. It was not so much that it made war inevitable. It was more that it illustrated how high the stakes were for Boer republicanism. Thereafter, republican mobilisation acquired the ideological cohesion and organisational will to ensure that if Britain wanted its way, it would have to be through war.

Meanwhile, while Chamberlain may have been too rash in throwing in his lot with Rhodes, he stayed in the game. Turning the Uitlander cause into a noisy British campaign for civil liberty and political freedom, the colonial secretary continued to force the pace in South Africa through tough diplomatic pressure. In 1897 he posted Alfred Milner as South African high commissioner. Aloof, arrogant and a self-proclaimed British Race Patriot, Milner was contemptuous of Boer republican claims. He also regarded the loyalty of the Cape Afrikaners as suspect, viewing them as part of a dangerous rump of 'Afrikanerdom' that would have to be flattened. This was not exactly a promising basis upon which to conduct reasonable settlement.

Anglo-Boer diplomacy

Along with his colonial secretary, Britain's prime minister Lord Salisbury was still wary of war itself and hoped that, once cornered, the ZAR would give in to threat or bluff rather than turn and fight. But the two were uncompromising on the assertion of British power. There was no question that the Boers would have to accept the imposition of imperial supremacy, if not peacefully then through force. If it came to war, it would have to be seen as unavoidable, as Boer refusal to compromise and accept political reform had made things intolerable for British interests. For his part Milner was soon scornful of what in 1898 he termed the waiting game. Accepting the inevitability of conflict, he worked hard to clear the decks for a war, which he wanted. In effect, the high commissioner and his political subordinates did whatever was necessary to undermine any remaining prospects of a republican-imperial compromise.

Fanning the fire with old and new complaints against the ZAR and denouncing it as a tyranny that had enslaved its resident British subjects, Milner turned a deaf ear to restraining voices. Pleas for respectful negotiation came not only from British colonial moderates, but also ZAR and Orange Free State reformists who favoured reaching an accommodation to avert war.

An intransigent Milner intensified demands backed by threats that the Kruger government give in on Uitlander franchise rights. But this only made the Boers dig in their heels. For the republic, that would amount to acceptance of British imperial supremacy over its internal affairs, and an end to its national autonomy. In a memorable observation, Paul Kruger declared that what the British really wanted were not franchise rights but his country.

By the last quarter of 1899, imperialists and republicans had reached the end of their tether. Milner concluded that the solution to Britain's problem in South Africa would have to be what he termed a purely military one. As in 1880, the republic would again have to take up arms to avoid being forced to submit to what in ZAR Attorney-General Jan Smuts's view would be a humiliating solution. British actions were certainly more than enough to force the Boers' hand. Ominously, by September the War Office had decided to despatch 10 000 troops to reinforce Natal and the Cape. This was accompanied by a brusque warning to the Orange Free State to remain neutral in the event of hostilities.

But this menacing brinkmanship strengthened Bloemfontein's support of Pretoria. With war unavoidable, both republics mobilised their forces at the beginning of October 1899 in readiness for a swift offensive in which they could have an advantage over enemy forces that were still assembling. Kruger and his Orange Free State ally President Marthinus Steyn then presented an ultimatum to London, demanding that Britain back off and consent to neutral arbitration to settle political differences. For the British Empire, long irritated at having to negotiate with what it saw as a primitive state run by Dutch farmers,

estimate formed of our power and influence in our colonies and throughout the world . . . [We], not the Dutch, are Boss.'

In September 1899 his cabinet agreed to a request from the government of Natal, engineered by Alfred Milner, high commissioner at the Cape, to defend it against a possible invasion by republican forces. He had been outmaneuvred. He was willing to hold a pistol against Kruger's head, but Milner and his colonial secretary, Joseph Chamberlain, forced him to pull the trigger. He remarked: 'We have to act upon a moral field prepared for us by Milner and his Jingo supporters.' Britain had to engage in 'considerable military effort – all for people whom we despise and for territory that will bring no profit or power to England'.

BOTTOM: *Marthinus Steyn, president of the Orange Free State. (Painting by Erich Mayer.)*

it was the last straw. On 10 October, republican terms were contemptuously rejected. Having resolved to land the first blow, the Boer republics declared war on Britain the next day.

It was what the British wanted, as they could now point to the Boers as the aggressors. For leading republicans such as Smuts and Jacobus de Villiers Roos, it was clear who was the aggressor and who the victim. In their passionate and imaginative 1899 propaganda piece, *A Century of Wrong*, they compared the British to vultures and jackals, motivated by greed to fall upon a peaceable and pastoral Boer society that lay before them like a wounded antelope.

For their part, having done so much to contribute to the outbreak of hostilities, Chamberlain and Milner were now full of confidence in the outcome. Along with so many others on the imperial side, it was their belief that the enemy consisted of simple farmers who could not possibly hold out for more than a moment against regular British troops. But the Boers were not about to roll over easily. A bitter and aged Paul Kruger told an American journalist that the war would amount to an apocalypse, as the price that Britain would have to pay to gain the Boer states would be far greater than it could ever have imagined.

Accounting for war

The path to a major Anglo-Boer clash was tortuous and involved conflicting interests and ambitions as well as ideologies. Exactly which forces were the dominant cause of war has long been a source of argument among historians. Still, there can be little doubt over some factors. The ultimate cause of war was not the responsibility of individuals like Rhodes or Milner, however powerful; all they did was light the flames. Nor was it all down to the Uitlander crisis; imperial concern over immigrant treatment and rights was essentially an excuse for British intervention to resolve the issue of absolute imperial authority over all of South Africa.

Even less was the war caused, as some imperial propaganda of the 1890s suggested, by Boer plans to exploit the ZAR's new strength to impose Afrikanerdom on the whole country. There was no basis for any such thing. Left alone, republican interests had no burning quarrel with British power and, as in the case of the Orange Free State, were quite willing to co-exist with it. Additionally, colonial Boers and republican Boers had their own regional political and social cultures and did not necessarily all wish to sing to the same tune.

Keeping gold supplies in view as a crucial factor, there is much to be said for a broad explanation of Britain's deliberate steps towards war in the 1890s. The ZAR had to be contained. Economic independence to back its republican sovereignty held out the troubling prospect of a wealthy and independent South African state beyond British reach. Its pursuit of policies of modernisation and economic protectionism spelled bad news for the preferential position of British financial interests and trade goods. The risk loomed of the British being squeezed out of Boer markets by German or French commercial rivals.

A parallel worry was the potential of the ZAR's new rail and port connection to Delagoa Bay. This opened a door for other great powers to deal with the Boers at British expense, including the nightmarish possibility of gold supplies being diverted to other European money markets.

These were not the only anxieties. Mozambican port development to service the ZAR had unsettling implications for naval strategy. With handy access to coal from the Boer state through Delagoa Bay, any rival European sea power could station its navy in the Indian Ocean and menace Britain's vital Cape maritime route. Finally, deep down, there was the issue of maintaining confidence in London as the world's financial and commercial centre and upholding the security and prestige of its empire. As the empire's global power began to decline in relative terms in the later nineteenth century, less and less could be left to chance. Given the critical significance of gold to Britain's international financial position, it needed the assurance of a friendly ZAR administration to look after the mining industry, just as much as it needed the assurance that South African bullion would end up in London.

No less assuredly, imperial supremacy could not be compromised anywhere, be it India or South Africa. As Chamberlain put it, if Britain's power in South Africa was challenged, it would put at stake its power and influence in its colonies and throughout the world.

Seeing off that challenge would mean war. Yet, as the British were about to discover, forcing war on a beleaguered enemy was not the same as being able to dictate its course.

The phases of the war

Although not responsible for bringing on hostilities, the Boer republics declared war first. Why? Going on the offensive was their best chance of attaining a reasonable settlement. It was vital to block a British advance on the republics as they had thousands of kilometres of exposed frontiers and too few soldiers and fortifications for an adequate defence of their territory. By acting quickly, before the British had properly reinforced their weak South African troop position, the Boers hoped to catch their enemy on the back foot. A deep invasion of the Cape and Natal before the November arrival of a large imperial expeditionary force would give the republicans an early advantage.

The Boer war plan was to carry the war to neighbouring British colonies and keep it going there, pinning down the British and checking their advance on the interior. That might produce stalemate. Leaders in Pretoria and Bloemfontein therefore gambled on inflicting a knockout blow, leaving a short war in which a weakened Britain would be obliged to make peace that would respect the ZAR's internal independence. Some in the Boer leadership, including Smuts, were hoping, too, for diplomatic intervention by European powers sympathetic to their cause to bring about favourable early peace terms. Should this strategy fail, Smuts anticipated a long and brutal struggle in which the Boers would have to be bled into submission. This bleak prophecy would prove to be accurate.

At first the conflict went well for the Boers. When war broke out, the republics were able to field around 50 000 well-armed and well-provisioned commandos against the precarious British, who had barely 20 000 troops at their disposal. Although an arrogant British command still expected a swift and smooth victory over what some imperial observers called a mob or rough tribe of Boer riflemen, they experienced a devastating shock. In the closing months of 1899, invading republican forces lunged deeply into British colonial territory, inflicting several major and humiliating defeats in battles with badly organised and poorly led British troops, and surrounding and laying siege to the Cape and Natal towns of Mafeking, Kimberley and Ladysmith.

A perceptive observer, Sol Plaatje, recorded the varied experiences of black and white townspeople trapped in Mafeking (*see box*). An assault on two fronts saw British garrison power knocked back and, with the assistance of colonial Boer rebels, the annexation of occupied frontier Natal and Cape districts as republican territory.

LEFT: *Lying low and shooting straight: Boer riflemen in battle.*

RIGHT: *In war, animals were a source of companionship as well as objects of luck and surreal humour: Boer commando with their armed mascot, a baboon.*

However, instead of exploiting their military successes by pushing on to gain more ground for political bargaining with the enemy, the Boers appeared to run out of steam. As their offensive ground to a halt and turned into holding positions within the British colonies, so conditions for forcing early negotiations evaporated. As the Boer armies eased up, they gave Britain time in which to mount a stiff counter-offensive.

As the Pretoria and Bloemfontein press celebrated the glorious gains of what they termed a just war blessed by God, the British were landing their first big Army Corps. London was determined to turn the tide quickly. Once again, though, an advancing imperial army found it unexpectedly hard going and had its nose bloodied. In battles at Modder River, Stormberg, Magersfontein and Colenso during November and December, most of the killing was done by the Boers and the dying by the British. Facing the grim spectacle of repeated defeats and a mounting toll of casualties, Salisbury's war secretary, Lord Lansdowne, described his country's war effort in South Africa as a national disaster on the greatest scale imaginable.

Still, for Whitehall it could be nothing but war to a victorious finish. Massive reinforcements were fed in to strengthen the campaign, forces were better organised, and ineffective generals were eased out of command. Early in the new year, Britain sent out a new chief commander, Lord Roberts, with Lord Kitchener as his chief of staff. Their arrival signalled a far more methodical and more ruthless campaign, supported by enormous resources. By early 1900, Roberts had amassed a field force of more than 180 000 soldiers, an invading army whose size was already not far off the combined white citizenry of the Boer states.

Rolling on relentlessly and breaking desperate republican resistance, overwhelmingly stronger British forces forced republican opponents back into their territory. In operations already becoming marked by increasingly indiscriminate harshness towards the Boer civilian population, by March 1900 Roberts's army was beginning to lay waste to the countryside, burning the homesteads, crops and livestock of Boers on commando service as punishment for not laying down arms.

SOL PLAATJE

On 17 November 1899, a resident of the besieged northern Cape town of Mafeking (now called Mafikeng) wrote in his diary:

> What a lovely morning after yesterday's rains. It is really evil to disturb a beautiful morning like this with the rattling of Mausers and whizzes and explosions of shells ... Goodness knows what these Boers are shooting: they kill on average only one goat, sheep or fowl after spending 5 000 rounds of Mauser ammunition – but very rarely a man.

This cool and ironic observation of life under siege came from Solomon (Sol) Tshekisho Plaatje, a 23-year-old black clerk employed in Cape government service. Confident, learned and witty, he had moved to Mafeking in 1898 and at the time of war was working as a court interpreter to Charles Bell, the town's resident magistrate and civil commissioner. During the Siege of Mafeking from October 1899 to May 1900, Plaatje maintained a diary. Written in elegant English, his daily observations provided a detailed record of siege conditions and an insight into the mind and feelings of a compassionate individual caught up in hostilities.

Only discovered and published in the 1970s as *The Boer War Diary of Sol T. Plaatje, an African at Mafeking*, this journal remains the only known eyewitness account of the war by a black observer. Plaatje's personal war chronicle vividly captured both the elation and the despair of wartime experience in Mafeking. In October 1899, he confided that in answer to the question 'of what I found war to be, I can say: no music is as thrilling and as immensely captivating as to listen to the firing of the guns on your side'. But as the siege began to take its grim toll on life, morale and possessions, Plaatje's mood grew more pessimistic and filled with distress by the deteriorating circumstances of black refugees trapped in the town. 'A miserable scene', he noted in March 1900, to be surrounded by 'hungry beings, agitating the engagement of your pity'.

While Plaatje did not mince his words in criticising Mafeking authorities for their high-handed dealings with blacks and lack of adequate emergency provision, his commitment to his varied official wartime duties remained firm, as did his loyalty to his employer. This put him on the spot, obliging him to maintain a difficult balance between sympathy for the grievances of his own Rolong people and his valued identity as a civil servant of the colonial government.

After the war, Plaatje went on to become the first secretary of the South African Native National Congress (later the African National Congress). In 1916 he published *Native Life in South Africa*, a book with several historical episodes illustrating African loyalty in South Africa to the British Empire. One of those was the war of 1899–1902 in which, Plaatje argued passionately, service as loyal subjects of the Crown had gone unrewarded.

Elsewhere, the republics' war effort experienced crushing blows in the field, such as defeat at Paardeberg and collapsing morale on the home front in the face of thousands of casualties and the loss of thousands of commandos taken prisoner. As Smuts had earlier concluded, the war had become little more than a seemingly endless retreat, led by disheartened Boer fighters who were abandoning their duty to defend their soil and fleeing homewards.

Intransigent Boer women, now often in charge of farms, condemned men for cowardice and urged them to return to the fight. Bloemfontein fell into British hands by mid-March 1900, and by June Pretoria and Johannesburg were occupied. Roberts assumed that the fall of their capitals would knock the heart out of the Boers, finally finishing them off. Yet some of his commanders were not so sure. They considered the republics to be too large, too rural, and their communities too scattered to be intimidated into surrender by the loss of distant symbols of urban identity.

So it proved to be. Although Roberts considered the conflict to have virtually come to an end by mid-1900, hostilities were anything but nearly over. Many parochial rural Boers felt little for the fate of their Afrikaner state capitals, seeing the conflict as a struggle to defend their homes, farming livelihoods and way of life. What this implied was grasped well by one British general, Sir Archibald Hunter. In his sceptical words, Roberts had annexed a country without conquering it.

It is, of course, equally true that the republicans had misgivings about the appalling costs of continued fighting. Early in June 1900 several influential Boer commanders,

ABOVE: *Author of the most moving and ironic African documentary record of the war, the Mafeking siege diarist, Solomon Tshekiso Plaatje.*

OPPOSITE TOP: *Victory for the Boers, defeat for the British: a tiled mural depicts the Battle of Colenso in December 1899.*

OPPOSITE BOTTOM: *The advantage for the Boers of holding the high ground is clear in this painting of the Battle of Colenso by Sylvester Reisacher (1862–1916).*

COMDT.-GENRL.
LOUIS BOTHA.
1900.

PAARDEBERG

among them Ben Viljoen and Louis Botha, had proposed to Kruger that the war be ended before Pretoria fell. Smothered by enemy superiority in men and equipment, the Boer armies were disintegrating, with thousands of commandos laying down their arms and accepting British surrender terms. If warfare continued, it could go on to devastate all of republican territory. A compromising Botha more than once wished to sue for peace without having consulted his southern Free State allies.

But younger and more tenacious generals like Koos de la Rey had no desire to throw in the towel. President Steyn, whose republic had suffered enormous destruction in its lost struggle for independence, sensed betrayal by the Orange Free State's ally. The ZAR's talk of peace was selfish and disgraceful, he concluded. Republican honour demanded that the Boers fight on, however bad the outlook. In the end, few were willing to break a combined ZAR-Orange Free State war undertaking. Yet Botha's underhand attempt at negotiations with the enemy left a troubling mark, sowing the seed of post-war mistrust of ZAR leadership.

If resisting Boers were down, they were not yet out. Although much of their military capability had been destroyed, surviving pockets of commandos remained committed to continuing armed resistance. Reorganising their combatants for irregular operations, the Boers switched to guerrilla warfare. By dispersing their mounted forces in small and fast-moving bands, republican generals planned a guerrilla campaign that would not only hurt British invaders on their territory, but again hit at the Cape and Natal by carrying the war back into the coastal colonies.

What ensued was nearly two years of effective guerrilla warfare. Staying on the run and living off what food and shelter they could scrape from the countryside, running commandos kept Britain's imperial army at bay with surprise attacks on columns, convoys and supply depots, sabotage of bridges, railway lines, telegraph links and other kinds of harassment. While they faced increasing strains and divisions over the costs of keeping up the fight, uncompromising nationalist patriots such as Koos de la Rey and Christiaan de Wet were of no mind to abandon hostilities. What they had left were the means to frustrate their enemy, denying Britain final victory for as long as possible. If war dragged on with no clear end in sight, there remained the faint hope of eventual diplomatic intervention, European aid or even a British loss of will to continue with so draining a colonial war.

Kitchener, who had replaced Roberts as Britain's commander-in-chief towards the end of 1900, grew both increasingly frustrated with this state of affairs and extreme in his view of what it would take to end the guerrilla struggle. In 1901 he even threatened to deport die-hard republicans to remote Indian Ocean or Pacific islands, and to banish Boer leaders from the country permanently, unless they surrendered shortly.

This was a wild bluff that in any event scared few commandos into giving in. Equally, by then Kitchener understood that the keys to victory lay not in threats but in a ferocious rural strategy to squeeze the life out of commando attackers. To isolate mounted bands from their essential agrarian lifeline of civilian food supplies, shelter and moral support, the British command adopted measures used in earlier colonial campaigns against Asian and black peasant opponents. These turned on the use of sweeping scorched earth tactics, destroying crops and livestock and burning thousands of farms. This policy, proclaimed in August 1900 by Lord Roberts, commander of the British forces, was intended to destroy Boer food supplies in order to starve the commandos into submission. Those who fell victim to this increasingly indiscriminate punitive policy included not only Boer families but also black farm tenants with their produce and animals.

Women and children, as well as a smaller number of older men who were uprooted from the land and turned into destitute, wandering refugees, were rounded up by British forces and deposited in a string of internment or concentration camps. The number of white and black inhabitants confined in this manner increased by many tens of thousands during the course of 1901. Even though not classed as combatants, their presence in hostile districts that housed roving commandos made them a target. In effect, by being placed in camps they were made prisoners of war. By removing embittered, anti-British civilians, burning homesteads and stripping the countryside of foodstuffs and other

LEFT: *A British prisoner of war camp. Although the war was waged with varying kinds of brutality by both sides, each regarded the other in the field as fellow human beings who could be taken prisoner. Black opponents, however, were shot if captured.*

OPPOSITE TOP: *Inspired by the American War of Independence, General Ben Viljoen waged a guerrilla campaign against the British in the eastern and northern Transvaal until his capture in January 1902.*

OPPOSITE MIDDLE: *General Louis Botha was one of the outstanding younger Boer commanders. His exceptional exploitation of terrain and mobility enabled him to hold out against the enemy to the very end of hostilities. Eventually accepting that the republican cause was lost, he advocated peace.*

OPPOSITE BOTTOM: *In the first major British victory of the war General Piet Cronjé's laager, containing women and children, was forced to surrender in February 1900. A British general remarked that after white flags were run up, so many men emerged from the ground that it resembled a mass resurrection. Here the Battle of Paardeberg is depicted in a tile mosaic.*

BELOW: *Paul Kruger. (Painting by Erich Mayer.)*

supplies, imperial commanders hoped to starve commandos of sustenance, breaking their will and compelling them to surrender.

The severity of clearance of rural areas was accompanied by more exacting methods of anti-guerrilla warfare. Kitchener's army vastly increased its intelligence capability and fenced off large sections of open countryside with barbed wire, blockhouses and other fortified posts, held together by sturdy lines of communication. By ensuring that fleet-footed Boers would increasingly run out of ground across which to operate, the British sought to counter the skilful and evasive guerrilla tactics in which their opponents, such as De Wet and De la Rey, had become so expert.

Squeezed into inhospitable terrain and caught between British lines through which escape became more and more difficult, shrinking bands of commandos were harried remorselessly by Kitchener's mounted columns, a strike force that at the beginning of 1902 consisted of well over 200 000 experienced troops.

To add to Boer woes, blacks on the southeastern and western fringes of the ZAR were turning on commandos seeking refuge on their lands, plundering provisions from homesteads and conscripting labour. Armed Zulu and Kgatla were growing increasingly sharp teeth. In April 1902 there was one ferocious confrontation in the southeast that had serious implications for the future of Boer fortunes. At Holkrantz near Vryheid a vengeful regiment of Zulu warriors fell upon a small commando camp, killing 56 burghers. It was an ominous indication of the deepening intensity of black resistance.

By early 1902 Britain's unrelenting pursuit of the war and intensifying Boer misery began inevitably to sap the will of the republicans to continue so ruinous and unequal a struggle. True enough, a hard core of commandos, backed by militant women in the camps and elsewhere, were committed to keeping combatants in the field. With lands cleared, homes burned and families locked away in camps, what was there to be saved by a compromising surrender?

Others like Smuts's close associate, the eloquent Deneys Reitz, perceived that the Boer cause was lost. Once a bitter *bittereinder*, with Smuts he had undertaken an epic commando trek deep into the Cape to assess prospects for prolonging the struggle. Reitz's powerful account of his war experiences, *Commando: A Boer Journal of the Boer War*, is probably the finest soldiering memoir of the conflict, and one of the great classics of twentieth-century war literature. In his painful view of early May 1902, there was nothing more that could be achieved by the remaining haggard commandos, short of clothes and equipment, and stumbling about in search of food.

By now, the Boers also had other nightmares to confront. Very high death rates for women and children in poorly run and unsanitary concentration camps appeared to threaten the very future of the Boer people. Awareness of such civilian suffering seriously eroded the morale of republican leaders. Then there was the deepening crisis of black hostility towards republican ownership and authority. Granted, the Boers could count on the loyalty of some personal farm dependants. But from the start of the war, black people had been collaborating with the British in ever-growing numbers, while high-handed and often brutal Boer conduct in the field towards blacks had gained them few friends.

Piet de Wet, younger brother of the more famous Christiaan, was born in 1861 on the farm Nuwejaarsfontein near Dewetsdorp in the Orange Free State. Although he began the South African War as a fairly prominent member of the Free State military command, he ended the war fighting on the side of the British against his own countrymen. He was not alone; 5 464 Boers labelled as 'joiners' by the *bittereinder* Boers enrolled with the British. Taking into account that the fighting Boers in the veld numbered 17 000 at the end of the war, the scale of what many Boers regarded as apostasy is clear.

De Wet's reasons for taking the drastic step were partly ideological. He argued that an early end to hostilities would save the volk from further ruin. He did not necessarily regard this as treason as he claimed that the republics' governments had ceased to exist after the British annexations and therefore he could not betray them. Although he was legally speaking in the wrong as the Boer governments did continue to exist as legal entities, de facto it appeared to many burghers like De Wet that the Boer governments were just being chased from pillar to post and had no real jurisdiction over their subjects.

His incentives were also materialistic because those who joined the British also shared in the looted cattle. As a keen cattle trader he welcomed the opportunity to build up his depleted stock.

In the post-war period Piet de Wet was widely despised by the *bittereinders* and particularly his brother, who refused to speak to him. For a while he served on the British appointed legislature of the Orange River Colony, but then disappeared into political obscurity. He died in 1929.

As conditions in the republics worsened, rural black resistance and assaults on farming communities and even isolated commandos became more serious and widespread. This produced, in the words of peace-minded Boer officials in 1902, an unbearable condition of affairs in many districts of both their territories.

As if that threat were not bad enough, the number of Boers who had lost faith in their war effort was growing fast. The really wounding development was collaboration with the British. Giving up by abandoning their arms and surrendering as *hensoppers* to sit out the rest of the war as peaceful neutrals was one thing. It was regarded as cowardice. Switching sides by enlisting in British ranks as joiners (as they were contemptuously termed) was another thing altogether. It was viewed as faithless treachery.

Boers who took up service with British forces and became rural guards and National Scouts, turning out against their former republican compatriots, were treated as traitors by die-hard *bittereinder* republican patriots. By the end of hostilities, there were no more than around 17 000 *bittereinders* still in the field. About 5 500 Boers had been recruited as collaborators by the British. Among them was Piet de Wet (*see box*), brother of Christiaan de Wet, one of the greatest Boer war heroes. In the last phase of the war, there was hardly a British column without its share of ex-commandos, teaching it the stealthy Boer way of war, such as muffling the hooves of horses. Like the black scouts and spies alongside them, they too had thrown in their lot with empire.

As searing divisions enveloped Boer society, coping with the burdening miseries of the war not only undermined the mood and allegiances of commandos. The challenge of continuing to fight and endure also affected relations between men on commando and Boer women. Much of the most militant anti-British resistance was sustained not merely by men but by nationalist Boer women. In farming areas, it was their domestic spaces that were invaded and wrecked by imperial forces, creating a sphere of female hatred and bitter resolve to continue resistance, despite the Orange Free State and ZAR being on their knees.

For the atrocities of scorched earth and the family sufferings of camp life created not merely cowering female victims but also female *bittereinders*, grimly determined to turn men from retreating or deserting and to stay in the patriotic fight. Indeed, there is an argument that the implacably hostile spirit of women more than matched that of more wavering male commandos, who at times had to be flogged into the front-line by their commandants or who would neglect duty to slip home to attend a cattle auction. In these uncertain circumstances, the moral fervour of irreconcilable women urging otherwise despondent men to stay in the battle was a notable element in sustaining resistance.

The end of the war

By 1902 leaders on both sides were prepared to end a wasting war and to conclude what would still amount to an honourable peace through a negotiated end to hostilities. The Boer war effort was all but flattened. In Britain, the public had become weary of the conflict, and for its government there was no political gain in its continuation. For Milner, the destruction of the conquered republics had gone far enough. Anything further would worsen prospects for reconstruction, and jeopardise an opportunity for reconciliation with the defeated Boers in order to prepare them for a post-republican future under the British Crown.

To achieve that, Britain was willing to accept that there could be no dilution of white political power. While Chamberlain had insisted previously that blacks be granted limited voting rights, Jan Smuts, not the British victors, drafted Article Eight of the Vereeniging peace terms. Clause Nine of the final peace proposals granted the former republics the authority to decide on franchise matters when they received a representative constitution of their own. This curtailed the political aspirations of those who were not white.

This was a pointer to the exclusivity of political power the Boers were soon to possess. Even if the Boers were unable to keep English out of schools and the courts, holding on to all the reins of voting power was a significant gain for them, providing some dividend for the agonising cost of keeping up hostilities.

With London willing to strike fairly generous surrender terms in return for the Boers signing away their claim to independence, Boer peace delegates accepted by 54 votes to six what became known as the Peace of Vereeniging in May 1902. Numbers of commando *bittereinders* who were still prowling the countryside were said to be shattered and distraught by this news, unable to believe that for all their sacrifice they had ended up as subjects of King Edward VII. Some even declared their loss of faith in God. Among other Boer fighters, now united with their families, there was rejoicing at the end of the dreadful conditions of the last months of the war. British troops were simply relieved that it was all over at last. Few wished to prolong their stay in South Africa, especially those who had been cursed and spat upon by enraged Boer women whose homes they had destroyed.

Almost three years earlier, a sombre Paul Kruger had warned that Britain would find conquering the Boer states no easy matter. In the sense that they were certainly not gained on the cheap, this was an accurate judgement. By the end of the war, the British had been obliged to mobilise almost 450 000 imperial soldiers to defeat Boer forces, which had been able to field roughly 80 000 combatants at most. Their extended resistance turned London's South African campaign into the largest and most costly war fought by the British between 1815 and 1914. This was a colonial war which Britain's Treasury estimated in September 1899 would require the despatch of at most 75 000 troops and funding of about £10 million for a campaign of two to three months. By the time the conflict finally ended, that cost had risen to £217 million. What this balance sheet reflected was the enormous military investment that the British Empire required to defeat two of the world's smallest agrarian states.

Unlike other African armies that had resisted imperial invasion, the Boers had been able to maintain a lengthy defence despite their huge numerical inferiority and economic

OPPOSITE: *General Piet de Wet not only surrendered, but was also subsequently accused of 'stabbing other Afrikaners in the back.'*

BELOW: *The January 1900 Battle of Spioenkop.*

THE WAR IN COMPARATIVE PERSPECTIVE

One view of the conflict is to see it as a confrontation between European enemies, which just happened to be fought on African soil. Like the American War of Independence a little over a century earlier, independent colonial patriots were forced to take up arms against an autocratic and bullying empire. Indeed, Boer generals studied the American war as an inspirational struggle for national independence. Just as the future position of Native Americans was never a factor in Anglo-American hostilities, so the overall maintenance of white supremacy was never a question for either side in South Africa.

Ultimately, it was an Anglo-Boer contest to decide who would have supreme authority over all of the country's minerals, productive lands and dispossessed black labour.

An alternative view of the war is that it represented a classic struggle of African underdogs against the greedy intervention of Great Power imperialism. After all, the most racist of imperial war propaganda stereotyped the Boers as a lower form of humanity. And British generals like Roberts and Kitchener knew well enough from crushing peasant resistance in Afghanistan

and the Sudan not to treat the republics' rural civilians with kid gloves.

In its way, therefore, Boer republican society was fighting essentially the same fight as other African peasant peoples like the Xhosa much earlier or, more recently, the Zulu. In this perspective, Boer commandos were a pale version of Zulu warriors, only with horses, rifles and corduroy jackets rather than spears, shields and leopard-skin.

Understandably, republican propaganda claimed that its war was an anti-colonial struggle, a message that attracted much sympathy in countries like Russia, Germany, France and the Netherlands where British imperialism was unpopular. *Land en Volk, De Republikein* and other Boer newspapers depicted mobilisation as the sacrificial struggle of a Christian, democratic nation in arms, its egalitarian citizen army of unpaid commando patriots upholding the best republican traditions of the eighteenth-century French Jacobins and American revolutionaries. For the Boers, too, it was a fight for liberties and independence against an old, aristocratic and degenerate foe.

Whether or not one agrees that there is something to be said for this argument, a

sceptical view might question the fragile basis on which the Boers were portraying their nationalist struggle. For citizens of the ZAR and the Orange Free State themselves represented a colonial society and could not escape its consequences. An independent republican existence rested not only on past seizures of African land and command of black labour. The Boer colonial position had to be sustained amid the upheaval of war.

Thus, in the mobilisation of October 1899, the armies fielded against the British represented only about 60% of republican fighting capacity. The other commandos were not resting at home; they were guarding farmlands against black intruders and garrisoning vulnerable Boer borders with potentially hostile black territories, such as Basutoland and Swaziland. Indeed, an atmosphere of fear and panic at spreading black hostilities against republican civilians and soldiers became one of the reasons given by Botha and Smuts for finally surrendering. In a region where four-fifths of the population was black, one could not fight a large-scale war without drawing blacks into the conflict.

ABOVE: *The reality behind the rhetoric – black riflemen with their white commander. Although both sides claimed to be conducting what they called a white man's war, thousands of black auxiliaries undertook armed duties.*

OPPOSITE: *The* agterryers *were blacks who served on the Boer side of the South African War. As servants of the Boers, they did menial tasks such as cooking food and tending horses. But quite often, they also performed combat duties and fought side by side with their masters. Many San men served their masters as* agterryers *out of loyalty, particularly in the former eastern Transvaal. But many others were provided for the burghers, commandeered by the governments of both Boer republics.*

limitations. The republics had been able to compensate for these drawbacks by exploiting their few advantages to the full. These included superb horsemanship which provided mobility and speed, an ample supply of modern firearms, excellent shooting skills and tactical flexibility that enabled Boer forces to duck away from damaging confrontations and to fight mostly at times of their own choosing and on terrain that suited them.

At the same time, the Boer armies also had disadvantages – for example, when it came to discipline and authority. Their democratic arrangement whereby officers were elected and commandos voted collectively to go into battle was not necessarily an asset when war began to go badly and soldiers became dispirited. Boer commandos were, after all, made up of citizen-soldiers: individual civilians with differing wants and priorities who did not even fight in uniform.

The more drilled, disciplined and obedient British army overcame its inferiority, but it took time to weed out bungling commanders and to get urban working-class recruits to stop feeding mutton to cavalry horses. When London prevailed at last, it came at the high moral and political cost of waging war against the rural families in the Boer states.

In spite of the severity of their losses, Boers did not come away from their traumatic struggle for a free existence entirely empty-handed – as the years after 1902 would prove. They would have the benefit of mild peace terms and generous reconstruction aid intended to foster Anglo-Boer conciliation. As a well-disposed Winston Churchill put it, Britain would welcome the day when it could take the Boers by the hand and watch them returning peacefully to plough their fields.

The second line of war: black involvement

In reality, whatever their sentiments towards the war, most rural and urban black people tried to steer clear of trouble and to stay neutral in the Anglo-Boer confrontation. At the same time, the increasingly total nature of hostilities made it difficult to avoid getting mixed up in the war, directly or indirectly. As warfare spilled through the countryside, many blacks found themselves in harm's way. Others were pulled into participating in military operations by the warring sides, choosing to serve in the war effort to escape extreme rural poverty or in the hope of gain or reward. Also,

ROLONG PARTICIPATION IN THE SOUTH AFRICAN WAR

On the eve of the South African War, the Tshidi branch of the Rolong was the largest group inhabiting the Mafikeng area of the northern Cape, numbering some 5 000 people. The Rolong sided with the British because of two decades of conflict with the Boers over land. Following a number of battles and six Boer sieges of Mafikeng during the 1870s and 1880s, most of Rolong-occupied land had been appropriated by the Boers. Consequently in October 1899 when Boer forces were about to invade Mafikeng, Rolong chiefs requested the commander of British forces in the area, Colonel Robert Baden-Powell, for arms and ammunition for their defence.

Initially, of course, the British military authorities prevaricated because this was a 'white man's war' and 'blacks should not be armed, and should not serve with British forces in a combatant capacity'. Eventually the 'massive threat' posed by Boer forces under General Piet Cronjé changed this policy and about 400 Rolong men were given Snyder rifles and ammunition. The coloured community formed their own defence contingent, the 'Cape Boys', while the Indians in the town were also armed and incorporated into the white Town Guard. Another two black groups, the Mfengu contingent and the Black Watch, were also given arms and ammunition. Each was assigned to defend a specific area of what is today greater Mafikeng.

Brian Willan has recorded that on 25 October 1899 the Rolong repulsed a Boer attack, killing an undetermined number of the attackers. Encouraged by this action, Baden-Powell gave the Rolong defenders extra rifles and ammunition and increased their number to some 500. 'On numerous occasions' the Rolong went on 'offensive operations against Boer positions, sometimes capturing guns and equipment'. Although nominally under the authority of Sergeant Sidney Abrams, the Rolong contingent conducted its own military operations, under its own command structure. It even used British-style military titles, such as field-marshal (Wessels Montshiwa), general (Lekoko Marumolwa), sergeant and corporal.

Blacks generally also acted as spies and dispatch runners, supplying the British military authorities in Mafikeng with vital intelligence about Boer commando activity. Those who got caught by the Boers, of course, ran the risk of being shot – and many of them were.

Although we now know a great deal about black and coloured participation in the South African War, San (or 'Bushmen') involvement is completely absent from the general historiography of the war. Recently, however, a few scholars, notably F. Prins, have begun the process of filling in this void, using mainly oral sources.

Oral accounts indicate that San participation occurred during the guerrilla phase of the war, following the implementation of Lord Kitchener's scorched-earth policy. In the Lake Chrissie area in the eastern Transvaal, for example, San farm labourers accompanied their Boer masters into battle as *agterryers*, but they were not armed for combat.

On 6 February 1901, during the battle of Lake Chrissie, Boer commandos under General Botha attacked the British forces that were deployed close to the little town of Chrissiesmeer. The Boer plan was to thwart the advance of the forces of General Smith-Dorrien into the eastern Transvaal. Oral tradition also relates that, using their intimate knowledge of the local terrain, San scouts constantly observed the movements of Smith-Dorrien's forces and reported them to the Boer commandos. For instance, they reported the location of British military camps. Although the death toll during the battle of Lake Chrissie was equally heavy on both sides, it should be noted that because of San intelligence, the British advance into the eastern Transvaal was delayed.

Oral tradition also relates that one night on Commandant Prinsloo's farm named Lake Banagher in the Lake Chrissie area, one of his servants, a San simply named Job, alerted Prinsloo's commando to the fact that 'he knew a secret way out of the lake and persuaded them to follow him through the mist ... In this manner the Boer commando managed to escape without any casualties.'

Only some San servants accompanied their masters to the war front, while the majority remained on their masters' farms. When the scorched-earth policy of the British forces came into practice, loyal San and Swazi servants took Boer livestock into Swaziland for safe-keeping – and herded the livestock back to their masters when the war ended. San servants who remained on the farms also carried out surveillance of the movement of British troops in the area and reported this to the Boer families on the farms. Such information was crucial because the movement of British forces around Boer farms was intended partly to pick up Boer women and children and take them into the much-dreaded concentration camps. Such information therefore enabled Boer women and children to hide as far away from British forces as possible, while being cared for and supplied with food by their San servants.

some became involved in hostilities with Boers on their own account, defending themselves against invading commandos, seizing opportunities to settle old scores over land losses or harsh treatment, and seizing opportunities for plunder.

Despite repeated – and hollow – declarations by both sides that the conflict was a concern of European opponents, British and Boer war efforts both made considerable use of blacks for skilled and unskilled labouring tasks and combat duties. Commandos were accompanied to the front by up to 12 000 black and coloured *agterryers*, or mounted personal servants. Loyal and trusted followers, these individuals served Boer masters as gun-bearers and ammunition carriers, and performed a variety of other field duties, including tending horses, maintaining weapons, scouting and dispatch riding, carrying rations and cooking, and treating and carrying wounded commandos.

Although of subordinate racial status, *agterryers* were often on intimate terms with their Boer masters, sharing the same clothing, food, tents and even musical culture. At times, under battlefield pressures and short of regular riflemen, Boer commandants swallowed hard and even posted armed skilled *agterryers* to front-line positions as combatants.

Understandably, black assistance to the imperial war effort was on a much larger scale, not least because the British military presence brought substantial wage employment. At least 100 000 black and coloured men, as well as Natal Indian medical corps volunteers under Mohandas Gandhi, were engaged by the army. Most served as transport workers, camp labourers and servants, scouts, dispatch runners, spies and depot guards.

Some women undertook domestic work for camps and garrisons, such as washing. Although the British conscripted some of these war workers for heavy labour, the majority were volunteers. These included migrant labourers who had lost mine jobs at the outbreak of war and peasants in desperate circumstances because of crop failures and livestock losses. Others were attracted by the prospect of relatively good wages or a belief in the rightness of the British cause. Many educated blacks were persuaded by British war propaganda that victory over the Boer states would bring more rights and a less discriminatory political and social order.

ABRAHAM ESAU

Abraham Esau was an independent coloured blacksmith and small transport driver in the northwestern Cape settlement of Calvinia. Educated in English at a Methodist mission school and strongly anglicised in character, Esau had established himself by the end of the 1890s as a lively, enterprising and articulate personality among Calvinia's coloured community. Through his small property ownership, his attachment to the non-racial Cape franchise and his entitlement to the status of a Crown subject and citizen, Esau in many ways embodied the essential character of the literate coloured artisan class of the liberal Cape Colony. Like many others of his kind, his loyalty to British rule and wholehearted support of a stable colonial order under Cape Liberalism was rock solid.

The war turned him into an individual of stature. By 1900 the spread of republican commandos raiding in the Cape was increasingly menacing the security of black civilians. As panic gripped Calvinia, its apprehensive coloured inhabitants became vociferously pro-British and anti-Boer republican. At the forefront of this increasingly anxious and belligerent mood stood an energetic and influential Abraham Esau, using his abilities as an orator and organiser to try to assemble resistance.

When the local magistrate refused to issue arms to coloured men on the grounds that the war exclusively involved whites, a dismayed and incensed Esau turned to another defensive tactic. He came to a clandestine arrangement with the British army's Namaqualand Field Force for his band of trusted followers to serve as a ring of spies and informers, providing information and intelligence on Boer movements and rebel activity. In reciprocation for this loyal and risky undertaking, a British military secret agent undertook to provide protection for Calvinia by imperial forces in the event of any Boer incursion.

It was a hollow promise. Calvinia was captured by an Orange Free State commando early in 1901. Being the district's most troublesome and detested British collaborator, Esau was a marked man. Brazenly defiant towards republican authority to the end, he was executed in February 1901. Although a minor incident in the war, the wartime conduct and killing of Abraham Esau became invested with political significance, his death turning him into a martyr and symbol of Cape coloured loyalty to the British cause.

ABOVE: *The Queen's coloured patriot, Abraham Esau of Calvinia.*

OPPOSITE: *Emily Hobhouse provided a powerful British voice against the inhumanity of total war against the civilian Boer population.*

As many as 30 000 men were armed volunteers with British columns or colonial town garrisons, and experienced deadly clashes with invading commandos. Others, like the coloured blacksmith Abraham Esau, were drawn into resistance through acting as spies and agents of the British (*see box*).

While warfare claimed the lives of about 7 000 Boer and 22 000 imperial troops, we will never know how many armed black participants perished in various actions. Nor, for that matter, is there a count of British collaborators summarily executed when caught by the Boers, nor do we know the number of republican collaborators who were the victims of irregular British reprisals, shot as spies. Yet the greatest human loss lay elsewhere.

For rural blacks, as for the Boers, it lay in Britain's concentration camps. Farm tenants, servants and peasant settlements whose livelihoods were destroyed by scorched earth tactics added thousands to the pool of war refugees. Interned in segregated camps where many inmates were compelled to provide labour service for nearby British forces, black refugees shared a fate in common with Boer families – atrocious conditions and high death rates. At least 20 000 blacks are now estimated to have died, mainly from epidemic diseases that cut down weakened camp inhabitants.

In this sense, the concentration camp experience could be seen as amounting to a common trauma for black and Boer societies, while not losing sight of proportion. Black civilian victims were a consequence of a British war waged against a Boer military and civilian front-line. Of the roughly 116 000 Boers housed in unsanitary and badly run white camps, some 28 000 died, largely from measles, dysentery and pneumonia. Almost all of the victims were women and young children. British humanitarian Emily Hobhouse did much to alert opinion worldwide to the appalling conditions suffered by interned Boers (*see box*).

In a highveld Boer society of little more than about 200 000 people, the impact of such enormous losses cannot be overestimated. In representing the lowest point of Boer

The terrible conditions in British internment or concentration camps were first brought to light in Europe by the pro-Boer British humanitarian and social worker, Emily Hobhouse, in dramatic and searing publications such as her 1902 *Report of a Visit to the Camps of Women and Children in the Cape and Orange River Colonies*. A staunch liberal pacifist, Hobhouse joined the anti-war South African Conciliation Committee at the outbreak of war and soon established the South African Women and Children Distress Fund in response to the first news of farm burnings and the evacuation of rural civilians to refugee camps. She first travelled to South Africa with clothing, food and other supplies at the end of 1900 and encountered rates of illness, suffering and mortality far worse than she had anticipated. On her return to London she produced a sobering account of camp conditions, distinguished for its cold factual reporting and restrained moral indignation.

Hobhouse soon found common cause with the leader of Britain's opposition Liberals, Sir Henry Campbell-Bannerman, who in 1901 drew on her revelations to de-

nounce his country's war policy as 'methods of barbarism'. While confining her probing to Boer camps, she was not unaware of the plight of refugees in black camps, and called for an investigation of conditions there. At the same time, Hobhouse was put out by the personal familiarity between some Boer families and the black servants who accompanied them in white camps. In 1902, in a rather racist tone, she deplored the 'undue familiarity' with which Boers and blacks were eating and sleeping together, 'all in the same tents'. But it is also interesting to note that, unlike the same conditions in the Boer camps, the conditions in the black refugee camps evoked no reaction either from the British government or from the British public. Similarly, in 1941, when the Dutch Reformed Church compiled the numbers of lives lost in the Boer camps during the war, Jacob Mohlamme records, 'it took no interest in the losses suffered by blacks, even though the Church had non-white members'.

In all fairness to Hobhouse, however, she did pass on information about conditions in the black camps to H. R. Fox-Bourne, sec-

retary of the Aborigines Protection Society of London, who suggested that the British government 'should secure for the natives who are detained no less care and humanity than are now prescribed for the Boer refugee camps'. The society suggested further that, because of the very high mortality rates in the black refugee camps, 'a committee of South African ladies should be appointed to visit and report upon them', just as the Fawcett Commission had recently done for the Boer refugee camps. Such noble suggestions seem to have been ignored.

Emily Hobhouse attempted another visit to South Africa in 1901 but on her arrival at the Cape was immediately arrested under martial law regulations and deported to Britain on Kitchener's personal instruction. Still, although her camp findings were dismissed as biased or exaggerated by pro-war critics, they created a political uproar in Britain, forcing the government into improving conditions. Hobhouse maintained a hallowed connection with Afrikaner people after the war, her ashes ending up appropriately at the foot of the Women's Memorial in Bloemfontein in 1927.

survival, the sufferings in the camps shaped one of this conflict's most enduring legacies – that of the pity of war, rather than of its imagined heroism or romance.

A violent engagement

While it would be misleading to call this a war in which everyone took part, the extent to which male and female civilians were drawn into hostilities, and the depth of black participation, demolish one older historical myth – that of 'a white man's war'. The brutality of the war's tactics, such as farm burnings, conditions in the camps and summary executions, overturns a second enduring myth – that the South African highveld saw the last of the European world's 'gentlemanly wars', fought with honour and mutual respect. It is more appropriate to view the South African War as the most violent and hostile battle between the British Empire and a South African community over more than a century.

For both sides the war was seldom a simple matter of a united national commitment to defeating a common enemy. British liberals like Emily Hobhouse and anti-war radicals such as Lloyd George denounced the inhumanity of their country's use of concentration camps as barbarism. Idealising the republics as a pastoral Eden in Africa, inhabited by virtuous white Protestants, militant British pro-Boers opposed the war as an unjust act of aggression. Their views were echoed in South Africa by prominent Cape English sympathisers such as Olive Schreiner (*see box*). Even in the British army there were soldiers who admired the Boers as worthy farmers and soldiers and disliked having to fight what they felt to be a war for the benefit of unscrupulous Johannesburg capitalists.

Republican leadership hoped constantly for a mass rebellion against British authority by Cape colonial Boers who, although British subjects, were expected to be largely disloyal to the Crown. But the idea of a big uprising by a rural fifth column turned out to be a

The Anglo-Boer crisis of the 1890s and the war it produced left a strong mark on Olive Schreiner, on the verge of making her reputation as a notable writer and feminist, and an acute commentator on South African life and politics. Forthright and impassioned, she lost no time in taking up cudgels and was well placed to do so, given her connections and the influences to which she was exposed.

Her brother W.P. Schreiner, the future Cape prime minister, resigned his post as attorney-general in Rhodes's government as a way of dissociating himself from the disastrous Jameson Raid. He subsequently did all that he could to try to avert what seemed after the Raid to be an increasingly inevitable war. Olive, meanwhile, turned on the aggression represented by Rhodes by contributing to a wave of pro-Boer literature inspired by the sordid Jameson episode.

Rising swiftly to prominence as a leading Cape pro-Boer, Olive Schreiner was a particularly powerful imaginative voice in exposing the brutalities and cruelties of the war, especially Kitchener's scorched earth and concentration camp policies.

Her views on the moral bankruptcy of the British cause were also influenced by the arguments of British liberal anti-imperialists like J.A. Hobson, for whom the war was a greedy expression of capitalist imperialism. Like other humanitarians or pacifists, Schreiner's admiration of the victimised Boers verged on patronising sentimentality, as in her memorable description of them as 'pure-blooded' Europeans 'descended from some of the most advanced and virile nations of Europe'. At the same time, her well-known wartime sympathies alienated Cape empire loyalists, both white and black. Writing from the Karoo at the end of the war, she grumbled about being unable to attract a domestic servant, despite offering a generous wage, for 'the natives here all boycott me'.

While a staunch advocate of Anglo-Boer conciliation, Schreiner remained wary of what she saw as the undesirability of a unified, centralised state emerging in the aftermath of the war. In letters to the *Transvaal Leader*, which culminated in the booklet *Closer Union*, she called for a loose, federal kind of South African union as a state more likely to preserve rights and freedoms. In the light of this, one of Schreiner's more telling warnings was of the danger of national circumstances in which 'nine-tenths of our community have no permanent stake in the land, and no right to share in our government'.

A writer who wielded her pen against the imperialist sword: Olive Schreiner.

pipe dream. Granted, some Cape Boers not only sent sons to serve in Orange Free State forces but also rebelled in support of invading commandos. In the course of the war about 12 000 men turned out as republican rebels, and the number of colonial collaborators might have been even greater if the thrust of republican invasion had been deeper. Yet their number remained too small to be of any decisive strategic consequence.

That said, the imposition of martial law to suppress rebellion did little to draw the angry sting of local pro-war Boers. The use of black and coloured witnesses in rough and ready special courts that tried and convicted rebels for offences such as high treason, murder and robbery, caused outrage. So did the practice of publicly executing convicted men, with rebel prisoners forced to watch. One execution, that of Commandant Gideon Scheepers in January 1902, despite his status as an Orange Free State burgher and a prominent officer, even prompted some British parliamentarians to question the propriety of the courts' martial procedures. Of the 30-odd Boers executed during Kitchener's command, most were rebel Cape citizens, as were the great majority of the other 500 who were sentenced to death but had the penalty commuted to varying terms of imprisonment.

Peace would bring further leniency. Under its terms, ordinary rebels in the Cape Colony lost only their right to vote for a brief period. Their rights as white citizens would eclipse misdemeanours like treason.

As for the war itself, too many Cape Boers were too realistic to fulfil republican expectations. For the most part, they found life as Crown subjects tolerable and remained reluctant to risk joining a republican war that they sensed could not be won. Tellingly, some colonial loyalists even enlisted in town guards and rural militia to defend their southern settlements against invading northern Boers.

Then there were the internal divisions of republican society. The source of deep animosity, their scars would remain long after the end of war. As the British onslaught cracked open Boer society, it opened up an increasingly raw gap between implacable *bittereinders* and compromising *hensoppers* about the acceptable terms of future survival.

This affected not only the conduct of the war itself. The issue of capitulation to, and collaboration with, British imperialism clouded even the conclusion of peace. More accommodating generals like Louis Botha were willing to break bread with the enemy, negotiating a surrender of their cause. More intransigent leaders, especially from the devastated

Orange Free State, remained contemptuous of what they considered to be weakness. To the end, for all Smuts's realistic assessment that what republicans faced was a catastrophic sacrifice of Boer people in a cause that could no longer be won, they were still all for going to the wire, resisting until they were battered into unconditional surrender.

The South African War ended clearly enough, with the Boers brought into line in a Transvaal Colony and an Orange River Colony, and British imperial supremacy victorious over the whole of South Africa. But its experience of agony and sacrifice would go on to haunt Afrikaner society in the twentieth century, providing the ideological tools of war remembrance that would play a part in the future rebuilding of an Afrikaner nationalist identity and republican political culture.

For the black majority, which was in theory not supposed to be party to the war, its outcome was mixed. True enough, it had for the duration of the war put bread in many mouths and even filled the pockets of those peasants who profited from the sale of livestock and crops to the British. Equally, for a great many others, there were grievous losses for which there was little if any compensation from the imperial side. Those who had been permitted to take up weapons were rapidly disarmed to ensure that they would not cause future trouble. But many others, such as the Kgafela-Kgatla, simply refused to hand in their weapons. Rebellious tenants who had seized stock or occupied land on the farms of the former republics would also be in store for an unpleasant surprise. All along, they had relished Britain's crushing of the Boers, believing that what they had seized would remain theirs. Instead, backed by the British South African Constabulary, returning Boers would be re-taking what they had lost.

In its reach into and across society, the South African War was the closest the country has ever come to experiencing the brutality of modern total war, in the sense that we might think of the lengthy industrial wars of the past century. The war's expression was stark, and it was not of ideals or high achievement. Its images – of dead Boer children in concentration camps, of blackened farmhouses and gutted livestock, of public executions of colonial Boer rebels under martial law, of British trench corpses mowed down by commando marksmen, of skinny black refugees wandering the countryside, or of colonial mission stations razed by invading Boers – all bring to mind the merciless nature of what for a time resembled South Africa's own war without end.

THE REV. A.I. STEYTLER AND OLIVE SCHREINER! BUSY AS EVER!

Fanning the flames of anti-British sentiment. This propaganda cartoon depicts a pro-Boer alliance between Karoo writer Olive Schreiner and Dutch Reformed Church clergyman Dominee A.I. Steytler, after whom the Karoo town of Steytlerville was named.

WHY 'SOUTH AFRICAN WAR', NOT 'ANGLO-BOER WAR'?

By the early 1980s the old belief that the second 'Anglo-Boer' War was a 'white man's war' had come to be viewed by many historians as a misconception. By that stage, research by Peter Warwick and Bill Nasson had revealed the very active participation by black people in a wide range of roles in the war, including armed combat on both the British and Boer sides.

Research by other historians, notably Jeremy Krikler, Jacob Mohlamme, Fred Morton and Bernard Mbenga, has added to the growing historiography on the theme of black participation in the war in the western Transvaal. All have shown that blacks were 'active shaping agents as well as victims' in the war. Many African communities that participated in the war, especially in an armed combat role, did so voluntarily. For example, when war broke out in the western Trans-

vaal, the Kgafela-Kgatla requested the British military authorities for arms, which they were given. The British thought they were using the Kgatla to fight the war merely on their behalf in the Pilanesberg. But in fact the Kgatla themselves had their own agenda and historical grievances and used the war to achieve their own objectives – for example, to regain the land they had lost to the Voortrekkers much earlier. Similarly, other communities – such as the Rolong of Mafikeng, the Zulu of the Vryheid district, the Shangaan of the eastern Transvaal and the coloureds of the Cape – consciously and wholly voluntarily took up arms to prosecute the war against the Boers for their own local reasons.

On the side of the Boers, too, many thousands of blacks served as *agterryers*. Apart from cooking their masters' meals, they

tended their horses and performed many other menial tasks, such as cattle herding, collecting wood and water, transport riding and digging trenches. In fact, as Pieter Labuschagne states, *agterryers* 'fulfilled almost the same duties as the burghers fulfilled during the war, that is, they played a military role. Thus they were much more than simply servants or lackeys of the burghers.' When necessary, *agterryers* 'switched from a quasi-menial role to a combatant role in the firing line. Especially towards the end of the war, when the numeric strength of the commandos was much depleted, they came to feature more prominently in a combatant capacity.'

For all these reasons it is appropriate to consider the war as the 'South African War' rather than the 'Anglo-Boer War'.

CHAPTER NINE

A new South Africa in the making

Milnerism and reconstruction

Among whites, English-Afrikaner divisions had become more pronounced as a result of the South African War. Among Afrikaners, *bittereinder*-joiner splits in the republics, as well as rebel-loyalist schisms in the British colonies, brought great bitterness within communities and even within families. Among English-speaking people, imperialistic and anti-imperialistic beliefs brought tensions to Cape society. Working-class and capitalist differences had been overshadowed by the clash of Boer and British interests during the war, but they were soon to resurface. There were also religious, cultural, racial, class and language affinities that stretched across state frontiers. It was from all these elements that a stable society and economy had to be reconstructed.

The vast task of reconstruction in the two colonies was controlled under High Commissioner Lord Alfred Milner and the lieutenant-governors, by executive councils consisting of the heads of departments. Milner's power was subordinate to that of Secretary of State for the Colonies Joseph Chamberlain (until September 1903, and his successor Alfred Lyttelton) and to the cabinet in London.

Milner realised that the defeat of the Boer republics and the establishment of British rule in the Transvaal and Orange River Colony did not ensure the triumph of the bureaucratic, agricultural, economic and social components of the British supremacy concept, which would mould South Africa into an efficient link in the imperial chain. Repairing the ravages of war and effecting economic recovery, together with consolidating the gains of conquest, were the priorities of the British rulers after the war. Milner's administration wanted to lay the groundwork for the creation of a stable, efficient capitalistic society and economy, which would be an asset and not a burden to the empire. For that the loyalty or subservience of Britain's former enemies was essential.

Milner relied heavily on a group of talented, inexperienced and often arrogant young Oxonians who became known as the Kindergarten, who were inspired by his view of imperialism. Members of the Kindergarten have been given great credit for their work in South Africa, but their influence may have been exaggerated or romanticised. Many Boers saw them in a different light. The Cambridge-educated Smuts, himself scarcely 32 at the end of the war, asserted in scathing terms that for Milner it was '... such a comfort to have a little kindergarten show of dolls – all your own, moving at your sweet will, not asking inconvenient questions, not making factious opposition . . . That is the way we are ruled here by the "finest flower of Varsity scholarship".'

The first task of the Milner administration was to return to their homes 31 000 Boer prisoners of war (the majority of whom were in overseas camps), 116 000 white and 115 000 black inmates of concentration camps, 50 000 Uitlanders, 21 000 *bittereinders* who laid down their arms within three weeks of the signing of the peace agreement and 5 400 joiners, together with the indeterminate thousands of black and coloured people who had served with the British army. The sheer logistics of this resettlement exercise posed enormous problems and the total cost of repatriation and resettlement was £16 500 000.

THE FIRST SOUTH AFRICAN CENSUS

The first simultaneous census in the South African states in April 1904 revealed that there were over 5.1 million people living in the four British colonies on that date, with 3.5 million blacks, 1.1 million whites, 445 000 coloureds and 122 000 Indians making up the population. The Cape with 2.4 million had the largest population, followed by the Transvaal with 1.2 million, Natal with 1.1 million and the Orange Free State (or Orange River Colony) with nearly 0.4 million people. The Cape had the largest number of white people (nearly 600 000) and Natal the least (less than 100 000). Natal had the largest number of black (nearly 1 million) and Indian inhabitants (more than 100 000). There were many more coloured people in the Cape Colony (nearly 400 000) than in the other three colonies combined.

The £3 million so-called compensation money to assist ruined farmers caused more resentment than anticipated. Allocating the money on the basis of wartime losses was a complex matter, which was further compounded by the fact that the *hensoppers* and joiners could also claim from an additional reserve fund. An exasperated Milner later exclaimed: 'Compensation has, on the whole, been rather a curse than a blessing. You give a man a pound and he hates you for it, because he asked for four and expected two, and all his neighbours who have not got anything hate you equally.' The general dissatisfaction about compensation eroded the divisions among the Boers as they now once again had a common enemy in the British.

Returning Boers had serious difficulties to overcome. British columns had destroyed all but a few farmhouses, dams and fences and had exterminated much livestock. Many blacks in both new colonies refused to leave farms they had occupied and worked – with the British turning a blind eye – during the war. Louis Botha reported that when he returned to his farm in the Vryheid district, black occupants on it told him that he should leave as he had no business there. From the end of the war, the authorities used the South African Constabulary, which functioned as a police force, to disarm blacks. Gradually the white landowner class regained their ascendancy over the countryside, as the Milner regime guaranteed property rights and emphasised the fact that the war had not altered master-servant relations.

In both the Transvaal and the Orange River Colony, however, significant changes in the agrarian economy occurred in the post-war period. Some black peasants were initially able to use the conditions to their advantage. Historian Tim Keegan has shown that immediately after 1902 many Sotho became involved in 'a form of colonising movement across the Caledon' as 'the white farmers welcomed with open arms any black family with stock and equipment who could plough and sow'. It was particularly in these arable eastern areas of the Orange River Colony that black sharecropping temporarily became

OPPOSITE: *Lord Alfred Milner: the unsmiling face of British imperialism. He did not heed the parting advice given to him by Hicks Beach, one of his superiors: 'I believe the greatest thing is patience. Impatience has been at the root of our difficulties in South Africa.'*

BELOW: *Triumphant imperialism? Euphoria in London at the time of the cessation of hostilities of the South African War.*

The South African Native Affairs Commission (SANAC) report used the term 'segregation' – which at the time was quite new in South Africa – only once, but the context is significant. It deplored the practice of blacks purchasing pockets of land among white-owned farms and recommended that blacks be denied access to 'white' land through purchase, lease or sharecropping. The state had to reserve for blacks the present 'locations' or other areas of concentrated African settlement. It proposed segregated townships and education for blacks appropriate to lower level jobs. The Cape's non-racial franchise was to be rejected. In a future federal Parliament blacks should be put on a separate voters' roll to elect a limited number of representatives, all white, as in the case of the Maoris in New Zealand.

Acting on the SANAC report, the British post-war administration of the Transvaal, under Sir Arthur Lawley, demarcated the black 'locations' in the Transvaal Colony. In the end only a million morgen, or about 3% of the Transvaal, was set aside for blacks, compared to, say, the holdings of three major land companies, which comprised 8% of the Transvaal. After the introduction of self-rule in 1907 Louis Botha's government accepted these recommendations. In the 1913 Natives Land Act the same areas demarcated in 1907 for blacks in the Transvaal were set aside. In the meantime, the number of blacks living in these locations had considerably increased and land shortages had forced out growing numbers to work elsewhere. An African chief commented: 'It is the same as if a hen was hatching eggs in a pigeon's nest, and the eggs keep rolling out.'

the standard system. This enabled white farmers to become productive again and enabled black peasants to prosper as well.

Milner hoped to bring considerable numbers of English-speaking settlers to farm on the Transvaal and Orange River Colony *platteland*. Mining companies, which had large tracts of land, supported the idea. But there was no marked influx of English-speaking immigrants (not many more than 1 000 families came) that could offset the Afrikaner numerical superiority in the new colonies. Nor did the Burgher Land Settlement Scheme, which aimed at making white *bywoners* 'sharecroppers of the state', achieve any significant results. Poor whites continued to stream to the towns, their rural livelihoods destroyed by the war, largely through the scorched-earth policy of the British forces.

Milner's educational policy also failed to achieve a dominance of pro-British views. He and his director of education, E.B. Sargant, decreed that English was to be the medium of instruction in state schools in the Transvaal and the Orange River Colony while Dutch was taught as a subject. Potential teachers were asked whether they would 'use their best endeavours to reconcile all Boers to their new position as citizens of the British Empire'. The curriculum had a strong imperialist bias.

The educational policy was not very effective, countered by the Christian National Education policy and practice of the private schools established by Boer political and religious leaders. More important was the fact that education was not compulsory: in the Transvaal in 1905 there were 28 500 white children enrolled at state schools and the enrolment of private schools was 9 000; more than 25 000 white children were not enrolled at any school at all.

The question of race

Milner did at times express views in favour of having a civilisation rather than a race barrier in the societies of the new colonies. He was, however, acutely aware of the views and prejudices of the white inhabitants and believed that it was vital not to alienate them. Commissioner of Native Affairs Godfrey Lagden was extremely paternalistic and condescending towards black people. Firm handling, he maintained, was essential 'otherwise they will become insolent, habitual idlers and a terror to the Dominion . . . they cannot be allowed to roam about without passes or the country will become untenable by a white race'.

The British authorities had indeed introduced a more strictly implemented pass system that compelled all black people to carry identification passes and to produce them

RIGHT: *A* bywoner *dwelling photographed for the Carnegie Commission's report of 1936.*

on demand for the duration of their service contracts. A limited number of blacks and coloureds were issued on application with 'letters of exemption' and 'certificates of registration' on grounds of 'civilisation'. They were exempted from producing pass books on demand, but now they had to show the letter or certificate instead. In reality it was a distinction without a difference.

Both Milner and Lagden believed it was necessary to proceed with extreme caution in the field of race relations. It was Lagden who was appointed by Milner to be chairman of the South African Native Affairs Commission (1903–1905), consisting largely of English speakers, to draft a common policy towards black people for all four colonies. Its recommendations included territorial segregation and the establishment of political separation by means of setting up separate constituencies for black people in each colony. In embryonic form the outline of South Africa's racial policies of the twentieth century can be discerned in the recommendations of this commission.

One of the most pressing matters confronting Milner was the scarcity of black mine labour. In 1903 there was a shortage of more than 129 000 unskilled workers in the gold mining industry due in part to disillusionment with British rule, but more importantly because of a reduction in wages from the pre-war 43 shillings per month to 30 shillings per month. The administration took the view that the importation of Chinese labourers was most likely to provide a solution because they had no social connections with any other groups in the country. The first Chinese labourers arrived in South Africa in June 1904.

This was a striking example of unity of purpose and co-operation between the forces of capitalism and imperialism. Of the nearly 64 000 Chinese who came to South Africa, the vast majority (62 000) were from the poverty-stricken agricultural northern Chinese provinces whose people had been prevented from going to work in Manchuria by the Russo-Japanese war of 1904–1905.

On the mines a high proportion of the Chinese were employed in the most productive and dangerous jobs such as hand-drilling in the stopes. Of the 3 192 Chinese who died on the Witwatersrand between 1904 and 1910, 986 died of causes directly attributable to their conditions of work. Chinese resistance to their working conditions and their accommodation in the mine compounds often took the form of desertion and crime. Economically the experiment of Chinese labour seemed to have been successful but it extracted a huge social cost.

In April 1905 Milner left South Africa and was succeeded as high commissioner by the Earl of Selborne. W.B. Worsfold, John Buchan and Leo Amery formed a first generation of

LEFT: *Chinese miners were brought to South Africa as part of mining capital's reach to the East in the unrelenting search for cheaper labour. Chinese workers were often employed in the most dangerous – and most productive – jobs. A high percentage were to lose their lives in the course of their work.*

The work regarded as the first significant demonstration of the creative potential of Afrikaans appeared in 1905. This was Eugène Marais' poem 'Winternag' (A Winter's Night). Capturing the bleakness of a cold highveld night, it can also be read as a metaphor for the post-war desolation and mood of bitter resignation. Translated by Guy Butler, it reads:

O cold is the slight wind
And sere.
And gleaming in the dim light and bare
As vast as the mercy of God
Lie the plains in starlight and shade.
And high on the ridges
among the burnt patches
the seed grass is stirring
like beckoning fingers.

O tune grief-laden
On the east wind's pulse
Like the song of a maiden
Whose lover proves false.
In each grass blade's fold
A dew drop gleams bold,
But quickly it bleaches
To frost in the cold!

O koud is die windjie
en skraal.
En blink in die dof-lig
en kaal,
so wyd as die Heer se genade,
lê die velde in sterlig en skade.
En hoog in die rande,
versprei in die brande,
is die grassaad aan roere
soos winkende hande.

O treurig die wysie
op die ooswind se maat,
soos die lied van 'n meisie
in haar liefde verlaat.
In elk' grashalm se vou,
blink 'n druppel van dou,
en vinnig verbleek dit
tot ryp in die kou!

commentators who depicted the work of Milner and his administration in glowing terms. A more balanced interpretation highlights the insensitivity to the views and interests of black, Afrikaner and (on occasion) English-speaking South Africans. As for Milner, even some of his devotees came to believe that he was cold and detached, obstinate and blinkered, resentful of criticism and inclined to ignore the faults of those who supported him.

Milner himself did not think that he had succeeded in achieving his aims. Historians Shula Marks and Stanley Trapido offered a quite different assessment: 'Milner succeeded in southern Africa better than he . . . realised . . . He laid the foundations for a state which not only reflected the demands of the twentieth-century British imperialism but also fulfilled them.' While such an evaluation of Milner's role does justice to the structural conditions for long-term capitalist investment that Milner cemented, in the short term he could not gain the upper hand in his political battle with Afrikanerdom.

Boer political revival

From the first day of signing a peace treaty the vanquished Boer leaders knew that Britain was in a hurry to bring about the unification of the four British colonies and intended this state to be a British South Africa.

But there were politicians who opposed Milner's aggressive imperialism and wanted a South African South Africa. They knew they could not lose any time in healing the divisions between the *bittereinders* and *hensoppers*, starting their own newspapers and establishing political parties. Financially crippled in the war, the Boer leaders looked to supporters in Europe to help their cause.

Botha, De la Rey and De Wet went to Europe to raise funds for Boer widows and orphans. They were able to raise only slightly more than £100 000. Of greater importance was their meeting with Paul Kruger and getting access to republican funds overseas, for use in the Transvaal and Orange River Colony. This money was spent not on relief work (which as Smuts privately explained, they were willing to leave to the British authorities), but on the acquisition of newspapers and on other projects that could promote an Afrikaner political revival.

Two of the most important Dutch-language newspapers that were established were *De Volksstem* (Pretoria), which was initially established in 1873 and reappeared in 1905 under the influential editor Dr F.V. Engelenburg, and *Het Westen* (Potchefstroom), which was first printed in November 1904 and had an influence far beyond the western Transvaal. The generals also made an unsuccessful bid for *Land en Volk* (Pretoria), edited by Eugène Marais.

The fervour of Afrikaners to ensure the survival and development of their culture and language, of which the Christian National Education schools were one manifestation, was also responsible for the second Afrikaans language movement. The movement was heralded by the revival of the Taalbond in 1903 by J.H. (Onze Jan) Hofmeyr and other Cape Afrikaners. The Taalbond aimed to develop the *volkstaal* (people's language) which some of these men regarded as Dutch rather than Afrikaans.

In the north, however, author and journalist Gustav Preller and the poets Eugène Marais, Jan F.E. Celliers and J.D. du Toit (Totius) pressed for the use of Afrikaans in literary works and public life. Two of the most haunting poems drawing on the folk memory of the suffering endured during their *Vryheidsoorlog* and the Boer predicament after Vereeniging were Marais' 'Winternag' and Celliers' 'Dis al'. The austere statement of bleak despair expressed in these poems stirred Afrikaners.

The serious rift between National Scouts and Volunteers on the one hand and *bittereinders* on the other was not healed with the coming of peace. In October 1902 Eugène Marais declared in *Land en Volk* that 'the feelings of hate are deep as the ocean and wide as God's earth'. The Dutch Reformed church required collaborators to confess their 'guilt' before being granted the sacraments. In 1903 some of the *hensoppers* and joiners established a separate Scout church, but by 1906 it had virtually ceased to exist. The Milner regime, many collaborators came to feel, had not lived up to their expectations. They joined *bittereinders* in condemning the British authorities. The new Boer leaders came exclusively from the ranks of the *bittereinders*.

After the death of Paul Kruger in Switzerland in July 1904, his embalmed body was taken to Pretoria and his funeral five months after his death further stimulated the Afrikaner political resurgence. In January 1905, under cover of agricultural societies, the political party Het Volk was established in the Transvaal under the chairmanship of Louis Botha, supported by Jan Smuts, C.F. Beyers and other South African War notables. A similar development occurred in the Orange River Colony with the formation of Orangia Unie in May 1906 led by J.B.M. Hertzog, Abraham Fischer and C.R. de Wet.

Milner was aware that the new colonies had to advance a form of self-government, but his proposal encountered strong opposition. It fell to Chamberlain's successor, Alfred Lyttelton, to anounce the grant of responsible government. Although based on the idea of promoting reconciliation between Boer and Briton, it should not be regarded merely as a magnanimous gesture. It was also designed to gain and ensure the loyalty of the majority of white South Africans to the imperial-commonwealth connection.

Recommendations on the details of the constitution were made in July 1906 by a commission of inquiry. At stake was the basis and nature of the delimitation of constituencies – there was never a possibility of anyone except white inhabitants obtaining the franchise. In retrospect it seems that nothing but gross gerrymandering could have prevented an electoral victory for the 'Boer parties' in the two states. No black or coloured people received the vote despite the representations of various organisations. The British government would appear to have been compelled by Clause Eight of the Vereeniging agreement not to grant black people in the new colonies the vote before self-government had been introduced; but no such restraint seems to have been necessary regarding coloured and Indian inhabitants.

In February 1907 Het Volk won the election in the Transvaal, obtaining 37 seats to the 21 of the main opposition, the Progressives, who were backed by gold-mining and financial interests. Louis Botha became premier and headed a cabinet responsible to the legislative assembly. In the Orange River Colony's election of November 1907 Orangia Unie won a massive victory by obtaining 30 seats to the Constitutional Party's eight. Abraham Fischer became prime minister. When Merriman's South African Party won the 1908 general election in the Cape Colony, three of the four states were governed by Afrikaner or Afrikaner-supported parties.

The road to Union

Part of the concept of British supremacy had entailed the incorporation of the different regions of South Africa into one state after the Union Jack had been hoisted over them. A united or federated South Africa would, it came to be believed, be of greater value to Britain in case of war than four separately governed colonies.

The reports of two commissions encouraged South African unity. The Selborne Memorandum, named after the high commissioner at the time, stressed the advantages to white South Africans of joining forces and establishing one government for the whole region. It initiated a movement that many white South Africans favoured. The Lagden Commission had been appointed to make recommendations regarding a common policy towards Africans for all the South African states. Race relations after 1905, particularly in Natal, made many whites in South Africa favour political amalgamation of the four colonies. The so-called Bhambatha Rebellion of 1906 was the largest and most violent manifestation of racial conflict since the Anglo-Zulu War of 1879.

The events leading to the Bhambatha Rebellion and its harsh suppression in 1906 made Liberals in Britain support federation. They thought that a strong central authority would alleviate the worst excesses of the way in which the Natal authorities treated their black population. Even in South Africa, M.T. Steyn, former president of the Orange Free State, had criticised the 'hysterical way in which Natal is dealing with the Native question'. Others interpreted the main lesson of the Bhambatha Rebellion to be the need for the establishment of a powerful South African defence force, for although the Natal militia had crushed the uprising, subsequent black revolts would perhaps not be subdued as easily.

ABOVE: *Chief Bhambatha (right) of the Zondi from Greytown with an attendant. In 1906, Zulu dissatisfaction about the arbitrary dismissal of African chiefs by the colonial authorities, labour, poll and hut taxes and the shortage of land came to a head. Bhambatha refused to pay the poll tax. Martial law was declared and the rebellion was crushed by force, resulting in many deaths, including that of Bhambatha himself.*

BELOW: *This cartoon shows mythical Britannia sealing the peace between former enemies by assenting to the Act of Union. With the benefit of hindsight, what is equally significant in this cartoon is that black people are completely absent.*

UNITED SOUTH AFRICA.

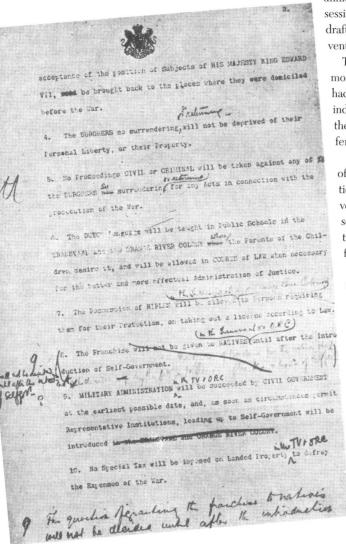

Fears of concerted black attacks on white authority continued and black resistance took a variety of forms. Historian Charles van Onselen has focused attention on the activities of the black Ninevite gangs whose operations (and crimes) in the Transvaal were often directed against black migrant workers and inhabitants of urban locations. Economic rivalry between the states, particularly epitomised by railway tariffs and customs policies, had not been eliminated when all the territories became British colonies, nor by the customs union of 1903, which was in essence a temporary compromise. Unification would ease this rivalry.

There were thus ample reasons why unification or federation appealed to many white South African leaders. Leaders like Steyn and J.B.M. Hertzog believed that it could strengthen Afrikaner nationalism, while Botha and Smuts were convinced that South Africa ruled by one government would provide the best opportunity of achieving self-determination within the framework of the empire. These views did not necessarily contradict each other. Yet these leaders were not initially impressed by Selborne's Memorandum. They were also concerned that the amalgamation of the South African states should not be hastily patched together by imperialistic forces.

A national convention

The attempts by South African politicians to bring about a union or a federation started when leading white political figures in South Africa – representing both the government and the opposition parties of the four colonies – were appointed by their respective parliaments to be delegates to the National Convention, which was to discuss the terms of unification. On 12 October 1908 it began its deliberations in Durban. Subsequent sessions followed in Cape Town from late November to February 1909. After the draft constitution had been referred to the colonial parliaments, the National Convention concluded its business in Bloemfontein in May 1909.

The constitution was drafted in the remarkably short time of less than eight months, compared to the period of about three years and ten years respectively it had taken Canada and Australia to draw up their federal constitutions. It was an indication of the unanimous agreement on the need to create one government for the sub-continent. It did not, however, mean that there were not formidable differences of opinion on various details of the constitution.

A basic matter to be settled, for example, was whether the constitutional form of the new nation would be a union or a federation. The only support for a federation was a vague, poorly presented case by the Natal delegates. Other controversial matters were the black franchise question, the division of parliamentary seats among the various provinces and the delimitation of constituencies within the provinces. But these matters were settled by compromise or by shelving them for future settlement.

The most dramatic moment of the convention was ex-President Steyn's intervention in the debate about an official language. Referring to the Boers and the British as different races, as was the custom at the time, he asked delegates to expunge 'the devil of race hatred' that had plagued the country for so long. The way to do that was to place the two languages on a footing of 'absolute equality in Parliament, in the Courts, in the schools and the public service – everywhere'. Smuts, who believed English should become the sole official language, kept silent. Steyn's view found expression in Article 137. It decreed:

> Both the English and Dutch languages shall be official languages of the Union and shall be treated on a footing of equality and possess and enjoy equal freedom, rights and privileges; all records, journals and proceedings of Parliament shall be kept in both languages, and all Bills, Acts and notices of general public importance or interest issued by the Government of the Union of South Africa shall be in both languages.

Hertzog was convinced that effective equality of treatment had been secured and that if necessary the government would use compulsion to achieve it. Writing in *The State*, Gustav Preller called the Union's promise to place the two official languages on a footing of 'most perfect equality' essential to Afrikaner support for the Union.

State feelings came so strongly to the fore in the discussions regarding the establishment of a capital city of the Union that a deadlock was only averted by another compromise, with Pretoria becoming the administrative capital, Cape Town the legislative capital and Bloemfontein the judicial capital.

Black rejection

Even before the first meeting of the National Convention, black South African political leaders organised a conference to discuss their attitude towards the white thrust for unification. After the war there was considerable disillusionment among black people in the Transvaal and the Orange River Colony about the terms of the Vereeniging peace agreement and their subsequent treatment by Milner's regime.

As historian André Odendaal has shown, a number of black political organisations emerged. The Transvaal Vigilance Association and a branch of the Cape-based South African Native Congress (which had been founded by Walter Rubusana and A.K. Soga) were established in 1903. In the following year the Transvaal Basotho Committee was started. The Bloemfontein Vigilance Committee was formed in 1903 and a larger organisation, the Orange River Colony Native Vigilance Association, came into being in 1904.

In the Cape the African Political (later People's) Organisation (APO) was founded in 1902 under the leadership of W. Collins and J.W. Tobin to further the interests of coloured people. In 1905 Dr Abdullah Abdurahman was elected president of the APO and its influence spread beyond the borders of the Cape Colony. Abdurahman announced in 1905 that the chief aims of the APO were to improve coloured education and to agitate for franchise rights for coloureds in the new British colonies in the north when they received responsible government.

At Queenstown in November 1907, 80 delegates from different parts of the Cape Colony, including members of the coloured organisation APO, resolved that federation was preferable to unification and that the Cape franchise should be the basis of the federal franchise. The Queenstown conference brought black and coloured leaders together and created greater cohesion between black newspapers although John Tengo Jabavu and his newspaper *Imvo Zabantsundu* continued to follow their own line.

Politically aware blacks knew that the formation of a united South Africa would have momentous consequences for them. When the deliberations of the National Convention started, blacks and white sympathisers as well as the APO sent petitions and messages to the Convention pleading that the rights of black and coloured inhabitants should be respected. When the draft Act was made public in February 1909 black newspapers were vehement in their rejection of the colour bar provisions and warned of 'a future filled with bitter hatred and even violence'.

Black delegates from all four colonies and representatives of the APO attended a South African Native Convention in Waaihoek location, Bloemfontein. In March 1909 they passed resolutions objecting to the colour bar clauses of the draft Act and decided to send a delegation to London if the National Convention did not heed their pleas. The Convention decided to continue to meet, and it may be considered to be the forerunner of the South African Native National Congress (formally established in January 1912), which later became the African National Congress. The APO conference in Cape Town in April 1909 condemned the colour bar clauses and forwarded its views to the final Bloemfontein session of the Convention. The National Convention ignored all representations from black and coloured sources, as they had also earlier ignored petitions urging votes for women.

A nine-man delegation led by W.P. Schreiner, which included Rubusana, Jabavu and Abdurahman, went to London to try to persuade the British government not to accept the form of Union drawn up by the National Convention. Gandhi and other Indians also went to the British capital to present the case of their people in South Africa. The colour

ABOVE: *Dr Abdullah Abdurahman, who led the coloured African Political (later People's) Organisation for 35 years, was one of the most important leaders in South Africa at the time. Elected to the Cape Provincial Council, he was a key figure in talks between leaders of the various racial groups from the mid-1920s to mid-1930s. As a member of the Wilcocks Commission that investigated the living conditions of the coloured population, he closely questioned a young professor, Hendrik Verwoerd, who was giving evidence to the commission on his ideas for a solution to the racial problem. These ideas later became known as 'apartheid'.*

bar aspects of the Act were criticised in the British press and also in Parliament, but no changes were mooted. A schedule to the Act laying down conditions on the colour bar for the possible future incorporation of Bechuanaland, Swaziland and Basutoland into the Union – which has been interpreted as a lever on white South African opinion – was the furthest the British government was prepared to go.

Launching the Union

It was decided that Herbert Gladstone, son of a prime minister of Britain and now the South African governor-general, would ask the politician who in his view had most support to form a cabinet. With ex-president Steyn not available due to ill health, the choice lay between Louis Botha and John X. Merriman. Neither was prepared to serve under the other. Gladstone decided on Botha, who formed a cabinet consisting of members of the ruling party in the four colonies. The Union of South Africa was inaugurated on 31 May 1910. In September 1910 the first election was held. The governing or ruling parties won 67 seats, the Unionist Party 39, the Labour Party four and independents eleven. In 1911 the South African Party (SAP) was formed to replace the coalition of ex-ruling parties.

Consolidation and centralisation were the most urgent priorities of the SAP government. It introduced a consolidated civil service to administer the various departments of state. Botha and Smuts commissioned the architect Herbert Baker to design new government buildings. These imposing Union Buildings, as they came to be known, were completed in 1913 on Meintjeskop less than two kilometres from the centre of Pretoria at a cost of £1 180 000. The result had a 'nobility of site and style', with two identical blocks and twin towers to symbolise the 'two races of South Africa' (that is, English- and Dutch-speaking whites). They were brought together in harmony in the central amphitheatre.

RIGHT: *South Africa's four provinces at the time of Union.*

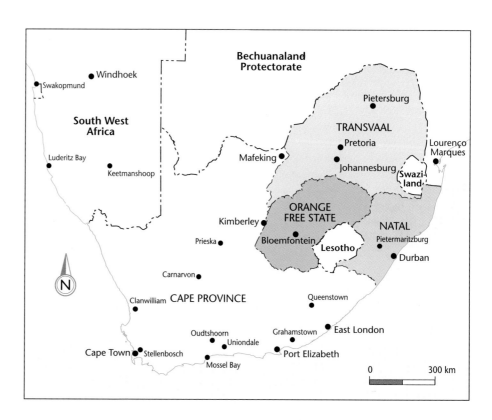

'Dividing' the land

The most contentious Act passed by the first Union Parliament – and the one that was to have the most far-reaching implications – was the Natives Land Act of 1913. The bill, initially drafted by J.B.M. Hertzog, who succeeded Burton as Minister of Native Affairs in June 1912, was in conformity with the segregation proposals of the Lagden Commission (1903–1905) and the 1912 report of the Native Affairs Committee headed by Burton. By December 1912 Hertzog was no longer a member of the cabinet, and yet another Minister of Native Affairs, J.W. Sauer, piloted the bill through Parliament. The Act provided for the purchase, leasing, ownership and occupation of land by blacks and whites in the Union of South Africa and defined the nature of black land tenancy.

These stipulations were to have important repercussions on labour conditions for blacks in rural and urban areas. A schedule to the Act declared which land was to be regarded as 'native areas'. These scheduled areas – all existing reserves, tribal locations and black-owned farms – comprised a total of some 8.9 million hectares or less than 8% of the Union's land area, with the promise that Parliament, advised by a commission, would subsequently make provision for more land for black ownership and occupation.

Except with the approval of the governor-general, no person other than a black person could acquire any land or interest in land in the scheduled areas. A black person was not permitted to purchase or lease land from a white person outside the scheduled areas. The Act further stipulated that all black tenants were to be defined as 'servants'.

The Act was not to be applied uniformly throughout South Africa. As it had not been passed by a two-thirds majority of both houses of Parliament sitting together, it could not be enforced in the Cape Province, where it impinged on the constitution. The franchise clause was entrenched and any curb on the right of people regardless of colour to own property would negatively affect the ability of people to qualify for the vote. In the Transvaal and Natal it was intended that no action would be taken against black tenants until extra scheduled land had been made available. In the Free State black sharecropping would immediately become illegal and black tenants could stay on white farms only if they or members of their family provided labour or services.

What were the forces responsible for the Act? There was pressure from white farmers from the Transvaal and Free State for the government to enact legislation to prevent further purchases of land by blacks in what were considered to be 'white areas'. This practice, often made possible by a number of blacks pooling their resources, was believed to be on the increase. It was seen as a threat to white supremacy on the land. The Natives Land Act was also an attempt to secure a supply of cheap black labour on the *platteland* and in the towns by checking the development of an independent black peasantry.

The formation of a new party

Divisions in the Afrikaner community soon surfaced. Much of the controversy in Afrikaner politics revolved around the figure of J.B.M. Hertzog from the Free State and a member of Botha's cabinet. Imperialism, declared Hertzog, was acceptable only when it helped South Africa; when it conflicted with the interests of South Africa, he opposed it.

BLACK VIEWS OF THE LAND ACT

The 1913 Land Act posed a major threat to black people. Yet, as Sol Plaatje's biographer has pointed out, it also provided the opportunity to mobilise black resistance in a way that no other issue had yet done. 'Unlike many of the earlier issues with which Congress had been concerned – travelling on railways, or employment in government service – the Land Act threatened the interests and well-being of virtually every section of the African population.'

Petitions and deputations were of no avail, and the bill became law in June 1913. The devastating effects that the Act would have on black people in areas of the countryside soon revealed themselves. Plaatje, who saw many families with their stock trekking from the Free State to the Transvaal in the belief that the Land Act would only apply to the former province, stated:

> I shall never forget the scenes I have witnessed in the Hoopstad district during the cold snap of July, of families living on the roads, the numbers of their attenuated flocks emaciated by lack of fodder on the trek, many of them dying while the owner ran risks of prosecution for travelling with unhealthy stock. I saw the little children shivering . . . and when the mothers told me of the homes they had left behind and the privations they had endured since eviction I could scarcely suppress a tear.

To him South Africa had to come first. Hertzog maintained that he was not one of those individuals who always talked of conciliation and loyalty for he considered them idle words.

Hertzog's speeches put Botha in a dilemma. With Hertzog in the cabinet, he would have little hope of winning English-speaking support. He reconstituted cabinet, excluding Hertzog. But Hertzog was not alone. Particularly younger Afrikaners under the leadership of lawyer Tielman Roos opposed Botha's conciliation policy. They were probably correct in their belief that 'conciliation' justly applied should mean a firmer recognition for Dutch as a language and for the rights of Afrikaners. Botha, however, was reluctant to countenance a diminution of the dominance of the English language and of the English-speaking people in South Africa, as his aim was to gain the confidence of this group.

Hertzogism soon assumed the stature of a political creed. Preliminary discussions in January 1914 were followed by the publication of a programme of principles and the formal establishment of the National Party of the Orange Free State in July 1914; subsequently Transvaal, Natal and Cape parties were formed.

Indian resistance

In the immediate pre-Union years there was considerable friction in both Natal and the Transvaal between the Indian inhabitants and the governments of those colonies. These South African Indians were originally workers who had been brought to Natal after 1860 to serve a five-year term of indenture or contract.

More than 152 000 Indians had come to Natal as indentured labourers by 1911 when the importation of Indian workers ceased. About half, most Hindu, stayed on in Natal after their contracts had expired. But half of those who decided to stay were nevertheless forced into second or third contracts of indenture in Natal. Ex-indentured labourers had to pay an annual tax of £3. If the labourers entered into another contract of indenture, payment of the £3 tax was suspended. The children of ex-indentured workers came to be known as 'the colonial-born' and from this grouping the Colonial Born Indian Association was formed in 1911.

From 1875 another category of Indians, Gujerati-speaking Muslim merchants, started arriving in South Africa. They were known as 'passengers' because they had paid their

BELOW: *Indian resistance to discriminatory laws, as personified by Mohandas Gandhi, dates back to the turn of the 19th century. Gandhi and other Indian leaders formed the Natal Indian Congress and launched a newspaper,* Indian Opinion, *to fight racial laws and demand better treatment of their people. They adopted forms of non-violent passive resistance to the racial laws. Gandhi and his associates often got into trouble with these laws, for example when they embarked on pass-burning demonstrations. Here Gandhi is addressing a crowd of supporters in Durban in 1914.*

own passages from India to establish trading concerns in Natal or the Transvaal. These men, some of whom arrived in South Africa with substantial capital, came to be the most prominent Indian traders and also dominated the political associations, the Natal Indian Congress (founded in 1894) and the British Indian Association (founded in 1903).

In theory, membership of the Natal Indian Congress was open to all, but the annual dues of £3 restricted its membership. The politically aware and active section of the Indian community was small and consisted mainly of a relatively privileged group.

The Union census of 1911 showed that Hindus were by far the largest religious group among South African Indians. Of the more than 150 000 Indians in South Africa at that date, more than 115 000 were Hindus compared to just under 21 000 Muslims. M.K. (Mohandas) Gandhi, whose family belonged to the merchant class, formed the British Indian Association. In 1903 the newspaper *Indian Opinion*, which became the organ of Indian merchants in Natal and the Transvaal, was first published. Gandhi determined the policy and often wrote the editorials.

Prior to Union all four colonies passed legislation that discriminated against Indians. Some of these laws remained in force after May 1910; others were amended by Union legislation. Indians were restricted in moving from one province to another, and were almost entirely excluded from living in the Orange Free State. No plural wives of South African Indians were admitted to any of the four provinces, and restrictions were imposed on domiciled Indians bringing their wives and minor children to South Africa. Indians were segregated in so-called bazaars in urban areas. Attempts by Indians to obtain business licenses were often blocked.

Gandhi developed and refined the political strategy of non-violent resistance known as satyagraha, or the power of truth. It involved a non-violent refusal to comply with an unjust law. In this he combined both the superior force of morality as well as the ability of a highly skilled tactician to shame adversaries. Satyagraha drew heavily on Indian philosophy and asceticism, which was part of the Jain tradition in which Gandhi had been raised.

The tactic of satyagraha was intensified from September 1913 to protest the question of the legality of Indian traditional marriages and soon broadened to include other concerns as well. Indians, including women, for the first time crossed the Natal-Transvaal and Natal-Orange Free State borders. In October a strike started among Indian labourers on the northern Natal collieries, which was supported by between 4 000 and 5 000 workers within two weeks.

Workers demanded the repeal of the £3 tax, but also had other economic and social grievances. Towards the end of October Gandhi led 200 strikers out of Newcastle towards the Transvaal border. Early in November the strike spread, apparently spontaneously, to the Natal coastal sugar plantations. Mass arrests of Indians, including Gandhi, were made.

The Union government appointed a commission to inquire into the strike. Gandhi and others who had been imprisoned were released and negotiations between Smuts and Gandhi started soon afterwards. The Smuts-Gandhi deliberations led to the Indian Relief Act being passed by the Union parliament in July 1914. The £3 tax was abolished and validity of Hindu and Muslim marriages was recognised. Gandhi, who left South Africa in the same month that the Relief Act was passed, claimed that it was the Magna Carta of Indian liberty in South Africa.

While certain gains had been made, Indians in the Union could still not own land in the two former republics and were not even allowed to live in the Orange Free State. Nor did the Act remove existing restrictions on Indian trading. Above all, Indians were still deprived of a voice in the election of members of Parliament. Union thus formally affirmed the insecure place they occupied in South Africa.

For coloured people too the unification of the four colonies was cause for trepidation. On behalf of the APO, Abdurahman issued a pamphlet calling 31 May 1910 a day of 'humiliation and prayer' for the coloured people. The Union 'deliberately curtailed their political privileges', and 'slammed the door to political freedom' to all those who were not white in the northern provinces.

ABOVE: *Before worldwide fame: lawyer and activist Mohandas Gandhi (seated in the middle) with a few of his colleagues.*

ABOVE: *Pixley Ka-Isaka Seme, a leading figure at the launch of the South African Native National Congress, later renamed the African National Congress (ANC).*

Black resistance continues

Black opposition also intensified. André Odendaal has argued that the South African Native Convention (SANC), which met in Bloemfontein's Waaihoek township in March 1909 to consider means of protesting against the draft Union constitution, was intended to be a permanent organisation to represent blacks on a national basis under Union. The SANC continued to be active in 1910 and in 1911 and its members wrote to Louis Botha and to the press to urge the government to consider black interests.

The main initiative to transform the SANC into a more dynamic body to represent black people in all parts of South Africa appears to have come from Pixley Ka-Isaka Seme. Educated at a mission school in Natal and the universities of Columbia and Oxford, he practised as an attorney in Johannesburg. After a considerable amount of preliminary organisation, the leaders of various local political bodies, as well as chiefs or their representatives, met at Bloemfontein on 8 January 1912.

There were 25 delegates from the Transvaal, representing not only the Witwatersrand and Pretoria but also the northern Transvaal. No other province was as strongly represented and only a few, including the influential Dr Walter Rubusana, came from the Cape. Chiefs or their representatives from Basutoland, Bechuanaland and various parts of the Transvaal were present.

The meeting was opened by a number of clergymen including a white man, the Rev. Rose, who made a plea for the acceptance of European auxiliary members in the organisation. Sol Plaatje, editor of the newspaper *Tsala ea Becoana* (The Friend of the Bechuana), emphasised the purpose of the conference:

> The white people of this country have formed what is known as the Union of South Africa – a union in which we have no voice in the making of laws and no part in their administration. We have called you therefore to this Conference so that we can together devise ways and means of forming our national union for the purpose of creating national unity and defending our rights and privileges.

The name South African Native National Congress (SANNC), which was to be changed to African National Congress (ANC) in 1923, was adopted but not without some disagreement. Plaatje thought the organisation should have an African name like Imbizo Yabantu (Bantu Congress). A special committee was appointed to draft a constitution. The five basic aims of the SANNC were spelt out in the draft constitution as follows:

- The promotion of unity and mutual co-operation between the government and the black people of South Africa.
- The maintenance of a central channel between the government and the black people.
- The promotion of educational, social, economic and political upliftment of the black people.
- The promotion of mutual understanding between the various chiefs and the encouragement to be loyal to the British Crown and to all lawfully constituted authorities and to bring about better understanding between white and black South Africans.
- To seek and to obtain redress for any of the just grievances of the black people.

Zulu politician John Dube was elected in absentia as president of the SANNC. Plaatje was elected general secretary and Pixley Seme became treasurer. Neither white newspapers nor Jabavu's *Imvo Zabantsundu* carried reports of the inaugural SANNC conference. A constitution was adopted only in 1919.

Dube was the 41-year-old son of a clergyman who was related to the Ngcobo chiefs. After studying at a mission school and in America, he returned to teach in South Africa and to launch and edit the newspaper *Ilanga laseNatal*. With Rubusana he had convened the South African Native Convention in 1909 and been a member of the delegation that went to London to protest against the South Africa Act.

A delegation of SANNC leaders saw the Minister of Native Affairs in Cape Town in March 1912 to voice their objections to the Natives Land Bill, without making any

impact. The SANNC delegation also met leaders of the APO. A newspaper, *Abantu Batho* (The People), the official organ of the SANNC, was partly sponsored by the Queen Regent of Swaziland, Labotsibeni. In parts of the eastern Cape, however, the followers of Jabavu, who believed that blacks were best advised to concentrate on winning the support of white politicians in the parliamentary spectrum, hesitated to give full support to the new organisation.

The SANNC considered the Natives Land Act as such a threat that it sent a delegation to Britain, consisting of Dube, Plaatje, Rubusana, Thomas Mapikela (who had acted as chairman at the Bloemfontein conference of 1912) and Saul Msane (a founder member of the Natal Native Congress at the turn of the century). It was granted an interview in London at the end of June 1914 with Secretary of State for Colonies Lewis Harcourt. Plaatje subsequently said: 'Mr Harcourt made no notes and asked no questions at the interview accorded to our deputation.' Relying on the assurances of General Botha, the minister told the delegation that it had not exhausted 'all South African remedies before coming to England'.

World War I

When war broke out in Europe in 1914 the British government requested Louis Botha's government to invade German South West Africa and to seize Swakopmund, Lüderitzbucht and the radio station at Windhoek. Botha, supported by Smuts and others, was in favour of agreeing to the British proposal. Four Afrikaner cabinet ministers opposed a South African expedition against German South West Africa, inter alia on the grounds that it was undesirable to test the loyalty of Afrikaners to the extent of becoming embroiled in a war on behalf of the British Empire. When Parliament sat in September of that year, Botha gained an overwhelming majority of 91 votes to 12.

The SANNC, which was holding its annual conference at Bloemfontein at the beginning of August, passed a resolution of loyalty to the empire and promised to suspend public criticism of the Union government for the duration of hostilities. Not all members of the SANNC agreed with that stance. J.T. Gumede considered it essential that the Union government should continue to be criticised. After the war Albert Nzula, who was then a member of the SA Communist Party, maintained that the decision of the SANNC to remain loyal to the empire during World War I was the 'first act of betrayal' by the

'chiefs and petit bourgeois native good boys', which weakened the 'liberationist struggles of the native people'.

At a meeting at Marabastad near Pretoria in the last week of August, addressed by the local native commissioner to influence black opinion, Transvaal SANNC leader S.M. Makgatho stated that he had read in a newspaper that Botha had informed Britain he could not spare men to assist the imperial war effort because 'he had to be ready to deal with the natives in this country'. Although no cable to this effect had in fact been sent to London, some members of the government had expressed such views in cabinet. Even the British Secretary of State for the Colonies initially had reservations about recalling the imperial troops from the Union because of his fears of African unrest. Makgatho went on to protest as follows:

> You shall not slander us before the Throne of King George for he is our King as well as yours. We too live under the Union Jack and we are proud of it and we are as ready to fight for it today as any white man in the land.

An Afrikaner rebellion

A substantial parliamentary majority voted in favour of the government's war policy, and it is probable that the majority of white voters were in favour of the decision to invade German South West Africa. There was also, however, no doubt about what Smuts called 'the people's genuine dislike of the German South West African expedition'.

Commandant-General C.F. Beyers of the Union's armed forces declared that he was not prepared to lead an invasion of German South West Africa. Shortly thereafter members of the government heard disquieting reports from the western Transvaal about the intentions of the highly respected and influential General J.H. (Koos) de la Rey who had been one of the most distinguished leaders of Boer forces during the South African War and who was an elected Transvaal senator representing the ruling South African Party in 1914 *(see box)*.

In August 1914 Nicolaas (Siener) van Rensburg, a frail 50-year-old man from the Wolmaransstad district who had impressed De la Rey and others with his apparent psychic powers during the South African War, 'saw visions' again. There is speculative evidence that Van Rensburg suffered from epilepsy that brought on these 'visions'. In his prophecies Van Rensburg made it clear that the war would lead to an easy recovery of Boer republican independence. In part this contributed to the restlessness among Afrikaners in the western Transvaal. It became known that De la Rey planned a meeting at Treurfontein (Coligny) on 15 August and that burghers had been told to come armed to the gathering.

In a meeting with Botha and other government officials De la Rey warned that the South West African expedition would have serious consequences. He talked of recovering republican independence and of Siener van Rensburg's prophecies. He told Botha, 'The prophet cannot see what month it is, but he can see it is the fifteenth.' De la Rey was apparently disillusioned that Botha and Smuts would not support him in a movement to regain the independence of the Boer republics, but he promised that he would do nothing rash.

De la Rey was killed on 15 September on the outskirts of Johannesburg when, in a case of mistaken identity, he was hit by a ricocheted bullet fired by a policeman trying to stop what he thought was a criminal gang. Unfounded rumours of government complicity swept the country and added considerably to the tension. Shortly afterwards Botha was compelled to proclaim martial law as former Boer generals Christiaan Beyers, J.G. Kemp, Manie Maritz and Christiaan de Wet went into rebellion with at least 11 472 men. Along with ex-President Steyn, De Wet was the greatest hero in the Free State with a considerable personal following *(see box)*. Thus the government had legitimate reason to fear the rebellion.

But the rebels were no match for the 32 000 troops the government pushed into the field and were further disadvantaged by the state's access to motorised transport, which rendered the Boer War tactics of fighting on horseback obsolete. Within four months the rebellion was suppressed.

Koos (as he was commonly known) de la Rey was born in 1847 close to the area now known as Winburg in the Free State. He showed an aptitude for military matters and from a young age participated in a leading role in the war against the Sotho in 1865.

His family later moved to the western Transvaal and De la Rey became a successful farmer in the Lichtenburg district. Despite a limited formal education, he was regarded as highly intelligent and also worked as a surveyor of farms and as Native Commissioner. He was well respected and through his work he gained a thorough geographical knowledge of the area – which was to come in useful at the time of the South African War. De la Rey had his reservations about Kruger's decision to take on the might of the British Empire in 1899. However, he made it clear that once war had started, he would be completely committed to the Boer cause.

He made his name as a master tactician and military strategist during the war. He successfully promoted the idea of trench warfare during the first stages of the war and during the latter phases he excelled as a guerilla leader in the western Transvaal. Through his exploits he became known in Afrikaner circles as the 'Lion of the Western Transvaal'. At Vereeniging De la Rey was prepared to continue the war, but ultimately realised that the odds against the Boer forces overall were just too heavy.

De la Rey went as a delegate to the National Convention in 1908–1909 and after Union was appointed as senator. Perhaps partly because of the influence of his maverick western Transvaal compatriot 'Siener' van Rensburg, who had prophesied that the outbreak of World War I would provide the opportunity for the restoration of the Boer republics, De la Rey was sympathetic to the idea of a Boer rebellion in 1914. However, before the rebellion proper started, he was killed by a ricochet police bullet while riding in a car outside Johannesburg. The police were looking for a criminal gang and when De la Rey's car did not stop at a police road block, he became the victim of mistaken identity.

Twelve years after the major 1994 political shift in South Africa, De la Rey made a somewhat unexpected return to Afrikaner consciousness when his name was invoked in popular Afrikaans music as a remarkable resistance leader. In 2006 De la Rey rode again – this time as an icon for a youthful and disenchanted Afrikaner youth in search of a leader of calibre who could help them find their way in what they increasingly seemed to regard as a bewildering 'new' South Africa.

A well-informed British official in South Africa who had close imperial ties believed that the rebellion 'came up like a thunderstorm out of a fairly clear sky, and was . . . an ebullition of midsummer madness rather than the result of a deep laid plot'. Cape politician John X. Merriman drew a parallel between the rebellion and the nineteenth-century Xhosa cattle-killing episode and the role of 'seers', finding it 'strange that two convulsions . . . should have largely been brought about by prophets'. But what made so many leading Afrikaners and their followers so susceptible to accepting rebellion as a credible course of action?

It would seem that the ill-planned coup d'état – scheduled to start on 15 September and to be led by De la Rey, Maritz, Kemp, De Wet and possibly Beyers – was aimed not only at changing the government's decision to invade German South West Africa, but also had as its goal the overthrow of the Botha government and the establishment of a Boer republic. Many Afrikaners followed the men, who had built up formidable reputations as leaders during the South African War, into rebellion without clear consideration. A fair number of the rank and file were indeed 'poor whites' lured by promises of a better future. In addition, there is evidence that family influences and kinship pressures also played a part in steering men towards rebellion.

But there was more to the rebellion than disenchantment with the government's war policy and a desire to regain republican independence. The rebellion had its greatest appeal in the western Transvaal, where De la Rey had strong personal support (*see box*), the northern Orange Free State and the northwestern Cape, all depressed areas that had suffered three years of disastrous drought before 1914. As Unionist politician Patrick Duncan, who was chairman of the parliamentary select committee of inquiry

ABOVE: *African soldiers who served in World War I against Germany. Although King George V praised the South African Native Labour Contingent for its contribution to the war effort, none of these troops received a medal or ribbon.*

into the rebellion, pertinently remarked, 'rebellion does not seem such a serious thing to desperate men'.

Hertzog sympathised with the motives of the rebels, but disapproved of the use of violence. He was not, however, prepared to repudiate the rebellion. Historian Noel Garson is probably correct in stating that 'the rebellion turned people into Nationalists who had not been Nationalists before'. The Nationalist cause gained martyrs, in particular as a result of the execution of Jopie Fourie, who had failed to resign his Defence Force commission before going into rebellion. Executing him was a grave political mistake on the part of Botha and Smuts, alienating vast numbers of Afrikaners from the South African Party.

Although the rebellion was in some respects a civil war among Afrikaners, all the inhabitants of the Union including black, coloured and Indian people were affected. The government appointed a so-called Native Intelligence Branch to report on rebel intentions and movements in the northern and western Transvaal. Black men were also used as scouts by the government in the Orange Free State. On the rebel side, black servants were used as *agterryers* and accompanied their masters in the field, as many black men had done before during the South African War. Other black men were intimidated and forced to act as servants to rebel commandos. Government forces and rebel commandos seized blacks' stock and supplies.

Black and coloured commentators found it difficult to understand why Afrikaners who had ample constitutional means at their disposal should have resorted to rebellion. They contrasted black loyalty with Afrikaner disloyalty. The APO newspaper declared that 'these very men who are now in rebellion have been loudest in proclaiming what they alleged was an ever-present danger, a Native rebellion'.

In the vortex

Before World War I South African military forces had never fought outside the region. During the war of 1914–1918 South Africans for the first time fought and died not only beyond the borders of the Union in Africa, but also in Europe.

From February 1915 the full weight of the military forces of the Union were directed against the Germans in South West Africa. More than 40 000 men were moved into the operational zone. These troops were not all volunteers; many of them had been commandeered to fight the rebels. Some of the oldest soldiers had fought against the British at Majuba. Black and coloured men were to render particularly valuable service in constructing railways, in transport work and as dock labourers.

Three columns, operating from Upington and Keetmanshoop, from Lüderitzbucht through Aus and from Walvis Bay to Swakopmund, were under the overall command of General Louis Botha. Outnumbered, the Germans surrendered by mid-1915.

The South West African campaign was one of the colonial sideshows that had little impact on the overall outcome of the war. It did have other significant implications, however. Botha's victory was extravagantly reported in the South African and British press. South Africa gained prestige in Europe. 'Bothaland' was suggested as a suitable new name for German South West Africa. The *Cape Argus* regarded the capture of Windhoek as 'the greatest blow which has ever been dealt to the German ambition of world dominance'. *The Times* of London commented that the conquest of German South West Africa 'will leave its mark in the history of the world'. It was pure hyperbole.

The conclusion of the South West African campaign freed the troops to support the Allied cause in other theatres of the war. In July 1915 the British government accepted the Union's offer to send an infantry brigade of 7 000 men to France. The required number was quickly raised. A spirit of jingoism had swept English speakers throughout the country. Historian John Lambert quotes the response of a young man from Natal who was proud to pronounce:

> We were the flag-wagging imperialistic jingoes, and how we loved it! We certainly did have something to shout about, and the present generation has no idea how we felt . . . We certainly had the courage of our convictions, because when the dogs of war were let slip we were ready in our thousands to uphold our beliefs.

A contentious issue was the inclusion of coloured and black men in contingents serving outside the Union. In August 1915 the government decided to form the so-called Cape Corps, consisting of coloured men, for combat duty in German East Africa. The Germans largely used black troops, called askaris, in the campaign. For most of their period in East Africa, from February 1916 to December 1917, the Cape Corps was assigned to duty in what was considered to be one of the unhealthiest areas in the territory, along the Rufiji River. The death rate attributable to malaria and other diseases among black and coloured troops in East Africa was high. In December 1916 the APO protested that the policy of assigning to local coloured troops areas regarded as dangerous to local white troops was contrary to all the spirit of sacrifice and determination with which the many sections of His Majesty's subjects had responded to the call of their king and country.

South African Indians served with honour as stretcher-bearers in that campaign. Smuts believed that the young white South Africans who fought alongside the troops from India in East Africa, returned 'with more kindly feelings than they had before' towards the Indian population of the Union. The use of coloured, Indian and black men in a non-combatant capacity in African campaigns seems to have caused little controversy. It was the use of coloured men as combatants in East Africa that met with strong disapproval from members of the National Party in South Africa.

The extremely heavy casualties on the Western Front led the British cabinet to approach the Colonial Office about the possibility of recruiting troops for trench warfare in France from 'the coloured races' in the empire. When the Colonial Office approached the Union government on the matter in late 1916 the Botha administration replied that there was no possibility of its agreeing to send black soldiers to fight in Europe. When the imperial authorities asked the Union government to send black labourers to France, it formed the South African Native Labour Contingent (SANLC). Some 21 000 black men were recruited for France. They were utilised as stevedores and worked on the railways, roads, in quarries and forests. Many blacks thought that the wage of £3 offered a month was too low. It was less than the Union rate of £4.50 for white privates, and 10% higher than the average mining wage for black workers.

The reasons of those who did enlist varied: they were peasants or labourers escaping from the drought-stricken northern Transvaal and criminals fleeing from justice, while others were attracted to the prospect of travelling overseas. A disproportionately small number were members of the black elite, who joined the SANLC 'to prove their loyalty to the civilising Imperial power in an hour of need'.

But many white South Africans objected to black men being sent to Europe. The *Natal Mercury* commented that 'more or less unsophisticated boys will come back to this country after contact with an altogether new environment very different individuals from what they were when they left'. The National Party member for Ficksburg, J.G. Keyter, who had been a powerful advocate of the 1913 Land Act, stated that when they returned 'they will have ideas above their station, will work for no white man and incite people to agitate for equal rights'.

For South African black society the most traumatic incident of the war was the sinking of the transport vessel, SS *Mendi*. In thick fog early in the morning of 21 February 1917 the *Mendi*, carrying 882 men of the SANLC, was steaming across the English Channel from Britain to France. Off the Isle of Wight another troopship, SS *Darro*, ploughed into the *Mendi*, gashing its hull open. The passengers mustered on deck and some lifeboats were lowered. Within 25 minutes the *Mendi* sank in icy water and 615 men of the SANLC drowned or died of exposure and exhaustion. Throughout the men behaved with great courage.

Delays occurred before the Union government was able to issue a statement and provide details of the disaster. Rumours abounded, black suspicions increased and it became more difficult to recruit black labourers for overseas duty. In time, black people came to regard 21 February 1917 with sorrow and pride. 'Mendi Day' also came to assume black nationalistic and libertarian overtones.

The white South African brigade was despatched to Flanders. South African participation in the 'big push' reached a climax during the battle of Delville Wood from 15 to

CHRISTIAAN DE WET

Christiaan de Wet, probably the most renowned and intrepid Boer general of the South African War, was born in 1854 near Smithfield in the Free State. He had gained military experience from a young age in campaigns against the Sotho and also against the British during the war of 1881. He became chief commandant on the western front in 1900 but could do little to stop the forces under Lord Roberts from entering Bloemfontein on 13 March 1900.

After the occupation of the Free State capital, he turned to guerrilla war and quickly excelled in harassing British convoys. He became chief commandant of all the Free State forces and along with President M.T. Steyn came to embody the spirit of Free State resistance.

Although speaking with a slight lisp, he was a fiery and forthright speaker who exerted strict control over his men. He was an astute tactician and based his strategy on rapid mobility. Calm under danger, he gained the trust and respect of a devoted band of men who managed to evade the British blockhouse and barbed wire system with impunity. To the British high command he became enemy number one.

At the peace negotiations at Vereeniging in 1902 De Wet was prepared to carry on, but it became clear that for the majority of the delegates it was simply not possible to do so. He signed the peace agreement as acting state president of the Free State and soon afterwards he left with other Boer generals to try to collect funds in Europe and Britain for Boer widows and orphans. On the voyage to Europe he recorded his memoirs of the war. The book became one of the war classics and was translated into several languages.

Twelve years after the war De Wet became involved in the ill-conceived Boer rebellion of 1914. The famous horseman of the South African War had to surrender in ignominious fashion when he was hunted down with the help of motor cars. The manner of his capture poignantly indicated the symbolism of a world that had moved on. He died in February 1922 and was buried at the foot of the Women's National War Monument in Bloemfontein.

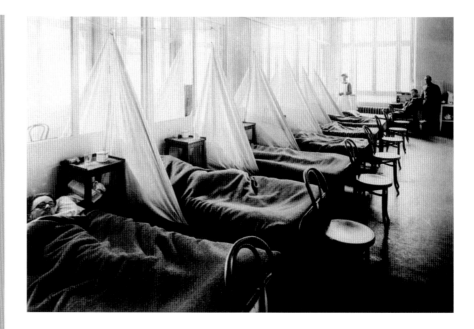

THE SPANISH FLU

South Africans did not escape the ravages of the greatest pandemic of modern times – the outbreak of Spanish influenza in 1918. Spanish influenza is considered to have started in Asia late in 1917 or the beginning of 1918 and spread to Europe and North America. It was called Spanish influenza because reports of its outbreak in central Spain were not censored, as was the case in other countries participating in the war.

The second and more virulent wave of the disease was spread throughout the world, including South Africa, by shipping. By mid-October people in all parts of the Union had been afflicted. Altogether some 20 million people throughout the world died of the disease. According to official statistics 11 726 white and 127 745 coloured, Indian and black people died as a result of the epidemic in South Africa. Howard Phillips's research has indicated that the toll was probably much higher than the official figure, and that between 250 000 and 350 000 deaths altogether in the Union would be a reasonable estimate.

Phillips also concluded that even on the official figures South Africa, particularly among the black and coloured people, had one of the highest per capita death rates from Spanish influenza in the world. If the figure of 250 000 to 350 000 deaths is correct, South Africa was one of the world's five worst affected countries.

Spanish influenza, Phillips has pointed out, 'almost at a stroke . . . radically altered the composition of the Union's population with regard to size, age-structure and ratio between the sexes. It was the most important episode in the country's demographic history, shaping the structure of the South African population fundamentally for the rest of the century.'

20 July 1916. Delville Wood was the strategic key to Longueval and the divisional commander ordered detachments of the South African brigade to clear the wood of the enemy at all costs. Despite fierce counterattacks from three German divisions the brigade refused to surrender. On 20 July it was relieved after six days and five nights of ferocious fighting. Led by Colonel E.F. Thackeray, just five officers and 750 men of the force of more than 100 officers and 3 000 men marched out of Delville Wood. According to recent research, 763 South Africans were killed in action or died of wounds sustained at Delville Wood.

A contemporary observer considered the battle of Delville Wood 'an epoch of terror and glory scarcely equalled in the campaign' and believed that 'as a feat of human daring and fortitude the fight is worthy of eternal remembrance by South Africa and Britain'. In an age in which war memorials were the norm, such sacrificial heroics did not go unnoticed and in 1926 an imposing monument to the fallen soldiers was erected on the Somme. The monument not only spoke of an indomitable martial spirit, but as historian Bill Nasson has alerted us, it was also a robust embodiment of white national political culture embracing Afrikaans and English speakers. It also confirmed South Africa's status as a member of the British Empire prepared to meet its obligations.

The war's aftermath

On 11 November 1918 an armistice ended the fighting between the Allied and the Central Powers. Thirty-two states were to attend a conference in Paris at the beginning of 1919 to draft treaties that, it was hoped, would ensure peace and stability. In addition to the Union government's official representatives at the Paris conference, two other groups of South Africans went to Europe in 1919 to voice their grievances and to express their views: an SANNC deputation headed by Sol Plaatje and an Afrikaner Nationalist delegation led by J.B.M. Hertzog.

There were members of the SANNC who believed that the outbreak of World War I had prevented the 1914 deputation from making a greater impression on the British government and public. They believed the time was ripe to press their demands, with both British Premier David Lloyd George and American President Woodrow Wilson having publicly emphasised the rights of small nations and the doctrine of self-determination.

In mid-December 1918 S.M. Makgatho, the president of the SANNC, summoned congress members to a special meeting in Johannesburg which was opened by the mayor of the city. It was agreed that a deputation should be sent to Britain and that a petition to King George V should be drafted and presented to the governor-general. The petition

cited numerous examples of African loyalty during the war and outlined the grievances of the black inhabitants of South Africa who, it was maintained, lived under a veiled form of slavery.

The petition asked the king to bring about a revision of the Union constitution to ensure the enfranchisement of blacks throughout South Africa. The congress stressed that not one of the protectorates should be transferred to the Union without the consent of the inhabitants of the territories. The petition further expressed the congress's strong feelings that neither German South West Africa nor German East Africa should be ceded to the Union of South Africa unless its constitution were altered to remove colour prejudice. The petition had, of course, no chance of changing the situation in the Union and was destined to never even reach the king. Its interest lies in reflecting the views of the SANNC.

In April 1919 R.V. Selope Thema and L.T. Mvabaza sailed from Cape Town to Britain to represent the SANNC. Thema had acted as national secretary-general of the congress during World War I and Mvabaza, who had been a member of the 1914 deputation to London, had been arrested in 1918 as one of the alleged instigators of the sanitary workers' strike in Johannesburg. They were later joined in London by Sol Plaatje, the well-known journalist and author, who had gone alone to Britain in 1914 to protest against the Natives Land Act, and J.T. Gumede from Natal, a founder member of the SANNC.

Thema and Mvabaza went to Paris, but their efforts to present their case to the peace conference were unsuccessful. They did, however, obtain a promise from Lloyd George that he would meet them on his return to London. Colonial Secretary Lord Milner responded to a memorandum detailing black grievances by reiterating that Britain could not interfere in the domestic affairs of a self-governing dominion. Plaatje, in particular, continued to publicise the grievances of his people and a number of members of the British Parliament spoke on the subject when the colonial office vote was discussed in the House of Commons in July 1919. The British government, however, stood by its doctrine of non-interference in South Africa's affairs.

In November 1919 the SANNC delegation met Lloyd George. The black delegates particularly criticised the pass laws, which they described as similar to the laws in the slaveholding southern states of the United States, and the Natives Land Act, which they said reduced them to the position of wanderers in the country of their birth. They faced large and powerful forces determined to enforce the colour bar and prevent the educational and economic advancement of the black population. To their chagrin, Lloyd George replied that the matters they raised were not within the powers of the British government to resolve.

ABOVE: *South African soldiers are buried at the Delville Wood cemetery, the last resting place of those involved in an 'epoch of terror and glory'.*

OPPOSITE: *Patients in an influenza ward in the US Army hospital in Aix-les-Baines, France, during World War I.*

Impressed by the delegates, Lloyd George wrote to Smuts that the black delegates were 'men possessed of very considerable oratorical gifts'. He urged him to meet them and satisfy their legitimate aspirations. He added a warning:

> If they do suffer under disabilities and if they have no effective constitutional mode of expression, it is obvious that sooner or later serious results must ensue . . . The colour question is now a world question. It is impossible for it to be treated in water-tight compartments. What South Africa does is of vital importance to the rest of us, just as what we do is going to be of vital importance to you.

This failed mission was the last serious attempt to obtain British intervention in South African affairs and it brought to a close the early period of black political activity. In the first flush of its formation and stimulated by the Land Act and the Native Administration Bill, the SANNC had become the widely accepted channel for black political protest. After this desperate gesture, the movement lost much of its coherence and initiative.

Louis Botha and Jan Smuts, who represented the South African government at the Paris peace conference that ended World War I, had attended a peace conference at Vereeniging seventeen years earlier as the representatives of a vanquished state. They may thus, in some respects, be said to have had sharper insights than other delegates into the implications of peace terms imposed by the victors after a war. They were also directly and deeply concerned about a specific territorial aspect of the settlement – the future control of German South West Africa. It was finally agreed that South West Africa would become a 'C class' mandate. It would be administered as an integral part of South Africa, as the mandatory state, subject to reports being submitted to the League of Nations.

On 28 August 1919 Louis Botha died in Pretoria a month short of his 57th birthday. The 49-year-old Smuts became the second prime minister of the Union of South Africa.

CHAPTER TEN

A turbulent decade

Post-war crises

In the aftermath of World War I the young South African state entered its most perilous phase. The state's security services were still weak and divided and the economy was stagnating. Between 1920 and 1932 the gross domestic product declined in monetary terms, with almost no increase in industrial output. The Industrial sector and the railways shed jobs. At the same time, largely as a result of the post-South African War baby boom, the number of white youths entering the job market jumped by 50% between 1921 and 1926, compared to the first two decades of the century. White unemployment rose sharply. In Johannesburg alone an estimated 3 000 families lived on the point of starvation. To compound matters, rampant inflation pushed prices up by 50% between 1917 and 1920.

The mines were the flashpoint. Large numbers of immigrant miners had left to return to Europe to fight in World War I, removing an ageing, more conservative element from the labour force. By 1918 Afrikaners formed the majority of white miners in the dangerous underground jobs. They would soon prove to be the most radical force the mines had ever employed. The distance between the workers and the government of the day widened after 1920 when the South African Party (SAP) absorbed the Unionist Party with its strong support of the mining houses. General Jan Smuts, who became prime minister in 1919 after General Louis Botha died in office, struggled to find his feet after a prolonged absence abroad fighting in World War I. He resorted to such tough methods that J.B.M. (Barry) Hertzog said his footsteps 'dripped with blood' after he put down the 1922 strike on the Witwatersrand.

Strikes and the Rand uprising of 1922

Post-war inflation and inadequate wage increases between 1918 and 1920 accounted for widespread labour unrest. In 1918 poorly paid Johannesburg sanitary workers agitated for higher wages; in 1919 Bloemfontein municipal and other workers struck for higher wages; and in 1920 there was a similar strike in Port Elizabeth, in which nineteen blacks were shot dead, and the Witwatersrand experienced the biggest strike in the history of the mining industry, with more than 70 000 workers demanding higher pay. The strike was put down forcibly and eleven miners were killed and 120 injured. In a way it was a portent of what was to follow.

Earlier, in 1913 another strike by whites on the gold mines had occurred over union recognition, with riots, arson, looting and near anarchy across the Rand. The police and the army were unable to contain the disturbances and the new Active Citizen Force (ACF) was still too poorly organised to be effective. The stability of the state itself would be at risk if strike leaders linked up with disaffected rural Afrikaners. Soldiers shot and killed 100 strikers and bystanders before the strike ended. The government had to sign a humiliating accord with the strike leaders, only to be challenged again six months later. A 1914 strike on the coal mines spread to the railways and harbours and culminated in a general strike. This time the government was ready. It declared martial law and sent in

BELOW: *The white miners' strike of 1922. Following the fall in the gold price on the world market, the mining companies were confronted with mounting production costs and declining profits. A number of mines faced imminent closure. In November 1921, the Chamber of Mines announced the elimination of the colour bar in semi-skilled work. Blacks would take jobs previously reserved for whites, thus replacing expensive white labour with cheap black labour and saving the mines a lot of money. This policy, which was to be implemented on 1 February 1922, would mean the loss of jobs of over 15 000 white miners. In January 1922, having formed their own armed commandos, the white miners took action. Not only did they go on strike, they also plotted to topple the Smuts government, which used the army to break the strike by force.*

units of the newly formed Permanent Force and ACF commandos. The English-speaking leaders of the trade union federation were arrested; Smuts deported nine of them summarily and illegally. To break the strike, Smuts relied on the support of men with whom he had fought the South African War. Rural Afrikaners called up for commando duty enthusiastically took up their weapons 'to shoot Englishmen' in Johannesburg.

In 1922 the most violent white miners' strike followed, leaving far-reaching political consequences in its wake. The strike began in January 1922 and lasted intermittently till March. It had its roots in rising production costs, a gold price that could not compensate for this, and ultimately in radical steps taken by the gold mining industry to try to remain profitable. Wages for certain categories of workers had been decreased and underground jobs reorganised so that blacks could be employed in semi-skilled positions. The colour bar would apply only to skilled jobs.

The strike leaders were mainly English speakers, but a fair percentage of Afrikaners were also involved. Committees, made up for the most part of Afrikaners, organised the so-called 'strike commandos', which gradually began to stray from their role as keepers of the peace and started instead to mete out violent treatment towards 'scabs'.

Although the class radicalism of the white miners cannot be doubted, it had firm racial boundaries. In the early twentieth century there was a marked fusion of class and white consciousness across the British Empire. The seemingly contradictory slogan emblazoned on the banners of the white militants – who marched under the slogan 'Workers of the world fight and unite for a white South Africa' – was therefore in keeping with the general trend at the time. Smuts was on the horns of a dilemma. He could not afford to alienate the Rand white working force from the government, but the gold mines were a vast source of income for the state. He did not wish to antagonise either party. Even so, on the day that the strike began he had already created the impression that he was unsympathetic towards the strikers by declaring: 'If a strike were to take place, the Government would draw a ring round both parties, do its best to maintain law and order, and let the two parties fight it out.' Although this was his official position, there were suspicions that he failed to put substantial pressure on the mine owners to negotiate.

Matters came to a head at the beginning of March. On 7 March all workers without exception went on strike, but a disruptive element took the law into its own hands. During the next week the Witwatersrand experienced unprecedented violence. People were assaulted in the streets while innocent and defenceless black miners were attacked because of rumours of a black uprising. Blatant sabotage and vandalism were rampant. Telephone lines were cut, cars overturned and a railway line was blown up. On 10 March Smuts declared martial law and rushed in government forces, supplemented by air support, bombs and artillery, machine guns and tanks. The Benoni strikers' position was machine-gunned from the air and the mine hall bombed. On 17 March the trade unions called off the strike.

The strike had exacted a high toll: 43 members of the army, 29 policemen and 81 civilians were killed, while more than 650 people had been injured. No fewer than 853 people were tried on various charges, 46 of them on murder charges. Eighteen were sentenced to death but the public outcry that followed was of such a nature that fourteen were reprieved and only C.C. Stassen, S.A. Long, H.K. Hull and J.D. Lewis were eventually hanged.

In an intriguing comparison, historian Jeremy Krikler argues that the white working class communities of the Witwatersrand in 1922 'did not look that different from black working class communities who participated in the anti-apartheid insurrections of the 1980s'. Both were alienated from the established order, both were determined to make themselves heard and both suffered at the hands of the state.

After the strike the wages of semi-skilled white workers were decreased and mine owners were free to allocate underground work as they saw fit. This meant that semi-skilled whites were replaced at an accelerated pace by cheaper black labourers. As a result the black-white ratio on the mines changed from eight blacks per white in 1918–1921 to nearly ten per white in 1923–1926. This position remained more or less constant until the late 1930s. Politically the strike was damaging for Smuts; his handling of the strike was widely criticised and cost him the 1924 election.

Bulhoek and Bondelswarts

In 1921 and 1922 the Smuts government also took harsh action against black people on two occasions. The first of these involved a black sect, the Israelites, under the leadership of Enoch Mgijima, who squatted at Ntabelanga near Bulhoek in the Queenstown area of the eastern Cape. The Israelites, numbering about 1 000, used to gather there to celebrate Passover, but in 1920 they erected a tabernacle and some huts without registering themselves or paying tax. Whites and blacks in the area protested to government that members of the sect were allowing their cattle to graze on neighbouring land, but these protests fell on deaf ears. In an explanation heavily infused with millenarian overtones, Mgijima insisted that he had had a vision that the end of the world was at hand and that Jehovah had instructed him to remain there.

Various attempts in December 1920 by the police, the government and moderate black leaders to persuade the Israelites to move failed to produce results. Mgijima requested that Smuts himself should negotiate with the sect but Smuts refused to do so. In response to the growing militancy of the sect a police unit of about 800 men was sent to Bulhoek in May 1921. The police issued an ultimatum demanding that the Israelites evacuate the area and warning that if they failed to comply, their leader would be arrested and their homes demolished. Undaunted, the Israelites replied that Jehovah would fight on their side.

Soon afterwards they launched an attack armed with clubs, assegais and swords. They were fired upon by the police and more than 180 people were killed and 100 wounded. The government refused to set up a commission of inquiry. In the consequent trial of Enoch Mgijima and his 'prophets' the judge came to the conclusion that the tragedy had been unavoidable but that the government had given the Israelites a false sense of confidence by waiting such a long time before acting. The management of the incident did Smuts's personal image a great deal of harm and his enemies later referred to him as the 'butcher of Bulhoek'.

The Israelites should not be seen as a totally isolated group. They were part of the movement of Ethiopian or Independent black churches in South Africa. They also represented black resistance towards white dominance, and their belief in an apocalyptic solution underscores the millenarian nature of the movement.

BELOW: *Enoch Mgijima, leader of the Israelite sect which was responsible for the unrest at Bulhoek outside Queenstown in the eastern Cape in 1920 to 1922. Police killed many of the members of the sect and Mgijima and some of his followers were charged with stoking unrest. Found guilty, they were sentenced to six years' forced labour, but were released in 1923. Upon his release, Mgijima laid the cornerstone of a large church in Queenstown. He died in 1928.*

The Industrial and Commercial Workers' Union of Africa (ICU) was indistinguishable from its flamboyant and eloquent leader, Clements Kadalie. He was assisted by T. Mbeki in the Transvaal and A.W.G. Champion in Natal, who were revered by many blacks for their outstanding abilities to perceive grievances and operate within the so-called white structures and institutions of society. Champion, for instance, concentrated on fighting issues in law courts and was able to win many of the workers' cases against white employers.

Blacks considered Kadalie their liberator. His audiences were enthralled by his words. One man recalled: 'Man, we thought we were getting our country back through Kadalie.' He was also a persuasive showman with a great appreciation for the dramatic. At times during his speeches he strode up and down, and built up to a climax by successively shedding his coat, waistcoat, collar, and finally his tie. In doing so he sought symbolically to strip away the trappings of Western civilisation and reassert his place with ordinary people. The historian of the ICU, Helen Bradford, has argued that the illiterate poor who communicated predominantly through voices, gestures and rituals could not have missed the social meaning of this performance.

Kadalie was once invited to attend an international trade union conference in Geneva, Switzerland, which gave the ICU added stature. Many of his, Champion's and others' ideas were also disseminated by the ICU newspaper, *The Workers' Herald*, to black workers in all types of employment.

Millenarianism is often the last resort of desperate people. These outbursts can be seen as a reaction against a steady tightening of white control in the 'native areas', running in tandem with greater industrialisation and increasing demands for cheap migrant labour from these areas for the Witwatersrand in particular.

The next year the government used excessive force once again – this time against the Bondelswarts, a group of mixed racial origin in the then South West Africa (Namibia). The Bondelswarts rebellion was the result of grievances that arose during the time of the German occupation. When South Africa was granted a mandate over South West Africa in 1919, the Bondelswarts were confident that their tribal status would be restored, that they would regain their lost land and that their leaders who were living in exile would be permitted to return and once again assume their positions of authority. None of these hopes was realised. Indeed, the South African government imposed further restrictive measures on the Bondelswarts, including a dog tax.

Conflicts erupted when two exiled leaders, J. Christian and A. Morris, returned to the community and were arrested by the police. The Bondelswarts resisted when the police tried to take Morris into custody. A force of 370 men advanced against the group and military aircraft started to bomb the Bondelswarts into submission. With the loss of only two people, the military force killed 115 Bondelswarts, including some women and children. The Bondelswarts had no option but to surrender.

Another religious 'prophet' appeared on the scene during the 1920s in the person of Wellington Buthelezi. Buthelezi was under the influence of Jamaican-born Marcus Garvey's doctrines propagating the 'back to Africa' notion in America. Buthelezi began to preach in the Transkei in 1925, telling blacks that on the Day of Judgment black Americans would drop glowing coals out of aeroplanes to free blacks from their oppressors. To ensure their deliverance, blacks were advised to paint their houses black and slaughter their pigs.

In 1930 the government introduced stricter measures against resistance groups. The Riotous Assemblies Amendment Act of that year made the incitement to racial hatred a criminal offence and also made provision for the banishment of political leaders from a district if it was found that they were disturbing public peace and order.

While these movements had no visible impact, their importance lies in the fact that they draw our attention to often hidden resistance in the rural areas. It counters the notion that black resistance was exclusively an urban phenomenon.

The SANNC/ANC and ICU

During the 1920s the South African Native National Congress (SANNC), which changed its name to the African National Congress (ANC) in 1923, did not accomplish a great deal to improve the life of black South Africans. Short of funds and poorly organised, it was overshadowed by a more dynamic trade union organisation. Called the Industrial and Commercial Workers' Union (ICU), it was established in 1920 by Clements Kadalie (*see box*), who was originally from Nyasaland (now Malawi).

The ICU started out as a trade union for the black and coloured dockworkers of Cape Town, but soon developed into a more general organisation, including in its membership skilled as well as unskilled workers from industry and the agricultural sector. Unlike the SANNC, the ICU did not officially petition the authorities, but adopted a more militant approach with a view to obtaining better working conditions and higher wages for its members. As a result its membership increased rapidly, mainly because the ICU held out hope for immediate change within the existing socio-economic system. Branches were opened throughout South Africa, and in 1925 the union moved its headquarters to Johannesburg. At some point during the 1920s at least 150 000 workers belonged to the union.

But the ICU was not restricted only to cities. It had a remarkable impact on the consciousness of black workers in some country towns and on farms. Many rural workers who lived as labour tenants on white-occupied farms found themselves in dire straits and were particularly susceptible to the millenarian undertones of the speeches made by ICU officials. It was the only movement that not only responded to their grievances, but also promised them freedom.

Some traditional authorities were exultant over the ICU's assurances of liberation and restoration of their land. A number of Swazi chiefs in the Nelspruit area, for example, went so far as to lead thousands of their followers into becoming members. 'Redemption has come and that is the ICU,' rejoiced one chief. The ICU was also widely perceived as the organisation that stood up for blacks against injustice. 'I see you' was often the way in which the name was interpreted. According to one white official, the letters ICU meant, 'I see you when you do not protect the Bantu.'

The ICU as an organisation largely failed to provide effective activist leadership. It demanded a redistribution of economic and political power, but had no clear idea of how to achieve that. Too often it equated protest with pressure and growing membership with increasing success. There was no consistent strategy. In 1924 Kadalie even flirted with Hertzog's National Party, despite the latter's alignment with the South African Labour Party, which openly advocated a policy of 'Workers of the world unite for a white South Africa'.

Kadalie stood to gain little from such involvement and, not surprisingly, was unable to extract any concessions. Similarly, he had unrealistic expectations of the ICU's connections with international trade unionism. Considerable energy and money were expended to protect farm labourers and although some small victories were registered, they were at the expense of consolidating and organising the workforce in the urban areas where the potential for success was greater.

Such flaws proved fatal. The ICU failed to promote strike action where it was clearly warranted, and when spontaneous strikes did occur on the Witwatersrand and in Durban in 1927 the organisation was unable to lend support. Consequently, the organisation lost considerable credibility, which, despite its militant rhetoric, it never really recovered.

The leaders had not developed organically from the working class and although they were by no means affluent they represented a trade union aristocracy. There were even more fundamental problems. Many workers were migrants and therefore not totally committed to the urban and industrial milieu. Compared to today, only a fraction of the total black population was absorbed in the small industrial workforce.

In due course two factions developed within the ICU. There were those who supported more militant action and those who advocated moderation. This, together with financial problems, was largely responsible for the gradual decline of the ICU and its final disappearance from the scene around 1930. Nonetheless, it occupies an important place in the history of black labour. Not only was it the first black trade union movement, but it also helped to make blacks more aware of their exploitation. In addition, it cut across traditional loyalties in its attempt to unite black people as workers.

The decline and disappearance of the ICU did not mark the end of the organised black trade union movement and joint workers' action in industry. Various black trade unions followed in its wake. A contributory factor was the introduction of a Wage Board to which organised labour could make representations on matters concerning wages and working conditions. In the years that followed, strikes and boycotts occurred frequently. One such example was an anti-pass campaign in Durban in 1930, during which the Durban leader of the Communist Party of South Africa, Johannes Nkosi, was killed in a skirmish

A REVOLUTION OF TWO STAGES

The South African Communist Party (SACP) was founded in 1921. Initially the leadership considered the white working class as the agent in forging a revolutionary alliance between white and black workers. In the final phases of the Rand Strike of 1922 the leadership was in the hands of a militant Council of Action consisting of Afrikaner nationalists and 'Marxist socialists'. The latter displayed a banner reading, 'Workers of the world fight and unite for a white South Africa'. The Communist Party gave tacit support in the 1924 election to the Pact coalition of Labour and Nationalists, but disillusionment soon set in. It now shifted its attention to blacks and began cultivating the ANC, which it hitherto considered a reactionary movement. By 1926 some 1 600 of its 1 750 members were black.

A major strategic change was initiated in 1927–1928 by James la Guma, secretary of its Cape Town branch, and Josiah Gumede, ANC president. Attending a Communist-sponsored conference in Belgium they proposed a motion endorsing the 'right of self-determination through the complete overthrow of capitalism and imperialist domination – the principle of Africa for the Africans'. On the invitation of the Communist International they visited Moscow.

Under pressure from Moscow, the SACP adopted a new policy in 1928 to work towards 'an independent native republic as a stage towards a workers' and peasants' revolution'. For the next 75 years this slogan informed Communist strategic thinking. According to this, South Africa found itself in a colonial situation in which socialism would be effected in two stages: a nationalist democratic revolution in which communists would forge an alliance with 'reformist' blacks to overcome white domination and, only after black power had been consolidated, a socialist revolution.

Gumede failed to win support for this in the ANC and was replaced as president in 1930. Over the next decade the ANC nearly became defunct. The communists initially also lost much of their popular following. But the core idea of an alliance between communists of all colours and black nationalists was born.

with the police. In the same year there was also a general strike of railway and harbour workers in East London.

In the meantime the South African Communist Party had undergone a fundamental change of course and was now proposing a Native Republic (*see box*).

A framework of segregation

The main white political parties still pursued the chimera of 'a white man's land'. Black people formed a growing urban presence. By 1912 there were already 420 000 blacks in the towns and cities in the common or 'white' area, a third of South Africa's urban population and 13% of the total black population. Shantytowns were springing up rapidly on the outskirts of the cities. The white municipalities ran these shantytowns in an unplanned way, usually making a profit; the residents themselves got little in return for their rent and taxes. Serious diseases like tuberculosis found an ideal breeding ground in the unsanitary and overcrowded hovels.

Smuts could not square this with his idea of whites acting as the trustees of blacks. He said: 'The natives have come to our towns unprovided for. They have picked up our diseases, and have found our white civilisation a curse to them . . . The Native question is so large. We know so little about it.' He believed that proper housing and proper control of blacks in the urban areas was an obligation of the state. If it accepted this obligation, South Africa would remove 'one of the biggest blots resting on our civilisation'.

In the meantime further segregationist pressures had built up. In 1922 a Transvaal local government commission headed by Colonel C.F. Stallard, one of the most prominent English-speaking segregationists, proposed that blacks were required in the urban areas only to 'minister to the needs of whites' and must depart from there when they 'ceased so to minister'.

Smuts depended on the judgment of his friend and leading Cape liberal, F.S. Malan, Minister of Mines, who probably had a leading hand in the bills dealing with urban blacks drafted between 1917 and 1923. Malan did not assume that collectively blacks constituted a threat. He had a vision of native 'villages' where black people who were 'civilised could feel at home and develop'. Because of their stake in the status quo they could become a bulwark against labour unrest and political agitation. Meeting an African delegation in 1920, he promised a better deal for regular and 'reliable' black workers, better housing and exemptions from the pass laws.

Smuts allowed Malan to speak in these terms because he himself believed in 'class legislation'. Such laws distinguished between the 'ordinary native', who had not yet emerged from 'barbarism', and the more 'advanced' blacks, who could take control of their own social problems in villages of their own. The Native Urban Areas Bill that the Smuts government submitted to a consultative Native Conference in 1923 envisaged that settled blacks could acquire freehold property. It aimed to improve the administration of black residential areas.

But white politics had reached the stage where any such improvement would be seen as undermining the claim to a white man's land. Barry Hertzog spelled out the claim in 1922: 'The [native] gets his own territory where all rights would be granted to him. He can live in our land, but can demand no rights here. The opposite is also true.' If blacks could get freehold property, acquiring 'white man's land', they would soon demand 'the white man's vote'. And that would be 'a matter of life and death for white civilisation'.

Smuts caved in and the provision to grant property rights was withdrawn from this bill, which was passed and promulgated as the Native Urban Areas Act. Confronted by an angry delegation from the South African Native National Congress, he pointed to the Bloemfontein location, where no freehold existed, but which was 'one of the most orderly and best run in the country'.

Black townships remained a neglected stepchild of urban administration. To add insult to injury the Act accepted the formula first developed by the municipality of Durban for funding the townships; its main source of revenue was the proceeds from the sale of sorghum beer to the captive market. The more black people drank, the more funds there would be for housing and other necessities.

The Union constitution of 1909, the Natives Land Act of 1913 and the Native Urban Areas Act of 1923 formed the basis of policy towards blacks for the rest of the century. The Natives Land Act was of paramount importance. Because it made no new land available, the reserves quickly became congested and the limited opportunities for individual tenure were further restricted by the strong support for communal tenure in the traditional African system.

Among some of the more liberal whites the belief persisted that with more land blacks would accept the policy. In 1923 Selby Msimang of the African National Congress said that blacks would be happy with territorial segregation if the Natives Land Act granted half of the land in the country for black occupation. But by now every white leader knew that giving half or even a quarter of the land to blacks would have severe political costs. Whites had come to believe that some 90% of South Africa was 'white man's land', and they were less and less inclined to sacrifice any part of it.

that test, do not differentiate, let him be treated as a full citizen of the country . . . You cannot divide the interests of a people, whether a man is black or brown or white.'

BELOW: *J.B.M. Hertzog, who founded the National Party in Bloemfontein in 1913. During his first term as prime minister, from 1924 to 1929, his party laid the foundation of the parastatal sector of South Africa by establishing the corporations Iscor (for steel production) and Escom (as electricity supplier). Along with Jan Smuts, leader of the South African Party, Hertzog formed the United Party, which in 1936 introduced a bill that removed the Cape Africans from the common voters' roll and doubled the land mass of the reserves.*

A framework for white labour

Although the Smuts government was badly shaken by the 1922 strike, it decided against extending the colour bar on the mines. It saw improved training for whites as a better option. Minister of Mines and Industry F.S. Malan explained to Parliament in 1923 that he did not wish to extend the colour bar. 'It is degrading to the white man to say that [he] should be artificially protected against the native and coloured man . . . The reason why a number [of white miners] are in danger today is that so many are not efficient miners.' The white workers had not availed themselves of the opportunities at the mining schools to become trained workers. They went into the mines as learners, Malan said, 'and learners they remained'.

While Smuts was prepared to accommodate white labour, he felt that they must not 'tyrannise everything'. A legal colour bar was an admission by whites that they could not compete against blacks, and had to take recourse to laws that violated human rights and fairness. He did not contemplate giving blacks the vote, but he also believed that 'no statutory barrier should be placed on the native who wishes to raise himself in the scale of civilisation'. It was necessary to see that 'no injustice [was] done to any other section of the community'.

The Smuts government nevertheless embarked on a major shift in the system of industrial bargaining that legalised a superior bargaining position for white workers. Under the old system, unions were barely tolerated and destructive strikes erupted over the colour bar. The Industrial Conciliation Act passed by the Smuts government in 1924 provided for reaching legally binding agreements in industrial councils consisting of employer associations and white or largely white trade unions. Employers could not lock out striking workers and workers could not strike before the council had tried to resolve a conflict. But unionised workers had to sacrifice the lightning strike, their major weapon.

On the other hand the industrial conciliation machinery favoured white and coloured workers by excluding 'pass bearers' (meaning blacks) from trade union membership, giving white-led unions a commanding role in determining occupational structures, and access to training and wages.

Before the 1924 election, the National Party (NP) and the Labour Party agreed to form a Pact to support each other's candidates against South African Party (SAP) candidates. Of the 135 seats, the NP won 63 and Labour 18 against the SAP's 53. Hertzog formed an NP-Labour government. The SAP had suffered a stunning defeat *(see box)*.

The Hertzog government that came to power after the momentous election of 1924 added a weapon that the state could use against employers who wished to undercut white labour – the Wage Act of 1925. It empowered the responsible minister 'to set the same minimum wages for whites and blacks'. The assumption was that if black and white wages were set at the same level employers would prefer whites. The government and its successors used these weapons sparingly. The priority was to enable the economy, particularly the mining industry, to grow and to provide jobs. Various trade-offs were made between the government and the mining industry. It was not expected that the latter would help solve the poor-white problem by employing them, or even to pay white miners particularly well. (White miners' wages only began rising towards the end of the 1930s, but those of black miners did not increase in real terms before the early 1970s.)

But the government would not tolerate unilateral decisions by the industry to reduce its white labour force sharply. An amendment to the Mines and Works Act was added to protect white mineworkers from displacement. In 1932 the Chamber of Mines told a commission that the mines could manage with 'a materially smaller number' of whites, but such a policy was no longer an option. White miners rose in number from 22 099 in 1922 to about 28 000 in 1930.

The Pact government and Afrikaner interests

Hertzog's Pact government sought to ensure that both Afrikaners and the Afrikaans language would be given ample support. The SAP had wanted to promote the Afrikaans language and culture without creating tension between Afrikaans and English speakers, but little actually came of the principle of bilingualism while it was in power. In the civil

There were both short- and long-term reasons for the defeat of the South African Party (SAP) in the 1924 elections. The SAP government's brutal suppression of the 1922 strike cost it much of its labour support. Segments of black opinion opposed the National-Labour Party Pact, but the black leadership also had little stomach for the SAP, which lacked a clear racial policy. 'No policy, no vote' was the call that went out from the Cape African National Congress (ANC). The national leadership of the ANC sent a telegram to leaders of the black and coloured voters in the Cape to cast their ballots against the SAP. *Die Burger* reported that most coloureds voted for the Pact.

Within the white community there was also some unexpected support. *The Star* reported that some communists had decided to back the Pact. These developments prompted Smuts to declare that 'the Red Flag has come to South Africa', which was being given a foretaste of what the country would be reduced to under a Pact government. Some white English speakers also looked sympathetically at the policy of the National Party (NP) on segregation. Edgar Brookes, later a prominent liberal, thought that Hertzog's policy rightly aimed at uplifting not a few individuals but 'the Bantu as a whole'. As late as 1927 he considered the reserves 'a useful subsidiary measure to facilitate administration'.

In the long term the defeat of the SAP of Botha and Smuts can be seen as the culmination of a process that had started as early as 1912. Initially the Afrikaners followed Botha and Smuts because of their leadership during the South African War. Both were generals in that war, as was Hertzog. From the time of Hertzog's exclusion from the Botha cabinet in 1912, the SAP began to lose Afrikaans speaking followers. Gradually the NP grew stronger, gaining more Afrikaner support in each election. In 1920 the SAP absorbed the Unionist Party, which meant that the English-speaking group was no longer as divided as before, but the price Smuts paid was a further loss of Afrikaner support, particularly in the rural areas.

Hertzog's position was further strengthened by two Afrikaans newspapers, *Ons Vaderland* in the Transvaal and *Die Burger* in the Cape. The latter became the most influential Afrikaans paper, a position it would retain for the rest of the century.

---

service in 1925 there were still 3 792 officials out of a total of 13 000 who could speak only English, while a mere twelve could converse only in Afrikaans.

In time D.F. Malan, Minister of Internal Affairs in the Pact government, saw to it that more bilingual officials were appointed to the civil service, which meant that the number of Afrikaans speakers increased. By 1931 the ethnic composition of the civil service had changed: it consisted of 36% Afrikaans-speakers and 64% English speakers, but there were considerably more English speakers in the higher-paid positions.

In the early 1920s the Afrikaans language and culture were still in their developmental phase. From the turn of the century, however, writers such as C. Louis Leipoldt, C.J. Langenhoven, Totius and Eugène Marais had shown that Afrikaans had the potential to be a lively and expressive medium. With the recognition of Afrikaans as an official language on 27 May 1925, its long evolution from spoken to written language was at last complete. A select committee of Parliament found that Afrikaans had developed sufficiently to be used as a legal and administrative medium. In Parliament a two-thirds majority was easily obtained on the acceptance of Afrikaans as an official language, although a significant number of English speakers – especially in Natal – could not disguise their indignation with regard to statutory bilingualism.

The Hertzog government also contributed £25 000 towards the creation of an Afrikaans dictionary, the *Woordeboek van die Afrikaanse Taal*. With government support the translation of the Bible into Afrikaans, which had been started in 1919, progressed so well that it was completed and published in 1933. By the late 1920s there was thus evidence of a distinct cultural drive as far as Afrikaans and the Afrikaner were concerned. This was to continue in the 1930s but a political angle was now added: a revival of the republican ideal, although it was seen as a long-term goal that had to be attained peacefully.

TOP: As the author of the new national anthem Die Stem van Suid-Afrika, *C.J. Langenhoven was 'the man who gave white South Africa a voice'.*

BOTTOM: *The descendant of German missionaries, Christian Frederik Louis (C. Louis) Leipoldt (1880-1947) was a medical doctor and Afrikaans poet. As medical inspector of schools in the Transvaal after Union, he drew attention to the shocking state of ill-health among* armblanke *children. In 1937 he published his memoir,* Bushveld Doctor.

CHAPTER ELEVEN

Diverse communities

Urbanisation and change

Between 1900 and 1930 South Africa had steadily become a more urbanised, integrated, Christianised and Westernised society. In the forefront of cultural change were the English-language missionary societies, which had begun to abandon segregation and were groping towards a common society using English as the linking language. The Afrikaans churches, by contrast, were laying the ideological base for apartheid. The English and the Jewish sections continued to dominate the urban economy, but were forced to abandon their close identification with the Empire and Crown as South Africa made progress towards a sovereign state.

The coloured people saw their hopes of benefiting from the 'civilised labour' policy dashed, prompting the educated elite to turn to radical politics. Those bearing the brunt of South Africa's rapid industrialisation were the poor – black, coloured and white – in the towns and in the rural areas. Missionaries found new fields among impoverished people who had begun their exodus from the reserves and farms. The education they provided to coloured and black children played an increasingly important role in the economy whose base was shifting towards manufacturing where black numbers increased by nearly eight times in the first half of the century. The manufacturing sector increasingly required a stable black and white work force, which lived with their families and became better skilled in order to increase their productivity.

While only one-tenth of the black population was urbanised in 1911, this jumped to a third by 1960. By 1946 the black population of Johannesburg stood at 400 000 – double

RIGHT: *An election poster for the South African Party shows Jan Smuts trying to prevent the Pact alliance plunging the country into chaos. After the Smuts government's brutal suppression of the mine workers' strike, the dominant classes were concerned that the new Pact government of Afrikaner nationalists and organised white labour, which had been backed in the 1924 election by elements in the Communist Party and the ANC, would embark on a radical form of populism by cutting ties with the British Empire, heavily taxing the mining corporations, pressing for high wages for white labour, offering unsustainable subsidies for struggling white farmers and cutting back on the limited rights of blacks and coloureds. Except for the latter these fears did not materialise.*

the figure of ten years earlier. The Afrikaners had also urbanised rapidly. By 1890 only some 10 000 lived in towns with a population of more than 2 000. By 1936 some 535 000 Afrikaners, comprising half the ethnic group, were urbanised.

Many of the first generation urbanised Afrikaners were devoid of any suitable labour skills or proper education for the urban economy. Only their skin colour distinguished them from recently urbanised black or coloured people. It was they who were the most visible of the so-called poor whites – a term borrowed from the southern states of the United States. It did not designate a measurable level of poverty but a condition deemed unsuitable for a white person in a white supremacist state. Parliament would consider the poor-white problem the most pressing issue in the early twentieth century.

LEFT: *Cape Town in the early 1930s.*

SELECTED POPULATION FIGURES			
	1904	**1930**	**1950/51**
WHITE POPULATION	1 117 234	1 801 000	2 641 689
BLACK POPULATION	3 490 291	5 585 000	8 556 390
TOTAL POPULATION	5 174 827	8 540 000	12 667 759

WORKERS IN MANUFACTURING			
	1916	**1930**	**1950**
WHITES	39 624	91 024	191 093
BLACKS	35 065	90 517	267 070

A new spiritual force

Missionary efforts continued steadily in the course of the nineteenth century, bringing about not only a large increase in converts, but also a major expansion of literacy. The colonial states had left the education of black and coloured children to churches and missionary societies. Protestant missionaries remained key players in racial politics in South Africa deep into the twentieth century.

By the mid-1930s the English-speaking churches and missionary societies would discard the hope that some good could come for blacks out of segregation. They would rally around the common belief of nineteenth-century missionaries that command of the English language and of Western culture and habits were the key to success in a society that was increasingly becoming economically and culturally integrated. Meanwhile, Afrikaner-funded missions would walk further on the road of segregation, stressing the education of blacks in their mother tongue and own culture. But it was only in the 1950s that the English-speaking and Afrikaner churches would come to a parting of the ways.

A challenge to old methods

A major challenge to missionary methods had occurred in the 1890s. The rapid expansion of the Protestant missionary enterprise was shaken when several black clergymen broke away from their missions to found their own black-ruled churches. The church founded by the Wesleyan, Mangena Mokone, later joined by James Dwane, was called the Ethiopian Church, in reference to the black nation of Ethiopia frequently mentioned in the Bible. The term was later attached to the whole movement. Most Ethiopian clergy were highly trained and deeply committed to the theological beliefs of their missionary mentors.

Though some tolerated polygamy, the Ethiopian rebels were not driven by a desire to alter doctrine or Africanise Christianity. Virtually every secession involved a dispute with a missionary – often over control of funds, or a symbolic slight to the dignity and professional standing of black clergy. 'No Native minister is honoured among the white brethren,' said Mokone; racial separation at clergy meetings showed that 'we can't be brothers'. Although some early Ethiopians were politically active, the mainspring of their movement was ecclesiastical, a desire for black-run churches.

White authorities were nonetheless alarmed by Ethiopianism, especially when Mokone and Dwane affiliated with the African Methodist Episcopal Church, the largest US black denomination, whose Bishop H.M. Turner, an outspoken pan-Africanist, toured South Africa in 1898. But, as the predominantly religious motivation of Ethiopianism became apparent, the panic died down. Dwane and his followers eventually joined the Anglican Church, as the separate Order of Ethiopia. Some other Ethiopian groups were reconciled to their missions, though most remained independent and spawned frequent new breakaways, as the Ethiopian movement spread over the African continent in a pattern of endless fission.

Missionaries experienced Ethiopianism as a personal betrayal by their closest African associates. They did not easily recover from the blow. James Stewart, the veteran Church of Scotland missionary and principal of the prestigious school for blacks at Lovedale,

suffered deeply from the rebellion of his colleague P.J. Mzimba, who broke away from the Scots mission to form the African Presbyterian Church. Stewart's legal adviser recalled that Mzimba's defection had 'left a scar that would not heal, a scar upon [Stewart's] heart that . . . he felt each day until he died'. Many missionaries, anticipating further struggles with their black colleagues and the loss of still more black followers, began to restructure their ministries. Surrendering their pastoral functions to black clergy, many redirected their energies from church management to social activism.

By the 1930s a new force, which would prove much greater than Ethiopianism, was altering much of African Christianity. Scores of new churches were being founded, deeply affected by African belief and spirituality, but with roots in the United States. At the turn of the twentieth century, a number of 'Zionist' and, later, Pentecostal mission-aries arrived from America with new teachings about 'baptism in the Holy Spirit', the power of the Spirit to effect physical healings and, among the Pentecostals, speaking in tongues. The emphasis on the Spirit proved highly congenial to blacks, who flocked to white evangelists, particularly to a revival at Wakkerstroom in the Transvaal, but quickly hived off to found churches of their own.

Before long, this movement (labelled 'Zionism' by scholars, after one of its main in-spirations, Zion City in Illinois) was growing more rapidly than Ethiopianism, especially in rural areas. African prophets tightly organised communities, often called Zion Cities. Attracting many followers, particularly through their emphasis on physical healing, most such churches owed much to the charisma of their founders or their founders' children. Numerous innovations appeared: elaborate garments, uniforms for members, adoption of Old Testament symbols such as the menorah candlestick, worship on Saturday instead of Sunday, and the shofar horn, and, in some cases, a toleration of polygamy.

For the most part rural (they would spread very rapidly in the cities after World War II), the prophetic African churches appeared rarely on the national scene. One important exception was the Israelites of Enoch Mgijima, whose clash with government forces and the subsequent deaths and injuries of his followers have already been noted.

As blacks flooded into the burgeoning cities of South Africa and poverty deepened in the African countryside, missionaries found vast new fields of ministry, providing social services and advocating political and social reforms for their black following.

ABOVE: *Established in 1842, Lovedale College had almost 400 students in 1874, of whom half were Christian. Initially pupils were taken through the first six years of the school curriculum, and there was a class that trained teachers for primary schools. Later Junior High School was added, but Lovedale long remained the only place in the country where blacks could attain this school level. By the end of the century more than 100 black students were studying abroad.*

To foster these aims they created a new region-wide body, the General Missionary Conference, in 1904. Responding to the crises of rural and urban blacks, missionaries turned increasingly to American ideas on race relations – particularly to the moderate views and politics advocated by Booker T. Washington and his colleagues at Tuskegee Institute – and to 'social gospel' influences emanating from the international missionary movement based in London.

Missionaries turned to the social gospel only after grappling with social disorders for which they could find no spiritual remedy. For example, American missionaries in Durban and Johannesburg concluded that the gospel of individual conversion that they had been preaching was inadequate to deal with the temptations of drunkenness, crime and sexual immorality to which black rural migrants were exposed in conditions of extreme poverty and racial discrimination.

D.F. Malan, the future prime minister and initiator of apartheid, began his career as a Dutch Reformed clergyman dedicated to missions and the social gospel. Unlike most of his missionary contemporaries, however, he slowly shifted his social concern from coloureds to poor white Afrikaners. In 1915, to foster the upliftment of poor whites, Malan resigned his ministry and became editor of *Die Burger* and a National Party politician.

Missionaries and social activism

By the 1920s there was still no prominent figure in the Dutch Reformed Church (DRC) who advocated the DRC practice of segregated schools, parishes and churches as a model for political or economic discrimination. Indeed Johannes du Plessis (no relation to J.C du Plessis), a towering figure in the DRC missions field from as early as 1910, was urging Afrikaners to govern blacks in a Christian manner. In 1921 Du Plessis, professor at the Theological School at Stellenbosch, edited a manifesto by ten leading figures in missionary circles who tried to defend the DRC against the charge of influential black academic D.D.T. Jabavu that it was 'an anti-native church'. The statement admitted that the DRC had fallen short in its ministries to black people, but pointed out in partial exculpation that it was the only large church in the country whose missions relied exclusively on funding from local whites. While the DRC writers regarded segregation as a 'most excellent theory', they were more aware of the ambiguities, contradictions and pitfalls of segregation than were many English-speaking theorists of the time.

The DRC mission leaders did not restrict themselves to vague expressions of goodwill towards blacks, but made striking concrete demands. Educated blacks should be exempted from the pass laws, black workers should have the right to strike, and 'Bantu tradesmen' should be able to compete unhindered against whites. They insisted, too, on

ABOVE: *John Tengo Jabavu and some English-speaking supporters. Jabavu was one of the first generation of missionary-educated westernised black leaders. He was educated at Healdtown and in 1884 started his own newspaper* Imvo Zabantsundu *with the help of white liberal friends. In 1898 he backed the alliance of the liberal faction and the Afrikaner Bond of Jan Hofmeyr in Parliament against the increasingly aggressive imperialist policies of Alfred Milner. In 1909 he was part*

expanded secondary education for blacks. In 1923 the DRC's Federal Council, a body created to deal with church issues across provincial boundaries, convened an inter-church conference of some 50 leaders, both white and black. This meeting marked the highest level of consensus on segregation that blacks, English-speaking whites and Afrikaners would ever attain. It called for 'differential development of the Bantu', but also rejected 'complete segregation'.

Though marginalised in white parliamentary politics, English-speaking missionaries strove to enhance their influence by allying with elite, extra-parliamentary networks. Three groups in particular became their allies: white paternalist theorists like C.T. Loram and Edgar Brookes, who expounded a mild form of segregation as a Christian alternative to blatant white domination; black nationalist leaders – including almost all the founders of the African National Congress – most of them educated in mission schools and committed to the tenets and language of the social gospel; and international missionary statesmen like the Scot J.H. Oldham, who enabled South African missionaries to raise funds from US charitable foundations and gain a hearing in the governing councils of the British Empire.

Protestant missionary influence in South African politics reached its peak in the years immediately after the inter-church conference of 1923, when an extraordinary Christian coalition – English-speaking missionaries in the centre, black nationalist leaders on the left, Afrikaner churchmen on the right – demanded reforms from the South African government. Johannes du Plessis led this alliance, which seemed to herald a concerted attack on the perennial injustices of South African society. A pugnacious controversialist, Du Plessis never hedged his provocative views for any audience, white or black. His complex political vision enabled him to hold together a motley alliance of interest groups. It was his mildly modernist theology, not his politics, which undid him in 1928 when authorities in his own church charged him with heresy.

Embroiled in a series of well-publicised ecclesiastical and civil trials, Du Plessis lost his ability to lead the DRC into ecumenical endeavours. At the same time many black leaders were turning away from missionary leadership. As a new ideology, labelled 'apartheid' from as early as 1929 (*see box*), gained ground in the DRC, the time for reform by an interracial Christian coalition had passed.

Many of the principal themes of apartheid were initially developed among missionary leaders in the DRC, who strove to reconcile the church's missionary obligation to blacks

of the delegation led by William Schreiner that lobbied the imperial government to change the colour clauses in the draft Union constitution.

OPPOSITE TOP: *Dr D.F. Malan took a keen interest in missionary work while serving as minister of the Dutch Reformed Church in Montagu between 1906 and 1912. This was later supplanted by his concern for poor whites and by his leadership role in the Afrikaner nationalist movement.*

ORIGINS OF THE TERM 'APARTHEID'

A pamphlet publishing the proceedings of a conference held in 1929 in the Free State town of Kroonstad to discuss the expansion of the missionary efforts by the Dutch Reformed Church (DRC) contains the first printed record of the term 'apartheid'. The term appears in a speech of the Rev. J.C. du Plessis of Bethlehem. It was made against the background of anxiety over the rapid spread of Ethiopianism.

Since the 1890s the Ethiopian movements had formed independent churches that attracted large numbers of Africans, frustrated with the fact that all the main Christian churches were loath to advance blacks quickly in church offices.

Another challenge to white supremacy was that of the Industrial and Commercial Workers' Union (ICU) of Africa, which in some Free State districts tried to recruit farm workers. A study noted that by the end of the 1920s 'the [Kroonstad] district was seething with rumours of pending unrest'.

In addressing the conference Du Plessis said: 'In the fundamental idea of our missionary work and not in racial prejudice one must seek an explanation for the spirit of apartheid that has always characterised our

[the DRC's] conduct'. He rejected a missions policy that offered blacks no 'independent national future'.

By 'apartheid' Du Plessis meant that the Gospel had to be taught in a way that strengthened the African 'character, nature and nationality' – in other words, the *volkseie* (the people's own). Blacks had to be uplifted 'on their own terrain, separate and apart'. Blacks and whites had to worship separately to 'ensure the survival of a handful of [Afrikaner] people cut off from their national ties in Europe'.

To justify the Afrikaners protecting their cultural and social exclusivity Du Plessis tried to turn the *eie* (own) or the *selfsyn* (being oneself) into a universal value. Implicit in this was the view that only identification with one's own ethnic community was authentic. Du Plessis envisaged the development of autonomous, self-governing black churches as a counter to English missionaries, who tried to gain converts by copying 'Western civilisation and religion'.

At a meeting in 1935 of the Federal Council of the DRC a common missions policy was formulated. The church was firm that 'education must not be denationalised',

but must be based on the group's national culture, giving a prominent place to its language, history and customs. It called for blacks and coloured people to be assisted in developing 'into self-respecting Christian nations'. Two aspects were new. For the first time coloureds were brought into the scheme as a 'separate nation'. And the church put the stress on the equal worth of all 'self-respecting nations', while before 1935 it had emphasised the equal worth of all individuals before God.

Thus DRC ministers and missionary strategists were first in the field to formulate an apartheid ideology. Church ministers and theologians were much less inclined than secular academics or politicians to condone blatant racial discrimination on account of a perceived racial 'inferiority'. For most of them there could be no question of a hierarchy of souls, churches or cultures. Yet the church also insisted that coloured and black people could be segregated because their cultures were different. Grateful for the opening the church had given them, Nationalist politicians and academics were careful not to offend the church's sensitivities.

OPPOSITE TOP: *In 1923 Z.K. Matthews (1901–1968) became the first student to graduate from Fort Hare College. A school for missionaries at a military fort in the town of Alice was turned into the South African Native College in 1916, later called the University College of Fort Hare. Matthews was on the staff for many years. As a member of the ANC, he played a major role in African politics and in the dialogue that took place in the 1920s between whites and blacks on the Joint Councils and the Bantu-European Conferences. Alan Paton, the biographer of Jan Hofmeyr, considered him at least the intellectual peer of the latter, and described him as a man who could mix diplomacy and bluntness with the greatest urbanity. He went into exile in 1960. His son Joe served as deputy minister in the first democratic government, and his granddaughter Naledi Pandor was appointed Minister of Education in 2004.*

with its attempt to build a *volkskerk* for white Afrikaners – a scheme to foster a form of separate 'development' among blacks that would fulfil the duty of white Christians but not threaten white supremacy. The word apartheid first appeared in print as part of the proceedings of a DRC missions conference in the Orange Free State (*see box*).

The first black challenges

Land hunger and labour demands prompted Africans during the 1920s and 1930s to take to Zionism or Ethiopianism in great numbers. In 1921 there were some 50 000 adherents of Zionist or Ethiopian bodies, out of a total of 1.3 million African Christian converts. By 1936 their numbers had jumped to over a million, the vast majority of whom were in the countryside.

One of the instigators of the aggressive expression of apartheid, which was allied to Afrikaner nationalism and originated in the 1930s in the DRC of the Orange Free State, was the missionary leader J.G. Strydom (no relation to the later prime minister). He was a truculent nationalist who believed that only the most aggressive evangelisation of blacks could save the Afrikaner 'volk and fatherland' from egalitarian notions propagated among blacks by communists and English-speaking missionaries. In 1935, the Union-wide DRC adopted as its official Mission Policy a more moderate version of apartheid; it hoped that the policy, which called upon whites to make significant sacrifices for blacks' advance, would win the support of blacks as well as international public opinion.

Both the Afrikaans-speaking and English-speaking missionaries continued to influence the government's racial policy and the resistance to it beyond 1948 (*see box*).

THE POST-1948 INFLUENCE OF MISSIONARIES

Many initiatives begun by English-speaking missionaries were perpetuated, even into the 1950s, by secular actors who retained a Christian idiom in their activities, along with a Christian commitment to non-violence. Among them were white researchers at the South African Institute of Race Relations; the novelist Alan Paton, whose *Cry the Beloved Country* moved an international audience with a Christian vision of racial reconciliation; several founders of the interracial Liberal Party; and black politicians such as Albert John Luthuli, secretary-general of the African National Congress from 1952 to 1967 and winner of a Nobel Peace Prize.

Similarly, the Dutch Reformed missionary-rooted vision of apartheid was secularised in the 1950s – a process exemplified in the life of G.B.A. Gerdener, the leading Dutch Reformed mission theorist, who helped draft the Nationalists' apartheid manifesto in 1948 and, increasingly, in the 1950s shifted much of his activity from the churches to SABRA, a secular Afrikaner think-tank. Gerdener, and also W.W.M. Eiselen, a missionary son who shaped the government's educational policy for blacks, powerfully expounded apartheid ideas in terms congenial to the Christian conscience of many Afrikaners.

In the mid-1950s, the Nationalist government forced the closing of mission schools and hospitals, thus depriving the missionary movement of its principal power base. Simultaneously in Europe and North America enthusiasm was waning for Protestant missions. Blacks, for their part, were drifting away from the accommodationist tactics of the white missionaries and confronted the government directly in the Programme of Action of 1949 and the Defiance Campaign of 1952. Radical missionary clergy like the English Anglicans Michael Scott and Trevor Huddleston, impatient with their churches' caution, involved themselves openly in black politics and, in consequence, were expelled or withdrawn from South Africa by their superiors.

In a series of conferences and colloquia, church leaders desperately tried to fend off a final rupture between the English-speaking Protestant churches and the DRC. In 1960 at the Cottesloe Consultation, convened by the World Council of Churches, representatives of the DRC valiantly signalled their disagreement with major contentions and policies of the Nationalist government. Yet soon after, denounced publicly by Prime Minister Hendrik Verwoerd and repudiated by their own synods, they recanted. The disappearance of missionaries as major players in South Africa coincided almost exactly with the opening of a gap between churches that would not be bridged for decades.

Alan Paton

The hopes for black education

Between the mid-1920s and the mid-1930s the African ability to exert pressure seemed to be slipping. The ICU, the only mass trade union, had collapsed and the ANC had lost its coherence. Whites drifted into the increasing acceptance of the Hertzog bills that demanded comprehensive segregation. Yet despite the Depression, black intellectuals had not abandoned the basic framework of the capitalist system and, more particularly, the core value of economic individualism and the belief that any individual could succeed through education, hard work and self-help. Instead of turning to socialism, most of them believed whites would reconsider the demand for black representation if they could back up their demand by black economic success. Yet success was impossible without good education, not to speak of equal education.

Z.K. Matthews, the first graduate from Fort Hare and an alumnus of the Yale and Harvard universities, remarked that education was the 'prime means of solving the problem created by the juxtaposition of White and Black'. But the state did not have a non-racial vision of education and was not prepared to move spending on white and black education towards parity.

All blacks paid taxes, but spending on education was limited to a fixed sum and a fixed portion of a general tax they paid. In 1930 Dr A.B. Xuma charged the government with grossly discriminating against blacks in spending. He argued that a common education brought out the best in white and black. While the government spent over £8 million on the education of the children of one and a half million whites, it committed only £500 000 for the education of children of five million blacks. Most of the money was taken from a tax imposed on blacks (*see box on page 262*).

As a result, black education was in a serious state of neglect. By 1928 only a quarter of black children received any schooling. Less than 1% were above the level of the first two school years. In the Cape Province, where education for blacks had reached the highest standards, two-thirds were without any school experience in 1939 and classes of 105 children per teacher were not uncommon.

There was some improvement in higher education. Before 1923 Lovedale was the only institution where black children could advance up to Junior High School, but missionaries subsequently established several new schools. By 1929 the number of children receiving junior certificates exceeded a hundred for the first time. Six years later the figure had jumped to 19 000.

For a long time Fort Hare was the only institution where blacks could prepare for matriculation. Between 1916 and 1925 a total of 42 got their matriculation certificates, rising to 130 in 1931–1934. Three students enrolled at the University College of Fort Hare in 1916. By 1935 enrolment had risen to 156.

Urban life

Living and working conditions for urban blacks were dismal. About one-third lived in informal houses. Few could get freehold tenure, so there was little incentive for those who lived in formal houses to improve them. Blacks in any event received such low wages that it was impossible for most to do so. Neither could they pay sufficient rent or taxes to enable the white municipalities to upgrade the locations under their control.

Blacks suffered a wide-ranging job colour bar. Apprenticeship committees excluded them from skilled jobs. Some white trade unions had black members, but most blacks were members of black trade unions, which could not take part in wage negotiations. Deficient education and training also formed major obstacles to advancement.

In a multitude of ways black urban life was demeaning. Family income on average was half the living wage and their diet was often disgracefully deficient. Blacks were subjected to numerous laws that applied only to them. The great majority of those convicted of criminal offences were guilty of contravening the pass laws and the possession of 'native' liquor, giving rise to what a government report called 'a burning sense of grievance and injustice'.

At the bottom of the labour market was a mass of migrant black workers without rights and with little choice but to sell their labour cheaply. The gold mines of the

ABOVE: *English writer Pauline Smith (1882 – 1959). Both Smith and Herman Charles Bosman (1905 –1951) produced remarkable short stories that evocatively depicted the life of the rural community. Smith's short story 'The Pain' (1924) and her novel* The Beadle *(1926) revealed what a literary critic called a 'strange, austere, tender and ruthless talent'. The most memorable character in Herman Charles Bosman's short stories is the shrewd and folksy Oom Schalk Lourens. The first of these stories appeared in the early 1930s. After the war the stories were republished in four volumes, of which* Mafeking Road *is the best known.*

DR XUMA'S CHARGE

In 1930, Dr A.B. Xuma, who ten years later became president-general of the ANC, addressed a conference of 'European and Bantu' Christian Associations at Fort Hare. This is what he had to say about education.

In the Cape Colony the earlier educational curriculum was identical for both Europeans and Bantu. Lovedale Mission Institution was opened with a class of 9 Europeans and of 11 Bantu students. [They] studied side by side. None seemed the worse for it. As a matter of fact, these generations of students produced some of the ablest and most prominent men in South Africa on both sides of the colour line . . . They were all being prepared and trained to play their part as citizens in their common country. It was in these generations that the best leaders among the Bantu were produced without any special system of education adapted to the African mentality and for the African mind . . . No one will deny that men like the Rev. Tiyo Soga, pioneer missionary, Mr John Tengo Jabavu, editor and journalist, the gifted Rev. Walter Benson Rubusana, and the versatile Rev. John Know Bokwe, were leaders, without regard to race or colour. They were educated as full citizens, able to stand alone, as men, in church, in the school, in public affairs, and not be assistants to someone else. The point worthy of note is that these boys when they began schooling were raw 'Kaffir boys'. They were primitive men, so-called. Not a day removed from savagery, or from the life of barbarism, and yet, side by side with white boys, they mastered the white man's education without special adaptation to Native mentality and needs and above all made best use of their education for the good of their country.

A.B. Xuma

Witwatersrand, the dynamo of the economy, were based largely on black migrant labour. By 1911 more than 90% of the black population of Johannesburg was male, working for very low wages; if they were paid more they would work less, so the justification went. Intending to return to the reserves, many blacks lived temporarily in wretched shacks or labour compounds. As a source of ultra-cheap labour, they were a constant threat to unskilled and even semi-skilled Afrikaner workers.

Black farm workers

On the white farms, where about a third of blacks lived, housing remained very poor and real wages, like those in the mines, did not improve until the early 1970s. For farmers, labour rather than segregation was the main issue. Until the 1920s the farmers' labour needs were met by 'resident natives' or squatters who worked for two or three days a week and in exchange received the right to build a hut, cultivate a garden plot and keep a few cattle. The squatters might also be paid some rations and a shilling a day. At this low rate of pay the white *bywoners* who lived on a farm could not compete.

The state named this arrangement labour tenancy and determined that a tenant should work at least 90 days a year and in some cases 180 days a year. But as in the case of the colonial states of the previous century these laws could not be enforced. Market forces were the real agent of change. Farming was fast becoming commercialised. Land values rose and intensive cultivation was introduced. A tenant was allowed less land, less time and fewer cattle on a farm. The farmers were also squeezed. The 1920s and 1930s were very tough. Throughout the 1920s agricultural prices fell and then dropped sharply as the Great Depression of 1929 hit the country. Prices for some agricultural products declined to 25% of their 1928 level.

The Native Economic Commission of 1932 described the change well:

> It is no longer economically possible for the farmer either to give the grazing which the Native wants or to allow him to work any portion of land . . . In such areas therefore labour shortage is beginning to be felt largely due to the farmers' inability to remunerate in the manner in which the Natives prefer.

Farmers now demanded the stricter application of pass laws. A pamphlet of the South African Institute of Race Relations (SAIRR) captured their mood: 'Native children should not be allowed to go to towns. [They] should not be allowed to leave the district without a pass from the Native Commissioner, and this pass should not be given if the farmer requires his services at a wage which satisfies the Commissioner.' 'Our natives must not be used,' a group of farmers demanded, adding that recruiting on farms for mines or public work should be prohibited. In response, the state issued a circular instructing officials not to issue passes without indicating the period for which a farm labourer was allowed to be absent.

Even more serious was the crisis in labour relationships. At the beginning of the war the liberal SAIRR noted a general deterioration of the racial situation in the rural areas, with farmers complaining that blacks 'had lost their respect for them', and that a 'strained relationship' had come to replace the old forms of co-existence. The average cash wage on a farm, including the value of food supplied in lieu of cash, was only a quarter of that in manufacturing. The outward-bound stream accelerated during the war years when the Smuts government relaxed the system of influx control that had kept many blacks out of the urban areas. In the mid-1950s a commission found that nearly half of the newly urbanised blacks had come from the farms.

A crisis in the reserves

A crisis was building up as a result of congestion in the reserves. The Native Economic Commission warned that pressure on land in the reserves was too severe to provide a home subsistence base for most migrant workers. Although half of the black population lived in the reserves, only a very small proportion was not connected to the 'white' economy, mostly through migrant remittances. Prominent liberal historian W.M. Macmillan wrote in *Complex South Africa* that the inhabitants of the reserves were 'dragging along at the very lowest level of subsistence, blighted by ill-health and starvation'. There was an appalling infant mortality rate. Families were more and more dependent on wage earning 'to relieve a dead level of poverty inside'.

By the 1930s the migration to the cities of the white and black poor had become the major social phenomenon. Addressing white and black students in 1930, Dr A.B. Xuma referred 'to the spirit of fear, of unrest, of uncertainty'. The mines and the farms demanded more labour, the municipalities wanted more power to deal with unemployed 'redundant natives' and the government adopted even more laws. More than half the adult male population of working age was employed as migrants. This not only eroded the subsistence farming in the reserves, but also weakened the ability of migrant labourers in the city to organise. It impacted very negatively on African family life and the prospects for a settled black urban society.

The Native Economic Commission concluded that the reserves could not support their populations, but was obdurate that the answer did not lie in allowing urbanisation. It was rather to control the movement away from the reserves and farms, and to develop the reserves. But the commission also accepted that there was a need for a population of permanently resident 'natives' employed by secondary industry. Their level of education and efficiency had to safeguard them against being undercut by the flow of cheap casual labour from the reserves.

OPPOSITE: *Migrant labourers in transit from the rural reserve to the city where they entered into labour contracts, usually for nine months or a year.*

TOP: *A picture of traditional Africans on a plot that allowed for some subsistence farming.*

BELOW: *A village in the reserves. The system of migrant labour originated as the main form of labour for the mines but in the twentieth century assumed an important additional function: it limited urban blacks to adult males engaged in migrant labour. By the 1930s the subsistence crisis, seen in this picture, had become so severe that people began streaming from the reserves to the cities.*

ABOVE: *A rural coloured woman bakes bread in a clay oven. The majority of coloured people were very poor, employed as unskilled labourers on farms or as domestic workers. Most of the trade unions refused to accept coloureds as members, and skilled workers earned less than half as much as their white counterparts. There were virtually no coloured people in senior administrative positions in the civil service and few in the professions. Coloured teachers, nurses and policemen serving the coloured population suffered discrimination with respect to their salaries and pensions. Coloured women, who mostly worked as domestic workers, received very low wages.*

RIGHT: *A yard in Vrededorp, Johannesburg, where many of Afrikaner workers lived in the 1930s. Many of the Afrikaner girls in employment supported their families and had a tough time making ends meet, often living in a back yard. E.S. (Solly) Sachs, who was secretary of the Garment Workers' Union, thought that the living conditions of some of the young Afrikaner women in Johannesburg were among the worst in the world.*

In some ways the commission foreshadowed the apartheid thinking of a decade later, but, as Macmillan argued in *Complex South Africa*, restricting blacks to remote reserves and imposing pass laws on them forced them to work for very low wages. It was not their blackness but their cheapness that threatened the permanent urban workers. If the curbs on blacks from the reserves were removed the domestic market would grow and the wages of whites as well as blacks would rise.

Coloureds: between white and black

The coloured community was a diverse one with, at the one end, farm labourers, domestic servants and unskilled labourers in the towns, who were generally poorly paid. At the other end were a very small stratum of skilled labourers and a small smattering of professionals, who were mostly teachers. Those who managed to urbanise after the emancipation of the slaves saw education as the major escape route from poverty.

Church and mission schools carried almost all the responsibility for coloured education. Although it had a non-racial constitution, the Cape Colony comprehensively discriminated against people on class grounds. In 1865 the government established non-denominational schools, funding them on a pound-for-pound basis. As a result these schools were financially much better off. Due to the poverty of the coloured people very few could afford them. The non-denominational schools became predominantly white, while almost all coloured and black children went to mission schools, which were free or asked only low fees.

By 1885 only 2% of mission school children were in standards higher than Standard Four. Since the schools were free or demanded only low fees and received little state funding, the quality of education suffered. Nevertheless, by the 1890s coloured and black children outpaced whites in the drive to get education. Segregated education continued, and by the time of Union there were only three non-denominational schools for coloured students in the Cape Town area.

For coloured people the demand was not so much integrated schools but equal state spending on white and coloured schools and compulsory education for all. In both respects they were rebuffed. In 1905 the Progressives under Leander Starr Jameson in the Cape Colony introduced compulsory and free education only for whites. Despairing of attaining equality, in 1922 a body of coloured teachers asked for a state subsidy of at least half the sum white children received. The South African Party government rejected the appeal, stating that it first had to attend to whites and that coloured people would have to wait their turn.

Other heavy blows fell in the first ten years of Union. The economic status of the coloured community was undermined by a number of laws designed to favour whites over blacks in the competition for employment. One of the most blatantly discriminatory laws was the 1911 Mines and Works Act that reserved a wide range of skilled and semi-skilled categories of labour in mining and industry for whites.

The 1921 Juvenile Affairs Act set up mechanisms for the placement of white youths into suitable employment while the Apprenticeship Act of 1922 put apprenticeships beyond the reach of the vast majority of coloured youths by stipulating a Standard Six pass as a minimum qualification for entry as an apprentice in 41 trades. It was an educational entry level that only a handful of coloured schools met, but that fell within the minimum educational standard set for white schools. The 1925 Wage Act, a pillar of the 'civilised labour' policy, subverted the ability of coloured labour to undercut white wage demands by setting high minimum-wage levels in key industries.

By the early 1930s the coloured community was marked by deepening poverty and growing political despondency. Because by far the greater part of this social group consisted of farm workers and a downtrodden urban proletariat, the Great Depression took a disproportionate toll in economic hardship. Additionally, coloured people, including the educated strata, suffered severe disadvantage in the workplace as a result of the Pact government's 'civilised labour' policy – despite promises that they would benefit from it by being included in the definition of 'civilised' and be protected from black competition along with whites.

A white skin became a better recommendation for a job than ability. Poor whites began displacing significant numbers of skilled and semi-skilled workers who were not white, especially in the public sector. Better-qualified coloured school-leavers found it progressively difficult to obtain suitable employment. The politicised coloured elite that aspired to acceptance within the dominant society was dealt a body blow in 1930 when only white women were enfranchised.

The immediate effect of this legislation was to reduce the coloured vote from 12.3% of the electorate to 6.7%. The Women's Enfranchisement Act of 1930 represented an about-face on the part of Prime Minister J.B.M. Hertzog. Throughout the latter half of the 1920s he had tried to entice coloured voters into supporting the National Party with the prospect of a 'New Deal' that would give them economic and political, but not social, equality with whites. This act was but the latest development in a decades-long trend of the erosion of coloured civil rights.

Coloured political organisation

Because of their marginality and the determination with which the state implemented white supremacist policies, the story of coloured political organisation through much of the twentieth century has largely been one of compromise, retreat and failure. The attrition started in the late nineteenth century with the raising of the franchise qualifications that struck thousands of black and coloured voters from the rolls. And from the 1890s white trade unions sought to subvert the prominence of coloured workers in the skilled trades in the western Cape. Discrimination intensified after the South African War of 1899–1902. The governments across South Africa made it their priority to reconcile English- and Afrikaans-speaking whites.

Because of their strong assimilationist impulse, politicised coloureds initially avoided forming separate political organisations, preferring to support white politicians who promised to promote coloured interests in return for their votes. By the early twentieth century, however, intensifying segregation forced coloureds to mobilise politically in defence of their rights. The first substantive coloured political body, the African Political Organisation (APO), was established in Cape Town in September 1902. The APO grew out of the 'Stone meetings' (named after the large boulders at which they were held) organised from May 1901 onwards by John Tobin, a leading personality in the coloured community. Held on Sunday mornings on the slopes of Table Mountain above District Six, these meetings provided a forum for the discussion of political issues affecting the coloured community. Stone meetings drew substantial crowds until they were superseded by the APO.

Tobin, who became vice-president of the APO, was expelled from the organisation in 1905 for his allegedly divisive behaviour. He continued to call Stone meetings sporadically till at least 1919, especially at election time. Tobin aligned himself with Afrikaner political interests and became a leading proponent of the idea that the coloured people should seek an affiliation within the fold of Afrikanerdom rather than within the English-speaking establishment.

The APO, which was liberal and Anglophile in outlook, dominated coloured politics until the mid-1930s. It became the main vehicle through which the coloured community voiced protest against the rising tide of segregation and pressed for reform. Although its constitution did not contain explicit racial bars, the APO was in effect a racially exclusive organisation, its aim being the advancement of coloured people. It did not seek to make common cause with black organisations or to recruit black members, despite its name. The term 'African' was meant to denote its geographical location and in a vague way to indicate international solidarity with black people.

In his 1910 presidential address, APO leader Dr Abdullah Abdurahman affirmed that the APO was 'an organisation of the coloured people only'. The APO felt it had little

RIGHT: *A 'Stone meeting'. In 1901 politically conscious coloured people began meeting on the slopes of Table Mountain to debate current affairs or to be addressed by white politicians. Soon Boland towns or mission stations began sending representatives to these meetings. The main organiser was businessman John Tobin, who stressed the themes of race pride and self-help within the context of equal rights for 'all civilised men', the ruling ideology of the Cape Colony.*

STRAATPRAATJES

Straatpraatjes, a satirical column that appeared in the African Political Organisation (APO) newspaper between 1909 and 1922, was written in vernacular Afrikaans characteristic of the coloured working class of Cape Town. Narrated with wit and ingenuity by the fictitious Piet Uithalder, it tells of his social experiences and political encounters as a voluntary worker at the APO's head office. Much of the humour derives from Uithalder's unsophisticated, rustic ways and rudimentary grasp of English. Among other things, Piet poked fun at the social pretensions of the coloured elite, lampooned rival political organisations and satirised the proceedings of Parliament, never shying away from sensitive issues. Besides inveighing against white racism, he took delight in ridiculing uncouth whites, especially 'rouwe boere van die backveld'. Uithalder's spirited rebuff of segregation and the novelty of addressing readers in the distinctive code of his community made Straatpraatjes one of the most effective weapons in the APO's journalistic arsenal. Evidence points to Abdullah Abdurahman, leader of the APO, as the author.

The idea of writing Straatpraatjes appears to have been prompted by the Parlementse Praatjes column, which appeared in *De Zuid-Afrikaan*, the leading Dutch newspaper at the Cape. Written in an urbane, lightly humorous vein under the pseudonym Jan Kieser, Parlementse Praatjes reported on the doings of Parliament in an educated, white, middle-class version of Afrikaans, which had not yet been formalised into a standard written form. Thus, just as the APO saw Parlementse Praatjes as representing the white supremacist interests of the Afrikaner in the language of the Afrikaner, so it instituted Straatpraatjes to voice coloured interests in the language of the coloured community. As the title of the column indicates, Uithalder consciously used this vernacular to contrast his Afrikaans of the street and kitchen with that of white speakers, which he associated with Parliament and parlour.

It is thus not surprising that Straatpraatjes adopted a defiant attitude. For example, Uithalder urged coloureds to assert themselves politically: 'Ons het lang genoeg gekruip net soes gediertes na die wit man. Dit is nou tijd dat ons moet reg op staan en nie met gebuide kneei "asseblief baas" en "ja baas" sê nie.' (We have crawled to the white man like animals for long enough. It is time that we stand up straight and no longer on bended knee say 'please boss' and 'yes boss'.) On one occasion he went as far as warning that there were coloureds '[wat] weet hoe om 'n boer agter die klip uit te haal' (who know how to remove a Boer from behind a boulder).

By 1913, however, a tone of despondency crept in with the inexorable advance of segregation. A frustrated Uithalder lost his sense of humour and assumed a hectoring tone, reflecting coloured disillusionment at their growing marginalisation.

It is ironic that Straatpraatjes used vernacular Afrikaans with such efficacy as the APO strongly advocated that coloured people 'endeavour to perfect themselves in English ... and drop the habit of expressing themselves in barbarous Cape Dutch'. English, an international language with a rich literature, which it identified with 'culture', 'progress' and liberal values, was contrasted with Cape Dutch, which it scorned as 'a bastard lingo' and 'vulgar patois fit only for the kitchen'. Afrikaans was also associated with the racism of the Afrikaner and with social inferiority within the coloured community itself.

Straatpraatjes represents an authentic replication of the Afrikaans vernacular spoken within the urban coloured community of the western Cape. It is also of interest as literature; not only the earliest known example of Afrikaans used to express black resistance to white domination, Uithalder is a pioneer of satirical writing in Afrikaans.

---

option but to follow a strategy of supporting the least racist of the white parties and one most likely to foster coloured interests. In the column Straatpraatjes in the APO newspaper, Abdurahman used the surprise weapon of satire against his Afrikaner nationalist adversaries *(see box)*.

Driven by the need for white allies against Afrikaner nationalists, Abdurahman was prepared to reconcile with his former political enemy Jan Smuts and support the South African Party, and later the United Party. The APO's politics of polite petitioning and moral suasion grew increasingly irrelevant as segregation became entrenched, leading to its demise in the mid-1940s.

There was a number of small, ephemeral, and generally more conservative, political organisations such as the South African Coloured Union formed in 1913, the United Afrikaner League of the late 1910s and the Afrikaanse Nasionale Bond of the latter half of the 1920s that competed for coloured support but failed to subvert the dominance of the APO. The latter two bodies were sponsored, if not started, by Cape National Party politicians who tried to woo coloured electoral support away from their more liberal opponents. The Afrikaanse Nasionale Bond and its associate, the Cape Malay Association, drew significant support especially among Afrikaans-speakers in the Boland towns on the basis of National Party promises of a 'New Deal' for coloureds. Both collapsed when Hertzog abandoned the much-vaunted 'New Deal' when an increased National Party

majority in the 1929 election made coloured support expendable. Fusion in 1933–1934 greatly strengthened the segregationist impetus in South African politics, further compromising the APO's strategy.

The failure of the APO's moderate approach to stem the torrent of discriminatory measures was instrumental in the emergence of a radical movement within the better-educated, urbanised sector of the coloured community during the latter half of the 1930s. During the 1920s coloured radicals such as John Gomas and James la Guma had organised individually in organisations such as the ICU, the SA Communist Party, which was founded in 1921, and the ANC, where they had a significant impact *(see box)*. Together with a new crop of activist leaders that included Goolam Gool, Cissie Gool and Ben Kies, they were at the forefront of this radicalism that injected a sense of purpose and excitement into coloured politics. Not only did Marxism provide these new recruits

LEFT: *Zairunissa (Cissie) Gool, daughter of Dr Abdullah Abdurahman and a member of the Cape Town City Council. A colourful personality in Cape politics, she established a reputation as a fearless champion of what was then known as the 'non-European cause'.*

DR ABDULLAH ABDURAHMAN

For three and a half decades before his death on 20 February 1940, Dr Abdullah Abdurahman was indubitably the most influential and popular political leader within the coloured community. His political acumen also won him widespread respect within the white political establishment and grudging acknowledgement from diehard opponents.

Abdurahman was born in Wellington in December 1872. Descended from grandparents who were manumitted slaves, he graduated as a medical doctor from the University of Glasgow in 1893 – a signal achievement. In 1904 he was the first person of colour to be elected to the Cape Town City Council, and represented Wards 6 and 7 (District Six) for the rest of his life. He chaired several council committees, wielding considerable clout. In 1914 he became the first coloured person to be elected to the Cape Provincial Council. He held the Castle Division seat until he died.

As president of the African Political Organisation (APO) between 1905 and 1940 he directed its growth from an insignificant, faction-ridden body into an organisation of several thousand members with a national network of branches by 1910, making it the country's largest black political organisation of the day. From 1909 it also published a bilingual newspaper 'to champion our just cause for political equality with whites'. Al-

though not editor, Abdurahman controlled editorial policy and contributed extensively to the paper, not the least of which was the Straatpraatjes column.

It was particularly in education that Abdurahman left an enduring legacy, having played key roles in the founding of Trafalgar High School in 1911, the Teachers' League of South Africa and the Rahmaniyeh Institute in 1913 and Livingstone High School in 1934, among many others. Although he of necessity focused on the advancement of coloured interests, Abdurahman recognised the need to foster interracial co-operation. His most notable contributions were participating in the 1909 South African Native and Coloured People's Delegation to Britain and jointly convening four Non-European Conferences with D. D. T. Jabavu between 1927 and 1934 to mobilise opposition to Hertzog's segregationist policies.

As the only black member of the Wilcocks Commission appointed in 1934 to enquire into the socio-economic condition of the coloured people, he consistently opposed the proposal to ban sexual intercourse between coloureds and whites, enforce the residential segregation of coloured people and establish a separate university for coloureds.

The mercurial Abdurahman was a gifted orator and a charismatic leader. In the earlier

part of his career it was his fiery rhetoric that animated supporters, as when he lambasted racist whites for regarding 'the coloured races as manual drudges [for] ministering to their ease and pleasure' and again when he denounced the educational authorities for exploiting coloured teachers: 'The pay of our mission school teachers is indeed a disgrace, and it is difficult to see how a civilised government . . . can have the audacity to ask publicly for the services of any individual at such wages.'

His indefatigable campaigning to improve their socio-economic condition and personal acts of generosity such as paying the school fees of destitute but deserving students, not charging indigent patients or taking time out of a busy schedule to secure apprenticeships for young men, won him a reputation as a champion of the poor.

Because he represented a marginal social group Abdurahman's achievement lies less in tangible gains than in the degree to which he was able to embody the aspirations of his constituency and unite them behind him in a stand against racism and autocracy over nearly four decades. In 1999 President Mandela honoured him by posthumously awarding him the Order for Meritorious Service, Class I (Gold).

with a novel and more credible paradigm for understanding the oppression of black people, it also advocated more forceful forms of resistance including mass action, civil disobedience and black political unity.

The National Liberation League established in 1935 and the Non-European Unity Movement founded in 1943 were the most important radical bodies. These organisations would, however, prove to be brittle and equally ineffective in overcoming the impediment of coloured marginality. Importantly, they failed to bridge the racial divisions within the society in their quest to unite blacks in the struggle against segregation and capitalist exploitation. Meanwhile, the moderate faction had little option but to continue with an increasingly bankrupt game plan of pleading for reform and supporting an openly racist United Party at election time. The coming of apartheid would cruelly expose the frailties of both movements.

April 1931 witnessed an event that foreshadowed the emergence of a new era in coloured politics by mid-decade. In her maiden speech, Cissie Gool, daughter of Dr Abdurahman, electrified an APO mass meeting called to protest the Women's Enfranchisement Act with her fiery rhetoric and led the gathering on an impromptu march on Parliament.

In 1935 a commission of inquiry under the chairmanship of R.W. Wilcocks reported on the condition of the coloured population. It found widespread poverty, malnutrition and alcoholism. The old-age pension was inadequate. Coloured people's life expectancy was half that of whites and infant mortality twice as high. The policy of 'civilised labour' was holding them back instead of helping as was the intention. On race relations the report concluded that whites treated coloured people as their inferiors although many of the more prosperous coloured people were of a higher intellect than many whites.

Segregation against coloured people had intensified and had failed to deliver opportunities for them above the level of manual labour. The 'civilised labour' policy, which was supposed to benefit them as well, had aggravated their position.

The Indians

The Indians in South Africa had long lived under the shadow of government policy that considered them as aliens against whom it was legitimate to discriminate. In one of their exchanges, Jan Smuts told Gandhi bluntly, 'Your civilisation is different from ours. Ours must not be overwhelmed by yours. That is why we must go in for legislation which must in effect put disabilities on you.' Yet the government did not have a free hand. Commonwealth ties, pressure by the government in India and the Indian Agent in South Africa, and after 1945 the United Nations, together with local Indian protests and resistance, all put pressure on successive governments. The result was a policy towards Indians that was confusing and contradictory, and satisfied no one.

The government's ideal solution would have been wholesale repatriation, but in the early 1920s an average of only 2 500 Indians left per year. At that point there were some 141 000 Indians living in Natal and 15 000 in the Transvaal. To placate the voters the Smuts government intended to segregate Indian trade and landownership, but he refused to give the Natal provincial government its way when it passed an ordinance abolishing the Indian municipal franchise. After 1924 the new Pact government passed the ordinance into law. The Indians were now completely disenfranchised.

In 1927 Dr D.F. Malan, on behalf of the Pact government, unexpectedly signed the Cape Town Agreement with the government of India. It offered some hope to Indians, although it was decidedly ambiguous. On the one hand, the Union government undertook to introduce a scheme of assisted emigration to India; on the other, it committed itself to settle the Indian question in a manner that 'would safeguard the maintenance of Western standards of life in South Africa by just and legitimate means'.

It stated that the Union government 'like every civilised Government' had the duty to take all viable steps 'for the upliftment of every section of their permanent population'.

THE UNITY MOVEMENT

The 1940s saw new challenges to white supremacy. The most militant movement was the Non-European Unity Movement (NEUM), founded in 1943. Its main support came from coloured and black teachers and other professional people. Although its membership was small and limited largely to Cape Town, NEUM became the strongest ideological opponent to the different varieties of black nationalism within the ranks of the oppressed. NEUM's coloured intellectuals linked up with the All-African Convention and a black man, Isaac Bangani Tabata, would later lead the movement. But NEUM would make no headway in the north.

Ideologically, NEUM was mostly influenced by the writings of Leon Trotsky. It rejected the ANC's notion of racially-based 'nations' that should work for a common political system in a predominantly capitalist society. It sought to overthrow the double oppression of capitalism and racial domination. Hence it sought to unite the working class, both black and white, in a struggle that would become a 'permanent revolution' that would ultimately bring about socialism.

On the more immediate level, NEUM called for universal franchise, compulsory education and full equality. Led by Ben Kies, an activist in the Teachers' League of South Africa, consisting mostly of coloured teachers, NEUM spearheaded the launch of the Anti-Coloured Affairs Department movement, calling for a boycott of all racial institutions, and reaching out to other 'non-European' institutions to build unity.

Although NEUM never gained mass support, it continued to make its voice heard among the intelligentsia in all liberation movements. It saw the duty of teachers and lecturers to lead students along 'the right road', and in particular reject the government's divide-and-rule strategy. By the 1950s the attempt to forge socialist unity among teachers and academics had foundered. NEUM nevertheless remained influential in Cape Town as a body of intellectuals that rejected any compromises with racially-based movements. Its strategy of the boycott destroyed the legitimacy of the structures of segregation.

LEFT TO RIGHT: *Members of the South African Indian community, some in traditional dress.*

Indian sugar cane workers.

A young Indian woman with a necklace made from the gold coins with which workers were at one stage paid.

Two Indian workers assist a white welder, photographed in December 1948. Blacks were not allowed to take on skilled work and the law forbade them to operate steam-powered vehicles.

It further asserted that the 'considerable section of the Indian community who will remain part of the permanent population should not be allowed to lag behind other sections of the population'.

To give effect to 'upliftment', the government undertook to launch an inquiry into the 'admittedly grave situation' of Indian education and to improve the facilities for Indians at the South African Native College in Fort Hare. It also would investigate housing and sanitary conditions in Durban.

Critics pointed out that in signing the agreement Dr Malan implicitly made the promise of upliftment conditional on growing numbers of Indians leaving. The latter did not happen, and discrimination continued but it was no longer possible to state categorically, as Malan did in 1922, that the Indians were an alien element. Using gaps in the law and the contradictions in the system of oppression, the Indians managed to take what chances there were. G.H. Calpin in his book *Indians in South Africa*, published in 1949, noted:

> Indians in South Africa often wonder whether it is not a disadvantage to be British subjects. They still feel, however, that to be British subjects in South Africa is preferable to being British subjects in India. Indeed after the Cape Town Agreement they settled down with a sense of security they had never before enjoyed . . . Some might have very vague ideas of what constituted Western standards of life, and the European example was not always good, but there was no doubt of their willingness to acquire the qualifications set for them and meet the demands made on them.

Education played a major role in the efforts at upliftment and private Indian initiatives formed an extraordinary part of the progress that was made as a result of education and training. Christian missionaries had started the first school for Indians in 1869, but schools established by the Indian community soon exceeded the number of mission schools. It was the Indian community that provided the local funds for their schools under the grants-in-aid system – unlike the coloured and black communities who relied on churches and missionary societies, and the whites who received their education virtually free from the state.

In the first half of the twentieth century four-fifths of the Indian schools in Natal were state-aided but the Indian community provided the sites and building for the schools. It was strong community support that made possible the establishment in 1930 of Sastri College, the first Indian high school in Natal. A large donation by Hajee M.L. Sultan went a long way to the founding of a technical college.

Despite the Cape Town Agreement, discrimination continued. The Durban City Council passed an ordinance denying Indians the right to purchase land the municipality owned.

Municipalities refused to issue trading licenses. The civilised labour policy was used to reduce the number of Indians employed on the railways from 3 000 in 1920 to 500 in the decade after the Pact government came to power. In the Transvaal the policy was a jigsaw puzzle making it very difficult for Indians to know where, outside their own 'locations', they could live, trade and own property. Yet despite the obstacles they could progress, particularly in Natal where Indians could own property anywhere from the early 1940s.

The white communities

Poverty was not a crisis only for people who were not white. It was part and parcel of a structural crisis that affected every community and made all except artisans and the more prosperous employers despair for the future.

C.W. de Kiewiet, one of South Africa's most gifted historians, writing in the 1930s, identified three major elements of the structural crisis: the country's 'low-grade ore, its low-grade land, and also its low-grade human beings'. Much of South Africa's low-grade gold ore, sold at a low, fixed price, could only be mined cost effectively by employing very cheap black labour. Low-grade land was responsible for much of agriculture's problems, with low-grade human beings the product of low spending on education and the extended distance many rural children had to travel to school. By 1917 one-fifth of white children were not in school.

De Kiewiet highlighted an important social aspect of a stagnant economy and small domestic market:

> It was not the natives alone who were depressed in their power to earn. The country could not afford a high standard of living for the entire population with the result that, in addition to the native population, a very large proportion of the white population was also depressed to a low level of income and livelihood.

White artisans, in fact, received better pay than their counterparts in any country of Europe. Real artisan wages were higher only in the United States, Canada and Australia. Ralph Bunche, a distinguished black American on a visit in 1937–1938, observed that the standard of living for whites was 'much too high for the poor-white group to live under'.

The three white communities – the English speakers of British descent, Jews and Afrikaners – were structurally located in different places in the economy. Jews were mainly in the professions and business; English speakers dominated the upper levels of the civil

RIGHT: *Until the end of World War II, white-owned farms tended to be labour-intensive, largely inefficient operations. In 1921 two-thirds of those employed worked on farms and by 1951 it was still more than a third. While industry increased output by more than 7% per year, that of the agricultural sector advanced by a mere 2%. Black sharecroppers were slowly eased out across the country to become wage labourers, subsisting on low wages supplemented by payment in kind. Between 1925 and 1939 farmers suffered the twin blows of depression followed by plunging producer prices and crippling drought. Agriculture slowly began to improve after major government intervention from 1937 to 1938, which favoured producers over consumers. The picture shows fruit-farmers producing raisins.*

OPPOSITE: *Sir Joseph Robinson was a rather eccentric Randlord and leading businessman until his death in 1929.*

service, the ranks of skilled labour and business; Afrikaners were farmers, lower level civil servants and semi-skilled and unskilled labourers.

Economic policy and particularly the position of the mining industry was often the topic of bitter political arguments between the South African Party and the National Party, but below the surface there was remarkable consensus between the two white communities to maintain white supremacy. Although Afrikaner nationalists resented the economic ascendancy of the white English speakers, they did not deny the fact that they had played a key role in the economic development of South Africa (*see box*).

Apart from their conflicts over the economic issues these communities also argued fiercely about status, and more particularly about South Africa's place in the British Empire, or Commonwealth.

General Barry Hertzog came to power in 1924 as an Afrikaner nationalist determined to establish South Africa's equal status with Britain and other members of the Commonwealth, each with its own flag, each conducting its own foreign relations. At an Imperial Conference in London Hertzog, with the co-operation of Mackenzie King, the Canadian prime minister, secured an unambiguous statement, issued as the Balfour Declaration of 1926, that Britain and the Dominions were equal in status and in no way subordinate one to another.

But a bitter controversy about a national flag showed how far from resolution the issue still was. Under the Balfour Declaration South Africa was entitled to have its own flag. In 1925 Dr D.F. Malan had proposed a 'clean flag' – that is, with no Union Jack or republican flags. The flag, Malan said, had to do 'with the nation itself . . . with the very existence as a separate entity'. Most English speakers would be satisfied with nothing less than the Union Jack displayed prominently on the new flag. After a bitter fight a compromise was reached in which the country chose two flags, a South African flag of blue, white and orange incorporating both the Union Jack and the flags of the ex-republics, and the traditional Union Jack, to be displayed at certain places to symbolise the country's Empire membership.

The Balfour Declaration was confirmed by the Statute of Westminster (1931), and by the Status Act, passed in 1934 by the South African Parliament. It affirmed the position of the Union as a sovereign independent state along with Australia, Canada and the other Dominions, tied by a common allegiance to the British crown. For Hertzog and many other Afrikaner nationalists the feelings of subordination and inferiority with respect to Britain had been largely removed.

In his essay in *English-speaking South Africa Today* (1974) Michael O'Dowd posed a key question: Why did South Africa succeed in advancing so remarkably economically in the twentieth century? South Africa was deficient in a favourable history, natural resources or proximity to large markets. Diamonds, gold and other minerals were discovered, but, unlike other countries that enjoyed a similar fortune, South Africa did not become a colony of exploitation that long remained mired in a state of backwardness. Instead it developed a secondary industry sufficiently dynamic to take off into self-sustained growth.

O'Dowd found that much of the credit had to go to English speakers. First, they 'brought every skill which was necessary for industrial development from financial and business expertise to the skills of miners, artisans and railway workers'. Second, after the South African War, Lord Alfred Milner created 'an administrative machinery altogether superior to what would normally have existed in a country like South Africa'. This civil service was independent and professional. English speakers dominated the senior levels but the rate of Afrikanerisation was very slow. Only by 1960 did the senior levels of the civil service reflect the white population composition.

Third, English-speaking immigrants came to stay and developed a loyalty to South Africa. Cecil John Rhodes opposed directives from London and wanted the Cape Colony to take the lead. He incorporated De Beers Consolidated in the Cape Colony, not England. The other mining tycoons took his lead and became South African entrepreneurs. The management of De Beers drifted back to London, but Ernest Oppenheimer, an immigrant, took control of it from its London directors, brought management back to South Africa and revitalised the company.

O'Dowd points out that an indigenous body of entrepreneurs is the most important asset a country can have. In countries developed by foreign capital, governments invariably at some stage try to nationalise some of the industries and establish local control over them. The main exceptions were the United States and South Africa. In World War I, the United States used the opportunity to repurchase control of sections of its economy from British companies. English speakers in South Africa did the same during and just after World War II. The fact that there was never a threat of nationalisation and that local control over the main corporations was acquired without any strife made South Africa very attractive to foreign investors and explains the large inflows of foreign capital.

Another crucial development was the political and economic independence Britain gave South Africa in 1910. The British government correctly assumed that the English-speaking community in South Africa and the pro-capitalist Botha government that took power in 1910 would protect British interests. Economic independence made it possible for South Africa to build up its local industries. It was the Afrikaner nationalists under General Hertzog who clamoured for the establishment of Iscor and Eskom, often against the opposition of the English-dominated mining industry, and for protection against cheap imports for the fledgling local industries. But once the battle for the idea that South Africa should have its own manufacturing sector was won, the mining corporations spearheaded the development of secondary industry in South Africa. The employment opportunities this created were to the benefit of all South Africans.

Much better than almost all other empires, the British Empire appeared to have evolved from a hierarchical structure to one based on equality and consent. As long as no war broke out in which Britain was involved there was no question of the Afrikaners' acceptance of South Africa's membership of the Empire, or the Commonwealth, as it was called by 1930.

English-speaking whites

Twenty years into Union, most English-speaking white South Africans identified in complex ways with both the country from which they or their ancestors had come and their country of residence. Over time, their identification with Britain declined and their identification with South Africa increased. Most were of British ancestry or descent and came from England. Relatively few were identified primarily as Welsh or Irish and even a separate Scottish identity tended to merge into a broader British identity.

Some identified with Britain as the home country, representing order, progress, civilisation, modernisation and philanthropy. For others, Britain meant aggressive imperialism based on self-interest or meddling interference. But even those English speakers who were critical of the British government and its agents in South Africa usually retained cultural ties with Britain. What they read came mainly from Britain.

Loyalties to South Africa and to Britain and the Empire could be combined in a host of different ways. Even those of jingoistic tendencies, who were active in the Sons of England Patriotic and Benevolent Society and continued to call Britain 'home', could at

the same time identify with the country in which they lived. After Union was created in 1910, many British South Africans were able to combine their loyalty to the Crown and Empire, their pride in British achievements and the imperial connection with a broad South Africanism. They hoped that Dutch/Afrikaners would join them in devotion to the Empire. The pro-Britishness of the ex-South African War generals Louis Botha and Jan Smuts, after Britain agreed to grant self-government to the former republics, seemed to show that that was possible. After the Unionist Party was incorporated in the South African Party in the early 1920s English speakers outside Natal gave strong and well-nigh unqualified support for Jan Smuts as their leader – and as a South African leader highly regarded in Britain and the United States (*see box*).

English-speaking whites were divided politically. While some of a working-class background voted for the Labour Party, most either belonged to an exclusively English party (first the Unionist Party, then in the 1930s the Dominion Party), or fully supported the broad South Africanism of the Cambridge-educated Smuts and the South African Party. A member of the Imperial War Cabinet in World War I, Smuts had come to support the civilising mission of the British Empire, and was trusted to retain the British connection. Another Afrikaner politician who was trusted and admired was J.H. (Jan or more familiarly Klein Jannie) Hofmeyr, Smuts's understudy in the South African Party.

JAN SMUTS, A WORLD FIGURE

Jan Smuts and Nelson Mandela were the two South Africans world opinion regarded most highly during the twentieth century. Smuts, born in 1870 on a farm near Riebeeck Kasteel in the western Cape, had studied at Victoria College in Stellenbosch before going to Cambridge University to take up law. The famous Cambridge legal scholar Frederick William Maitland called him the most outstanding student he had taught, coming 'not only first but brilliantly first' in both parts of the law tripos.

Together with John X. Merriman, he laid the groundwork for the Union of South Africa in 1906–1907. British Prime Minister David Lloyd George appointed him to his war cabinet in 1917. Smuts proposed the basic structure and principles for the League of Nations, which President Woodrow Wilson introduced in 1919 as a vital part of the post-war international order.

Smuts used the period in which he found himself in the political opposition (1924–1933) to make some important scientific contributions. He proposed the concept of holism, defining it as 'the tendency in nature to form wholes that are greater than the sums of the parts through creative evolution'. His *Holism and Evolution* (1926) developed it as a philosophy that emphasised the supreme worth of the human personality and its evolution to perfection.

Contemporary thinkers in different fields considered holism a key contribution to the human sciences. Alfred Adler translated the work into German and called his theory of 'individual psychology' holistic. Karl Popper attacked holism as a variant of the 'organic philosophies', to which fascism also belongs, but according to Smuts's Dutch biographer Martin van Meurs holism made a strong comeback in the United States during the 1980s. Marilyn Ferguson, poet, best-selling writer and proponent of the New Age, called holism 'a brilliant breakthrough by the Boer General Jan Smuts that preceded many of the breakthroughs of the late twentieth century'.

In 1930 the British Association for the Advancement of Science honoured him by asking him to become president in its centenary year. Smuts gave his address the title of 'The Scientific World Picture of Today'. His contribution touched on recent developments in physics, nuclear physics and astronomical theory. Thirty-three years later, W.K. Hancock, his Australian biographer, asked ten highly competent scientists to examine the text. All ten gave Smuts credit for descriptive accuracy in the wide fields of his scientific interest.

Smuts stayed in England for extended periods during World War II as a member of Winston Churchill's war cabinet. Harold

Macmillan, a cabinet member, remarked that this 'was most fortunate for all of us'. Churchill wrote that 'my faith in Smuts is unbreakable' and consulted him regularly.

It is remarkable that the uniquely gifted Smuts could not make a breakthrough in addressing the white-black conflict. Hancock wrote that his cosmological outlook, reinforced later by studies of palaeontology and pre-history, excluded crude notions of racial inequality. In a letter to Mohandas Gandhi during the 1920s Smuts insisted that his policy towards Indians was not based on prejudice. 'Let alone the question of superiority . . . your civilisation is different from ours. Ours must not be overwhelmed by yours.' (Gandhi commented: 'I understood what he said.')

With respect to blacks, he favoured a Fabian approach of incremental change. But the problem with this was that South Africa had two white communities within the dominant bloc competing politically against each other. Racial reform could not be introduced in such a way that the newly enfranchised tilted the battle in the favour of one of them. When Harry Oppenheimer in 1948 suggested a bolder racial policy for the United Party, Smuts replied: 'It would be impossible until the prior question of creating unity between white South Africans had been achieved.'

Though those who served in World War I saw themselves as British soldiers fighting for the Empire, the terrible slaughter in the battle of Delville Wood in France in 1916 – the South African equivalent of Gallipoli – helped to strengthen ideas of white South African nationalism because those who died were regarded as South African heroes.

While for most English speakers there was no conflict of interest between Britishness and South Africanness, the rise of Afrikaner nationalism seemed likely to threaten both. The year after Barry Hertzog defeated Smuts and came to power in 1924, with republican ambitions, the visit to South Africa by the Prince of Wales occasioned a vast outpouring of pro-royal sentiment. As Hertzog reduced South Africa's imperial commitments, English-speaking whites were increasingly worried about their cultural survival in an Afrikaner-dominated country.

But while some English became more jingoistic in the face of the rise of Afrikaner nationalism, most, while retaining a sense of loyalty to the Crown, accepted that South Africa was no longer a British colony, and that Afrikaners would remain a majority of whites and never adopt English culture.

Even when South Africa became effectively independent within the emerging British Commonwealth, thanks to the Statute of Westminster of 1931 and then the Status Act of 1934, most English speakers did not see their position as threatened. They assumed that South Africa would enter any war on Britain's side. After all, while they lacked political power as a group – though English speakers were prominent in all South African Party/ United Party governments – they seemed likely to retain their dominance of the economy. 'God Save the Queen' continued as one of the two national anthems, and the Union Jack was to remain part of the national flag until 1957. The King's Birthday and Empire Day were still public holidays, and leading newspapers and schools promoted Britishness, which often went with an attitude of superiority that others bitterly resented.

Pro-British sentiment was most intense in Natal, sometimes called 'the last outpost of the British Empire', where English-speaking whites outnumbered Afrikaners, and blacks vastly outnumbered both groups. In 1920s Natal 90% of children who were asked to write about 'winter' wrote of an English winter of ice and snow, and a general knowledge examination in 1935 asked such questions as what was the Flying Scotsman, and what was meant by the King's Silver Jubilee. Royal occasions were still celebrated all over South Africa, and with special and exaggerated fervour in Natal. The English in Natal, who had voted in 1909 against entering the Union of South Africa, were to reject the idea of a republic in 1960.

The Jewish community

During the 1920s increasingly strident calls were made in the press to curb the influx of East European Jews, based upon the purported 'unassimilability' of the newcomers and their 'alien' values and practices. These culminated in an Act that abruptly severed the half-century-old umbilical connection to the Lithuanian wellsprings of the community. The Quota Act of 1930, which set out to halt Eastern European Jewish immigration to South Africa, came as a major blow to a Jewish community that considered itself well integrated into the white population of the Union.

Jewish settlement in South Africa preceded the Litvak (Lithuanian) influx of the late nineteenth century by some decades. As non-Protestants, Jews were denied the right to settle at the Cape during the rule of the Dutch East India Company (1652–1795). But the extension of religious tolerance by the Batavian Republic and its entrenchment by the British after 1806 allowed a handful of Jews, mainly of English, German and Dutch origin, to settle at the Cape and beyond. Among them were the adventurer Nathaniel Isaacs, an associate of the Zulu kings Shaka and Dingane, and a contingent of eighteen Jews who, with their fellow 1820 Settlers, set up home in the remote eastern reaches of the colony.

Only in 1841 was the community formally established, with the foundation in Cape Town of Tikvath Israel (Hope of Israel), the mother congregation of South African Jewry. The Anglo-German founding fathers were mainly merchants, acculturated and comfortably ensconced in a tolerant English-speaking white middle-class milieu in which religion

ABOVE: *A Johannesburg shopping arcade. The rise in prosperity for the upper classes following the sharp increase of the gold price in 1933 was reflected in the construction of new shopping centres.*

ABOVE: *Jewish immigrants arriving in Cape Town, where they came to make a new life. Unlike their counterparts who went to London or New York, most Jewish immigrants to South Africa escaped the meagre wages and harsh working conditions which waited in these cities. Their descendants mostly joined the white professional and business classes.*

OPPOSITE TOP: *Sammy Marks and his father (see box on page 190).*

OPPOSITE MIDDLE AND BOTTOM: *The flamboyant Barney Barnato, born in London's East End, arrived in South Africa in 1873. With his love of the stage (he often acted in plays himself) and spirited personality, he was one of the most colourful of the early mine magnates, initially in Kimberley and later at the Witwatersrand. In 1897 he committed suicide by jumping overboard while sailing to England, presumably in a bout of depression.*

was considered a domestic concern and Jews were accorded full respect. All religious denominations, declared Governor Harry Smith in 1848, were 'equally valid'. The 170 Jews in Cape Town in 1855 and the increasing number of Jewish traders in the hinterland thrived in a society that separated church and state.

Through their trading activities these merchant capitalists accelerated the transition from a subsistence to a cash economy. The Mosenthals, for example, were instrumental in creating a trading network throughout the wool-producing districts of the Eastern Cape. Jewish entrepreneurs, such as Jonas Bergtheil in Natal and the De Pass family in the Cape, also played a pioneering role in attempts to exploit the natural resources of the region.

The discovery of diamonds in the late 1860s attracted a trickle of Jewish fortune-seekers, mainly from England and Germany. Though few in number, they played a significant part in the rapid evolution of the industry. Jews traded in diamonds, in some cases illicitly, owned and operated mining claims and floated mining companies both locally and in Europe. Among the most successful were the flamboyant Londoner Barney Barnato, Sammy Marks from Lithuania and his cousin Isaac Lewis, and Hamburg-born Alfred Beit.

Unforeseen events in the 1880s, both near and far away, dramatically transformed the demography and character of South African Jewry. The assassination of Russian Tsar Alexander II in 1881, followed by a wave of pogroms and the anti-Semitic 'May Laws' of 1882, prompted mass emigration from the 'Pale of Settlement'. Although the United States was the premier destination, some 40 000 (out of a total of approximately three million) chose South Africa in the three decades before World War I, attracted by the economic opportunities created by the discovery of gold on the Witwatersrand in 1886.

While the majority gravitated towards the urban centres, some dispersed into the countryside, either to the dorps or to isolated locations along the transport routes. Some initially tramped the countryside as *smouse* (itinerant pedlars), where pious Boer farmers who regarded them as the 'People of the Book' often received them warmly. As with other whites, the racial ordering of the economy and the availability of cheap unskilled black labour inclined Jews towards non-manual occupations. Unlike New York or London at this time, the South African Jewish immigrant by and large avoided the gruelling sweatshop experience.

In Cape Town as in Johannesburg the newcomers gravitated to inner city precincts such as District Six or Ferreirastown. These ethnic enclaves provided companionship and psychological comfort for the *grieners* (greenhorns). While women were initially outnumbered – typical of a new immigrant community – the gender balance gradually equalised. From the start South Africa was seen as a destination of settlement, a new and permanent home where wives and children soon followed in the wake of the male migrant rather than a transient opportunity for enrichment.

Jews in Johannesburg and Cape Town straddled the social spectrum. At one extreme a few played a conspicuous part in the underworld, most notably in the illicit liquor trade on the Witwatersrand during the 1890s. These members of Johannesburg's lumpenproletariat acquired the pejorative label 'Peruvian'. The great majority, however, anxiously pursued respectability, with a small but highly visible minority rapidly achieving public eminence – among them mining magnates like Lionel Phillips and Barney Barnato and civic notables like Hyman Lieberman and Harry Graumann, mayors of Cape Town and Johannesburg respectively.

Jews were similarly visible in the rural landscape. They were significant agents of the commercial revolution that transformed the South African countryside in the late nineteenth and early twentieth centuries. Jews acted as informed and energetic intermediaries – as they had for centuries in Eastern Europe – between the new markets of the town and the producers, both black and white. Jewish storekeepers and *smouse* bought wool, maize and skins from Boer landowners and black sharecroppers alike, and then forwarded these to urban markets and wholesalers. In turn, the Jewish country store met the growing needs of these emergent rural consumers.

Some of these activities attracted negative comment and even calls to curtail the Eastern European Jewish influx. For some hostile observers, including J.A. Hobson of the *Manchester Guardian*, Jews were over-represented among the Randlords and dominant in Johannesburg. Others – most notably the journalist and author Eugène Marais – accused Jews and 'Hollanders' of undue influence in Paul Kruger's republic. Despite this alleged favouritism Jews, like other non-Protestants, faced a range of religious disabilities, albeit of limited consequence. The South African War of 1899–1902 swept these away. During the conflict a few Jews fought with the Boer commandos, a greater number served with the British forces, while the majority sat out the war as refugees in the coastal cities.

In the dozen years between the cessation of hostilities and the outbreak of the Great War in 1914 Jews constructed a network of communal institutions, including the South African Jewish Board of Deputies, the representative voice of the community. A South African Zionist Federation had already been established in 1898, a year after the historic first Zionist Congress in Basel, Switzerland. As in *der heim* (the old country), most Lithuanian Jews in South Africa (unlike some of their local Anglo-Jewish co-religionists) enthusiastically supported Theodor Herzl's vision of a Jewish national renaissance.

Although a process of homogenisation – the merging of Anglo-Jewish and Litvak streams – was well under way by 1914, it was far from complete. As wars often do, the Great War starkly exposed rifts within the community, uncovering the fissures beneath the facade of growing homogeneity. This was apparent in the community's uneven response to the plight of Russian Jews caught up in the East European theatre of war. These divisions were even more apparent when it came to the issue of broader loyalties beyond the strictly Jewish, with Russian-born Jews unwilling to fight in the imperial cause because of Britain's alliance with Russia.

The Bolshevik Revolution of 1917 was greeted with enthusiasm in Johannesburg's Jewish immigrant neighbourhoods, soon leading to accusations of Jewish Bolshevism. These accusations had particular resonance because of fears of rising worker consciousness associated with wartime industrialisation, and the growth of a restive and increasingly radicalised black proletariat, especially on the Witwatersrand. Despite assurances in 1919 by Bernard Alexander of the Board of Deputies that 'every Jew is not a Bolshevist and every Bolshevist is not a Jew', the Rand Revolt three years later was depicted in leading newspapers as a 'Russian-Jewish' conspiracy.

ABOVE LEFT AND RIGHT: *Two photographs of Jewish* smouse *(pedlars) doing their rounds on farms. The one on the right is Michael Hurwitz, selling a watch to a farmer. Jews often began their working lives as* smouse, *travelling around country districts. Success enabled them eventually to set up their own stores, and even to start manufacturing goods. In this way they pioneered the furniture, mattress and garment industries in South Africa.*

For all the conspicuous presence of Jewish immigrants among the radical agitators – including a Yiddish-speaking branch of the International Socialist League, the forerunner of the SA Communist Party – the overwhelming majority of Jews rejected radicalism and identified with the status quo. Most embraced the capitalist order and some contributed significantly to the economy's post-war growth. The Jewish newcomer was the classic *homo economicus*.

Commercial occupations ranged from the chain-store pioneer through the general dealer to the lowly *kaffireatnik*, the exploited shop assistant in the concession stores and rough dining halls on the mines. Among the retailing innovators were the South African-born Gustave Ackerman and the Lithuanian-born Morris Mauerberger, joint founders of the Ackerman's chain, and the London-born Sam Cohen who with Michael Miller was the joint founder of the O.K. Bazaars retailing empire. Jews in manufacturing had benefited from the disruption of imports during World War I and continued to benefit from the protectionist policies of the Pact government. In addition to commerce and manufacturing, Jews were entering the professions in significant numbers by the 1920s, with medicine and law particularly favoured.

Contrary to the contemporary accusations of 'unassimilability', Jews were increasingly embedded in white urban English-speaking society. This was reflected in their political preferences for the party of Jan Smuts, a more comfortable home than Barry Hertzog's Afrikaner-dominated National Party. Behind this preference lay an abiding loyalty to and respect for British 'fair play' and goodwill, dating back to the nineteenth century. This made the support of English speakers for the Quota Act of 1930 all the more galling.

The Act ushered in a decade of profound difficulty and discomfort for South African Jewry. A 'Jewish Question' emerged against a backdrop of economic depression and a burgeoning, exclusivist Afrikaner nationalism. This was evident in the formation in 1933 of the Greyshirts, led by Louis T. Weichardt. The message that it and other far-right movements propagated was that Jews had fomented the South African War, incited blacks against white civilisation, controlled the press, dominated the economy and exploited Afrikaners. These accusations resonated beyond the ranks of the radical right. For those wrestling with the effects of drought and depression, and fearful of black economic competition, the Jews provided ideal scapegoats.

Anti-Jewish ideas rapidly penetrated the Afrikaner nationalist mainstream. Hostility was exacerbated by the influx of German-Jewish refugees in the wake of Hitler's ascent to power. The groundswell of anti-Jewish feeling prompted demands not only for the ending of Jewish immigration but also for action against recent arrivals, including restrictions on property rights and on access to the professions.

These calls for the unequal treatment of Jews came from the opposition Purified National Party, led by Dr Malan. Fearful of being outflanked, the ruling United Party introduced an Aliens Act in 1937, designed to restrict Jewish immigration from Germany. The Act failed to appease the Purified Nationalists. The 'Jewish Question' now became an important plank in their political platform. Malan, under pressure from the radical right, focused increasingly on the Jew as an explanation for the Afrikaners' misfortunes.

South African Jewry fully supported South Africa's entry into World War II. More than 10% of the entire Jewish population served in the Union Defence Force and other Allied forces. During the war the Board of Deputies had to contend with a powerful anti-Semitic mood orchestrated by the paramilitary Ossewa-Brandwag organisation and the avowedly pro-Nazi New Order founded in 1940 by Oswald Pirow.

Most Jews were shocked by the defeat of Jan Smuts's United Party in the 1948 general election. The victory of the National Party, which had opposed the war effort and which harboured individuals who had previously articulated stridently anti-Semitic views, was a cause of great alarm and of concern for the future. Nonetheless, Jewish leaders rapidly managed to effect a rapprochement with the National Party, which had distanced itself from the anti-Semitic sentiments of the recent past, and South African Jews were soon able to enjoy the comfort and confidence they had experienced before the 1930s.

The Afrikaners

By 1930 the output of Afrikaner farmers still represented more than 80% of agricultural production. But until World War II the position of most farmers was far from secure. They still looked to government to stabilise prices and help them further tighten their control over labour. But Afrikaners were rapidly becoming urbanised, from 29% in 1910 to 50% in 1936 and 75% in 1960. In 1936 they constituted a quarter of the white population of both Cape Town and Johannesburg, and half of that of Pretoria and Bloemfontein. The entrepreneurial activities of the Afrikaners were extremely modest. In 1937 the Johannesburg newspaper *Die Transvaler* estimated that there were in total only twenty Afrikaner enterprises in the city.

Educational standards of Afrikaners were still low. Out of 100 who started school together 44 left without passing the eighth year (Standard Six), seventeen passed the tenth year (Standard Eight), and only eight completed the twelfth or final year (matriculation). Fewer than three went on to university.

Afrikaners were poorly represented in many of the white-collar occupations; in 1939 only 3% of people in the professional category with the most prestige (owners of companies, directors and self-employed manufacturers) were Afrikaners. Of the white population Afrikaners made up 3% of engineers, 4% of accountants, 11% of lawyers, 15% of medical doctors, and 21% of journalists. Less than a quarter of senior civil servants spoke Afrikaans as a first language.

LEFT: *The re-enactment of the Great Trek in 1938 sparked mass Afrikaner enthusiasm as the wagons passed through towns across the land. Men and women, often clad in Voortrekker dress with the men sporting Voortrekker beards, met the wagons. Streets were renamed for Voortrekker leaders. From that time* braaivleis *(barbecue), a re-enactment of how the Voortrekkers cooked their meals on the veld, became fashionable among city people.*

Early unskilled road workers.

Afrikaner labourers working on the railways.

Whites living in poverty in the towns. The Carnegie Commission tried to describe and define the phenomenon of poor white-ism. J.R. Albertyn, author of a report on poor whites, described them as people who were law-abiding, religious and anxious to keep the family together, but also lacking in ambition, thrift and prudence, and inclined to be gullible, dishonest, deceitful, irresponsible, lazy and listless. In his education report E.G. Malherbe defined a poor white as a person 'who has a mental attitude towards life, owing for example to lack of intelligence, lack of education, temperamental defects or to physiological conditions, which prevents him rising to or maintaining a decent standard of living when exposed to the economic forces around him'. But he also defined white poverty in relative terms. 'A very appreciable portion of our white population,' he wrote, 'is sinking below the economic standard of living which we consider that a white man should maintain by virtue of his white skin over the native.' Poor white-ism, in other words, was a racial problem as well as a social one.

Only a quarter of apprentices in skilled trades were Afrikaners. A third of the employed Afrikaners were blue-collar workers whose white skin, rather than their skills, was often the only protection against competition. Some artisan unions excluded Afrikaner workers from certain occupational categories, fearing them as a source of potential undercutting. In 1939 almost 40% of adult male Afrikaners in Johannesburg were clustered in four job categories: unskilled labourer, mineworker, railway worker and bricklayer, compared to 10% of non-Afrikaner males in these occupations. Railway workers earned five shillings a day or less, compared to the widely quoted 'civilised' minimum of eight shillings a day. English was overwhelmingly the language of success and aspiration. As a result, many working-class Afrikaners had low self-esteem.

The semi-skilled and unskilled Afrikaner workers mostly belonged to general unions. Although Afrikaners made up 80% of the members of the white unions, only 10% of the secretaries were Afrikaners. E.S. (Solly) Sachs, a communist who ran his union of predominantly Afrikaner female garment workers superbly, commented scathingly on the refusal of the unions to respect the Afrikaner workers' culture and traditions.

The crisis of 'poor white-ism'

By 1930 the one million strong Afrikaner community held political power, but its intelligentsia had grave fears that the large proportion of Afrikaners who were desperately poor threatened white survival. The question of white poverty had been an issue in white politics since the 1890s. Poor white is a term, like segregation, that was imported from the United States. It was never defined satisfactorily and was generally taken to refer to whites so desperately poor that they could not maintain themselves as members of the dominant group.

There had long been only informed guesses about the numbers of South African poor whites. In 1916 the number was thought to be 106 000. In 1932, the Carnegie Commission report found that there were 300 000 poor whites (17% of the white community). Hendrik Verwoerd, a future prime minister who first gained national prominence through his analysis of the Carnegie report for the 1934 conference held to discuss the study, stated that the poor whites were 'for a very large part of Afrikaans-speaking descent' and put the figure at 250 000, or a quarter of the Afrikaner population.

E.G. Malherbe, one of the authors of the Carnegie report, did not share Verwoerd's nationalist sentiments, but he also thought that the problem of Afrikaner poverty was huge. He found that if those in the categories 'very poor' and 'poor' were added together, more than half of white pupils were recruited from homes not in a position to provide them with proper food and clothing. Malherbe formulated the general white thinking that poor whites were 'a menace to the self-preservation and prestige of the white people, living as we do in the midst of the native population, which outnumbers us 5 to 1'.

The most obvious explanation of Afrikaner poverty was their large-scale participation in subsistence farming, which required a relatively low level of education. In the second half of the nineteenth century several disasters hit cattle farmers, in particular drought, disease (particularly the rinderpest in the 1890s), the deterioration of the land through overstocking and the devastating losses as a result of the South African War. Afrikaner urbanisation was often a chaotic affair, pushing large numbers of Afrikaners onto the urban labour market with few or no qualifications.

But there were all kinds of other 'explanations' of Afrikaner poverty. Most hurtful to Afrikaners was the myth that there was something genetically wrong with their poor. Newspaper reporter M.E. Rothmann heard Sir Carruthers Beattie, vice-chancellor of the University of Cape Town, blithely tell a public meeting that poor whites were 'intellectually backward and that there was something inherent in the Afrikaners that resulted in the phenomenon [of poor white-ism] assuming such alarming proportions in their case'.

From the beginning the Union government gave serious attention to the crisis. Between 1912 and 1926, spending on education as a proportion of the budget and the number of white pupils had doubled. By 1931 vocational and industrial schools were functioning all over the country. Boarding schools for indigent children helped ensure that virtually no white child was out of school.

But the issue once again seemed to reach crisis proportions in the late 1920s. The main reason was the global economic crisis that began in 1929 and the prolonged drought that destroyed crops and livestock in the early 1930s. Desperate to avoid a huge wave of impoverished farmers leaving the land, the Hertzog government made loans available to farmers. At the same time it boosted unemployment relief and subsidies for temporary employment on public works. Relief measures, 2.6% of the budget in 1930, rose to an astounding 15.8% in 1933.

These schemes provided some training for unskilled labourers, educated and trained their children so they might escape the poverty cycle, and provided free housing and medical services for those working on public projects. Many schemes contributed significantly to strengthening the infrastructure of the country – for example, forestry settlements, irrigation works, and road and rail construction.

After the Carnegie Commission report, in 1934 the Dutch Reformed Church organised a *volkskongres*, or national conference, and subsequently published a report called 'Verslag van die Volkskongres', in which the findings were discussed and ways suggested to make white poverty one of the top priorities on the national agenda *(see box)*.

Occasionally the idea was floated that quotas should be introduced to help the Afrikaners to enter into the professions and business. The main proponent of this idea was Hendrik Verwoerd, who arrived in Johannesburg in 1937 to become editor of *Die Transvaler (see box on page 282)*.

SAVING THE AFRIKANER POOR

The question of white poverty had been an issue in white politics since the 1890s, but came to a head in the 1930s. Some main themes in the Afrikaner debate over white poverty could be isolated. It was recognised that black poverty was as acute as white poverty. To justify a focus on whites only, it was suggested that solving the poverty of whites would also benefit other communities. The 1934 Dutch Reformed Church Volkskongres stressed that attempts to rehabilitate the white poor had also to be seen as 'fair and healthy' towards blacks. But that perspective would soon fade. The recommendations for alleviating white poverty would widen the gulf between whites and blacks.

The report of the Carnegie Commission of Inquiry into the poor white problem in South Africa, published in 1932, recommended better education and particularly better vocational guidance, and more opportunities for the acquisition of skills and work opportunities in the towns and cities. But it also concluded that increased self-sufficiency for whites was vital for the resolution of the problem. Researchers strongly warned against the tendency of the poor to demand charity and government help. But National Party politicians, particularly Dr D.F. Malan, took an opposite view. During the 1938 commemoration of the Great Trek Malan said: 'South Africa expects of its poor whites that they remain white and live white', but in the labour mar-

ket the competition for the white man was 'killing'. The National Party was committed to help the poor whites 'to live white'.

The Afrikaner intelligentsia began disseminating the view that Afrikaner poverty could only be addressed if the community also took responsibility for the Afrikaner poor. Speaking at the 1934 Volkskongres, Malan stressed the Carnegie report's recommendation that the poor had to be rescued from their isolation. 'They must not be merely objects of study and even less objects of charity . . . We must consider them and treat them as part of our volk.'

During the centenary celebrations of the Great Trek in 1938, the Rev. J.D. ('Father') Kestell of Bloemfontein called for a mighty *reddingsdaad*, or 'rescue action', to save the descendants of the Voortrekkers 'living in hopeless poverty, sunken materially, morally and spiritually'. No government charity or outside help would solve the problem; the an-

swer lay in ethnic solidarity. 'A people is an integrated whole – the poor and rich. There is no unbridgeable gap between them. If pauperism is not curtailed it will mean the ruination of the entire nation. *'n Volk red homself.*'

Rapid economic growth after 1933, when South Africa devalued the currency, helped to soak up white poverty. The Department of Labour reported in 1939 that it could offer work to every able-bodied white male willing to accept unskilled labour on specific projects designed to relieve unemployment. During the war years the demand for labour was so high that the government could stop supplying jobs specifically for unskilled whites.

This call that the Afrikaner people had to 'rescue themselves' became a leading theme in the ideology of the nationalist movement. But while it was true that the social integration of the poor into the Afrikaner community played an important role, the slogan overlooked the state's major contribution.

HENDRIK VERWOERD AND QUOTAS

When the first edition of *Die Transvaler* was published in 1937 Hendrik Verwoerd, the editor, wrote a long article entitled 'The Jewish Question as seen from an NP viewpoint'. It claimed that a conflict of interests existed between the 'disadvantaged Afrikaner majority and a privileged Jewish minority'. The main problem according to Verwoerd was that the Jews relative to the Afrikaners were over-represented in commerce and industry because they had entered the towns and cities long before the Afrikaners and now dominated commerce and industry along with people of British descent.

As a result the Afrikaner was compelled 'to become a *handlanger*', or subordinate,

often at a meagre wage. Jewish dominance of the economy enabled the younger generation of Jews to crowd out Afrikaners in the professions and business. Afrikaners were beginning to feel 'that Jews have a chokehold on their continued existence'.

Verwoerd recommended legislation to ensure that each white section (Afrikaners, English speakers of British descent and Jewish South Africans) should enjoy 'a share of the major occupations according to its share of the white population'. Since Jews held a disproportionate share of the wholesale and retail trade, a future National Party government would refuse further trading licenses until the Jewish share was brought back in

line with their share of the white population (popularly estimated at 4%). Verwoerd described this as *ewewigtige verspreiding*, or balanced distribution, but added that 'this has also been called a quota system'. He added: 'Any discrimination has to disappear once the right balance has been achieved.'

During the mid-1950s some speakers at a secret conference of the Afrikaner Broederbond proposed that cabinet ministers be lobbied to assist Afrikaner enterprises 'to a greater or lesser extent through the allocation of quotas'. Anton Rupert and Andreas Wassenaar, two Afrikaner business leaders who were members of the Bond, rejected this and the idea was discarded.

CHAPTER TWELVE

The Great Depression and war

Economic woes and political reaction

Reflecting on the South Africa of the late 1920s and early 1930s S.P. Viljoen, a leading economist, observed that few appreciate how poor South Africa as a mining and agricultural country was before the sharp rise of the gold price in 1933. By 1925 South Africa had a gross domestic product (GDP) of only R537 million, agriculture contributing 21%, mining 16.2%, and secondary industry just 7.8%. Viljoen added: 'Since secondary industry tends invariably to act as the growth sector in a newly developing country, South Africa's economic structure was then [in the 1920s] as undeveloped as those of most African countries now [during the early 1980s].' By the late 1920s industry was still starved of capital; more than half the profits from the mines were sent abroad as dividends. The government levied a tax of only 5% on the value added by the gold mines. Under the next government, based on a fusion of the parties of Hertzog and Smuts, the tax on the mining industry rose sharply to 15% by 1936.

In 1929 the economy received a hammer blow – the Depression, which started with the crash of the New York Stock Exchange, quickly spread through the developed world. It rapidly widened the gulf between fascists and communists, between socialists and nationalists. It gave Adolf Hitler the final push he needed to capture power. South African exports plummeted and a crisis in economic confidence developed on a scale never experienced before. In South Africa the despondency was compounded by a prolonged drought. By 1933 the output of manufacturing had dropped by one-fifth since 1929, and 22% of all coloured and white males were registered as unemployed. Workers resisted wage cuts and employers tried to smash unions. Agricultural income dropped by half; wool farmers now had to export four times as much wool to earn the same amount of foreign exchange as they had five years before.

By the mid-1930s the Depression and drought had reduced sheep flocks by fifteen million head. The price of maize, the major agricultural product, dropped by half between 1929 and 1933. Rising operating costs as a result of South Africa's overvalued currency and lower prices drove numerous farmers into debt. Some threatened to repudiate their debts. There was a real danger that a number of the commercial banks might be forced to close.

The coloured vote

In the 1929 election the National Party (NP) for the first time won power on its own. It had mobilised the great majority of Afrikaners, but had not succeeded in attracting more than 10% of the coloured voters in Cape Town. Cape NP leader D.F. Malan backed off from an earlier view that the coloureds represented one of three 'races', stating that he did not favour a policy that created 'a definite racial group' out of the coloureds, who were then supposed to vote according to their own racial interests. Coloureds, he declared, should go to the polls as citizens of South Africa.

Two developments prompted a rethink. The one was the white female franchise. In 1930 a bill was passed extending the vote to white women but not to coloured women.

ABOVE: *In 1932 and 1933 South Africa experienced severe drought. Faced also by a worldwide depression, farmers were challenged like never before. Agricultural income dropped by half; wool farmers had to export four times as much wool as five years before to earn the same amount in foreign exchange. By the mid-1930s the Depression and drought had reduced sheep flocks by fifteen million head. The price of maize, the major agricultural product, dropped by half between 1929 and 1933. Rising operating costs as a result of South Africa's overvalued currency and lower prices drove numerous farmers into debt. Some were threatening to repudiate their debts, and there was a real danger that commercial banks might be forced to close.*

As a result the proportion of coloured voters in the Cape Province electorate dropped from 11% to 6%. Previously the NP could not afford not to compete for the coloured vote. In the 1929 election a minority of coloured voters had assisted the party to win the seats of Paarl and Stellenbosch. After the election coloured supporters of Bruckner de Villiers, the victorious Stellenbosch candidate, carried him shoulder high into the Parliament building.

The other development was fusion and the establishment of the United Party (UP). The middle-of-the-road UP stood poised to draw almost all the coloured support that Malan's party earlier had attracted. The coloured share of the vote was so small that the NP could afford to attack it rather than try to win some limited support.

Coalition and fusion

In September 1931 the British government announced that in order to deal with the economic crisis that the Depression had generated it had decided to abandon the gold standard and to form a national crisis government across party lines. Although Britain was South Africa's main trading partner, the Hertzog government refused to abandon the gold standard, mainly to demonstrate the country's economic independence. This compounded the economic crisis. Agricultural exports plummeted, gold producers contemplated closing marginal mines and a major flight of capital occurred.

During the course of 1932 the pressure from the mining industry and farmers to devalue steadily mounted. A delegation of both NP and South African Party (SAP) farmers urged Hertzog to form a coalition to deal with the crisis. The announcement that Tielman Roos, an ex-NP leader of the Transvaal and now a judge, was re-entering politics threw party politics into disarray and threatened the leadership positions of both Hertzog and Smuts. In the final days of 1932 the Hertzog government announced that the country was leaving the gold standard. Hertzog and Smuts agreed early in the following year to form a coalition government. In the general election of May 1933 the coalition won 136 of the 150 seats.

Smuts easily gained the support of his party, and the NP of the Transvaal, Orange Free State and Natal also accepted fusion with large majorities. The only serious resistance was in the Cape NP under the leadership of Malan. Some of the Parliamentary represen-

tatives in the Cape party rejected absorption in the new UP in which Smuts and 'Klein Jannie' Hofmeyr – and through them, the mining industry – would have a major say.

Die Burger, the most important Afrikaans newspaper – and Nasionale Pers, which published it – also rejected fusion. It recognised the fact that the NP had been held together to win an equal place for Afrikaans as an official language, and expressed its opposition to the influence of the mining capitalists, and the 'civilised labour' policy. All this would come under pressure in the newly formed party.

The scene was set for a fusion of the NP and SAP. In December 1934 the UP was formed, with Hertzog as leader and Smuts as deputy leader. It was based on the common acceptance of an independent South Africa, equal language rights, 'civilised labour' and the need for a solution of the 'native question'.

In response Malan and eighteen members of Parliament (fourteen elected in Cape seats, four in the OFS and one in the Transvaal) founded the Gesuiwerde (Purified) National Party, which became the official opposition in 1934. It retained the old federal structure of Hertzog's old NP, with the provinces acting almost as autonomous entities, but the Cape NP, which Malan and his closest followers controlled, dominated the new NP until 1954.

Fusion: 'The great experiment'

For Smuts the fusion of the NP and SAP was 'the great experiment', representing a triumph for the principles of universality steadily progressing in the world. 'The driving force in this human world should not be morbid fears or other sickly obsessions, but . . . [an] inner urge towards wholesome integration and co-operation.' Smuts frequently warned against a spirit of isolation. To counter the new fascist states in Germany and Italy, South Africa needed the Commonwealth bonds more than ever.

It was not impossible for the UP to placate English fears at the same time as advancing Afrikaner interests. The overwhelming majority of English speakers flocked to the UP and soon accepted Hertzog as leader. He was convinced that the right of Afrikaans as an official language was now entrenched. South Africa enjoyed national sovereignty, with the right to secede from the Crown and to stay neutral in any war which Britain itself had entered. Hertzog knew that Smuts disputed this interpretation, but he, not Smuts, was the leader. The challenge now was to build a safe, 'white South Africa' on the foundation of white unity.

Hertzog brought with him into the UP several leading Afrikaners with nationalist credentials, the most outstanding being Henry Allan Fagan (as a young man an activist for the Afrikaans language movement), Attie Fourie (who as Minister of Labour spearheaded the efforts to rehabilitate the poor whites) and General Jan Kemp (who headed the agriculture ministry at a time when the state spent massively to make farming viable). The Marketing Act of 1937, which established marketing councils to undertake single-channel marketing and fix prices, greatly helped to stabilise farming.

Non-European conferences

General Hertzog's announcement in 1926 that his government intended to remove the Cape African vote and enlarge the land set aside for blacks met with prompt black opposition. In 1927 the annual conference of the ANC proclaimed Africans' right to own unlimited land and strongly defended the Cape black vote. Blacks were 'an integral and inseparable element in the population and should not be denied a say in the government of the nation'.

In the same year Dr Abdullah Abdurahman, leader of the African Political Organisation (APO), called the first Non-European Conference to forge a united response from black, coloured and Indian organisations. It gained its main impetus from a 'European-Bantu' Conference convened by the Dutch Reformed Church in March 1927, during which delegates who were not white decided to meet again later. The first Non-European Conference met in June 1927 in Kimberley. Davidson Don Jabavu, Professor of Classics at Fort Hare and leader of the Cape Natives Voters' Association, Dr W.B. Rubusana, a former member of the Cape Provincial Council, and Sol T. Plaatje, a delegate from

Kimberley, were among the leading black figures who attended. There were 45 black delegates, 39 coloured and 14 Indian.

Delegates were angered by the series of laws since 1910 that favoured whites and reduced blacks and coloured people to a second-class citizenship. Yet they preferred to hold up a positive vision of a single nation working together for the common good. Jabavu pleaded for mutual respect among the different black groups so that they 'could combine better with Europeans'. He rejected the government attempt to portray South Africa as a land of different races and nations. With remarkable prescience he warned, 'A nation within a nation is an impossibility.'

Abdurahman – the main figure at this and three subsequent conferences – deplored the government's attempts to divide and rule by treating blacks, coloured people and Indians differently. To achieve the unity that the delegates so firmly desired it was necessary to start the process of drawing people together.

Sol Plaatje pointed out that for co-operation between white and black to come about the blacks, coloured people and Indians first had to come together. Jabavu suggested co-operation at local level between all 'non-European organisations and recognised communities'. But it was not a clear-cut issue. At a subsequent conference Abdurahman opposed the idea of the different black groups losing their identity: 'It is not the aim of the conference to attempt to break down group consciousness. That would be fatal.'

The first warning of resistance that went beyond verbal protests was also issued. At the 1927 conference A.W. Champion of the Industrial and Commercial Workers' Union (ICU) asked pointedly: 'Had they no right, if a man were cutting them politically with a knife, to take the knife from him and retaliate?' He pointed out that the ICU had helped the Pact government into power in the 1924 election and thus had every right to criticise it.

In the meantime white liberals and black leaders had begun discussing race relations at meetings of the Joint Councils of Europeans and Africans, out of which the South African Institute of Race Relations grew in 1929. By the early 1930s the leadership of the Anglican Church, Catholic Church and most of the other churches had become critical of segregation and was making racial justice a central demand without, however, spelling out an alternative political order. In 1930 the Anglican bishops asked for full citizenship for all, regardless of colour. They challenged the Afrikaans churches to offer a Christian alternative to the liberal stand of the other churches, but they received no reaction to the challenge.

With the extension of the vote to white women in 1930 the proportion of Cape black voters dropped from 7.5% of all South African voters to a mere 3%.

Dr Abdullah Abdurahman and his mainly coloured APO played a leading part in the conferences in the mid-1930s, but the APO was now a conservative organisation. Abdurahman's leadership was increasingly under attack by a new, much more militant generation of teachers. A fifth Non-European Conference scheduled to be convened by an APO member for 1936 was never held.

A convention

By 1935 the United Party government's drive to remove the Cape black voters from the common roll had gathered momentum. Fusion and the establishment of the UP had strengthened Hertzog's hand. His political base was now much wider. General Smuts and Jan Hofmeyr, who had strongly opposed Hertzog's bills, were now members of his cabinet, with a much reduced ability to attack his policy.

To spearhead black resistance Davidson Jabavu (see box) and Pixley Seme, president of the ANC, decided to form an umbrella organisation. On 16 December 1935, 400 delegates from political movements, trade unions, churches and other branches of civil society met in Johannesburg to establish the All-African Convention (AAC). Its purpose was 'co-ordinating the activities and struggles of all African organisations in their fight against oppression and as a mouthpiece of the African people'. Jabavu was elected president and Dr Alfred Xuma vice-president. Jabavu called the Cape black vote 'a key experiment' in the attempt to solve the race question, while Xuma called on whites to accept blacks 'capable of rising to its standards' and able to enrich their institutions.

The convention opposed the bills and in particular the proposal for a Union Native Representative Council. It also objected to setting aside only seventeen million morgen of land for blacks out of the 143 million morgen of land in South Africa. The resolution that was accepted declared that ignoring the reality of a rapidly growing black population could only be interpreted 'as an attempt to force them into a position of economic dependency'.

But the problem confronting the convention was that partly as a result of the difficult economic times most of the organisations that were represented were in a state of disarray. Particularly the ANC and the ICU were little more than shells. Indeed, most of the delegates represented little more than themselves. The proposals of the communists and other radicals for militant action were rebuffed. Most delegates favoured moderation, prayer and protest meetings, and discussions with government leaders. There was no mass action. An Afrikaans newspaper headline summed up the impression whites had gained: 'Naturelle stil' (Natives quiet).

Curbing the black franchise

After nearly ten years of discussion of various bills, Hertzog submitted a bill to Parliament in 1936, confident of securing the necessary two-thirds Parliamentary majority (*see box*). According to the bill Cape blacks would have to vote on a separate roll to elect three whites to represent them in the House of Assembly. Four white senators, elected by electoral colleges, would represent other blacks in South Africa. There would be a Natives Representative Council to discuss issues touching on blacks in both the reserves and the common area of South Africa. An additional 7.25 million morgen of land would be bought up for the reserves – now 13% of the country's land instead of the 7% previously offered.

The bill was accepted with only eleven members voting against it. The legislation split the leaders of the All-African Convention. Some proposed a black boycott of the election of twelve members of a Natives Representative Council, a body of 21 members who could express an opinion on bills affecting blacks. Jabavu rejected a boycott, calling it 'bottled revenge'. It could only work if no one disobeyed the call.

ABOVE: *John Tengo Jabavu with his son, Davidson Don Tengo Jabavu, who continued his father's political involvement.*

D.D.T. JABAVU: RALLYING WHITE AND BLACK

In the 1920s and 1930s, when the missionaries' hopes of influencing South African policy waxed and then waned, their principal black colleague was Davidson Don Tengo Jabavu. The son of John Tengo Jabavu, a respected black newspaper publisher and politician in the eastern Cape, Jabavu bore the names of both his father and of Scottish missionary John Davidson Don. In 1885, the year of Jabavu's birth, Don had electrified black opinion by publicly denouncing the failure of government to prosecute a white man who had murdered a black man. The younger Jabavu's life would reflect the duality of his name: a desire to honour and extend the political legacy of his father, of whom he wrote a reverential biography, and close ties with missionaries, in particular those dedicated to fighting injustice.

A graduate of the University of London, Jabavu served from 1915 to 1944 as a lecturer, later professor, at the South African Native College at Fort Hare. His activities embraced farmers' associations, the Cape African Teachers' Association and the temperance movement, and he wrote and spoke widely on religious and political affairs. He was tirelessly active in interracial organisations, a speaker at interracial conferences and a founder of the South African Institute of Race Relations in 1929. In black politics he was not a member of the ANC. Yet in 1935 he founded the All-African Convention, taking the lead in rallying black and liberal white opinion against the government's plan to remove Cape blacks from the common roll.

In public Jabavu resembled many of his British missionary colleagues: unemotional, practical, rational, diplomatic. He had close ties with white missionaries at Fort Hare, in the church and in interracial organisations, and he addressed numerous missionary conferences in South Africa and abroad. A third-generation Methodist and a lay preacher, Jabavu regarded himself as 'a missionary with remarkable opportunities to carry on mission work according to the needs of my environment'. He credited white missionaries with laying the foundations 'for the modernisation of the African, not to mention the supreme gift of the gospel', reducing African languages to writing and founding schools. 'All our Native leaders today in every sphere of life are men who owe their education and training to some missionary school or college.' But Jabavu also criticised missionaries for an undiscriminating condemnation of African culture and their reluctance to perpetuate the belief in racial equality expressed by early missionaries like John Philip.

From 1914, when he returned to South Africa from his British studies, until 1936, when his influence among blacks began to wane, Jabavu was the missionaries' most powerful African ally, the chief link between the white and black sections of the interdenominational Christian movement for social reform.

Almost all the principal speakers in the 1936 debate on disenfranchising blacks asked the question whether all this was fair, just and Christian. Deputy Prime Minister Jan Smuts disliked the bill, but he thought that it had sufficient elements of 'justice and fair play and fruitfulness for the future'. Invoking the principles of self-preservation and self-defence, Prime Minister Barry Hertzog argued that no one could prove that the white fear of superior black numbers was unfounded.

Jan Hofmeyr, the leading liberal in Parliament, strongly differed from both. He opposed any law based on fear; it would fail to secure self-preservation. No nation, 'save at the cost of honour and ultimate security, can take away [franchise] rights without adequate compensation'. The bill reduced black people to an inferior, qualified citizenship. 'The puny breastworks that we put up must be swept away, but I do believe that the mere putting up of those breastworks is going to accelerate the day that the tide will

turn . .'. He believed that there was an opposing current, 'a rising tide of liberalism', among young whites in South Africa.

Another liberal, F.S. Malan, proposed extending the Cape Province's qualified franchise to the other provinces, arguing, 'You cannot divide the interests of a people, whether a man is black or brown or white.' He appealed to the Cape liberal tradition, upheld by its leader J.H. (Onze Jan) Hofmeyr, who, as far back as 1887, had laid down the broad principle: 'Have one principle for your voter, make the test as high as you like, but when a man comes up to that test do not differentiate, let him be treated as a full citizen of the country.'

Leader of the Opposition D.F. Malan differed strongly. To him the qualified franchise for Cape blacks was a bluff, and it 'was not seriously intended that it actually was seriously intended (sic)'. The overriding principle was white security. Even in the supposedly liberal Cape Colony, politicians altered the franchise qualifications in 1887

and 1892 in the belief that it was a risk to have too many blacks who had qualified. If you made the qualification for the franchise too low, they argued, you got a black man's country in which 'white civilisation' could not survive. Raising it ever higher would produce 'a small restricted coterie' of white people governing the country. Less affluent whites denied the vote on that account would have insufficient protection against exploitation. 'The poor [white] man's vote is the bulwark against exploitation.'

J.G. Strijdom, who would later become prime minister, argued that instead of spending money on land for blacks, the government should buy land for poor whites, who 'needed it much more'. Heaton Nicholls from Natal pointed out that both poor whites and poor blacks were streaming to the cities where they competed for work. Other than buying more land for blacks, it would be impossible to implement a policy of territorial segregation or try to rehabilitate the poor whites.

N.P. van Wyk Louw (above) and Elisabeth Eybers (opposite), two of the most important Afrikaans poets of the 1930s.

One of the Cape representatives elected to Parliament was Margaret Ballinger, who became one of the most effective Parliamentarians of the twentieth century. Her dilemma was that in serving as 'native representative' and exposing the harshness of racial oppression she also served to strengthen the system that black leaders increasingly considered intolerable.

A resurgent Afrikaner nationalism

A resurgent Afrikaner nationalist movement drew its dynamism mainly from three sources: the development of Afrikaans as high-culture language, the propagation of a nationalist history and the effort to promote Afrikaans businesses.

The government had recognised Afrikaans as an official language in 1925, but only a few respected works, fiction or non-fiction, had as yet appeared in the language. In 1932 only a quarter of the secondary white schools used Afrikaans as the sole medium of instruction against half that used only English and another fifth that used both. It was feared that English would quickly crowd out Afrikaans in the 20% of schools that used both languages.

English-language newspapers, particularly *The Star*, tended to denounce any Afrikaner attempts to insist on parity for the two official languages as 'racialism' that impaired the relationship between the two white 'races'. When F.W. Beyers rendered the first judgment in Afrikaans in the Appeal Court in 1931, *The Star* identified him as an ex-politician who pursued 'an extreme form of nationalism, particularly on the language question'. In exasperation C.J. Langenhoven, the most outstanding Afrikaans popular writer, once asked an English speaker: 'Why is my politics always racialism to you and your racialism always politics?' The Afrikaner Broederbond, together with its public arm the Federasie van

The Afrikaner Broederbond was founded in 1918 in Johannesburg. In 1929 the Bond founded the Federasie van Afrikaanse Kultuurvereniginge (Federation of Afrikaans Cultural Associations), or FAK as it was known generally, to promote the Afrikaans culture and Afrikaner economic action in a coordinated way. Almost all Afrikaner cultural associations eventually affiliated with the FAK. Also in 1929 the Broederbond became a secret organisation.

By 1933 the Bond had 1 003 members in 53 branches, or divisions, of which only four were in the Cape, the rest in the Transvaal and the Orange Free State. A quarter of the members were farmers and a third were teachers and lecturers.

The principal influence was wielded by Potchefstroom academics steeped in neo-Calvinist thought. Throughout its history the Bond exercised its greatest influence in the spheres of education and culture. It orchestrated some of the pressures that helped to transform the bilingual university colleges in Pretoria and Bloemfontein into Afrikaans language institutions. It helped to found the Afrikaanse Nasionale Studentebond, an Afrikaans student organisation with a radical nationalist programme.

It took an active part in establishing the 'people's bank' Volkskas in 1934 and in organising an Ekonomiese Volkskongres, or people's economic congress, in 1939. Several of the future Afrikaner business leaders, such as Anton Rupert, Andreas Wassenaar and W.B. Coetzer, became members. However, they used their membership to exert influence on the Bond and its members, rather than the other way round. The Bond's efforts to form Afrikaner trade unions or take over the leadership were ineffectual.

When D.F. Malan rejected fusion in 1933–1934, Barry Hertzog focused his wrath on the institutions with which he was associated. Malan had indeed become a Bond member in August 1933, but moved in the circles of the Cape National Party and Nasionale Pers and none of his main advisers was a Broederbonder. Hertzog latched on to a Broederbond circular of April 1934 in which it was stated: 'The Afrikanerdom shall reach its ultimate destiny of domination in South Africa ... Brothers, our solution for South Africa's troubles is not that this or that party shall gain the upper hand, but that the Afrikaner Broederbond shall rule South Africa.' He accused the Bond of spreading a 'Potchefstroom fanaticism' intent on excluding the English as true citizens of the country.

Hertzog never gave evidence for the influence he attributed to the organisation. It was in fact a small organisation slowly building itself up, struggling to make its influence felt and mostly serving as a debating forum for an elite often far removed from the real political action.

It reflected the divisions in Afrikaner nationalist ranks and encouraged debate until a consensus was reached. It played no significant role in the development of apartheid as an ideology. In the National Party government most cabinet ministers were also members of the Bond and they used it as a sounding board and early warning system about dissent in Afrikaner nationalist ranks. The organisation tried to influence the cabinet but in general the cabinet used the Bond rather than the other way around.

Afrikaanse Kultuurvereniginge, would become the main organisation in civil society committed to promoting Afrikaner economic and cultural interests (*see box*).

From the early 1930s Afrikaans surged ahead as a public and literary language and medium of instruction. For poets and novelists, and also for historians and other writers of non-fiction, the challenge was to build up a national literature with its own character. The syntax and vocabulary of Afrikaans had to a large extent assumed its present form. The translation of the Afrikaans Bible appeared in 1933 and was widely acclaimed – in contrast to the first draft, which was considered to be written in a *stompstert Hollands*, or broken Dutch, that was 'neither fish nor fowl'. Dr D.F. Malan welcomed the new translation as the greatest event in the life of the Afrikaner people in the field of culture and religion. Between 1934 and 1937 W.E.G. Louw, Elisabeth Eybers and Uys Krige published their first volumes of poetry, a flowering of talents (*see box*).

During the 1930s a new generation of Afrikaners sought to rediscover themselves through acknowledging both the heroism and the suffering of the Great Trek and the South African War. A spate of popular books on the war suddenly appeared, along with numerous articles in popular magazines and newspapers, almost all glorifying the Boer fighters, particularly the heroic resistance of the *bittereinders*, and almost all attacking the deplorable conditions in the concentration camps, largely responsible for the death of 26 000 Boer women and children.

The Great Trek also received much attention from both popular and academic historians, especially as the commemoration of the event in 1938 approached. N.P. van Wyk Louw's choral play *Die Dieper Reg* (The Higher Justice) portrayed the Voortrekkers as heroes and heroines who followed the 'call of their blood'. The celebrations handed

RIGHT: *The re-enactment of the Groot Trek led to a surge in enthusiasm for the 'Afrikaner cause'.*

D.F. Malan and his party a unique opportunity to broadcast the message that the Afrikaners as a people had had to fight their own battles for survival and could still rely only on themselves.

By the second half of 1938 the celebrations organised by the Afrikaanse Taal- en Kultuurvereniging were attracting mass enthusiasm among Afrikaners. Nine ox-wagons staged a trek from Cape Town. One route went to Pretoria, where the cornerstone of a massive new monument in honour of the Voortrekkers was to be laid on 16 December. This was the date of the Battle of Blood River, where a commando under Andries Pretorius decisively defeated a large army of the Zulu king Dingane in 1938. The other route led to the scene of the battle in northern Natal.

The re-enactment of the Trek turned out to be an electrifying event, sparking mass Afrikaner enthusiasm as the wagons wound their way through hamlets, villages and cities across the land. Afrikaner men and women, often clad in Voortrekker dress with the men sporting Voortrekker beards, met the wagons. At solemn ceremonies wreaths were laid on the graves of Afrikaner heroes, and streets were renamed for Voortrekker leaders. 'Die Stem van Suid-Afrika' (The Call of South Africa) for all practical purposes was elevated to the Afrikaners' national anthem, while the *volksliedjies* – folk songs from the FAK volume – became part of popular culture. From that time *braaivleis* (barbecue), a re-enactment of how the Voortrekkers cooked their meals on the veld, became fashionable among city people.

A crowd of over 100 000 attended the culminating event in Pretoria on 16 December. Writing 30 years after the event, journalist Schalk Pienaar, who accompanied the wagons from Cape Town, remarked: 'It brought about positively the same result as that which occurs negatively when war breaks out or is being waged, when the volk feels its very existence being threatened. The peaceful wagons made the volk mightily aware of its own existence.'

The celebrations were meant to be above party politics, but the National Party was the great beneficiary. At the mass meeting on 16 December at Blood River, Malan spoke in vivid historical images, singling out the plight of the urban poor Afrikaners as the greatest challenge to Afrikaner survival. Smuts attended the celebration in Pretoria, but did not speak. Hertzog did not participate at all.

Z.K. Matthews, a black intellectual and leading figure in the ANC, tried to strike a positive note. The centenary, he wrote, could demonstrate a 'large-heartedness and a generous attitude towards former foes'. He pointed to a statement made at a recent Dutch Reformed Church conference that the Voortrekkers had advocated social separation without implying that blacks, in consequence, were to 'be oppressed or hindered in their development'. For Matthews, the best Voortrekker monument, apart from an improvement in black health services and education, would be training blacks 'for work among their own people in services *for their benefit*' (his emphasis). The architects of apartheid would soon take up this challenge in a way that Matthews in all probability did not anticipate.

Afrikaner economic mobilisation

In the first four decades of the century English companies completely dominated the mining, manufacturing, financial and commercial sectors. It is estimated that by 1938, nearly three decades after Union, the share of Afrikaner companies in the different sectors was 1% in mining, 3% in manufacturing and construction, 8% in trade and commerce and 5 % in the financial sector.

After the South African War Afrikaner savings started flowing into trust companies, boards of executive and agricultural co-operatives. In 1914 the company Nasionale Pers was founded in Stellenbosch, which began publishing *De Burger* in 1915 and *De Huisgenoot* in 1916. The latter unexpectedly soon became very profitable. Called the Afrikaners' 'people's university', it was at one stage read by a fifth of all Afrikaner families. In 1918 the Suid-Afrikaanse Nasionale Trust en Assuransie Maatskappy (Santam) was founded and it established the Suid-Afrikaanse Nasionale Lewens Assuransie Maatskappy (Sanlam) The two insurance companies marketed themselves as 'genuine Afrikaner people's institutions'. The Sanlam motto became: 'Born out of the volk to serve the volk.' After major setbacks in their early years, Sanlam and Santam steadily expanded. In 1925 a journal covering the insurance industry called the rise of Sanlam 'extraordinarily rapid'. In agriculture the first major advance was the founding in 1918 in Paarl of a wine co-operative, the Ko-operatieve Wijnbouwers Vereniging (KWV).

In the north the Afrikaners took long to recover from the devastation of the South African War. Here the state corporations, Iscor and Escom (a steel and iron plant and an electricity supplier), founded in the late 1920s, provided avenues for Afrikaner managers.

The few Afrikaner enterprises were very modest undertakings. The Afrikaner-Broederbond had a key hand in the establishment of the savings bank Volkskas in 1934, which 60 years later became part of Absa. Driving Afrikaner businessmen was not profit alone, but their determination to prove that Afrikaners could succeed in the world of business, which was considered the domain of English or Jewish South Africans.

Albert Wessels, a successful future entrepreneur, wrote that when he arrived in Johannesburg in 1936, he found only three Afrikaner businesses of any significance: 'the

TOP AND ABOVE: *Front pages of* De Burger *and* De Huisgenoot *in 1916.*

BOTTOM LEFT: *Two of the companies founded by Afrikaner capital. Sanlam was established in 1918 in Cape Town while Volkskas was started in 1934 in Pretoria by 60 members of the Afrikaner Broederbond. By the end of the 1930s English companies still controlled considerably more than 90% of each of the mining, trading, manufacturing and financial sectors.*

publishing company Afrikaanse Pers, with its struggling pro-United Party daily, *Die Vaderland*; the bank Volkskas . . .; and a shop for men's clothes, soon to fold.' He added: 'We remained aware of the fact that our parents had been defeated, and deep in our consciousness there was a craving for rehabilitation and the urge to prove that we were at least the equals of the conquerors and their descendants.'

By the late 1930s Afrikaner farmers had recovered from the Depression and drought. They were aided by farming co-operatives, which had grown rapidly since the 1920s, offering a service without the profit motive and a low-interest advance on the coming crop. The government stabilised the prices of the principal products through new control boards. A considerable part of the risk of farming was removed by the guarantee of a minimum price. By the late 1930s and early 1940s farmers still vociferously complained of labour shortages but the most enterprising among them were ready for the great boom period that followed. Many had built up savings that they were keen to invest.

The 1938 centenary celebrations of the Great Trek provided a spur for the raising of capital, with D.F. Malan and the Free State church leader J.D. ('Father') Kestell suggesting that the best tribute to the Voortrekkers would be to save poor Afrikaners through a *reddingsdaad*, a rescue act.

The Afrikaner Broederbond decided to assign the FAK the task of organising a congress to discuss setting up a large *volksfonds* (people's fund) for the rehabilitation of the Afrikaner poor. Early in 1939 the Broederbond's Executive Council had made up its mind against a 'charity plan'. It preferred deploying Afrikaner savings and capital in enterprises that could 'save' the Afrikaner poor by employing them. In this way the Afrikaners could also become 'autonomous economically'.

Senior executives at the Cape Town-based insurance company Sanlam came to a similar conclusion. Sanlam was eager to escape from the narrow limits of insurance and agricultural credit to which it was subjected, and to establish its own finance house to centralise efforts to attract Afrikaner savings for investment in promising enterprises.

The driving force of the South African economy were the mining houses obtaining investment funds through their financial corporations, which, as listed companies on the Johannesburg Stock Exchange, attracted funds from investors worldwide. The Afrikaner nationalists took this as their model, but they wanted their finance house to marry three

OPPOSITE TOP: *Lucas Majozi, one of the thousands of blacks who served in the Union Defence Force as stretcher-bearers. He was awarded the Distinguished Conduct Medal (DCM) for bringing in countless wounded while under hostile fire at El Alamein.*

RIGHT: *The opening of the OK Bazaars, which became a South African institution and for decades was the most recognisable brand name in South Africa, after Coca-Cola. As the urbanisation of South Africa accelerated in the 1920s and 1930s a mass market for affordable food and drink of reasonable quality developed. Meeting this demand was SA Breweries founded in 1895 by Jacob Letterstedt and OK Bazaars, fathered in 1927 by two shopkeepers, Michael Miller and Sam Cohen. Both firms were among the first to recognise the value of regular advertising in newspapers.*

quite different objectives: to make profit for its shareholders, to promote the collective advancement of the Afrikaners and to help Afrikaners escape from poverty by Afrikaner employers offering them respectable jobs.

Tienie Louw's proposal for a finance house to the Sanlam board captured the spirit of Afrikaner entrepreneurship at that time. It was self-evident that an Afrikaner finance house would have to observe sound business principles, and that the profit motive would not be excluded. 'But while management would try to make the greatest possible profits for its shareholders, the main purpose will always be to enhance the Afrikaner position in trade and industry.'

The initiatives of Sanlam and the Bond would not make much impact as separate enterprises. The Bond leadership had little business experience and, acting on its own, Sanlam would be seen as furthering its own interests. The Bond-Sanlam alliance that came about provided the credibility vital in a campaign to attract Afrikaner savings for investment. It can hardly be a coincidence that several Sanlam senior executives accepted invitations to become members of the Bond at this point.

The alliance's first step was to hold an economic congress, called the Eerste Ekonomiese Volkskongres (First Economic Congress of the People). It met in October 1939 in Bloemfontein and was attended by politicians, businessmen and academics. The poorwhite problem received little attention. Church ministers and populist politicians were conspicuous by their absence. The list of speakers read like a 'Who's Who' of future Afrikaner entrepreneurs.

Considerable effort was made to break down the prevailing opposition among Afrikaners to a form of capitalism in which individuals were enriched without the community benefiting. In his opening address L.J du Plessis defined the goal as mobilising 'the volk to conquer the capitalist system and to transform it so that it fits our ethnic nature'. This adapted capitalist philosophy was later called *volkskapitalisme*, or capitalism of the people. It meant that free enterprise was not intended primarily to create wealth for individuals for their own sake, or for a handful of individuals. It had to help the Afrikaners escape from their economic thrall and gain for the people their legitimate share of the economy.

The Volkskongres created three institutions: a finance house, a chamber of commerce and an organisation to assist in a 'rescue action'. The most important was the finance house, Federale Volksbeleggings (FVB), controlled by Sanlam. Afrikaners were asked to engage in conventional investment in shares in sound Afrikaans enterprises. By 1943 more than £2 million of new investment had gone to buy shares in Afrikaner companies, mostly of FVB. By the end of World War II, FVB had major investments in fishing, wood, steel, chemicals and agricultural implements. Bonuskor, an investment corporation in the Sanlam group, was the first Afrikaans company listed on the Johannesburg Stock Exchange, posted on 26 May 1948, coincidentally also the day when the National Party captured power.

One of FVB's first loans to a small Afrikaner enterprise was to a company belonging to a young entrepreneur, Anton Rupert. Within two decades, Rupert would build up the Rembrandt group of companies as a world-scale conglomerate with interests in tobacco manufacturing, wine production and luxury goods. It is estimated that the Afrikaner share of certain sectors of the private sector rose between 1938 and 1975 as follows: mining 1% to 18%, manufacturing 3% to 15% and trade 8% to 16%.

The watershed of war

South Africa inevitably became embroiled in the war that broke out in Europe in September 1939. The right of South Africa not to participate in Britain's wars was one of the most burning issues among Afrikaner nationalists during the first three decades of Union. After the Statute of Westminster of 1934 was passed General Hertzog, for one, believed that South Africa's autonomy was assured. In September 1938 he cemented this by tying the cabinet to a position of firm neutrality if Britain joined the war. Jan Smuts seemed to have gone along with this, but changed his

BELOW: *A recruitment poster in the aftermath of Tobruk.*

BELOW AND MIDDLE: *Scenes from the Battle of El Alamein: Sidi Rezegh in the aftermath of battle and, below, the Gazala line.*

BOTTOM: *The* Cape Times *announces the war.*

mind after the German invasion of Czechoslovakia. He believed that South Africa, regardless of the political cost, was obliged to help stop Germany under Adolf Hitler. For him South Africa's freedom and the future of Western civilisation, even of the human race, was at stake. Yet it was inconceivable by mid-1939 that he would take the country into a war on a very small majority in Parliament, and with most of the electorate in all probability opposed to it.

When, just before a session of Parliament on 4 September 1939, Hertzog proposed that South Africa remain neutral, Smuts and half the cabinet favoured intervention. In the Parliamentary debate Hertzog blundered by ignoring any malevolent and aggrandising purpose in Nazi foreign policy. To him Britain and France had brought the war on themselves by imposing the humiliating peace treaty of Versailles on the Germans in 1919, much as had been the case with the republican Afrikaners at Vereeniging in 1902.

But the other part of his speech carried great force: entry into the war on a split vote would severely damage the trust between the two white communities. 'The Afrikaner people twice tried to bring together the Afrikaans speakers and the English speakers into one nation,' he said, referring to the formation of the South African Party at the time of Union, and fusion, which brought about the establishment of the United Party. He warned that if the second attempt also failed the shock to the Afrikaner people would be so severe that it would take years for it to recover. 'But if it comes as a result of a war with which we have nothing to do it will affect our national life for fifty or even a hundred years.'

D.F. Malan formulated his support for Hertzog in telling terms. If South Africa had no ties with Britain it certainly would not have entered into a war caused by a conflict in distant Eastern Europe. If South Africa were to be sucked into every war into which Britain entered, he would say out loud: 'You can talk as much as you wish about freedom, but we are a country of slaves.' Smuts was also blunt. Hertzog's speech sounded like a justification for 'Herr Hitler's actions'. He had no doubt that what was at stake was the same as that at the time war broke out in 1914: the quality of the system of government, 'the fate of humanity and the future of our civilisation'.

Hertzog's motion was defeated by a vote of 80 to 67 that went largely along the ethnic division in the white community. The governor-general refused his request to dissolve Parliament and to call a general election. *Round Table*, an authoritative journal, considered it likely that the anti-war faction would have won such an election at that time. Instead the governor-general asked Smuts to form a government, and he took South Africa into the war. It was a watershed event in white politics, also destroying the middle ground with respect to the issues of race and colour well before the National Party announced its apartheid programme. Without the political polarisation brought about by

CAPE TIMES, THURSDAY, SEPTEMBER 7, 1939.

SOUTH AFRICA DECLARES WAR ON GERMANY

PROCLAMATION ISSUED LAST NIGHT

GENERAL SMUTS OUTLINES HIS POLICY

"STAND FOR DEFENCE OF FREEDOM"

ENEMY AIRCRAFT NEAR ENGLAND

FAILURE TO PENETRATE DEFENCES

the war, which from the time of the war vote in 1939 was increasingly drawn on language lines, Malan's National Party would have been unlikely to come to power in 1948.

South Africa at war

When South Africa entered the war it had a standing army of only 260 officers and 4 600 men. There was no navy to speak of and only six modern aircraft. Jan Smuts took command, almost personifying the war effort. He was not only the prime minister, but also Minister for Foreign Affairs, Minister of Defence and Commander in Chief of the armed forces. Together with outstanding men such as Pierre van Ryneveld and Hendrik van der Bijl, he set about putting the Defence Force on a war footing.

The war was one of the most divisive issues ever in the white community. In general Afrikaners strongly opposed the war. O.D. Schreiner, a senior judge, recounted years later the reply given by an Afrikaans witness in court when he was asked what meaning he attached to the term Afrikaner, which he had used several times. His answer was: 'Someone who is against the war.' The reasons for the opposition to the war were complex: the slender victory in Parliament for the war vote and the refusal of the governor-general to call an election after Hertzog's fall; resentment at becoming embroiled in 'England's war'; sympathy for Germany; and, among some of the intelligentsia, support for national socialism.

Yet more than half of the white soldiers who enlisted were Afrikaners. Mindful of the divisions, the government relied solely on volunteers. Those prepared to serve beyond the country's borders took a special oath of loyalty and wore a special tab, called the *rooi lussie* (red tag), on their uniform. Members of rabid anti-war factions sometimes assaulted them. Nevertheless, a total of 190 000 out of a possible 570 000 white men enlisted.

While a desire to defend freedom and democracy spurred some on, others were keen to escape from the stranglehold spiral of poverty. The wage of £19 per month to a white soldier, the highest in the Commonwealth, was an attractive proposition.

Only a small proportion of the men who volunteered for service were deployed as frontline combatants. South Africans fought in East Africa (July 1940 to November 1941), North Africa (May 1941 to November 1942), Madagascar (June to November 1942) and Italy (April 1943 to May 1945). The momentous battles were at Tobruk, where a South African division had to surrender to the German Afrika Korps under General Erwin Rommel in June 1942, and at El Alamein, where the Afrika Korps was forced to retreat. South African troops were among the first to enter Rome.

During the war South Africa lost 152 men in East Africa, 2 104 in North Africa and 753 in Italy. Apart from the Springbok Legion, an association of ex-volunteers, no organisation was formed after the war to promote the ideals of democracy and freedom in South Africa. The men returned to their different social stations in life. The war did not transform political outlooks. Some disenchantment set in after the war, helping to tip the electoral balance against Smuts. For blacks who enlisted, the war opened new worlds but once again demonstrated their inferior position at home (*see box*).

The home front

The war effort disrupted the lives of white South Africans particularly. Petrol rationing restricted each car to travel only 640 kilometres per month. All consumer goods became scarce. The building of private dwellings was discouraged and only a limited amount could be spent on building materials. Civilians had to hand in their arms and ammunition.

The war opened up opportunities for white women. At the height of hostilities some 65 000 worked in radar sets, munitions factories and in the Defence Force administration. The war stimulated diversification of the economy. The government established the Industrial Development Corporation to help finance new industrial undertakings. Major new opportunities opened up because the war virtually halted the flow of imported manufactured goods from Britain. The manufacturing sector employed a small but growing number of black workers living with their families on a stable basis.

During the war the government relaxed the pass laws in order to meet labour shortages in a fast-growing economy. People poured into the towns and cities. Between 1936 and

'FIGHTING WITH KNOBKIERIES'

Black support was much more conditional than in the case of World War I. The ANC made it clear that its sympathies were with Britain but it insisted on a change in racial policy and made it clear that if blacks had to enlist in the Defence Force it had to be on exactly the same terms as whites.

The government did not feel it could agree to this, but soon found it necessary to raise an auxiliary corps in a non-combatant capacity. In order not to offend whites, it was decided to arm the recruits with assegais and knobkieries. Although the blacks did not serve as frontline combatant troops they still had to perform their duties in the actual battle zone. Outraged, Dr A.B. Xuma exclaimed, 'They are expected to fight aeroplanes, tanks and army artillery with knobkieries and assegais. What mockery!' In practice, however, commanders did not hesitate to arm black soldiers under their command.

Blacks were in no rush to enlist. After an intensive recruitment effort in Richmond, Natal, the magistrate reported in racist and paternalistic parlance, 'Only two old boys of between 60 and 70 said they would like to go and wash dishes.' Eventually some 76 000 blacks and 45 000 coloured people were recruited.

Very few blacks were from the ranks of the educated and by far the most were from poor rural areas. Material considerations were decisive. Serving in North Africa and the Middle East, members of the Native Military Corps were used as batmen, loaders and guards and the more skilled men as transport drivers, cooks, carpenters and telephone operators.

Black soldiers who expected some recognition for their services were sorely disappointed. When they were discharged they received a cash allowance of £2, a civilian suit and a gratuity for length of service. Most had to return to the rural areas from where they came. Coloured troops were generally treated better, but they also received no great benefits on their return to South Africa.

ABOVE: *Blacks who are about to serve as transport drivers in World War II are being taught the rudiments of gear changes.*

TOP RIGHT: *The 'Desert Rats', as infantry troops in the desert were nicknamed.*

1946 the proportion of urbanised whites jumped from 68% to 75% while that of coloureds rose from 57% to 61% and that of blacks from 18% to 24%. The number of urbanised African women nearly doubled. By 1948 there was a black population of 8.5 million, approximately two million of whom lived in towns and cities, compared to 1.6 million urban whites.

The rapid influx stretched the already inadequate and racially based infrastructure to breaking point. Very few houses were built during the war years, which led to an acute shortage and appalling living conditions. This gave rise to the illegal occupation of the land and the growth of large shantytowns. Black workers who lived with their families earned somewhat more than they had in the past, but they continued to struggle for survival in deplorable conditions. It produced a potentially explosive mix for dramatic political and social action, but the daily struggle to eke out an existence also sapped the energy for mass action.

The borders between white and black had become much more porous. Fears of interethnic violence mounted. In 1944 Hendrik Verwoerd's *Die Transvaler* wrote that living in racially mixed areas had become increasingly dangerous and that the government should take action.

In 1948, in Verwoerd's first speech in Parliament, he referred to 'Europeans and non-Europeans scattered and mingled about the whole of South Africa'. 'Europeans and non-Europeans have been working up to a crisis,' he said, 'with more and more trouble blowing up, clashes in the towns, the creation of all sorts of hamlets on the borders of the towns full of poverty and misery, clashes on the trains, assaults on women.' The Witwatersrand region had become 'one vast breeding place of injustice and crime'. Increasing white-black competition in the urban labour market would produce 'the most terrific clash of interests imaginable'.

Verwoerd told the Natives Representative Council after the 1948 election that the only way to avoid a clash was 'to adopt a development divorced from each other'. A major shock was the clash between Zulus and Indians in Durban in 1949, ending in 147 deaths, the destruction of 300 buildings, and damage to an additional 1 700.

The ANC regroups

Black political leaders saw tensions not as the result of blacks and whites sharing an urban space or working together, but as the product of the systematic discrimination against blacks. After becoming nearly moribund in the 1930s, the African

National Congress (ANC) was revived by the threat that D.D.T. Jabavu's All-African Convention (AAC) posed as an umbrella organisation for all black movements after spearheading the resistance to the United Party segregation legislation of 1936. The AAC decided to recognise the new Natives Representative Council (NRC), which made provision for sixteen elected black members and six white officials who were to advise the government on issues affecting blacks. It also backed white candidates for three Native's Representative Seats in Parliament and two in the Cape Provincial Council. Soon the ANC followed suit.

The ANC's survival started with the Jubilee Conference of 1937 which had been proposed by men like James Calata (an Anglican priest), Selope Thema (NRC member and editor of the *Bantu World*), and the communists J.B. Marks and Moses Kotane. It gained momentum when some exceptionally fine Native Representatives were elected to Parliament, especially Margaret Ballinger and Donald Molteno, who found they shared the ANC ideals and began to work closely with ANC leaders. The real breakthrough came when Dr Alfred Xuma, a medical doctor, was elected president in 1940.

Often using his own funds, Xuma began to transform the somewhat chaotic organisation into a more efficient body which in 1952 would have a paid-up membership of close to 10 000. He changed the constitution, drew the black intelligentsia into the body and established branches for the masses. The plaintive nationalism of the ANC made way for an aggressive and confident assertion of the rights of all individuals regardless of colour.

Although the revived ANC did not initially reject separate representation, it insisted on black participation at all levels of government, the removal of all restrictions on black land ownership and the phasing out of migrant labour. A range of socio-economic demands was made: a living wage, the eradication of the colour bar, the recognition of black unions, trading rights and the training of blacks for graded positions in the civil service. Underlying it all was the comprehensive repudiation of the notion that this was a white man's land.

The early war years offered hope after the bleak decades of repression. The victories of the Axis powers had impressed on government the need for black allies. In 1942 Jan Smuts spoke of segregation that had fallen on 'evil days', and denounced the National Party leader who spoke of the country as one of a population of only two million 'while the native was carrying the country on his back' and was clearly an integral part of the common economic order. The Secretary of Native Affairs called for the eradication of the economic colour bar.

Government social policy was moving in a reformist direction. It gave the moderate black leadership some cause for cautious optimism. Midway through the war the government put provision for old-age pensions, grants for invalids, and unemployment insurance on a firmer footing, and established the principle that blacks had to be included in any social security scheme and in any legislation conferring such benefits. Blacks could be trained as medical doctors, dentists and social scientists and for some other professions at some of the existing white universities. (They normally first went to Fort Hare College, the only tertiary institution for blacks.)

The government also no longer limited government spending on black education to the revenue from direct taxes collected from blacks. It provided free education, free books and free school meals in primary schools and increased its spending on secondary education. By the end of the war, spending for black education was three times higher than ten years before. Despite increased spending, most black children were not at school by 1948.

Nevertheless, all the changes under the Smuts government indicated an enhanced sense of government responsibility towards blacks and a more concrete recognition of their citizenship. Blacks experienced greater freedom during the war years than they had known before. Real black wages in the manufacturing sector were rising sharply.

The ANC pressed for further reforms. It adopted 'African Claims in South Africa', which, based on the Atlantic Charter, included a Bill of Rights and rejected all discrimination. It joined in the Anti-Pass Campaign of the SA Communist Party. An anti-pass march in Johannesburg in 1944 drew 20 000 members.

ABOVE: *J.B. Marks reports to members in 1946. Marks became a communist in 1928 after listening to a speech by S.P. Bunting at a meeting of mineworkers. He became chairman of the African Mineworkers Union (AMWU) and served on the executive of both the ANC and the Communist Party. Along with two other communists, Moses Kotane and Dan Thloome, Marks influenced the ANC to fight for the repeal of the pass laws and to demand adult suffrage. When Africanists in the ANC tried to expel them, the communists were supported by the more conservative members of the ANC executive, who valued their sterling contribution. In 1945 Marks became chairman of the Council for Non-European Trade Unions (CNETU), which was the most powerful African trade union grouping ever to exist in South Africa, with 158 000 members belonging to 119 unions and accounting for more than two-fifths of black workers in commerce and manufacture. He led the AMWU in the momentous strike of 1946. Due to brutal repression the AMWU was destroyed and the CNETU seriously weakened. In the 1950s Marks was detained and restricted for several periods. In 1962 he was elected leader of the illegal Communist Party. In 1972 he died in exile in Moscow.*

The war years also saw several strikes by black workers, who had become better organised in the late 1930s. Tired of trying to work with white unionists, black labour leaders formed the pro-Africanist Council for Non-European Trade Unions (CNETU) in 1938. Max Gordon, a white Marxist with Trotskyist leanings, who had organised several trade unions, accused the organisers of racism. CNETU Chairman Gana Makabeni, a Marxist who had turned Africanist, replied that whites dominated every institution and then asked: 'Must we have European leaders even in our own establishments?'

In 1941 two communists, Edwin Mofutsanyana and Gaur Radebe, organised a conference at which the African Mineworkers Union (AMWU) was formed, with J.B. Marks as the first president. Despite harassment by the Chamber of Mines it could claim a membership of 25 000 by 1944. It demanded recognition, regular wage increases, the abolition of the compound system and the tribal divisions of the workforce, and the statutory minimum wage.

The Chamber of Mines argued before the Lansdowne Commission that the basic pay of just over two shillings a shift was adequate because the mines fed and housed the workers in compounds and because the workers had an additional source of income from their plots in the reserves, which fed their families. But after investigating, the commission found that the production in the reserves was a 'myth' and 'cause for grave concern'.

The commission recommended a marginal increase of wages, but, taking into account the profitability of the mines, did not see how it could propose the recognition of black unions or the abolition of migrant labour. Labour relations on the mines quickly deteriorated.

A 'last God-given opportunity'

Reaction in government ranks had set in as early as 1942 when the war had begun turning in favour of the Allied powers. Thrown on the defensive by National Party allegations that black strikes and other protest actions were communist-inspired (which was partly true), the Smuts government took an increasingly tough stand against ANC demands. After the United Party electoral victory in 1943 Xuma asked Smuts to use this 'last God-given opportunity' to bring about freedom and prosperity for the non-white section. But Smuts had begun to speak of uniting the white population in order to address 'native' policy. He refused to give Xuma an interview to discuss black claims. All black strikes were outlawed and trade union activity made impossible.

In December 1942 the ANC national executive authorised the formation of a Youth League. Before it could act, a group of young men took the initiative. They were prepared, in Xuma's words, 'to march barefoot against race oppression'. They included Jordan Ngubane and Nelson Mandela, still in his twenties, Anton Lembede, the philosopher of the group, who had just turned 30, and Ashby Peter Mda and Walter Sisulu, who were in their thirties. Initially the League was exclusively Africanist, setting itself the goal of eradicating all racial discrimination. It proclaimed the goal to be the assertion of the black numerical majority. Although it was prepared to tolerate racial minorities, it rejected cooperation with other minorities or with the communists, which the leadership saw as proclaiming a non-Africanist agenda. But that view soon would change.

In 1946 some 60 000 black mineworkers struck, demanding a minimum wage of ten shillings a day. The state set out to crush the strike. J.B. Marks and several other trade unionists were arrested, the trade union offices were raided and twelve strikers died in police action. More than 1 000 were injured. It took three years before the mine owners granted blacks an extra three pence a shift.

The Natives Representative Council (NRC) at Dr Xuma's behest decided to adjourn if the pass laws were not abolished and black trade unions were not recognised. When the government refused, the council adjourned itself. It had come to the end of the road. As one of its members remarked, it was like using a 'toy telephone' in trying to engage government. The council now demanded direct African representation at all levels.

When the National Party came to power in 1948 the ANC had not yet formally abandoned participation in the NRC, but the All-African Convention, which had joined forces with the Non-European Unity Movement, rejected in principle any participation in racial structures. This was the context in which Isaac Bangani Tabata, leader of the Unity Movement, addressed a letter to the young Nelson Mandela, a member of the ANC Youth League (see box).

Nationalist divisions

General Hertzog's break with the United Party did not immediately unite nationalist Afrikaners; instead came a bitter deepening of divisions in nationalist ranks. In January 1940 Dr D.F. Malan's National Party and Hertzog's supporters merged in a party called the Herenigde (Reconstituted) National Party under Hertzog's leadership. But while Malan supported Hertzog with enthusiasm, the more radical nationalists in the north constantly undermined him. Hertzog was apathetic towards the idea of a republic and rejected the plan of some of the northern nationalists to consign the English language, and perhaps even English speakers, to a subordinate place. After a showdown at a party congress Hertzog withdrew from the party and Malan became leader.

Thirteen of Hertzog's followers in Parliament went on to found the Afrikaner Party under the leadership of N.C. Havenga, Hertzog's most loyal ally. Hertzog himself was now a disillusioned and embittered man, and before his death in 1942 he said that national socialism's 'true character' was closely attuned to the 'spiritual and religious outlook of the Afrikaner nation'. He opposed a form of democracy that made it possible to declare war against the people's will. He had not given up his commitment to a form of democracy that was modelled not on the Westminster system, but on that of the old Boer republics. He also discouraged militant action against the war effort. To future entrepreneur Anton Rupert and some other Afrikaner students who privately asked his advice about militant resistance he suggested they return to their studies. The Afrikaners would take over after the war by way of the ballot booth, he assured them.

Hertzog's views revealed the crisis for democracy, but also the initial appeal of the Nazi model. In 1933 Louis Weichardt had founded the South African Christian National Socialist Movement, popularly known as the Greyshirts. It was inspired by the outbreak of violent anti-Semitism and Brownshirt thuggery in Germany under Adolf Hitler. Although membership apparently never rose to more than 2 000, it put greater pressure on the

A LETTER TO MANDELA

The rise of the Youth League exacerbated the divisions between the ANC and the All-African Convention (AAC). The ANC continued to participate in structures the government set up for blacks, like the Natives Representative Council. The AAC, which stood for unity on a non-racial basis, rejected participation in any racial government structure. The AAC was part of the Non-European Unity Movement, which in the war years was led by I.B. Tabata, a Xhosa who grew up in Cape Town. In 1948, just after the National Party came to power, Tabata attacked the ANC's inconsistencies in a letter to Nelson Mandela.

Can you give me any good reason why you joined the ANC? – apart from the fact that your father and your father's father belonged to it and it was supposed to be an organisation for African people – an argument that is purely sentimental and falling outside the realm of politics . . .

An organisation, if it's true to its principles, will seek to unite the oppressed people and will at the same time follow a course of non-collaboration with Government. But I am totally opposed to any organisation whose policy is to collaborate with the Government and disunite the people . . . You and all your fellow members of the Congress Youth League are talking with two voices at one and the same time. As members of the Youth League you speak the language of the modern intellectual, progressive, independent and rejecting inferiority. But as members of the ANC your language is the negation of all these things. You accept the theory of inferiority and trusteeship with all its manifestations. For example, segregated institutions like the NRC (where leaders of the Congress serve), voting for the three whites to 'represent' Africans in the whites-only Parliament, and sitting on advisory boards, and the Bunga, etc.

I think it of paramount importance that a man, and especially a young man like yourself entering politics, establish the habit of basing his action on principles. He must be ready, if necessary, to swim against the stream. Thus armed he is protected against the temptations of seeking popularity and ephemeral success.

Ossewa-Brandwag (OB) guard of honour for its leader J.F.J. (Hans) van Rensburg, who was a strong admirer of Nazi Germany and rejected parliamentary politics. He hoped to establish an authoritarian Afrikaner-dominated republic should Germany defeat the Allied forces. The OB, with a membership of over 100 000 at its height, had its own division of storm troopers called the Stormjaers, which committed several acts of sabotage. Van Rensburg, however, refused to assist Robey Leibrandt, a saboteur, sent from Nazi Germany. Support for the OB declined after D.F. Malan instructed his followers to choose between the National Party and the OB.

right flank of Malan's party. The party nevertheless was not in any significant way influenced by the far right.

During the early war years two more organisations that were openly pro-German and pro-dictatorship operated. One was Nuwe Orde, or New Order (NO), formed in September 1940 under the leadership of Oswald Pirow, a member of Hertzog's cabinet before the 1939 split. In 1942 it had seventeen Parliamentary representatives, all elected in 1938 on a United Party (UP) ticket, advocating an Afrikaner variant of national socialism.

But the most important anti-war movement was the paramilitary Ossewa-Brandwag (OB), founded to perpetuate the 'ox-wagon' spirit of the 1938 celebrations. In January 1941 the OB came under the leadership of J.F.J. (Hans) van Rensburg, who had served as administrator of the Orange Free State. He was a strong admirer of Nazi Germany and considered himself a man of action rather than a 'cultural fire-eater' (a reference to the National Party). He campaigned for 'a free Afrikaner republic based on Nationalist-Socialist foundations'. Explicitly rejecting Parliamentary politics, the OB insisted that as the only mass movement, it represented all Afrikaners. It pinned its hopes on a victory for the Axis powers and on German help in establishing an Afrikaner republic. The OB had its own division of storm troopers, called the Stormjaers, who actively resisted the war by acts of sabotage and a handful of assassinations.

As a quasi-military organisation, the Ossewa-Brandwag rode on the wave of Afrikaner disillusionment with 'British-Jewish' democracy to acquire a mass membership, estimated by some to be as high as 100 000. It was soon widely ridiculed for its efforts to inspire enthusiasm by uniformed military drills and the introduction of military distinctions of rank. In the Transvaal several prominent members of the Nationalist intelligentsia were not only OB members, but even prominent Nazi supporters. Editor of *Die Burger*, Albert Geyer, dismissed Nico Diederichs, chairman of the Broederbond's executive council from 1938 to 1944, as a 'Nazi through-and-through'. L.J. du Plessis, perhaps the most influential of all Broeders, H.G. Stoker, the leading Calvinist thinker, and Piet Meyer, deputy secretary of the Bond, all published books and articles that represented thinking close to Nazi ideology.

Malan's National Party (NP) continued to support Parliamentary politics and rejected all violent resistance to the war effort. But on almost every occasion Malan declared that South Africa should pull out of the war. The government, operating on the assumption that most Afrikaners were anti-war, took the necessary security precautions, including internment on a large scale.

One war measure that outraged the anti-war camp was the order that civilians, including farmers, had to surrender their arms and ammunition. Malan protested: 'The Afrikaner is turned into an alien in his own land and is disarmed.' The government also instructed civil servants and teachers to resign from the OB and, at the end of 1944, from the Broederbond as well. But the most hated measure was internment without any prior trial, which was used on a large scale. John Vorster, a young lawyer who would become prime minister, was among the internees. In 1944 J.G. Strijdom, also a future prime minister, expressed his outrage. English speakers and their Afrikaner supporters were using internment against Afrikaner nationalists despite the fact that the country's security was not at stake. It had also happened in 1914–1918 and in the South African War. 'What right have [they] to call for racial peace and co-operation if every time England is at war the Afrikaans-speakers are humiliated and crushed?'

Afrikaners were generally victimised by the way in which the government issued its wide array of special permits, especially for rationed petrol and rubber, regardless of whether or not they opposed the war. The Smuts government in effect had suspended the non-partisan civil service; it turned the security forces and civil service into instruments of war policy, blurring all distinctions between the ruling party and the civil service. It gave the assurance that no one would be commandeered to fight overseas or beyond the equator, but those who volunteered for service there wore a highly visible orange tab on their shoulders. It was a political distinction; one section of the white population considered the tabbed soldier loyal, the other section saw him as disloyal. Within the armed forces the lives of those who refused to fight were made miserable, and scores were compelled to resign, finding it difficult to get jobs afterwards in any branch of the civil service. One practice that inflamed relations between political parties was the Department of Military Intelligence's transmission of intelligence reports to Louis Esselen, secretary of the UP, who used them not only for the war effort but also against the NP.

Other controversial war measures also politicised the civil service. Because large numbers of civil servants had joined the army, the government had to relax the bilingual requirements for new recruits; it promoted to graded posts a number of people who could speak only English. 'Security requirements' also led to denial of promotion to a large number of Afrikaners suspected of anti-war sympathies, often on the word of an informer. So widespread were complaints from Afrikaners on the railways that in 1948 the NP government appointed a Grievances Commission to investigate. Some 2 875 railway employees testified that although innocent of anti-war activities, they had been denied promotion for posts ranging from clerical posts to that of general manager.

A key question in the early war years was whether the NP would be outflanked by the OB and NO, or whether it would become a pro-Nazi party. A recent study by Patrick Furlong argues that Malan's NP, the OB and NO formed an 'interconnecting web', and that the Nationalists in the Transvaal, in particular, were a 'hybrid variant' of 'authoritarian and populist ingredients, reminiscent, although never an exact facsimile, of European fascism'. There were, indeed, some NP leaders whose speeches in the early war years were thinly veiled attacks on democracy and the rights of English speakers, and Malan himself at one stage accepted a draft constitution for South Africa drawn up by Hendrik Verwoerd as a party discussion document. It proposed a Christian-National republic in which Afrikaans would be the first official language and English a second or supplementary official language.

But attempts to depict the Nationalist leaders as proto-fascists lack conviction. It represents a poor understanding of both the Nazi and the Afrikaner nationalist movement. The fascist and other radical right-wing movements were driven by a singular commitment and blind obedience to a leader whose authority could only be challenged at one's peril, by a clear political creed, and by an operational ideology prescribing action.

It is far-fetched to describe the NP as fascist or proto-fascist in this sense. Malan, and J. G. Strijdom in the Transvaal, were elected leaders and could be outvoted. Their party was divided over a key issue like the republic, and apartheid had not yet become one of the pillars of party unity. Followers were free to express their views, to join or leave the party, and even to denounce it or the leaders without fear of retaliation. Almost without exception the NP leaders found the efforts to imitate the paramilitary style of the fascist movements distasteful. Furlong offers no convincing evidence that radical right-wing movements like the Ossewa-Brandwag or the Greyshirts had anything but a fleeting impact on the Afrikaner nationalist movement or on apartheid as an ideology.

From early in 1942 Malan and other NP leaders, including Verwoerd and Strijdom, unequivocally rejected national socialism as an alien import into South Africa, and endorsed Parliamentary democracy. They condemned sabotage by the Stormjaers, the OB's paramilitary wing. The major Afrikaner churches expressed a similar view. The influential *Kerkbode*, official journal of the Dutch Reformed Church, declared in March 1941: 'The Church could never associate itself with any form of state domination or intervention as is found in the European totalitarian system, which undermines the Church in its freedom.' In 1945, a day after Germany capitulated, the pro-war and pro-government daily *The Star* declared: 'We do not suppose Dr Malan and his disciples were ever Nazis at heart, or that they had any real affection for the Hitler regime.' The Herenigde Nasionale Party (HNP) was pro-German and anti-Britain. What it wanted was not so much a German victory, as denial of a decisive victory for Britain.

Between 1941 and 1948 Malan displayed shrewd strategic abilities in first outmanoeuvring and ultimately crushing the NP's opponents on its right. The party, he often said, was the 'mother' and the 'ballot box' the only proper political course. In 1941 NP members were instructed to resign from the Ossewa-Brandwag. Support for it and the New Order steadily dwindled, and in the 1943 election the NP felt confident enough to reject an electoral pact with these organisations.

The 1943 election was fought on the war issue. Smuts asked his followers for a mandate to see the war through and to make the world safe for democracy. The NP, for its part, asked voters to reject UP 'imperialism' and to express themselves in favour of democracy for South African whites. The UP won 89 seats, the NP 43. Many Afrikaner voters had abstained, but Malan could claim that the opposition was once again one consolidated whole. *Die Burger*, the party's most influential supporter, summed up the significance of the election in a sentence: 'There is no other model than the ballot booth for [our] aspirations.'

Thus one of the most important political battles of the early war years was that won in the Afrikaner nationalist movement by those who favoured a democratic system over those who preferred or would accept a dictatorship. After the 1943 election the NP was no longer a small party, but had achieved the status of an alternative government. In the 1938 election 40% of Afrikaners were estimated to have voted for the UP; approximately 30% did so in 1943. Another drop of ten percentage points for the UP would bring the NP within reach of victory. Malan now began to assuage the fears of English speakers by stressing that both white sections would have equal language and cultural rights. 'We have to live together in this land, also after the war,' he observed early in 1942. A republic would be declared only after a mutually acceptable test of the opinion of the white public, such as a referendum.

The consolidation of nationalist unity

The orthodoxy among historians is still that the NP victory in 1948 was the outcome of the Broederbond's manipulative abilities, the upsurge of mass nationalist sentiments in the 1938 commemoration of the Great Trek and, above all, the formulation of apartheid as an ideology in the early 1940s. But these factors, separately or jointly, were not decisive. The crucial turning point was the Afrikaner nationalists' outrage over the country being taken into the World War on a split vote, confirming in their eyes South Africa's continuing subordination to British interests, and the disruption brought about by the war effort.

This was the catalyst that enabled the NP to draw together diverse people in a powerful alliance: cultural nationalists seeking cultural autonomy, farmers seeking labour, businessmen seeking investment capital and clients, and workers seeking racial protection and opportunities for training; and all of them seeking to secure Afrikaner political survival and a changed relationship between South Africa and Britain. This nationalist alliance formed the basis of the NP victory in 1948.

ABOVE: *Sophiatown in the 1940s. Anglican priest Father Trevor Huddleston, who lived there, gave this eyewitness account: 'Sophiatown is not, and never has been, a slum . . . in the evening light, across the blue grey haze of smoke from braziers and chimneys against a saffron sky, you see close-packed, red-roofed little houses. You see moving up and down the hilly streets people in groups: people with colourful clothes, people who, when you come up to them, are children playing, dancing and standing around the braziers.'*

LEERDAM

4

From an Afrikaner state to an African state

(1945–2005)

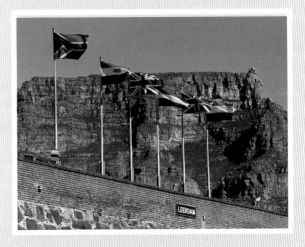

Flags the Castle in Cape Town has known since 1679 when the first flag – that of the Dutch East India Company – was raised. The flags are, from right: the Company flag, the British flag before the incorporation of Ireland, the Batavian flag, the Union Jack, the Union flag and the flag of a democratic South Africa, which was raised for the first time on 10 May 1994.

1946: Black mineworkers' strike.

1947: Natives Representative Council demands removal of all discriminatory laws.

1948: Fagan Commission recommends stabilising the black urban population; Sauer Committee established by National Party (NP) recommends apartheid. NP under D.F. Malan wins the election.

1949: Congress Youth League publishes its Programme of Action.

1950: Communist Party dissolves itself.

1948–1953: Most of the apartheid legislation is passed.

1951–1956: Removal of coloured voters from the common roll triggers a prolonged constitutional battle.

1952: ANC-led Defiance Campaign starts.

1955: Freedom Charter is presented to a Congress of the People.

1956: Tomlinson Commission report is published. Treason Trial of 156 anti-apartheid activists begins.

1957: Union Jack is abolished as official national flag.

1958: H.F. Verwoerd succeeds J.G. Strijdom as prime minister.

1959: Verwoerd announces the plan to remove all African representation in Parliament and moots the idea of independent 'homelands' for blacks.

1959: Pan-Africanist Congress (PAC) is formed under Robert Sobukwe; apartheid is introduced in university education.

1960: British Prime Minister Harold Macmillan makes 'wind of change' speech. Police kill 69 protestors in Sharpeville. Government declares a State of Emergency. ANC and PAC are banned; most leaders go into exile.

1961: Republic of South Africa is proclaimed after a referendum; Nelson Mandela forms Umkhonto weSizwe; international economic, diplomatic and sport sanctions begin to tighten.

1961–1973: South Africa experiences a period of strong economic growth.

1963: Mandela and nine others stand trial; most receive life sentences; the government introduces partial self-government for the Transkei.

1966: Verwoerd is assassinated and succeeded by B.J. Vorster.

1967: Steve Biko and allies break with the National Union of South African Students and start the Black Consciousness movement.

1972: Biko begins to work full-time for the Black Community Programme.

1973: First independent trade unions are formed in Durban.

1974: A coup in Portugal leads to independence for Angola and Mozambique and the transfer of power the following year.

1975: A contingent of South African forces invades Angola before the transfer of power.

1976: Soweto uprising; Theron Commission criticises government neglect of the coloured population.

1977: The government bans all the organisations associated with the Black Consciousness movement; Biko dies of injuries inflicted while in police custody.

1978: South Africa produces the first highly enriched uranium and a year later the first fully assembled nuclear device; P.W. Botha becomes prime minister and eleven months later Vorster is compelled to resign as state president after being implicated in the Information Scandal.

1979: The government abolishes the curbs on black labour, permits black trade unions and accepts the inclusion of trade unions with black members in the formal bargaining system; an ANC study group visits Vietnam, leading to a shift away from the armed struggle to the establishment of a domestic political underground providing leadership to an array of popular organisations.

1981: South Africa embarks on a campaign of destabilisation of the region to achieve its security objectives.

1982: A new system of black local government is introduced but widely rejected; the Conservative Party under Andries Treurnicht is formed.

1983: United Democratic Front is formed as a pro-ANC extra-parliamentary organisation.

1984: A new constitution is introduced. A Tricameral Parliament, with separate houses for whites, coloureds and Indians, triggers widespread resistance; an urban uprising begins in Sebokeng on the East Rand.

1985: Major unrest in several parts of the country leads to the imposition of a partial State of Emergency; foreign banks refuse to roll over loans. Congress of South African Trade Unions is founded.

1986: Worsening of the security situation prompts government to impose a general State of Emergency.

1988: An informal group of government officials begins talks with Mandela in prison.

1989: F.W. de Klerk becomes state president; several ANC leaders are released from jail.

1990: De Klerk lifts the ban on the ANC and several other organisations; Mandela is released.

1991: All-party negotiations begin; government abolishes all apartheid laws.

1992: Two-thirds of whites approve of the continuation of negotiations in an all-white referendum; ANC embarks on rolling mass action and withdraws from formal negotiations; when talks resume it is widely seen as holding upper hand.

1993: Chris Hani is assassinated; agreement reached on interim constitution.

1994: ANC wins election, drawing nearly two-thirds of vote. Nelson Mandela becomes first president of a democratic South Africa heading a Government of National Unity (GNU).

1996: Final constitution is accepted; NP withdraws from GNU.

1999: Thabo Mbeki succeeds Mandela as president.

2004: Mbeki elected for a second term.

Introduction

When peace was concluded at the end of World War II in 1945, South Africa was among the victorious powers. It had made great sacrifices in the battle against one of the greatest threats ever to Western freedom and democracy. But while the Allied powers prevailed, Western assumptions of political and cultural superiority received a major blow. Third World leaders began pressing in world bodies for rapid decolonisation and they also urged the West to isolate South Africa. With India receiving its independence from Britain in 1947, the decolonisation of Africa and Asia began. The United States started to integrate its defence force and other institutions. South Africa was left isolated as the last major country whose racial policy was based on white supremacy and racism.

But the West did not abandon white South Africa. This was because it considered its battle against the Soviet Union to be of paramount importance. South Africa's exports of strategic minerals and its control over the Cape sea route shielded it from Western economic and diplomatic sanctions.

Europe's post-war reconstruction triggered two decades of strong economic growth, only coming to an end with the oil crisis of the early 1970s. South Africa also benefited from this and during the 1960s managed to attain one of the highest growth rates in the world. The strong growth accelerated the processes of steady urbanisation and racial integration that had begun in the mid-1930s. Apartheid as a system tried to limit these processes and even turn the stream of blacks back to the reserves. Instead of trying to meet the aspirations of the urban black elite, it sought out the traditional leaders in the reserves as the state's main allies.

The African National Congress (ANC) became the dominant force challenging apartheid. Spurned by the West, it was compelled to link up locally with members of the SA Communist Party, banned by the government in 1950. Joint participation in the Defiance Campaign of the early 1950s and Soviet Union support offered after the ANC banning in 1960 strengthened the bonds. The ANC represented a classic form of territorial nationalism striving for the liberation of a people, not a class.

The National Party was an ethnic nationalist movement built on the Afrikaner people. The enthusiasm the party generated derived from its determination to realise the goals of South African sovereignty and the economic and cultural advancement of the Afrikaner people. Apartheid served as an operating ideology of that nationalism, spelling out the relations between the white and other groups in a way that at least partly concealed Afrikaner domination. The proclamation of a republic and the realisation of other nationalist goals, together with the high growth of the 1960s, caused the nationalism to lose its coherence.

From the early 1970s apartheid was steadily eroded as a result of the growing predominance of the manufacturing sector with its demand for skilled labour, the demographic weakness of whites, the collapse of the resource base of the black 'reserves' and the rapid urbanisation of blacks.

Until the late 1970s the ANC pursued the strategy of armed struggle with very limited success. Its major breakthrough came in the second half of the 1970s when black youth who fled the country joined the organisation. After learning the lessons of other struggles, particularly that in Vietnam, the ANC began applying the much more effective strategy of popular mobilisation and mass protests.

The state remained stable but by the final years of the 1980s a stalemate had developed between it and the ANC and its internal proxy, the United Democratic Front. The idea of a peaceful settlement was born. The negotiations for a democratic South Africa took place in conditions of political turbulence but the goal was reached without major bloodshed or outside assistance.

CHAPTER THIRTEEN

The Afrikaner nationalists in power

ABOVE: *General Jan Smuts in his military uniform during World War II. South African forces saw action primarily in four regions: East Africa (July 1940 to November 1941), North Africa (May 1941 to November 1942), Madagascar (June to November 1942) and Italy (April 1943 to May 1945). The two greatest battles in which they were involved were at Tobruk in North Africa and El Alamein. At Tobruk they were part of an Allied army that suffered a heavy defeat at the hands of the German army under General Erwin Rommel; at El Alamein Allied troops forced Rommel's Afrika Korps to surrender. Smuts was actively involved in the conduct of the war. He attended meetings of the British war cabinet and was gazetted a field-marshall in the British Army. He nevertheless remained known as 'die generaal' to his friends; he said he was too old to change names.*

The post-war era

In 1945 South Africa under the leadership of General Jan Smuts was among the victorious powers at the end of World War II. It had played its part and made great sacrifices in the battle against one of the greatest threats to freedom and democracy. But while the Western powers had won the war, their dominance over the so-called Third World – and with it the assumptions of white supremacy – would soon be challenged as leaders of nationalist movements in Africa and Asia began mobilising support for independence and freedom.

The war effort also accelerated the steady urbanisation and racial integration of South Africa. Apartheid as a system tried to reverse these trends: to limit black urbanisation and even turn the stream back to the reserves, and to base the economy as far as possible on migrant labour. Blacks had to exercise their political rights in their respective 'homelands'.

Midway through the war the idea of apartheid had become crystallised in the leadership ranks of the Afrikaner nationalist movement. In 1943 *Die Burger* first used the term 'apartheid' when it referred to the 'accepted Afrikaner viewpoint of apartheid'. In January 1944, D.F. Malan, speaking as leader of the opposition, became the first person in Parliament to employ it. A few months later he elaborated: 'I do not use the term "segregation", because it has been interpreted as a fencing off *(afhok)*, but rather "apartheid", which will give the various races the opportunity of uplifting themselves on the basis of what is their own.' Blacks, notably the intellectuals, reacted to the growing racial discrimination.

'The Natives want rights'

In 1947 the Natives Representative Council (NRC) demanded the removal of all discriminatory laws. The main liberal voice in the United Party (UP), Jan Hofmeyr, who was also acting prime minister, told Z.K. Matthews, a major intellectual figure in ANC ranks, that the UP government could do nothing that 'would be interpreted as a surrender' by its white constituency. He wrote to Jan Smuts, who was attending a meeting of the United Nations: 'Hitherto moderate [black] intellectuals are now committed to an extremist line against colour discrimination and have carried the chiefs with them. We can't afford to allow them to be swept into the extremist camp, but I don't see what we can do to satisfy them which would be tolerated by the European public.' 'The Natives want rights, not improvements,' Smuts noted in a private letter, but for him effective political power for blacks was unthinkable.

The Smuts government ignored the NRC's resolutions on the removal of discrimination in the labour market, the repeal of the pass laws and the extension of political rights to blacks. It prompted the NRC to describe itself as a 'toy telephone'. It now demanded direct representation, from the municipal council level up to Parliament, and effectively disbanded itself. When the new National Party (NP) government closed it down in 1952 it was a mere formality.

The Sauer report

In 1947 Malan appointed his closest associate, Paul Sauer, to head a party commission to turn apartheid into a comprehensive racial policy. The report was characterised by apartheid's peculiar combination of racism and rectitude. It rejected the domination and exploitation of blacks on the one hand and, on the other, equal rights and social *gelykstelling* or 'levelling' between the races. This, it asserted, would result in the national suicide of whites. In accordance with its professed principle of 'Christian trusteeship,' the National Party claimed to protect and help non-white groups so that they would 'develop along their own character and calling'.

The report proposed wide-ranging segregation between whites and coloured people and a ban on mixed marriages. Coloureds had to be protected against competition from blacks. The report considered Indians as inassimilable and suggested that as many as possible should be repatriated.

With respect to blacks it formulated the ultimate ideal as complete apartheid between 'whites and natives', which would be implemented as far as practically possible but without disrupting agriculture, industry and general interests. Blacks would receive all opportunities to develop in their own territories. A concentrated effort, with a Native Industrial Development Corporation at the helm, had to be made to develop the reserves as 'the fatherland of the natives' where, the Nationalists claimed, the best social services for blacks would be provided. Blacks should receive Christian National Education under control of the state.

Qualifying its call for total apartheid, the report also stated that the economy would depend on blacks for 'many years'. The whole thrust of the report was the elimination of 'surplus' black labour, not all black labour, and the channelling of sufficient labour to the mines, farms and industry. In many ways the Sauer report presaged the policies of the National Party (NP) introduced over the next ten years.

The Fagan report

In 1946 the government appointed Henry Fagan, a former United Party cabinet minister and now a judge, to head a commission to investigate the question of black urbanisation.

The Fagan report, published in February 1948, considered three options: a policy of apartheid, or the comprehensive territorial separation between white and black; a policy of not discriminating between white and black; and the policy which accepted that whites and blacks had to co-exist and adopted laws that took into account the similarities and differences between them.

It rejected the first two options as impractical and opted for the third. It concluded that black urbanisation was inevitable. This trend could be 'guided and regulated, and may be perhaps also limited . . . but cannot be stopped or turned in the opposite direction'. Any policy based on the proposition that the blacks in the towns were all temporary migrants was 'a false policy'. The reserves were so overcrowded and overstocked that it was unrealistic to believe they could accommodate urban blacks as well. It favoured a policy that recognised that whites and blacks 'will continue to exist side by side, economically intertwined . . . and part of the same big machine'. Black workers had to be encouraged to bring their families with them to their places of work. The old slogan 'send them back' was outdated.

The report was ambivalent about the pass laws and migrant labour, but in the end accepted them. It nevertheless hoped that the pass laws could be replaced by a system that linked firm employment to identity cards. The main feature of the report was its uneasiness with the idea of a firm blueprint and fixed policy parameters. It wrote that what was needed was 'the constant adaptation to changing conditions, constant regulation of contacts and smoothing out of difficulties between the races so that all may make their contribution and combine their energies for the progress of South Africa'.

The Fagan report pointed to a road South Africa did not take. It represented a gradualist approach that would allow the forces of economic growth to sweep aside outdated policies and prejudices over time, to a point where a form of political accommodation became possible. It made the kind of recommendations one would expect in a pre-democratic

BELOW: *Henry Fagan followed his leader, General J.B.M. Hertzog, into the United Party, and served in his cabinet as Minister for Native Affairs. Fagan won the Stellenbosch seat for the UP in the 1938 election before he left politics for the bench. He was widely respected across party lines for his relatively liberal views on racial policy. With increasing hostility building up among blacks over the restrictions they faced, Jan Smuts asked Fagan to head a commission to report on the pass laws, migrant labour and the position of blacks in industry and the urban areas. The National Party and several academics in Stellenbosch savaged Fagan's report, published just before the 1948 election, which the UP lost. It is uncertain how much of the more flexible approach to racial policy the Fagan Commission recommended would have been implemented by a UP government. Fagan went on to become chief justice and subsequently leader of the National Union, a small party that contested the 1961 election in alliance with the UP, on the platform of a racial federation.*

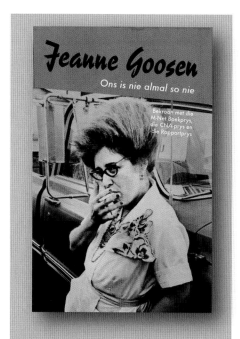

ONS IS NIE ALMAL SO NIE

Jeanne Goosen's short novel *Ons is nie almal so nie* (We are not all like that) brilliantly captures the idea that apartheid also classified and dehumanised whites, even those who opposed it. The main character in her novel, set in the 1950s, is Doris, who is more sensitive to the injuries inflicted on the coloured people than her fellow working-class Afrikaners. When her coloured neighbours are forced to move out of the 'white area' under the Group Areas Act, she runs after the truck carrying their belongings with a cake as a gift, shouting '*Ons is nie almal so nie*' – We are not all like that. The man at the wheel turns up the truck's window. Apartheid has made Doris one of 'them'.

society where some of the most burning issues were put beyond democratic contestation. In post-war South Africa, however, a large part of the electorate would see the accommodation of urban blacks as a process that would lead inexorably to bringing whites and blacks in direct competition with each other. The question was whether Fagan's approach could work in a society like South Africa where only the members of the dominant group were enfranchised and where the very deep socio-economic inequalities corresponded with the racial divisions.

The NP savaged Fagan's report. After the 1948 election Fagan wrote that the NP now had a mandate to test its apartheid policy. 'If the attempt succeeds,' he continued, 'well and good. If not, it will nevertheless be a preparatory step to bring the mentality of the public to maturity and to get people to acquiesce in a policy which concedes the impossibility of territorial segregation and . . . to find the best way of adapting ourselves to what is possible.'

A momentous election

When the 1948 election campaign started, the UP failed to see that it was in serious trouble. Afrikaners had been seriously alienated from the UP by the split decision in 1939 to take South Africa into the war and by the disruption the war effort caused. By 1948 there was growing irritation with wartime restrictions that were still in place. Living costs had increased sharply. White farmers in the northern provinces were particularly unhappy that black labour was leaving the farms and moving to the cities. They demanded the strict application of pass laws.

In the election of 26 May 1948, D.F. Malan's National Party, in alliance with N.C. Havenga's Afrikaner Party – formed during the war from General Hertzog's core support – won with a razor-thin majority of five seats, and only 40% of the overall electoral vote.

Malan said after the election: 'Today South Africa belongs to us once more. South Africa is our own for the first time since Union, and may God grant that it will always remain our own.' When Malan said that South Africa 'belonged' to the Afrikaners he did not have the white-black struggle in mind but the rivalry between the Afrikaner and the English community (led politically by Jan Smuts and a few other Afrikaners).

Many Afrikaners felt victimised by the way in which the wartime measures had been applied. Rumours were rife of Afrikaners who had been refused promotion merely on the say-so of informers. According to an analysis of the letter columns in the Afrikaans papers, *Die Burger* and *Die Transvaler,* the most salient matter was the belief that the UP government had discriminated against Afrikaners in the previous eight years; next were food shortages and rationing and the treatment of ex-servicemen. Editorials, by contrast, frequently raised the racial question.

The NP that came to power in 1948 was two parties rolled into one. The one was a party for white supremacy that introduced apartheid, promising the electorate it would secure the political future of whites; the other a nationalist party that sought to mobilise the Afrikaner community by appealing to Afrikaans culture – their beliefs, prejudices and moral convictions, a sense of a common past and shared hopes and fears for the future.

Immediately after the 1948 election the government began removing the remaining symbols of the historic British ascendancy. It abolished British citizenship and the right of appeal to the Privy Council (1950), scrapped *God Save the Queen* as one of the national anthems and the Union Jack as one of the national ensigns (1957) and took over the naval base in Simon's Town from the Royal Navy (1957). The removal of these symbols of a dual citizenship was seen as a victory for Afrikaner nationalism.

The NP's advance was the story of a people on the move, filled with enthusiasm about the 'Afrikaner cause', putting their imprint on the state, defining its symbols, and giving their schools and universities a pronounced Afrikaans character. Political power steadily enhanced their social self-confidence. In the world of big business Rembrandt, Sanlam,

Volkskas and other Afrikaner enterprises would soon begin to earn the respect of their English rivals.

The NP as a ruling party stood mobilised and ready for action. An English editor described its style in the 1950s: 'Activity is ceaseless; the contact continuous. There is rarely a weekend without a party or public meeting somewhere in each province. Not a week goes by without one or other Minister speaking to the people and participating in their group activities, easily and spontaneously.'

Yet the apartheid part of the policy steadily marginalised the part that appealed to culture and took pride in the achievements of the ethnic group. For other people it looked as if the Afrikaners were obsessed with fears about their own survival, and thus did not care about the damage and the hurt apartheid inflicted upon others in a far weaker position.

The novelist Alan Paton made the pat comment: 'It is one of the deep mysteries of Afrikaner nationalist psychology that a Nationalist can observe the highest standards towards his own kind, but can observe an entirely different standard towards others, and more especially if they are not white.' It came as a shock to those Afrikaners who rejected the harsh policies that blacks and coloured people nevertheless saw them as part of an intransigent dominant group.

Transition troubles

For a short spell after 1948 serious strife existed in the armed forces between those whites who had refused to fight in World War II (almost all of them Afrikaners) and those who had fought (about 50:50 Afrikaners and English). Some senior military officers were openly contemptuous of the Nationalist Party leadership, who to a man opposed the war effort.

F.C. Erasmus, the new Minister of Defence, was particularly unwilling to forget the injustices he believed Afrikaner nationalists had suffered as a result of the war. The co-operation between the United Party and some military units still rankled. Erasmus sidelined Major-General Evered Poole, first in line to become Chief of General Staff. Several other members of the top command who were pro-war, including Afrikaans-speakers, were demoted or sidelined.

Nat Nakasa

The mining industry adapted remarkably well to the racial restrictions on labour by professing the repugnance of apartheid. This is well illustrated by the attitude of the founder of Anglo American Corporation, as portrayed in Lewis Snowden's autobiography *Land of the Afternoon (1968).*

Sir Ernest Oppenheimer, last of the great magnates, was then [in 1957] in his seventy-seventh year, living in a great house in Parktown, Johannesburg. He received me once in a large, beautiful room that was hung with Renoirs, and talked of the Diamond Corporation's new headquarters he was to open in London on his next birthday, and then of the apartheid laws. 'They are no trouble to us, you know ... I mean on the mines, we have all the native labour we need. You know why? The natives come to us because they know that on the mine they are sheltered. No pass law raids. No chivvying by the police. We look after them ...' As the magnate explained, holding a long-stemmed glass, he spoke with a shrug and a smile. 'The government's restrictive laws – apartheid and all that – don't touch them ... So we have no labour problems. That's how it works out for us ... That's how it is.'

ABOVE: *Sir Ernest Oppenheimer (1880–1957) was born in Germany and arrived in South Africa in 1902. He founded Anglo American Corporation in 1917 and won control of the De Beers Consolidated Mines, a diamond monopoly.*

Erasmus also embarked on a major effort to South Africanise the Defence Force, which imitated Britain in its uniforms, the names of the officer ranks, and its medals and colours. Afrikaner traditional ranks like commandant were introduced, the uniforms were changed and new medals of honour were created.

Blacks were by law excluded from all army ranks except in menial, lowly paid civilian roles.

Before 1948 correspondence and instructions were conducted almost exclusively in English. Erasmus instructed the Permanent Force to alternate between Afrikaans and English every month in its communications. Members of the force would no longer be promoted without first passing a strict bilingual test. A spate of resignations occurred as a result of this, especially in the Air Force. By 1956 three-quarters of the recruits in both the Army and the Air Force were Afrikaners. The Defence Force was becoming an Afrikaner preserve.

The strict application of the bilingual requirement upset many English-speaking civil servants, and many rightly or wrongly believed that their chances of promotion had diminished greatly after the NP victory, particularly if they had been strongly pro-war. There was, however, no massive purge of English civil servants after May 1948. It took more than ten years before the upper ranks reflected the composition of the white community. New recruits were, however, predominantly Afrikaans-speakers and the number of Afrikaners in the civil service doubled in the first twenty years of NP rule.

Affluent but powerless

Retaining their economic dominance, English-speakers continued to hold the key to future domestic fixed investment and to foreign fixed investment. By 1948 the per capita income of English-speakers was more than double that of Afrikaners, their level of education was much higher and they identified with a culture that was vastly richer and more diverse than the Afrikaans culture.

After the 1948 election the English community in South Africa found itself in the political wilderness. Patrick Duncan, son of a South African governor-general, wrote: 'English South Africans are today in the power of their adversaries. They are the only English group of any size in the world today that is, and will remain for some time, a ruled, subordinated minority. They are beginning to know what the great majority of all South Africans have always known – what it is to be second-class citizens in the land of one's birth.'

For English-speaking business leaders the NP victory came as a major shock. The Smuts government had been ideal for English business. After 1948 English business leaders contributed substantially to the United South African Trust Fund that funded the UP with a view to unseating the NP government. Ernest Oppenheimer, the magnate controlling the giant conglomerate Anglo American Corporation, was the main donor. But business was hardly liberal. It refused to back the Liberal Party that Alan Paton helped to form after the 1953 election with a programme of a multi-racial democracy based on universal franchise.

By the mid-1950s English business leaders had come round to accepting and working with the government. Manufacturers enthusiastically welcomed the government's policy of promoting growth and boosting import substitution through protection. Mining magnates reaped the benefits of a very cheap, docile labour force while blaming the government for the system (*see box*).

The West and National Party rule

The 1948 election result dismayed Britain, South Africa's principal foreign investor and trading partner. But with the shadow of the Cold War falling over the world, the priority for Western governments was to prevent South Africa, with its minerals and strategic location, from falling under communist influence. The British Labour government under Clement Attlee concluded that this aspect was more important than its revulsion for apartheid. He would soon offer South Africa access to the intelligence secrets of Britain and the United States.

In the southern states of the United States segregation still held sway. A survey in 1942 found that only 2% of whites favoured school integration, and only 12% residential integration, while only one-fifth thought the intelligence of blacks was on the same level as that of whites. Even among northern whites only 30–40% supported racial integration.

The West did not insist on a popular democracy in South Africa, arguing that such a system was impossible for the time being. During the 1950s it was not uncommon for Western leaders to express racist views. In 1951 Herbert Morrison, foreign secretary in the British Labour government, regarded independence for African colonies as comparable to 'giving a child of ten a latch-key, a bank account and a shotgun'.

Still, the defeat of Nazi Germany and the horror of the Holocaust had discredited racial ideologies and speeded up pressure for racial integration, particularly in the United States. The granting of independence to India in 1947 was a major turning point in world history that intensified the pressure to allow black and brown people to be free. The General Assembly of the United Nations became an effective platform for the nations of the Third World to vent their anger over centuries of Western domination. Apartheid soon became the focus of their wrath.

The National Party in the ascendant

The United Party was unable to capitalise on the provincial and other divisions in the National Party. Jan Hofmeyr, Smuts's heir-apparent, died in 1948 and Smuts in 1950. J.G.N. Strauss, his successor, failed to make any political impact. In 1956 Sir De Villiers Graaff replaced Strauss. He was personally popular across the party divisions, but failed to develop an alternative to apartheid that could attract electoral support.

The NP fought the 1953 election with Malan as leader, now nearly 80 years old, and an apartheid policy that was still very crude. It again drew the minority of votes, but pushed its majority up to 34. In 1954 J.G. Strijdom succeeded Malan as leader and prime minister, signalling the new dominance of the Transvaal in the NP caucus. In the 1958 election the NP won 103 seats, the UP just 53. It was now clear that the NP was unlikely to lose power as long as whites controlled politics.

Hendrik Verwoerd became prime minister in 1958 when Strijdom died in office. Although he had studied and taught at Stellenbosch he was never popular among the opinion-formers in the south and more particularly the academics and journalists. They disliked his rigid, doctrinaire approach, especially his intransigent views towards the coloured community.

Albert Luthuli

Albert Luthuli was elected president-general of the ANC in 1952. The government imposed several bans on him, including one in 1957 limiting him to a radius of 24 km from his home. It was lifted briefly to allow him to receive the Nobel Peace Prize. On the left he and his wife are shown on their way to Oslo to receive it. Above he makes his acceptance speech.

Hendrik Verwoerd was two years old when his parents emigrated from the Netherlands to southern Africa. A brilliant student, he received his doctorate at the University of Stellenbosch in 1924 and then visited universities in Germany and the United States.

There is no evidence that he was influenced by Nazi racial ideology. In his academic career he would often draw on the work of social scientists in the United States, which he visited after Germany, and in particular on the work on modern business management. As a politician he would be described as a social engineer, but he rarely referred to the extensive literature on social engineering. What he did learn was that research and the aura of social science could be used to shape and defend social policies. When he became Minister for Native Affairs in 1950 he quickly established a research division.

His lecture notes and memoranda while working as Professor of Sociology at Stellenbosch shows that he rejected the notion of biological differences between the big racial groups. He added that since there were no differences 'this was not really a factor in the development of a higher social civilisation by the Caucasian race'.

He acquired national prominence when he organised a conference about the problem of poor whites in 1934, following a report by the Carnegie Commission. Verwoerd was energetic, hugely ambitious, exceptionally well organised and methodical in anything he undertook. He had an unshakeable confidence in the right of the state to make decisions not only for whites, but for the rest of the population as well. All that was required to solve the problem of white poverty,

he believed, was a leadership with the necessary drive, vigour and commitment.

He had a great ability to marshal arguments for white privilege so as to make it appear that it was not actually the intention for whites to be the principal or even the sole beneficiaries. Throughout his career he would advance contentious arguments with great intellectual composure.

Along with a few other Stellenbosch professors he staged a public protest in Cape Town in 1936 against the arrival of Jewish immigrants escaping from Nazi Germany on the ship the *Stuttgart*. Their argument was that an influx of Jews would make it even more difficult for Afrikaners to make headway in business and the professions.

He became editor of *Die Transvaler*, a new Johannesburg daily, in 1937 and entered politics in 1948. Over the next ten years he developed apartheid into a coherent policy that arose from the assumption that man is a social being who finds fulfilment only in his association with his particular *volk*, or ethnic group, and that the task of the state is to regulate the co-existence of different nations defined and set apart by the state. Under him the cabinet discarded the offensive racial terminology for the subordinate communities.

Before Verwoerd South Africa's racial policies were harsh but there were many loopholes, inconsistencies and compromises that made living under it slightly more tolerable. However, as *Die Burger* editor Piet Cillié remarked, Verwoerd's spiritual make-up was 'overwhelmingly intellectual: ordered thoughts, clear doctrines, fixed future patterns. What was justified and correct in principle, had to be capable of im-

plementation.' Verwoerd brought this essentially academic approach to the racial problem. Apartheid was a vast scheme of social engineering that perhaps only an academic could conceive. Once he put his tight system in place, he refused to allow tinkering with it. Exceptions, he believed, would only bring everything crushing down.

Rykie van Reenen, a perceptive journalist from *Die Burger*, was struck by 'his immense charm' and 'razor-sharp brain power' when she interviewed him. But the lasting impression was his answer when she asked him if he could sleep at night, given the awesome responsibility in executing his policy. 'Oh, yes,' he replied, he slept very well, and added: 'You see, one does not have the problem of worrying whether one perhaps could be wrong.'

The ruthless application of apartheid, ignoring the gross harm and humiliation it inflicted, could be traced to this kind of ideological certitude, which Verwoerd conveyed to his followers.

Hendrik Verwoerd

Constructing the apartheid system

Apartheid rested on several bases. The most important were the restriction of all power to whites, racial classification and racial sex laws, group areas for each racial community, segregated schools and universities, the elimination of integrated public facilities and sport, protection for whites in the labour market, a system of influx control that stemmed the movement of blacks to the cities, and designated 'homelands' for blacks as the basis for preventing them from demanding rights in the common area.

In 1948 Afrikaner voters outnumbered English voters by only 135 000, and while virtually no English-speakers voted for the National Party in its first fifteen years of power, more than 20% of the Afrikaners had cast their vote for the United Party in the 1943 election. It was generally accepted that the large majority of the approximately 46 000 coloured voters supported the UP. With its slender majority of five, the NP insisted that these voters be removed from the voters' roll because they held the balance of power in several constituencies. Apartheid as a policy was directed at uniting all Afrikaners behind a policy that appealed to both racists and reformers and addressed the interests of all the constituencies in the Afrikaner people. It promised undiluted white supremacy and firm control over black labour.

Political apartheid

According to the constitution the coloured vote could not be changed without a two-thirds majority of the House of Assembly and Senate sitting together. In 1951, Parliament passed the Separate Representation of Voters Act, which put all coloured voters on a separate roll. It was declared unconstitutional by the Appeal Court. A prolonged constitutional struggle ensued. In 1956 the government enlarged the Senate by appointing sufficient members from its own party ranks to get the necessary two-thirds majority to remove the coloured vote, violating not the letter but the spirit of the constitution. Four whites now represented the coloureds in Parliament.

The government's action aroused strong opposition, particularly by veterans of World War II, who saw it as an assault on the values they had fought for. It led to the establishment of the Torch Commando, led by a highly decorated soldier, A.G. ('Sailor') Malan. By 1952 it boasted 125 000 paid-up members. Organising some of the largest demonstrations the country had ever seen, it offered spirited resistance to the violation of the Union constitution. But it made little impression on the government, which saw it as a disguised protest against the elimination of the UP voters. The Torch Commando lost its momentum after disputes erupted over whether coloured ex-servicemen could become full members.

BELOW: *War veterans formed the Torch Commando to protest against the government's attempt – in violation of the constitution – to remove coloured voters from the roll without a two-thirds majority. The first Torch Commando meetings held in 1951 attracted surprisingly large crowds. Its leader, A.G. ('Sailor') Malan, a much-decorated fighter pilot, pledged 'every constitutional step to enforce an immediate general election'. He warned that 'if the political rights of so large a group as the coloured people are diminished without effective protest, the status and rights of no other group in the community are safe . . .' English-speaking South Africans were briefly roused, but after sharp National Party gains in the 1953 election interest started to wane.*

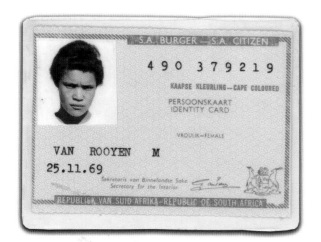

The cornerstone of apartheid was the Population Registration Act of 1950, which classified whites and blacks by race and coloured people by appearance or general acceptance as well as by descent. The picture above shows the identity card coloured people were required to carry. The signs illustrate 'petty apartheid', a term coined in 1959 when Piet Cillié, editor of Die Burger, *referred to measures that 'irritated without achieving anything' and detracted from the ideal of 'grand apartheid' – the success of the independent homelands.*

OPPOSITE TOP: *The 'pass' or reference book for blacks had to show that the bearer was legally employed and qualified to be in an urban area.*

The government made no effort to attract the urbanised black elite. Instead it decided to build its apartheid system upon the chiefs in the reserves, which would soon be called 'Bantu homelands'. The reserves were also part of the pre-1948 segregation policy but now they were turned into substitutes for representation in the common area. In 1951 Minister of Native Affairs Hendrik Verwoerd piloted the Bantu Authorities Act through Parliament, providing for three tiers of authority in the reserves, all under his control via the Department of Native Affairs.

At this stage the system of traditional rule was in an advanced state of decay. But the chiefs emerged from the shadows to inherit the kingdom in the reserves. Many of the chiefs were little more than stooges, but that did not bother government. It favoured subservient chiefs who were prepared to uphold and enforce government policy even at the cost of whatever popularity they had.

Communal apartheid

In terms of the Population Registration Act of 1950, the state classified every citizen in statutory groups with whites, Indians and blacks as the main groups. Each 'population group' had to live in its respective group area and attend schools and other facilities set aside for its group.

Classifying coloured people was particularly difficult. The Act's main criteria for classifying them were where a person belonged in terms of social standing and white public opinion. Whites hired as classifiers passed judgment on a person's race, falling back on white beliefs and stereotypes about racial difference. People were questioned about their descent and, in extreme cases, their fingernails were examined and combs pulled through their hair (if the combing encountered tough curls a person was identified as coloured, or not white).

The existing ban on marriages between whites and blacks was extended to whites and coloured people. The Prohibition of Mixed Marriages Act of 1949 banned all marriages between white people and those not deemed white. The Immorality Amendment Act of 1950 outlawed carnal intercourse between a white person and one who was not white.

To prosecute offenders under the Immorality Act the police used binoculars, tape recorders and cameras, burst into bedrooms, and instructed district surgeons to examine the genitals of suspects. Those caught included not only ordinary people but also church ministers, schoolteachers, and even a private secretary to a prime minister. By 1985 when the law was repealed, some 11 500 people had been convicted and many more had been charged. Some white offenders committed suicide or emigrated.

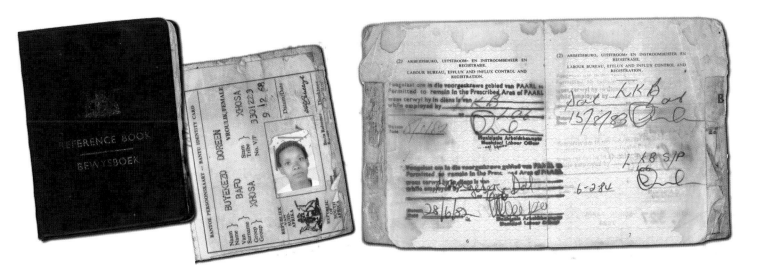

RACIAL CLASSIFICATION AND HUMAN TRAGEDY

The havoc that racial classification could wreak in people's lives is illustrated by a 1974 newspaper report written by Stanley Uys, one of the most outstanding journalists of his time.

The suicide of a 20-year-old Coloured boy in Cape Town has brought to light an apartheid tragedy almost unparalleled in South Africa's history. The boy threw himself under a train at a suburban station when he learnt that his white girlfriend was pregnant. He could not marry her, because the Mixed Marriages Act prohibits marriage across the colour line ... The girl tried to commit suicide by cutting her wrists, but failed. She was unaware that her boyfriend was Coloured ... The boy's identity is not being revealed, because his family is leading an illegal try-for-white existence. The father, who is white, met the mother, who is Coloured, in 1950 – the year in which the Mixed Marriages Act was passed. They lived together, defying the Immorality Act, which prohibits sexual relations across the colour line. They have five children, and the family lived as whites in a white suburb. They could not send the children to school, because their birth certificates classified them as Coloured, and they would have been refused admission to a white school. This would have begun events that would have led to their exposure, their expulsion from the white suburb, and the loss of their white friends ...

18 DRUM, October 8, 1973

This is petty apartheid

"Only nannies" is the sign on this bench so the young man who wanted to have a chat with the woman who looks after the White children is asked to move off.

Group areas

Apartheid extended the pre-1948 practice of developing a suburb or a township for a particular racial group only. What was new was breaking up racially integrated areas. By 1950 almost a third of coloured people in Cape Town lived in mixed areas. In virtually every town there were *onderdorpe* where whites, blacks and coloured people lived interspersed. The Group Areas Act of 1950 restricted ownership and the occupation of land to a specific statutory group.

The Reservation of Separate Amenities Act segregated public facilities; it provided for segregated entrances, buses, train coaches, parks and public toilets. Blacks and coloured people could only be served over a counter and not at a table in restaurants in the so-called white business areas and were excluded from white theatres and cinemas, hotels (except segregated bars) and swimming pools. Beaches were also segregated. Eventually one out of every four coloured people and one out of six Indians (against only one in 666 whites) across the country was forced to move.

One of the most controversial actions occurred in the mid-1950s when blacks living in Sophiatown, Johannesburg, were compelled to move along with many others to a vast

CONTRASTING VIEWS ON RESIDENTIAL SEGREGATION

D.F. Malan, 1950

[It] is only on the basis of apartheid in regard to residential areas that we shall be able to achieve sound relationships between the one race and the other. Only on that basis will we be able to secure justice for both sides. What justice is there for the non-European if he is in the position in which he is today? He will always have a sense of inferiority. He is unable to do justice to himself. On the basis of apartheid, however, with his own residential area, he will be in a position to do justice to himself. There he will be able to live his own life – there he can develop what is his own, and only by the main-

tenance and the development of what is your own can you uplift yourself and uplift your people.

Allan Hendrickse, 1988

Last year, when I asked him [President P.W. Botha, who had been the minister responsible for the removal of people from District Six in the late 1960s] to give District Six back to the coloured people, he wanted me instead to thank him for what he had done. He said he never heard of such ingratitude, that those people had been living in houses owned by whites, that they were exploited and living in slums, and that now they were home-owners in Mitchells

Plain. 'You must thank me for what I have done,' he said, 'because now you are living in dignity.' That was his approach. It was typical of that gap in their thinking that just cannot be overcome.

These extracts highlight the two completely different worlds of those who made the policy and those on whom it was imposed. The first is from a speech by Prime Minister D.F. Malan; the second is from a speech by Allan Hendrickse, leader of the Labour Party in the Tricameral Parliament, on the removal of coloured people from District Six in the heart of Cape Town to Mitchells Plain on the outskirts.

new black township southwest of Johannesburg, called Soweto. Sophiatown was rezoned for whites only and renamed Triomf (Triumph). Another removal that caused particular outrage occurred in the second half of the 1960s, when 65 000 coloureds from District Six, a vibrant but crime-infested inner city ward of Cape Town, were forced to leave. It was virtually razed.

The new townships failed to develop any economic or social dynamism. Neighbourhoods and even families had been broken up in the removals and people were dumped in new areas that lacked infrastructure. The group areas removals put the poor at a considerable distance from their places of work, often without adequate public transport. The absence of established social norms gave rise to high crime rates.

In the first fifteen years of apartheid there was large-scale construction of dwellings for black groups. By 1958 many former slums in and around the major cities had been cleared and some 100 000 houses for blacks had been built under the supervision of Verwoerd's department. As in most township developments, the abodes were small and the township architecturally monotonous, with few public amenities.

Apartheid education

By 1948 the education of black people was still for more than 90% an extension of the church and missionary enterprise. Illiteracy was widespread. Although a few mission schools provided good education, the overall state of black education was extremely poor: only 3% of blacks had received post-primary school education by 1952 and only 8 488 blacks had a matriculation qualification. By contrast, more than 40 000 whites passed the highest school standard every year. In 1947 there were only four coloured high schools and 182 candidates who sat the examination of the final school year.

In 1949 the new government established a commission of inquiry into black education, under the chairmanship of Werner Eiselen. It proposed a new state-controlled system. No mention was made of any theories of racial inferiority. The report concerned itself with the worrying lack of a *groepsgevoel* (group feeling) among blacks. It pointed out that African cultures were dynamic and could provide the context for the modernisation of entire peoples. Instead of imitating English culture, the system had to inculcate pride in the *volkseie* – the history, customs, habits, character and mentality of the ethnic group of pupils. The report also evinced a strong belief in the superiority of mother-tongue education. As a result, the government made the ethnic language compulsory during the entire primary schooling, and subsequently in most of secondary school as well.

OPPOSITE: *District Six during the forced removals in the 1960s. When the government introduced the Group Areas Act in 1950, it claimed that 80– 90% of residential areas were occupied by people of a single group and that separation should not be too difficult. But the law had a dramatic impact. When the government announced its proposals for Cape Town, the UP-controlled City Council was so shocked that it boycotted the public hearings. Eventually one out of every four coloured people and one out of six Indians (against only one in 666 whites) across the country had to move. Coloured families across the Cape Province were driven out of the* onderdorpe *to townships on the fringes of the town or even further away.*

BELOW: *The new, state-controlled system of education for blacks, called 'Bantu education', was an attempt to provide mass education for an industrialising economy. While it made for a definite improvement in mass literacy, it came under heavy criticism from white liberals and the black elite on account of inadequate government funding. For nearly two decades the government pegged its spending on black education at the same level. Although total expenditure on black education grew, the sharp increase in the number of students resulted in per capita spending on black children falling by a third in this period. In Brakpan, Benoni, Germiston, Natalspruit, Alexandra township and Moroka, children were taught in leaking halls, dilapidated cinemas and even on the open veld.*

In 1953 the government took control of black education. It was keen to eliminate the church and mission schools whose teachers mostly rejected the apartheid policy and had extended English influence. This assumption of control went hand in hand with a major extension of inferior mass education to blacks. In 1948 only 24% of blacks of school-going age were enrolled in schools; by 1994 the proportion had risen to 84%, a steady increase in black pupils of an average of 5.8% per year.

Verwoerd got the National Party caucus to accept the introduction of mass education with the promise that there would be 'no place for Africans above the level of certain forms of labour'. He added that within their 'own community all doors are open'. These words reverberated through the years. They were blunt and callous, epitomising the mean spirit of apartheid. It came as a shock because the war years had kindled the hope that the straitjacket of segregation was slowly slipping from the body of blacks.

The fact was, however, that Verwoerd did not announce new policy. There had long been a consensus among the white parties that skilled and semi-skilled jobs were reserved for whites. As Jonathan Hyslop remarks in *The Class Room Struggle*, '"Civilised labour" had a long and broadly based history in white politics. What *was* new was Verwoerd's aim of opening up new structures of black incorporation through the homelands.' The state was never a white state. Even in the 1950s there were more blacks in the civil service than whites. The number of black civil servants in the various apartheid structures 'serving their own people, as the policy would have it', steadily increased over the next three to four decades.

Verwoerd provoked particular hostility by saying that it did not serve any purpose to teach a black child mathematics if he or she could not use it. Despite these words, analysts found that syllabuses in black schools were very much the same as in the white schools and an improvement on those used previously in many of the private black schools.

The small, urbanised professional class of blacks strongly rejected mother-tongue education. They saw the sole purpose of 'Bantu education', as it came to be called, as that of preventing the advance of blacks in the Western economy and culture. They wanted jobs in the modern economy, not to be restricted to serving white society. They saw the emphasis on distinct 'Bantu' cultures as an attempt at divide-and-rule not based on a genuine concern for these cultures.

'Bantu education' suffered from inadequate funding. For nearly two decades the government pegged its own statutory spending on black education through the general budget at the same level. The sharp increase in the number of children absorbed by the system resulted in per capita spending on black children falling by a third in this period.

The system paid very little attention to the need for secondary education until the early 1970s. The number of blacks who passed the highest standard with what was called a school-leaving certificate remained stagnant between 1954 and 1961 (ranging between 279 and 338). As late as 1966 there were only 1 615 black children in the final school year.

In 1959 the government introduced legislation to segregate universities by race. 'White' universities could accept no black or coloured students for any course also offered at designated black or coloured universities. One of the main objectives of the new policy was to remove black students from the influence of liberal academics and the city environment. But students at the 'bush colleges' did not become the leaders of their respective ethnic communities, as the apartheid system envisaged, but the most disaffected elements in the subordinate population. The system failed to produce the pliant 'apartheid man', without which it could not survive.

Labour and influx controls

Black unions had been excluded since 1924 from the industrial councils where bargaining for wages occurred. The apartheid system elaborated these curbs. In 1953 blacks were barred from belonging to registered unions. Employers were pressured to ignore black unions. Those who tried to organise black workers ran the risk of being banned or detained. By 1960 most black unions had been smashed.

The Industrial Conciliation Act of 1956 made it possible to reserve certain jobs for members of racial communities. Such determinations, while symbolically important, did

not affect more than 2% of jobs. More important was an informal colour bar. The government put strong pressure on employers not to replace white workers with blacks, to avoid putting blacks in a position of authority over whites, and not to rely too much on black labour.

Influx control, which underpinned the migrant-labour system, was the most severe constraint on black workers. The modern system was introduced in 1923 and was further elaborated in 1937. The Native Laws Amendment Act of 1952 imposed even stricter influx controls. As in the past the key was the pass book, a document that had to prove its holder was legally in a 'white area'. A migrant labourer had to register at a labour bureau in his 'homeland' and accept whatever job was offered him. Separated from their families for the greatest part of the year, such workers lived in degrading conditions in single-sex hostels.

A black person who did not possess a proper pass and remained in an urban area for more than 72 hours could be arrested and was likely to be deported back to his 'homeland' in due course. If a pass-holder's wife did not have a pass she could be deported with their children to her 'homeland'. From 1957 women, too, had to carry passes. Prosecutions for pass law offences rose from an average of 318 700 per year in the 1950s to 541 500 per year in the early 1970s.

The government's tough influx control measures failed in their goal of stemming the tide of black urbanisation. The urban black population grew from 2.4 million in 1951 to 3.5 million in 1960 – an increase of nearly 45%.

Intervention and resistance

Apartheid turned blacks into foreigners in their own country. They could not own land except in the 13% designated to them, could not move without their passes, could not

resettle in another district and could not do skilled work. They could be arrested at any moment and there was always some law under which they could be charged and found guilty. The black prison population as a percentage of the total black population was among the highest in the world.

Apartheid was slightly less onerous for coloureds and Indians since they did not have to carry passes and had more labour mobility, but they too could only live in their 'group areas', were denied access to all white schools, prohibited from using most public facilities, could not join the Defence Force, were excluded from white competitive sport, also on international level, and were likely to be punished more severely than their white partners if they transgressed the racial sex laws.

Such massive intervention in the lives of people invited resistance. Among those who did resist, communists – both white and black – were prominent. The government quickly moved against them, particularly those active in trade unions. In 1950 Parliament passed the Suppression of Communism Act, banning the South African Communist Party, and giving the government the power to ban publications that promoted the objectives of

WORKING-CLASS ICONS

Emil Solomon (Solly) Sachs (1899–1976) and Rachel (Ray) Alexander (1913–2004), both Jewish immigrants from eastern Europe, became iconic figures in the workers' struggle in the mid-twentieth century in South Africa. Sachs grew up in a poor household in a *shtetl* (small town) in Lithuania before leaving for South Africa in 1914 to join his ne'er-do-well father in Johannesburg. The family lived in a slum area on the fringe of the Robinson Deep Mine, and experienced considerable hardship.

Ray Alexander came from a more respectable and cultured home. Growing up in a small town in Latvia, Ray was exposed at an early age to socialist ideas and was a precocious recruit to the communist underground. Afraid that her daughter would be arrested for her political activities, her mother sent her to join her brother and sister in Cape Town at the age of sixteen. Five days after landing in November 1929 she joined the SA Communist Party. She later became deeply involved in union activity, and worked from 1941 till 1953 for the militant Food and Canning Workers' Union in the western Cape, a non-racial union serving workers in the fruit canning and fishing industries.

Sachs's route to socialism and the SA Communist Party was via Malay Camp – where he had first-hand experience of the poverty of its multiracial inhabitants – and through working as a *kaffireatnik*, an exploited shop assistant in a concession store. After interrupted spells as a student at the University of the Witwatersrand and a trip to the Soviet Union, Sachs settled as general secretary of the Garment Workers' Union (1927–1950) where he devoted himself to the interests of its predominantly white Afrikaner women membership – much to the chagrin of Afrikaner nationalists competing for the loyalty of the same constituency. Hester Cornelius, a prominent union organiser, would later recall:

> At first I could not understand why Mr Sachs, who was a Jew, fought so hard for the Afrikaner daughters . . . I also learnt that Mr Sachs fought not only for garment workers, but for all the workers. It took a Jew to make me understand that poverty could be wiped out in sunny South Africa . . .

Inevitably both the 'Jew Communist' Sachs and Alexander were targets of the repression that followed the National Party's victory in 1948. Sachs was banned under the Suppression of Communism Amendment Act in 1952 and went into exile in Britain the following year. Alexander was repeatedly banned, was forcibly prevented from taking her place as the elected 'Native Representative' in Parliament, and eventually went into exile with her husband, noted academic Jack Simons, in 1965.

communism, and the power to 'name' people who could be barred from holding office, practising as lawyers or attending meetings.

The Act, extended in 1976 through the Internal Security Act, defined communism as any doctrine that aimed at bringing about 'any political, industrial, social or economic change in the Union by the promotion of disturbances or disorder, by unlawful acts or omissions or by the threat of such acts and omissions'. This definition of communism was so broad and crude that its liberal opponents suspected it was seeking also to trap liberals in its net.

The NP's homelands obsession

Among the supporters of apartheid were several church leaders, academics and professional people who wanted apartheid to offer expanding opportunities for black and coloured people in their own areas. They argued that apartheid would only become credible if it sought to develop at least some of the reserves into self-sufficient states.

However, a gargantuan effort was needed. The reserves had no industries, factories or towns of any significance, and no proven mineral deposits. Most of the residents were women, children and the elderly, all mostly dependent on the earnings of males working in the common area. Only massive expenditure would push up the capacity of the reserves so that they could become a real home for more than half their populations.

In 1950 the government appointed a commission under Prof. F.R. Tomlinson, a Pretoria academic and acknowledged expert in agricultural economics, to investigate the development and growth potential of the reserves. The Tomlinson Commission report was presented to Minister for Native Affairs Hendrik Verwoerd in October 1954 and published in 1956. It argued that the 'homelands' could become economically self-sufficient on the basis of small-scale labour-intensive farms, the remittances of migrant labourers, and industrial development based on both white private capital and state investment.

OPPOSITE TOP: *Solly Sachs.*

OPPOSITE BOTTOM: *Ray Alexander, surrounded by comrades.*

BELOW: *A homestead in the Transkei, one of the reserves or 'homelands'. For the homelands to be considered a solution of even a very limited kind, a gargantuan effort was needed. The reserves had no industries, factories, towns of any significance, services nor mineral deposits. Most of the residents were women, children and the elderly, all depending on the earnings of males between the ages of sixteen and 60 working in the common area. Not even a tenth of the permanent population enjoyed an economic existence. Only massive expenditure would push up the capacity of the reserves so that they could become a real home for more than half their population. Even if the proposals for agricultural and industrial development in the reserves were implemented, there would still be large-scale migrant labour, causing a major disruption of black family life.*

It recommended that the government should spend £104 million (R10 billion in 1998 values) over the next ten years to develop the reserves. The commission calculated that if these steps were taken, 50 000 new jobs would be created per annum in the reserves, and if this could be sustained until the end of the century the reserves would carry a black population of ten million.

Verwoerd rejected all the key Tomlinson proposals. Most importantly, he refused to commit the government to any large-scale development expenditure or to permit any white private capital to help develop the reserves. To him white private enterprise could make no contribution 'towards keeping the Native Areas truly Bantu'. However, without the involvement of private capital all hope for a dynamic development of the reserves was extinguished. Even with private investment the chances of dynamic development were remote.

Verwoerd's shift in policy

In 1959 the National Party government abolished the four white representatives of blacks in Parliament. To Verwoerd they kept alive the black hope of better representation in the common political system. But abolishing them would make it necessary to offer some alternative form of political representation at a time when more and more colonial peoples worldwide were receiving their freedom. Ghana, for example, had become independent in 1957, followed by one African colony after the other.

Verwoerd, almost as an aside, stated that 'when the white man is given full authority only in his own areas . . . the Bantu will acquire full authority elsewhere in the course of time'. Later Verwoerd spelled out his vision that each of the major black nations had its own historic 'homeland' and that their destiny was to exercise 'self-determination' there. Initially the policy made provision for Territorial Authorities in eight homelands.

The policy pronouncements masked the hardship and massive disruption it would entail. It would require the uprooting of black communities – called 'black spots'– in rural white areas and the forced resettlement of the hapless people in the reserves. Land would be excised from one tribal area and transferred to another to bring about greater

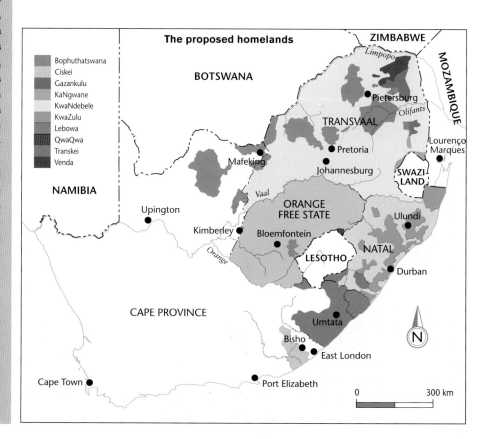

ethnic homogeneity. Productive white-owned farmland would be acquired and transferred to a 'homeland' in order to facilitate its 'consolidation'. It was social engineering on a massive scale.

Opposition politics

In 1954 the United Party tentatively moved away from old-style segregation. Politically it stood for the leadership of the white race, but it also believed that black political rights went hand in hand with an increase in black economic power. As Fagan had done, the UP accepted the economic integration of all races as a dynamic process that would continue and that the government had to guide and control. Socially it considered blacks part of a unitary South African state and it pledged to give them 'a more definite and secure place in our Western way of life'. This policy pointed in a different direction from apartheid, but it was so vague and open to conflicting interpretations that the UP remained a house divided.

Among the organisations that tried to remedy an almost total lack of political white-black dialogue were the South African Institute of Race Relations, a liberal organisation founded in 1929 in Johannesburg, and the Black Sash in Cape Town, founded by white women to give voice to their outrage over the violation of the constitution. In 1959 the Black Sash invited Albert Luthuli, president-general of the ANC and a future winner of the Nobel Peace Prize, to address several house meetings in Cape Town. His audiences saw him as a wise and balanced man determined to bring about black liberation. He was against violence but warned that there was such pent-up black frustration and rage that bloodshed had become almost inevitable.

Luthuli's vision was that of a society in which whites and blacks would consider each other as equals in a common fatherland (*see box*). Shortly after this visit, the government

Zachariah Keodirileng (Z.K.) Matthews

imposed a banning order on him, which restricted him to a magisterial district and prohibited him from attending or addressing meetings.

In 1959 the tension in the United Party came to a head over Verwoerd's new policy towards blacks. The UP tried to outflank the National Party on its right by rejecting the purchase of additional land, as envisaged in the 1936 legislation, as long as the NP proposed to grant independence to the reserves. Eleven of the 53 United Party MPs walked out to form the Progressive Party (PP) because they felt that in terms of the 1936 law blacks were entitled to the land. The UP failed to find a clear alternative to apartheid until its demise in 1977.

The Progressives proposed a form of qualified franchise. Nine-tenths of the seats in the lower house would be elected by people with relatively high educational and wealth qualifications. It also proposed a Bill of Rights and the devolution of considerable power to the provinces. The party received little support. In the 1961 election only Helen Suzman retained her seat. For the next thirteen years she was the sole PP representative in Parliament.

A resurgent African National Congress

In the mid-1940s the transformation of the ANC into a mass organisation began. President A.B. Xuma devised a constitution that laid the foundations for a grassroots structure, allowing branches to retain a portion of subscriptions and paying from his own pocket for full-time officials. A young group of Fort Hare graduates established the Congress Youth League in 1944. Its objectives were to reorient the ANC towards a militant nationalism emphasising black race pride and cultural autonomy, and to persuade their elders to endorse a militant mass-based strategy. Youth Leaguers were inspired by the emergence of black labour organisations, as well as the collective force represented by the direct action of the urban poor manifested in bus boycotts and squatter movements.

A black mineworkers' strike in 1946, though crushingly defeated, helped to foster within the League the conviction that organised black workers constituted a potentially powerful force that could be harnessed to a nationalist programme. Youth Leaguers won commanding positions in the 1949 ANC executive elections and succeeded in winning the organisation's support for their Programme of Action.

Towards an activist movement

The ANC's embrace of the Youth Leaguers' strategic vision was one factor in its transformation into an activist movement. As important was the influx into its branches of local Communist Party organisers, many of them with skills and experience derived from the trade unions that had built a black membership during the war. Communists were especially critical in constructing a well-organised popular membership for the ANC in the main towns of the eastern Cape.

In Port Elizabeth the relatively liberal local government favoured the development of a permanently urbanised black workforce. This facilitated the growth of durable black trade unions. Communists had already developed a presence within the better-established coloured unions in Port Elizabeth by the late 1930s. Communist trade unionists also helped to encourage the creation of a strong set of ANC branches in the townships of the East Rand and in Alexandra. By contrast, the nationalist and generally anti-communist Youth Leaguers predominated in the ANC following in what was to become Soweto.

The 1950s witnessed the implementation of the methods advocated by the League, beginning in May 1950 with a well-supported stay-away strike to protest the prohibition of the Communist Party. Former Congress Youth League principals Nelson Mandela, Oliver Tambo and Walter Sisulu revised their earlier advocacy of black exclusiveness, as well as their antipathy towards collaboration with white communists and Indian Congress officials. Sisulu actually joined the communist underground in 1953 or shortly thereafter. In 1952, a Joint Planning Committee composed of representatives of the ANC and the Natal and Transvaal Indian Congresses appointed a 'volunteer-in-chief', Nelson Mandela, and an Indian deputy, Ismael Cachalia, to lead three stages of civil disobedience.

The long-term influence of Mohandas Gandhi proved to be strong (*see box*).

The Defiance Campaign

The 'Defiance Campaign' ostensibly sought the abolition of 'five unjust laws' that embodied the National Party's apartheid programme. These laws elaborated urban segregation, imposed passes on black women, banned the Communist Party, removed mixed-race coloureds from the common voters' roll and gave to rural chiefs new authoritarian powers to implement highly unpopular land conservation measures.

The first stage of the campaign opened in June 1952 with small bands of black resisters in the main towns, broadening the movement to embrace smaller centres and larger groups. In subsequent stages it was intended to extend the movement to the countryside and to support passive resistance with general strikes.

Action began with groups around Johannesburg challenging curfew regulations and for six months civil disobedience mainly targeted 'petty apartheid' regulations in railway stations and post offices, as well as the rules governing entry into black townships.

More than 8 000 people were arrested countrywide in the Defiance Campaign, nearly 6 000 of them in the eastern Cape. In Port Elizabeth, a one-day strike in November to

SATYAGRAHA AND THE DEFIANCE CAMPAIGN

Mohandas Gandhi's presence in South Africa between 1893 and 1914 left an indelible mark on the wider political culture and forms of resistance. Satyagraha, which entailed a firm but non-violent struggle for a good cause, continued from serving as a tool to address the interests of the Indian community, such as the 1946 campaign against the Asiatic Land Tenure and Representation Act, to a broader strategy encompassing all groups in the country.

Most notable was the 1952 mass campaign in which African, Indian and Coloured organisations collaborated in defiance of the pass laws, the Group Areas Act, the Separate Representation of Voters Act, the Bantu Authorities Act and the policy of stock limitation. This non-racial initiative raised the con-

troversial issue of the different 'locations' of the diverse communities it aimed at mobilising, in contrast to the more homogeneous nature of the earlier campaigns, comprising Indians only.

Nelson Mandela describes a discussion between the ANC and the South African Indian Congress (SAIC) after the joint Defiance Campaign had been announced. 'We discussed whether the campaign should follow Gandhian principles of non-violence, or what the Mahatma called Satyagraha, a non-violence that seeks to conquer through conversion. Some argued for non-violence on purely ethical grounds, saying it was morally superior to any other method.'

Others argued in favour of a tactical approach, and that the method of resistance should be dependent on the prevailing conditions. Mandela's own view was: 'I saw non-violence in the Gandhian model not as an inviolable principle but as a tactic to be used as the situation demanded ... I called for non-violent protest for as long as it was effective.'

In his autobiography, Mandela comments on his feelings about the futility of passive resistance in the face of the increasing repressiveness of the government in the wake of the Defiance Campaign. 'I said that the time for passive resistance had ended, that non-violence was a useless strategy and could never overturn a white minority regime bent on retaining its power at any cost. At the end of the day, I said, violence was the only weapon that would destroy

apartheid and we must be prepared, in the near future, to use that weapon.'

Comparing the situation with India, he saw 'Gandhi . . . dealing with a foreign power that ultimately was more realistic and farsighted. That was not the case with the Afrikaners in South Africa. Non-violent passive resistance is effective as long as your opposition adheres to the same rules as you do. But if peaceful protest is met with violence, its efficacy is at an end. For me non-violence was not a moral principle but a strategy; there is no moral goodness in using an ineffective weapon.' However, he acknowledges in retrospect that his thoughts had not been fully formed and that he might have spoken too soon.

In a racialised context, visible minorities are always more vulnerable. As Leo Kuper, one of the most astute analysts of passive resistance, expressed it: 'The racialism of all groups converged on the Indian, who became all things to all men – the communist, the capitalist exploiter, the imperialist adventurer, the Oriental, the Jew surrogate.'

Yet, Indian South Africans exercised great influence in the South African anti-apartheid struggle, both as providers of strategic ideas, fundraisers and active participants in exile and mobilisers at home. Indian South Africans continued disproportionally to serve the post-apartheid governments in leading positions, although the community is presently split equally between support for the ANC and its parliamentary opposition.

Mohandas Gandhi

protest curfews and a ban on meetings brought armoured cars onto the streets. Thousands lost their jobs afterwards.

But protest was not confined to workers. In the eastern Cape nearly half the volunteers were women. In parts of the Ciskei the campaign attracted peasant participants. Reaching a peak in August, the movement lost impetus after violent riots in its main two centres, East London and Port Elizabeth.

In December, just before the campaign's end, a particularly well-publicised act of defiance took place in Germiston when 40 volunteers entered the black township without the required permits. The group included seven whites and was led by Mahatma Gandhi's son Manilal and Patrick Duncan, the son of a wartime governor-general. The seven whites also served prison sentences, the first white South Africans convicted for civil disobedience against the NP government.

Despite some expressions of sympathy for black grievances in English-language newspapers, though, the campaign elicited either hostility or indifference within most of the white community. The black press helped to extend the campaign's impact, particularly given the advent of photojournalism with the appearance of *Drum* magazine in 1951. *Drum* was to provide generally sympathetic coverage of the ANC's undertakings through the decade, helping to develop the messianic status of its leaders, especially Chief Albert Luthuli, the ANC president, and his deputy, Nelson Mandela.

During the campaign the ANC began to receive funding from sympathisers in Britain, the first signals of the international support that would later play such an important role in anti-apartheid resistance. In early 1953, the Criminal Law Amendment Act was passed. The new law prescribed a prison term, as well as whipping, for 'offences committed by way of protest'. Younger volunteers had already been subjected to floggings in several towns. Most activists were unprepared for such severe punishment. For ANC leaders, despite their command of an organised following now swollen to 120 000, civil disobedience no longer seemed a practical option.

Mobilised resistance

For the remainder of the decade, ANC campaigning only occasionally evoked the same intensity of popular commitment that was evident in at least the eastern Cape during the Defiance Campaign. From mid-1953 until early 1955 national leaders were strongly committed to attempts to mobilise resistance to the first removals of families from Sophiatown. This was an inner city district in Johannesburg in which blacks had retained freehold landownership and which the government was determined to expropriate because of its symbolic significance as a centre of cosmopolitan black urbanity. Towards the end of 1954 the ANC also began planning for protests against the implementation of the Bantu Education Act.

At the same time the movement was engaged in preparations for a Congress of the People. This event was held in June 1955 outside Johannesburg, and drew an assembly of 3 000 delegates drawn mainly from ANC branches that approved a Freedom Charter, which the ANC itself adopted the following year. Unambiguous in its commitment to a nonracial South Africa, the Charter envisaged liberal political freedoms accompanying land reform and the break-up of 'monopoly' industry.

The Freedom Charter

In 1954 the ANC and its allies established a National Action Council for the Congress of the People. An army of Freedom Volunteers began collecting 'demands' nationwide for inclusion in a Freedom Charter. ANC leaders reviewed a draft version of the Charter assembled from these demands only on the eve of a Congress of the People held on 26–27 June 1955. The document had been written very hurriedly by Lionel Bernstein, who belonged to the Congress of Democrats, a body of white sympathisers of the ANC established during the Defiance Campaign. Many of them, including Bernstein, were also members of the clandestine Communist Party.

At the Congress of the People, 3 000 delegates assembled on an open patch of ground in Kliptown, on the borders of Soweto. They approved all the draft clauses with a show of hands before police brought proceedings to a halt. The police announced that they believed treason was being contemplated and sent everybody home. The Charter was adopted more formally by the ANC in 1956; this was despite objections from a group of 'Africanists', members of the ANC Youth League.

The Charter contained a list of basic democratic rights. It began by reaffirming that 'South Africa belongs to all who live within it, black and white', and went on to argue for the transfer of the mines and monopoly industry to the ownership of 'the people as a whole', to guarantee equal opportunities to all who wished to trade and manufacture, to advocate the redivision of land 'among those that work it' and the ending of restrictions on labour and trade unions, as well as proposing a comprehensive range of welfare provisions.

For remaining 'African nationalists' within the ANC the inclusion of the racial minorities in a broad notion of South African citizenship was unacceptable. They would eventually break away from the ANC to form a rival Pan-Africanist Congress (PAC) in 1959.

Among supporters of the Charter, there were interpretive differences. In June 1956 Nelson Mandela published an exposition of the Charter. He explained that although it was a revolutionary document, it was 'by no means a blueprint for a socialist state'. It proposed the transfer of power to 'the people', not a single class 'but all people of this country, be they workers, peasants, professional men, or petty bourgeoisie'. The breaking up and 'democratisation' of 'monopoly' enterprises would 'open fresh fields' for the development of a non-European bourgeois class which would for the first time own productive property in its own name. As a consequence 'private enterprise' would 'flourish as never before'.

Not everyone agreed with this interpretation of the Charter. Communist Party member Ben Turok was allowed to strengthen the commitment to public ownership at a preliminary meeting that reviewed the draft Charter. As a keynote speaker at the Congress, he suggested that after the Charter's enactment, workers' committees would themselves manage the mines and the other big industries. He managed to persuade his comrades that these proposals accorded with the Party's vision of a 'national democracy', a transitional stage in the road to communism, during which capitalists would exist but would not predominate politically or economically.

Another criticism of the Charter arose from its references to 'National Groups'. In a liberated South Africa, 'National Groups', or races, the Charter promised, would enjoy equal status in state bodies and they would have equal cultural rights. Both Africanist opponents of the Charter at the time of its adoption and later critics have suggested that these passages, as well as the more general usage by the ANC of the term 'multiracialism', implied that in a South Africa governed under the terms of the Freedom Charter racial distinctions would continue to matter politically.

The Africanists claimed that the ANC's programme implied a politics of 'partnership' in which, as in the Central African Federation, representatives of different racial groups would be equally represented in Parliament, with the minorities accorded the same representation as the black majority. This was clearly not what the Charter's drafters had in mind. It is quite likely, though, that at that stage they perceived South Africa to be a 'multinational' state in which the different racial groups constituted nations; this was implied in the SA Communist Party's political theory, which certainly helped to influence the way in which the Charter was written.

From this sort of perspective, the 'equal status' that the Charter refers to would most likely have been confined to protection and support for minority languages and certain aspects of folk culture. During the 1960s, the ANC began referring to a 'non-racial' rather than a multiracial future society, following the usage of both the PAC and the Liberal Party. The ANC's tendency to conflate race with nation persisted, however, and

ABOVE: *The Congress of the People met at the Kliptown football ground on 26 June 1955. It consisted of the ANC, the Indian Congress, the Coloured People's Organisation and the Congress of Democrats. The Freedom Charter was read and signed by delegates. Many speakers noted that the day might not be far off when the Freedom Charter's demands would be met; the road might be long, but a united democratic front was the only solution.*

On 9 August 1956, 20 000 women from the cities and towns, reserves and villages, some with babies on their backs, took a petition addressed to the prime minister to the Union Buildings in Pretoria. He was not in. The petition demanded that the pass laws be abolished. The top picture shows women waiting patiently, with the Union Buildings in the background. Above they board a bus.

whites were only admitted to full membership of the organisation in 1985.

The Charter retained its status as the ANC's programmatic vision for the next 40 years and even today government policy often echoes its phraseology. However, the disagreements about its meaning have also persisted.

'Strijdom, you have struck a rock'

Meanwhile, a Federation of South African Women to which the ANC's Women's League was affiliated began organising protests against the extension of pass laws to black women. This opposition was orchestrated especially dramatically in August 1956 when 20 000 women assembled outside the Union Buildings to sing their triumphant anthem: 'Strijdom, you have tampered with the women, you have struck a rock.' The movement proliferated and as it spread it became more confrontational. In Johannesburg, township branches of the ANC Women's League persuaded 1 200 women to deliberately court arrest before an alarmed ANC leadership directed that women should not break the law.

Despite such strictures, women's protest expanded well beyond the boundaries of organised politics. In mid-1959 anger about passes and soil conservation regulations helped to generate a series of revolts led by women in the Natal countryside. Mostly, participants concentrated on destroying cattle-dipping tanks, but they also set fire to sugar fields and marched on police stations and magistrate's courts.

Even the former Youth Leaguers who now predominated within the ANC's national executive believed that the organisation was unready for protest of the scale and the

ROBERT SOBUKWE: A VISIONARY

Robert Mangaliso Sobukwe (1924–1978) was born in Graaff-Reinet, of which it has been said that 'even the dogs bark in Afrikaans'. His labourer father and domestic worker mother were determined that their children should have the education they themselves had never had. After a Methodist Church primary school, he went to the Methodists' Healdtown School in 1940. His intellectual gifts drew the attention of white teachers who helped him financially, especially after tuberculosis forced him into hospital in 1943. They saw him as a future Healdtown teacher and helped him to attend Fort Hare Native College. Studying 'Native Administration' for a BA awakened Sobukwe to laws of racial discrimination.

His leadership qualities emerged with election as Students' Representative Council president: his end-of-year speech, with a stirring call to African nationalism, made it 'a night not to be forgotten' in student memory. It also alienated his white teachers. He joined the college's ANC Youth League branch and later became national secretary, but struggled to find work after a cool testimonial from Fort Hare.

Jandrell Secondary School in Standerton employed him and he was there during the 1952 Defiance Campaign. He was seemingly told not to defy, to avoid the fate of teachers who were fired. In 1954, newly married to Veronica Zodwa Mathe, he moved to Johannesburg as a Language Assistant in the Department of Bantu Languages at the University of the Witwatersrand (Wits) – a prestigious post for a black man. He graduated with BA (Hons) in 1957 and continued as a Methodist lay preacher.

The ANC was in turmoil with disputes over ideology and internal mismanagement. Sobukwe joined the Africanist group, accusing ANC leaders of abandoning the non-collaboration of the 1949 Programme of Action, and being influenced by white and Indian communists. The Africanists broke away, founding the Pan-Africanist Congress in April 1959. As president Sobukwe articulated PAC policy: commitment to 'positive action' to destroy apartheid, a vision of a United States of Africa, and anti-communism.

The bedrock belief was African Nationalism (later called Black Consciousness) together with non-racialism (in contrast to the ANC's multiracialism). The aim was government of Africans, by Africans, for Africans, 'with everybody who owes his only loyalty to Africa and who is prepared to accept the democratic rule of an African majority being regarded as an African'. The contradiction between black exclusiveness and ignoring skin colour was evident and not satisfactorily explained. But it was seen inside the PAC: Sobukwe was a non-racist to the core of his being, yet the leadership included some who spoke in fiercely anti-white terms.

On 21 March 1960 Sobukwe urged blacks to leave their passes at home and offer themselves for arrest at the nearest police station. He went first to Orlando police station, together with most PAC leaders. Despite his plea for non-violence, the police opened fire and killed 69 people in Sharpeville, setting off countrywide protests. Proscription of the PAC and ANC followed, driving resistance underground and into violence and solidifying international pressures against apartheid.

Robert Sobukwe

Sobukwe was jailed for three years for incitement. As his sentence was ending the government, fearing his power, rushed the 'Sobukwe Clause' through Parliament to detain him on Robben Island without trial. He passed the time by studying for a BA in Economics from London University.

With six years of virtual solitary confinement taking its toll, the government released him in 1969 – and banished, banned and house-arrested him in Galeshewe township, Kimberley. He died of lung cancer nine years later. Treatment that might have saved his life was delayed because of the restrictions on him.

Twenty-five years afterwards, Wits posthumously conferred on him a Doctor of Laws, lauding his visionary view of Africa: 'What better embodiment could there be of the best of Africa's aspirations than Robert Mangaliso Sobukwe?'

---

intensity of this spontaneous rural rebellion. This was despite their efforts to implement a programme of street-level cellular organisation, the so-called M-Plan, first developed by militants in Port Elizabeth during the Defiance Campaign and later adopted nationally in a rather uneven fashion. From December 1956, national leaders would be limited in the actions they could initiate or direct after they were arrested and charged with treason.

For the rest of the decade, the ANC would depend on its allies in the labour movement to mobilise protest. In 1957 the ANC's trade union affiliate the SA Congress of Trade Unions led an 80%-effective (among black workers) 'stay-away' in Johannesburg and Port Elizabeth in support of its call for a 'One Pound a Day' minimum wage. Encouraged by this success, the following year the ANC leadership called for a similar three-day protest to coincide with parliamentary elections in April. Generally low rates

Nelson Mandela was a key personality in shaping the course of black resistance to apartheid in the 1950s, in particular in fostering a multiracial 'Congress Alliance'. Initially, though, Mandela adhered to a racially exclusive nationalism, helping to establish the ANC Youth League in this vein in 1944. In 1948 as secretary of the Youth League, he called for the expulsion of communists from the ANC, a motion that was defeated.

Walter Sisulu

Mandela opposed the ANC's participation in a general 'stay-away' on 1 May 1950 to protest the prohibition of the Communist Party. Between 1950 and 1952, however, Mandela's friendships with Indian activists and white communists, as well as his growing familiarity with Marxist theory, encouraged him to revise his conviction that African nationalists should not co-operate across race lines and doctrinal divisions. That year Mandela helped to plan a Defiance Campaign against 'unjust laws'. Appointed 'volunteer-in-chief', Mandela was among the first to be arrested.

Throughout the decade, as the ANC's deputy president, Mandela decisively influenced ANC strategy. He lent his name to a scheme to establish the ANC's popular organisation on a street-based cell system, the M-Plan. Mandela adapted this approach from existing practice in the eastern Cape, anticipating a time when the ANC would have to work in a more clandestine, insurgent fashion. He helped lead ANC opposition to the removal of the inhabitants of Sophiatown, an inner city neighbourhood where blacks owned property. He was prominent in the leadership of most of the other ANC campaigns during the decade.

As early as 1953 he and Walter Sisulu started considering the possibility of the ANC embracing a programme of guerrilla warfare, but he remained among the more cautious figures in the ANC leadership during the 1950s, supporting the early curtailment of protests and opposing the use of picketing during strikes. Unusually among ANC leaders, he maintained contact with rural leaders, particularly in the Transkei, for he was anxious that the ANC should retain support from the chieftaincy despite the latter's incorporation into the government's 'tribal authorities'.

Mandela's moderation at this time was partly motivated by tactical circumspection, a consequence of a general recognition that he shared with communists in the movement that action needed to be supported by well-structured organisation. He was more aware than many of his fellow leaders of the weaknesses in the ANC's organisation.

Throughout the 1950s he remained optimistic that the ANC's pressure might induce liberal predispositions among whites, a conciliatory attitude that was reinforced by his more civil encounters with officials and his friendships with white activists. For example, in 1960, in the course of cross-examination during the Treason Trial, he described a hypothetical scenario in which – in return for government commitment to a phased incorporation of blacks into Parliament – he would

Oliver Tambo and Nelson Mandela

consider suspension of militant campaigning. Until 1960 Mandela was convinced that most ANC rank-and-file supporters remained morally unready for direct and forceful confrontation with state authority.

Mandela already enjoyed iconic national stature by the mid-1950s, a status boosted by traditional praise poetry and more modern photojournalism, and he deliberately assumed a messianic role. His imposing physical presence – he was unusually tall – his sartorial style, his professional distinction as one of the country's very few black lawyers, and from 1958 his marriage to Winnie Mandela, an articulate and glamorous partner, were all ingredients in his emergence as a modern media celebrity. Mandela was probably the first black South African politician to fulfil such a role.

Nelson Mandela burning his pass

of absenteeism persuaded the ANC's Johannesburg-based National Working Committee to end the protest on the evening of its first day.

On 26 June 1959, the ANC announced 'a second phase' of the anti-pass campaign which up to then had confined itself to opposing giving passes to women: a series of nationwide protests and demonstrations intended to reach a climax on 26 June 1960. Its plans were pre-empted by its new rival, the Pan-Africanist Congress (PAC), founded in April 1959 and led by a group of former Youth Leaguers who considered that the ANC's 'multiracialism' had diminished its appeal to blacks. Robert Sobukwe and other PAC leaders believed that the ANC's adoption of the Freedom Charter was evidence of the ANC's subordination to communist leadership.

1960: A fateful year

The eventful year 1960 witnessed Harold Macmillan's 'wind of change' speech in Parliament, the massacre at Sharpeville, the march from Langa on Parliament, a state of emergency, an attempted assassination of the prime minister and a white referendum on a republic. There was also the traumatic decolonisation of the Congo – the newspapers were full of dramatic accounts of the flight of whites from the Belgian Congo and of rampaging soldiers after the granting of independence.

On 3 February 1960 British Prime Minister Harold Macmillan addressed Parliament in Cape Town at the tail end of a visit to several African states. Macmillan stated: 'The wind of change is blowing through the continent. Whether we like it or not, this growth of national consciousness is a political fact. We must all accept it as a fact. Our national policies must take account of it.' The speech was made against the

BELOW: *On 3 February 1960 Harold Macmillan, the British prime minister, addressed Parliament in Cape Town at the tail end of a visit to several African states. Macmillan warned that the 'wind of change'– the storm of African nationalism – was blowing across the continent. It meant that Britain, acting in terms of both moral commitments and material interests, was now siding with the forces of African nationalism against apartheid. Macmillan is shown here in a motorcade in Durban.*

background of a fierce rivalry between the West and the communist bloc for the allegiance of the African states and other parts of the Third World. It meant that Britain was now siding with the forces of African nationalism against the dominance of whites in any African state.

In reply, Verwoerd presented his government's policy in terms far removed from the crude apartheid ideology of the preceding decade. The whites were Europeans but also part of Africa. They had brought to Africa both industrial development and the Gospel and the ideals that inspire Western civilisation. Blacks were entitled to all the rights the people of all other colours claimed. The whites in Africa wanted to co-operate with blacks and help them to secure their rightful place in South Africa. But Verwoerd's vision for a place for blacks was limited to the reserves.

Sharpeville and its aftermath

Early in 1960 the PAC announced a campaign to defy the pass laws. One of the few centres where it was well organised was Sharpeville, an eastern Witwatersrand township where blacks were particularly upset by the sharply increased rentals. On 21 March a PAC demonstration there turned into a major tragedy. A crowd had turned up at the police station. It was peaceful, with most simply wanting to heed the PAC injunction to be arrested without a pass.

But the police were jumpy after a recent event in Durban where a crowd had murdered nine policemen. They panicked and fired into the crowd, killing 69 blacks. On 30 March Philip Kgosana, PAC regional secretary for the western Cape, led a march of 30 000 protesting blacks from Cape Town's townships to Parliament.

That evening Afrikaner entrepreneur Anton Rupert met Kgosana at a dinner organised by Patrick Duncan, a PAC supporter. He was shocked that a young man without laces in his shoes could bring out such a multitude. He told Verwoerd this the next day and suggested that the best guarantee for stability was to grant property rights to urban blacks and to enable them to buy their houses, and at a discount. It was the last thing Verwoerd wanted. In his view property rights and even a leasehold system would make blacks feel that they had a permanent stake in the common area. They would soon de-

RIGHT: *A long procession of people shouted slogans as thousands converged on Langa on 28 March 1960 for the funeral of three black protestors who had been shot by the police.*

mand the vote at a point where the demands of the majority and minority were far from being reconcilable.

ANC leader Albert Luthuli burned his pass and asked people to stay away from work. The stay-away was nearly total, and brought the many businesses dependent on black labour to a standstill. Many whites were terrified; the Stock Exchange plummeted, followed by a massive capital outflow. With worldwide condemnation of the killings and of the harshness of the apartheid policy, international isolation seemed a real possibility.

On 30 March the government called a state of emergency and detained more than 18 000 people over the next few weeks. On 8 April it banned the ANC and PAC. The

BELOW LEFT: *The aftermath of the Sharpeville massacre of 21 March 1960, when 69 people were killed by police fire after a crowd had assembled at the police station to protest against the pass laws.*

TOP: *Grief-stricken women being taken home after the woman in the middle had viewed her husband's lifeless body, twisted by police gun-fire, opposite the Sharpeville police station.*

ABOVE: *The campaign to burn passbooks was spearheaded by the ANC after the PAC called on people to hand their passes in at police stations.*

TOP: *A few days after the Sharpeville killings Oliver Tambo was in Cape Town when he heard that the government was about to ban the ANC and PAC. The ANC had already decided that if it was banned, Tambo should leave the country to continue the struggle abroad. His friend Ronald Segal (left) drove him to Johannesburg and then to Botswana.*

ABOVE: *Govan Mbeki and comrades in the 1940s. Mbeki received a bachelor's degree from Fort Hare in 1937 and a teaching diploma the following year. He worked as a teacher and was a member of the editorial board of the radical journal* New Age. *Shortly after being sentenced to life imprisonment in 1964 his best-known work,* South Africa: The Peasants' Revolt, *was published. He was released in 1987 after 24 years on Robben Island and served in South Africa's post-apartheid Senate. Thabo Mbeki is his son.*

next day a mentally deranged white man, David Pratt, shot Verwoerd in the head and seriously wounded him.

Macmillan's speech made a major impact on the English-speaking community. Historian C.W. de Kiewiet summed it up well:

> As the grim truth became evident that Great Britain was, in impolite language, scuttling the traditional responsibilities of empire, the English-speaking South Africans entered a strange and lonely world. Familiar symbols faded; the comfort of having the Union Jack at hand was gone. As the pace of change in the rest of Africa increased, they pondered Dr Verwoerd's warnings that South Africa was on its own and had to defend itself by its own strength.

The prospects for a liberal democratic alternative in Africa seemed to be in decline. In the newly independent African states there was a growing influence of socialist ideas and talk of democratic centralism or one-party democracy by the new nations of Africa and Asia. The leaders started challenging the notion that Western liberal ideals were inherently enlightened, and would naturally prevail.

The ANC, as with most other nationalist organisations on the continent, was seeking not just a broadening of rights and freedoms to encompass the entire population, but rather a radical transformation of the economy and society.

The campaign for a referendum

Verwoerd recovered remarkably quickly and soon began campaigning for a referendum on a republic that was scheduled for 5 October. He had taken a great risk because the National Party had not yet secured the majority of votes in any general election, but he never seemed to doubt victory. He argued that only a republic could bring about white unity, which in turn was imperative for an effective response to the racial problem and to pressure from within and without.

The republican vote won by a narrow margin of 74 580 votes. In a deft move Verwoerd told a victory celebration that the whites were now a united people:

> We have risen above pettiness and selfishness . . . The English-speaking and the Afrikaans-speaking sections have become like the new bride and bridegroom who enter upon the new life in love to create together and to live together as life-mates.

Thus Verwoerd ended the old animosities between the two white communities and buried the politics of ethnic resentment. There were, in his mind, more important things to turn to.

The ANC turns to the armed struggle

After the suppression of a three-day strike in May 1961 to challenge the transition to a republic and to call for a constitutional convention, Nelson Mandela and other younger ANC leaders, in conjunction with the SA Communist Party, formed an insurgent wing, Umkhonto weSizwe (MK). In December 1961 MK exploded the first home-made bombs in a two-year sabotage campaign. Intended as a last resort 'to bring the government to its senses', the bombs were targeted against property not lives. Meanwhile the ANC's external mission headed by Oliver Tambo began its efforts to secure military training for guerrilla recruits and to win international backing for a South African trade embargo.

For the ANC the turn to violence was decisive. Though it remained committed to maintaining its own clandestine organisation separate from MK and though it intended to continue organising mass protests, the key local activists, especially those with trade union experience, joined MK. Several senior ANC officials, including Mandela and Sisulu, had been thinking about the possibility of embracing armed tactics since 1953.

At the same time, though, they retained hopes that protest might induce political reform, hopes encouraged by the extent to which they had succeeded during the 1950s in eliciting international sympathy and support. Could they have achieved more if they had pursued civil disobedience more vigorously during the 1950s? Probably not, for the ANC's organised following was fragmentary and the movement was desperately short of resources.

For the most part, outside Port Elizabeth and the East Rand, ANC members lived and worked on the margins of the industrial economy so they possessed very little leverage. The ANC's achievements during the 1950s in mobilising popular support around an articulate and personable leadership group were significant enough: they helped to nurture an international audience for the struggle against apartheid and they supplied a dramatic narrative of heroic events that as myth would shape later movements and struggles.

Mandela and Umkhonto weSizwe

Mandela was arrested near Pietermaritzburg on 5 August 1962. CIA officials apparently informed the police about Mandela's journey from Durban to Johannesburg that day but from whom they derived their information remains a mystery. He was on his way back from visiting Chief Luthuli. While in Durban he had also briefed members of the regional command of Umkhonto weSizwe (MK) about the lessons he had brought back from his travels across Africa between January and July.

MK operations had barely started when Mandela, the organisation's commander in chief, left South Africa. For the first four months of MK's history after June 1961, he had stayed hidden in various 'safe houses' in suburban Johannesburg before moving in October to Lilliesleaf farm in Rivonia, then on the outskirts of the city, a property purchased by the SA Communist Party for MK's use.

While staying in Rivonia, Mandela undertook a reading course on the theory and practice of guerrilla warfare, and helped plan the initial phase of MK's offensive. This would take the form of a sabotage campaign, a last-ditch effort to bring the government and its supporters 'to their senses' before the onset of a full-scale guerrilla war. With Joe Slovo, Mandela drafted a constitution for the new organisation, and he also witnessed at least one of its early experiments with home-made explosives.

At the end of December, though, an invitation to the ANC to send a representative to a conference in Addis Ababa diverted Mandela from these military preparations. MK needed assistance from African governments to provide training facilities for its recruits. Another reason for sending Mandela abroad was so that he could counter the PAC's diplomatic success in Africa.

Mandela left Johannesburg after spending six months working mainly with SA Communist Party (SACP) leaders. During that period he had become strongly influenced by at least their strategic ideas. While travelling in Africa, though, he discovered that the ANC's association with the Communist Party puzzled African leaders and officials and sometimes engendered hostility. He returned to South Africa convinced that – at least in public – the ANC should play down its relationship with the SACP and that it should emphasise its dominant role in any alliances it formed with other organisations.

These insights provided the substance of Mandela's conversation with Chief Luthuli in the days just before his arrest. Luthuli was unhappy for he felt that Mandela's message might be interpreted as a weakening of the ANC's non-racialism. Chief Luthuli had other grounds for being unhappy. He had initially opposed the ANC's adoption of violence and remained uneasy about the decision. He remained the ANC's president-general but Mandela increasingly rivalled his authority. This was partly a consequence of Mandela's growing prominence as an activist leader in Johannesburg while Luthuli was immobilised in Natal by banning orders, but it was also a reflection of a deliberate effort by communists within the ANC to promote Mandela's popularity.

Mandela agreed with the Johannesburg communists on the necessity to move to violence and he appeared to be in more general sympathy with their views. On his return from his African tour, though, Mandela demonstrated that he very much remained his own master.

The young Walter Sisulu. Sisulu, six years older than Nelson Mandela, was also born in Thembuland. Born in 1910 out of wedlock, his father was Victor Dickenson, a white government official, and his mother was Alice Sisulu, a member of the Gcina clan. In 1928 he dropped out of school and left for Johannesburg to work on the mines. Considered too young for mine work, he turned to selling advertising for Bantu World, *the leading black newspaper, and then became an estate agent, selling property in Alexandra and Sophiatown, the two Johannesburg neighbourhoods where blacks could own property. He settled in Orlando and joined a Xhosa cultural association whose members read aloud and discussed Xhosa epic poetry. When Mandela sought help to realise his ambition to become a lawyer, it was to Sisulu that he turned. Finding Mandela 'a man with great qualities', Sisulu introduced him to the partners of the firm Witkin, Sidelsky & Eidelman. In 1940 Sisulu became chairman of the local ANC branch after the president-general Dr A.B. Xuma asked him to get the youth actively involved in the organisation. A firm friendship quickly developed between Sisulu and Mandela, with the latter staying for long periods at the Sisulu home. A man who inspired warmth, affection and trust, Sisulu was Mandela's closest ally in the turbulent years before their imprisonment and for more than 25 years on Robben Island.*

Mayibuye and arrests

The High Command that Mandela helped to establish survived his arrest by less than a year. Between December 1961 and July 1963, MK units undertook just over 200 operations, which were mainly home-made incendiary bomb attacks intended to damage public facilities. On the whole these were undertaken in such a way as to minimise the risk of hurting or killing people though MK members were also accused and convicted of attacking policemen and suspected informers. In addition, the organisation despatched more than 300 recruits abroad for military training.

The police captured Walter Sisulu, Govan Mbeki and most of the other key leaders in a raid on the Rivonia farm on 11 July 1963. At the time of their arrest, MK's commanders had met to discuss Operation Mayibuye, a proposal prepared by Joe Slovo and Mbeki for a guerrilla insurgency. The unfolding of the scheme depended on the 'simultaneous landing . . . by ship or by air' of four groups of 40 highly trained combatants in four different rural areas of South Africa. In each of these locations these external forces would assume control over a much larger body of several thousand recruits whom they would then arm and train.

The scheme envisaged an initial stage of dispersed rural operations that would be supported by externally derived supplies. The scheme's prospects would depend on the collaboration of foreign governments capable of transporting guerrillas into South Africa by air and by sea.

At the time of the Rivonia raid both Slovo and Mbeki believed that they had already convinced their colleagues to embrace the scheme. Slovo had left South Africa two months beforehand, travelling to the ANC's exile headquarters to brief Oliver Tambo about the plan. Tambo was enthusiastic about the project, according to Slovo, and certainly the ANC's guerrilla strategy for the next decade or so would reflect many of the strategic presumptions that were evident in Operation Mayibuye.

Other important MK leaders, including Mandela, maintained that Mayibuye was just a proposal and an impractical one at that, a view shared by several SACP authorities, including Bram Fischer. Understandably, this was the line taken at the trial of the Rivonia leaders, but it may have been true. Later in prison Mandela would have a heated disagreement with Govan Mbeki over the merits of Operation Mayibuye.

When the Rivonia raid occurred Mandela was already in prison. He had been convicted in November for incitement and leaving South Africa illegally, and was sentenced to three years. In mid-July he was taken from his prison cell on Robben Island to join the group arrested at Rivonia.

During the raid the police had discovered documentation implicating Mandela in MK's activities, including notes he made from his readings about guerrilla warfare and a diary he had kept during his African trip. According to Mandela during his trial in late 1962, he had asked Joe Slovo to destroy this material but unaccountably Slovo had failed to do so.

In October 1963 ten accused, including Nelson Mandela, Walter Sisulu and Govan Mbeki, appeared in what subsequently came to be known as the Rivonia Trial before Justice Quartus de Wet on charges of sabotage, attempting to start a guerrilla war and the promotion of communism.

At the trial, Nelson Mandela chose to make a statement from the dock rather than the witness stand. It provided the scope for a clear and uninterrupted statement of principle. He, his co-accused and their lawyers may also have been worried that if he had submitted himself to cross-examination he would have faced awkward questions. For example, among the documents that the police discovered at Rivonia was his diary of his African journey, with entries indicating that the ANC's plans for guerrilla warfare were already quite advanced by early 1962. In their defence, the accused were going to insist that Operation Mayibuye, the guerrilla warfare blueprint, was only a draft and that it had yet to be adopted by the Umkhonto weSizwe (MK) command. In a case in which the accused were risking the death penalty, convincing the judge that Mayibuye was not policy was important.

In his statement, Mandela defended the ANC's alliance with the Communist Party in what was certainly the most explicit commentary on this subject by an ANC leader to date. However, this topic was one which he and the other accused – most of them party members – would be reluctant to discuss in an unscripted fashion.

In the opening passages of his defence, Mandela admitted much of the substance of the state's case. He had helped to form MK and he had helped to plan its sabotage campaign. 'Civil war', though, remained an optional 'last resort', one that had yet to be decided upon. The ANC had formed an alliance with the multiracial Communist Party, though the two organisations did not share 'a complete community of interests'.

Mandela said he had been influenced by Marxism but unlike communists he retained admiration for the Western and particularly the British parliamentary system, 'the most democratic in the world'. MK was an African movement, fighting for dignity, for decent livelihoods, and for equal rights.

Mandela ended his statement with an exposition of his personal standpoint:

> Africans want to be paid a living wage. Africans want to perform work which they are capable of . . . Africans want to be allowed to live where they obtain work, and not be endorsed out of an area because they were not born there. Africans want to be allowed to own land in places where they work . . . Africans want to be part of the general population and not confined to living in their own ghettoes. African men want to have their wives and children with them where they work . . .
>
> Above all, we want equal political rights . . . I know it sounds revolutionary to the whites in this country, because the majority of voters will be African. But this fear cannot be allowed to stand in the way of the only solution which will guarantee racial harmony and freedom for all . . .
>
> During my lifetime I have dedicated myself to the struggle of the African people. I have fought against white domination, and I have fought against black domination. I have cherished the ideal of a democratic and free society in which all persons live together in harmony and with equal opportunities. It is an ideal which I hope to live for and to achieve. But if needs be it is an ideal for which I am prepared to die.

This eloquent testimonial was reproduced in virtually every important newspaper worldwide. It would remain for decades to come the definitive expression of liberal African nationalism, cementing Mandela's iconic status in South Africa and – as importantly for the ANC – internationally.

The court sentenced Mandela and seven others to life imprisonment.

Few attempts to influence Hendrik Verwoerd made any impact on him. But one did: an official visit from Dag Hammarskjöld, secretary-general of the United Nations, who arrived in South Africa in January 1961. Verwoerd considered the visit important enough to arrange six off-the-record meetings with him in a visit of six days. Hammarskjöld's memorandum of the meetings noted that he had told Verwoerd the UN favoured speedy integration in South Africa, but the prime minister had called this totally unacceptable.

Hammarskjöld then posed the crucial question: was there a chance of apartheid being turned into what he termed a 'competitive alternative' to integration? Verwoerd replied that the homelands policy constituted such a key arrangement, to which the UN secretary-general responded that for the homelands policy to be considered a 'competitive alternative' the government must set aside a sufficient and coherent territory for blacks, publish a plan for their economic development, and introduce institutions based on the will of the people that would lead to independence if the people so wished. The government also had to accept the fact that the homelands could not be a complete solution. Blacks working outside the homelands had to be entitled to similar rights and protection as those that Western countries gave to foreign workers and, in particular, be entitled, after prolonged residence, to citizenship in South Africa with full civic rights.

Verwoerd had a unique opportunity at hand to develop a plan that could gather sufficient international support for the 'decolonisation' of South Africa. But tragically Hammarskjöld was killed a few months later in a plane accident in what is today Zambia, robbing the South African government of a valuable interlocutor.

The 'fabulous years'

After the tumultuous years of 1960 and 1961 South Africa settled down to a political reality that was quite different from what had gone before. On the one hand South Africa was without firm allies in the world and isolation seemed set to grow; on the other hand the state's ruthless repression of black protests and of black labour made it unlikely that there would soon be another challenge to the political order. The creating of black 'homelands' initially raised hopes that these could become growth points for black political participation.

During the 1950s the National Party government's conservative macro-economic policy, along with suppression of black labour, laid the foundations for steady growth. Budget surpluses were used to retire debt. The NP dropped its earlier plans to nationalise the mines. Excessive wage demands from white workers were resisted. Investors nevertheless remained wary. The question was whether the state could handle a major black challenge.

By 1961 the doubts were removed: the government had ruthlessly crushed black resistance. The political turbulence in the first months of 1960 had caused a massive outflow of capital. The government had countered that by imposing strict controls on the repatriation of profits. This led to the accumulation of a large amount of private capital in the country. Foreign firms had little option but to reinvest in South Africa, and local companies followed suit. All this resulted in a sudden, major economic boom. Outside South Africa, however, it was not this new economic boom that attracted the attention of the international community. It was the policy and practice of apartheid.

International isolation

Since the end of World War II the international isolation of South Africa had got steadily worse. At first there was a dispute in the United Nations (UN) between South Africa and India and Pakistan over the treatment of Indians. In 1952 the policy of apartheid was placed on the agenda despite South Africa's protests. A UN commission found that apartheid was creating 'a dangerous and explosive situation' that threatened international peace. After the massacre at Sharpeville the Security Council requested South Africa to abandon apartheid. Sanctions were proposed for the first time. Early in 1961 the UN secretary-general visited South Africa to investigate charges of the violation of human rights (see box).

A particular bone of contention was South Africa's administration of South West Africa in terms of a mandate received from the League of Nations after World War I. In 1959 the UN General Assembly charged South Africa with administering the territory in a manner that conflicted with the mandate. In 1960 Ethiopia and Liberia, the only African states that were UN members, instituted proceedings at the International Court to withdraw the mandate. This attempt failed but the Trusteeship Committee continued to urge South Africa to repeal the apartheid laws in South West Africa and to allow a UN committee to visit the territory.

From 1962 the UN General Assembly regularly passed resolutions almost unanimously asking member states to impose diplomatic sanctions and to bar South African ships and planes from their territory. The Security Council agreed on an arms embargo.

Resistance, repression and censorship

In 1961 Verwoerd appointed tough politician John Vorster as Minister of Justice, who took the view that the security of the state was the highest priority, trumping personal freedoms. A new law gave the government the power to place people under house arrest, and supplemented its power to list, ban or banish individuals or organisations. The police could now detain suspects without a charge under conditions of solitary confinement for successive periods of twelve days. This was soon expanded to 90, then to 180, then to an unlimited period. Newspapers could not report on any torturing or third-degree methods since legislation prohibited unauthorised articles on prison conditions.

A new Publications Control Board was introduced in 1963 with a team of censors authorised to ban films and books considered to threaten public morals or security. The press remained relatively free, but subject to constant pressure from the government and curbs on reporting on the ANC and other similar organisations.

With the arrest of Bram Fischer (*see box on page 342*) in 1965 both the ANC and SA Communist Party ceased to function. Better organised than the PAC, the ANC managed to set up structures in exile and had begun to receive funding from the Soviet bloc.

By 1963 the ANC's strategy of multiracial alliances, an inclusive South Africanism and relative moderation was widely seen to have failed. The question was whether Africanism, alive since the late 1940s, could fill the void. With Robert Sobukwe in jail or detained or forced to live under house arrest until his death in 1978, the mantle of Africanism fell on the shoulders of Potlako Kitchener Leballo.

Gail Gerhart observed in her book *Black Power in South Africa: The Evolution of an Ideology* (1978) that Leballo clung to Lembede's ideas that black people had to rely on themselves to achieve psychological emancipation in the pursuit of political liberation. He became increasingly critical of the growing influence of communism among ANC leaders and was expelled from the movement in 1954 when he criticised Youth Leaguers who attended a communist-sponsored youth festival in Bucharest in 1953.

Leballo heeded the call of Lembede to embrace the cause of nationalism with 'the fanaticism and bigotry of religion'. He was a born rebel, ready to spring into action at the slightest provocation. Pouring scorn on the pronouncement of the Freedom Charter that South Africa belonged to all, both white and black, he wrote that if all whites were engaged in 'the maintenance and retention of the spoils passed on to them by their fore-fathers, then they were traffickers in stolen goods, none could escape responsibility for the original "theft"'. There were only two combatants in the conflict: the conquered and the conqueror, the invaded and the invader, the dispossessed and the dispossessor.

Leballo moved the PAC offices to Maseru in Basutoland. Off-shoots or 'cells' of the PAC had sprung up, but were poorly organised and had little or no formal links with the office in Maseru. These cells were called Poqo (roughly translated it meant 'We Africans go it alone'). One existed in Langa, Cape Town, another in Paarl, and others in the Transkei. There was little revolutionary theory among the mostly young activists, only a vague idea that mass killing of whites would bring white supremacy to an end.

The most publicised incident occurred in Paarl in 1962 where five policemen and three coloured women were murdered before a mob surged into the town, killing two whites and burning down some shops. Five whites were murdered at Bashee Bridge in the Transkei. An attempt to assassinate Kaiser Matanzima, a supporter of the homelands policy in the Transkei, was foiled. By the end of 1962 more than 3 000 PAC or Poqo members had been arrested and more than 1 000 sentenced.

The PAC's attempt to set up a base in exile was even less successful than the ANC's. The links with the Chinese government yielded much less than the support the ANC derived from Moscow. By the end of the 1960s the governments in Lusaka and Maseru closed down PAC bases in their respective countries. The impetuousness of Leballo was one of the main reasons.

In the early 1960s radical whites, mostly lecturers and students, organised themselves in the African Resistance Movement and committed random acts of sabotage, hoping that this would force government to change course. They were all quickly caught and sent to jail. The most shocking act was committed by John Harris, who set off a bomb in the concourse of the Johannesburg station, killing a woman and seriously injuring fourteen others. He was sentenced to death and executed.

By the mid-1960s South Africa was teeming with police spies and informers. People with radical ideas kept their heads down and refrained from political activity. In terms of a 1967 law the police could detain any person deemed a terrorist until he provided what the police considered satisfactory answers to questions put to him. No persons other than officials of the state were entitled to have access to him. From the police cells disturbing information emerged of torture ending in the death of inmates while being questioned, driving people to suicide or causing nervous breakdowns.

ABOVE: *P.K. Leballo, a colourful Africanist, was born in 1914 in the rural eastern Free State. After seeing action in World War II, Leballo studied at the Lovedale teacher training college, where he was expelled after a student strike. He settled in Orlando, working as an insurance salesman, and quickly made his name as a lively and colourful orator and a dogmatic enemy of the ANC's alignment with white communists. As chairman of the Orlando East Youth League he charged Youth League officers who accepted invitations to the 1953 World Youth Festival with being 'Eastern functionaries'. In 1953 he started a journal,* The Africanist, *and in 1959, after parting ways with the ANC, he was elected first national secretary of the PAC. He was widely blamed by PAC members for prematurely disclosing details of the PAC's anti-pass campaign to the press, warning police of the planned protests and leading to severe repression, including his own arrest. After his release, he continued to serve the PAC in various positions until he was ousted in 1979 following serious internal tensions.*

In the 1977 inquest into Steve Biko's death, the officer in charge of the security police in Port Elizabeth was asked where he got the authority to keep an injured man naked and in chains in his cell for 48 hours. He replied: 'We have full authority. It is left to my sound discretion . . . We don't work under statutory authority.' Between 1963 and 1977 when Biko was killed in a violent scuffle, 45 people who were imprisoned without trial died in jail.

The homelands vision falters

Transkei offered to the government the best opportunity to implement its so-called Bantustan strategy. During 1962–1963 there was armed resistance to the policy in Thembuland and Chief Sabata Dalindyebo emerged as a strong opponent of the faction headed by Kaiser Matanzima, who supported the policy. In 1963 the NP government introduced partial self-government for the Transkei, with a promise of full independence over time. Matanzima's party defeated that of Sabata in the elections for the assembly. He would soon begin to show a measure of independence of thought and action. A process had been set in train that Pretoria could not completely control.

At first some Western countries watched the 'Bantustan' experiment with interest.

BRAM FISCHER, AN AFRIKANER COMMUNIST

When security police arrested Abram ('Bram') Fischer in November 1965 after ten months in hiding it seemed to signal the destruction of the SA Communist Party (SACP) and ANC inside South Africa. Fischer had tried – and failed – to put together again those few pieces of the two organisations that had survived devastatingly effective state repression following the formation of Umkhonto weSizwe in 1961. Until the early 1970s there would be no internally based ANC and SACP activity, apart from sporadic pamphleteering by a handful of isolated young intellectuals.

At the time of his arrest in 1965, Fischer was the acting chair of the outlawed Communist Party and the most senior communist at liberty inside the country. He had been living under a number of false identities and in disguise in a variety of Johannesburg suburbs. On capture, he was sentenced to life imprisonment for sabotage and Communist Party activity, and died in May 1975 from cancer, still a prisoner though he was released into the care of his brother in Bloemfontein in his final days.

That Fischer found himself a political fugitive testified to his exceptional life. He straddled the conflicts and contradictions of South Africa during one of the bitterest chapters in the struggle against apartheid.

Most who were influenced by Afrikaner nationalism in the early twentieth century became segregationist conservatives. But Fischer, from a leading Afrikaner family in the Free State, was driven to an anti-imperialist analysis of political and economic power in South Africa that led him to communism and identification with the black struggle against white minority domination. Though his membership of the staunchly orthodox SACP implied support for Stalinism, he upheld the basically liberal social democratic vision of the ANC, with which the SACP was in alliance. Despite being one of South Africa's leading jurists Fischer defied the law that banned the SACP in the 1950s by helping to rebuild it underground after 1953. He defended many of the ANC's and SACP's leading figures in the most significant of South Africa's political trials in the 1950s and 1960s, including the Rivonia Trial (see box on page 339) of Nelson Mandela and others.

Although many of Fischer's ANC and SACP comrades chose exile in the course of the severe repression between 1960 and 1965, he steadfastly refused to obey their entreaties that he should do the same. Fischer believed the liberation struggle had to be led and pursued inside the country. It was in the service of this perspective that he went into hiding in January 1965 – and then to jail for life.

In the course of his exceptional life, Fischer was condemned as a traitor by

Bram Fischer

many Afrikaners and other whites. Among blacks, however, he was greatly admired, achieving a remarkable status. In the democratic era since 1994 appreciation of him has broadened further, as Mandela noted in 1995 when delivering the first Bram Fischer Memorial Lecture: 'In any history written of our country, two Afrikaner names will always be remembered.' One, said Mandela, was Beyers Naudé, the Afrikaner churchman who played a leading though still largely unexplored role in the underground struggle against apartheid. 'The other is Bram Fischer. The people of South Africa will never forget him. He was among the first bright beacons that attracted millions of our young people to fervently believe in a non-racial democracy in our country.'

Early in 1962 *The Sunday Times* of London wrote that the ruling Afrikaner minority seemed intent on an alternative to fighting a multiracial democracy to the death. If there had to be apartheid, the paper continued, the Transkei represented a courageous step as a visible alternative. *The Guardian*, further to the left than the *Times*, accepted the principle of separate viable white and black spheres of influence, leading ultimately to full partition.

In 1964 liberal historian C.W. de Kiewiet, then living in the United States, published an article in *Foreign Affairs* after a visit to South Africa. Noting the hopelessness of the situation and the increasing repression, he nevertheless argued that it was unwise to reject out of hand the possibility of the Bantustan experiment offering 'an enlarged political experience' and relief from political subordination in the common area. Verwoerd, De Kiewiet wrote, was addressing the country's grave problems with 'boldness, shrewdness and even imagination'. It was 'by no means absurd' to suggest a comparison between Verwoerd and Charles de Gaulle, 'the stern, headstrong but deeply imaginative leader of France'.

But the economic development of the homelands moved at a snail's pace. Between 1956 and 1966 fewer than 45 000 jobs were created in the reserves and in the adjacent border areas. Black family incomes in the larger towns were on average three to four times the average homeland income. The average output per head in the homelands was twenty times lower than in the remainder of South Africa.

Although the pace of development quickened after 1970 the function of the homelands had changed. The government now considered them as places where 'surplus' blacks could be settled and where black teachers, nurses and other government officials could provide social services to blacks. Even more important: the homelands provided an ideological justification for the exclusion of blacks from the political system in the rest of the country.

A massive boom

By 1966 the costs of apartheid were not yet prohibitively high, measured in purely economic terms. The economy was still largely based on agriculture and mining. Employers used large numbers of unskilled or poorly skilled black and coloured labour wastefully and with little concern for productivity. Pass laws and curbs on black political and labour organisations severely restricted the ability of blacks to bargain for higher wages. The government spent little on the development of the homelands or on the rehabilitation of the poorest communities.

By the mid-1960s the economy was growing at a phenomenal rate of 6% while the inflation rate stood at only 2%. Attracted by the cheap labour, a gold-backed currency and high profits, investors from all over the world had ploughed money into the country. The magazine *Time* wrote: 'Production, consumption and the demand for labour [are] soaring.' South Africa 'is in the middle of a massive boom'. In an otherwise highly critical assessment of apartheid, it called Verwoerd 'one of the ablest leaders Africa has ever produced'. The *Financial Mail*, the premier financial magazine of South Africa at the time, celebrated the period 1961 to 1966 as the 'fabulous years' when South Africa's gross national product rose by 30% in real terms.

1966, the heyday of apartheid

By 1966, the final year of Verwoerd's term in office, the scheme for a white South Africa was never more forcefully pursued. All housing construction in the black townships had been frozen since the early 1960s, and in 1964 the government introduced extremely harsh influx controls that expanded the system to peri-urban areas and made possible the eradication of the so-called 'black spots' (black settlements in the supposed white rural areas).

In many ways Verwoerd's policies represented a holding action, not a settlement. As a result of influx control in South Africa, the system kept one to 1.5 million people in the reserves who otherwise would have become urbanised by the end of the 1960s. But the numerical preponderance of blacks steadily grew. There was now a black population of

There is an assumption that economic growth under apartheid did nothing for black people. This is not correct. It is true that the gap between whites and blacks remained enormous and that a maze of restrictions blocked black progress. But on average in the two decades after Verwoerd gained power the disposable personal income of all the politically subordinate groups improved (albeit from a very low base) at a rate higher than that of whites. As the calculation by J.L. Sadie in the table shows, the income of all black groups doubled between 1960 and 1980, while that of whites grew by less than half and stagnated between 1970 and 1980.

Disposable personal income (at 1990 prices)			
	1960	1970	1980
WHITES	R12 114	R17 260	R17 878
INDIANS	R 2 171	R 3 674	R 5 655
COLOUREDS	R 2 000	R 3 033	R 3 933
BLACKS	R 1 033	R 1 439	R 1 903

In 1964 Harry Oppenheimer, head of the Anglo American Corporation, by far the largest conglomerate in the country, remarked that in the previous five years the average wages of 'non-white' workers in secondary industry had risen by 5.4% (against those of whites at 3.7%) per year. To him this explained why the country was 'so much more stable than many people are inclined to suppose'. This was of little comfort to those blacks living on a pittance in the reserves. But for them the glimmer of hope was the prospect of a job, albeit one with a very low wage. In 1965, 73.6% of new entrants to the labour market were absorbed in the formal sector, a rate never achieved before. It would rise to 76.6% in 1970, but would drop to 43.4% in 1998.

Percy Qoboza

Schalk Pienaar

fourteen million compared to fewer than four million whites. Because of the rapid black population increase, the supposedly white state even in the 1950s had to appoint more blacks (as policemen, teachers, nurses, etc) than whites in the civil service. Despite the restrictions, economic growth drew large numbers of blacks into secondary industry. In declaring in 1958 that in twenty years' time the stream of blacks to 'white' South Africa would be reversed, Verwoerd seemed to believe that political conviction could prevail over economic realities.

There were still no major breaches in the white ideological support for apartheid. In a study undertaken in the late 1960s of political, business and bureaucratic elites, between 83% and 96% of Afrikaners agreed with the following statements: that 'Bantu [blacks] should remain Bantu', that a 'doctorate is a veneer', that they were not inferior but 'different by nature', and that multiracial democracy was not practicable. Upwards of 80% disagreed with the statement that there were no differences in abilities between whites and blacks, only a difference in opportunities. Between two-thirds and three-quarters of the English elite agreed with these propositions.

Verwoerd's assassination

Muted opposition to Verwoerd in Afrikaner nationalist ranks again was evident in 1965. Schalk Pienaar, a brilliant editor of Sunday newspaper *Die Beeld*, gently mocked Verwoerd's prediction that the policy of homeland development would succeed in reversing the flow of blacks to the cities by 1978. He urged the government to accept that the permanently urbanised blacks could not be accommodated by the homelands policy. His newspaper reported that businessmen questioned the viability of most of the reserves.

But Verwoerd seemed untouchable. In a general election on 30 March 1966 the National Party won 126 of the 166 seats and 58% of the votes cast. The liberal Progressive Party suffered heavy setbacks. For the first time the NP had attracted a significant share of the English vote. On 31 July 1966 the *Rand Daily Mail*, the liberal daily most critical of the government, wrote: 'Dr Verwoerd has reached the peak of a remarkable career . . . The nation is suffering from a surfeit of prosperity.' It saw him as a leader who had refined the crude ideology of white supremacy 'into a sophisticated and rationalized philosophy of separate development'.

At the height of Verwoerd's power, on 6 September 1966, white parliamentary messenger Dimitrio Tsafendas assassinated him on the floor of the House of Assembly just before he was to make a speech that was said to have contained important policy announcements. Schalk Pienaar of *Die Beeld* assessed its significance as follows:

> Man and policy, creator and creation had grown so much together in the crisis of our time that the one cannot be easily seen as separate from the other. And now in the midst of a dynamic growth process the man suddenly is no longer there . . . Verwoerd never sketched the end of the road as he saw it . . . He walked a high and lonely road without people he really trusted. In that sense he left without a will.

It is unlikely that anyone else would have stood as firm as Verwoerd in the aftermath of Sharpeville. He said that abandoning apartheid would, as in the rest of Africa, lead to the white and other minorities being 'expelled or absorbed'. Experiments with socialism or state capitalism would follow, which would wreck the economy. While this view can be contested, it certainly cannot be dismissed out of hand. It is difficult to believe that the high growth of the 1960s could occur in a climate of uncertainty.

But Verwoerd's political intransigence was also a stumbling block. It is unlikely that he would have been capable of accommodating the demands of a new, more assertive and better skilled black labour force. As his power grew, he himself became much more assertive and ever less willing to tolerate adjustments to apartheid that the high growth rate, made possible by his political clampdown on black protests, had made imperative.

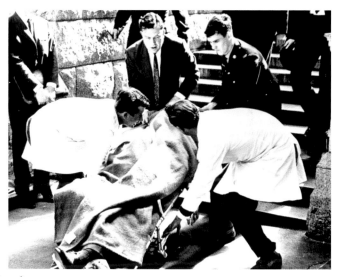

Verwoerd's attempt to develop apartheid as a form of decolonisation fell far short of his earlier promise. He did not put in place any structures in which he could meet with politicians from the Transkei and other homelands in the form of a 'commonwealth of confederation' to address grievances and discuss common interests. Verwoerd's most significant contribution in this regard was to help whites think about race in terms other than biological superiority/inferiority and to present the problem as a political problem where different ethnic groups had to find a way to co-exist. But in practical terms the homelands policy was a pipe dream unless the government was prepared to part with a large part of the land and some of the metropolitan centres.

A complex society

By the mid-1960s South Africa had come a considerable way from the poor and struggling country of the 1950s. White English speakers, forming less than 10% of the population, were by far the most successful. In 1965 they controlled more than 80% of the companies in the financial sector, 90% of those in the mining sector and the same proportion in the manufacturing sector. The percentage of English-speaking children who passed the highest school standard was twice as high as that of Afrikaners, and there were twice the number of English university graduates in the white community. Afrikaners, who formed nearly 60% of the white community, earned only 45% of the total white income.

A small but significant black lower middle class had appeared. Shrewd observers noted that it consisted of urban people who had skills and qualifications, and were becoming increasingly Western in their consumer patterns and cultural tastes. They had become South Africans, acquiring, with whites, an emotional identification with a country they shared with other people. Although oppressed and humiliated they were steadily acquiring expertise, knowledge and political acumen. The laws had crushed many but below the crust there was a ferment and a yearning that no decree could stifle. But the people in the homelands experienced increasing poverty and hardship. The exception was a new stratum of black civil servants who would spearhead the advance of blacks into public administration.

ABOVE: *Prime Minister Hendrik Verwoerd's body on 6 September 1966, after his assassination by a parliamentary messenger who was later found by a court to be deranged.*

OPPOSITE TOP: *Percy Qoboza, editor of the Johannesburg daily tabloid* The World. *Donald Woods, editor of the* Daily Dispatch, *remarked that until 19 October 1977 editors of the English-language press knew the statutory limits within which they could criticise apartheid. On that day, however, the government tore up the rules, detaining both Woods and Qoboza, and closing down* The World.

OPPOSITE BOTTOM: *Schalk Pienaar, editor of* Die Beeld, *a Sunday newspaper that was the most enthusiastic supporter in the Afrikaans press of reform.*

CHAPTER FOURTEEN

In search of a new order

A state of change

The white-dominated political system appeared to be invincible in 1966, the year that Hendrik Verwoerd died. Yet a 'silent revolution' was under way that would steadily undermine apartheid stability. During the 1950s a demographic change of historic importance began to manifest itself. Up to then whites constituted 20% of the total population and could fill all the middle-level and top positions in the public and private sectors. But the proportion of whites to the total population began to fall fast. In 1969 bold headlines in the Afrikaans newspaper *Die Beeld* announced 'a new factor' in South African politics: 'Verwoerd's figures wrong: South Africa will be much blacker.' The black population was growing much more rapidly than antici-pated. The white population, which stood at approximately 20% of the total popula-tion between 1910 and 1950, was projected to fall to 15% by 1985 and to below 10% early in the new century.

The economy had moved decisively away from the early phase of industrialisation, characterised by the predominance of mining and agriculture that relied heavily on uneducated and poorly trained workers, many of them migrants. Employers could use large numbers of unskilled or poorly skilled black and coloured labour wastefully and with little concern for productivity. Pass laws and curbs on black political and labour organisations severely restricted the ability of workers to bargain for higher wages. From the 1960s, however, the manufacturing, construction and services sectors became increasingly dominant. These sectors demanded a skilled and productive workforce, settled on a family basis in the cities.

By the 1970s there was an acute shortage of skilled workers. Whites could no longer fully supply the demand for skilled labour. By the beginning of the 1960s whites still made up 82% of middle-level manpower. This dropped to 65% in 1981. Increasingly, employers trained coloured people, Indians and blacks in more senior positions.

The state had over-reached itself in terms of its capacity to control blacks. The mammoth Department of Bantu Administration and Development found itself incapable of stemming the flow of blacks to the cities.

In order to meet the growing demand for skilled labour, the government began to expand black education. The dramatic advance of black pupils into the more senior school levels can be seen in the table below.

At the same time, however, there was a large and steadily expanding pool of labour that was 'surplus' to the needs of the modern economy. Black children advanced to school standards their parents could only dream about, but had far less chance of getting a formal job. In the 1960s, 97% of school-leavers could expect to find employment, but this declined to 72% in the 1970s. In the Soweto uprising of 1976 the majority who participated were school children and the unemployed – marginal groups who could withdraw from the system without sacrificing income.

OPPOSITE: *Children find their own playgrounds in the rain puddles of Crossroads, the sprawling informal settlement outside Cape Town that sprang up in the 1970s. By the early 1980s it housed more than 50 000 black workers, about a third of them illegally. The government planned to move them to a new township called Khayelitsha, 30 kilometres from the city centre, but unrelenting resistance forced them to abandon these plans. This proved to be the decisive defeat for the pass laws and the government's attempt to limit the number of black people living in the western Cape. The pass laws were abolished in 1986.*

Black enrolment in higher education since 1960			
Year	Secondary school	Highest school standards	University students
1960	54 598	717	1 871
1965	66 568	1606	1 880
1970	122 489	2 938	4 578
1975	318 568	9 009	7 845
1980	577 584	31 071	10 564
1985	1 192 932	34 733	49 164

Total population by statutory groups, 1951–1987				
	1951	1970	1980	1987
Black	8 560 083	15 057 952	21 307 749	26 313 898
White	2 641 689	3 752 528	4 453 273	4 911 000
Coloured	1 103 016	2 018 453	2 554 039	3 069 000
Indian	336 664	620 436	794 639	913 000
Total	12 641 452	21 449 369	29 109 700	35 206 898

BELOW: *In the 1970s South African cities became increasingly black. Below is an aerial view of Soweto, which, like other urban centres, saw an impressive increase in the number of formal dwellings but no marked improvement in the quality of town planning. No real neighbourhoods were created, but rows of modest houses with cramped interiors were dotted along regimented street blocks.*

OPPOSITE: *John Vorster resigned in 1978 as prime minister to become the ceremonial state president of South Africa. He is seen here taking the salute with his wife (right).*

As a result of a rapid black population increase the cities became increasingly black. By 1970 five million blacks lived in the towns and cities in the South African common area (compared to two million in 1946). The white population, both urban and rural, was fewer than four million. As consumers, blacks transformed the marketing strategies of business and as labourers they broke down the colour bar in industry.

By the end of the 1970s huge informal settlements had sprung up on the perimeters of cities: 500 000 were housed in greater Inanda adjoining Durban, 250 000 in Edenvale-Zwartkops near Pietermaritzburg, 300 000 in Winterveld near Pretoria, 100 000 in Mdantsane near East London, and approximately the same number in Crossroads near Cape Town's airport. More than half the black population was under the age of sixteen and many were increasingly beyond the control of government or family.

'A strong state and weak subjects'

Repression was not random or unpredictable but properly legalised. In 1971 prominent anti-apartheid activist Fatima Meer wrote: 'The government preserves its structure through a highly sophisticated administrative technique which carefully mixes personal benevolence with the impersonal and hence "impartial" mystique of the law . . . The non-white victim is beginning to believe that he has the sympathy and support of minor and senior officials, including the prime minister, and that both white and black are equally the victims of South African custom and the law of apartheid.' Meer referred to the 'awe-inspiring strength of the state', but added that this was only possible 'because of the complementary weakness of its subjects'.

A police state?

South Africa of the 1960s and 1970s was often glibly described as a police state, but the picture was more complex. As for the draconian security legislation, influx control and other curbs on the movement of blacks, and the lack of black freedom, the statement was true. On the other hand, many features of the classic police state were absent. South Africa was, in fact, a remarkably under-policed state. As late as 1984, after serious unrest, it was reported that there were only 1.4 policemen per 1 000 of the population, compared to roughly 2.4 for the United Kingdom, 4.4 in Ulster, 5.7 in Algeria, and 16 for the Soviet Union.

So, too, the number of political dissidents suffering persecution was small for a country whose population by 1970 stood at 22.5 million. Almost 1 000 people had been banned since 1950, 350 of them with banning orders still in force by 1970. In 1970 some 800 South Africans were serving prison sentences for contravention of the security laws. Hundreds had left the country on exit permits, while many had their passports withdrawn or refused. But by April 1976 only about 74 people were believed to be in detention without trial.

The degree of militarisation of society was still low. In 1967 the government passed legislation introducing military conscription for all white males, and in 1972 the period of service was extended to one year. Until unrest in the townships broke out there was little resistance to this service, and even after 1976 the number of those who refused to do military service was small.

Under P.W. Botha, who became Minister of Defence in 1966, the country modernised its military equipment and greatly expanded local arms manufacture. It was France and to a lesser extent Germany that stepped into the breach when a Labour government in Britain announced it would stop supplying arms to South Africa.

Particularly valuable to South Africa was the supply of helicopters and Mirage fighter-bombers. France also supplied the technology for the Koeberg nuclear power station. After the mandatory United Nations arms embargo of 1977 the arms manufacturing corporation, called Armscor, greatly reduced the dependence on arms imports and even began exporting arms. South Africa's military spending was very low in the early 1960s, and remained modest until the early 1980s.

Judges in the higher courts prided themselves on their impartiality, although blacks invariably received stiffer sentences. The few newspapers that supported the black struggle were banned and their staff harassed, and the government increasingly clamped down on criticism of the police force and prisons, but the main newspapers were remarkably free.

A different kind of politician

One of the first cracks in the National Party's base was the split that occurred in the mid-1960s between *verligtes* and *verkramptes* (*see box*). Initially, the right wing, or *verkramptes*, in the ruling party had reason to be confident that Hendrik Verwoerd's rigid system of apartheid would continue. In a state of deep shock after Verwoerd's assassination on 6 September 1966, the National Party caucus elected B.J. (John) Vorster as his successor. He was the candidate of the right wing, who applauded his attacks on communists and liberals as subversive elements undermining the social order. Vorster had been interned during World War II as an active supporter of the Ossewa Brandwag, which supported the Germans.

Although Vorster retained the draconian security legislation and extended apartheid by removing all vestiges of coloured representation, he took on the *verkramptes*. The ultraright wing in the NP gathered around Albert Hertzog, son of General J.B.M. Hertzog and a member of his cabinet. From this position he attacked Vorster's cautious

reforms – the somewhat more liberal sports policy, the acceptance of black ambassadors and efforts to bridge the gap between the two white communities. In 1969 Vorster dismissed him from the cabinet. Hertzog left the party and founded the Herstigte (Re-established) National Party. It was crushed by the National Party in the general election of 1970, when it drew only 4% of the votes polled (but close to 10% of the Afrikaner votes), and failed to win a single seat.

As a result of his stand against the *verkramptes* Vorster attracted the strong support of the main Nasionale Pers newspapers (*Die Burger* and *Die Beeld*). He was less aloof than Dr Verwoerd, played golf regularly, met the press frequently and made witty after-dinner speeches. The liberal *Rand Daily Mail* soon described him as the most popular prime minister South Africa had ever had.

A sport lover, Vorster was much keener than his predecessor to maintain international sport contacts. They had been jeopardised by Verwoerd's refusal in 1965 to allow a New Zealand national rugby team that included some Maoris to visit. As a result the tour was cancelled. Under Vorster a tortuous process of the desegregation of sport started but took more than fifteen years to complete.

As committed as Verwoerd to white supremacy, Vorster introduced a different note: the Afrikaners craved acceptance by Africa. 'We have a duty towards Africa . . . Africa is our mother . . . You want to do your level best to get your people accepted by Africa, accepted as an African people with every right to be in Africa, as opposed to the here-today-gone-tomorrow idea of the colonialists.'

Keen to break out of South Africa's deteriorating relationship with the world community, Vorster launched his 'Outward Movement'. The first step was to establish diplomatic and economic ties with African states to the north. They constituted South Africa's natural market but took only 10% of its manufacturing exports. He also wished to persuade African states in the region to deny bases to the ANC and the Pan-Africanist Congress (PAC).

But the only tangible success was the establishment of diplomatic relationships with Malawi. When President Hastings Banda of Malawi paid a state visit to South Africa Vorster was photographed sitting between two black female guests at a state banquet. The white press wrote that in doing so he made a major statement against racism.

Homelands or dumping grounds?

The homelands policy provided for different levels of authority – tribal and regional, and territorial or national. It operated on the premise that all blacks, even those living in an urban area, could exercise their rights only through their respective homeland governments. When an ethnic group like the Xhosa received its 'independence' a Xhosa would lose his South African citizenship and become a citizen of the Xhosa 'homeland' even if he had never lived there.

A constitution was drafted for the Transkei and in November 1963 the first election for a partly self-governing Transkei was held. Subsequently the legislative assembly elected Kaiser Matanzima as chief minister. The Ciskei received a legislative assembly in 1971. Only 54% of the Xhosa lived in the two Xhosa homelands.

Between 1963 and 1971 the following other groups designated by the state also received a legislative assembly and a form of self-government: the Zulu in KwaZulu, the Pedi and Northern Ndebele in Lebowa, the Venda in Venda, the Shangaan and Tsonga in Gazankulu, the Tswana in Bophuthatswana, and the Sotho in Basotho Qwa Qwa. Subsequently some form of 'representation' was also given for the Swazi and the South Ndebele although the respective homelands were not more than a district (370 square kilometres in the former case and 2 090 square kilometres in the latter).

The Transkei had the advantage of contiguous territory but its resources and infrastructure were meagre. Bophuthatswana consisted of nineteen tracts of land and only a small minority of its inhabitants had access to roads, railways and telecommunications. Mines near Rustenburg produced large quantities of platinum, and other mineral deposits were also mined. Although the territory had more material resources than the other homelands it was, like all the others, largely dependent on financial transfers

decided upon by central government and voted by the South African Parliament. Only a third of its putative citizens – mostly women, children and old men – lived there. In the first election approximately half voted, compared to only 15% of those who worked and lived in Pretoria. KwaZulu was the most fragmented of all the homelands, consisting of 29 major and 41 minor enclaves. Its resources were poor, with most of the territory hilly and lacking in any mineral deposits. Approximately half of its 'citizens' lived there.

Although the homelands were at the very heart of the apartheid policy, development of the areas was painfully slow. Fewer jobs were created in the first ten years than the Tomlinson Commission had required for one year. In 1966 total production of the homelands was only 1.9% of that of the Republic as a whole. The homelands were not becoming industrialised, nor were they ringed with border area factories that could absorb surplus workers, as had earlier been envisaged.

The developmental aspect of the homelands policy was largely replaced by a policy to use the reserves as dumping grounds where the government resettled blacks from 'white' South Africa. People from black rural settlements (called black spots), redundant farm labourers and some of the urban unemployed were forcibly moved to the homelands. Between 1962 and 1982 a total of 1.9 million black people, in the government's own estimate, were relocated. When group areas removals in the towns and cities and evictions of farm labourers were added, 3.5 million people were resettled as a result of apartheid.

Conditions in the resettlement camps were bleak, with little or no hope of getting a job. Between 1970 and 1980 the population of the homelands territories increased by 57%, a doubling of the population density since 1950. Agricultural production largely collapsed and the homelands became overwhelmingly dependent on the earnings of migrant labour.

The homeland style of politics

Only three of the homelands, the Transkei, Bophuthatswana and KwaZulu, figured prominently in the white-dominated political debates of the 1970s and 1980s. The Transkei's Kaiser Matanzima soon revealed that he was more interested in enjoying the spoils of power than using his limited power base to confront the central government. Confident that it posed no security threat, the central government in 1976 granted 'independence' to the Transkei.

Despite the extremely unpromising economic context, Lucas Mangope, who was elected chief minister of Bophuthatswana in 1972, and Chief Mangosuthu Buthelezi, who became chief minister of KwaZulu in 1975, used the few opportunities to try to improve the position of blacks.

Mangope pursued an ambivalent policy, combining collaboration with apartheid with attempts to find a Tswana territorial base in a new federation. After initially backing Buthelezi in rejecting the goals of separate development, he eventually steered Bophuthatswana to 'independence' in 1977.

Buthelezi opted for more open confrontation. A shrewd, proud and prickly individual with great staying power, he used his exceptional political skills to put together a platform that formally rejected the homelands system, but also used it as a cover for building a mass movement.

In 1975 he relaunched the Inkatha cultural movement, originally founded in the 1920s. It soon had between 150 000 and 200 000 members. To promote supra-ethnic nationalism he established the Black Unity Front for nationalists both inside and outside the

homelands system. In 1977 a careful assessment by Gail Gerhart, a balanced American scholar, concluded: 'To argue that Buthelezi is a net asset to the regime because he lends credibility to the Bantustans is seriously to undervalue his role as propagandist for nationalism. Buthelezi is in fact the strongest evidence that black initiatives can lead to the backfiring of the best-laid plans of the apartheid strategists.' Educated blacks viewed Buthelezi with suspicion. They saw him as representing largely the elderly, the traditional, and those in the government's pay.

A fresh voice in the mid-1970s was that of Bishop Desmond Tutu, representing a new generation of black clergy who had risen to leadership positions in the principal English churches and were committed to black liberation. In his view the choice was stark: whites and blacks 'will survive together or be destroyed together'.

The Black Consciousness movement

While the Black Consciousness (BC) movement that emerged in the 1960s was distinct, it was nevertheless an integral part of an evolution of black resistance stretching back to colonial times. The distinctiveness of the BC movement lay in its incorporation of growing numbers of black university students, its interaction with the National Union of South African Students (Nusas) as an anti-apartheid student group, and its response to the relentlessness of discriminatory practices at the hands of an increasingly confident white government.

A separate black organisation

Whereas in the past there was one university – Fort Hare – to which blacks could be admitted with relatively few difficulties, by the early 1960s this number had grown to six. Blacks from all groups now also had access to the University of Durban-Westville, University of the North, University of the Western Cape, University of Zululand and the Medical School at the University of Natal.

In the mid-1960s Steve Biko, a student at the University of Natal, was a member of Nusas, the dominant student union at the time. Nusas was mainly white and active at English-speaking universities. By 1966 Biko had developed the idea of founding a separate black student organisation. In his view white students could not possibly identify in the fullest meaning of the word with the experience of oppression and thus with the aspirations of black students.

By the late 1960s Nusas had toned down its opposition to apartheid in the face of an aggressive government. This greatly annoyed the emerging black constituency of university students who were massing at exclusively black institutions. The final straw was the annual conference in 1967 held at Rhodes University at which black delegates were housed in degrading conditions outside the university campus.

Biko's rejection of a single body for both black and white students did not mean that he also rejected liberal ideas. In elaborating his views about the future, Biko never sought to rid South Africa of whites, accepting that they were part of the reality of South Africa. Their role should focus on convincing their community to stop apartheid, he argued.

Biko's task was facilitated by the existence of the University Christian Movement (UCM), an organisation that had become predominantly black by 1968. The idea of creating a black student organisation was discussed and endorsed at a UCM meeting in 1968. Biko's early writings showed he had by this time worked out a set of ideas that would later congeal into the theory of black consciousness.

The first organisation Biko founded was the South African Student Organisation (Saso) in July 1969. He was elected the first president. He also played an important role in other Black Consciousness formations, including the Black People's Convention (BPC), South African Students' Movement (SASM) and the National Youth Organisation (NAYO). Projects included the Black Community Programme, for which Biko worked in the early 1970s, and Zanempilo, a health facility outside King William's Town. The clinic, which employed Dr Mamphela Ramphele as a house doctor, was a BC-inspired project.

After Biko was banned in 1973 the Black Community Programme continued to support

BELOW: *Neville Alexander speaking at a 1983 meeting of the National Forum, an alliance of black consciousness-inclined and independent socialist organisations. A leading intellectual, he had a doctorate in German literature from Germany. He was a prisoner on Robben Island from 1964–1974 along with Nelson Mandela and others.*

In 1983 he threw his weight behind the National Forum (NF). Although poorly funded, the NF posed a stiff theoretical challenge to the United Democratic Front (UDF). It rejected the UDF's attempt to style itself as 'non-racial' while allowing ethnic organisations into its fold and many whites into leadership positions. It deplored the 'reckless' inclination in the UDF to commit activists to futile attempts to overthrow the state. It was also much more explicitly anti-capitalist. Alexander argued strongly that South Africa's capitalism had acquired such a profound racial character that there was no possibility for black workers to find common cause with white capitalists in a post-apartheid order. The NF took a socialist line and looked to an organised black working class to take the lead in both the anti-apartheid struggle and a future government. In the end the UDF and ANC prevailed over the NF because it was better funded and more pragmatic on economic policy. Yet many of the issues the NF highlighted would come back to haunt the ANC in power, in particular the close alliance between a black bourgeoisie and white big business.

THE DISTINCT VOICE OF STEVE BIKO

Steve Biko's father Mathew Mzingane worked as a clerk and his mother Alice Nokuzola as a domestic servant. Born on 18 December 1946 in King William's Town, Biko was exposed to politics at an early age when his brother was arrested for involvement in the activities of the PAC in 1963. He himself was expelled for political activities from Lovedale College in the eastern Cape where he was enrolled for his high school education. He matriculated at a Catholic school in Natal and was admitted to the medical school at the University of Natal (Black section). He discontinued his studies in 1972 to work full-time for the Black Community Programme (BCP) in Durban. When he was banned in 1973 he set up a BCP office in King William's Town where he continued to work.

This was stopped by a new order that banned him from working for the BCP.

Black Consciousness ideology posited that black people needed to take pride in their black identity. Biko argued that years of white oppression had imposed views of beauty on blacks that were rooted in white experiences. Blacks had accepted this and ended up hating themselves for being inadequate because they were black. He argued that blacks did not require the guidance of whites to oppose white oppression. Liberals – as Biko called whites who participated in opposing apartheid and sought a better deal for blacks – could not be beneficiaries of apartheid and at the same time oppose it.

The task of opposing apartheid should fall on black people who were its victims. Only blacks, Biko argued, understood the pain of oppression. Whites who felt a need to contribute to alleviating the pain resulting from apartheid oppression of blacks should channel their energies into convincing other whites that apartheid was wrong and allow blacks to fight apartheid in the best way they knew how. The ideology was captured in what later became a popular slogan within Black Consciousness circles: 'Black man, you are on your own.'

About the phrase 'black is beautiful' Biko wrote: 'It has been meant to serve and I think is serving a very important aspect of our attempt to get at humanity. You are challenging the very deep roots of the Black man's belief about himself. When you say "black is beautiful" what in fact you are saying to him is: man, you are okay as you are, begin to look upon yourself as a human being ... So in a sense the term "black is beautiful" challenges exactly that belief which makes someone negate himself.'

Steve Biko with his son Samora

him. His banning order persisted until his arrest in 1977. Even while banned, he served and promoted the organisations he had founded. Until his death in 1977 in police custody he remained a leader of the Black Consciousness movement he had helped to form.

The mobilising agenda

Organising the black population was made relatively easy by the common experience of a single racial group living in segregated townships. Black universities provided fertile ground for propagating Black Consciousness views and fashioning a powerful student organisation. Initially the state allowed the movement some respite.

Black Consciousness imbued blacks with the conviction that blacks alone could end racial oppression. The pride that blacks took in themselves contributed to a growing self-confidence among adherents of the creed.

Once established, Saso grew very rapidly at black university campuses. For the first time since the banning of the ANC and the PAC, open black resistance was reignited.

Spreading the ideas

The spread of Black Consciousness ideas through the community occurred principally through the Black People's Convention. Other important organisations that spread BC ideas were the Students' Christian Movement and the South African Students' Movement. The former was an old university-based Christian movement patronised by black students even when Nusas was the dominant student body on black campuses. The latter was formed to provide an organisation for high school pupils. It gained a presence in a number of schools, including Morris Isaacson High School and Naledi High in Soweto. These schools provided the epicentre of the 1976 uprisings. Healdtown in the eastern Cape was another major centre of activism.

Brimming with newfound confidence, these groups never truly mastered the art of enlisting the masses of people into organised resistance. Black Consciousness groups tried but failed to organise workers. They were unable to build the kind of civic associations that later succeeded in reaching out to people other than activists or students. Rooted in educational settings as they were, their style reflected their origin and they mainly concerned themselves with the consciousness of people rather than building strong organisations that could be thrown into the battle against apartheid. By focusing on consciousness they nonetheless built resistance capital that would be put to work later.

Into the schools

In 1976 Soweto pupils refused to co-operate in their own oppression. The rejection of instruction by means of Afrikaans triggered a revolt that culminated in numerous ground-breaking victories for the oppressed people and the final removal of apartheid.

The leaders of the student uprisings in Soweto were politically socialised by groups like the South African Student Organisation (Saso) and the Black People's Convention. Their immediate points of reference were individuals associated with Black Consciousness. Onkgopotse Abram Tiro, a Saso leader who was expelled from the University of the North for attacking the racially segregated university system, had taught at Morris Isaacson High School in Soweto where the uprising started in 1976. He was venerated by his pupils. Other teachers with involvement with Black Consciousness groups taught for brief periods at the school.

Biko's generation was familiar with the early resistance of the ANC and the PAC. Their critical thinking and actions laid the basis for a process that would help the black community to overcome the debilitating defeats of the early 1960s. The bulk of the 1976 leaders and marchers were at first only vaguely aware of these early struggles. They soon learnt, though.

The strikes that changed South Africa

The early 1970s was a watershed period in the factories of South Africa. After the 'silent sixties' black labour suddenly hit back at apartheid through strikes, starting in present-day Namibia – then South West Africa – in 1971–1972 and culminating in a wave of strikes in Durban in 1973. At the lower end of the labour market wages were abysmally low. In the early 1970s a fifth of the workers in Durban and other cities received less than R10 per week at a time when the monthly subsistence level stood at just under R80. A worker told a reporter: 'When we asked for increases our boss gave 55 cents. I would like to give my boss 55 cents and ask him to buy his children a piece of meat for 55 cents.'

On the mines and farms the position of black workers was, if anything, worse. Real wages in these two sectors had not improved since the early decades of the century. By the 1970s the average farm wage (not including food and housing) was only a third of the manufacturing wage. In the early 1970s the government still pledged to reserve the skilled, better-paid jobs for whites and in other ways preserve white dominance.

The Durban strikes of 1973

No proper machinery existed that black workers could use to negotiate better wages. There were industrial councils or conciliation boards where employers and white unions bargained collectively for wages and investigated labour disputes, but black unions were prohibited from participating in these so there was no legal way for them to bargain collectively or to strike legally. Blacks were not considered employees according to the law.

On 9 January 1973 some 2 000 workers in the Coronation Brick and Tile factory in Durban struck for a wage of R30 per week after the employers had rebuffed them. Other

workers followed. Suddenly workers all over Durban demanded higher wages and better working conditions.

Particularly hard hit was the British-controlled Frame group with several textile plants. In Britain a growing anti-apartheid lobby seized upon the extremely poor wages and the victimisation of workers to demonstrate the iniquity of the system.

The Afrikaans paper *Rapport* reported: 'Most whites silently sympathised with the workers with their low wages, but very few whites did anything about it.' Vorster said in Parliament that the strikes were a lesson to all – one he was prepared to learn. The worker was somebody with a soul and normal needs and not a mere unit who had to labour so many hours per day. Employers, Vorster said, were ready to criticise the government, but they were unaware of the beam in their own eye.

The police kept a low profile. The most senior police officer in the region, Brigadier Bisscoff, declared that the police 'have nothing against people asking for higher wages' although he added that the strikes were illegal. The employers did not victimise strikers: during the whole of 1973 only 3% of the Durban strikes ended in dismissals. The head of the local security police force claimed that he could find no evidence of an organisation behind the strike.

The rise of independent unions

May 1973 saw the formation of the first independent trade unions. The first was the Metal and Allied Workers Union, followed by the National Union of Textile Workers and the Chemical Workers Union. By 1975 there were five independent unions with 11 000 members. Soon the independent unions spread to other parts of the country.

The political scene had changed and new players had appeared. In the absence of any state-recognised unions, office-bearers from the KwaZulu administration entered the void. Chief Mangosuthu Buthelezi acted as the first patron of the Institute of Industrial Education and pioneer of worker education.

Leaders from the Black Consciousness movement became involved, in particular Mosiuoa Lekota and Strini Moodley. So did Mewa Ramgobin and others from the revived Natal Indian Congress, and Jacob Zuma and Harry Gwala, members of the SA Communist Party recently released from Robben Island. Among the white academics active in worker education were Johnny Copelyn, Eddie Webster and Alec Erwin. The tension between these groupings and Buthelezi had begun, first because of his support for the capitalist system and later because he was seen as an obstacle to the ANC.

By the second half of the 1970s the government began to urge employers to relax the curbs on blacks doing skilled jobs or black supervisors giving instructions to whites. It also tried to set an example. Already in 1975 the Defence Force had announced that black soldiers would enjoy the same status as whites of equal rank, and that whites would have to take orders from blacks. By the end of the 1970s more and more companies in the private sector had accepted the principle of merit-based promotion. A 1979 survey revealed that blacks supervised whites in one-fifth of a sample of companies.

Acting on the recommendation of the Wiehahn Commission in 1979, the government abolished the curbs on black labour, permitted black trade unions and accepted the inclusion of trade unions with black members in the formal bargaining system.

The way was now clear for the independent unions to form federations to enhance their bargaining power. In 1979 the strongest of these, the Federation of South African Trade Unions (Fosatu), was established. Black workers now had industrial rights but no political rights. From its base of industrial rights, labour power would increasingly challenge political power.

The government's bold labour reforms stood in sharp contrast to its timidity in reforming social apartheid, particularly segregated schools and the racial sex laws. What made it even stranger was the lack of sustained pressure from either employers or organised black labour. What then motivated the reforms? Government thought that mobilisation on the shop floor would provide a outlet for frustations and that organised labour would prioritise economic over political demands. It also believed that it could refuse labour rights to the workers of independent homelands. These expectations proved to be wrong.

The retreat of white rule

The mid-1970s witnessed a major retreat of white rule. Following a coup in April 1974, power in the Portuguese colonies in southern Africa was quickly transferred to black liberation movements. On 24 November 1974 South African ambassador to the United Nations, R.F. (Pik) Botha, told the UN Security Council that South Africa was moving away from discrimination by all the means at its disposal. These developments briefly stirred the hopes of the subordinate population in South Africa for substantial changes to apartheid. But a huge chasm existed between what blacks saw as reasonable demands and what whites were prepared to yield. The cornerstones of apartheid were still intact.

A commission not heeded

For the coloured people, the group closest to Afrikaners in culture, language and church affiliation, the National Party government had no coherent policy. The four white representatives the coloured people could elect on a separate roll all opposed apartheid, giving rise to increasing frustration on the part of government. The coloured people found themselves in limbo.

In 1968, with John Vorster now prime minister, government abolished the vestiges of coloured representation in the House of Assembly (four whites elected on a separate roll by coloureds), the Senate, and the Cape Provincial Council. As a substitute he introduced a Coloured Persons' Representative Council consisting of nominated and elected members with extremely limited powers.

Another law passed in the same year made it illegal for parties to be active in the political affairs of another racial group. Also in 1968, the South African Indian Council Act was passed to create an advisory, wholly nominated body to deal with Indian affairs in three provinces (in the fourth, the Orange Free State, Indians were still not allowed to settle). In 1971 all coloured voters were removed from municipal voters' rolls and the terms of office of coloured councillors in Cape Town and some other towns in the Cape Province ended the next year. However, the intention to set up segregated coloured municipalities was ill conceived, since none would prove to be financially viable.

Both councils failed to make any impact. The Labour Party, which won most of the seats in the coloured council, set out to wreck it, and its alienation increased when the government fabricated a pro-government majority by appointing nominated members who had been defeated in the election.

To stem the unease in its own ranks in 1973 the government appointed a commission of inquiry into the coloured population, headed by Erika Theron. For the first time since the National Party came to power, a commission included coloured members. The report signed by the majority of the Theron Commission did not denounce apartheid in totality.

TOP: *R.F. (Pik) Botha first became prominent in 1974 when as South African ambassador to the United Nations he stated that his government was 'moving away' from discrimination. He was referring to aspects of social and economic apartheid rather than political apartheid. As Minister for Foreign Affairs between 1978 and 1994 Botha played a key role in finding a settlement in Namibia.*

ABOVE: *Erika Theron with R.E. van der Ross and Sam Motsuenyane. She did her doctoral degree at the University of Stellenbosch under Hendrik Verwoerd, who was Professor of Sociology and Social Work before moving to Johannesburg in 1937. Heading a commission on the coloured population, her role was decisive in getting majority support for recommendations for reform that displeased the political leadership.*

LEFT: *The Theron Commission highlighted the need to address the huge backlog in coloured housing. The picture shows the Chicago residential block in New Orleans, a low-income housing estate outside Paarl in the western Cape.*

OPPOSITE, FROM THE TOP: *Harry Gwala, Mosiuoa Lekota, Strini Moodley and Jacob Zuma. All served time on Robben Island and played a leading role in extra-parliamentary organisations after their release.*

Some of its findings, however, amounted to devastating criticism of government neglect of the coloured population. 'Chronic community poverty' affected more than 40% of the population. In the cities between 10% and 20% lived in squatter camps and many of the rest in overcrowded houses. A high rate of infant mortality had hardly changed from the 128 deaths per 1 000 births in the period 1946–1951, to 120 in 1965–1970.

In the urban labour market coloureds were reported to be suffering from pervasive discrimination since they could not join mixed trade unions without government permission. Even in its own terms apartheid had failed because whites, particularly Afrikaners, dominated the senior positions in all state institutions that served coloureds.

The government accepted the Commission's recommendation for a direct coloured say in the white-dominated political structures, but also declared that the principle of white self-determination remained paramount. The tone of its response was so churlish that it satisfied no one. After the Sharpeville shootings, coloured people had been conspicuous in their absence from the demonstrations that followed. It was different when the Soweto uprising of 1976–1977 broke out, as the ideology of Black Consciousness had attracted considerable support among coloured lecturers and teachers. Large numbers of coloured children in Cape Town participated in public demonstrations and school boycotts in 1976 and subsequent years.

A sharp weakening of white power

By the mid-1970s the period of continued high economic growth since the early 1930s had come to an end. The average annual rate of growth fell from an average of 4.5% in the first 30 years of apartheid to an average of only 1.65% between 1976 and 1994 – well below the 3% annual population increase. In these final eighteen years real per capita income slumped by about 25%, with the poorest people the hardest hit.

The reasons for the economic crisis were complex. By the early 1970s the costs of apartheid were manifesting themselves. They included curbs on the training of black and coloured workers, the lack of proper funding for black and coloured education, the poor productivity of workers, and the long distances the poorest of the workforce had to travel because of the group areas. Inflation had become a serious economic problem.

But much of the economic crisis of the final two decades of apartheid was independent of apartheid. It included factors such as the sharp rise in energy prices after 1973, weaker prices for South African gold and other commodity exports, and the slowdown of the growth of South Africa's main trading partners. The 1980s saw a slump that affected middle-income countries worldwide. South Africa did not fare particularly badly. The World Bank rated South Africa's performance, measured in GDP growth between 1980 and 1985, as twelfth out of twenty comparable developing countries.

A serious problem confronted policy makers. The economy needed a flexible labour market and wage restraints to enable the formal sector to employ as many people as possible. But for political reasons it was important to increase black wages and narrow the huge gap between whites and blacks. Effective trade union organisation forced employers to push up wages. By the end of the 1970s South Africa's labour costs were outstripping those of its competitors and its competitive advantage in most sectors began to dwindle.

The National Party government was also weakened by its inability to attract any significant support from the emerging middle and lower-middle class of blacks in the urban areas. At the heart of the government's policy lay a form of political schizophrenia. On the one hand it wished to create a stable and contented black middle class; on the other hand it wanted policies in place that controlled all blacks. The pass laws that were the symbol of black subordination affected migrant workers and black professionals alike.

To facilitate the former objective, in 1977 the government allowed blacks to take out a 99-year leasehold on their houses, implying recognition of their permanence in the common area. The Riekert Commission of 1979 proposed a two-tier approach towards blacks, dividing them between outsiders (mainly migrant labourers from the homelands) and insiders (mainly professional people and skilled labourers). The insiders were supposed to enjoy more rights and privileges, but they too lacked political rights, freedom of movement and a sense of full citizenship.

South Africa's diplomatic position also weakened. During the 1960s sports boycotts began to bite. South Africa did not receive an invitation to the 1964 Olympics; in 1968 international cricket ties were ended when an English team cancelled its visit after Vorster objected to the inclusion in the team of a South African-born coloured person, Basil D'Oliviera; and at the end of 1969 a tour by the South African rugby team to Britain was severely disrupted.

High noon in southern Africa

On 25 April 1974 a coup in Lisbon heralded the end of Portuguese rule over its colonies of Angola and Mozambique. The new government in Portugal announced that within the next eighteen months it would cede power to the guerrilla movements.

On 25 June 1975 Portugal handed over power in Mozambique to Frelimo, a left wing movement that showed Marxist leanings. Vorster pledged that South Africa would leave the new government in Mozambique in peace as long as it was stable and did not provide bases for South Africa's own guerrilla movements.

In Angola, which was scheduled to become independent on 11 November 1975, the spectre of a civil war loomed as three movements jostled for power. They were the Frente Nacional de Libertacao (FNLA), a northern-based nationalist movement led by Holden Roberto; the Uniço Nacional para a Independência Total de Angola (Unita), based on a large ethnic group in the central highlands and led by Jonas Savimbi; and the Movimento Popular de Libertacao de Angola (MPLA), a movement of Portuguese Marxists and other leftists and indigenous mestizos, based in Angola's capital, Luanda.

By mid-1975 the MPLA controlled less than a quarter of the country's territory, but it was being supplied with arms by the Soviet Union from Central Africa. It also received a steady trickle of Cuban advisers. Angola promptly became the site of one of the proxy wars the Soviet Union and the United States fought in distant corners of the Third World. Soon the CIA in Washington – with the concurrence of US Secretary of State Henry Kissinger – sought ways of helping the FNLA and blocking Cuban support for the MPLA. It asked South Africa to assist the anti-Marxist movements in Angola (FNLA and Unita) to prevent the MPLA from being recognised as the sole *de jure* government of Angola.

A secret operation

While still waiting for a reply from Vorster for permission to assist Unita, the South African Defence Force (SADF) launched an operation, codenamed Savannah, into Angolan territory. SADF troops were well north of the border by 9 August 1975.

LEFT: *A rolling maul of a different kind In response to the disruption of the Springbok rugby tour to the British Isles in 1969-1970 the popular Afrikaans rugby commentator, Gerhard Viviers, described the protestors as the scum of British society, 'pink British sewerage rats, whose protests should be summarily dismissed by all civilised people'. These demonstrations were to herald an era of increasing sporting isolation for South Africa. As international anti-apartheid opinion hardened, at least nine official rugby tours involving South Africa were cancelled between 1970 and 1989. Similar exclusionary practices applied to other sporting codes.*

South African forces went as far as 120 kilometres south of Luanda, and awaited the outcome of a battle between the FNLA, moving in from the north, and the MPLA. But the FNLA attack on Luanda on the morning of 9 November failed as a result of poor discipline and co-ordination. Two days afterwards an MPLA government was installed in Angola. At the meeting of the Organisation of African Unity a month later the member states were deadlocked over recognising the MPLA as a legitimate government. Finally, Idi Amin of Uganda, the chairman, used his casting vote in favour of the MPLA. In December the US Congress cut off all American aid to the FNLA and Unita.

South Africa's military adventure had resulted in a massive increase in the number of Cuban soldiers in Angola. Vorster signalled that he had learnt a bitter lesson: 'When it comes to the worst South Africa stands alone.'

What explains South Africa's actions? Vorster later gave a rather unconvincing explanation in Parliament: the SADF was protecting the Ruacana-Calueque hydro-electric scheme on the border between Angola and South West Africa (SWA) and the safety of South African workers there. Closer to reality was South Africa's interest in not acceding to the UN wish to install the South West African People's Organisation (Swapo) as SWA's government. South Africa did not think it possible to prevent South West African independence; it simply wanted to control political change there. With the MPLA in control of Angola that would be more difficult. South Africa's plan was to keep Swapo off balance for as long as possible.

The early actions and reactions would shape the war in Angola in four ways. First, the Soviet Union kept up arms shipments at least until Mikhael Gorbachev's reform policies started in the late 1980s. It flew in advisers and an estimated $200 million of armoured cars, rocket launchers and heavy artillery pieces. Cuba rushed combat troops to assist the MPLA, reaching a total of 14 000 by early 1976.

The Angolan Constitution recognised only one political party, the MPLA, which believed it could militarily defeat its enemy, Unita. This belief would prove false: every

BELOW: *A Unita parade before a patrol, photographed in 1988. The Unita movement headed by Jonas Savimbi controlled a large part of southern Angola.*

winter, when the ground was sufficiently hard, the MPLA would launch a southerly offensive and every time it would fail to defeat Unita.

Second, the principals in the Cold War continued to support opposing sides. Once American aid had gone to the FNLA, this encouraged Cuba and the Soviet Union to increase their support of the MPLA. The Ford administration would have gone further in aiding and abetting its proxies but was prevented by the US Congress. During the Carter administration, the Americans became more critical of the South African government, but the Soviet Union's invasion of Afghanistan in 1979 brought anti-communism back in full force. In the subsequent Reagan administration, a policy of Constructive Engagement emerged; for Prime Minister (later President) P.W. Botha it meant that, no matter what was done in Angola, the Americans would never completely isolate the South African government.

Third, with the patrons prepared to ship arms, a spiral of escalation was born. What began as unconventional war would in time become increasingly conventional. This hardly suited South Africa. The military budget increased in leaps and bounds. Affected by an ever-tightening noose of sanctions, the South Africans struggled to get enough relevant equipment. Heavy armour was limited mainly to a modest supply of World War II-vintage tanks. Armoured cars were produced quite successfully, but worked best on tarred roads; a reliable locally-produced off-road vehicle, the Casspir, became available later. In the air, transport helicopters were few and far between and light attack aircraft, including attack helicopters, were available but, like the heavy armour, limited in number. Automatic rifles were plentiful, as were machine guns.

Fourth, the local press revealed only scant details of Operation Savannah. But that was enough to alert parents of national servicemen. The secrecy surrounding cross-border operations could not conceal a basic political fact: the SADF was dependent on national servicemen whose presence in Angola had to be retroactively legitimated through an act of Parliament. Were harm to come to them in high numbers, the SADF as a regional military instrument would be neutralised.

Sheltered from air strikes in the southeastern corner of Angola, Unita attacked the MPLA military, Fapla, and its Cuban allies and at first kept Swapo off balance. But Swapo was not kept off balance for long. In 1976/77, the strength of its armed wing, Plan, was estimated at 2 000. By 1978 one estimate put the number at 10 000, another at 16 000. Plan units in Ovambo, formerly typically consisting of about ten soldiers, expanded to groups of between 80 and 100. Contacts with security forces increased to an average of 100 per month. In August 1978 came Swapo's boldest strike, a mortar and rocket attack on the base at Katima Mulilo, headquarters of the SADF in eastern Caprivi. It was retaliation for the SADF's attack on Cassinga in May 1978, when many civilians were killed.

The fall of Rhodesia

Having left its allies in the lurch in Angola, the Ford administration now shifted its attention to Rhodesia, which was an outcast in the world community. Vorster was still reluctant to pressurise Smith, but when he met US Secretary of State Henry Kissinger in July 1976 his hand had been weakened by the outbreak of the Soweto uprising a month earlier.

South Africa now accepted a solution of the Rhodesian question on the basis of 'majority rule with adequate protection for minority rights', and began exerting pressure on Rhodesia by delaying the supply of oil and other strategic supplies that reached Rhodesia via South Africa. This pulled the plug on white rule. Ian Smith later wrote bitterly of the eagerness of the South Africans 'to throw us to the wolves in their desperate desire to try to buy time and gain credit for solving the Rhodesian problem'.

In 1979 the Rhodesian regime held internal elections on the basis of universal franchise. Although the election had a 64% poll and was won by a predominantly black party, Western countries refused to recognise it, because the principal liberation movements had refused to participate. A precedent had been set and it would be reaffirmed in SWA/Namibia. For the West the key question was whether the parties with the capability to wage war and cause major disruption had participated in an election (and had won). The

BELOW: *Robert Mugabe inspects a guard of honour in Harare shortly after becoming prime minister of Zimbabwe. Mugabe was born in 1924 on a mission station, where he went to school. He received a degree from Fort Hare, five from the University of South Africa and ten honorary doctoral degrees. He entered liberation politics as early as 1961 after a brief career as a schoolteacher. He was elected secretary of the Zimbabwe African National Union (Zanu) in 1961 and became president in 1977. He led the Zanu delegation to the negotiations at Lancaster House in London, which set the table for independence. After an overwhelming Zanu victory in the first election he became prime minister in 1980.*

OPPOSITE: *On 16 June 1976 high-school students in Soweto protested, demanding better education. Police fired teargas and live bullets into the marching crowd, killing innocent people and igniting what is known as the Soweto uprising, the bloodiest episode of riots between police and protestors since the 1960s.*

game was all about backing the future winners in the region and re-establishing trade and investment under the successor government it had anointed.

In 1980 a socialist-inclined liberation movement headed by Robert Mugabe took power after a landslide election victory. White South Africans did not share the benign view of the West of the new government that came to power on its northern border. As political scientist Deon Geldenhuys wrote at the time: 'South Africa is far from encouraged by [Zimbabwe]. Mugabe is hardly the personification of a friendly, co-operative neighbour or a leader who offers his white subjects a safe and happy haven.' The question was whether the same pattern would unfold in South Africa.

The Soweto uprising of 1976

Despite the turmoil on the northern borders resulting from the collapse of the Portuguese empire in 1974 and the increased activities of Swapo on the northern border of South West Africa, the political system in South Africa seemed remarkably stable on the surface. Speaking in court a month before the Soweto uprising in June 1976, Black Consciousness leader Steve Biko was adamant about one thing: 'The masses of black people within the country will increasingly become defiant.' They faced a police force ill-equipped to deal with large demonstrations – something later remarked on by General Magnus Malan, a leading figure in the military establishment. The cabinet at the time did not even know that the police were at liberty to use live ammunition in suppressing protests.

The underlying causes

Afrikaans was the trigger that brought Soweto pupils out in protest (*see box*); the reckless use of live ammunition by the police was the immediate cause that transformed a protest by school children into a massive uprising. As the comments by the paper *Ilanga* show (*see box*) there were certain deep-seated structural factors that caused the situation to explode once the first deadly police bullets were fired.

At the core of it all was the lack of political rights and freedom. Tsietsi Mashinini, the first leader of the Soweto students that the press identified, put it simply. Black students, he stated, were not only tired of the education system, but of 'the system of the country, the way laws are made by the white minority'.

Blacks in the urban areas enjoyed virtually no political rights, except on local level. The Urban Bantu Councils introduced in 1961 had very few political powers or financial resources. In 1972 Administration Boards, mainly staffed by white officials on the senior levels, were introduced to take over most of the running of the townships. Later the subsidies paid over to the townships from the (white) city council were also stopped. As a result the townships increasingly had to be funded by the rates and levies residents paid, supplemented by the income from the beer halls. Because this source of revenue was quite inadequate, frustration began to mount.

Next to the lack of political rights, the pass laws and the larger system of influx control were the main causes of discontent. These had been identified in a study of Soweto matriculants by Melville Edelstein, a welfare officer in Soweto. Ironically, he was killed by black students on the first day of the uprising. The causes were confirmed by Vic Leibbrandt, one the most senior officials in the department that administered the townships. He told the *Financial Mail*: '[I]nflux control is by far the greatest grievance that Africans have. They cannot understand why other racial groups are allowed the privilege of movement in South Africa while they are subject to rules and regulations which make life intolerable and above all create a positive hatred of the white man.'

In Soweto, opposition to 'Bantu education' introduced in 1954 was the strongest. It was here that the use of mother-tongue instruction and the disparities in per capita spending were resented most. In 1975–1976 fifteen times more was spent on a white child than a black child. Hand in hand with this went growing uncertainty about securing a job after leaving school.

AFRIKAANS AND THE SOWETO UPRISING

In the two decades before the uprising of 1976, Afrikaans had become identified among blacks in Soweto as the language of the oppressor – the medium used, for example, when white policemen arrested pass offenders or when white civil servants issued permits or ordered blacks out of their houses or out of the urban areas. The Black Sash gave this evidence to the Cillié Commission that investigated the causes of the Soweto uprising: 'We suspect that . . . Afrikaans has tragically come to be seen as the language of the minority oppressor who enforces the pass laws upon the subject majority.'

The formal policy towards the language of instruction outside the homelands was that Afrikaans and English had to be used on a 50-50 basis in black secondary schools, but it was not rigorously applied.

Vorster himself did not object when homeland leaders in 1974 requested that the official language in the homelands (in practice, English) also be used in black schools elsewhere.

Yet some of the officials of the Department of Bantu Administration and Development had almost become a law unto themselves. Andries Treurnicht, leader of the National Party's right wing and deputy minister of Bantu Administration and Development, held the view that the government had the right to decide the medium of instruction in black schools because white taxpayers subsidised the schools. This position was sure to provoke hostility, particularly in Soweto, now with a population of well over a million. Most jobs in Johannesburg required a command of English, and a 1972 survey of young

Sowetans found that 98% of them did not wish to be taught in Afrikaans. Half of those polled considered Afrikaners 'the most cruel and least sympathetic people in South Africa'.

Ignoring all this, the Department of Bantu Administration and Development early in 1976 decided to push ahead. Inspectors in Soweto and other schools in the southern Transvaal area gave instructions that mathematics and arithmetic had to be taught in Afrikaans alone, despite the fact that most teachers and pupils probably had no command of Afrikaans. Teacher organisations and black parents on school boards in the townships protested strongly, but the government ignored these protests and the warnings by the official opposition that a volatile situation was building up in Soweto.

The uprising

The defiance of children who had put fear behind them expressed itself in the demonstration of the morning of 16 June 1976. John Kane-Berman, a *Financial Mail* journalist, sketched the scene on that morning.

Twenty thousand Soweto schoolchildren marched in protest against a decree by the South African government's Department of Bantu Education that Afrikaans had to be used as one of the languages of instruction in secondary schools . . . Newspaper photographs and several eyewitness accounts suggest that the marching students were good-humoured, high-spirited and excited. Some were giving the clenched fist 'Black Power' salute. Others were carrying placards bearing slogans 'Down with Afrikaans,' 'We are not Boers,' and 'If we must do Afrikaans Vorster must do Zulu.'

Police vehicles rushed to the scene . . . The pupils taunted them and they responded with teargas . . . Apparently no order from the police to the marchers to disperse was heard, and a senior police officer admitted at the time that no warning shots had been fired either. The first child to be killed was evidently a thirteen-year-old schoolboy Hector Petersen, apparently by a bullet fired at him directly from behind. Several other youngsters were also shot dead. Then, in the words of one newspaper, 'All hell broke loose.'

Most of the leaders of the protesting black youth were inspired by the Black Consciousness movement. The protestors attacked and burned down Administration Board buildings, beer halls, schools, clinics and libraries and organised several work stoppages. A reporter who flew over Soweto wrote that he felt like 'a war correspondent flying over a city after a bomb attack'. After a lull the protests, particularly against Bantu education, flared up again despite the relaxation of the Afrikaans decree.

On 4 August some 20 000 students tried to march on the centre of Johannesburg but were turned back. In the subsequent months students tried to organise stay-aways of workers on several occasions. There was a successful campaign against rent increases, which forced the resignation of the Soweto Urban Bantu Council.

In the vacuum two important new bodies emerged. The one was the Committee of Ten, which was broadly representative and tried to present a plan for a Soweto city council that would enjoy widespread legitimacy. The other was the Soweto Students Representative Council, which tried to co-ordinate the action of the pupils.

RIGHT: *Schoolchildren protesting in the streets of Soweto on 16 June 1976.*

The security police increasingly targeted teachers and students in an attempt to quell the revolt. But it was only partly successful because of the mass nature of the participation. Jimmy Kruger, Minister of Police and Prisons, estimated that one-fifth of the residents of Soweto participated. More than 500 teachers resigned in the first year of the uprising. Secondary education in Soweto had been brought virtually to a standstill.

Violent protests in townships spread throughout the Transvaal, the northern Free State, Natal and KwaZulu, and the northern Cape. In August the Bophuthatswana legislative assembly in Mafeking was burned down. In the same month unrest in Port Elizabeth claimed 33 lives on the campuses of black universities. In the first four months after the events of 16 June some 160 communities demonstrated their anger and frustration. In the first six months 176 died, most shot and killed by the police.

Apart from Soweto, the most important centre of the revolt was Cape Town. There were huge demonstrations in Guguletu, Langa and Nyanga. Coloured pupils and university students demonstrated. Marches by both coloured and black children to the centre of Cape Town ended in bloody clashes with the police in the city centre. In December clashes broke out between youths and hostel dwellers, causing the destruction of numerous houses and the flight of thousands.

Black local councillors resigned in several towns and there were prolonged school boycotts. By October 1977, when the uprising finally subsided, between 600 and 700 people had been killed. The uprising had rocked South Africa and changed the political landscape. Thousands of children fled the country to continue the struggle. Most of them enlisted in the ANC, with many joining Umkhonto weSizwe.

In October 1977, Jimmy Kruger, now Minister of Justice, banned all the organisations associated with the Black Consciousness movement, Johannesburg's leading black newspaper *The World*, and the Christian Institute headed by Beyers Naudé.

In September 1977, Steve Biko died in horrifying circumstances of injuries inflicted by security policemen while in police custody. Despite the seriousness of his condition, he was given no proper medical treatment and was transported naked and shackled, 800 kilometres on the floor of a van to Pretoria, where he died. On hearing of Biko's death Kruger (apparently under the wrong impression that he had died following a hunger strike) declared to a party congress that Biko's death 'left him cold'. If the death illuminated how many political prisoners were at the mercy of the security police, the callousness of the responsible minister's response, and the failure of Vorster to dismiss him, betrayed the government's indifference, or worse.

TOP AND MIDDLE: *Anger explodes in Soweto on 16 June 1976.*

ABOVE: *The 1976 Soweto uprising spread to Cape Town, where police dragged away a man they shot during the protests.*

LEFT: *Jan Hamman won the press photographer of the year award in 1977 with this picture of two Soweto youths during the uprising, kneeling in front of the police and holding their hands in the air, showing the peace sign.*

RIGHT: *'Another cup of tea, sir?' This 1978 cartoon by Tony Grogan shows Connie Mulder, Minister of Information, trying to make light of the Information Scandal by describing it as a storm in a teacup.*

The uprising, Biko's horrific death and the banning of the black organisations accelerated the international isolation of South Africa. In 1977 the UN Security Council accepted a mandatory arms embargo and a voluntary oil embargo of South Africa.

Leadership crisis

The years 1976–1978 constituted a fundamental crisis for National Party rule. Apart from the worsening situation beyond the northern borders, there was the uprising in Soweto that spread throughout the country. Unlike at the time of the 1960 Sharpeville uprising, South Africans now had television and the images on the screen left little doubt about black hatred for the white system of rule. Especially disconcerting was the fact that black youths appeared to be much angrier and disaffected than their parents.

A second shock for the Nationalist elite was the publication in 1978 of two books on the Afrikaner Broederbond, one of which included an almost complete list of the secret organisation's members. It listed 13 262 members in 914 divisions. The organisation's influence, always overrated by scholars, was already on the wane, and the publication of members' lists removed the aura of secrecy (*see box*). Still, in a society that had become modern, secular and increasingly committed to transparency, the Bond was seen as outdated.

Yet another blow hit the Nationalist leadership in 1978, when the so-called 'Information Scandal' broke. The growing international rejection of apartheid had created something similar to a persecution complex among members of the government, who tended to see the world as divided between 'friends of South Africa' and its enemies.

South Africa still followed the conventional route to influence opinion, to the increasing irritation of Eschel Rhoodie, a brash and ambitious administrative head of the Department of Information. He felt that the greatest threat to the state was the growth of the anti-apartheid lobby in the West where a divestment campaign was rapidly gaining support, especially in universities and churches. To change the negative perceptions of South Africa, the country had to embark on an unconventional propaganda war with large financial resources.

From the start he had the backing of Connie Mulder, Minister of Information and heir-apparent of Vorster, and Hendrik van den Bergh, the head of the Bureau for State Security (Boss). Early in 1974 Vorster and Nic Diederichs, the Minister of Finance, promised to give financial and tacit support.

Over the next five years, as numerous secret projects were launched, a history of sleaze, corruption, violation of exchange control regulations, murder and lies in Parliament accumulated. Since one of the thorns in the government's side was the English press, one of the main projects was to found a sympathetic newspaper.

To launch *The Citizen*, the Department of Information employed secret state funds, using Afrikaner fertiliser tycoon Louis Luyt as its front. Its circulation figures were falsified from the start. Luyt, in turn, unsuccessfully tried to buy one of the two English newspaper chains.

Through other fronts the Department attempted to buy *The Washington Star*, the French journal *L'Equipe*, and a British investors' journal. A fictitious club of businessmen, called the Club of Ten, placed advertisements in overseas publications.

Things turned deadly serious in late 1977 when Robert Smit, an Afrikaans-speaking National Party candidate for the upcoming election, and his wife were murdered in what looked like a deed perpetrated by hired killers. As a government official Smit had previously attended meetings of the International Monetary Fund. When the Information Scandal burst it was widely speculated that Smit had been on the point of revealing the currency control violations. No one was ever arrested for the murders.

A leader toppled

By early 1978 rumours about the projects of the Department of Information were rife. Vorster seemed distracted, while Mulder, ahead in the race for his succession, was confronted in Parliament with the question of whether the government was funding *The Citizen*. He answered in the negative, which, as a commission later found, was a public lie. He was soon forced out of the party. Vorster tried to hide his complicity and later resigned as prime minister to become state president, hoping that his colleagues would stand by him as he so often had done for them.

On 28 September 1978 Pieter Willem (P.W.) Botha narrowly defeated Mulder to become the next prime minister. Eleven months later Vorster was compelled to resign as state president. A Commission of Inquiry found that he had known for a long time about the irregular activities of the Department of Information.

Vorster had removed some of the cruder aspects of apartheid but he failed to use the ten years of stability between the mid-1960s and the mid-1970s to develop a new strategic approach that could possibly set South Africa on a course of fundamental but peaceful change.

A 'total onslaught'

In 1977 the Department of Defence published a White Paper spelling out the belief of P.W. Botha and the military that South Africa faced a 'total onslaught' in virtually every area of society. Threats could only be countered by a 'total strategy' against subversive elements.

The battle had to be fought on two fronts. There were the challenges of liberation organisations with Marxist leanings coming to power in neighbouring states. Internally there were the grievances of a subordinate black population that was poor and without rights. Improving socio-economic conditions in the townships was seen as essential for the white-dominated political order and the free-enterprise system to prevail.

From the mid-1970s the speeches of senior generals had as their recurring theme that the struggle against revolutionaries was 20% military and 80% socio-economic. As one phrased it: 'If South Africa lost the socio-economic struggle we need not bother to fight the military one. The objective is no longer territory but the hearts and minds of men.'

ABOVE: *Louis Luyt, a fertiliser tycoon, was used by the Department of Information as a front for the newspaper* The Citizen, *which it published with secret state funds. The paper's circulation figures were falsified from the start. Luyt also unsuccessfully tried to buy one of the two English-language newspaper chains on behalf of the department. Through other fronts, the department attempted to buy* The Washington Star, *the French journal* L'Equipe, *and a British investors' journal, to no avail.*

'Adapt or die'

In September 1978 P.W. Botha became prime minister of South Africa. His politics were formed by two quite different influences. He was a career politician who had started as a full-time organiser for the National Party, where he learned the importance of organisational efficiency. The other influence was the military. As Minister for Defence he rapidly built up the South African army, based on a relatively small permanent force and a large annual intake of white conscripts.

In 1979 he was reported to have said: 'We are moving into a changing world, we must adapt otherwise we shall die.' Adapt or die – these striking words seemed to encapsulate the approach of Botha, who injected a much greater dynamism into the process of reform than B.J. Vorster had done.

He was determined, energetic and purposeful, but also brash and impetuous, the kind of leader that was willing to adapt but was also spoiling for a fight. He seemed to signal that far-reaching change was on the way. He called blacks 'fellow South Africans', visited Soweto with 'a message of hope', and toured all the homelands. *The Washington Post* wrote that these changes astonished blacks and kindled hopes of an alternative to violence and despair.

Like the security officials and military, Botha was inspired by the work of counter-revolutionary strategists who argued that states had to defend themselves against communist subversion not only by military means but also by combating political and ideological attacks.

Botha soon embarked on wide-ranging administrative reforms to improve the capacity of the state. He thoroughly overhauled the machinery of the government; he strengthened the prime minister's office and established a proper cabinet secretariat. He turned the State Security Council, established in 1972, into a key body to discuss and resolve matters in the field of security and foreign policy. He now chaired the body on which ministers dealing with security and other strategic interests sat, together with the heads of the various security agencies.

The council supervised the working of a National Security Management System, with Joint Management Centres (JMCs) for twelve national regions, sub-JMCs for metropolitan centres and mini-JMCs for each town, where officials and businessmen met under the chairmanship of a military or police officer. The JMCs provided information on local security and acted as an early warning system by spotting areas of friction and identifying

RIGHT: *A 1979* Cape Times *cartoon by Tony Grogan, showing Piet Koornhof (left), minister of the department that dealt with most matters affecting blacks, and who proclaimed apartheid dead in 1979. He is with P.W. Botha, who supported trade union rights for black workers, but rejected the abolition of residential segregation and population registration. On the right is Andries Treurnicht, who propagated the restoration of apartheid.*

bureaucratic obstacles to improvements in living conditions in the townships. Behind this lay a managerial approach that assumed blacks were primarily interested in having their social needs met.

In pursuit of settlement in South West Africa

From the 1960s South Africa's administration of South West Africa (SWA) – now Namibia – threatened to bring it into direct confrontation with the world community. The UN recognised Swapo as the 'sole legitimate representative of the Namibian people', and in 1974 the Security Council unanimously asked South Africa to transfer power as soon as possible.

A contact group of major Western powers was established to negotiate with South Africa about handing over power to the indigenous population. South Africa faced extensive sanctions if the matter were not resolved. The Vorster government now accepted the principle of self-determination in SWA, but it also argued that the internal parties (non-Swapo) had the right to spell out its future vision. In September 1975 representatives of all the major parties except Swapo met in the Turnhalle in Windhoek to deliberate on a constitution. In 1977 they agreed on a document that tried to combine ethnic and individual rights. Dirk Mudge, who broke away from the National Party and formed the non-racial Democratic Turnhalle Alliance, played the key role.

In February 1978 the Vorster government committed itself to independence for SWA before the end of 1978, and two months later accepted a plan drawn up by Western powers (United States, Canada, Britain, France and Germany) for a settlement that would be presented to the UN Assembly after all the parties, both internal and external, had agreed. South Africa would remain in control until April 1979, when an election would be held for a government to steer SWA to independence.

Minister of Defence P.W. Botha was a dissenting voice in the cabinet, but he got permission to attack a large Swapo base in Cassinga, Angola, 250 kilometres north of the SWA border. In the battle as many as 600 Swapo fighters and other followers died. After Botha became prime minister he and the military hawks could set the agenda. South Africa pulled out of the UN plan and announced that it would sponsor internal elections in SWA in December 1978. The obvious aim was that of building an internal counter to Swapo.

For the December election in SWA, 78% of the potential electorate and 85% of those registered voted. The Democratic Turnhalle Alliance (DTA), a multiracial moderate alliance, emerged as the victor. But, as in the case of the internal election held in Rhodesia in 1979, the international community refused to recognise the election. Swapo had not participated and South Africa had given strong financial backing to the DTA, which had failed to attract any significant support among the Ovambos, the largest ethnic group.

The number of Cuban troops in the region had increased from 14 000 in 1977 to 25 000 by 1983; in addition there were 5 000 military personnel from the Soviet Union and other East Bloc countries. A US delegation led by Judge William Clark visited South Africa in 1981, offering a quid pro quo that South Africa quickly seized. In exchange for South Africa working towards an internationally recognised election in SWA, the conservative Reagan administration in Washington would commit itself to get the Cubans out of the region. The common idea was that South African and Cuban troops would withdraw simultaneously and there would be no partisan UN role. Only then would an election be held.

The Botha government continued to attempt to weaken Swapo so that it would disappear as a significant factor in a future election. In successive operations in the early 1980s South African troops established a buffer zone in the southern part of Angola and launched military attacks against Swapo bases. Across the border in Angola, large-scale aid flowed to Unita. With South African assistance it had become an efficient force, controlling large parts of the south and putting the Angolan army under pressure in the central region. Kept far out by a South Africa-controlled zone in the south of Angola,

BELOW: *P.W. Botha, prime minister of South Africa from 1978 to 1984 and executive state president from 1984 to 1989. Botha and his namesake Louis were the only prime ministers who did not hold university degrees. P.W. Botha dropped out of undergraduate studies in Bloemfontein to become a full-time organiser for the National Party in the Cape Province. He soon became part of the inner circle of the Cape National Party. As Minister for Defence between 1966 and 1978 he played a large part in the modernisation of the defence force.*

4 / GRASSROOTS / SEPTEMBER 1989

Comrade Sam Nujoma returns after 30 years

ABOVE: *Samuel Daniel Nujoma was born in northern Ovamboland in 1929. He worked as a manual labourer in the then South West Africa before fleeing into exile. In 1960 he became president of the South West African People's Organisation. In 1989, when Swapo won the UN-supervised election, he became the first president of Namibia.*

Swapo was unable to infiltrate guerrillas in any significant numbers. But there was no indication of a weakening of the will of either Cuba's Fidel Castro or the Swapo leadership, or a wavering of Swapo support.

Through providing veterinary services, drilling boreholes, building clinics and other 'hearts-and-minds' operations, the South African troops tried to win the support of the population in Ovamboland. Some observers considered it 'one of the most successful counter-insurgency campaigns in history' undertaken by a military force. But this was undercut by *Koevoet* ('Crowbar'), a special counter-insurgency unit operating as part of the police force, which developed a frightening reputation for cruelty and ruthlessness in capturing and killing Swapo guerrillas.

Destabilisation

Fighting had intensified in southern Africa from the mid-1970s and explosives, rockets and automatic rifles had poured in. The security establishment in South Africa wanted permission to hit guerrillas as far beyond the border as possible. It also wished to put pressure on neighbour states to refuse sanctuary to ANC guerrillas.

By 1980 South Africa and the black states in the region were not yet on a collision course. Botha had invited them to become part of his Constellation of States, but they rejected the offer and formed the Southern African Development Co-ordinating Council (SADCC), which aimed to reduce their economic dependence on South Africa. There were early signs that their lessened dependence translated into increased support for ANC guerrillas, at that point infiltrating into South Africa through neighbouring countries, particularly Mozambique, Lesotho, Swaziland and Botswana.

From 1981 South Africa embarked on what became known as a campaign of destabilisation of the region to achieve its security objectives. In fact, the campaign had two objectives: both talk and thump. One was to convince Africans in the region of the 'folly' of Marxist policies. The other was military intervention to drive ANC guerrillas from the region. In 1982 the National Intelligence Service was instrumental in arranging a visit from CIA head William Casey, who met with Botha and his security advisers. They agreed that it was possible to build a new *cordon sanitaire* by forcing neighbouring states to expel guerrillas within their borders in exchange for South Africa ending their destabilisation.

To force its neighbours' hands South Africa bombed ANC facilities in Matola, Maputo and Maseru and supported dissident factions in eastern Zimbabwe, Lesotho and particularly in Mozambique, which had become the main route of ANC guerrillas into South Africa. Under severe pressure from Pretoria, the Frelimo government was compelled to sign the Nkomati Accord in 1984 (*see box*).

The ring of pliant states around South Africa and the destabilisation measures made it difficult for the ANC to pursue its armed struggle with any great effect. An ANC insider calculated that approximately half of a total of 12 000 trained guerrillas were infiltrated into South Africa. Of these, a third abandoned their mission, and many of the others were turned by the security forces, killed or convicted and sent to jail. In 1987 Zulu Chief Mangosuthu Buthelezi commented on the lack of any significant success in the armed struggle. 'After twenty-five years of endeavour every bridge in the country is still intact and there is not a single factory out of production because of revolutionary activity. The classical circumstances in which the armed struggle wins the day . . . are just not present in South Africa.'

But this success in stemming the armed struggle was not decisive. For blacks engaged in resistance, any evidence of ANC-directed armed activity – even if negligible and intermittent – raised the morale. The knowledge that the ANC had a military organisation that could retaliate was enough for many young people to fight back, even with stones.

A precious unity lost

The Soweto uprising imparted a body blow to white complacency, and precipitated an urgent search for allies. The major question confronting government was whether constitutional change should be piecemeal – initially incorporating only the coloured and Indian communities, which formed 8% and 3% of the population respectively – or

The Front for the Liberation of Mozambique (Frelimo) government under Samora Machel was an easy target for destabilisation by South Africa, using as its instrument the Resistencia Nacional de Mocambique (Renamo).

Unlike Unita, Renamo was not based on an ethnic group or rival liberation movement; it also lacked a charismatic leader and its system of command and communications was primitive. Its numbers were estimated to have reached 15 000 by the mid-1980s, but it was never much more than a band of brigands. It could operate so successfully only because Frelimo had very tenuous control over large parts of the country. With South African help it cut railway lines, mined roads, blew up fuel depots, destroyed grain stores and disrupted the export and import routes of the border states. More than a million people were displaced.

In addition, parcel bombs sent by operatives in the South African security services to Maputo killed Ruth First (a prominent academic and estranged wife of Joe Slovo, one of the ANC's principal military strategists) and seriously injured Albie Sachs (a leading ANC-supporting academic).

By 1984 the pressure on the Machel government in Mozambique was so intense that it signed the Nkomati Accord with South Africa. Both sides pledged to deny sanctuary to irregular forces and not to support violent actions against the neighbouring state. Effectively this meant that the ANC would be prohibited from operating from Mozambique, and that South Africa would stop backing movements that sought to overthrow the Frelimo government.

The Machel government expelled 800 ANC activists, and South Africa returned 1 000 Renamo guerrillas. But nothing much had changed. Since South Africa had liberally supplied Renamo with arms before the signing of the accord, it was not seriously weakened. At the same time Frelimo did not cease its help to ANC guerrillas, although this now occurred in greater secrecy.

After the introduction of the Tricameral Constitution and the signing of the Nkomati Accord between South Africa and Mozambique, conservative Western governments bestowed great praise on President Botha.

Both British Prime Minister Margaret Thatcher and German Chancellor Helmut Kohl described it as a triumph for the peaceful solution of problems. President Reagan called it an extraordinary agreement that would deny opportunities to the Soviet Union, 'which has sought to profit from violence and confrontation'.

Ruth First

Albie Sachs

whether it should, from the start, include blacks. The fateful road that it took was to bring coloureds and Indians into Parliament, but not blacks.

To the more enlightened voters it explained that demolishing the symbolism of white supremacy and exclusivity could not happen in one fell swoop, and that the incorporation of blacks would soon follow. To its more conservative supporters the government stressed the need for winning support beyond white ranks for the struggle against blacks. The National Party's chief information officer appealed to the right wing's survival instincts. He wrote to Andries Treurnicht, leader of the right wing faction in the NP caucus: 'I would like to know your view on the idea that we at any price have got to associate the Coloureds as a bloc of 2.5 million with the whites in order to broaden our own power base, and not surrender them to the "black-power" situation.'

By 1980 acute tensions had developed in the NP between the factions under Botha and Andries Treurnicht. The conservative faction was prepared to accept coloured and Indian representation in separate houses of Parliament, but Botha insisted that there could be only one government and one parliament in one country (*see box*).

On 24 February 1982 Treurnicht and 21 other NP members of Parliament left the

ABOVE: *Ruth First, who was married to Joe Slovo, and Albie Sachs (as painted by Marjorie Wallace). Both Sachs and First were respected academics who combined their research and teaching with active involvement in the ANC-led movement. Both fell victim to bomb attacks in covert action by South African government agents.*

The National Party (NP) presented the new more inclusive constitution as a form of 'healthy power-sharing', one in which the NP could never be outvoted by a coalition of the white opposition, coloureds and Indians. There was now a Parliament with a white, a coloured and an Indian chamber elected on separate rolls according to a fixed 4:2:1 ratio that corresponded with population size. An electoral college drawn from all three houses elected an executive state president.

Each house had its own cabinet and budget to deal with the 'own' affairs of its community, mainly education, housing and social welfare. There were also 'general' affairs – defence, security, and economic policy. Bills were discussed and passed separately by each house. The 'power-sharing' element was introduced by the requirement that all houses had to approve a bill and that coloured and Indian ministers could serve in the general affairs cabinet (Botha appointed the leaders of the coloured and Indian chambers to his cabinet).

But the lever of white control was retained; the NP as the largest party in the white chamber effectively elected the state president, who could use a President's Council, a multiracial advisory body of experts mostly supportive of him, to break any deadlocks if a house refused to pass a bill. It was, as the saying of the time went, a form of 'sharing power without losing control'.

caucus and formed the Conservative Party (CP). Previously the NP had suffered 'splinters', but this was the end of Afrikaner nationalist unity, cultivated over so many decades.

The NP presented the constitution as merely a first step in an unspecified 'right direction'. The liberal opposition opposed the constitution as a provocation to blacks by underlining their political exclusion, and Buthelezi slammed it. But Chris Heunis, the tough, resourceful and overbearing Minister for Constitutional Development, managed to persuade the Labour Party, the main coloured party working within the system, to participate, which set the ball rolling.

In 1983, the NP held a referendum of white voters in which two-thirds approved the draft constitution. Subsequently elections for the coloured and Indian chambers were held, which showed a lack of broad-based legitimacy. Only 30% of the registered coloured voters and 24% of Indians bothered to vote. The system was introduced in September 1984 with Botha as the first elected state president.

Blacks in general saw the partial incorporation of coloured people and Indians as a blunt rejection of their demand for common citizenship. Their alienation was aggravated when the government offered the homelands system, together with a new system of segregated black local authorities, as a reason for denying blacks any representation in Parliament.

A fatal attraction

For the government the apartheid model of ten black homelands, each with its own government, held a fatal attraction that blinded it to the need for imaginative responses to escape from a blind alley. The homeland governments, each with its own chief minister, cabinets, legislatures and fully fledged civil service, offered channels for black advancement that did not threaten whites. In general these governments concerned themselves with homeland affairs, and did not attempt to extract meaningful concessions from Pretoria.

In 1976 the South African government granted 'independence' to the Transkei, although it was the only government in the world that recognised it. This was followed by

Bophuthatswana in 1977, Ciskei in 1979 and Venda in 1980. With independence, their citizens, even if they lived permanently in the common area, lost their South African citizenship. Xhosa-speakers living in squatter camps in Cape Town were deported to their 'independent homeland' under laws covering aliens. Similarly, a homeland government could expel from its territory any person who belonged to an ethnic group outside the homeland. The government classified funds supplied to the homelands as 'foreign aid'.

As the homelands became 'independent', the basis of discrimination, in the government's eyes, would shift from race, which was objectionable to the world, to citizenship of an 'independent country'. Connie Mulder, who became Minister for Plural Relations (previously Bantu Administration and Development) in 1978, openly stated that once all the homelands had become independent there would be no black South Africans left.

The progressive parliamentary opposition

Between 1961 and 1974 Helen Suzman was the lone representative of the Progressive Party (PP), which proposed a non-racial qualified vote and the constitutional protection of minorities. With many African states in the 1960s quickly abandoning the spirit if not the letter of their constitution and starting to experiment with socialism and state capitalism, white voters in general saw little to attract them to the PP's policy.

After the 1974 election six newly elected PP members joined Suzman in Parliament. Although the United Party won 41 out of 169 seats, and close to a third of the votes cast, it was rudderless. It collapsed in 1977 with some of its representatives forming the New Republic Party and others joining the PP, which was now reconstituted as the Progressive Federal Party (PFP) under the leadership of Colin Eglin.

In 1979 Frederik van Zyl Slabbert became leader of the PFP. Like Jan Smuts, he was an Afrikaner leading a predominantly English party. He was also a very different, modern kind of politician – an ex-academic widely respected for his analytical abilities and

Elected for the first time to Parliament in 1953, Helen Suzman was a determined and eloquent voice for a democratic non-racial alternative. Fully engaged and fiercely committed to her cause, she used a probing mind, parliamentary questions, and personal visits to prisons, including Robben Island, to expose the iniquities of apartheid and the way in which the policy affected ordinary people.

She was often the only dissenting vote in Parliament when the government proposed draconian security bills that gave the police much scope to grill and even torture detainees. By holding up a consistent and committed view of liberal democracy, she began to attract a younger generation of whites who were relatively affluent and well qualified. The English-language newspapers began to shift allegiance from the United Party to the Progressive Party.

The large majority of National Party members in Parliament found Suzman's views on racial policy abhorrent. Yet the general respect for Parliament as an institution was such that they allowed her to use the system to the best of her ability. Ministers regularly replied to her parliamentary questions and the Speaker of the House of Assembly gave her ample time to speak.

Hendrik Verwoerd called her an 'outstanding parliamentarian with well-considered arguments'. Black leaders also paid tribute. For Albert Luthuli she was 'a bright star in a dark chamber', and Nelson Mandela remarked that when he and his comrades were in captivity in Robben Island 'it was a wonderful sight to see this courageous woman peering into our cells'. The poet Breyten Breytenbach, in jail in Pollsmoor for opposing apartheid, called her 'Our Lady of the Prisoners'. She clashed bitterly with National Party leaders before 1989 but with F.W. de Klerk she enjoyed a relationship of mutual respect.

Suzman left Parliament in 1989, having won the respect of large numbers of people outside the ranks of the ANC in exile. She had incurred the organisation's wrath by consistently opposing sanctions and the armed struggle as likely to increase white-black polarisation.

Helen Suzman

distaste for the horse-trading and messy compromises of party politics. Slabbert concluded that apartheid had irreversibly failed. Time and again he ridiculed the huge gap between the promises of apartheid ideology and the sordid reality.

Slabbert also recognised the need for a thorough review of his party's racial policy. The qualified franchise had become outdated in an era of mass movements and mass democracy. The Soweto uprising of 1976, which imparted a severe shock to the system of white rule, expedited the search for an alternative. In 1978 the PFP accepted a new policy. The Lower House, the seat of legislative power, would be chosen on the basis of general adult franchise on a common roll on a system of proportional representation. The Upper House would consist of representatives of several federal states, and 10% of the representatives in the Lower House would be able to veto all measures, except certain financial and administrative matters and the election of the prime minister. Except for the minority veto, which the party never vigorously defended, it was a classic liberal-democratic policy that normally works only in ethnically homogeneous societies.

Initially the PFP did well, although the white electorate had little enthusiasm for its policy. Before the 1987 election it had 25 out of 166 seats and 16% of the votes cast. But as a party the PFP was under intense pressure. In January 1986, the uprising that had started in September 1984 showed no sign of abating. Slabbert resigned from Parliament, calling the institution irrelevant.

Buthelezi: ally or foe?

A stumbling block in the government's homelands strategy was Mangosuthu Buthelezi, chief minister of the KwaZulu homeland in Natal. More than any other opposition his tough stand against independence for the Zulu people, forming 20% of the total population, destroyed the government's hope to construct 'a constellation of black states' out of the homeland system. But in 1979 he fell out with the ANC in exile over sanctions and the armed struggle.

The ANC-Inkatha relationship deteriorated into bitter enmity, with the ANC branding Buthelezi as a counter-revolutionary force. It correctly saw him as much more dangerous than the other homeland leaders, who were, it said, mere puppets. Buthelezi thought that the armed struggle and sanctions were destroying the chance for peaceful change. Yet he also told Botha that violence could not be averted 'by marching to anti-communist drums'. Violence would flow not from Marxist subversion but from white and black leaders losing control of their constituencies.

Buthelezi offered a clear alternative to the National Party approach by proposing a multiracial federation. In 1981 a commission he had appointed proposed the integration of the white-controlled province of Natal and the KwaZulu homeland, to be run by an assembly elected by proportional representation and a multiracial executive making decisions along power-sharing lines. A single body would control education, the local economy and welfare services. These proposals were given flesh by a multiracial Natal *indaba* in the mid-1980s, and received the backing of the business leadership in the province and the liberal opposition.

ABOVE: *Mangosuthu Buthelezi served as chief minister of the KwaZulu homeland. He used his exceptional political skills to put together a platform that formally rejected the homelands system, but also used it as a cover for building a mass movement. He projected himself as both a Zulu nationalist and an African nationalist and there is reason to believe that Nelson Mandela, in jail in Robben Island, secretly encouraged him to use the Zulu homeland structures in order to promote African nationalism. In 1979 Buthelezi fell out with the ANC over sanctions and the armed struggle.*

Here was a last opportunity for the government to avoid losing control over the process of change. If it backed regional integration in KwaZulu-Natal (without trying to control it), it could spark similar initiatives in other regions of the country. From these regions properly elected black leaders could be elevated to the national cabinet. But Botha's response was in the classic apartheid mode. Buthelezi was welcome to investigate matters that concerned 'his own country', but had no right to deal with matters under the control of central government.

By the late 1970s the idea of economically viable homelands had hopelessly faded. Even the Transkei, the best prospect, could meet only 10% of its own food requirements and provided for only 20% of its budgeted expenses out of its own resources. The great majority of people in the homelands were dependent on pensions and the money migrant labourers sent back to their families, most of which flowed back to shops in the common area. Migrant labour thus served as an engine that generated an ever-greater dependency and poverty of blacks in the homelands.

Fears for the future

Botha had considerably more leeway than his predecessors, since large numbers of English-speakers were up for grabs. A new fluidity in white politics had developed after the United Party, led by Sir De Villiers Graaff for more than twenty years, disintegrated in 1977. Between 25% and 40% of English-speakers were sympathetic to the National Party's cautious approach to reform.

The solutions the Conservative Party under Treurnicht offered had all been totally discredited. There was no black homeland or black or coloured township that was financially viable.

Yet because conservatives increasingly distrusted the National Party government, Treurnicht was able to take large numbers of Afrikaners with him. By 1987 the votes of all the right-wing parties in the general election amounted to almost 30% of all votes, and the Conservative Party had become the official opposition. By the end of the 1980s nearly half of the Afrikaners voted for right-wing parties. In general, Afrikaner expectations of black rule were negative. More than four-fifths of Afrikaners in polls taken in 1979, 1984 and 1987 believed that under black majority rule there would be reverse discrimination, and that the Afrikaans language and culture would be threatened.

ABOVE: *Andries Treurnicht, born in 1921, was first a church minister, then a conservative newspaper editor, and later a National Party minister. As Deputy Minister for Bantu Education he participated in the decision to enforce Afrikaans as a medium of instruction in Soweto, which triggered the uprising. He founded the Conservative Party in 1982.*

OPPOSITE BOTTOM: *Frederik van Zyl Slabbert with his first wife, Mana.*

There was also another dimension: fear. More than 80% believed that the physical safety of whites would be threatened, that white possessions would not be safe, and that white women would be molested. Less than 10% thought that life would continue as before. The extent of the fears was visible in the ownership of firearms – at least one firearm per white adult. These fears translated into growing right wing support.

In the meantime support for the ANC had grown. As part of its armed struggle the ANC had carried out 362 violent acts between 1976 and 1983. Guerrillas had struck at

some high-profile targets, including a Sasol (oil from coal) plant in 1980, the Voortrekker-hoogte military base in Pretoria in 1981, and the Koeberg nuclear reactor near Cape Town in 1982. An ANC car bomb exploded in 1983 at the Air Force headquarters in Pretoria's Church Street, killing nineteen people.

The ANC in exile

For most of its 30 or so years in exile to 1990, the ANC's choice of strategy did not match the quality of its will to confront the apartheid state. ANC exiles spent the first two decades imprisoned within an unhelpful set of assumptions about what means of struggle were sufficient to achieve the outcomes they sought. Over this period, they conducted clandestine operations as if armed struggle was not merely a necessary condition to achieve fundamental change in South Africa but as if it alone was sufficient to do so. This entailed disregarding a cornerstone of insurgent strategy. Insurgents who resort to armed struggle usually stress the need to redress the asymmetry between their own initial military weakness and the enemy state's strength.

For two decades, ANC exiles substantially disregarded mobilisation by political means as a way of achieving some kind of symmetry with the enemy. In the process, not only did they forego the possibility of a political base able to sustain guerrilla operations inside South Africa; they also disregarded legal and semi-legal space inside the country for building popular political organisations of various types. These failings curtailed the pressure they could apply against the apartheid state.

As a result of the particular strategy that was followed, the years in exile of members of the different liberation movements proved to be a longer and more difficult learning experience than they might otherwise have been. They were sustained through the fifteen-odd years to 1976 and beyond largely by a mix of fortitude and the broad foreign support they developed. The ANC, through its overlapping relationship with the SA Communist Party, received military training and equipment from the Soviet Union and its allies. The Organisation of African Unity and its Liberation Committee mobilised what diplomatic and material support they could from young, poor and often badly led member states.

Anti-apartheid movements in Western countries, drawing support from liberal and communist alike, became sources of pressure on their governments and on businesses with South African interests. Later, generous funding reached the ANC from some Western governments, notably Sweden's.

A failed military strategy

Assorted early ANC attempts to return a military presence to South Africa failed. ANC exiles faced two major problems: they had no domestic political base, and in the early 1960s apartheid enjoyed a huge land buffer to its north. In these circumstances, ANC exiles at one point planned a sea-borne landing by guerrillas. But the plan was aborted after problems with the boat and its crew.

A disastrous setback in Rhodesia (*see box on page 378*) – the second in eight years – led to ANC leadership and strategy being questioned, though not fundamentally. In 1969, senior members gathered in Tanzania to resolve the situation. Little changed. Tambo's leadership was confirmed. Nobody was seriously censured for the Rhodesian debacle. White, coloured and

Indian activists who had been working in exile with the ANC – invariably communists from former Congress Alliance organisations – were now allowed formally to join the ANC external mission, though not the ANC itself. And strategy remained fixed. The core conference document on strategy and tactics claimed that armed struggle was 'the *only* [emphasis added] method left open' to the ANC. Nods towards political mobilisation were more rote than meaningful. The ANC had to plan for 'future all-out war' ending in 'conquest of power'. A new Revolutionary Council was established to oversee operations, and drew in individuals who would become significant later. They included Thabo Mbeki, Joe Slovo and Chris Hani.

The military emphasis in strategy from 1961 seems to have had two main origins. The first was a questionable, though briefly fashionable, doctrine developed by Che Guevara and Regis Debray out of the Cuban revolution. It suggested guerrilla activity by a small group could induce mass political mobilisation and detonate revolution. A second influence appears to have been the bitter Sino-Soviet split in 1965 in which the SA Communist Party and, in its wake, the ANC backed Moscow. But, in the revolutionary canon, the main champion of political mobilisation by political means in guerrilla warfare was the Chinese communist leader Mao Zedong. The Soviet Union was suggesting an alternative: mobile warfare, an intermediate form between guerrilla and conventional warfare. Hence the form of the Rhodesian campaigns.

Winning hearts and minds

Between 1969 and 1975 several developments improved the exiles' prospects. The Revolutionary Council deployed talent to states adjacent to South Africa, including Thabo Mbeki briefly to Botswana and Swaziland, and Hani to Lesotho. They made cross-border contact with ANC veterans released from Robben Island, among them Jacob Zuma, who were rebuilding an underground network inside South Africa and linking up with Black Consciousness activists, many of whom were won over to the ANC when they arrived in exile. The ANC external mission survived a potentially disastrous breakaway by eight leaders who alleged the ANC had been taken over by communists. And a coup in Portugal in April 1974 led a year later to the independence of Angola and Mozambique under liberation movements allied to the ANC. This would give the exiles military training camps in Angola and a new forward capacity via Mozambique.

When the assertiveness of Black Consciousness encountered harsh state repression in June 1976, resulting in uprisings in Soweto and elsewhere, the ANC in exile was uniquely placed to benefit. However embryonic its networks inside South Africa and in adjacent countries, the ANC won over most of the thousands of young students who flooded into exile seeking new weapons against apartheid. The ANC's rivals in exile, chiefly the Pan-Africanist Congress, lacked comparable energy and organisation after years of chronic infighting and corruption.

But one factor above all others made the ANC the organisation that fleeing students wanted to join. It was the ANC's earlier attempts to confront apartheid militarily. No rival group could claim comparable efforts. The ANC might be criticised for the ineptitude of its military campaigns. But now, paradoxically, its earlier efforts, most manifest in their failure, bought it crucial political advantage: the hearts and minds of a new generation. Soon ANC membership in exile had multiplied into the thousands. International supporters, appalled at increased repression in South Africa, poured resources into it.

These new conditions allowed the ANC to resume military activity inside South Africa. But the new military campaign, despite the sensation it caused, was soon in trouble. From 1977, first handfuls then scores of new young recruits were returned into the country. But their targets were invariably symbolic, their periods of survival inside the country were short – seldom more than a few days or weeks – and the intensity of the campaign remained very low. In the Mafikeng-Zeerust areas, for example, there were occasional firefights between MK guerrillas and Bophuthatswana Defence Force and SADF soldiers. The result was an increasingly fractious search in exile for the reasons armed struggle was failing to take root domestically and grow. Eventually, a commission was set up to inquire into strategy.

THE ANGUISH OF EXILE

By late 1965, the ANC and SA Communist Party inside South Africa had been destroyed. Their popular support was cowed. The steadfast numbered a few hundred in exile and in prison. Apartheid had survived the ANC's challenge. The white supremacist National Party was again firmly in control of the country. The economy resumed healthy growth. The state closest to South Africa from which the exiles could operate freely in 1965 was thousands of kilometres to the north – in Tanzania.

An ANC external mission led by Oliver Tambo based itself in Dar es Salaam and London. The ANC was cash-strapped, particularly in Africa, and conditions in its camps harsh. What optimism survived relied heavily on notions of national or class destiny that so often lie at the heart of nationalist and communist belief systems: notwithstanding grave setbacks, history ordained that victory was 'certain'.

Exiles' lives were often anguished. Many were cut off from family. They were uncertain about the fate met by comrades left behind. And they often experienced feelings of dislocation and irrelevance, with some resorting to heavy drinking. Ronnie Kasrils was among a few hundred Umkhonto we-Sizwe recruits undergoing military training in Ukraine in the early 1960s as the Rivonia Trial in Pretoria decapitated the ANC and Communist Party internally. He recalls how, as they goose-stepped around with commands being barked out in Russian, he and his comrades 'firmly believed that capitalism was in decay and that monopolistic contradictions would bring the system down . . . With the help of the Soviet bloc, the former colonies would find a non capitalist path to socialism.'

OPPOSITE TOP: *Joe Slovo in Zambia in October 1986.*

OPPOSITE MIDDLE: *Thabo Mbeki in discussion with Johnstone Makatini.*

OPPOSITE BOTTOM: *Oliver Tambo, Thabo Mbeki and Alfred Nzo in exile.*

When Southern Rhodesia's white minority unilaterally declared independence from Britain in November 1965 rather than cede further powers to the black majority, this represented a challenge both to local liberation movements, such as the Zimbabwe African People's Union (Zapu), and to the ANC. In response, Zapu and the ANC planned a joint military campaign in then-Rhodesia. After little reconnaissance or political preparation, sporadically over the year from August 1967 several score of Zapu and ANC fighters crossed the Zambezi River from newly independent Zambia into the northwest of Rhodesia in columns bigger than would normally be deployed in the early phases of a guerrilla war.

The initial ANC force – named the Luthuli Detachment following the death of the ANC's president in South Africa a month earlier – was to split: the smaller force was to help Zapu develop a guerrilla war inside Rhodesia; the larger to head for South Africa. South African government forces joined battle inside Rhodesia against ANC-Zapu forces. What the ANC called its Wankie and Sipolilo campaigns ended in routs. One ANC fighter eventually reached South Africa. The remainder were killed, captured or fled west into Botswana where they were promptly jailed by Seretse Khama's government.

ABOVE: *The flag used by Zapu during the liberation struggle in the then Rhodesia.*

The Vietnamese model of success

In 1979 an ANC commission visited Vietnam, then the pre-eminent instance of insurgent success. Its report represented a turning point. In line with Vietnamese advice, the 1979 report challenged the ANC's disregard for political organisation by political means. Henceforth, the report suggested, the ANC's stress should fall on developing new political organisations inside South Africa – underground and popular – and working with what already existed. The challenge was to establish a domestic political underground providing leadership to an array of popular organisations and to armed struggle.

Implementation of the new perspective was repeatedly undermined by old habits and vested interests. Disagreements often centred on what the relationship should be between political and military operational structures, with the political side pressing for integration and the military for a significant degree of separation. But Revolutionary Council political work directed into the country, now better resourced and led by innovative strategist Mac Maharaj, rapidly influenced the domestic landscape. More often than not, the ANC achieved this by, so to say, leading from behind. Maharaj realised exiles seldom had the grasp of detail necessary to provide close tactical guidance to domestic ANC-inclined activists who had – often autonomously – started building popular organisations inside the country.

Therefore, exiles largely limited themselves to encouraging more domestic activists to take the initiative, to providing broad strategic direction and to steering funds from international donors towards domestic organisations they favoured. Many millions of rands began flowing into the country to support what became known as 'the movement'. By the early 1980s, crypto-ANC popular campaigns were being mobilised, drawing in tens of thousands.

In this ferment, a small group of leading ANC-aligned activists inside the country called for the formation of a broad alliance of political organisations that became the United Democratic Front (UDF) in 1983. Although the formation of a front along similar lines was prefigured in the 1979 strategy report, the idea of the UDF's formation was originated internally and called for without reference to the leadership in exile.

Reading the omens well

Some ANC leaders in exile, particularly Thabo Mbeki, read the omens more clearly than others. He, Maharaj and others immediately recognised the possibilities of linking up with certain organisations, pressure groups and opinion formers.

Among the most important of these was one with trade unions, some of whose leaders were unconvinced by ANC commitments to working-class interests, and with a group of Afrikaner academics and journalists in Dakar, Senegal. Mbeki's strategy in these meetings was to optimise the array of forces amenable to the ANC and negotiations, and to isolate those elements that were not.

He encountered similarly sophisticated thinking on the other side – among a group of civilian state intelligence officials. This group, which included Dr Niel Barnard, head of the National Intelligence Service, was formulating state options in the unfolding security crisis. They wanted to know whether enough of the sting could be drawn from the ANC to make negotiations a plausible option. A result was that, during meetings between the external mission and some domestic groups, the first oblique exchanges of signals over possible 'talks about talks' occurred between Pretoria and ANC exiles. Later, there were indirect contacts. And Mbeki and Zuma eventually met two of Barnard's group clandestinely in Switzerland in 1989.

The success of this political offensive boosted the ANC internationally. Doors in Western capitals hitherto shut were opened for Oliver Tambo, a manifestly reasonable man, and the urbane Thabo Mbeki. By contrast, Western confidence in the Pretoria government's amenability to negotiations became somewhat shaky after 1986 when it sabotaged a Commonwealth negotiating initiative, the so-called Eminent Persons Group, by mounting military raids into neighbouring states.

A hero in jail and a democratic front

The Nkomati Accord and the Tricameral Parliament lifted Western pressure on white-ruled South Africa only partially. Soon it would be confronted by a twofold internal challenge; the one by a man now more than twenty years in jail on Robben Island, and the other by a democratic front that in many ways constituted the friendly face of the ANC.

By the mid-1980s the campaign for the release of Nelson Mandela and his comrades from incarceration on Robben Island had become a global matter about which there was virtually no dissent. Even friendly governments like that of Margaret Thatcher in Britain put pressure on Botha to release Mandela and his comrades and to find a settlement with the ANC and other parties excluded from regular politics in South Africa. The problem was that the National Party leadership, Botha included, had long told their followers that the ANC was dominated by communists and resolutely committed to the armed struggle. 'We have painted ourselves into a corner,' Botha told his Minister of Justice, and asked: 'Is there a way out?'

The United Democratic Front

The United Democratic Front (UDF) was founded on 20 August 1983 in Mitchells Plain, Cape Town, following a call by Allan Boesak that a front of all opponents of the government be formed (*see box on page 382*). Earlier many small and localised groups had launched protests over local concerns such as increased rates and service charges, rent or bus fare increases, inferior education and shack demolition. These struggles were not co-ordinated and thus their efforts were dispersed.

The UDF was conceived and formed as a means to unite these struggles and bring together people from around the country who opposed apartheid. The UDF claimed that some 575 organisations were affiliated to it. It was vague about the number of people represented by these organisations but left the impression that it was a great multitude.

Youth, student, civic, trade union, religious, professional, political and women's groups were affiliated to the UDF. Many of the campaigns that came to be identified with the UDF in the public mind were rooted in some affiliate organisations. School boycotts, for instance, were associated with the UDF though they were driven by the Congress of South African Students, one of the UDF's militant affiliates. Mass stay-aways and consumer boycotts too were often attributed to the UDF when they were driven by civic associations and trade unions.

LEFT: *Community leaders Mac Maharaj, Cheryl Carolus, Allan Boesak and Trevor Manuel at a UDF rally in Cape Town on 11 March 1986.*

THE WEAKNESS OF THE UNDERGROUND

The ANC's grasp of the importance of domestic political organisation came, from its perspective, not a moment too soon. When the Nkomati Accord between Pretoria and Maputo (*see box on page 371*) threatened to strangle the flow of Umkhonto weSizwe (MK) guerrillas through Mozambique via Swaziland into South Africa in 1984, the ANC was not hobbled. Already, armed activity involving externally trained guerrillas was playing a role secondary to popular political pressures. This was not surprising. The ANC's chronic inability to build a pervasive and reasonably secure internal underground meant that various attempts to integrate MK fighters within popular struggles before 1984, and later with popular insurrectionary violence, failed.

Other consequences flowed from the weakness of the underground. One was that the external mission had difficulty curbing sometimes anomic – and politically damaging – violence by sections of domestic youth, most evident in the practice of 'necklacing'. Another was that the ANC retained an extraordinary reputation for restraint in its armed struggle. Occasional lapses aside, MK fighters met an external mission ban on the targeting of non-combatants. It is unlikely they could have done so, however, had the armed struggle been conducted more effectively.

Yet these military weaknesses were no serious disadvantage for ANC exiles when, from about 1987, they had to cope with the consequences of changes in Moscow's foreign policy, and later with the incipient collapse of the Soviet Union. Moscow now joined the West in favouring negotiated settlements across the subcontinent: in Angola and Mozambique, where South African-sponsored civil wars raged, in South West Africa and in South Africa.

The creation of the UDF immediately transformed the nature of black opposition politics. In one stroke, its co-ordinating role gave many small groups from around the country a national presence and the struggle against apartheid also took on a national character.

The UDF deliberately chose to be a non-racial group striving to end a system in which race determined access to power and privilege. Many affiliates adopted the Freedom Charter that went beyond describing what was unacceptable to offer a distinct alternative to the system. Opposing apartheid, a race-based policy, invariably gave the actions of the UDF a racial character. The UDF constantly had to clarify its views on race. The leadership accepted racially based organisations, but a faction rejected it on the grounds that it implied accepting the structures imposed by apartheid.

Combating the constitution

The immediate target of the UDF was to oppose the new constitution enacted in 1983, and more particularly the election of representatives for the (coloured) House of Representatives and the (Indian) House of Delegates in Parliament, as well as the black local authorities.

The government soon abandoned its original idea of a referendum and instead decided to hold elections for the (coloured) House of Representatives on 22 August 1984, and for the (Indian) House of Delegates on 2 September. Polls of 30% and 24% were recorded for the two houses respectively.

The average poll for the elections for the black local authorities held in late 1983 was even lower. The UDF claimed victory on account of the low voter turnout in these elections. The government claimed that the poll was sufficient to introduce the new apartheid institutions.

By launching itself at the time it did, the UDF was first in the ring among radical opponents of the government. It captured the attention of the country and gave hope that something might happen to change the system fundamentally. Moreover, its success in attracting well-known individuals gave it a considerable advantage. They included Allan Boesak, Desmond Tutu, Helen Joseph, Archie Gumede, and Smangaliso Mkhatshwa. They were big attractions at rallies.

Initially the UDF was strongest in Natal, Transvaal and the western Cape, but its focus soon shifted to the African townships in Port Elizabeth and East London, from where it rapidly spread to small towns. This shift occurred at the same time as the onset of school, consumer and rent boycotts.

The UDF leadership stressed that the movement was not a mere stalking horse for the ANC. Increasingly, however, the UDF used the same language and symbols as the ANC. At the funeral of four activists from Cradock who were assassinated by the security police, Stone Sizane was probably the first leader on a UDF platform to explicitly extol the armed struggle led by the ANC. The flags of the ANC and SA Communist Party were in full display during the funeral.

A rival front

The Azanian People's Organisation (Azapo), an offshoot of the Black Consciousness movement, and organisations loosely connected to the Unity Movement in Cape Town had made calls for a united front in 1981 and 1982. When Azapo leaders again made a call for a national front two weeks after Boesak, it looked as if they were copying what had already been done. The National Forum was formed in June 1983 – the main opponent of the UDF among extra-parliamentary organisations, but its failure to attract equally well-known and respected names added to the view that it was second best.

A shift soon occurred in popular sentiment away from affiliates of the National Forum towards the UDF. Newspapers gave much bigger coverage to UDF activities. The UDF consolidated its position by building and maintaining a sound relationship with journalists in the commercial media and encouraging the creation of alternative media organisations, which were either friends of the UDF or even affiliates. Mosiuoa (Terror) Lekota did sterling work as publicity secretary.

Between the end of 1977 when the Soweto revolt subsided, and 20 August 1983 when the United Democratic Front (UDF) was founded in Cape Town, several calls were made for a united front against apartheid. Yet at the start of 1983 there appeared to be more divisions than ever. In 1979 Chief Mangosuthu Buthelezi had broken with the leadership of the ANC in exile over sanctions and the armed struggle. The South African Black Alliance, with the Zulu-based Inkatha and the (coloured) Labour Party as main allies, collapsed when the Labour Party decided on 4 January 1983 to participate in the Tricameral Parliament.

ANC leader Oliver Tambo criticised the Labour Party for its decision and urged people 'to organise all democratic forces into one front for national liberation'. Howard Barrell, after interviewing Mac Maharaj and Joe Slovo in connection with these matters, commented that the formation of a front along similar lines was prefigured in the 1979 strategy report of the ANC. However, the idea of establishing a united democratic front 'originated in South Africa and the call

was made without reference to the leadership in exile'.

The man whose call set the process in motion was Allan Boesak, a minister in the Nederduitse Gereformeerde Sendingkerk, with a rapidly growing reputation as an orator and activist. Although he was viewed with suspicion by Freedom Charter supporters in view of his ties with the Black Consciousness movement, some Charterists in the Indian community invited him to address a mass meeting of the Transvaal Anti-South African Indian Council Committee in Johannesburg. Here Boesak stated: 'People must say no to apartheid . . . In order to do this we need a united front.' It was just a brief, almost casual aside, but the effect was electric. Cas Saloojee remarked: 'He moved people . . . he just created a helluva sensation.' Immediately the Charterists sprang into action. Thus, the ground was well prepared when Boesak spoke at the official launch of the UDF in Mitchells Plain, Cape Town, on 20 August 1983.

The formation of the UDF, largely unplanned, was the single greatest windfall the ANC enjoyed. The UDF soon eclipsed

Allan Boesak

Inkatha, which was not invited, as the most important internal opposition movement, it absorbed virtually all the Black Consciousness movement followers in the coloured and Indian communities, and it injected the Freedom Charter – largely forgotten by the late 1970s – into the heart of the political debate.

ABOVE: *By mid-1985 the urban uprising that had started in September the previous year had escalated dramatically. There were frequent clashes between large crowds and the police, and government structures had collapsed in many of the black townships. People were killed almost every day. Here members of the South African army patrol the streets of a township in a Casspir.*

OPPOSITE: *Police throw teargas at defiant marchers and residents of Alexandra township during pre-election violence between residents and Inkatha supporters.*

An urban uprising

To compensate for the lack of any black representation in the Tricameral Parliament the government adopted a law in 1982 that introduced a new form of black local government. Although the formal powers differed little from those of the white bodies, these institutions had major flaws. First, the government presented them as a quid pro quo for the exclusion of Africans from the Tricameral Parliament. It was widely seen as adding insult to injury.

Second, these authorities were without a viable revenue base. Few township residents owned property, with the result that the revenue that could be raised by rates and levies was extremely limited. In many townships the beer halls, a main source of revenue, had been destroyed in the Soweto rebellion of 1976. The government even channelled some of the funds that should have gone into improving the infrastructure of the townships into homeland development.

Third, the authorities were elected in polls with a low voter turnout. Many residents had stopped paying house rent and the charges for water and electricity. Undeterred, the new councils sharply increased the price of rent and electricity.

In September 1984 an open rebellion broke out in Sebokeng township in the Vaal Triangle southeast of Johannesburg (*see box*), on the very day that coloured and Indian representatives in the new Tricameral Parliament were being sworn in. The chairman and deputy mayor were among the first to be killed by the crowd. The uprising continued with great intensity until the middle of 1986, spreading across the country.

The protests were much more broadly based than in 1976, when the Black Consciousness movement, the main source of inspiration to children and students, lacked the organisational capacity to sustain protests. Now clergy, students, teachers, lecturers, business people, women's groups and workers were mobilised for the dismantling of the apartheid system. There was better strategic thinking and a far more successful appeal to international opinion.

Since the press itself was freer than in 1976, the protests were also much better reported in the local and international media, until the state clamped down on these reports. ANC leaders, particularly Oliver Tambo (who had been in exile for 25 years) and Nelson Mandela, Walter Sisulu and Govan Mbeki (who had each spent more than twenty years in jail), had acquired almost mythical status in the eyes of the people engaged in the struggle, as well as large sections of the international community.

The protests spread

The protests in the townships of the Vaal Triangle in September 1984 quickly spread to other parts of the Transvaal, and to Natal and the eastern Cape. There were numerous symbolic stay-aways and strikes by workers, rent and service charge boycotts, consumer boycotts and marches, often headed by churchmen with mass student participation.

In many townships crowds attacked the houses of black town councillors, forcing their resignation and eventually the collapse of the system of local government. They also burned government buildings, shops and liquor outlets. Activists firebombed the houses of black policemen to drive them out of the townships and killed many suspected informers, sometimes by the so-called necklace – lighting a petrol-soaked rubber tyre placed around the victim's neck. This grisly form of reprisal soon led to the police's sources of information drying up. The funerals of people who died in clashes with the police became highly charged occasions, with coffins often covered by an ANC flag. Foreign diplomats attended the funerals of prominent activists suspected of being murdered by the security forces.

After police opened fire on a peaceful funeral procession in March 1985 in Uitenhage, killing twenty, the protests spread into the eastern Cape and then to Cape Town and other parts of the western Cape. Bombs exploded in Durban and Johannesburg on 16 June, the anniversary of the Soweto uprising. On 20 July the government declared a state of emergency in some magisterial districts. Two days later the ANC responded by

On 8 January 1985 Oliver Tambo first issued a call to 'Render South Africa ungovernable' – a concept originally conceived
by his close assistant Thabo Mbeki. After
the proclamation of a state of emergency
in July he repeated the call as a reply to
President Botha. 'We have to make apartheid unworkable and our country ungovernable. Prepare the conditions for the
seizure of power by the people.'

Tambo stated that great progress had
already been made in the 'weakest link' –
the black local authorities – but the offensive had to be spread throughout the country. 'In all our localities, wherever they may
be, we must rise now and destroy apartheid
organs of government that are used to hold
our people in bondage. We make this call
to all people – African, Indian and so-called
coloureds.' The call was extended to white
people too. 'To guarantee its [sic] own security, white South Africans must come
over to the side of the forces fighting for a
democratic non-racial society.'

way of a call to make South Africa ungovernable (*see box*). But severe repressive measures by the state steadily decimated the leadership of the uprising.

In August, when the rebellion was in its eleventh month, Chase Manhattan Bank suddenly announced that it would not extend its large short-term loans to the South African
government, setting in train a process that would soon lead to South Africa's default on
its international debt.

By November 1985 some 8 000 UDF members had been detained. Many leaders of
its national and regional executives had been killed, were in jail or had fled the country.
In Natal and KwaZulu the competition for turf between Inkatha and the ANC reached
the intensity of a low-level civil war.

In the angry disappointment that followed President Botha's 'crossing the Rubicon'
speech in August 1985 (*see box*), scorn was poured on his words. The speech fell so far
short of the quite unrealistic expectations that had built up that a wave of new sanctions
and disinvestment hit South Africa.

The Reagan administration in the United States announced a mild sanctions package,
but the US Congress soon went much further by banning all new investments and loans
to the South African government. In Britain, Margaret Thatcher's Tory government held
out, but the Commonwealth accepted measures that included a ban on all agricultural
and manufacturing imports from South Africa, and on any new loans and investment.
Even Thatcher signalled in 1989 that she could not resist for much longer if Mandela
were not freed. One-fifth of British firms left South Africa, and total British direct
investment halved between 1980 and 1986.

In March 1986 the government briefly lifted the partial state of emergency, but on
12 June 1986 it declared a national state of emergency, which would remain in place until 1 February 1990. The state used massive force to crush the revolt. More than 20 000
people were detained, and the state activated its National Security Management System
in many townships. The State Security Council became the main decision-making body
on security matters.

Democratic struggles

The UDF had no central organisation planning and directing the protests on a national
scale. In general the UDF eschewed violence and opted for a democratic struggle in
which access to the masses of the people was critical. Taking up arms or openly advocating the armed struggle would have jeopardised this strategy. It was also in the interest of

RIGHT: *Desmond Tutu at a UDF rally in
Cape Town's St George's Cathedral in
1988, addressing the new Defiance
Campaign gathering. Behind him sits Dean
Colin Jones.*

OPPOSITE: *Winnie Mandela, then still
Nelson Mandela's wife, and Desmond Tutu
in a protest march calling for the release
of Nelson Mandela as part of the new
Defiance Campaign. With them are Mosiuoa
Lekota (left), Popo Molefe and Valli Moosa
(right). Trevor Manuel is right behind them.*

the ANC to protect the UDF from repression that would have been triggered by clear evidence that the UDF was engaged in armed activity. The UDF leadership accepted that it had most to gain by focusing on relatively peaceful campaigns, although violence often erupted in enforcing strikes or stay-aways.

The UDF suffered considerably from detentions during the state of emergencies imposed in 1985 and 1986. The eastern Cape was the hardest hit, but all regions suffered the detention of leaders. Popo Molefe and Terror Lekota, Valli Moosa, Trevor Manuel and Stone Sizane were among the regional leaders who were detained at different times during the emergency period.

The state tried to tie up most of the leadership through prolonged trials, the one in Pietermaritzburg and the other in Delmas, east of Johannesburg. While the UDF denied any formal alliance with the ANC it used the same symbolism. It had established itself as the major organisation challenging the state.

One of the UDF goals that remained elusive was an alliance with the trade unions, in particular the Federation of South African Trade Unions (Fosatu). In 1983 the UDF failed to convince the federation to affiliate to the Front. Fosatu leaders viewed it as being led by a bourgeois group heading up a multi-class alliance, and thus incapable of worker-based solutions to questions of immediate concern to working people.

The creation of the Congress of South African Trade Unions (Cosatu) in 1985 laid the foundation for better co-operation. Sydney Mufamadi, who became deputy secretary of Cosatu, was a UDF leader. The National Union of Mineworkers, led by Cyril Ramaphosa, had not been part of Fosatu, but now joined Cosatu.

Gradually the UDF and the trade unions reached rapprochement. It was mainly white trade union officials who had insisted on remaining outside a multi-class alliance like the UDF. Elected black leaders never shared their reservations. After the ANC had assumed the status of the major challenger of government it had become ever more urgent for the trade union movement to choose its allies. There was little space or time for the unions to build their own political party. They ran the risk of political isolation if they spurned an alliance with the ANC-UDF. In 1986 a meeting between Cosatu and ANC leaders established common ground on several matters. A resolution committed the two organisations to 'work together and consult each other in order to establish maximum unity'.

When the government imposed severe restrictions on the UDF and 16 other organisations on 24 February 1988 the Mass Democratic Movement was founded to take its place. It was led by Cosatu, which was more immune to harassment by government.

THE 'CROSSING THE RUBICON' SPEECH
With President Botha scheduled to open the Natal Congress of the National Party on 15 August 1985, there was intense international speculation that he would announce the release of Mandela, among other far-reaching steps. Angered by the unrealistic expectations raised by Minister of Foreign Affairs Pik Botha, President Botha used the occasion to display all the defiance of an old-style white supremacist. He was not prepared to lead white South Africans on 'a road to abdication and suicide'. Without white South Africans and their influence, President Botha asserted, the country would drift into 'faction strife, chaos and poverty'. He had no respect for revolutionaries who had turned Africa into a dying continent. Mandela and 'his friends' were in jail, he said, because they had planned a revolution, and would only be released if they renounced violence.

Hardly noticed was the fact that, in terms of his party's policy, President Botha had in fact taken a major step: he had buried much of the homelands policy and with it the attempt to deny blacks political rights in the common area. He said that his government accepted the permanence of the urban blacks and that they should participate along with other groups in negotiating matters of common concern. He added: 'The policy which I announced today will have far-reaching consequences for us all. I believe we have crossed the Rubicon today. There can be no turning back.'

In the 1980s, the militancy of black labour increased greatly. There was a steady growth in black membership of registered trade unions, and assertive labour federations – of which the Congress of South African Trade Unions (Cosatu) was the strongest – became a force to be reckoned with. Unions became more politicised, taking up not only industrial but also community issues. There was a steady escalation of work stoppages and strikes. The days lost through strike action rose from 0.18 million in 1980 to 0.68 million in 1985, 1.31 million in 1986 and 5.83 million in 1987.

Leading from jail

In mid-1985, with riots raging across South Africa, Mandela wrote to Kobie Coetsee, Minister of Justice, requesting a meeting. He did so without consulting the leaders of the ANC in exile and ignoring the precept that prisoners could not negotiate with their jailors. Mandela would later explain: 'I knew my colleagues upstairs would condemn my proposal and kill my initiative . . . There are times when a leader must move out ahead of his flock, go off in a new direction.'

The representatives of the state immediately recognised Mandela's stature and lack of bitterness despite having spent 25 years in jail. He came across to government officials as a pragmatist who resorted to the armed struggle as a last resort rather than a doctrinaire revolutionary glorying in violence for its own sake. His intention and that of the movement he led was not to overthrow the state but to draw attention to the legitimate aspirations of the long-oppressed African people.

An acute assessment by a prison official stated that Mandela believed in his cause and was certain about eventual victory. It concluded that he 'commands all the qualities to be the Number One black leader in South Africa'. He was no moderate in National Party terms, but consistently argued that majority rule, which he considered non-negotiable, had to be balanced by guarantees that ensured white domination would not be replaced by black domination.

Mandela soon indicated that any attempt to get him to forswear violence on behalf of the ANC was misguided. As he told distinguished foreign visitors allowed to visit him in jail, the National Party government had forced the armed struggle on the ANC. There was only one solution: 'The ball is in their court. They must legalise us and treat us like a political party.' Early in 1985 he had his daughter Zindzi read out a statement to a crowd in Soweto where he told Botha that it was the government that had to renounce violence. He, Mandela, cherished his freedom, but what freedom was he being offered while the organisation to which he belonged remained banned?

In May 1986 Coetsee joined Mandela in a discussion with the Eminent Persons Group, a Commonwealth fact-finding team visiting South Africa to explore negotiations as an alternative to further sanctions. Mandela suggested that the ANC might be prepared to suspend violence if the troops and police were withdrawn from the townships. Subsequently Coetsee privately proposed to Mandela that he and a few government officials under the leadership of Dr Niel Barnard begin discussing the possibility of negotiations. The informal committee began its work in May 1988 and would hold 47 meetings. When Mandela met Botha secretly in 1989 he prepared a statement of ten pages in which he summarised what he had discussed in these meetings. Mandela now formulated the key challenge for the negotiations that would take place over the next seven years: the black demand for majority rule reconciling with the white demand that this should not mean subjugation of the white minority.

Stability gradually returned. Fatalities had risen from 879 in 1985 to 1 298 in 1986, but declined to 661 in 1987. They would rise again in 1988 to 1 149 and to 1 403 in 1989. The state had suppressed the political challenge, but South Africa had irrevocably changed. US Assistant Secretary of State for Africa Chester Crocker summed up the state of play: '[The] government and its opposition had checkmated each other. Neither could move unilaterally: the black resistance had no hope of forcing the government to capitulate, but the government could no longer hope to regain the legitimacy it lost.'

A security assessment

Top police force officers had come to believe that suppression of dissent offered only a temporary respite in a situation where a rapidly growing black population would offer ever stiffer challenges. Adriaan Vlok, who became Minister for Police in 1986, would later describe the situation as follows: 'It was like a pot of water with a lid on. It could not go on forever. Eventually the steam would blow the lid off.' Mike Louw, second in command of the National Intelligence Service, remembered the situation in the late 1980s as follows: 'Nowhere was the situation out of hand, but it was clear that politically and morally we were losing our grip. Everywhere in the townships we encountered intimidation and

The government continued with reform in order to regain investor confidence. It kept those pillars of apartheid it considered essential (population registration, segregated education, and the exclusion of blacks from Parliament), while it removed those parts of apartheid deemed to be 'unnecessary'. In 1985 it granted urban blacks across the country full residential rights and repealed the racial sex laws. In 1986 it scrapped the pass laws and other forms of influx control. In 1987 it allowed blacks full freehold rights to property. It turned a blind eye to inner city areas that were becoming integrated. Public facilities were desegregated on a broad front.

Most forms of formal job discrimination had been ended. There was still a gap in the spending per capita on pupils, with the greatest disparity between the amounts spent on white and black children. It stood at 1:7 in 1954 when 'Bantu education' was introduced, rose to an average of 1:10 in the 1960s and after a peak of 1:19 in 1971 steadily dropped to reach 1:3.5.

But the demands of the leaders of the uprising were much more radical than the cosmetic reform of apartheid. They wanted the scrapping of apartheid as a system and negotiations for a fully inclusive democracy. The worldwide campaign for the release of Mandela had built up an irresistible momentum. It was almost universally accepted that negotiations had to be preceded by the release of Mandela and other leaders in jail.

a strong political consciousness. The political system had become obsolete, and a long bloody struggle lay ahead. It had become clear that the sooner we negotiated a new system the better.' Repression could only buy time for the politicians to find a political solution, not provide a permanent settlement.

Business and the political crisis

The new political militancy of the black workers forced a reassessment on the business community, which had long adapted to white supremacy and financially did quite well out of it (*see box*). When strike activity began to intensify in the 1970s employers admitted that it was inconvenient – 'it felt like trying to negotiate with 1 500 workers on a football field', remarked an employer – but the business lobby did not take the initiative in proposing the extension of industrial rights to black workers. The labour reforms of 1979 largely emanated from the state and met with only qualified business approval.

This complacency received a rude shock in the 1980s. Blacks now enjoyed industrial rights but no political rights. As the only black legal institutions backed by mass membership and a strong leadership that could not be easily banned, the unions quickly filled the political void in the country. In March 1986 Cyril Ramaphosa, leader of the powerful mineworkers' union, said: 'We have a very strong base, maybe stronger, for instance, than the ANC . . . We would like to see a country that is going to be ruled in the interests of the workers who produced the wealth of the country.' Cosatu, the trade union federation, soon claimed half a million members.

As the urban uprising plunged white South Africans into a deep cloud of gloom, some English business leaders embarked on the highly symbolic step of meeting with the ANC leadership in Zambia in September 1985. Here Oliver Tambo, president of the ANC, called Gavin Relly, chairman of Anglo American Corporation, which controlled more than half the companies on the Johannesburg Stock Exchange, 'Gavin' – and asked to be called 'Oliver'.

Relly later called it 'one of the nicest days I have ever spent', although Tambo had insisted that some of the major corporations had to be taken under state control and warned that the ANC might attack economic installations. Two Afrikaans business leaders, Anton Rupert of Rembrandt and Fred du Plessis of Sanlam, opted out of the visit at the last moment. Rupert would later write privately to President Botha about his profound misgivings regarding the prevailing political order (*see box on page 391*).

BUSINESS, GOVERNMENT AND UNIONS

Since the establishment of the Union in 1910 the business-government relationship was highly unusual due to the fact that Afrikaners wielded political power and the English community economic power. More than 80% of the private sector (excluding agriculture) was in English hands as late as 1975. That no government ever seriously contemplated nationalisation was due to the strong economic ties with Britain and the existence of several large state corporations in which Afrikaners could advance in managerial positions.

Even more unusual was the relationship between business and black labour. From the 1930s most workers in industry were black, but business adapted to a political order that did not recognise them as political and industrial citizens.

English business briefly spoke up in times of national crises, but soon shut up when slapped down. In 1960, after Sharpeville, the Associated Chambers of Commerce (Assocom), the most outspoken of business associations, asked that blacks be allowed greater freedom of movement and the opportunity to own their houses in the townships. Prime Minister Verwoerd reacted harshly, accusing Assocom of being part of an organised campaign against the state. When Assocom called for the restructuring of the racial order after the Soweto uprising, John Vorster warned it against the proposing of a new socio-economic order that would 'do away with the private enterprise system and destroy the democratic rights of the electorate'.

Although English business leaders were well represented in the prime minister's Economic Advisory Council they were seen as people mostly interested in economic indicators and indices and rarely in the total picture. They rarely spoke up about the need to train black workers and provide them with housing.

In 1977, in the wake of the Soweto uprising, big business founded the Urban Foundation to improve the quality of life of blacks in the cities. Headed by Jan Steyn, a highly respected ex-judge, it encouraged the implementation of labour codes and pressed for extended rights for urban blacks by fighting court cases and lobbying government.

In general, however, the business leaders were reluctant to commit themselves. They were very uneasy about the ANC's economic policies. The ANC's Freedom Radio in Addis Ababa continued with its blood-curdling threats against whites. On 7 October 1985 it declared: 'We must attack them at their homes and holiday resorts, just as we have attacking [sic] black-boot-lickers at their homes.' A series of deadly bombings polarised public opinion. At Musina a landmine in a rural road killed six whites, a bomb in a shopping centre in Amanzimtoti three Christmas shoppers, and one in the Magoo's Bar on the Durban beachfront three clients. By the end of 1986 there seemed no prospect of a settlement in which the ANC played a leading role.

On a local level, business had to deal with the consumer boycotts that hit cities and towns in several regions. In the eastern Cape UDF activist Mkhuseli Jack spearheaded several actions that forced shopkeepers to reach a settlement. When he was detained, local business pointed out that this left them with no one with whom to negotiate. After boycotts had spread throughout the Transvaal, the Associated Chambers of Commerce discussed the need to set up a communications system that could defuse inflammatory situations.

But the large enterprises rode out the storms of the eighties. It did not prevent them in the 1990s from re-inventing themselves as life-long foes of apartheid.

The most important impact business had in bringing about an end to apartheid was in failing to make new investments in machinery and plant. From 1983 the outlook for

SACRIFICING SCHOOLING

Turmoil in the black, and sometimes also coloured, schools continued for more than fifteen years after the protests that marked the Soweto uprising of 1976. At the heart of it was a rejection of Christian National Education that made the child's identification with his ethnic group a prime goal. Other grievances included disparities in government spending on the different racial groups (per pupil in 1982 the state spent R1 385 on whites, R871 on Indians, R593 on coloureds and R192 on blacks – due mostly to the higher salary white teachers received on account of their higher qualifications), poor school facilities, and the lack of qualifications of black teachers.

After the Soweto uprising the government soon dropped the insistence that both English and Afrikaans had to be used as languages of instruction and it allowed private white schools to admit blacks. But black children began boycotting schools in 1980. The Congress of South African Students (Cosas) became increasingly important as a mouthpiece of the protesting children. In October 1984 Cosas, which was an affiliate of the UDF, organised a major school boycott in consultation

with the Transvaal Regional Stay-away Committee. On 5 and 6 November 1984 nearly 400 000 students from more than 300 schools stayed away and engaged in protest action. Coloured schools were also affected and there were clashes between the police and coloured pupils and students.

By 1985 it looked as if a radicalised black and coloured youth had become a potent new political factor. But the movement soon lost its coherence and a real threat of disintegration of black school education loomed. The UDF leadership admitted that 'while regional structures exist, regional and national co-ordination has broken down and organisation at the level of the local student congresses is weak'. Slogans like 'Liberation Now, Education Later' and the ANC-inspired 'People's Education for People's Power' were often heard but there was little sign of a coherent alternative system.

In 1986 the National Education Crisis Committee (NECC) was founded with the aim of promoting 'People's Education' to resolve the crisis. Parents attempted to break the cycle of school boycotts while continuing to press for reform.

high growth looked grim. For business this was no time to expand. Private fixed capital formation dropped from 26.1% of the Gross Domestic Product in 1983 to 10.3% in 1993 (it would return to the earlier mark only in 2005). The government knew that this was a major blow to economic growth and that fixed investment, and with that employment figures, would improve only after the government had created a more stable political system than apartheid. Anton Rupert, doyen of Afrikaner business, spelled this out in no uncertain terms to government (*see box on page 391*).

A dirty frontier war

Between 1978 and 1984, the SA Defence Force (SADF) launched seven major codenamed operations in the south of Angola: Sceptic (June 1980), Protea (August 1981), Daisy (November 1981), Super (March 1982), Mebos (July–August 1982), Phoenix (February–April 1983) and Askari (December 1983). Each succeeded in many ways. Their collective strategic failure was the inability to prevent the build-up of MPLA/Cuban air power, which, if used, would have exposed SADF national servicemen to rising casualties. Askari claimed the highest number of SADF casualties of any operation to date – 21. The deaths inspired critical commentary from home about casualties on distant battlefields.

BELOW: *A military exercise with an armoured car (MK2) and soldiers in the mid-1980s.*

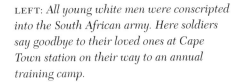

LEFT: *All young white men were conscripted into the South African army. Here soldiers say goodbye to their loved ones at Cape Town station on their way to an annual training camp.*

Between 1985 and 1988 the white nightmare of simultaneously suppressing a continuing internal uprising and fighting a frontier war materialised. There were now more than 30 000 Cuban troops in Angola, and new Russian aircraft gave South Africa's enemies a degree of air superiority that threatened to make the war for South Africa ever more costly in both lives and equipment. Much was at stake. Confronted by an aggressive right wing accusing it of selling out, the government would be severely hit by a humiliating retreat in Angola. The Soviet Union and Cuba were determined to record a victory in Angola and win a battle in the Cold War. Victory could open the way for a Swapo incursion in the northern parts of what was then South West Africa.

Although heavily outnumbered, South Africa scored a major, largely unheralded military victory in Angola. In a large-scale formal battle at Lomba, the forces of South Africa and Unita inflicted a crushing defeat on the Cuban and Angolan forces, together with their Russian military advisers. The Cuban-Angolan force retreated to Cuito Cuanavale. The South African/Unita force laid siege to the town, but did not attempt to take it because the strategic value was limited. A master of revolutionary myth-making, Fidel Castro fabricated the legend that the entire war turned on this battle at Cuito Cuanavale, and that South Africa had lost it.

Castro also made exaggerated claims about the final battle just beyond the SWA border. The reality was that the battle was inconclusive. South Africa proved that a Cuban attempt to breach the border would exact a toll far higher than it seemed prepared to pay.

Early in 1988 the Reagan administration received word from the Soviets that they were eager to get out of Africa. Both South Africa and Cuba now prepared to withdraw. For South Africa the financial costs had been high: Between 1985/86 and 1988/89 military expenditures increased by 25% at constant prices to make up 17.7% of the budget. The fruits were ambiguous. South Africa had helped Unita to become a formidable force, it had thwarted Swapo attempts to establish a military presence in South West Africa and ultimately prevented some illusion of Cuban success that could have created very unfavourable conditions for a settlement in Africa. However, Swapo had managed to survive politically and was sure to win a free election.

Moreover, the South African government had exhausted one of its important instruments of survival: military supremacy in the region. It had relied on the SADF as a military instrument to control political change in SWA but the cost of using the SADF in such a manner eventually exposed the Achilles heel of the military – a rising number of white conscript deaths. It was a force that the government politically could not afford. For Angola too, the costs were extremely high. Much of its infrastructure had been destroyed, many towns had been laid waste and hundreds of Angolan army soldiers (along with some of their Cuban allies) killed, not to mention all the civilians killed, maimed or misplaced.

THE PENALTY OF SANCTIONS

The international community used sanctions against South Africa as the main way to express its rejection of the policy of apartheid. South Africa's significant degree of integration into the international economic and financial systems represented a double-edged sword: South Africa was hurt by sanctions but its main trading partners sought to limit their scope for fear of injuring their own economies.

Oil and arms sanctions hurt South Africa most. By 1980 South Africa was dependent on foreign oil for 80% of the needs of its transport sector. The oil-producing cartel, Opec, imposed sanctions in 1973. It was ignored by Iran, which supplied 90% of the oil, but after the fall of the Shah in 1979, it joined ranks with Opec. South Africa had to incur large costs related to stockpiling and the development of nuclear energy and synthetic fuels programmes.

During the early 1960s the first United Nations arms embargoes were introduced. These compelled South Africa to diversify its purchases away from Britain and the United States at considerable cost. Its own arms industry produced small arms, missiles, electronics and communications equipment, but was unable to supply aircraft, tanks and other armoured vehicles. In the second half of the 1980s South African troops had to face Angolan soldiers who had the advantage of Soviet-built T55 tanks, MiG23 jets and SA8 and A9 aircraft.

The economic sanction that caused most damage was not introduced as a result of anti-apartheid activism, but because South Africa was seen as too big a risk. This was the decision of Chase Manhattan Bank in July 1985 not to roll over its outstanding loans. The South African rand plunged from 54 cents to 34 cents to the dollar. Subsequently South Africa was starved of foreign capital. The ban on new foreign loans and investment severely dented business confidence. Mainly as a result of a disinvestment campaign by churches and universities the total of nearly 400 American companies with direct investments in South Africa plunged to 136 at the end of the 1980s. Local companies snapped them up at low prices but important technological know-how was lost.

The main products affected by trade sanctions were iron, steel, uranium, coal, fruit and textiles. The country's precious and strategic minerals were sanctions proof. Trade ties with the West weakened, but those with Asia improved, with the result that the overall volume of foreign trade grew. By the end of 1986 the country had a trade surplus of R15 billion.

Sport sanctions and academic sanctions were minor irritants, but they contributed to a sense among white South Africans that they were moral outcasts.

Sanctions exacted a high price but on their own would not have forced the South African government to seek a settlement. Once negotiations started, the question of when sanctions should be lifted was one of the major levers in the ANC's arsenal.

The road was now clear for South West African independence without the South African government being seen to be selling out. P.W. Botha probably thought until near the end that Swapo could be eliminated as the dominant political force, but most military commanders felt the main aim had been achieved, namely the elimination of the Cuban presence and conditions for a peaceful election. In 1989, the election for a constituent assembly took place peacefully in SWA, which became Namibia. The demonstration effect on white voters in South Africa was generally positive.

Weakening control

National Party rule of 40 years was based on a party united behind an ideology, strong support of the Afrikaner-Broederbond and the Afrikaans churches, disciplined security forces (except for the prisons where a blind eye was turned to non-lethal torture) and the fragmented state of the black opposition. From the mid-1970s these pillars of support began to crumble.

As late as 1974 the Dutch Reformed Church (DRC) synod reaffirmed the stale story of Babel as a parable of God's creation of distinct peoples. On this basis it justified apartheid and rejected non-racial membership for the DRC. But by 1982 the church had suffered painful blows. In 1982 the World Alliance of Reformed Churches, a body whose membership it prized, expelled it.

The blow that hurt most was a step the Dutch Reformed Sendingkerk (the 'coloured' DRC) took in 1982. It drafted the Belhar Confession, which left little doubt that the church's theological support for apartheid was in conflict with the Christian message. It called on the DRC to confess its guilt for 'providing the moral and theological foundations of apartheid'. The DRC finally broke with apartheid at its 1986 and 1990 synods by stating that such a system clashed with the Bible, and was sinful and a major error.

The Afrikaner-Broederbond also came round to abandoning apartheid. In 1986 it sent a memorandum, entitled 'Basic Constitutional Values for the Survival of the Afrikaners', to its divisions for comment. It stated that blacks had to be incorporated in government at all levels. The head of the government did not necessarily have to be white. These steps would entail 'calculated risks', but as Executive Council chairman Piet de Lange stated: 'The greatest risk we currently run is not to take any risks. Our will to survive as Afrikaners and our energy and faith are the strongest guarantee.'

Anton Rupert

TOP: *Cartoonist Derek Bauer's view of P.W. Botha's stand on political prisoners.*

By the mid-1980s the disarray extended to the cabinet. At a meeting of a cabinet committee held in March 1986, Botha remarked that he did not favour one-man one-vote in a unitary or federal state. 'I thought we had clarity, but I do not think we have it any more, because you want me to say we stand for a unitary South Africa. You allow me to say it, you write it in my speeches and I accept it, but what do you mean by that?' Chris Heunis, Minister for Constitutional Development, remarked that the government did not know where it was going.

On the grassroots level, support for the apartheid system was still strong. A 1984 survey found that upwards of 80% of Afrikaners (and 35–45% of English-speakers also) supported the key pillars of apartheid: the ban on sex between white and non-white; segregated residential areas, schools and public amenities; separate voters' rolls for coloureds and Indians; and homelands for blacks.

Yet those in decision-making and opinion-forming positions realised that apartheid as a policy to defend white domination had run its course and that things could not continue as before. A vivid illustration was provided when the Conservative Party, after winning most towns in the Transvaal in the 1988 local government elections, tried to reintroduce forms of social apartheid that had fallen away. Blacks immediately responded by consumer boycotts that crippled local businesses. The central government overruled the local authorities.

Another major pillar of white power, namely black political fragmentation, had also begun to disintegrate in the 1980s. The turmoil in the townships eliminated most of the black councillors. The ANC in alliance with the UDF had succeeded in establishing itself as the dominant and cohesive force in black politics. When the government began seeking a new model for incorporating blacks into the political structures in 1986, it discovered that it had run out of moderate black leaders as negotiating partners. Buthelezi insisted that the government first stated that it was prepared to consider power-sharing between whites and blacks and that it would release Nelson Mandela. Botha refused both demands. Strong enmity remained between the ANC in exile and Buthelezi, but the government was no longer able to play black leaders off against one another.

While the security forces had showed no sign of any loss of will during the 1984–1986 uprising, they could not wipe out black dissent. Police methods to control crowds were often unsophisticated. After the police had shot and killed twenty protesters on 21 March 1985 in Uitenhage in the eastern Cape, a judge found that they had acted provocatively towards the black crowd and were armed solely with lethal weaponry. The judge commented that 'the use of more lethal weapons is not the answer to a lack of numbers'. During the second half of the 1980s the state employed large numbers of *kitskonstabels*, 'instant constables', who were given limited training and rushed into situations where they sometimes had to control angry crowds.

Even more seriously, with officers close to the top either turning a blind eye or giving covert support, elements in both the army and the police had embarked on a series of 'targeted killings' to destroy the coherence and effectiveness of the ANC. The most notorious was Unit C-10, a secret police unit, that used a farm called Vlakplaas near Pretoria to 'turn' ANC guerrillas into security police agents and then sent them out to kill state enemies.

Another was a military unit, the Civil Co-operation Bureau, which operated mainly abroad but also had an internal cell comprised mainly of ex-policemen, who murdered or severely injured political opponents. A state bureau researched chemical and biological weapons, and was probably responsible for several assassinations. On a regional level some security force officers took the law in their own hands, either ordering their men to kill activists or summoning Vlakplaas operatives. Ten years later several security policemen would ask for amnesty for 'targeted killings' related to the 'Pebco Three', the 'Guguletu Seven', the 'Cradock Four' and several other activist groups.

There was intense speculation whether the cabinet or State Security Council gave explicit orders for assassinating opponents of the state. There was no evidence that explicit instructions were given, but the truth was complex. As Adriaan Vlok and Johann van der Merwe, head of the police, pointed out, the politicians deliberately used ambivalent language. Vlok recounted that he instructed police officers in hot spots to 'make a plan', that is to 'eliminate' or 'neutralise' key activists. Botha was also reported as having given similar commands. There were also clear cases where government leaders approved illegal action. President Botha told the Minister of Police he was happy with the bombing of Khotso House in the centre of Johannesburg where activists often met.

Exploring negotiations

From mid-1986 the National Intelligence Service (NIS) began to talk to members of the ANC in exile, while on a separate track secret discussions took place with Mandela in prison. The idea of a negotiated settlement had become unassailable. Botha took no action when a large group of Afrikaner academics under the leadership of Van Zyl Slabbert publicly met with leaders of the ANC in exile in Dakar, Senegal, in 1987, though he did attack them as 'useful idiots'.

In 1988 NIS officials met with ANC leaders in exile. Conditions for negotiations with the ANC were much more favourable than they had been six or seven years earlier. The war in Angola was over, the transition to an internationally recognised transfer of power in SWA/Namibia was proceeding smoothly, the Soviet Union was anxious to withdraw from Africa, and the African states in the region were eager for a settlement that would bring peace to the entire region. In South Africa a semi-stable deadlock existed between the security forces and their challengers.

A stroke and its consequences

Early in 1989 Botha suffered a stroke. He decided to resign as party leader but to stay on as president. F.W. de Klerk was elected new party leader. As the government stumbled on with two centres of power rallying around De Klerk and Botha, its electoral base was steadily eroded from both the left and the right. The Democratic Party, formed in April 1989 after the Progressive Federal Party incorporated several independents who had broken away from the National Party, now challenged the ruling party as the only genuine vehicle of reform.

In the general election in September 1989 the National Party lost 27 seats but retained enough to avoid a hung parliament. Its main platform was a vague promise to negotiate a new political system within five years. Botha had resigned after a showdown with his cabinet a few weeks before the election. De Klerk became acting president and was formally elected as president after the election.

LEFT: *Breyten Breytenbach, Thabo Mbeki and Frederik van Zyl Slabbert in Dakar. After Slabbert left Parliament in January 1986 because he considered the institution politically irrelevant he set up the Institute for a Democratic Alternative in South Africa (Idasa) to explore ways in which democracy could be broadened. The idea of a conference attended by 50 or 60 Afrikaner academics and journalists and an ANC delegation was born when Slabbert and Breytenbach attended a cultural festival in Dakar, Senegal, where black South African singer Miriam Makeba sang. At the conference in Dakar in July 1987, Slabbert declared his aims were threefold: to introduce Afrikaners to Africa, to introduce Afrikaners to the ANC and to make the ANC aware that 'not all Afrikaners go around shooting blacks'. The conference unanimously expressed preference for a negotiated resolution of the political question; as a first step, this required the release of political prisoners and the unbanning of political organisations.*

F.W. de Klerk was the model Nationalist whose family history was interwoven with that of the Afrikaner nationalist movement. One grandfather was a Gereformeerde (Dopper) minister; another was elected to the Transvaal Provincial Council. An uncle was J.G. Strijdom, prime minister from 1954–1958, and his father was a cabinet minister. De Klerk studied law at Potchefstroom University. His approach was the typical neo-Calvinist one of starting with abstract principles and taking them to what he saw as their logical conclusion. For much of his political career he considered apartheid as morally and politically sound.

In his parliamentary career, which started in 1972, he carefully avoided becoming part of any National Party caucus faction. Intelligent, self-confident and a good debater, he glibly explained away the inconsistencies and injustices of apartheid. He attacked the liberal opposition as short-sighted on survival without offering a plausible alternative. Until the end of the 1980s there was nothing that suggested that he was able to provide transformative leadership.

But the prolonged unrest that started in September 1984 and the demographic weakness of the white minority prompted him to change his views fundamentally. He was not prepared to walk over corpses to retain power. To those who advocated shooting it out, he answered in the stark terms he used in an address to senior police officers just before unbanning the liberation movements: 'For if this Armageddon takes place – and blood flows ankle deep in our streets and four or five million people lie dead – the problem will remain exactly the same as it was before the shooting started.'

Moreover, De Klerk resisted using the might of the state in negotiations. He soon alienated the military by disbanding the National Security Management System and sidelining the State Security Council. He also cut military expenditure and halved conscription.

De Klerk's simple but fundamental conclusion was that there could never be peace unless there was a political system accepted by the majority. He had not undergone a conversion in a shattering moment of truth. For all his search for principles, he was an adaptable politician weighing alternatives in a shifting demographic and political balance. He abandoned apartheid because the

F.W. de Klerk

homelands policy had failed to achieve 'separate freedoms', not because it was wrong. He told a television interviewer, 'If one believes a policy is unworkable, it becomes immoral to advocate it.' Pragmatic survival instincts preceded morality in De Klerk's decision to abandon apartheid. In his own words, he was a peacemaker.

OPPOSITE: *The Berlin Wall came down in November 1989, signalling the end of the Cold War. On three occasions external wars brought about a fundamental realignment of South African politics. South Africa's entry into World War I triggered the Rebellion of 1914–1915, the suppression of which boosted the fledgling National Party. South Africa's entry into World War II in 1939 split the United Party and led to most Afrikaners breaking away to support the NP, which won the election nine years later. The fall of the Berlin Wall signalled the end of the Cold War, the end of Soviet intervention in the Third World, and the beginning of communism's death throes. It presented De Klerk with what he described as a 'God-sent opportunity'. But the fall of the Wall was a double-edged sword. Anti-communism had long been the main reason why Western governments accepted and even bolstered white rule in South Africa. The disappearance of the communist threat and the ANC's retreat from nationalisation*

The Wall disintegrates

In September 1989 the extent of the informal talks between some government representatives and ANC leaders was known only to President Botha, one or two trusted ministers and a few senior National Intelligence Service officials. There was no sign of a breakthrough on the deadlock. Even De Klerk was not fully informed. After coming to power he privately criticised his brother, Dr Willem de Klerk, for meeting abroad with ANC office bearers a few weeks earlier. In June Thabo Mbeki had chaired a congress of the SA Communist Party where it was decided to continue with the armed struggle until victory and introduce socialism thereafter. There was animated talk of 'building East Germany in Africa'.

The dismantling of the Berlin Wall, which began on 9 November 1989, dramatically heralded the end of the Soviet Union's sway over eastern Europe, and also contributed to the breaking of the deadlock in South Africa. Communism as a political and economic system was rapidly beginning to disintegrate. These developments presented De Klerk with what he termed a 'God-sent opportunity'. The National Party could tell its constituency that without Soviet backing the ANC, with its ally the SA Communist Party, no longer constituted a major threat to stability and private ownership. He could also argue that communism was so discredited that the ANC would be compelled to accept the free market, property rights and other investment-friendly policies.

For the National Party government the fall of the Wall was a double-edged sword. Anti-communism had long been the main reason why Western governments accepted and even bolstered white rule in South Africa. But the disappearance of the communist threat and the ANC's retreat from nationalisation had made the South African govern-

ment's anti-communism old-fashioned, and deprived it of its strongest argument for Western pressure to force the ANC to accept power-sharing.

By the end of 1989 De Klerk had made a great leap. In April 1987 he had told people in his constituency that it was necessary for whites to take the 'slight risk' of building a system of power-sharing in order to get 'a substantial portion or even a majority of blacks to join them in forging a bastion against the ANC'. Now he decided to invite the ANC into the bastion and work out the power-sharing system with it. In December 1989, he persuaded his cabinet to accept the need to unban the ANC, the Pan-Africanist Congress and other liberation movements, and to begin all-party negotiations for a new constitution without preconditions. On 2 February 1990 he announced this decision to a startled Parliament.

Without the fall of the Wall, it is difficult to conceive of the ANC coming to power five years later.

made the South African government's anti-communism old-fashioned. It also deprived it of its strongest argument for Western pressure to force the ANC to accept power-sharing to enable the NP to insist on market-oriented policies.

CHAPTER FIFTEEN

Towards an inclusive democracy

Negotiating in turbulent times

The government's lifting of the ban on the African National Congress (ANC) and other liberation and extra-parliamentary movements on 2 February 1990 triggered a surge of political activity. Mass meetings attended by multitudes, particularly to hear Nelson Mandela, freed on 11 February 1990, together with strikes, street protests, demonstrations and violence of all kinds ushered in a period of profound uncertainty and potentially dangerous instability. Yet the security forces believed they could deal with any immediate challenge. In November 1992, the ANC leadership pointed out that while the regime had been weakened, the ANC was unable to overthrow it. 'The regime still commands vast state and other military resources', it stated. The time to talk had begun.

In meetings with senior police and military officers in early 1990 President F.W. de Klerk stated that it was no longer expected of them to promote certain political aims or to suppress others. The task of the police and the military was now solely to fight crime and protect all South Africans. Rejecting the undue influence of military and intelligence advisers on the Botha government, De Klerk rarely consulted the commanders of the security forces. There would be no calling up of the reserves or military parades or targeted assassinations. There would also be no angry withdrawal from the negotiating table, unlike the ANC, which would suspend negotiations and embark on rolling mass action.

Rogue units

In January 1990 President F.W. de Klerk first heard of rogue units within the security forces that had committed assassinations. The Civil Co-operation Bureau (CCB) was a military unit staffed mainly by ex-policemen who murdered or severely injured political opponents. A similar secret police unit also existed. It was formally called Unit C-10, but because it used the farm Vlakplaas near Pretoria, it became known as the Vlakplaas unit. The government appointed the Harms Commission to investigate allegations of hit squads and political murder. Due to a lack of co-operation from the leadership of the security forces, as well as the fabrication of evidence, it could not prove the complicity of state agents in deaths of activists. At most it appeared that some individuals were guilty of common law crimes. Evidence of a much more comprehensive involvement of operatives with their base at Vlakplaas was only submitted to the De Klerk government in March 1994. There was also Project Coast, which studied the use of chemical and biological weapons, ostensibly for defensive purposes. It was later alleged that this operation provided poisons for the assassination of activists.

A time of unrest

The core area of the conflict in the late 1980s was in the KwaZulu-Natal area where battles between Inkatha and the ANC raged. In 1989 more than 90% of the deaths occurred here. In 1990 the number of deaths outside Natal and KwaZulu rose from 124 to 1 888, mainly as a result of a fierce political turf battle between the ANC and Inkatha on the Witwatersrand. Hoping to create an aura of normality De Klerk lifted the state of emergency outside Natal on 7 June 1990. Violence escalated.

There were some 20 000 political fatalities between 1984 and 1994, 70% of them between February 1990 and April 1994. Between 14 000 and 16 000 of the 20 500 fatalities involved clashes between supporters of different predominantly black organisations, mostly between supporters of the Inkatha Freedom Party (IFP) and those of the ANC. But the media put by far the greatest emphasis on rogue organisations existing within the security forces. The police killed an estimated 3 000 people in riots or fighting guerrillas in actions deemed lawful by the state. Members or ex-members of the police asked the Truth and Reconciliation Commission (TRC) for amnesty for the unlawful death of some 150 people.

The ANC leadership alleged that a paramilitary force of 200 trained by the Defence Force in the Caprivi Strip was responsible for many deaths in Natal. The cabinet had formally approved the unit in 1986. Commanders of the security forces insisted that the

OPPOSITE TOP: *Dr Gerrit Viljoen was chief negotiator of the National Party until his resignation in mid-1992 due to ill health. He was previously vice-chancellor of a university, head of the Afrikaner Broederbond and a cabinet minister. At the negotiations at the Convention for a Democratic South Africa he was respected across party lines and his departure was considered a major blow to the NP government, from which it never recovered.*

OPPOSITE BOTTOM: *A poster for the 1994 election on the gate to a remote farm.*

BELOW LEFT AND RIGHT: *A fierce battle for political turf erupted between the ANC and Inkatha in KwaZulu and Natal, and on the Witwatersrand. Inkatha claimed to have lost several hundred office-bearers in Natal through assassinations. In the country as a whole the death toll mounted steadily. Between September 1984 and December 1993, 18 997 people died. In a period of eight years the police recorded more than 80 000 violent incidents. Of the violent deaths, by far the greatest proportion occurred in clashes between Inkatha and ANC members.*

Between 1984 and 1994 approximately 20 000 people died in the conflict in South Africa. As the table shows, this figure is very low in comparative terms. (These figures do not take into account the deaths in clashes between the South African armed forces and guerrilla fighters beyond the South African borders, particularly in Angola and Mozambique.)

All over the world, ethnic conflicts with high death tolls often occur in one of the following two contexts. One is an invasion by a foreign army or irregular forces accompanied by the destruction of crops, the looting of towns and the hounding of people into camps. The other is when a government loses control over its armed forces or uses such forces to attack communities in ethnic-cleansing operations.

In South Africa the judicial system remained independent and policemen who killed someone illegally knew, particularly by the beginning of the 1980s, that there was

a chance they would stand trial. There was no encouragement from the general public, black or white, for racial killings.

That did not mean the hands of all the pre-1990 political leaders were clean. President P.W. Botha and some of the senior ministers in charge of security affairs never gave explicit instructions to assassinate leading activists, but they did give subtle and not so subtle hints to 'remove' or 'eliminate' some of them. Even at the level of the State Security Council there was loose talk of this kind. All this stopped after De Klerk came to power in 1990. But after the transition to democracy the politicians were quite happy to let the police and its leadership virtually alone carry the burden of guilt for assassinations and to allow the military and the other security agencies to profess their innocence. But other than in the case of the Vlakplaas police unit, the Army's Special Forces, and the Caprivi trainees operating in KwaZulu-Natal, the departmental heads of the police and

the army never really lost control over their respective forces. The number of 'targeted assassinations' informally authorised by people in command was low, comparatively speaking.

The ANC practised a relatively greater degree of restraint than its counterparts in other parts of the world. In Nelson Mandela it had a leader who in the 1980s concluded that a successful armed uprising was impossible over the short to medium term. Oliver Tambo, leader of the ANC, also urged restraint. The government forces, the ANC and Inkatha all committed atrocities, but the death toll never rose so high that a settlement became impossible.

DEATHS IN SELECTED ETHNIC CONFLICTS (APPROXIMATE FIGURES)

COUNTRY	DEATHS	POPULATION (MILLIONS)	YEARS OF CONFLICT	DEATHS AS PERCENTAGE
Cambodia*	2 400 000	7.2 (1971)	1975–1978	33.3%
Rwanda	800 000	8.0 (1990)	1994	10.0%
Chechnya	90 000	1.1 (2002)	1994–2005	8.2%
Guatemala	200 000	3.8 (1962)	1960–1998	5.3%
Bosnia	200 000	4.0 (2002)	1992–1995	5.0%
Algeria**	300 000	10.0 (1965)	1954–1962	3.0%
East Timor	18 600	1.0 (2006)	1974–1999	1.9%
N. Ireland	3 500	1.4 (1961)	1968–1998	0.25%
South Africa	19 000	26.0 (1988)	1984–1993	0.07%

* The deaths in Cambodia are estimated to be in a range of 1.7 million to 3 million.

** The Algerian government that came to power in 1962 put the death toll at a million.

introduction of the force was a response to the assassination of more than 100 Inkatha leaders or chiefs by ANC operatives. In ANC and United Democratic Front (UDF) circles there was a widespread perception that it was a government-sponsored hit squad. Shortly after the introduction of the unit in KwaZulu-Natal a massacre occurred in Kwa-Makutha, Durban, in which thirteen people died. In 1995 the state charged eleven military officers including two ex-Defence Force heads and a previous Minister of Defence (General Magnus Malan) as accessories to the massacre. The court found them all innocent and President Mandela accepted the judgement.

Wouter Basson, who was in charge of Project Coast, faced trial on the charge of providing substances used to murder or poison activists. General Malan testified to the TRC that there was never permission for the offensive application of this capability. In a controversial judgement, the court found Basson innocent.

Many of the killings were attributed to ANC sympathisers. It was in fact still partly a revolutionary organisation with its own army, Umkhonto weSizwe. In 1986 some senior leaders approved Operation Vula, headed by Mac Maharaj, which would aim at building an underground in the country, infiltrating arms and staging an insurrection should negotiations fail. When De Klerk legalised the ANC in 1990 Maharaj set about implementing the plan. The operation was uncovered and he was arrested.

Activists aligned with the ANC or its auxiliary force, the UDF, enforced some of the strikes and the school and consumer boycotts with great severity. They targeted policemen, soldiers, local councillors, informers and all other kinds of 'regime puppets'. More than 400 suspected informers were killed through the gruesome 'necklace method' – a burning tyre around a person's body, to which the leadership often turned a blind eye. As a result the township sources of the police quickly dried up.

Anthea Jeffery, who researched the conflict in Natal, noted:

> The violence that the ANC generated quickly spiralled out of control. And because it targeted so many in the black community it also provoked a violent backlash. Once the retaliation had begun, it developed its own momentum and among other consequences evolved in a civil war between the ANC and IFP.

The ANC furiously rejected the view that it, along with the IFP, was primarily responsible for the violence. It claimed that a Third Force in the security forces was directly responsible for most of the violence or for instigating it. Mandela repeatedly accused De Klerk of personally directing the violence or having lost control over his security forces. De Klerk responded that if he acted against the security forces without out evidence, they could lose all confidence in him.

The ANC's allegations, supported by some newspapers, kept the government on the defensive. They also whittled away the considerable black support that the polls had revealed for De Klerk. In 1991, after evidence had been produced that the police were secretly funding Inkatha to counteract the ANC, De Klerk felt compelled to remove General Magnus Malan and Adriaan Vlok from the portfolios of Defence and Police respectively.

Relations between the government and the ANC were strained after 17 June 1992 when Inkatha-aligned hostel-dwellers killed 48 residents of Boipatong, an ANC-supporting township 100 kilometres southeast of Johannesburg. Claiming police complicity, the ANC suspended its participation in the negotiations indefinitely. Both a court and the Amnesty Committee of the Truth and Reconciliation Commission later could find no evidence that the police were involved, as the ANC claimed. However, at the time the ANC managed to make it seem that the state, perhaps even De Klerk, was to blame.

ABOVE: *The cover of a book written on Operation Vula, showing some of the operatives in disguise. During the first years of the 1990s the ANC was still partly a revolutionary organisation with its own army, Umkhonto weSizwe (MK). Back in 1986, while still in exile, some senior leaders approved Operation Vula, headed by Mac Maharaj. This aimed to build an underground in the country, infiltrating arms and staging an insurrection should negotiations fail. When De Klerk legalised the ANC in 1990 Maharaj set about implementing the plan. The operation was uncovered and Maharaj was arrested.*

BELOW: *Violence erupted in 1985 in the Crossroads informal settlement between residents and the police.*

The rumours of police complicity at Boipatong added fuel to the ANC's campaign of 'rolling mass action' over several weeks. The aim was to challenge the system of political control and to topple the homeland governments, including that of KwaZulu, by force. The first target was the Ciskei. An ANC march on the government building was brutally ended when Ciskei soldiers opened fire, killing 29 people.

Talks between the government and the ANC resumed but the violence continued. The ANC continued to blame a Third Force within the police or the military for murders of activists and commuters on trains. In November 1992 the Goldstone Commission raided a clandestine agency of Military Intelligence and found some evidence of efforts to undermine the ANC's military arm, Umkhonto weSizwe. De Klerk asked Pierre Steyn, a general in the Defence Force, to investigate the allegations. Steyn did not produce a written report but in a presentation to De Klerk in December 1992 tabled what he called 'unverified allegations'. His report claimed that members of the Defence Force's Directorate Reconnaissance (Special Forces) were involved in 'murder, terrorism, destabilisation abroad . . . corruption, promotion of factional party political objectives and blatant disregard of government policy'. None of the allegations was proved, but De Klerk dismissed 22 military officers. However, the attorney-general found the evidence too scant to prosecute.

While the ANC and National Party began marching in lock step towards a negotiated settlement, the Pan-Africanist Congress tried to subvert the process. It broke off negotiations and unleashed violence aimed at destroying the 'colonial settler state'. Its armed wing, the Azanian People's Liberation Army (APLA), attacked farmers, residents in hotels and patrons of country clubs.

Some particularly gruesome attacks horrified the country. In July 1993 APLA operatives attacked the congregation at an evening service in St James Church, Cape Town. They tossed hand grenades and fired automatic rifles. Eleven people were killed and many injured. American exchange student Amy Biehl was murdered in the township of Guguletu in Cape Town, hacked to death by members of the Pan-Africanist Students Organisation after they had stoned her car. In the final weeks before the election Afrikaner Weerstandsbeweging (AWB) members committed several racially motivated murders on blacks. Right-wingers were responsible for a car bomb that went off in the centre of Johannesburg two days before the April 1994 election, killing nine, including an ANC candidate.

The Mandela factor

Nelson Mandela's contribution to the political settlement of 1990–1994 was decisive. Firstly, in 1985 he began the 'talks about talks' that were an indispensable preliminary to the formal negotiations. Acting on broad approval from Oliver Tambo but deciding on his own on the content of his conversations with officials, he met 47 times with senior government officials in discussions that led some National Party leaders to believe that an acceptable settlement could be negotiated with the ANC.

Mandela laid down two conditions for negotiations: the ANC would not accept any preconditions set by government, and it was interested only in negotiating for a unified South Africa that would meet black aspirations for majority rule. That an ANC leader whom the government believed was relatively conciliatory was saying these things was of critical importance.

Secondly, it is difficult to imagine any other ANC official enjoying the authority that Mandela could exert in disciplining the ANC's following. By the time of the ANC's return, its president, Oliver Tambo, had been incapacitated by a stroke. Mandela's moral authority was especially important after the assassination of Chris Hani in 1993. The assassination was followed by riots in which 70 people were killed. Observers agree that Mandela's televised address after Hani's death ensured that the casualties were not much higher and much more politically disruptive.

In this crisis, Mandela's assumption of the role of national conciliator demonstrated his own and the ANC's political authority. Public support among both black and white people for a political settlement increased. He tended to delegate decisions about the

Chris Hani (left) with Tokyo Sexwale.

details of this settlement, though significantly he intervened personally in the bargaining to deny the National Party a minority veto in cabinet decision-making.

Thirdly, Mandela's willingness to confront the ANC's adversaries during the negotiations and his tactics of brinkmanship were important in extracting concessions. His capacity for risk-taking was especially evident in obtaining government consent to the ANC's conditions for resuming negotiations after their suspension in mid-1992. In September 1992 he forced De Klerk to release political prisoners in return for the ANC's resumption of the constitutional talks, telling him that he had to make this concession, 'Because you know in the end you are going to give in. Because if you don't we are going to humiliate you. And I will see to it that that happens.'

By 1992, Mandela had convinced himself that De Klerk was a 'dishonourable' partner in the transition, complicit in the continuing attacks on ANC supporters by what ANC leadership believed to be a covert Third Force directed by intelligence officials. Mandela certainly believed that De Klerk was at least guilty of failing to act decisively to curtail such activity.

While De Klerk saw himself as an equal partner in creating the new South Africa, Mandela could not acknowledge the president or his government as equals. As a realist, he was aware of the government's coercive power and hence the necessity to 'do business' with it. This was a necessity many influential ANC personalities were unwilling to accept. Mandela would not concede, though, that his adversary's actions were in any way morally worthy. When the two men were jointly awarded the Nobel Peace Prize Mandela's anger was obvious.

The right wing blusters

White organisations that committed themselves to wrecking the negotiations proliferated. By 1990 there were an estimated 20 paramilitary groups and 30 fundamentalist organisations. By 1993 their combined figure had risen to nearly 200. The most prominent was the Afrikaner Weerstandsbeweging (AWB), an ill-disciplined paramilitary organisation under Eugène Terre'Blanche, which claimed to have 15 000 men under arms.

The AWB acquired prominence during the 1980s when the Conservative Party made strong headway, throwing the National Party on the defensive. It wrecked several National Party meetings, but its aim of restoring the Boer republics and restricting citizenship to people with right-wing beliefs, together with its racist rhetoric, repelled all but a small white fringe. Terre'Blanche was a bombastic orator imitating the political style of Afrikaner leaders in the heyday of apartheid. His theatrical town meetings received excessive coverage from foreign television teams only because they confirmed the foreign stereotype of reactionary whites ready to plunge the country into a bloodbath.

Realistically there was only one major threat in the white community that could seriously threaten the negotiations. This was the possibility of General Constand Viljoen, ex-head of the Defence Force, leading an uprising of men from the Defence Force and Citizen Force. This never materialised (see box).

In the months before the election, scheduled for 26–28 April 1994, it looked as if the political centre was unable to hold. The traditional Zulus under King Goodwill Zwelithini and Mangosuthu Buthelezi demanded independence rather than tolerate 'Xhosa domination' under the ANC. On 28 March between 30 000 and 40 000 Zulus marched past the ANC headquarters in the centre of Johannesburg. ANC security guards opened fire. At the end of the day eighteen people lay dead.

Lucas Mangope, president of Bophuthatswana, bent on retaining 'independence', refused to allow registration for the election in the territory and resisted the homeland's reincorporation in the republic. The situation in Mafikeng spiralled out of control after

ABOVE: *The historic 'Groote Schuur Minute' was the signing of a document between Nelson Mandela, then president of the ANC, and State President F.W. de Klerk at Tuynhuis in Cape Town on 4 May 1990. The document was a commitment between the two parties towards resolving the existing climate of violence, as well as to stability and peaceful constitutional negotiations.*

Uncertainty about what General Constand Viljoen might be planning was constantly in the background while the negotiations continued. Viljoen had served as chief of the South African Defence Force before retiring in 1984. He had been the model of the disciplined soldier faithfully executing the commands of the political leadership, but became convinced that the ANC was pursuing a revolutionary agenda and that F.W. de Klerk had caved in to its demands.

Called the last of the Boer generals, he was widely respected in the Defence Force for his professionalism and personal integrity. Blunt, determined and committed to the Afrikaner cause, he was the sort of leader to whom many Afrikaners would have flocked if he had had a credible plan of action. Viljoen and his followers joined The Afrikaner Volksfront, a coalition of right-wing organisations, which all rejected participation in a democratic election and demanded an Afrikaner *volkstaat,* or ethnic state.

Most of the Volksfront favoured a 'white' state with Pretoria as its capital and including parts of the western Transvaal, eastern Transvaal and northern Free State. But while approximately two-thirds of the Afrikaners resided in this area, the great majority of people there were non-Afrikaners. A 1993 poll showed that only one-fifth of the Afrikaners would consider moving to a *volkstaat* and more than half either opposed it or were uncertain about it.

By 1993 Viljoen began to plan to disrupt the elections, have De Klerk removed as president and restart the negotiations. Some believed that he could raise 50 000 men from the Auxiliary Citizen's Force and also some Defence Force units. In a briefing, General George Meiring, chief of the Defence Force, warned the government and the ANC of the ghastly consequences of Viljoen's opposing the election.

To dissuade Viljoen, for whom he had

'the highest regard', Meiring had several meetings with him. At one meeting Viljoen said, 'You and I and our men can take this country in an afternoon,' to which Meiring replied, 'Yes, that is so, but what do we do the morning after the coup?' The white-black demographic balance, the internal and foreign pressures, and all the intractable problems would still be there. After a debacle in Mafikeng, Viljoen abandoned all plans for an uprising.

the ANC initiated mass action. Mangope sought help from Viljoen, with whom he was in a loose alliance. This was Viljoen's moment of truth. He undertook to assemble a force of 3 000 men, while Mangope promised to supply arms.

But before Viljoen could act, an AWB vigilante mob arrived, wreaking havoc and shooting blacks in the streets at random. Bophuthatswana troops returned fire. The *Sunday Times* would later publish a dramatic photograph of three AWB men prostrate next to their car moments after they were shot dead by a black soldier.

It epitomised the fall of white supremacy. Viljoen and his men quickly withdrew from the tragic farce and disassociated themselves from it. A few days later he announced his intention to participate in the election as leader of the Freedom Front. In a way the AWB's intervention was fortuitous. It prevented a situation where troops of the Defence Force would be asked to shoot at Viljoen, their previous commander.

A new constitution

Nearly two years went by between State President F.W. de Klerk's epoch-making speech on 2 February 1990 and the start of formal constitutional talks at the Convention for a Democratic South Africa. The intervening period was devoted to removing the obstacles to negotiation. The first – the apartheid laws – were removed on 1 February 1991 when De Klerk announced the intention of his government to abolish them all.

None of the other obstacles to negotiation was easy to resolve. In a series of agreements (the Groote Schuur Accord, May 1990; the Pretoria Minute, August 1990; and the D.F. Malan Accord, February 1991), the government and the ANC agreed to seek a negotiated political settlement. The ANC agreed to suspend the armed struggle, but not to disband its armed wing Umkhonto weSizwe.

The Convention for a Democratic South Africa (Codesa) opened on 20 December 1991 at the World Trade Centre in Kempton Park. The two major parties, the National Party and the ANC, had differing ideas of what purpose it should serve. The ANC insisted that only an elected constituent assembly could draw up a constitution, while the National Party and the Inkatha Freedom Party opposed this, fearing that an elected body, with a probable ANC majority, would have a blank cheque to draft a constitution that suited ANC political needs.

Nevertheless, nineteen of the twenty delegations – the Bophuthatswana government declined to sign – agreed to a Declaration of Intent committing them to 'a united, democratic, non-racial and non-sexist state in which sovereign authority is exercised over the whole of its territory'. The concept of 'sufficient consensus' was employed, meaning that the process could go forward if the National Party and the ANC reached agreement.

Codesa resumed its labours early in 1992, separate tasks being allocated to each of five Working Groups, but another threat loomed to imperil the process. This was the menacing rise of the ultra-right wing, signified by the Conservative Party's victory in a by-election in the historically safe National Party seat of Potchefstroom on 19 February. It was the climax of a series of by-elections in which the Conservative Party had either beaten the National Party or slashed its majorities.

De Klerk needed to determine whether his initiative retained the support of the white electorate, so he called a referendum for 17 March in which voters were asked whether they wished the reform process aimed at negotiating a new constitution to continue.

LEFT: *Codesa – the Convention for a Democratic South Africa – opened negotiations at the World Trade Centre in Kempton Park outside Johannesburg in December 1991.*

OPPOSITE TOP: *Constand Viljoen being congratulated by the then Minister of Defence, P.W. Botha, after being handed an award in 1977.*

OPPOSITE BOTTOM: *Three AWB members were shot dead next to their Mercedes Benz in Mafikeng, Bophuthatswana, on 9 March 1994. They had intended to assist President Lucas Mangope's government, which was under threat of being toppled by demonstrations organised by the ANC.*

Over 68% voted 'yes', and the ultra-right wing, which had contributed to the violence, was thrown into disarray. The National Party (NP) leadership tacitly assumed that with this victory it was no longer necessary to refer any major constitutional change to the electorate, although De Klerk had promised to seek the voters' endorsement of the constitutional principles after the completion of the negotiations.

The breakdown of Codesa

By mid-May 1992 the negotiations stalled over what appeared to be fundamental differences. The NP's constitutional proposals included enforced coalitions, a collegiate presidency composed of the leaders of the major parties, serving as president on a rotational basis, and a senate that gave generously weighted representation to minority parties. It advocated a federal system with strong regional and local governments. The Democratic Party, the Inkatha Freedom Party and some of the homeland administrations also advocated federalism.

The ANC strongly opposed the NP's proposals, rejecting enforced coalitions and minority vetoes, and insisting that minority parties would be adequately protected under majority rule by their assured representation under proportional representation, their ability as opposition to keep the government on its toes, and the development of a vigorous civil society. It was also suspicious of federalism, regarding it as a means whereby wealthier regions could protect their advantages.

De Klerk had previously conceded the principle of an elected constitution-making body, but with the proviso that there should be a two-phase process in which an interim constitution would be drafted by a multiparty conference and enacted into law by the existing Tricameral Parliament. A fully inclusive Parliament, elected by universal

ABOVE: *Out of the 20 political groups at Codesa in December 1991, 19 agreed to sign the Declaration of Intent stating that they would begin writing a new constitution for South Africa.*

RIGHT: *Gerrit Viljoen, F.W. de Klerk and Pik Botha at the opening of Codesa in December 1991.*

franchise under the interim constitution, would act as a constitution-making body and draft and adopt a final constitution. A new body, the Constitutional Court, would have to certify that the constitution incorporated pre-agreed principles laid down by the original multiparty conference. De Klerk's proposal, it transpired, became the template for the future trajectory of the constitutional negotiations.

The ANC ascendant

The ANC walked out of Codesa in mid-May 1992 after failing to reach agreement with the NP on substantial questions. The bleakness of the political situation was compounded shortly thereafter by the Boipatong massacre on 17 June 1992.

After breaking off negotiations, the ANC embarked on a campaign of 'rolling mass action', declaring that what it could not get at the negotiating table, it would gain by

Martin Thembisile ('Chris') Hani was an exact contemporary of Thabo Mbeki. Hani was born on 28 June 1942 in the tiny village of Sabalele in the Cofimvaba district in rural Transkei, the fifth of six children. His father was a semi-literate migrant worker on the Rand mines; his mother worked on a subsistence farm. He and his siblings walked 25 kilometres to school each weekday and the same distance to church on Sundays. Hani was a devout Catholic and wanted to become a priest.

Mbeki was born in the little village of Idutywa nearby on 18 June 1942, one of Govan and Epainette Mbeki's four children. Both Hani and Mbeki imbibed their radical politics at the same school, Lovedale College, at the same period. At Lovedale the brash Hani was early on noticed as a leader. In contrast Mbeki, although involved in politics, was more reclusive. Mbeki's behind-the-scenes leadership style was even then

apparent. For example, although Hani, Mbeki and Sam Nolutshungu, who later became a renowned political scientist, were all involved in organising a strike that would shut down the mission school, the school principal and teachers only noticed Hani and Nolutshungu – and singled them out for reprimand.

Hani joined the ANC's youth league in 1957, a year after Mbeki. Hani studied classics at the universities of Fort Hare and Rhodes, graduating with a bachelor's degree in Latin and English from Rhodes. In 1963 he joined the ANC's armed wing and left the country. In the 1960s he fought on the Rhodesian front in skirmishes with fighters from the Zimbabwe African People's Union (Zapu). He was appointed chief of staff of Umkhonto weSizwe in 1987.

Hani rose swiftly through the ranks of the South African Communist Party (SACP). A major influence was Thabo's father, Govan, who introduced him to Marxism-Leninism – a philosophy he adhered to throughout his life. He was the first choice when Oliver Tambo, the ANC's president-in-exile, cast around for an aide-de-camp, but Hani saw himself more as a fighter in the mould of Che Guevara than a bureaucrat and politely declined.

After Lovedale College, Thabo Mbeki pursued his studies in the United Kingdom, eventually completing a master's degree in economics at Sussex University, later also undergoing the obligatory military training for talented ANC cadres in the Soviet Union. He rose to senior positions in the SACP but cut his ties with the party following its unbanning in 1990. Just as the ANC moderates prepared Mbeki for a future leadership role, the SACP helped craft Hani, who be-

Thabo Mbeki

came general secretary of the SACP, into a left-wing, socialist alternative.

By now it was clear that Mandela would become the ANC's next leader; the question that vexed all was who would succeed him – Mbeki or Hani?

Hani's assassination on 10 April 1993 by a white right-winger opened the door for Mbeki to capture the presidency. Before his untimely death, Hani was the protégé of SACP chairman Joe Slovo, and such internal kingmakers as Winnie Madikizela-Mandela urged him on to the presidency at the height of her charm and influence. The powerful security network built up by the ANC in exile was at his disposal, he was revered by the radical youth and he was gifted with a natural charm, charisma and intelligence. Given his popularity at the time of his assassination – only Nelson Mandela was more popular – many ANC supporters, especially those on the left, still believe that he would have beaten Mbeki to succeed Mandela.

Chris Hani

demonstrating its popular support. Boipatong was the turning point in the negotiations: whereas previously the ANC and the NP had been fairly evenly balanced, the scales now tipped in the ANC's favour. Pessimism was deepened by an episode at Bisho, capital of Ciskei, where 29 people died.

After the Bisho massacre the dangerous downward spiralling of the economy and heavy diplomatic pressure forced the ANC and the government to resume bilateral negotiations. This resulted in De Klerk and Mandela signing the Record of Understanding on 26 September 1992, opening the way for the resumption of formal negotiations in 1993. The Record followed De Klerk's suggested model, but added that an elected constitution-making body should have a fixed time frame and adequate deadlock-breaking mechanisms. Moreover, the elected body would act as an interim Parliament, and an interim government of national unity would govern the country. The ANC wanted as short a time frame as possible, whereas the National Party was holding out for an open-ended period of multiparty government.

But the major change was symbolic, underlining the ANC's new ascendancy. It got a reluctant De Klerk to agree to the release of political prisoners, the fencing and policing of hostels and the prohibition of carrying dangerous weapons. The latter two decisions seemed to pin the blame for the political fatalities mainly on Inkatha. Buthelezi was enraged that he was not consulted. He joined the Concerned South Africans Group (Cosag), consisting of various homeland governments and ultra-right wing organisations, including the Conservative Party. Its aim was to act as a counterweight to what it regarded as an 'unholy' alliance between the ANC and the National Party.

The final hurdles

Formal multiparty negotiations were resumed in April 1993. The name Codesa was dropped since it was associated with failure, and was replaced by 'Multiparty Negotiating Process' (MPNP). The MPNP was more streamlined and, in view of the political tension prevailing, was imbued with a sense of urgency. The country was again brought to the brink of widespread violence by the assassination of popular SACP leader Chris Hani on 10 April. It took Mandela's public appeals for calm to prevent disaster.

An important bridging of the differences between the NP and the ANC had occurred in November 1992 when the ANC accepted the need for a form of joint rule (or joint decision-making) before majority rule. Joe Slovo, leader of the SACP and one of the ANC's leading theoreticians, devised the strategic repositioning. He recommended a 'sunset' clause whereby a government of national unity, comprising the major parties, would govern for a five-year period, with the proviso that parties that had lost the election would not be able to paralyse the government. Slovo also drew attention to the 'vast potential' of the bureaucracy and security forces to destabilise a fledgling democracy unless guarantees of job security or retrenchment packages were offered.

The NP was still holding out for permanent multiparty government, but the ANC's concession went some way to meeting its demand. Roelf Meyer, the Minister of Constitutional Development and the government's chief negotiator, acknowledged subsequently that the government of national unity (GNU) concept was not a coalition 'but a forced agreement of co-operation between opponents and not between two parties who have found common ground'. The GNU proposal was to be temporary, which some of Meyer's colleagues opposed, wanting it to be permanent. With De Klerk's backing, Meyer's view prevailed.

Although the principle of a GNU was accepted, agreement on how it should take decisions proved elusive. The NP wanted two-thirds support for cabinet decisions, which the ANC rejected. It was not until November 1993 that agreement was reached when the NP abandoned its demand. De Klerk recognised that an impossible situation would be created if the cabinet had to vote on every decision: 'If the minority parties consistently thwarted the will of the majority it might in the end impose intolerable strain on the whole constitutional edifice.'

It was agreed that every party winning at least 80 seats (out of 400) would be entitled to a deputy presidency and every party winning at least 20 seats would be entitled to cabinet seats proportionate to the number of seats held by it in the National Assembly.

Slowly and painfully the ANC and the NP edged closer together. Initially, while the NP wanted maximum decentralisation of government, the ANC wanted a strong central government. In the end the ANC accepted regional governments whose powers the central government could not remove. This should have cleared the way for an IFP return to negotiations, but Buthelezi still demanded a form of confederation and rejected the principle of an elected constitution-making body. He feared that a victorious ANC would destroy the scaffolding of his power-base in KwaZulu, namely the traditional leaders.

ABOVE: *Roelf Meyer replaced Gerrit Viljoen as chief negotiator of the National Party. He and Cyril Ramaphosa, his counterpart in the ANC, developed a 'back channel' through which the two sides kept talking after formal negotiations had broken down in the winter of 1992.*

OPPOSITE: *Election scenes from across the country.*

The assassination of Chris Hani enabled the ANC to exert fierce pressure on government to fix a date for the election. On 2 July 1993 the MPNP agreed to 27 April 1994 as the date. The deadline meant that many outstanding concerns needed to be resolved speedily since the interim constitution had to be enacted into law by Parliament before the end of 1993. The parties had to agree on three main matters: constitutional principles to be incorporated in the final constitution, the demarcation of regions (later called provinces) and the legislation for 'levelling the playing field' before the election.

The constitutional principles on which further agreement was reached were the following: a constitutional democracy free of discrimination, the separation of powers, an independent judiciary, a public service that was to be non-partisan and broadly representative of the public, and equality before the law, making allowance for affirmative action.

To appease the seemingly intransigent white right wing, Constitutional Principle number 34 was added. It acknowledged the right of a cultural community to self-determination, provided there was substantial proven support for this within the community concerned. General Viljoen and the Freedom Front were now drawn into participating in the election by an ANC promise that the new government would appoint a council of his followers to consider the prospect of an Afrikaner *volkstaat*.

At a late stage Buthelezi and the IFP agreed to participate in the election after assurances were given about the constitutional position of the Zulu monarchy. A promise was also made that outstanding constitutional problems would be resolved later through international mediation.

The independent 'homelands' of Transkei, Bophuthatswana, Ciskei and Venda had little option but to be reintegrated into South Africa. Transkei and Venda, whose military dictators supported the ANC, agreed willingly. Bophuthatswana and Ciskei were still reluctant, but – faced with popular unrest and pressure from the South African government – were forced to acquiesce.

Significant legislation drafted by the MPNP and passed into law by Parliament created institutions designed to level the playing field in the run-up to the election:

- The Transitional Executive Council came into operation in January 1994. It was a multiparty body with a wide brief to facilitate the transition to democratic government at all levels of government.
- The Independent Electoral Commission (IEC) chaired by Judge Johann Kriegler was required to ensure that the election was free and fair, to determine the result, to adjudicate disputes, and to supervise the conduct of parties during the campaign.
- The Independent Media Commission's task was to contribute to a climate that was conducive to free and fair elections and, particularly, to ensure that state information services and the South African Broadcasting Corporation were impartial in their treatment of the parties.

The founding elections

The NP and the ANC had agreed that the electoral system for both national and provincial elections should be based on a list system of proportional representation. This had the advantage of simplicity and of enabling minority parties to obtain some representation. The details of the system were set out in Schedule 2 of the interim constitution: the National Assembly was to consist of 400 members, 200 of whom would be elected from national lists submitted by registered parties, and 200 from provincial lists. Pressure from the Democratic Party led to an amendment requiring separate ballot papers for the national and provincial elections.

An unavoidable weakness was the absence of voters' rolls for the 1994 election because there was insufficient time to compile them. Instead, eligible voters were required to produce an identity document – which millions did not possess. Accordingly, the IEC was empowered to issue temporary voting cards. Its statistics showed that by 29 April over 3.5 million such cards had been issued, nearly 1.5 million during the four voting days. It was obviously a system liable to abuse since many applicants were unable to provide proof that they were at least 18 years old.

The election was held over three days, 26–28 April, and extended to 29 April in six areas that had been seriously affected by logistical problems. The challenges facing the IEC were formidable. The magnitude of the task is conveyed by some of the statistics: an estimated 22.7 million people were eligible to vote (according to the dubious figures in the 1992 census), for which 10 000 voting stations were required.

The problem of violence haunted the country. There were reports of housewives stockpiling food in case there was a general breakdown of law and order. The IEC was especially worried by the possibility of intimidation: research reports before the election suggested that there were 165 'no-go' areas across the country. But the worst did not happen. The IEC's official account of the elections said that 'the incidence of frustration of political activity was minimal and that the degree of election violence was negligible throughout the country'. That there were irregularities is undoubted. De Klerk claimed, plausibly, that as many as one million illegal votes were cast, mostly because towards the end of the election, temporary voting cards were being issued virtually on request.

Yet the first elections had proceeded remarkably peacefully.

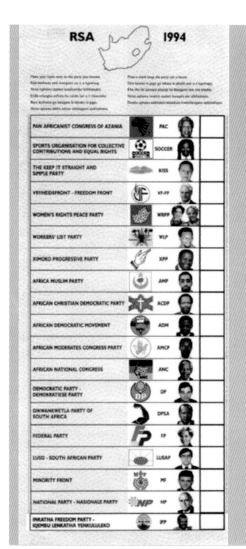

THE ELECTION RESULT

Of the 22.7 million eligible voters, 19.7 million voted in the national election and 19.6 million at the provincial level. These figures indicated a poll of 86%. Very few spoilt votes were recorded in spite of the substantial number of illiterate voters, especially in the rural areas. The ballot papers were simple: they depicted each party's name and crest in party colours, together with a photograph of the leader. Perhaps the major reason for the remarkably high turnout was that for many voters, especially blacks, the election was a joyful catharsis and a symbolic affirmation of their newfound rights as citizens.

The results were announced by the IEC on 6 May, although the National Party had conceded defeat on 2 May. The seven parties that gained representation and their percentage share of the vote and seats were:

At the provincial level, the ANC won outright control of six provinces, the NP winning in the Western Cape and the IFP in KwaZulu-Natal. In the Northern Cape, the ANC won a plurality of the votes (49.7%), fractionally more than the combined total of votes won by the NP, FF and DP.

Among black and white voters, votes cleaved largely to the racial divide. According to Andrew Reynolds's estimates, 94% of the ANC's national votes came from blacks, with only 0.5% from whites. Proportionately to its overall vote, the NP showed the widest spread of cross-racial support: 49% white, 30% coloured, 14% black, and 7% Indian. Approximately two-thirds of coloured and Indian voters voted for the NP.

Party	Percentage	Seats
African National Congress (ANC)	62.65%	252
National Party (NP)	20.39%	82
Inkatha Freedom Party (IFP)	10.54%	43
Freedom Front (FF)	2.17%	9
Democratic Party (DP)	1.73%	7
Pan-Africanist Congress (PAC)	1.25%	5
African Christian Democratic Party (ACDP)	0.45%	2

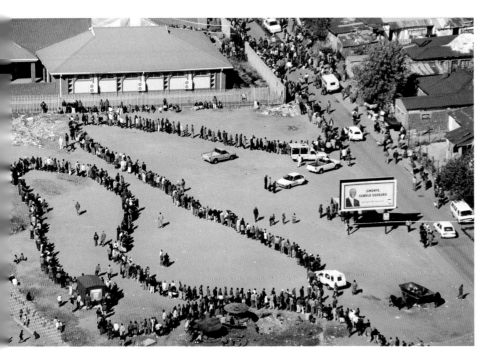

The final constitution

The Constituent Assembly (CA), consisting of 400 members of the National Assembly and 90 members of the Senate, met for the first time on 24 May 1994 and elected Cyril Ramaphosa (ANC) as chairperson and Leon Wessels (NP) as deputy chairperson.

It had to pass a new constitutional text within two years of the first meeting of the National Assembly, namely 9 May. A deadlock-breaking mechanism could be invoked if required. The CA required a two-thirds majority for passing the text. The ANC let it be known publicly that if agreement on the full draft could not be reached it would invoke the deadlock-breaking mechanism, going all the way to a referendum – which it knew it would win – and thereafter consider reverting to its own original draft, and not the negotiated text.

With over 62% of the votes in the founding election, the ANC possessed considerable weight in the CA's deliberations, but even with the possible support of the PAC, its majority fell short of two-thirds. Compromises would be necessary.

The 34 principles, already largely woven into the text of the interim constitution, provided a framework, but many details required to be elaborated or expanded – and in those details lurked many devils.

The difficult questions in the negotiations related less to the structure of the executive and the concept of a Government of National Unity, which had been resolved at the Multiparty Negotiating Process, than to a range of seemingly more technical matters, which turned out to be important and difficult to resolve. The deadline of 8 May 1996 imposed great stress on the principal negotiators. The discussions focused on:

- The relationship between the national and provincial governments.
- The extent to which – if at all – property should enjoy constitutional protection.
- Matching the rights of trade unions to bargain collectively and to strike with a right of employers to enforce lockouts.
- The death penalty.
- The procedure for appointing judges, the attorney-general, the auditor-general and other officials, whose posts required strict impartiality and security of tenure, in such a way that the political factor in their appointments was circumscribed.
- The official language(s).
- Whether the constitution should allow single-medium schools (which in practice meant Afrikaans-medium schools).
- Whether the Bill of Rights should include 'second-generation' or socio-economic rights, and whether rights could be limited during states of emergency.

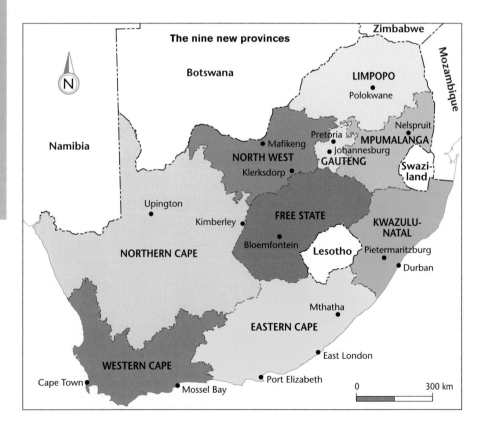

Fudging the main concerns

General agreement was achieved partly by fudging matters, by ambiguous clauses or qualifying principles by means of 'escape' clauses. For example, the text appeared to have certain federal characteristics, such as the vesting of some exclusive powers in the provinces; but these were largely negated by 'over-rides' that could be employed by the national government to ensure that provinces stayed in line.

Moreover, the revenue-raising capacity of provinces was severely circumscribed. The description of the constitution as a hybrid federal-unitary model was misplaced – it was little more than a unitary constitution with federal fig leaves.

The agreement on the medium of instruction in schools, which in effect meant Afrikaans as a single medium of instruction, is an example how the 'escape' clause was used to paper over real differences. Schools were permitted to offer single-medium tuition, but subject to considerations of equity, practicability and the need to redress the results of past discrimination.

Comparable clauses qualified the principle of equality and non-discrimination by permitting affirmative action, and the right to own property, which was subject to expropriation but only in terms of a general law and with payment of compensation.

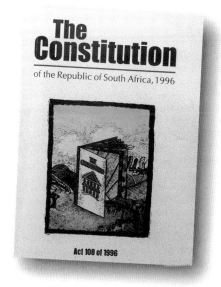

The text of the constitution was put to the vote on 8 May 1996. The ANC, NP, DP and PAC voted in favour – 421 votes (327 votes were required for a two-thirds majority). The Freedom Front abstained, the IFP boycotted the proceedings as it had done for much of the CA's negotiations; and the ACDP voted against.

The text was submitted to the Constitutional Court, made up of some of the finest legal minds in the country. It concluded that the basic structure of the constitution was sound. After some technical amendments were made, the Constitutional Court approved the revised text, and President Mandela signed it into law as The Constitution of the Republic of South Africa, Act 108 of 1996.

The Mandela presidency

The Mandela presidency attempted to pursue three goals, each of which contained major contradictions. First, President Nelson Mandela made a sincere attempt to bring about reconciliation but also introduced a Truth and Reconciliation Commission which many in the white minority did not believe was conducive to nation-building. Second, his presidency strongly committed itself to human rights as a basis for foreign policy, but Mandela himself was hostile to the idea of a vigorous and assertive opposition at home. Third, under the leadership of Deputy President Thabo Mbeki, a market-oriented economic policy was firmly established as the basis for both growth and redistribution. At the same time, government pressure for affirmative action together with relatively rigid labour laws produced severe skills and capacity problems and unemployment.

The National Assembly elected Nelson Mandela as president and F.W. de Klerk and Thabo Mbeki as deputies. The new South Africa formally dawned with the inauguration of Mandela as president of the Republic of South Africa on 10 May 1994. The ANC dominated the cabinet with eighteen ministers. The National Party had six ministers and two deputy ministers in the Government of National Unity. Also in the cabinet were Mangosuthu Buthelezi and two other ministers from the Inkatha Freedom Party.

TOP: *The new South African constitution was printed in booklet form in each of the eleven official languages, with the idea that citizens should know it and use it. But the effectiveness of the constitution as a living document was undermined by the reluctance of government to enforce the judgements of the courts, including the Constitutional Court, especially with respect to socio-economic rights. However, the Constitutional Court was seen as the main bastion in the defence of first-order human rights, such as freedom of speech – a position the government did not challenge.*

ABOVE: *F.W. de Klerk and Nelson Mandela share a light moment.*

TOP: *27 April 2004 saw the inauguration of President Thabo Mbeki, seen here with Nelson Mandela, the former president.*

ABOVE: *The Rugby World Cup final of 24 June 1995. One of the major controversies in the democratic government's new sport policy revolved around the Springboks and the Springbok colours (green and gold with a jumping antelope), which historically were tied most closely to the sporting code of rugby. The new government insisted on a new name (Proteas) and new colours but some voices in the ANC argued for an exception being made for rugby. The issue was resolved when President Nelson Mandela arrived at Ellis Park, Johannesburg, for the final of the 1995 Rugby World Cup dressed in a No. 6 Springbok jersey. Here he is congratulating Springbok captain Francois Pienaar after South Africa beat the All Blacks by 15–12 to win the cup.*

A spirit of reconciliation

A spirit of reconciliation marked the start of the democratic era with Mandela its symbol. He did not spend much time attending cabinet meetings or dealing with the looming crises of spiralling unemployment and the slump in the efficiency of the criminal justice system. He led as a wise statesman, a dignified peacemaker, a consummate politician and an imaginative unifier of people across racial lines, to the point of having tea with Betsie Verwoerd and other widows of NP leaders. He showed no sign of bitterness over the more than 27 years he had spent in jail.

Mandela captivated the whites; he cast a spell that produced a state of 'charismatic bewilderment', as one commentator described it. The culmination was his appearance at the final of the Rugby World Cup tournament held in Johannesburg in 1995, having decided that the national rugby team could retain its green and gold jersey with the springbok emblem despite the fact that for many it symbolised apartheid in sport. Before a crowd of 70 000, Mandela donned the jersey and appeared on the field to wish the players well. Fired up, the Springboks went on to win against the odds.

The NP's decline

The National Party's attempt to assert itself in the new government soon foundered. The ANC had no desire to give it any credit for its part. Its own electorate base started to crumble, with increasing numbers of supporters defecting to the Democratic Party, which was seen as a more effective opposition.

De Klerk still hoped that after the first democratic election his party could exert power as the gatekeeper to some strategic sectors. However, its ability to act as the agent for them was soon questionable. When the ANC renounced nationalisation as a policy option, big business quickly accepted it as a future government with which it could do business and scaled down its support for the NP. Most white civil servants had decided at an early stage that the negotiations would result in black majority rule and the replacement of many of them by blacks. They gave up on the NP as the guarantor of their interests, particularly after the ANC promised to pay out pensions and satisfactory retirement packages for those it wished to retrench.

The alienation of the security forces turned to dismay when the chance was missed to negotiate amnesty for the members of all parties. In a visit to South Africa early in 1992 ex-US Secretary of State Cyrus Vance urged the different parties to accept a general amnesty to get the problem out of the way. Inexplicably the De Klerk government procrastinated. In the final round of the negotiations a clause was hurriedly inserted compelling violators of human rights to ask for amnesty to avoid prosecution. As the future majority party the ANC would have the most say in the composition of the commission that would deal with amnesty and coming to terms with the past.

The NP was also strongly criticised for leaving the future status of Afrikaans very uncertain. No one expected Afrikaans to retain its former status, but few thought the NP would leave Afrikaans schools and universities as vulnerable as it did. The constitution recognised the right of single-medium education where feasible, but also provided for the right to access (in practice, access in the medium of English). The new government soon indicated that it considered the latter right superior to the former. The first two education ministers made it clear that they considered Afrikaans universities unacceptable.

Within ten years some 40% of Afrikaans schools that were single medium in 1990 became parallel or dual medium. Some schools became English medium. The steady penetration of English into the old single-medium Afrikaans universities put Afrikaans on the defensive. On state television Afrikaans was abruptly relegated from sharing a channel on a 50-50 basis to a slot in a channel on which it was allocated less than 10% of prime time. State institutions ignored the constitutional provision that the state should use at least two of the eleven official languages. The Pan South African Language Board, set up in terms of the constitution to watch over the implementation of the language clauses, warned that this practice would lead to general disrespect for the constitution.

In the Government of National Unity, NP cabinet ministers were expected to work within the ANC's policy framework. No conventions were laid down for the cabinet. The

ANC strongly criticised De Klerk when in public he aired disagreements over questions that the cabinet had addressed.

The major source of disagreement between the ANC and NP was over entrenching a power-sharing cabinet in the final constitution. When the ANC refused, De Klerk took the NP out of the government at the end of 1996. In January 1997, in a speech in London, he declared that no balanced political settlement of the kind the NP had sought had occurred; instead there had been surrender of power and with it the loss of 'sovereignty'.

> The decision to surrender the right to national sovereignty is certainly one of the most painful any leader can be asked to take. Most nations are prepared to risk war and catastrophe rather than to surrender this right. Yet this was the decision we had to take. We had to accept the necessity of giving up on the ideal on which we have been nurtured and the dream for which so many generations had struggled and for which so many of our people had died.

In response *Die Burger*, under the heading '*Oorgawe*' (Surrender), asked whether the leader of a party that had fared so poorly in the negotiations could continue in a leadership position. In his defence De Klerk pointed out that he had never promised a white minority veto. He weathered the storm, but his political role had come to an end. With NP support dropping steadily in the polls, he retired from politics in August 1997, accelerating the NP's decline.

The Truth and Reconciliation Commission

The Truth and Reconciliation Commission (TRC) was established in 1995 to investigate human rights violations since 1960. It was authorised to grant amnesty to those perpetrators who made a full disclosure. The commission also had to foster reconciliation and unity among South Africans.

The TRC's mandate charged it with the responsibility to be even-handed, but its composition was hardly balanced. The chairman, Archbishop Desmond Tutu, was a patron

BELOW: *Scenes from the Truth and Reconciliation Commission. On Human Rights Day, 21 March 2003, the final meeting of the TRC took place and Archbishop Desmond Tutu handed over its report to Thabo Mbeki.*

AN ELUSIVE SEARCH FOR TRUTH

Three books illuminate the difficulty of finding and dealing with the truth about South Africa's tortured apartheid past. In her *The Truth about the Truth Commission* (1999), Anthea Jeffery takes the Truth and Reconciliation Commission (TRC) to task for downplaying the notion of factual or objective truth. She argues that by not allowing cross-examination, the TRC based key findings on untested and uncorroborated statements.

Yet court cases often leave behind a sense that while legal procedures have been followed, the search for truth and justice might have been thwarted. This is the thrust of Marlene Burger and Chandré Gould's *Secrets and Lies* (2002), about the military doctor Wouter Basson and the chemical and biological warfare programme he headed. In 1981 Basson was appointed to head Project Coast, tasked with developing a counteraction to the possible use of chemical and biological weapons by enemy forces in Angola. He and several scientists in military employ testified before the TRC about projects or suggested projects using biological methods to prevent or stifle resistance to the state. Basson stood trial on charges that he provided members of the security forces with toxic substances to assassinate the regime's enemies. He was acquitted in a controversial judgement.

In her prize-winning *Country of My Skull* (1998), Antjie Krog, a leading Afrikaans poet who covered the TRC proceedings for radio, considers the indisputable evidence of horrific abuses under apartheid rule. She asks: 'How can I live with the fact that all the words used to humiliate, all the orders to kill, belonged to the language of my heart?'

Antjie Krog

of the United Democratic Front, the ANC internal front since the early 1980s. Deputy Chairman Alex Boraine had been an NP opponent in Parliament in the 1970s and 1980s and was considered by De Klerk as a 'hothead and inquisitor'. None of the seventeen members had been a member of either the NP or the IFP. Almost all members were considered to be tacit or overt ANC supporters.

It was not so much the body's composition, the way in which it performed its task or the reports of a largely sycophantic press that inspired confidence, but the fact that both Nelson Mandela and Desmond Tutu, two leaders of great moral stature, gave the proceedings authority. Blacks felt free to approach the commission to tell painful stories of injury to themselves or the death of their beloved. The saturation media coverage of the hearings made it impossible for anyone thereafter to deny the atrocities of the previous regime. The TRC was not afraid to criticise human rights violations by the liberation movements.

The commission received some 21 300 victim statements that recorded some 38 000 gross violations of human rights. More than 1 000 perpetrators received amnesty after full disclosure. An analysis published by the South African Institute of Race Relations argued that the commission's staff was overwhelmingly sympathetic to the ANC and that it tended to seek out victims of human rights abuses the government or IFP forces had perpetrated. The study also found that in many cases the level of corroboration of the victims' evidence was not high. Instead of concentrating on the context of a deed the commission focused on the perpetrator or victim, with the result that the context was in most cases only scantily sketched. Cross-examination of victims was not normally allowed in the victim hearings, but hearsay evidence was.

The result was decidedly mixed. Where there were inconsistencies in the evidence the result was, as Pierre du Toit remarked in his *South Africa's Brittle Peace* (2001), 'an amicable interchange between commissioners and deponents, which may have furthered the process of healing, but was not necessarily conducive to establishing factual truth'. The TRC did not investigate 60% of the killings and based key findings on untested and uncorroborated statements. It may have overreached itself in taking on the task of perpetrator findings.

On the positive side the TRC performed an important therapeutic role, giving victims the opportunity to tell their story and have their suffering acknowledged. It revealed the truth in some notorious cases. Vlakplaas operatives or local security policemen asked for amnesty for the murders of Matthew Goniwe and three friends outside Port Elizabeth, the 'Pebco Three', the 'Guguletu Seven', and several other 'targeted killings'. ANC

operatives asked for amnesty for the Church Street bomb in Pretoria in 1983 where eighteen people were killed.

There was intense interest in the controversial question of whether the cabinet or State Security Council gave orders for assassinating opponents of the state. Although no evidence was found of explicit instructions, the truth was complex. General Johann van der Merwe, head of the police, pointed out that the politicians deliberately used ambivalent instructions to members of the security forces, telling them to 'make a plan', or to 'eliminate' or 'neutralise' key activists.

Senior policemen rightly felt that politicians who denied any role in abuses left them in the lurch.

Ex-President De Klerk made an apology on behalf of the NP and the previous government (*see box*). The apology failed to satisfy the TRC. What it also wanted to hear was if the State Security Council (SSC), of which De Klerk had been a member, had authorised or condoned the murder and torture of 'state enemies'. De Klerk denied that the SSC had ever given such instructions and insisted that the terms recorded in the minutes ('eliminate' or 'exterminate' opponents) did not mean that the security forces were given permission to murder or torture.

At a press conference Desmond Tutu rejected De Klerk's claim that he did not know about the atrocities and other crimes, and maintained that the NP government's policy gave the security forces 'a licence' to commit murder. Accusing the TRC of bias, the NP sought a court injunction against Tutu, who retracted his claim.

The TRC did not find evidence of a centrally directed Third Force but found that security force operatives, with the connivance of senior officers, had engaged in violence and killings. It also found the ANC accountable for some human rights violations as some of its members had at times blurred the distinction between soft and hard targets. The UDF too was guilty of widespread excesses, including necklace executions and attacks on black councillors. The PAC targeted primarily civilians for killing. Finally it found that the white right wing – and specifically the Volksfront – committed random attacks on black people and tried to instigate a revolution to replace the black government with a white one.

The TRC's attempt to get the major interest groups and professions, such as the business sector, the press and the judiciary, to state whether they promoted or opposed apartheid encountered resistance. It tended to underestimate the opposition in civil society to the effort to put them on trial.

On 18 February 1998 TRC Chairman Desmond Tutu called on 'all whites, especially the Afrikaners', to acknowledge that 'dastardly things' had happened in the past. 'You white people – if you reject the TRC you will carry the burden of guilt to your graves,' he said. After an outcry Tutu qualified his statement to exempt those Afrikaners who had opposed apartheid or who had confessed to the TRC.

In its report the TRC singled out the NP government, assisted by the IFP, as the main perpetrators. The report satisfied none of the main parties, including the ANC, which tried to stop publication of the interim report since it criticised some of the methods the ANC had used.

Yet the TRC was a cathartic event. South Africa, whites in particular, was suddenly forced to confront a past that in many ways was dark and tragic. The commission reduced the number of official or semi-official lies about white rule to a minimum. The truths that were revealed probably destroyed the NP and severely damaged the Dutch Reformed Church, both intimately associated with apartheid.

The ANC benefited most but it too could no longer sustain its claim that its violent acts could be justified because it fought a just war. When some of its leaders hesitated to ask amnesty for the bomb blast in 1983 in Church Street, Pretoria, where some eighteen people died, Tutu threatened to resign. The point was made that even people who saw themselves as liberators had to admit guilt if they had used excessive methods.

One of the best-known accounts of the TRC is to be found in *Country of My Skull* by Antjie Krog, a renowned Afrikaans poet who reported on the commission's hearings on the radio.

OPPOSITE: *An ANC member hangs posters in the southern Cape town of George on 22 January 1998, the eve of the court appearance of former president, P.W. Botha, on charges of failing to appear before special hearings of the Truth and Reconciliation Commission.*

Mandela's presidency: how good was it?

Nelson Mandela consolidated the democracy by setting important precedents in acknowledging the constitutional limitations on his executive power. His good-tempered acceptance of Constitutional Court judgements that ruled against the government was particularly important in this respect. In 1998, his willingness to endorse the TRC's findings despite their angry repudiation by Thabo Mbeki, then his deputy, was another major instance of his ability on occasion to distance himself from the more partisan perspectives of some of his comrades.

His famous gestures of reconciliation and empathy with white South Africans fostered among white South Africans broad acceptance of the new government's moral authority. His role in shifting ANC policy perspectives in the direction of a pro-market policy – in particular in weakening the ANC's commitment to public ownership – undoubtedly helped to reassure white South Africans and foreign business. In choosing to serve only one term and presiding over an orderly succession procedure within the ANC he certainly strengthened ANC commitment to constitutional procedures.

He suggested that 'human rights should be the core of international relations'. His attempt to mobilise African and Commonwealth statesmanship to boycott the Abacha dictatorship in Nigeria was one of the most obvious expressions of this predisposition. But he also defended repressive administrations that had aided the ANC, thus subverting his human rights-based foreign policy.

What were the main failures of his presidency? While Mandela deferred to liberal constitutional proprieties, he is also partly responsible for the survival within the ANC of the strong authoritarian predispositions it brought back to South Africa from exile. Between 1990 and 1994 Mandela attempted to restrict internal electoral procedures within the organisation. Mbeki's ascendancy as deputy president under Mandela was not the outcome of any election, but of secret deals between ANC leaders.

The more authoritarian dimension of Mandela's personality was also often evident in his attacks on independent journalists and other critics, especially if they were black. His treatment of his coalition partners revealed his dislike of liberal parliamentary opposition. F.W. de Klerk was marginalised in the Government of National Unity from its inception, partly a consequence of Mandela's personal hostility to the former president.

Mandela may have helped to foster the venality that has become so conspicuous in South African public life. He included in his administration individuals with an established record of venality – notably his former wife Winnie, as well as Stella Sigcau.

Mandela himself has been retrospectively critical of his government's slowness in responding to the HIV-Aids crisis. In the outcry over inappropriate spending following *Sarafina*, an expensive musical promoting HIV-Aids education, Mandela vigorously defended Minister of Health Nkosazana Zuma. Aside from the *Sarafina* debacle, the 'Virodene scandal' when the minister decided to promote the use of an industrial solvent as an HIV-Aids cure, raised serious concerns about the quality of leadership within the Department of Health. To be fair, though, since his retirement Mandela has become an important ally of HIV-Aids activism, willing in 2001 to confront the ANC's leadership over its reluctance to support the full-scale prescription of anti-retroviral medication.

Will these flaws in Mandela's leadership completely overshadow his achievements? The long-term answer to this question depends upon what happens. If South African politicians continue to adhere to the political rules they adopted in the mid-1990s, then Mandela will be honoured for his role in creating a successful democracy. If that democracy becomes a lost cause, historians will emphasise his record's shortcomings. The balance of evidence still favours the first scenario but both corruption and a possible unruly succession contest within the ANC increase the risks of the second option becoming a reality.

BELOW: *Thabo Mbeki played only a minor part in the constitutional negotiations but positioned himself well enough to be appointed deputy president in 1994. This opened the way to the presidency in 1999. He established a highly centralised form of executive rule, sidelining Parliament and concentrating power in the office of the president. He could make appointments to virtually all the strategic posts on different levels of government. He soon showed that he was unable to emulate Nelson Mandela's easy rapport with the public; instead of public speeches, he preferred to communicate through a weekly letter on the Internet, which tended to be too abstract to appeal to a wide audience. His ambition to improve delivery to the masses was frustrated by a too-rapid transformation of the civil service, giving rise to serious capacity problems.*

The Mbeki presidency

In some ways the Mbeki presidency had started in 1994 already, with Mbeki assuming more than the powers normally associated with a prime minister. It was in this capacity that Mbeki spearheaded the drive to centralise power, forced through a market-based economic policy, and oversaw the restructuring of the educational system. His term as president also marked a much more determined attempt to Africanise the civil service and the managerial ranks of the parastatal corporations.

Thabo Mbeki became president after the 1999 election in which the ANC won 66.4% of the votes against the 9.6% of the Democratic Party, 6.9% of the New National Party (NNP) and 8.6% of the IFP. By 2001 Mbeki's popularity regularly trailed more than 20% behind the ANC's in polls, but he recovered after a strong expansion of social welfare to the poor. The opposition was weakened when changes in the defection clause made it possible for a large part of the NNP to join the ANC and retain their seats after an unhappy liaison with the DP, called the Democratic Alliance (DA), had foundered. In the 2005 election the ANC won 69.7% of the vote, the DA 12.3% and the IFP 7%.

The world was dominated at this time by the Washington consensus, which stressed growth driven by the private sector and the maintenance of monetary and fiscal discipline. Mbeki's most highly rated achievement was the introduction of an economic policy that curbed inflation, kept a firm control over state expenditure and promoted trade liberalisation. As a result the economy surged ahead at a rate last seen more than 30 years earlier. He introduced two major African initiatives, the New Partnership for Africa's Development (Nepad) and the replacement of the Organisation for African Unity by the African Union (AU).

Both were vastly overambitious. The AU set itself the impossible long-term goals of a single continental currency and army. Over the shorter term, Nepad rested on the prospect of large-scale capital inflows from the First World into Africa should African states rid their administrations of corruption and other ills. It foundered because of a lack of commitment by many African states. The most serious blow was Mbeki's failure to speak

Evidence of an epidemic of heterosexually transmitted HIV-Aids surfaced by the end of the 1980s. Among the patients attending public antenatal clinics – largely less affluent, black women – the 1990 prevalence of heterosexually transmitted HIV-Aids was 0.7%. By 1994 this had risen to 7.6%, and by 2005 to 30.2%, with an estimated 5.5 million of South Africa's 47 million people infected. An estimated 1 000 new HIV infections and 900 Aids deaths occurred each day.

Many believe it could have turned out differently. By 1991 the urgent need for a credible, effective Aids strategy was clear. In November 1991, the health secretariat of the recently unbanned ANC and the Department of National Health and Population Development held meetings to formulate a strategy, leading to the formation of the National Aids Convention of South Africa (Nacosa), which drew together a wide range of organisations and professional people.

Nacosa convenor Mary Crewe wrote that the National Aids Plan was 'a reflection of years of experience' and that the bulk of the plan 'could have been effectively implemented in less than two years'. Instead, by 2000 she would write that the Plan 'remains unconsulted, unimplemented and largely ignored' – this despite the fact that the first two health ministers under South Africa's new dispensation, Dr Nkosazana Dlamini-Zuma and Dr Manto Tshabalala-Msimang, had been key members of the drafting team.

Had the Plan been fully implemented by its many enthusiastic, dedicated supporters, and had Nelson Mandela with his immense moral authority backed it, South Africa, like Uganda, may have become one of Africa's Aids success stories. Instead, the programme floundered. First, under Dr Zuma, the matter was dogged by controversy. The *Sarafina* debacle – an inappropriate, all-star musical staged by the government as an Aids education vehicle – outraged people and also signalled the beginning of a rift between the Department of Health and civil society.

The 1997 scandal around Virodene, a toxic industrial solvent (dimethylformamide), touted as a treatment for Aids by researchers who had ignored all the established ethical and procedural protocols for drug research, only exacerbated the tensions. Dr Zuma and the entire cabinet, including Deputy President Thabo Mbeki, became entangled in the affair as they sought endorsement for its approval by the Medicines Control Council, which refused to oblige.

The following year, the minister's refusal to make the drug AZT available to pregnant HIV-positive pregnant mothers, despite its proven efficacy in cutting mother-to-child transmission, was a factor in the formation of the Treatment Action Campaign. This activist group grew in passion and influence as South Africa's Aids policies became even more fraught with controversy under Dr Manto Tshabalala-Msimang, the health minister appointed by Thabo Mbeki when he became president in 1999.

In 1999 President Mbeki openly questioned the 'science of Aids'. His scepticism led him into the arms of the largely US-based Aids dissidents, who questioned whether HIV existed, suggested that Aids was caused by the use of recreational drugs (or even AZT), and speculated that the epidemic in Africa was simply poverty aggravating old disease patterns. Mbeki's response remained a mystery. Perhaps he feared that admitting millions of South Africans were infected with a sexually transmitted disease would reinforce racial and sexual stereotypes – what he referred to as beliefs that blacks were 'natural-born, promiscuous carriers of germs'.

His health minister openly questioned the safety and efficacy of antiretroviral drugs, promoting instead the therapeutic value of bizarre 'nutritional' items, such as beetroot, garlic, olive oil and lemons, mega-dose multivitamins offered by quacks, and scientifically untested 'traditional' African remedies. The players that once united behind the 1992 Nacosa plan became almost unanimous in their criticism of the Mbeki government.

Manto Tshabalala-Msimang

out on President Robert Mugabe's human rights transgressions in Zimbabwe. Following a defeat in 2000 in a constitutional referendum, Mugabe proceeded to rig the next elections and unleash his thugs on the opposition. He seized most of the white farms, causing a precipitous economic decline. Mbeki remained silent.

Mbeki also failed to give leadership in the HIV-Aids pandemic (*see box*). This provided the spur for a vigorous challenge by the Treatment Action Campaign, ultimately forcing the state to provide treatment. Its leader Zackie Achmat became one of the heroes of the first decade of democracy (*see box*). In addition, under Mbeki the perception developed that crime, particularly violent crime, had escalated out of control, and that he was unable to face up to the magnitude of the crisis.

ZACKIE ACHMAT AND THE TREATMENT ACTION CAMPAIGN

Launched in December 1998, the Treatment Action Campaign (TAC) grew out of the National Association of People Living with Aids/HIV (Napwa) SA, as a pressure group to demand that government and the pharmaceutical industry make drug treatment for HIV/Aids increasingly accessible. The initial call was for free AZT (azido-thymidine) for HIV-positive pregnant mothers to reduce the chances of passing the virus on to their babies. Over time the campaign has increasingly called

Zackie Achmat

for antiretroviral (ARV) treatment for all those who need it. It has also widened to include other aspects such as prevention, treatment literacy and the debunking of Aids myths and unproven treatment claims, and, more recently, to campaigns for 'access to affordable and quality health care for all people in South Africa'.

The TAC in its first seven years was synonymous for many with its dynamic chairperson Zackie Achmat. Born Abdurazzack Achmat to a Cape Town Muslim family in 1962, Achmat's adolescence coincided with turbulent years in the anti-apartheid struggle, which he embraced, foregoing education (setting fire to his school in 1976 during the widespread school boycotts), and being arrested and detained five times between 1976 and 1980. His style as an activist in a democratic system combined community mobilisation and civil disobedience with the militancy and street theatre of Western Aids activist groups like ACT-UP.

Openly gay and HIV-positive, he founded the National Coalition for Gay and Lesbian Equality in 1994, helping to ensure the recognition of their rights in the post-apartheid constitution. He became director of the University of the Witwatersrand's Aids Law Project (ALP), which had started in 1993, and moved on to co-found the TAC in 1998. With the legal backing of the ALP, the TAC has since waged a relentless campaign to force the government to provide ARVs through public health facilities, where necessary pursuing cases up to the level of the Constitutional Court.

As card-carrying members of the ruling African National Congress, Achmat and many TAC members found the often-bitter battles, especially with Health Minister Dr Manto Tshabalala-Msimang, distressing. But their tenacious campaigns served not only to ensure that the government was forced to begin to provide ARVs, but also to demonstrate the critical role of civil society.

The ANC's centralisation of power

Before 1990, both the ANC and National Party had in one way or another been firmly committed to authoritarian ideologies. The ANC in exile looked towards eastern Europe for inspiration for the type of society it planned to build in South Africa. The legal scholar Raymond Suttner, after 1994 an ANC representative, noted that the ANC in exile had difficulty getting support outside of the Eastern Bloc. As a result 'much political thinking was conditioned by Soviet training and exposure to life in the former socialist states'. The experience of exile and the success of the South African forces in infiltrating the organisation also created a narrow and closed circle of decision-making. Once it was in power, the ANC soon centralised power in the president's office and imposed tough discipline on the party.

During the negotiations and beyond the ANC remained committed to the idea that democracy meant the transfer of power from the white ruling class to 'the people', as embodied in the ANC. Initially, however, the ANC was acutely aware of the disruptive threat the white right wing posed to the new order. To offset this threat Mandela reappointed Afrikaners to senior positions, reiterating that the skills of the white minority were valued by the ANC, and would be needed for the reconstruction of society. The constitution required that state institutions should act impartially and without 'fear or favour'.

After the National Party left in 1996, the government toughened its stance towards opposition parties. At the ANC's 50th conference in Mafikeng in December 1997, in a speech made by Mandela but to all accounts written by Mbeki, a warning was issued about a counter-revolutionary offensive against the government that sought to maintain the 'privileges of the white minority'. It attacked the 'mainly white' opposition parties for defending 'white privilege'. The white-led parties had decided 'against the pursuit of a national agenda'; they were propagating a 'reactionary, dangerous and opportunist position'. The statement rejected the view that the 'legitimate responsibility' of opposition was to oppose the ruling party and seek to gain power through the ballot box.

Imposing leadership control

At the Mafikeng conference of 1997 the ANC leadership received a formal mandate to bring all centres of power under its control. According to a high-level ANC document adopted the following year, transformation of the state entailed extending the power of the national liberation movement 'over all levers of power: the army, the police, the bureaucracy, intelligence structures, the judiciary, parastatals, and agencies such as regulatory bodies, the public broadcaster, the central bank and so on'.

The ANC began to 'deploy' ANC 'cadres' to key positions in the state and required that they remain under party discipline. This policy met with very little public opposition. There was a widespread assumption in the press that it was democratic for such a dominant ruling party to control the levers of state power. No serious resistance developed outside the ANC. The government had adopted a prudent fiscal and monetary policy and had sought to increase the black share of the economy by setting sectoral charters in which white-dominated companies' leaders willingly sold off part of their stockholding to black companies.

By the mid-1990s the ANC was commonly described as having a long 'tradition' of internal democracy, and this was seen as one of the key constraints against any move towards authoritarianism. But once power had been secured, much stricter party discipline was imposed – and the organisational principles of 'democratic centralism' reasserted. The feeling inside the movement was that if South Africa was to be 'transformed', what was required from the ANC was cohesion, discipline and central direction. All party activists wherever they were located were now required to do the bidding of the leadership, and to place loyalty to the party over loyalty to the institution to which they had been 'deployed'.

The ANC's alliance partners, Cosatu and the SA Communist Party, accepted seats on the party's new deployment committees. As Carol Paton later observed, the ANC's deployment strategy was enthusiastically embraced by them: 'It seemed inconceivable to everyone in the alliance that the interests of the movement could be anything other than the interests of the nation.' The effect was that Cosatu was sidelined in the decision-making processes.

The ANC had quite willingly handed Mbeki control over appointments to all spheres of government in the expectation that this would be used to drive the movement's agenda forward. Yet he had been given the ability to 'reward his friends and punish his enemies' and he used this power to consolidate his authority over both party and state.

By the time Mbeki formally assumed the South African presidency in June 1999 government legislation, the ANC's electoral dominance and its internal party rules all combined to create a highly centralised system. Ministers, directors-general, premiers and mayors of ANC-controlled provinces and municipalities, the speakers and heads of committees in Parliament, were all appointed by the ANC leadership. By 2000 most key positions in state institutions – from the Reserve Bank to the news service of the public broadcaster, to the prosecution service and the police – were now filled with political appointees. Even the Constitutional Court had a high quotient of former party members among its judges. Only the lower courts of the judiciary remained to the greater part free of ANC influence.

Opposition to the growing ANC hegemony was weak. Two of the most important centres of power outside direct ANC control were business and the newspapers. Big business became adept at providing 'spontaneous support' for ANC policies. Many journalists promoted into senior editorial positions in the two largest English-language newspaper groups initially identified strongly with the ANC.

By 2000, which can be seen as the high-water mark of the political power and moral authority of the ANC, critical discourse was sustained by a handful of individuals and institutions, most notably the left-leaning *Mail & Guardian*, the liberal Democratic Party led by Tony Leon, which had become the official opposition the previous year, and the SA Institute of Race Relations.

The extent of the erosion of South Africa's constitutional checks and balances was fully exposed in early 2001 when the ANC leadership acted to control and limit the inquiry, launched earlier by Parliament, into the exorbitant spending on a multibillion rand arms deal. The Special Investigating Unit headed by Judge Willem Heath was excluded from the inquiry. Andrew Feinstein, the independent-minded head of the ANC caucus on the public accounts committee, was removed from his position and the committee packed with more reliable party loyalists.

The various political appointees in the other investigative agencies closely watched the progress of the inquiry, and the final report of the investigators was watered down after President Mbeki met with Auditor-General Shauket Fakie. Nor was the ANC caucus in Parliament, firmly subordinate as it was to the leadership, effectively able to hold the executive to account. On his resignation as Member of Parliament in August 2001 Feinstein stated that it had 'become increasingly difficult, if not impossible, for independent-minded MPs to work for the ANC in Parliament'.

Although formally vested with comprehensive powers over the organisation there was a decline in the influence of the ANC's National Executive Committee. Most members of that elected body were appointed to their salaried positions by the ANC leadership, over which they were supposed to exercise some kind of oversight. What fully exposed the decline in the ANC's culture of internal debate was the reluctance of senior ANC figures to oppose, let alone reverse, Mbeki's damaging HIV/Aids policies.

BELOW: *Tony Grogan's 2003 cartoon of Minister of Health Manto Tshabalala-Msimang. While in exile Tshabalala-Msimang received medical degrees in Russia, Tanzania and Belgium. Returning to South Africa in 1990, she quickly rose in the ANC ranks and in 2002 occupied the fifteenth place in the election for the National Executive Committee. Her position was further strengthened by her marriage to Mendi Msimang, who served as the ANC's treasurer-general for many years, acquiring intimate knowledge of the financial transactions in which the leadership was involved. Appointed as Minister of Health in 1999 and chairperson of one of the five sectoral cabinet committees in the Mbeki cabinet, she quickly became the most often lampooned cabinet minister as a result of her dissident views on the link between HIV and Aids and the treatment of the pandemic. It was widely believed that she retained her portfolio because President Mbeki shared her views.*

Residents of Walmer township in Port Elizabeth protest about housing in May 2005. Between 1994 and 2004 the government made considerable strides in providing housing and services. There was a 40% increase in the number of formal houses, of which many were built for low-income households, a 69% increase in the number of formal houses that used electricity for lighting, a 47% increase in households with access to clean water, and a 36% increase in households whose refuse was removed by the local authority. Yet a huge backlog and rapid population growth made it difficult to satisfy especially the poor, the ruling party's main constituency. By the end of 2006, some 30% of families did not live in formal houses, more than 60% of households were without water in their dwellings and 20% of the households were without electricity. There were 4.2 million people living on less than R10 a day in 2007. More than 200 of a total of 284 municipalities in the country could not provide electricity, sanitation, refuse removal and water to the majority of the inhabitants under their jurisdiction. There were 42 municipalities who could not execute half of their functions. From 2000 onwards numerous protests erupted because of poor service delivery.

In December 2002 the ANC's national conference passed constitutional amendments that further strengthened the power of the party leadership. The section on discipline was tripled in length and a clause introduced that stated that all members 'without exception' were subject to party discipline. In the 2004 national and provincial elections the ANC leadership appointed their premiers after the vote, while in 2006 the same happened with the mayors of ANC-controlled municipalities. The comprehensive powers of the national leadership, and its control over all avenues of patronage, meant that its position was unchallengeable from below for as long as it remained united. It was only in 2006 that serious opposition to Mbeki's iron control of the party began to build up.

The decline of state capacity

The government also moved rapidly to remove white civil servants, claiming that many of them were hostile to transformation. At the start of 1996 the ANC government acted to reduce the power of the Public Service Commission over civil servants. It introduced early retirement and voluntary severance package schemes to encourage the departure of the existing incumbents of the state.

The constitution stipulated that public administration should be 'broadly representative' of the South African people, but added that 'ability, objectivity and fairness' should also be considered. It did not require the application of demographic representation in the private sector and civil society. The government, however, watered down individual merit as the main criterion for appointment to – or promotion within – the state and gave great discretion to the political heads of departments in the making of appointments.

Large sums were spent to remove white staff from posts in the civil service. By the end of 1998 the state had granted 56 985 early retirement packages to predominantly white civil servants (these figures exclude members of the Defence Force). Another 60 000 were removed in the next four years.

The effect on the racial composition of the civil service was dramatic. In 1994 whites held 44% of all posts in the civil service; by the beginning of 1999 they held 18%. Of the top management of the civil service (directors-general and their deputies), 56% by 1999 were black, coloured or Indian, and 42% of the other managerial posts (chief directors and directors) came from these three communities. The government declared that it still considered whites to be over-represented, particularly at the level of senior management.

The system of deploying political appointees to state institutions without the necessary skills to do the job often served to disrupt organisational hierarchies, and resulted in a

blurring of lines of accountability. It also signalled to the bureaucracy that henceforth advancement would proceed through political favouritism, not individual application or merit.

By 2006 there were 40 000 vacant posts out of a total of close to 400 000 posts in the national departments of the civil service. If the Department of Safety and Security was excluded an average of one out of every five posts in the national government departments was not filled. The drive to concentrate power and bring about racial transformation did not bring about a stronger and more efficient state but a weaker and more incoherent one.

The judiciary and crime

The government upheld the judgement of the courts but also pressed hard for the racial transformation of the bench to reflect the population composition. In January 2005 the ANC accused the country's judges of 'popular antagonism' towards the judiciary and the courts. It accused them of not being in line with the 'vision and aspirations of the millions who engaged in the struggle to liberate the country from white minority domination'. It acknowledged that some progress had been made to change the racial and gender profile of the bench, but said the reality was that many judges and magistrates did 'not see themselves as part of the masses'.

The new government's insistence on rapid transformation of the bench and its refusal to devolve policing functions to the provinces added to the weakening of the justice system. It had already started showing serious strains in the early 1980s. Between 1980 and 2000 the number of crimes reported for every 100 000 people increased by a third but the conviction rate also fell by a third. By 1999 the number of criminal convictions in absolute terms was the lowest in 40 years, despite dramatic increases in the population and crime rate.

By 2003 the chance of murderers being convicted was less than one out of five, compared to one out of two in Europe or the United States. The chances of a person being murdered in South Africa were 50 times greater than in western Europe.

An important reason was the loss of expertise. A third of the prosecutors resigned in the first two years of the democratic government. Personal security had to a large degree been privatised. By 1999 personnel in the private security industry was twice that of the police service and, ironically, at least one police personnel building in Pretoria was being guarded by a private security company.

In a national poll conducted towards the end of 2006 three-quarters of South Africans said they wanted an urgent referendum on the death penalty because they felt the crime required it. A majority said that crime was 'severe and out of control'.

Pursuing growth and redistribution

At the heart of the transition lay an informal pact that bound the black and white communities together. Political power would be transferred to blacks but property rights would enable whites with wealth to retain it. While white big business would assist black business people in acquiring stock in their corporations, whites with advanced skills would be assured of jobs in an economy aiming for high growth and more efficiency. The task of selling the economic side of the pact to the victorious ANC fell on the shoulders of Thabo Mbeki. It was a huge task. Many ANC and Cosatu leaders had embraced the doctrines of socialism and expected wholesale state intervention to assist the poor, rapidly narrow the gap between white and black, and provide a better life for all.

The two decades from 1973 to 1994 had seen a dramatic decline in economic growth. There was a staggering drop in fixed investment, rising unemployment and high levels of poverty and inequality, with blacks the worst affected. Moreover, physical and social infrastructure – housing, health, education, sanitation, water, electricity – for the majority black population was hopelessly inadequate following decades of neglect. The budget deficit in the last year of the National Party government ballooned to 10.8% of GDP; the total national debt to GDP ratio stood at 52.5%; inflation at 8%.

Baptism of fire

The task facing the ANC in assuming power in 1994 was well formulated by Alan Hirsch: 'How could the new SA balance the tasks of setting the economy on a path of economic growth, to lay the basis for prosperity and, simultaneously, redistribute income, wealth and other resources such as human capital to meet the objectives of social justice and long-term sustainability?'

It soon became clear to Nelson Mandela and the first ANC cabinet members that there were just not enough resources to make good on the ANC's promises to its voters

THE ANC'S MEDLEY OF MODELS

In 1955 the ANC adopted the Freedom Charter with its call for public ownership and nationalisation in key sectors. From the period following its banning in the 1960s to the 1980s, the ANC's economic policies were firmly on the Left. The ANC's first important policy document in exile – the 'Strategy and Tactics' document adopted at the movement's conference in Morogoro, Tanzania, in 1969 – suggested a 'capitalised socialism'. However, by the mid-1980s some leading thinkers were won over by Scandinavian social democracy – Scandinavian countries had now become major funders of the ANC. ANC economists also noticed successful East Asian industrialisation, which was market-based and within the broad rubric of capitalism, but under state direction. The failure of Soviet bloc communism pushed the ANC towards economic orthodoxy.

The ANC's important Constitutional Guidelines in 1988 proposed a mixed economy with a 'public sector, a private sector, a co-operative sector, and a small-scale family sector'. It stated: '[T]he private sector shall be obliged to co-operate with the state in realising the objectives of the Freedom Charter in promoting social well-being.' An ANC statement after a meeting with white civil society organisations in 1989 noted: 'The exact forms and mechanisms of state control are left open in our programmatic perspectives. Nationalisation . . . does not advance social control.'

When released, Nelson Mandela asserted that nationalisation was still a cornerstone of the ANC. The unions, a major component of the ANC alliance, were deeply sceptical about the ANC exile and prison leadership becoming 'soft' on economic policy. ANC policy documents released in 1990 argued for a limited economic role for the state, but

both referred to nationalisation as a possibility. Business and mainstream white political parties strongly attacked these documents for their alleged 'socialist' undertones.

The ANC's seminal policy conference of 1992 adopted the ANC's Ready to Govern document. The draft document released before the conference was stripped of references to higher corporate taxes and restructuring of the financial sector, and hinted of privatisation and the need for a property rights guarantee. The Left – including Cosatu and the SA Communist Party – was determined that the ANC should adopt nationalisation, reject privatisation and focus the ANC's economic programme on 'growth through redistribution'. In the heated three-day discussion that followed, the centrists under Thabo Mbeki won a crucial victory against the movement's Left.

In the final resolutions, nationalisation was dropped as a cornerstone of ANC policy, and the way was left open for privatisation under an ANC government. Furthermore, the ANC resolved to work with the

World Bank and International Monetary Fund, and to commit itself to trade liberalisation. Importantly, the slogan 'growth through redistribution' was dropped. However, the debate over economic policy continued unabated. The Ready to Govern document formed the basis of the ANC's 1994 election platform – the Reconstruction and Development Programme (RDP).

The ANC's final election manifesto tried to please both the ANC's Left and the market. Most importantly, it shifted back to the emphasis on growth and development through redistribution. However, the RDP stressed that macro-economic stability would be at the heart of policies. For example, it stated that 'the largest proportion of RDP projects . . . will be financed by the better use of existing resources', rather than through increasing taxes. Mandela, Mbeki and other ANC leaders widely consulted business leaders such as the Oppenheimer family. Many aspects of the final RDP document were amended several times to reassure suspicious business leaders.

of a better life for all. And worse, investment was not forthcoming from domestic businesses or from the international front.

The ANC had believed that the world's revulsion of apartheid would result in developed countries pouring resources into the South African economy along the lines of the Marshall Plan that rescued western Europe after the devastation of World War II. In addition, there was a widespread belief that in return for not having their assets seized via nationalisation, local business would quickly make investments that would create jobs. Both failed to materialise in the first two critical years (1994–1996) of the new democratic government.

President Mandela tried to reassure whites fearful of black retribution and appease blacks impatient for change. Investors adopted a wait-and-see policy before making investments in the new democracy. Privately, many local businesses were talking of 'capital flight' if the ANC pursued a radical redistribution programme. Markets viewed the government's ability to manage the economy with scepticism; financial indicators showed that both a fiscal and monetary crisis was imminent; and the condition of the economy was even worse than initially thought. The ANC's Left groupings called for more expansionist economic and social policies, which led to a further sag in market confidence.

Two approaches

There were roughly two approaches that developed within the ANC family over how to proceed, and these differences were still manifest ten years later. The groups on the ANC's Left – most notably Cosatu and the SA Communist Party – demanded a quick programme of radical redistribution, whatever the market backlash. They wanted growth through redistribution.

By contrast, Thabo Mbeki, then deputy president and the ANC's chief economic strategist, proposed stabilising the rapidly deteriorating macro-economic situation and putting the emphasis on growth and market confidence. Supporting him were the key centrist economic reformers in the ANC, including Alec Erwin, Tito Mboweni, Trevor Manuel (who became finance minister in March 1996) and Joel Netshitenzhe (one of the key policy advisers).

Mbeki's idea was that the industrial part of the economy, dubbed the first economy, which consisted of companies that could already compete internationally, should be supported and that the business environment for them should be improved. Once the first economy was improved, it would trickle to the second economy – where the majority of black South Africans eked out a living in the informal sector. Furthermore, once the country reached macro-economic stability and improved the business environment for companies in the first economy, the government could embark on redistribution, the expansion of welfare and the improvement of services to the poor.

Mbeki's vision assumed that improved performance by companies would boost market and investor confidence and start a positive cycle of new investment from both local and foreign investors.

In essence the policy meant that stability and growth should come before redistribution, service delivery and the expansion of welfare to the poor. The ANC's market-oriented reformers set about persuading the ANC, which had to be dragged kicking and screaming to accept these dramatic changes in policy. Not surprisingly, it outraged the ANC's Left.

This new approach was formalised in 1996 in a new policy framework – Growth, Employment and Redistribution Strategy (Gear). Gear stipulated policies that would focus on 'sound money', export-orientated growth, privatisation of public services, public finance austerity, labour market flexibility, and a reliance on foreign investment as a key for prosperity.

Gear's taxation policy aimed to reduce corporate taxes to attract investors. It also called for a reduction of the state's role in the economy and stipulated that the civil service had to be reduced by a third. It aimed to liberalise trade and open South Africa's economy. As part of the attempts to shore up business confidence in the new black government, South Africa lifted tariff barriers further than the World Trade Organisation demanded.

Gear was sold to the ANC's constituency as a continuation of the RDP, not as a replacement. The key people assisting Mbeki and Manuel were their allies in Cosatu and

The emergence of a new black middle class of consumers, who contributed massively to the economic boom in South Africa, was one of the most prominent themes in newspapers in the first years of the new century. How big was this middle class? The more cautious analyses warned against including in this category people in routine white-collar occupations, such as cashiers, clerks and sales assistants, who would be hard hit by a recession. If international definitions were used some 200 000 blacks in South Africa formed part of the 'core middle class', measured by a combination of lifestyle and an income of at least R120 000 per year. Their numbers increased by 23% a year in the first decade after apartheid, but their total number still fell far short of the 1.3 million whites in the core middle class. By 2004 blacks formed 11% of the core middle class, but this represented less than 1% of all blacks.

FROM LEFT TO RIGHT: *An office worker, a shopper at Southgate mall outside Soweto, and stockbroker Mpho Mojalefa at work at the Johannesburg Securities Exchange.*

the SA Communist Party (SACP), including the key figures of Mbhazima Shilowa (then Cosatu general secretary), Charles Nqakula (then SACP secretary general) and Mlungisi Hlongwane (then South African National Civics Organisation general secretary). At its national conference in Mafikeng held in December 1997 the ANC adopted a resolution that made macro-economic stability the centrepiece of the movement's policy blueprint.

Mandela and Mbeki went out of their way to show to the markets and business that the ANC leadership was not hostage to dogged leftist ideology. Both publicly attacked the SACP and Cosatu. Mbeki saw big business – with its extensive skills base, access to capital, resources, infrastructure and mechanisms of delivery – as a key partner in addressing the country's development objectives.

Enhancing competitiveness

Measured against most international benchmarks, the competitiveness of the economy improved in the fifteen years after the normalisation of politics. The country indeed achieved a level of macro-economic stability not seen for 40 years. The ANC cut budget deficits to less than 3% of GDP and reduced inflation and national debt. As a result the economy began to grow steadily.

In addition, the government allowed large companies, such as Anglo American Corporation and South African Breweries, to leave local shores and get a primary listing on stock exchanges abroad. Mbeki and Manuel believed that as a quid pro quo companies allowed to go abroad would make huge local investments and embark on equity programmes within their companies. This was not to be the case.

To a remarkable extent – and anticipated by few – the ANC leadership realised its ambition to come to be seen as a party of economic prudence, and so eliminate widespread perceptions of African governments as spendthrift by nature. However, in terms of redressing the inequities of the past and reducing unemployment – the single most important political concern among the ANC's core support groups – the record remained mixed.

On the one hand the black middle class expanded dramatically, but on the other hand the gap between the white rich and their new black cousins and the rest of the black poor widened. The degree of racial segregation in residential areas, schools, lifestyles and clubs loomed disturbingly large. Poverty, unemployment and inequality remained extraordinarily high. Furthermore, redistribution has often benefited blacks in the middle classes who, it could be argued, with their education and skills would have done well, even under apartheid.

Despite Gear, investment levels remained low. This was because of high real and nominal interest rates that inhibited investment, the volatility of the rand over the period, perceptions of labour market inflexibility, as well as continuing negative perceptions about a variety of topics such as the high crime rate, the Aids pandemic and the crisis in Zimbabwe.

At a meeting with the country's senior business leaders, Mbeki expressed dismay at the 'doom and gloom' view of the country's economic prospects, the continual business criticisms of the government and the lack of new investments. At that meeting business leaders promised to tone down the criticism and initiate a domestic investment drive.

Deracialisation and redistribution

From an early stage in the 1990s Mbeki saw the formation of a black capitalist class as the key to a deracialised South African society and building a sustainable democracy. Empowerment had two aspects: increasing the historically oppressed communities' ownership in companies and bettering their prospects in the workplace. The ANC adopted Black Economic Empowerment (BEE) at its seminal conference in December 1997. From just one BEE transaction on the Johannesburg Stock Exchange in 1993, there were 238 in 2005. These transactions increased in value from R140 million in 1993 to R56.2 billion in 2005.

In 1998 the Employment Equity Act was passed. It increased pressure on employers to implement affirmative action. In the public sector affirmative action and other interventions had already brought about a rapid change in the racial composition. The government put pressure on the private sector to follow suit.

The 'self-enrichment of the few'

Although the government talked of 'broad-based empowerment', there was little evidence that it benefited the small business sector. Moeletsi Mbeki, the president's brother, stated that BEE meant 'the enrichment of the few'. Many BEE transactions typically involved the same handful of politically well-connected people.

Economists such as Nicoli Nattrass argued that there was no evidence that BEE increased employment or stimulated the small business sector. The effect on the racial ownership of the private sector remained small. By 2002 black-controlled firms accounted for only 3% of the Johannesburg Stock Exchange market capitalisation.

Pressure to change the BEE process came from various quarters. As a result, in 2000 Mbeki set up the Black Economic Empowerment Commission, under the chairmanship of former ANC secretary general Cyril Ramaphosa. The commission was charged with revisiting the effectiveness of BEE. As a direct result of the commission, a new way of measuring BEE was introduced – the 'balanced scorecard' approach. Charters were worked out by the different sectors of industry, which set BEE minimum targets. The Mining Charter finalised in October 2002 set the benchmark. A major tenet of the Mining Charter stated that 26% of mining assets must be transferred to BEE companies within ten years.

Various attempts were made to broaden participation in BEE away from a few well-connected oligarchs. Even so, by late 2004 BEE companies were still dominated by a

THE BEE 'NEW ESTABLISHMENT'

A notable dimension of Black Economic Empowerment (BEE) was the phenomenon of politicians and senior officials in the public service using their presumed influence and network of contacts to switch careers by entering business. The Institute for Justice and Reconciliation's *Transformation Audit* for 2006 contained an 'indicative chart' for what it termed the 'New Establishment'. The chart listed some 120 names of black leaders in controlling positions in the state, private sector and parastatals. Of these at least 43 were former politicians and bureaucrats, while a number of others listed were close relatives (including spouses) of leading politicians.

Several of the politicians-turned-businessmen remained active in the ANC. The names that stood out in this category were Cyril Ramaphosa, formerly the ANC's chief constitutional negotiator and secretary-general; Tokyo Sexwale, formerly premier of Gauteng; Mathews Phosa, formerly premier of Mpumalanga; Popo Molefe, formerly premier of North West; and Saki Macozoma, formerly an ANC Member of Parliament.

Another significant category consisted of directors-general who had left public service for business. Prominent examples included former directors-general Ketso Gordhan (transport), Andile Ngcaba (communications), Sipho Pityana (foreign affairs and labour), Alister Ruiters (trade and industry) and Robinson Ramaite (public services and administration).

One of the biggest BEE deals occurred when US-based company Thintana Communications decided to sell its 15.1% stake in Telkom. Smuts Ngonyama, ANC head of the Presidency, was one of the successful bidders. Key members of the ANC, including the president, Minister of Communications Ivy Matsepe-Cassaburi and the ANC's treasurer-general Mendi Msimang, did much to facilitate the deal. There was nothing illegal in the transaction, but the lack of transparency surrounding it evoked considerable adverse comment. Questions were raised about the propriety of former senior officials, such as Ngcaba, using their insider knowledge so soon after leaving the public service to secure lucrative deals.

ABOVE: *Tokyo Sexwale, the son of a washerwoman, who spent many years on Robben Island before becoming the first premier of Gauteng in 1999. He left politics for business, where he achieved spectacular success.*

few prominent political names. In December 2005 government released a draft of BEE codes, which aimed to finally make broad-based BEE more of a reality. It moved BEE away from the initial government emphasis on black equity ownership requirements to a more flexible approach. Companies could score in areas like preferential procurement, skills development and small business development.

There remained the danger that the burden of financing BEE deals would actually lower growth, or that a focus on BEE would replace both government and private efforts to slash poverty, unemployment and inequality. It did not seem to fit coherently into the government's Accelerated Shared Growth Initiative, announced in 2006, which aimed to lift growth to 10% over the next few years.

The ANC's Left baulks

Although the new government was anxious to improve the condition of the poor, and did a lot to narrow the gulf between the rich and the poor, its record was mixed. The main reason was increasing unemployment because of a tightening of the labour market and a stronger position for the trade unions. A study conducted by a Norwegian institute and partly funded by the Department of Labour found that 32% of the economically active population was unemployed on the strict definition of unemployment and 45% on the expanded definition.

Mbeki's introduction in June 2005 of another wave of economic reforms aimed to take off from Gear and lift economic growth even further. This triggered a revolt by the party's left wing. It used as a rallying point Mbeki's firing of Jacob Zuma as deputy president because of alleged corruption. Zuma promised to reverse the changes and turn the ANC back to its pre-1994, pro-redistribution roots.

By the beginning of 2005, resentment among ANC grassroots members grew to the extent that they demanded a change in Mbeki's stern leadership style. A prelude to this was the widespread rebellions in the provinces by ANC members against premiers handpicked for their loyalty to Mbeki's reform project, often at the expense seemingly of their local constituencies. Ordinary black South Africans started increasingly to demand the economic dividend of the democracy. They wanted 'delivery', whether it were jobs, houses or social services. Moreover, ANC members started to demand a greater say in the election of local leaders and policies.

Many could see that Gear and BEE were visibly benefiting some individuals, who only ten years ago were their neighbours in the townships but were now 'empowered', apparently because of their political connections. At the same time, they could see that better-educated whites thrived in a market economy where good education counted.

This was the background to the 2004 protests against slow delivery in rural towns and townships. Observers increasingly urged that for the sake of social stability, there had to be a greater effort to look beyond growth and BEE and to find ways to reduce poverty, secure social justice and racial unity – and to make South Africa more competitive.

Trying to fashion educational equality

When the new democratic government took power in 1994 the legacy of apartheid education loomed as a daunting symbolic and policy challenge. Racial inequality in education was indeed massive. It was imperative that the economy grew more rapidly to provide jobs for its population. For a higher growth the country had to become better at fostering and using knowledge and skills. That required schools to become more efficient in producing a growing proportion of learners who completed school and went on to university.

The new government tackled the task of restructuring education with zeal. But in that zeal, coupled with the readiness with which it rejected the advice of experienced educators, lay the germs of some large new failures.

The chasm to bridge

Between 1975 and 1985 the overall number of black children in secondary schools grew from 319 000 to 1 193 000, and the number in the final two years of schooling increased

tenfold from 27 000 to 266 000. The system was racked by protests of school children, starting in 1976, which soon escalated into school boycotts.

After a lull, disturbances erupted again from 1983 onwards, and large areas of black education were sucked into a nakedly political struggle, epitomised by the slogan 'liberation now, education later'. In this phase school principals and inspectors were cowed by the anger of the black youth, and administrative authority in black schools was critically undermined. In some ways the culture of learning and teaching never really recovered.

New tasks, new ideals

The new democracy in 1994 inherited a very uncertain framework of discipline and respect for educational authority. The major educational challenge perceived by the new government, however, was that of racial inequality of provision and outcomes. Like politicians with revolutionary idealism the world over, but very understandably after apartheid, their reaction was to bulldoze the old structure.

Notwithstanding the earlier progress in narrowing the racial gaps, the relative performance and output of black schools still lagged behind badly. Racial segregation had meant that the black educational community was alienated from the more successful white and Indian education. While a measure of integration had taken place at tertiary educational institutions, at school level it was minimal. In 1992 nearly all white schools were reclassified as so-called Model C schools and were allowed to determine their own admissions policy. But less than 1% of children attending these schools were black, and the administering authority was still white.

The ANC government was confronted with the complex task of integrating a multitude of education departments and systems in the former black homelands, the provinces and the racially structured systems in the common area of the country. In addition, there was the mammoth task of addressing massive backlogs in resource provision in black schools. By the early 1990s, 80% of schoolchildren were black. Black schools had large numbers of under-qualified teachers, high pupil-teacher ratios and school infrastructure that was positively dilapidated compared with former white schools.

These realities, coupled with the poor socio-economic circumstances of most black and coloured pupils, meant that rates of progression through educational grades were appallingly low. By 1993/94, of every cohort of 1 000 pupils entering the school system, only 489 black pupils and 326 coloured pupils survived to Grade 12, compared with 616 Indian and 853 white pupils. For every one black pupil in secondary school there were 2.7 in primary grades, while for coloured pupils this ratio was even worse at 1:2.8. For Indian and white pupils, on the other hand, the ratios were 1:1.7 and 1:1.5 respectively.

Pass rates in the school-leaving examinations mirrored these disparities. In 1993, they ranged from 39% among blacks to 86% among coloureds, 93% among Indians and 95% among whites. Slightly less than 2% of black and 4% of coloured candidates were earning higher-grade passes in mathematics, compared with 21% of Indian and 24% of white candidates.

The new government was under immense pressure to improve equity, efficiency and quality of educational provision. Compulsory schooling was extended to black pupils and spending on education increased substantially from R22 billion in 1992/93 to R37 billion in 1997/98 and R82 billion in 2005/06. Enhanced funding was allocated to the provinces with the greatest backlogs. Average expenditure per pupil increased from R1 360 in 1991 to R3 336 in 2001, and provincial disparities narrowed.

In order to address high pupil-teacher ratios, the number of teachers was also increased in the disadvantaged provinces; with the consequence that personnel expenditure consumed the lion's share of budgets, leaving little with which to improve facilities and infrastructure.

Bridges too far

An overly ambitious attempt in 1996 to correct inequalities in pupil-teacher ratios between the provinces had disastrous consequences. The government redistributed teaching posts, offering surplus teachers either transfers to disadvantaged schools or retrenchment packages. The most skilled, experienced and employable of the affected teachers chose the latter option, resulting in a significant net loss of human resources in a skills-starved system.

Despite having prioritised infrastructure, particularly classrooms, sanitation and water, progress was inadequate. By 2002, 28% of schools had no water, 43% no electricity and 78% no libraries. In order to increase spending on school building, infrastructure and learning support materials, provinces were instructed to start limiting personnel spending to 80% of total budgets. By 2003/04, however, some provinces were still spending almost 87% on personnel.

In a search for greater efficiency, the government introduced admission age and age-by-grade regulations in 2000, as well as placing limits on repetition. As a consequence, enrolment in the lowest and highest grades dropped as under- and over-aged children were excluded from the system.

Despite these strict regulations, flow-through remained a problem and primary schools were still over-enrolled and secondary schools under-enrolled relative to the appropriate age proportions. The Department of Education expressed concern about the high dropout rates among boys in the secondary grades, in poorer rural communities in particular. This was producing a growing army of redundant and unemployable youth, with painfully predictable consequences.

Among many other initiatives and changes, one deserves particular mention – a new curriculum and teaching methodology. 'Curriculum 2005' was implemented from 1998, to be in place in all grades by 2003. It encompassed a new approach of 'outcomes-based education' (OBE), involving radically changed teaching methods and syllabus content. The new approach was meant to discourage rote learning and routine tests and usher in ongoing class assessments, self-assessments and independent effort by pupils, with teachers acting as 'study facilitators' rather than imposing a regimen of notes and facts.

It ran into problems almost from the start, due to inadequate teacher training and a lack of resources and study facilities in schools. Its introduction in the higher grades was subsequently postponed, and a revised, simplified version was launched in 2004, stipulating achievement markers for pupils as they progressed through school. Predictably, however, OBE tended to work well mainly in better-resourced schools with trained and motivated teachers.

Research found that the gap between good and weak learners, and hence between the races, was in fact widening in the senior school phase. In 2005 there were reports of secondary school principals complaining that the majority of weaker learners could not read and write or do arithmetic properly. Moreover, many parents, and even some of the teachers themselves, objected to OBE.

The persistence of inequality

The irony of the school system as reformed and restructured was that some of the policy measures taken by government had a negative impact on precisely the schools that most needed to improve – those in impoverished areas. While standards at most formerly white and Indian schools tended to be high and improving, they could accommodate only a very small proportion of black children, who benefited enormously. In the 2003 Senior Certificate examinations over a third of black pupils in former black schools failed compared with only one tenth of blacks in the former white schools.

The teaching of mathematics and science was a problem of near-crisis proportions in many schools, as illustrated by the Senior Certificate examination results in the Western Cape. Of the 10 144 black candidates who wrote the exams in 2005, only 4% passed higher grade mathematics compared with 30% among white candidates. In 2003, the former white schools produced 82% of the successful school leavers with higher grade mathematics in the province. Quality problems were also apparent at primary level because Grade 6 assessments in the Western Cape in 2005 produced an average mark of a mere 42% for literacy and a very disturbing 17% for numeracy.

Another major factor impacting on the quality of learning was that of language. Up to the end of 1992, mother tongue had to be used as medium of instruction until Grade 5. From 1993, however, black schools could use any of the 11 official languages, and parents could decide which language(s) should be used and from what grade. This policy of parental choice of language medium has remained largely unchanged, and all children also had to learn at least one additional language from Grade 1 upwards.

The parents, transfixed by the image of English as the language of economic progress, international achievement and perhaps even of liberation, eschewed the proven benefits of home language learning during the early years of schooling, and the use of English has well-nigh exploded. The number of primary schools using English as medium of instruction increased from 33% in 1991 to 55% in 1998 and then expanded even further.

A number of experts attributed the poor results in literacy and numeracy at Grade 3 and 6 levels over the past few years to the lack of opportunity to learn these crucial skills first in a familiar home language. The government declared an intention to encourage mother-tongue instruction but here again a massive task of teacher and materials development and administrative co-ordination lay ahead.

Some non-African children had to pay a price for inequalities established long before they were born. These were the pupils in many of the 2 000 formerly Afrikaans-medium schools in which the implications of school integration meant the introduction of English tuition in addition to or instead of Afrikaans. The use of English in these schools expanded so rapidly that the eventual loss of Afrikaans as a medium of instruction in many or most of these schools was inevitable.

A system in crisis

South Africa was unlikely to continue its impressive economic performance of the first few years of the century, with an education system that failed to produce the kind of recruits for a labour market that required growing numbers of applicants with a sound grasp of mathematics and science. South Africa spent more on education as a proportion of the Gross Domestic Product than most other countries but its return on this expenditure was worse than that of several other countries.

The performance of the educational system (*see box*) was cause for such concern that some analysts began categorising it with the other major crises: HIV-Aids, crime and unemployment.

ABOVE: *Christina Mulemba, 11, in front, on her way to buy airtime for her mother's cell phone. Christina walks seven kilometres to school every day and her mother recharges her phone off a car battery.*

For most tourists visiting a free South Africa it was a paradise of natural beauty, exotic animals and friendly people. To the Western world, South Africa represented a microcosm of global harmony. Not so for visitors from Africa, particularly the millions of illegal migrants who eked out a living as street hawkers or car guards. Denounced as competitors for scarce jobs, drug dealers or criminals, these invisibles – pejoratively dubbed *makwerekwere* by black South Africans – bore the brunt of xenophobia.

The image of post-apartheid South Africa was inextricably linked to Nelson Mandela. Even bitterly opposed ideological foes praised Mandela. People in power, from the Iranian regime to the Israeli prime minister, from Cuba's Castro to the Bush administration, endorsed him uncritically.

Mandela's glowing reputation was greater abroad than at home, where by 2006 the picture was decidedly mixed. The country was struggling with the world's highest HIV infection rate, was riddled with crime, and the Mbeki government persistently refused to act against or even condemn the atrocities of Robert Mugabe's regime in Zimbabwe. Well-disposed foreign governments were stunned by the South African government's ineffective response to the HIV-Aids pandemic. At the same time they were impressed by South Africa's remarkably robust media debate and a truly free press – comparable and even better than most parochial US counterparts.

Left-liberals in the West bemoaned the widening inequality between a small non-racial economic elite still largely dominated by whites and a vast impoverished underclass almost exclusively consisting of an unemployed and under-educated black youth. Some considered a fragile democracy rooted in such disparities as inherently unstable.

International business, on the contrary, praised the neo-liberal policies of the post-apartheid government. Levelling inequality required a growing economy, to which fiscal discipline, prudent privatisation of state assets and unpopular market-oriented policies were seen as essential foundations.

Even if Mbeki's centralisation of decision-making violated left-liberal tenets of participatory democracy, it was recognised that a developing country needed a strong executive. Influential foreign media – from the *Wall Street Journal* to *The Economist* or the *Frankfurter Allgemeine* – lauded the progress made in socio-structural reforms, from the provision of some basic housing, clean water and electricity to access to rudimentary health services for many. This economic perspective rightly celebrated the success that was achieved.

Post-apartheid legitimacy opened the gates of Africa for South African business. The self-declared southern 'engine of growth' was not yet half as resented as comparable US multinationals in their backyard of Latin America. In the first decade of inclusive democracy South African companies invested an estimated R200 billion in the continent. Only eight of the top 100 firms listed on the Johannesburg Stock Exchange did not operate in the rest of Africa. The areas of investment included retail, financial services, telecommunications and transport. Shoprite Checkers, Pep Stores and other South African companies began to sprout in African capitals like Lusaka and Kampala.

Probing the growing international disillusionment a dozen years after liberation, not one event, but an accumulation of moral turnarounds, can be blamed. Not all of these can be attributed to the short-sightedness of leaders. Many deficits derived from structural conditions that the new power holders inherited.

Among the most serious blotches on the South African image among informed foreign observers were HIV/Aids, crime and inaction against Zimbabwe, followed by the government's arms purchases, seen as wasting resources on frigates and fighter planes when South Africa did not face external enemies.

Next on the list was corruption. Corruption of high-ranking officials partly stemmed from the arms deals, but pervaded other sectors as well, such as massive social welfare fraud and patronage arrangements.

Parliamentarians, managers and executives allocated themselves disproportionately large salaries and perks in the face of widening income gaps. Ordinary South Africans were dismayed. When Desmond Tutu criticised this practice, an ANC spokesperson replied: 'The Archbishop should stick to religion.'

The end of the apartheid morality play normalised South African politics. Pragmatic compromises and the politics of expediency robbed the country of its former moral stature. The costs of such moral losses were difficult to calculate, but showed up in a reduced influence in the arenas of international diplomacy.

A final word: a perplexing, challenging country

After the first free election in April 1994 South Africans shared a single nationality, a common citizenship and a commitment to tackle the future together. The preamble to a widely acclaimed constitution called on citizens to remember both the suffering and the achievements of the past. The national flag and the anthem successfully blended historic symbols and songs. Slowly becoming racially more diverse, the national teams in the different sporting codes won the enthusiastic backing of all but a smattering of diehards.

Early in the new century overwhelming majorities of both blacks and whites declared that they were proud to be South Africans. They considered being a South African an important part of their social identity. At the heart of this sentiment lay the fact that blacks of all groups were finally free and that whites no longer were oppressors. To this was added the immense relief over the achievement of South Africa in negotiating a generally accepted constitution without any foreign assistance, thus proving expectations of a bloodbath wrong. As president, Nelson Mandela played his role as the great conciliator with aplomb and became the most admired living ex-politician in the world.

But the past still bore down heavily on the present. South Africa remained a challenging, perplexing, bewildering country. Wealthy people flaunting their riches lived close to large and growing numbers of people who were dismally poor and with little or no prospect of a regular job. A small number of public schools able to hold their own against the best public institutions in the world co-existed in a system in which four-fifths of public schools were found to be 'performing poorly'. Wealthy urbanites perversely persisted in buying the newest car models despite the fact that South Africa had one of the highest rates in the world for car hijacking.

Tied together by an expanding economy

The prospects for social stability were closely tied to those of an expanding economy creating new jobs and some welfare benefits for the very poor. Since the early 1930s South Africa had burst the bonds of a struggling, neo-colonial economy in a race against time to provide food and work for its rapidly growing population. The gold mines were becoming less and less profitable, the manufacturing sector sluggish and agriculture was

GROWING INEQUALITY

Inequality between white and black was a burning issue in the struggle against apartheid. One of the most commonly used indicators, the 'Gini coefficient', measures income inequality. It can vary from 0 (complete equality) to 1 (complete inequality). In 1978 the Gini coefficient for the South African population was 0.66. This was the highest – i.e. the worst inequality – out of the 57 countries for which data was available. The values for Mexico and Brazil, which never knew any formal segregation, came a close second and third. Inequality among whites in South Africa was modest (0.39) and on a level with that in Western democracies, but among Africans (0.55) it was already high.

In the new democratic system the groups that started out with the highest basic incomes (whites at 0.45 and Indians at 0.48) were also the groups that experienced the least change in terms of inequality. The same is not true for African (0.64 in 2005) and coloured people (0.56 in 2005), with increases in measured inequality of 21% and 17% respectively since 1996. This points to rapidly rising incomes for a small section of these groups, with relatively little financial benefit experienced by the lowest-income earners. By 2004 three-fifths of blacks lived below the defined poverty income, against only 4% of whites. In this year some 4.3 million people (9% of the population) lived on less than $1 a day compared to 2 million in 1996.

LEFT: *Children from Sterretjie nursery school in Witpoortjie marched against crime in September 2003, a few months after their principal was killed in a hijacking.*

OPPOSITE: *One of many MTN stalls in Abudja, Nigeria.*

nearly swamped by its problems. Liberal historian C.W. de Kiewiet wrote that the backward economy of the early 1930s suffered from three factors that constrained growth: 'its low-grade ore, low-grade land and low-grade [poorly educated] people'. The South African economy at this point was not much different from the struggling economies that would characterise independent African states in the 1970s.

The 40 years of high growth between 1933 and 1973 were followed by stagnation after the Soweto uprising of 1976 and declining per capita incomes. After the first democratic election the economy picked up. Private fixed capital formation rose from 10% of Gross Domestic Product in 1993, to 26%, a level last seen in 1983 before serious unrest had begun.

By 2003 the South African economy had grown almost beyond recognition. It was now 33rd in the world for the largest industrial output, 27th for services output, the 21st biggest economy measured in purchasing power and the 18th largest in market capitalisation. But it was also in the top four for the highest rate of unemployment in developing economies, in the top three of the Gini coefficient league of inequality, in the top three for the murder rate and, because of the incidence of HIV-Aids, the one with the 21st highest death rate.

But in some respects the fundamental weaknesses of the economy and the political system remained. First, like other economies whose growth was driven by commodities (in the South African case it was minerals and agricultural products), South Africa failed to develop an exports-driven manufacturing sector. By 2006 it was recognised that South Africa could find itself in serious economic trouble if the worldwide boom in commodities suddenly faltered.

Second, the ruling party overspent in a dramatic effort to change materially the welfare of all segments of its constituency. Before the mid-1970s there was grossly disproportionate social welfare spending on whites. Having promised 'a better life for all' in 1994, the ANC government tried to address the plight of the poor. It built on a fairly well-developed welfare system. In the final years of apartheid South Africa was

already spending more, as a percentage of GDP, on social assistance in the form of non-contributory schemes than developed countries and more than almost any country in the developing southern hemisphere.

Between 2001 and 2005 the ANC government increased social security by an average annual rate of almost 26%. The recipients of all types of social grants jumped from just under three million in 2000 to just under eight million by the time of the 2004 election. By 2004 as many as 56% of households in the lowest living-standard category received grants and pensions. With twelve million people, or around a quarter of the population, receiving a direct cash transfer from the state, South Africa easily had the largest welfare system in the developing world. Mexico and Brazil paled in comparison. South Africa had become virtually the only welfare state in the developing world.

But without high economic growth, such a welfare net – and even more so, any extension of it – was unsustainable. Also hampering the economy was the tendency of government, like its predecessor, to put ideological goals before efficiency, merit and growth. Before 1970 the obsession was with segregating society, after 1994 it was with black empowerment and the attempt to bring about demographic representation. Neither promised to accelerate job creation or reduce crime, the major preoccupations of the citizenry. Similarly the government's efforts to address the developmental problems of Africa deterred foreign fixed investment, which showed a downward trend.

The state steadily expanded services in water, electricity and sanitation, but with half the economically active population out of work, many were unable to pay for the services and had them terminated.

Return of political stability

After the transition in 1994 political stability soon became the order of the day. The main explanation was a demographic one. By 2000 whites had dropped to less than 10% of the population and the Afrikaners to barely more than 5%. The transfer of political power from whites to blacks was abrupt, decisive and irreversible. The approximately

30 000 whites in the standing army in 1994 did not voice their resentments with the new order for the sake of career and retirement planning. Initially, self-censorship rather than any lack of press freedom stifled criticism. The pension proved to be mightier than the pen. The idea of a tax revolt by whites quickly dissipated with the introduction of a revenue service much tougher and efficient than the pre-1994 one.

South Africa was in many ways a new country, hardly resembling the old one in which whites filled all the top and middle-level positions. At the top a rapid process of de-racialisation was under way. In the richest 20% of the population whites fell from 87% in 1975 to less than 54% in 1996 and then dropped further. But the poorest tenth of the population was still more than 90% black.

In the public schools, where middle and lower-middle class parents paid fairly high fees, racial integration increased steadily and peacefully. Although whites still predominated in these schools, a new generation was playing and learning together. The student bodies of the previously largely white universities were transformed, with blacks making up most of the undergraduate students, except on the Stellenbosch and the Potchefstroom campuses.

A hybrid state

The new state was a curious hybrid of a weak and a strong state. The central government faced no rivals as a source of authority in the form of warlords, private armies, multi-national corporations, ethnic communities or regional governments. On the other hand there was evidence of widespread corruption among state officials, drug lords who remained above the law and the proliferation of criminal gangs.

South Africa enjoyed what the analyst Van Zyl Slabbert in *The Other Side of History* called 'predominantly consensual stability'. The constitution was liberal and the political machinery a collection from models from the most advanced industrialised countries. What was sorely lacking was an efficient state with the ability to enforce laws and bring criminals promptly to book in order to arrest a serious incidence of violent crime that most people, if not the president, considered out of control.

The executive's efforts in the first ten years to centralise as much power as possible had backfired. The ruling party found itself in a serious state of crisis as a large section of the party rebelled against a system in which the president had great scope to use and abuse the system to punish his enemies and reward his supporters. But apart from intimidation he had limited means with which to suppress dissent. The liberal constitution prevented anyone from going outside the law to silence a faction or to bludgeon critics or rivals into submission. The police and the military were so thinly stretched that any suggestion of a coup was farcical. The only way to deal with crises was to build support.

Corruption was spawned by the blurring of the lines between party and state, and by an unseemly scramble of politicians and civil servants to benefit personally from black economic empowerment policies. In an interview with a financial journal early in 2007 Kgalema Motlanthe, the ANC's national secretary-general, declared that corruption was 'far worse than anyone imagines'. He added: 'This rot is across the board. It is not confined to any level or any area of the country. Almost every project is conceived because it offers opportunities for certain people to make money.'

The ANC had squandered its moral high ground. Ironically, this had salutary consequences. By the late 1990s the moral authority with Mandela at the helm was so overwhelming that people outside ANC ranks were afraid of voicing criticism or organising protest action. South Africa's liberal democracy almost suffocated at birth.

But the disappearance of Mandela from the scene, the Mbeki presidency's blind eye to the crises of Zimbabwe, the Aids pandemic, rampant violent crime and the flourishing of state corruption sapped the authority of the political leadership. The result was a reawakening of civil society – a direct result of the decline of that moral authority. Businessmen told government that corruption and crime were negatively affecting the economy's ability to attract new fixed investment and retain high-skilled people. People began to put pressure on the government to deal with the spiralling crises. They were less and less willing to tolerate government excuses. In newspapers of all languages there was a marked decline in the race consciousness of the press commentators.

People unexpectedly rediscovered their communal and cultural identities. Among Afrikaners there were attempts to retain Afrikaans as language of instruction, but with it came the realisation that this battle concerned all minority languages in the struggle against English cultural hegemony.

'The worst never happens'

In 1949 the elderly Jan Smuts, recently defeated in a momentous election, observed: 'The whole world is moving into a Colour phase of history, with results none can foresee and South Africa should dread most. Still, the worst, like the best, never happens.' This may have ignored some of the cruellest episodes in South African history – the extermination of the San, the subjugation of the Xhosa and their national suicide, the suffering of migrant workers on the mines and the deaths of women and children in concentration camps during the South African War. During the 1930s the slums in the South African cities were among the worst in the world. Apartheid destroyed many tight communities and closed off career chances.

But the worst did not happen in the 1980s and 1990s. The feared bloodbath did not occur in the transition from white to black rule. South Africans proved to be resilient and innovative. Urbanisation, better health care, the provision of mass education and a narrowing racial gap in education saw not only rapid population growth, but also a proliferation of skills across the colour spectrum.

Society was changing. Increasingly, performance and incompetence were judged in non-racial terms. Through the overuse and ultimately abuse of the race card to deflect criticism, government itself had discredited the card. Whites were much less guilt-ridden and blacks much less inclined to accept poor performance from the government. Racial prescriptions were slowly reduced in the national and provincial sports teams, and not only because the market demand for merit and achievement could not be ignored.

A society whose components from the start struggled to live with each other were joining forces to attempt, against considerable odds, to forge a new nation from the bottom up, eschewing government's attempt to do it from the top down. They were slowly coming to terms with their own and each other's histories. They were also beginning to sing new songs and tell different stories in a fresh identification with their land, people and culture.

ABOVE: *The Johannesburg skyline. Economic growth in the first decade of fully democratic government was spurred particularly by a boom in commodities and by construction. In the main cities numerous construction sites created the impression of a country confident of the future and sure of its ability to confront the challenges it faced. Despite the signs of growth and prosperity, however, real progress was still painfully slow. In 2006 the per capita Gross Domestic Product topped the 1981 level for the first time. There were major obstacles to rapid progress: rampant crime, an HIV/Aids pandemic, a huge skills shortage, a lack of capacity in the state administration, a looming crisis in the education system and millions of unemployed people lacking the skills for a modern labour market. Yet progress had undoubtedly been made: the private sector was resilient, the tax system was efficient and trade was being liberalised. Above all there was confidence among South Africans, black and white, that South Africa could achieve the near impossible, emulating the peaceful political settlement of 1994.*

Glossary

Agterryer – An African or coloured male who accompanied his Boer master during the South African (or Anglo-Boer) War of 1899–1902. He cooked for him, tended his horse, dug trenches and generally did all the menial tasks. He also acted as a spy and scout, and sometimes performed a combat role for the Boer commando.

Amabutho – Male age-based regiments in Zulu army; at times work parties.

Amagogotya – The Xhosa name given to the 'unbelievers' who rejected the prophecies of Nongqawuse. The word implies 'hardness' or 'stinginess' and that the unbelievers put their own selfish interests ahead of the interests of the nation as a whole.

Amagqoboka – Xhosa expression with the literal meaning 'those who have been pierced' by the Christian message, i.e. converts to mission Christianity. The implication is that they have a hole in their hearts and that Christianity has entered through that hole.

Amakholwa – Literally 'believers', i.e. believers in the Christian teachings of the missionaries. Historically, the word is usually used to describe the African communities of the Natal mission stations whose Christian beliefs encompassed love of education and peasant production for the market.

Anthropogenic – Caused by humans.

Anthropomorphic – Attributed with having the characteristics of a human being.

Apartheid – Term used in 1929 for the first time by a Dutch Reformed Church minister to propagate segregated churches and church services. Later extended to political and economic institutions and to many spheres of social interaction. It was government policy between 1948 and 1992.

Arboreal – Living mainly in trees.

Assegai – Spear used by Khoikhoi and Bantu speakers.

Bandiet – 'Convict', i.e. person convicted by the VOC of a crime, generally non-political, in the East and sentenced to hard labour at the Cape.

Bastaard – In the Cape district, a person born out of wedlock; in trekboer and frontier regions, a person of mixed Khoikhoi-European or, less frequently, slave-European descent; any person accepted as a member of a Bastaard community.

Bijwoner – Normally a white Afrikaner man living on the farm owned by another farmer, and exchanging his services for a wage or part of the yield.

Bipedal – Walking on two legs.

Bittereinder – Fighting a war to the end against great odds. First used for Boers fighting in the guerrilla phase of the South African War.

Carbon dating – A method for dating organic materials found in archaeological excavations. It is based on the fact that all living plants and animals contain the radioactive isotope carbon-14 in equilibrium with the atmosphere. When they die and stop breathing, the carbon-14 decays at a fixed and known rate. By measuring the amount left in the shell, charcoal, bone or other organic matter, one can estimate how long ago the plant or animal died. It is reliable for samples less than 35 000 years old.

Clientship – A system/practice used by stronger and wealthier men to control and influence poorer and weaker men in a way that benefits both.

Commando – A mounted unit consisting of burghers supplemented by Khoikhoi and, later, by Bantu-speaking Africans. It was used on the frontier for both offensive and defensive purposes.

Corps Pandoeren – An auxillary corps (1791–1799) of Khoisan and 'Bastaards' formed by the VOC; under the British it became the Cape Regiment.

Dagga – *Cannabis sativa*, smoked as a drug; introduced from the East by the Portuguese.

Difaqane – See **Mfecane**.

Dopper – A member of the smallest and theologically the most conservative of the Reformed churches in South Africa.

Drostdy – Area of jurisdiction of a landdrost; also his official residence.

Droster – A slave, soldier or servant who left service without permission; also indigent persons in general.

Eenlopende – An officially unmarried white man, living on his own or with a woman who was not a European.

Fiscal – Public prosecutor.

Freeburgher – (*vrijburger*); person not employed by the VOC and free to own or rent land, to practise certain trades and hold office.

Gracile – Slender or graceful; used as the opposite of robust for early hominid fossils.

Griener – 'Greenhorn', new Jewish immigrant.

Groepsgevoel – Phrase often used in the ideology of apartheid to denote a feeling of solidarity with the ethnic group.

Heemraad – (pl. *heemraden*); member of the board of *heemraden* aiding the landdrost in the administration of a district.

Hensoppers – Republican burghers who surrendered voluntarily in the South African War.

Heren XVII – 'The Lords Seventeen', the central board of directors of the VOC.

Imam – Muslim religious leader.

Impi – Nguni word for regiment.

Inboek – Apprenticeship of a Khoisan or African youth as farm labourer until he or she reached a certain age; usually given no wages but food and clothes.

Inboekseling – Term used in the Boer republics in the period 1850 to 1870 for indentured African children, a status considered by some to be close to slavery.

Induna – Zulu word meaning overseer or headman appointed by the chief.

Ithola – Xhosa word denoting the war doctor who doctors the army for military operations; believed to have the ability to predict the outcome of battles, and frequently assists in the formulation of military strategies.

Izigodlo – Female age-based regiments, usually work parties.

Joiners – Republican burghers who fought on the British side in the last phase in the South African War.

Kaffir – Common name used both by officials of the Dutch East Company and burghers for convicts acting as auxiliary police in Cape Town.

Kaffireatnik – Shop assistant in mine concession stores and dining halls.

Kaptyn – Person of authority in Griqua political institutions.

Kaross – A cloak made of skin or leather and worn over the shoulders.

Knecht – Man, usually white, employed by someone else, usually as overseer.

Knobkierie – A stout stick with a round knob at one end, used as a weapon.

Kraal – a settlement, usually in circular form, of Khoikhoi huts; later also used freely to refer to traditional black settlements; a livestock enclosure.

Labour tenancy – A form of farm labour in which the labourer receives cultivation and grazing rights in addition to wages.

Landdrost – Chief administrator and magistrate of a district.

Leningplaats – Land given out by government for occupation subject to payment of rent.

Lineage – A line of ancestors.

Litvak – 'Lithuanian' Jew.

Lumpenproletariat – Part of the working class that does not earn regular wages, often finding itself in a subsistence crisis.

Madrasah – School for Muslim children.

Mafisa system – African practice of chiefs or well-to-do men loaning cattle to poorer men for temporary use.

Manumission – The process of setting a slave free.

Mardijker – Free black from VOC's Eastern territories.

Maroon – A settlement of fugitive slaves, usually in a mountainous area.

Mfecane – A series of wars leading to massive disruption and restructuring of African society in Natal and on the highveld in the 1820s and 1830s.

Midden – A rubbish dump. Shell middens formed when hunter-gatherer people lived on shellfish along the coast and discarded the shells with other debris, such as bones, stone tools and ostrich egshell.

Muid – Dry measure roughly equivalent to one hectolitre.

Ngwato – Refers to the Bamangwato, then under the rule of Sekgoma I, based at Shoshong in modern Botswana.

Onderdorp – Poorer section of a town, often racially integrated before the 1950s.

Oorlam – On the Northern frontier, a person usually of Khoikhoi descent, previously in colonial service.

Opgaaf – Enumeration of freeburghers, free blacks and their property for tax purposes.

Opstal – A homestead.

Ordonnantieruiter – A mounted police officer subject to the landdrost.

Pacht – Trading rights in certain commodities; monopoly rented by the VOC to *pachters* in return for *pachtgeld* (lit. 'monopoly money').

Pastoralists – People who farm mainly with livestock such as sheep, goats and cattle.

Peruvian – Pejorative South African term for 'undesirable' Eastern European Jewish immigrant.

Plakkaat – Proclamation with the force of law during the VOC era.

Platteland – Countryside; during the seventeenth and eighteenth centuries effectively the entire interior of the Cape Colony beyond the limits of Cape Town.

Quitrent – A form of land tenure in the Company period guaranteeing occupation for at least fifteen years.

Renosterbos – Invasive shrub (*Elytropappus rhinocerotis*).

Request – Petition to the Council of Policy for burgher rights, manumissions, monopoly rights, etc.

Secunde – Second-in-command to the governor or commander; later lieutenant governor or deputy governor.

Segregation – Term borrowed from the American South to denote a policy of racial separation.

Sjambok – A heavy whip, usually of rhinoceros hide.

Slachtersbrief – Letter given by butchers or their servants in lieu of cash for cattle and sheep purchased in the interior. These letters had to be cashed in Cape Town.

Smous – Itinerant peddler.

Socialism – Collective or popular ownership of the means of production and distribution.

Tikvath Israel – Hope of Israel.

Transhumance – Moving seasonally with livestock from one place to another to obtain good grazing.

Transport – Deed of transfer.

Trekboer – Semi-nomadic livestock farmer.

Uitlander – (Mainly) English-speaking immigrants at the turn of the nineteenth century on the Rand who were opposed to President Paul Kruger's government because they were not allowed to vote and could not become citizens of the ZAR (South African Republic, or Transvaal).

Veldschoenen – Leather shoes, usually without heels.

Veldwachter – Police officer at the drostdy assisting the landdrost; later ordonnantieruiter.

Veldwachtmeester – Freeburgher militia officer in rural areas; also responsible for some civil administrative duties in the division to which he was appointed.

Verkramptes – Arch-conservatives during the later years of National Party rule in South Africa.

Verligtes – 'Enlightened' faction in National Party proposing reform (but not abolition) of apartheid.

Vicariance – Ecological term for the dividing of an ancestral population into geographically distinct daughter populations.

VOC – (*Verenigde Oost-Indische Compagnie*); the Dutch East India Company.

Volkseie – Key word in apartheid ideology denoting special pride in distinctive ethnic characteristics.

Volkskapitalisme – Form of capitalism that would suit the needs of the Afrikaner people as a group struggling to capture a share of the economy in the entrepreneurial function.

Volksraad – Parliament of the ZAR (Transvaal); Official Afrikaans name for the lower house of the South African Parliament after 1910.

Volkstaat – Afrikaner ethnic state.

Bibliography

PART ONE

Blundell, G. (ed.). *Origins: The Story of the Emergence of Humans and Humanity in Africa*. Cape Town, 2006.

Botha, H.C. *John Fairbairn in South Africa*. Cape Town, 1984.

Dart, R. *Adventures with the Missing Link*. New York, 1959.

De Wet, C.G. *Die Vryliede en Vryswartes in die Kaapse Nedersetting*. Cape Town, 1981.

Diamond, J. *Guns, Germs and Steel – a Short History of Everybody for the Last 13 000 Years*. London, 1997.

Du Toit, A. and H. Giliomee. *Afrikaner Political Thought, 1780–1850*. Cape Town, 1983.

Dunbar, R. *The Human Story – a New History of Mankind's Evolution*, London, 2004.

Elphick, R. and H. Giliomee (eds.). *The Shaping of South African Society, 1652–1840*. Middletown, 1989.

Elphick, R. *Kraal and Castle: Khoikhoi and the Founding of White South Africa*. New Haven, 1977.

Fredrickson, G.M. *White Supremacy: a Comparative Study in American and South African History*. New York, 1981.

Gerstner, J.N. *The Thousand Generation Covenant: Dutch Reformed Covenant Theology and Group Identity in Colonial South Africa*. Leiden, 1991.

Gould, S.J. 'Our Unusual Unity', in *Leonardo's Mountain of Clams and the Diet of Worms*. New York, 1998.

Gould, S.J. *Wonderful Life*. New York, 1989.

Gribbin, M. and J. Gribbin. *Being Human: Putting People in an Evolutionary Perspective*. London, 1993.

Guelke, L. and R. Shell. 'An Early Colonial Landed Gentry: Land and Wealth in the Cape Colony, 1682–1731', *Journal of Historical Geography*, 9, 3, 1983.

Hall, M. *The Changing Past: Farmers, Kings and Traders in Southern Africa, 200–1860*. Cape Town, 1987.

Hammond-Tooke, D. *The Roots of Black South Africa*. Johannesburg, 1993.

Heese, H.F. *Groep Sonder Grense: die Rol en Status van die Gemengde Bevolking aan die Kaap, 1652–1795*. Bellville, 1984.

Huffman, T.N. *A Handbook to the Iron Age: the Archaeology of Precolonial Farming Societies in Southern Africa*. Pietermaritzburg, 2007.

Huffman, T.N. *Mapungubwe: Ancient African Civilisation on the Limpopo*. Johannesburg, 2005.

Huffman, T.N. *Snakes and Crocodiles: Power and Symbolism in ancient Zimbabwe*. Johannesburg, 1996.

Keegan, T. *Colonial South Africa and the Origins of the Racial Order*. Cape Town, 1986.

Klein, R. *The Human Career*. Chicago, 1999.

Lewis-Williams, J.D. *The Mind in the Cave: Consciousness and the Origins of Art*. London, 2002.

Lewis-Williams, J.D. *Images of Mystery: Rock Art of the Drakensberg*. Cape Town, 2003.

Maggs, T. *Iron Age Communities of the Southern Highveld*. Pietermaritzburg, 1976.

Marks, S. and A. Atmore (eds.). *Economy and Society in Pre-Industrial South Africa*. London, 1980.

Mason, J.E. Jnr. *Social Death and Resurrection: Slavery and Emancipation in South Africa*. Charlottesville, 2003.

Maylam, P. *A History of the African People of South Africa: from the Early Iron Age to the 1970s*. London and Cape Town, 1986.

Milone, P.D. 'Indische Culture and its Relationship to Urban Life', *Comparative Studies in Society and History*, 9, 1967.

Mitchell, P. *The Archaeology of Southern Africa*. Cambridge, 2002.

Mithen, S. *After the Ice: a Global Human History*. Phoenix, 2003.

Newton-King, S. and V.C. Malherbe. *The Khoikhoi Rebellion in the Eastern Cape, 1799–1803*. Cape Town, 1981.

Newton-King, S. *The Enemy Within: the Struggle for Ascendancy on the Cape Eastern Frontier*. Cambridge, 1999.

Oppenheimer, S. *Out of Africa's Eden: the Peopling of the World*. Johannesburg, 2003.

Phillipson, D.W. *African Archaeology*. Cambridge, 1985.

Ross, R. *Adam Kok's Griqua*. Cambridge, 1976.

Ross, R. *Cape of Torments: Slavery and Resistance in South Africa*. London, 1983.

Ross, R. *Status and Respectability in the Cape Colony 1750–1870: a Tragedy of Manners*. Cambridge, 1999.

Saunders, C. (ed.). *Black Leaders in Southern African History*. London, 1979.

Schama, S. *The Embarrassment of Riches: an Interpretation of Dutch Culture in the Golden Age*. London, 1987.

Schoeman, K. *Armosyn van die Kaap: Voorspel tot Vestiging, 1415–1651*. Cape Town, 1999.

Schoeman, K. *Die Wêreld van Susanna Smit, 1799–1863*. Cape Town, 1995.

Shell, R. C.-H. 'Islam in Southern Africa, 1652–1998', in Nehemia, L. and R.L. Pouwels, (eds.) *The History of Islam in Africa*. Athens, 2000.

Shell, R. C.-H. *Children of Bondage: a Social History of the Slave Society at the Cape of Good Hope, 1652–1838*. Johannesburg, 1994.

Shell, R. C.-H. et al. (eds.) *Bibliographies of Bondage: Selected Bibliographies of South African Slavery and Emancipation*. Cape Town, 2006. CD-ROM.

Shell, R. C.-H. *From Diaspora to Diorama: the Old Slave Lodge in Cape Town*. Cape Town, 2006. CD-ROM

Skotnes, P. (ed.). *Miscast: Negotiating the Presence of the Bushmen*. Cape Town, 1996.

Soodyall, H (ed.). *The Pre-history of Africa: Tracing the Lineage of Modern Man*. Johannesburg, 2006.

Sutton J.E.G. (ed.). 'The Growth of Farming Communities in Africa from the Equator Southwards', a special volume of *Azania*, 29–30, 1994–95.

Tobias, P. *Into the Past – a Memoir*. Picador, 2005.

Van der Merwe, P.J. *Die Noordwaartse Beweging van die Boere voor die Groot Trek, 1770–1842*. Den Haag, 1937.

Van der Merwe, P.J. *The Migrant Farmer in the History of the Cape Colony, 1657–1842*. Athens, 1995.

Van Schalkwyk, J.A. and E.O.M. Hanisch. *Sculptured in Clay: Iron Age Figurines from Schroda, Limpopo Province, South Africa*. Pretoria, 2002.

Watson, R.L. *The Slave Question: Liberty and Property in South Africa*. Hanover, 1990.

Westra, P.E. and J.C. Armstrong. *Slave Trade with Madagascar: the Journals of the Cape Slaver Leijdsman, 1715*. Cape Town, 2006.

Wolf, E. *Europe and the People Without History*. Berkeley, 1982, 1997.

Worden, N. *Slavery in Dutch South Africa*. Cambridge, 1985.

PART TWO

Akenson, D.H. *God's Peoples: Covenant and Land in South Africa, Israel and Ulster*. Ithaca, 1992.

Beinart, W., P. Delius and S. Trapido (eds.). *Putting a Plough to the Ground*. Johannesburg, 1986.

Bhana, S. and J. Brain. *Setting Down Roots: Indian Migrants in South Africa, 1860–1911*. Johannesburg, 1990.

Boeyens, J.C.A.'Die Konflik tussen die Venda en die Blankes in die Transvaal, 1864–1869', *Argiefjaarboek van Suid-Afrikaanse Geskiedenis*, 1990.

Bonner, P. *Kings, Commoners and Concessionaires*. Cambridge, 1983.

Bozzoli, B. (ed.). *Town and Countryside in the Transvaal*. Johannesburg, 1983.

Brookes, E.H. and C. de B. Webb. *A History of Natal*. Pietermaritzburg, 1965.

Bundy, C. *The Rise and Fall of the South African Peasantry*. London, 1979.

Cobbing, J. 'The Mfecane as Alibi: Thoughts on Dithakong and Mbolompo', *Journal of African History*, 29, 3, 1988.

Delius, P. *The Land Belongs to Us: The Pedi Polity, the Boers and the British in the Nineteenth Century*. Johannesburg, 1983.

Du Toit, A. 'No Chosen People: The Myth of the Calvinist Origins', *American Historical Review*, 88, 4, 1983.

Du Toit, A. 'Puritans in Africa?', *Comparative Studies in Society and History*, 21, 2, 1983.

Dubow, S. *Illicit Union: Scientific Racism in Modern South Africa.* Johannesburg, 1995.

Duminy, A. and B. Guest (eds.). *Natal and Zululand: from Earliest Times to 1910, a New History.* Pietermaritzburg, 1986.

Dwane, S. *Ethiopianism and the Order of Ethiopia.* Cape Town, 1999.

Eldredge, E. and F. Morton (eds.). *Slavery on the South African Frontier.* Pietermaritzburg, 1994.

Eldredge, E.A. *A South African Kingdom: the Pursuit of Security in Nineteenth Century Lesotho.* Cambridge, 1993.

Etherington, N. *The Great Treks: the Transformation of Southern Africa, 1815–1854.* London, 2001.

Guy, J. *The Destruction of the Zulu Kingdom: the Civil War in Zululand, 1879–1884.* Pietermaritzburg, 1994.

Guy, J. *The View Across the River: Harriette Colenso and the Struggle Against Imperialism.* Charlottesville, 2001.

Hamilton, C. *Terrific Majesty: the Powers of Shaka Zulu and the Limits of Historical Invention.* Cape Town, 1998.

Hamilton, C. *The Mfecane Aftermath: Reconstructive Debates in Southern African History.* Johannesburg, 1995.

Innes, D. *Anglo American and the Rise of Modern South Africa.* Johannesburg, 1984.

Jordan, A.C. *Towards an African Literature.* Berkeley, 1973.

Keegan,T. 'The Making of the Orange Free State, 1846–1854', *Journal of Imperial and Commonwealth History,* 17, 1, 1988.

Kirk, T. 'Progress and Decline in the Kat River Settlement', *Journal of African History,* xiv, 1973.

Laband, J. *Rope of Sand: the Rise and Fall of the Zulu Kingdom in the Nineteenth Century.* London, 1995.

Liebenberg, B.J. *Andries Pretorius in Natal.* Pretoria, 1977.

Lye, W.F. and C. Murray. *Transformations on the Highveld: the Tswana and the Southern Sotho.* Cape Town, 1980.

Molema, S.M. *Montshiwa 1815–1896: Barolong Chief and Patriot.* Cape Town, 1966.

Morris, D.R. *The Washing of the Spears: a History of the Rise of the Zulu Nation and its Fall.* London, 1966.

Mostert, N. *Frontiers.* New York, 1992.

Newbury, C. 'Out of the Pit: the Capital Accumulation of Cecil Rhodes', *Journal of Imperial and Commonwealth History.* 1981.

Odendaal, A. *Vukani Bantu: the Beginnings of Black Protest Politics in South Africa to 1912.* Cape Town, 1984.

Omer-Cooper, J.D. *The Zulu Aftermath: a Nineteenth Century Revolution in Bantu Africa.* London, 1966.

Peires, J. *The Dead Will Arise: Nongqawuse and the Great Cattle-Killing of 1856–7,* 2nd ed. Johannesburg, 2003.

Peires, J. *The House of Phalo: a History of the Xhosa people in the Days of their Independence.* Johannesburg, 1981.

Poland, M., D. Hammond-Tooke and L. Voigt. *The Abundant Herds: a Celebration of the Nguni Cattle of the Zulu people.* Cape Town, 2003.

Pretorius, J.C.C. *Molokwane, an Iron Age BaKwena Village: early Tswana Settlement in the Western Transvaal.* Pretoria, 1992.

Rasmussen, K.R. *Migrant Kingdom: Mzilikazi's Ndebele in South Africa.* London and Cape Town, 1978.

Ross, A. *John Philip.* Aberdeen, 1986.

Shillington, K. *The Colonisation of the Southern Tswana, 1870–1900.* Johannesburg, 1985.

Slater, H. 'The Changing Pattern of Economic Relationships in Rural Natal', in Marks, S. and S. Trapido (eds.). *Economy and Society in Pre-Industrial South Africa.* London, 1980.

Soga, T. *Journal and Selected Writings of Rev. Tiyo Soga,* D. Williams (ed.). Cape Town, 1983.

Stockenstrom, A. *The Autobiography of the Late Sir Andries Stockenstrom.* Cape Town, 1887.

Thompson, L. *Survival in Two Worlds: Moshoeshoe of Lesotho.* Oxford, 1975.

Trapido, S. 'The Friends of the Natives: Merchants, Peasants and the Political and Ideological Structures of Liberalism in the Cape, 1854–1910', in Marks, S. and S. Trapido (eds.). *Economy and Society in Pre-Industrial South Africa.* London, 1980.

Trapido, S. 'The Origins of the Cape Franchise Qualifications of 1853', *Journal of African History,* 1964.

Trapido, S. 'Landlord and Tenant in a Colonial Economy: the Transvaal, 1880–1910', *Journal of Southern African Studies,* 5, 1978.

Turrell, R. 'The 1875 Black Flag Revolt on the Kimberley Diamond Fields', *Journal of Southern African Studies,* 7, 1981.

Van der Merwe, P.J. 'Die Matabeles en die Voortrekkers', *Archives Yearbook of South Africa,* 1986.

Worden, N. and G. Groenewald, (eds.). *Trials of Slavery: Selected Documents, 1705–1794.* Cape Town, 2005.

Worger, W. *South Africa's City of Diamonds.* Johannesburg, 1987.

Wright, J.B. and A. Manson. *The Hlubi Chiefdom in Natal: a History.* Ladysmith, 1983.

PART THREE

Karis, T. and G. Carter (eds.). *From Protest to Challenge.* Stanford, 1972.

Adhikari, M. (ed.). *Straatpraatjes: Language, Politics and Popular Culture in Cape Town, 1909–1922.* Pretoria, 1996.

Alfred, T.Q. *A Working Life: Cruel Beyond Belief.* Johannesburg, 1989.

Ally, R. *Gold and Empire.* Johannesburg, 1994.

Ashforth, A. *The Politics of Official Discourse of Twentieth-Century South Africa.* Oxford, 1990.

Beinart, W. et al. (eds.). *Putting a Plough to the Ground.* Johannesburg, 1986.

Bickford-Smith, V. *Ethnic Pride and Racial Prejudice in Victorian Cape Town.* Johannesburg, 1995.

Bonner, P. et al. (eds.). *Apartheid's Genesis, 1935–1962.* Johannesburg, 1993.

Booyens, B. *Die lewe van D.F. Malan: Die eerste 40 jaar.* Cape Town, 1969.

Bottomley, J. '"Almost Bled to Death": the Effects of the Anglo-Boer War on Social Transformation in the Orange River Colony', *Historia,* 44, 1999.

Bozzoli, B. (ed.). *Class, Community and Conflict: South African Perspectives.* Johannesburg, 1987.

Bradford, H. *A Taste of Freedom: The ICU in rural South Africa, 1924–1930.* Johannesburg, 1987.

Bradlow, E. 'Capitalists and Labourers in the Post-Emancipation Rural Cape', *Historia,* 31, 1986.

Bradlow, F. 'Islam at the Cape of Good Hope', *South African Historical Journal,* 15, 1981.

Bredekamp, H. and R. Ross. *Missions and Christianity in South African History.* Johannesburg, 1995.

Callinicos L. *Gold and Workers 1886–1924.* Johannesburg, 1981.

Campbell, J.T. *Songs of Zion: the African Methodist Episcopal Church in the United States and South Africa.* New York, 1995.

Comaroff, J.L. (ed.). *The Boer War Diary of Sol T. Plaatje: an African at Mafeking.* London, 1973.

Comaroff, J.L. and J. Comaroff. *Of Revelation and Revolution.* Chicago, 1991, 1997.

Coplan, D. and T. Thoahlane. 'Motherless Households, Landless Farms: Employment Patterns among Lesotho Migrants', in Crush, J. and W. James (ed.s) *Crossing Boundaries: Mine Migrancy in a Democratic South Africa.* Cape Town, 1995.

Couzens, T. *Murder at Morija: Faith, Mystery and Tragedy on a South African Mission.* Charlottesville, 2005.

Crais, C. *The Making of the Colonial Order: White Supremacy and Black Resistance in the Eastern Cape, 1770–1865.* Johannesburg, 1997.

Crush, J. and W. James, 'The Politics of Normalisation: Mine Migrancy in a Democratic Society', in Crush, J. and W. James (eds.). *Crossing Boundaries: Mine Migrancy in a Democratic South Africa.* Cape Town, 1995.

Cuthbertson, G. et al. (eds.). *Writing a Wider War: Rethinking Gender, Race and Identity in the South African War 1899–1902.* Athens, 2002.

Davenport, T.R.H. and C. Saunders. *South Africa: a Modern History.* Johannesburg, 2000.

Davenport, T.R.H. *The Afrikaner Bond, 1880–1911.* Cape Town, 1966.

Davids, A. 'The Afrikaans of the Cape Muslims from 1815 to 1915: a Socio-Linguistic Study', masters dissertation, University of Natal, 1991.

Davies, R. *Capital, State and White Labour in South Africa.* Brighton, 1979.

Du Plessis, E.P. *'n Volk staan op: die Ekonomiese Volkskongres en daarna.* Cape Town, 1964.

Dubow, S. 'Afrikaner Nationalism, Apartheid and the Conceptualisation of "Race"', *Journal of African History,* 33, 1992.

Dubow, S. *Racial Segregation and the Origins of Apartheid in South Africa.* London, 1989.

Dubow, S. *Scientific Racism in Modern South Africa.* Cambridge, 1995.

Edgar, R. *Because they chose the Plan of God: the Story of the Bulhoek Massacre.* Johannesburg, 1988.

Elbourne, E. *Blood Ground: Colonialism, Missions and the Contest for Christianity in the Cape Colony and Britain, 1799–1853.* Montreal, 2002.

Elphick, R. and R. Davenport (eds.). *Christianity in South Africa: a Political, Social and Cultural History.* Cape Town, 1977.

Etherington, N. 'Recent Trends in the Historiography of Christianity in Southern Africa', *Journal of Southern African Studies,* 22, 1996.

Etherington, N. *Preachers, Peasants and Politics in Southeast Africa, 1835–1880: African Christian Communities in Natal, Pondoland and Zululand.* London, 1978.

Evans, M.M.E. *Encyclopaedia of the Boer War.* Oxford, 2000.

Feinberg, H. 'The Natives Land Act in South Africa', *International Journal of African Historical Studies,* 26, 1993.

Furlong, P.J. *Between Crown and Swastika: the Impact of the Radical Right on the Afrikaner Nationalist Movement in the Fascist Era.* Johannesburg, 1991.

Giliomee, H. 'Aspects of the Rise of Afrikaner Capital and Afrikaner Nationalism in the Western Cape', in Wilmot, J. and M. Simons (eds.). *The Angry Divide: Social and Economic History of the Western Cape*. Cape Town, 1989.

Giliomee, H. 'The Beginnings of Afrikaner Ethnic Consciousness', in Vail, L. (ed.). *The Creation of Tribalism in South Africa*. London, 1989.

Gooch, J. (ed.). *The Boer War: Direction, Experience and Image*. London, 2000.

Gordon, C.T. 'Aspects of Colour Attitudes and Public Policy in Kruger's Republic', in Kirkwood, K. (ed.). *St Anthony's Papers*. Oxford, 1969.

Gordon, C.T. *The Growth of Boer Opposition to Kruger, 1890–1895*. Cape Town, 1970.

Grundlingh, A.M. *Fighting their own War: South African Blacks and the First World War*. Johannesburg, 1987.

Grundlingh. A.M. *The Dynamics of Treason: Boer Collaboration in the South African War of 1899–1902*. Pretoria, 2006.

Hancock, W.K. *Smuts: the Fields of Force, 1919–1950*. Cambridge, 1968.

Hexham, I. *The Irony of Apartheid: the Struggle for National Independence of Afrikaner Calvinism against British Imperialism*. New York, 1981.

Hofmeyr, I. 'Building a Nation from Words: Afrikaans Language, Literature and Ethnic Identity', in Marks, S. and S. Trapido (eds.). *The Politics of Race, Class and Nationalism in Twentieth-Century South Africa*. London, 1987.

James, D. *Songs of Migrant Women: Performance and Identity in South Africa*. Johannesburg, 2000.

James, W. *Our Precious Metal: African Labour in South Africa's Gold Industry*, Bloomington, 1992.

Johnstone, F. *Class, Race and Gold*. London, 1976.

Kallaway, P. 'F.S. Malan, the Cape Liberal Tradition and South African Politics, 1908–1924', *Journal of African History*, 15, 1974.

Katz, E. *A Trade Union Aristocracy: a History of White Workers in the Transvaal*. Johannesburg, 1976.

Keegan, T. 'Crisis and Catharsis in the Development of Capitalism in South African Agriculture', *African Affairs*, 84, 336, 1985.

Keegan, T. 'The Making of the Orange Free State, 1846–1854', *Journal of Imperial and Commonwealth History*, 17, 1988.

Keegan, T. *Rural Transformations in Industrializing South Africa*. Johannesburg, 1986.

Krikler, J. *The Rand Revolt: the 1922 Insurrection and Racial Killing in South Africa*. Johannesburg, 2005.

Laband, J. *The Transvaal Rebellion: the First Boer War, 1880–81*. London, 2005.

Labuschagne, P. *Ghostriders of the Anglo-Boer War: the Role and Contribution of Agterryers*. Pretoria, 1999.

Lacey, M. '"Platskiet politiek": the Role of the Union Defence Force, 1910–1924', in Cock, J. and L. Nathan (eds.). *War and Society: the Militarisation of South Africa*. Johannesburg, 1989.

Marais, J.S. *The Fall of Kruger's Republic*. Oxford, 1961.

Marks, S. and S. Trapido, 'Lord Milner and the South African State Reconsidered', in Twaddle, M. (ed.). *Imperialism, the State and the Third World*. London, 1992.

Muller, C.F.J. *Sonop in die Suide: Geboorte en Groei van die Nasionale Pers, 1915–1948*. Cape Town, 1990.

Nasson, B. 'Civilians in the Anglo-Boer War 1899–1902', in Laband, J. (ed.). *Civilians in Wartime in Africa*. London, 2007.

Nasson, B. *Abraham Esau's War: a Black South African War in the Cape 1899-1902*. Cambridge, 1991.

Nasson, B. *The South African War 1899–1902*. London, 1999.

Omissi, D. and A. Thompson (eds.). *The Impact of the South African War*. London, 2002.

Phimister, I. 'Unscrambling the Scramble for South Africa', *South African Historical Journal*, 28, 1993.

Porter, A. 'The South African War: Context and Motive Reconsidered', *Journal of African History*, 31, 1990.

Porter, A. *The Origins of the South African War*. Manchester, 1980.

Pretorius, F. *Kommandolewe tydens die Anglo-Boereoorlog, 1899–1902*. Cape Town, 1991.

Rich, P.B. *White Power and the Liberal Conscience: Racial Segregation and South African Liberalism, 1921–60*. Johannesburg, 1984.

Roberts, M. and A.E.G. Trollope. *The South African Opposition*. London, 1947.

Roux, E. *Time Longer than Rope: a History of the Black Man's Struggle for Freedom in South Africa*. Madison, 1966.

Saron, G. and L. Hotz (eds.). *The Jews in South Africa: a History*. Cape Town, 1955.

Schreuder, D. 'South Africa', in Eddy, J. and D. Schreuder (eds.). *The Rise of Colonial Nationalism*. Sydney, 1988.

Schreuder, D.M. *Gladstone and Kruger: Liberal Government and Colonial 'Home Rule'*. London, 1989.

Schreuder, D.M. *The Scramble for Africa, 1877–1895*. Cambridge, 1980.

Shain, M. *The Roots of Antisemitism in South Africa*. Johannesburg, 1994.

Shimoni, G. *Jews and Zionism: the South African Experience (1910–1967)*. Oxford, 1980.

Simons, R.A. (ed. Raymond Suttner). *All my Life and all my Strength*. Johannesburg, 2004.

Smith, I. *The Origins of the South African War, 1899–1902*. London, 1996.

Spies, S.B. 'The Outbreak of the First World War and the Botha Government', *South African Historical Journal*, 1, 1969.

Spies. S.B. *Methods of Barbarism? Roberts and Kitchener and Civilians in the Boer Republics*. Cape Town, 1977.

Steinberg, J. with G. Seidman. 'Gold Mining's Labour Markets: Legacies of the Past, Challenges of the Present', *Labour Studies Research Report 6*, Sociology of Work Unit, Johannesburg, 1995.

Stultz, N. *The Nationalists in Opposition, 1934–1948*. Cape Town, 1975.

Sundkler, B. *Bantu Prophets in South Africa*. London, 1961.

Surridge, K. *Managing the South African War*. Woodbridge, 1998.

Swan, M. *Gandhi: the South African experience*. Johannesburg, 1985.

Swanson, M.W. 'The Sanitation Syndrome: Bubonic Plague and Urban Native Policy in the Cape Colony, 1900–1909', *Journal of African History*, 18, 1971.

Swart, S. '"You were Men in the War Time": the Manipulation of Gender Identity in War and Peace', *Scientia Militaria*, 28, 1998.

Swart, S. 'Desperate Men: the 1914 Rebellion and the Politics of Poverty', *South African Historical Journal*, 42, 2000.

Tamarkin, M. *Cecil Rhodes and the Cape Afrikaners*. London, 1996.

Taylor, J. '"Our Poor": the Politicisation of the Poor White Problem', *Kleio*, 15, 1992.

Teulié, G. 'A Portrait of the Boer as an Enemy in British Juvenile Literature in the Anglo-Boer War', *South African Journal of Cultural History*, 18, 2001.

Thompson, L.M. *The Unification of South Africa*. Cape Town, 1961.

Van Aswegen, H.J. 'Die Verhouding tussen Blank en Nie-Blank in die Oranje-Vrystaat', *Argiefjaarboek*, 1971.

Van der Merwe C. and M. Rice. *A Century of Anglo-Boer War Stories*. Cape Town, 2000.

Van der Ross, R. *The Rise and Decline of Apartheid*. Cape Town, 1986.

Van Heyningen, E. 'The Relations between Sir Alfred Milner and W.P. Schreiner's Ministry, 1898–1900', *Archive Yearbook of South Africa*, 1976.

Van Jaarsveld, F.A. *The Afrikaner's Interpretation of South African History*. Cape Town, 1964.

Van Jaarsveld, F.A. *The Awakening of Afrikaner Nationalism*. Cape Town, 1961.

Van Onselen, C. *Studies in the Social and Economic History of the Witwatersrand, 1886–1914* (two volumes). London, 1982.

Van Onselen, C. *The Seed is Mine: the Life of Kas Maine – a South African Share-cropper, 1894–1985*. Cape Town, 1996.

Walshe, P. *The Rise of African Nationalism in South Africa*. Berkeley, 1971.

Warwick, P. (ed.). *The South African War*. London, 1980.

Warwick, P. *Black People and the South African War, 1899–1902*. Cambridge, 1983.

Wickens, P.L. 'The Natives Land Act of 1913', *South African Journal of Economics*, 49, 1981.

Willan, B.P. *Sol Plaatje: a Biography*. Johannesburg, 1984.

Wilson K. (ed.). *The International Impact of the Boer War*. London, 2001.

Yudelman, D. *The Emergence of Modern South Africa*. Westport, 1983.

PART FOUR

Adam, H. (ed.). *South Africa: Sociological Perspectives*. London, 1971.

Adam, H. and H. Giliomee. *Ethnic Power Mobilized: Can South Africa Change?* New Haven, 1979.

Adam, H. et al. *Comrades in Business: Post-Liberation Politics in South Africa*. Cape Town, 1997.

Adam, H. *Modernizing Racial Domination: South Africa's Political Dominance*. Berkeley, 1971.

Albertyn, J.R., P. du Toit and H.S. Theron. *Kerk en Stad*. Stellenbosch, 1947.

Alexander, P. *Alan Paton*. Oxford, 1994.

Andrews, P. and S. Ellman (eds). *Post-Apartheid Constitutions: Perspectives on South Africa's Basic Law*. Johannesburg, 2001.

Bakker, R.J. *De Boycott Beoordeeld: Een Etische Studie over Internationale Dwangmaatregels teen Suid-Afrika*. Zoetermeer, 2007.

Barnard, F. *Dertien Jaar in die Skadu van dr. H.F. Verwoerd*. Johannesburg, 1967.

Beinart, W. *Twentieth-Century South Africa*. Cape Town, 1994.

Bell, T. and D. Ntsebeza. *Unfinished Business: South Africa, Apartheid and Truth*. London, 2002.

Berger, P. and B. Godsell (eds.). *A Future South Africa*. Cape Town, 1988.

Bloomberg, C. *Christian-Nationalism and the Rise of the Afrikaner Broederbond*. London, 1990.

Bonner, P. et al. (eds.). *Apartheid's Genesis, 1935–1962*. Johannesburg, 1993.

Brink, A.P. *Mapmakers: Writing in a State of Siege*. London, 1983.

Brits, J.P. '"The Voice of the People": Memoranda presented in 1947 to the Sauer Commission', *Kronos*, 22, 2000.

Brits, J.P. *Op die Vooraand van Apartheid: die Rassevraagstuk en die Blanke Politiek in Suid-Afrika, 1939–1948*. Pretoria, 1994.

Callinicos, L. *Oliver Tambo: Beyond the Engeli Mountains*. Cape Town, 2004.

Calpin, G.H. (ed.). *The South African Way of Life*. Melbourne, 1953.

Carter, G. *The Politics of Inequality: South Africa since 1948*. London, 1958.

Cillié, P.J. *Tydgenote*. Cape Town, 1980.

Clingman, S. *Bram Fischer: Afrikaner Revolutionary*. Cape Town, 1998.

Cock, J. and L. Nathan (eds.). *War and Society: the Militarisation of South Africa*. Cape Town, 1989.

Coetzee, J.M. 'The Mind of Apartheid', *Social Dynamics*, 17, 1991.

Coetzee, J.M. *White Writing*. New Haven, 1988.

Coetzer, P.W. (ed.). *Die Nasionale Party, Deel 5: 1940–1948*. Bloemfontein, 1994.

Crocker, C. *High Noon in Southern Africa*. New York, 1992.

D'Oliveira, J. *Vorster: the Man*. Johannesburg, 1977.

Davenport, T.R.H. *The Transfer of Power in South Africa*. Cape Town, 1998.

De Gruchy, J.W. *The Church Struggle in South Africa*. Cape Town, 1979.

De Kiewiet, C.W. 'Loneliness in the Beloved Country', *Foreign Affairs*, 42, 1964.

De Klerk, F.W. *Die Laaste Trek: 'n Nuwe Begin*. Cape Town, 1999.

De Villiers, B. (ed.). *Birth of a Constitution*. Kenwyn, 1994.

De Villiers, D. and J.M. de Villiers. *PW*. Cape Town, 1984.

Deegan, H. *South Africa Reborn: Building a New Democracy*. London, 1999.

Du Pisanie, J.A. *John Vorster en die Verlig/Verkrampstryd*. Bloemfontein, 1988.

Du Toit, P. *South Africa's Brittle Peace*. London, 2001.

Dugard, J. *Human Rights and the South African Legal Order*. Princeton, 1978.

Ebrahim, H. *The Soul of a Nation: Constitution-making in South Africa*. Cape Town, 1998.

Edelstein, M.L. *What do Young Africans Think?* Johannesburg, 1972.

Eglin, C. *Crossing the Borders of Power: the Memoirs of Colin Eglin*. Johannesburg, 2007.

Fourie, J.J. *Afrikaners in die Goudstad, 1924–1961*. Pretoria, 1986.

Friedman, S. and D. Atkinson (eds.). *The Small Miracle: South Africa's Negotiated Settlement*. Johannesburg, 1994.

Friedman, S. *The Long Journey: South Africa's Quest for Negotiated Settlement*. Johannesburg, 1993.

Gagiano, J. and H. Giliomee (eds.). *The Elusive Search for Peace: South Africa, Northern Ireland and Israel*. Cape Town, 1990.

Gann, L.H. *South Africa: War? Revolution? Peace?* Cape Town, 1979.

Geldenhuys, D. *The Diplomacy of Isolation*. Johannesburg, 1984.

Gerhart, G. *Black Power in South Africa*. Berkeley, 1977.

Gerwel, G.J. *Literatuur en Apartheid*. Kampen, 1983.

Giliomee, H. and L. Schlemmer (eds.). *The Bold Experiment: South Africa's New Democracy*. Halfway House, 1994.

Giliomee, H. and L. Schlemmer (eds.). *Up against the Fences: Poverty, Passes and Privilege in South Africa*. Cape Town, 1985.

Giliomee, H. and L. Schlemmer. *From Apartheid to Nation-building*. Cape Town, 1990.

Giliomee, H. and Simkins, C. (eds.). *The Awkward Embrace: One-party Domination and Democracy*. Cape Town, 1999.

Greenberg, S. *Race and State in Capitalist Development*. New Haven, 1980.

Guelke, A. *South Africa in Transition*. London, 1999.

Gumede, W.M. *Thabo Mbeki and the Battle for the Soul of the ANC*. Cape Town, 2005.

Hadland, A. and J. Rantao. *The Life and Times of Thabo Mbeki*. Johannesburg, 1999.

Hamann, H. *Days of the Generals*. Cape Town, 2001.

Hanf, T. et al. *South Africa: the Prospects of Peaceful Change*. Bloomington, 1981.

Hanlon, J. *Beggar your Neighbours: Apartheid Power in Southern Africa*. London, 1986.

Hartshorne, K. *Crisis and Challenge: Black Education, 1910–1990*. Cape Town, 1992.

Hartshorne, K. *The Making of Education Policy in South Africa*. Cape Town, 1999.

Hirsch. A. *Season of Hope: Economic Reform under Mandela and Mbeki*. Pietermaritzburg, 2005.

Horowitz, D. *A Democratic South Africa? Constitutional Engineering in a Divided Society*. Cape Town, 1991.

Horwitz, R. *The Political Economy of South Africa*. London, 1967.

Hyslop, J. *The Classroom Struggle*. Pietermaritzburg, 1999.

Jaster, R. *South Africa's Narrowing Security Options*. London, 1980.

Johnson, R.W. and L. Schlemmer (eds.). *Launching Democracy in South Africa*. New Haven, 1996.

Johnson, R.W. *How Long will South Africa Survive?* London, 1977.

Kane-Berman, J. *Soweto: Black Revolt and White Reaction*. Johannesburg, 1978.

Kenney, H. *Architect of Apartheid: H.F. Verwoerd – an Appraisal*. Johannesburg, 1980.

Kloss, H. *The Unfolding of Afrikaans in its Germanic, African and World Context*. Pietersburg, 1977.

Krog, A. *Country of My Skull*. Johannesburg, 1999.

Kuper, L. *Passive Resistance in South Africa*. New Haven, 1957.

Lipton, M. *Capitalism and Apartheid*. Aldershot, 1986.

Lodge, T. *Black Politics in South Africa since 1945*. Johannesburg, 1983.

Lodge, T. *Mandela: a Critical Life*. London, 2006.

Lodge, T. *Politics in South Africa: from Mandela to Mbeki*. Cape Town, 2002.

Lyman, P. N. *Partner to History: the US Role in South Africa's Transition to Democracy*. Washington DC, 2002.

Mandela, N. *Long Walk to Freedom*. London, 1994.

Mandela, N. *No Easy Walk to Freedom*. London, 1994.

Marais, H. *South Africa: Limits to Change: the Political Economy of Transition*. Cape Town, 1998.

Mbeki, T. *Africa: the Time has Come*. Cape Town, 1998.

Meer. F. *Higher than Hope: the Authorised Biography of Nelson Mandela*. New York, 1990.

Moll, T. 'Did the Apartheid Economy Fail?', *Journal of South African Studies*, 17, 1991.

Nattrass, J. *The South African Economy*. Cape Town, 1981.

Neame, L.E. *The History of Apartheid*. London, 1962.

O'Meara, D. *Forty Lost Years: the Apartheid State and the Politics of the National Party*. Johannesburg, 1996.

Pogrund, B. *How Can Man Die Better? The Life of Robert Sobukwe*. Johannesburg, 2006.

Posel, D. 'Whiteness and Power in the South African Civil Service: Paradoxes of the Apartheid State', *Journal of Southern African Studies*, 25, 1, 1999.

Posel, D. *The Making of Apartheid, 1948–1961*. Oxford, 1991.

Pottinger, B. *The Imperial Presidency: P.W. Botha, the First Ten Years*. Johannesburg, 1988.

Rantete, J. *The African National Congress and the Negotiated Settlement in South Africa*. Pretoria, 1998.

Rees, M. and C. Day. *Muldergate*. Johannesburg, 1980.

Reynolds, A. (ed.). *Election '94: South Africa*. Cape Town, 1994.

Robertson, J. *Liberalism in South Africa, 1948–1963*. Oxford, 1971.

Sachs, A. *Justice in South Africa*. London, 1973.

Sadie, J.L. *The Fall and Rise of the Afrikaner in the South African Economy*. Stellenbosch, 2002.

Sampson, A. *Nelson Mandela: the Authorised Biography*. London, 1999.

Scholtz. G.D. *Verwoerd*. Johannesburg, 1974.

Schrire, R. (ed.). *Leadership in the Apartheid State*. Cape Town, 1994.

Schrire, R. *Adapt or Die: the End of White Politics in South Africa*. London, 1992.

Seegers, A. *The Military in the Making of Modern South Africa*. London, 1996.

Seekings, J. and N. Nattrass. *Class, Race and Inequality in South Africa*. New Haven, 2005.

Seekings, J. *The UDF: the United Democratic Front in South Africa, 1983–1991*. Cape Town, 2000.

Serfontein, J.H.P. *Brotherhood of Power*. London, 1979.

Serfontein, J.H.P. *Die Verkrampte Aanslag*. Cape Town, 1970.

Shepherd Smith, J. *Buthelezi: the Biography*. Melville, 1988.

Sisk, T.D. *Democratization in South Africa*. Princeton, 1995.

Sparks, A. *Beyond the Miracle: Inside the New South Africa*. London, 2003.

Sparks, A. *Tomorrow is Another Country: the Inside Story of South Africa's Negotiated Revolution*. Sandton, 1994.

Spitz R. and M. Chaskalson. *The Politics of Transition: a Hidden History of South Africa's Negotiated Settlements*. Johannesburg, 2000.

Thompson, L.M. *The Political Mythology of Apartheid*. New Haven, 1985.

Van Rooyen, J. *Hard Right: the New White Power in South Africa*. London, 1994.

Vatcher, W.H. *White Laager: the Rise of Afrikaner Nationalism*. New York, 1965.

Verwoerd, W.J. (ed.). *Verwoerd: Só Onthou Ons Hom*. Pretoria, 2001.

Vigne, R. *Liberals against Apartheid: a History of the Liberal Party, 1953–1968*. London, 1997.

Waldmeir, P. *Anatomy of a Miracle: the End of Apartheid and the Birth of a New South Africa*. London, 1997.

Walker, C. *Women and Resistance in South Africa*. New York, 1991.

Webb, V. and T. du Plessis (eds.). *The Politics of Language in South Africa*. Pretoria, 2006.

Western, J. *Outcast Cape Town*. Cape Town, 1982.

Wilkins, I. and H. Strydom. *The Super Afrikaners: Inside the Afrikaner Broederbond*. Johannesburg, 1978.

Wilson, F. and Ramphele, M. *Uprooting Poverty: the South African Challenge*. Cape Town, 1989.

Wilson, Francis. *Labour in the South African Gold Mines*. Cambridge, 1972.

Hermann Giliomee   Bernard K. Mbenga

About the authors

HERMANN GILIOMEE studied and taught at the University of Stellenbosch and served as Professor of Political Studies at the University of Cape Town from 1982–1998 before resigning to write full time. He has held fellowships from Yale University, Cambridge University and the Woodrow Wilson Centre for International Scholars in Washington. From 1995–1997 he was President of the South African Institute of Race Relations. He is presently Extraordinary Professor of History at the University of Stellenbosch.

He has written extensively on South African history and contemporary politics. He is author or editor of more than a dozen books, including *The Shaping of South African Society, From Apartheid to Nation-building* and *The Awkward Embrace: One-Party Domination and Democracy.* His *The Afrikaners: Biography of a People* was a bestseller in both English and Afrikaans and was co-published by Virginia University Press in the United States and Christopher Hurst & Co in the United Kingdom. His most recent book is *Nog altyd hier gewees – Die storie van 'n Stellenbosse gemeenskap.*

BERNARD K. MBENGA, an Associate Professor of History, has been lecturing at the North-West University, Mafikeng, since September 1987. He has an M.A. in Southern African Studies from the University of York in the United Kingdom and a doctorate in the history of the Bakgatla-ba-Kgafela in the Pilanesberg from Unisa. His research interests include the role of black societies in the South African War of 1899–1902, the acquisition of land by black communities in the Transvaal, missionaries, chiefly authorities and black societies in the Transvaal. He also lectures on Indigenous Knowledge Systems.

He has delivered papers at international conferences in South Africa, the US, England and Australia. He is co-editor and co-author (with Professors Carolyn Hamilton and Robert Ross) of the *Cambridge History of South Africa, Vol.1, c. 200 AD to 1886 AD.* He is a member of the editorial boards of the *South African Historical Journal*, the *Journal of African History* and the online e-journal *History Compass*, [www.history-compass.com].

HERIBERT ADAM is Professor of Sociology at Simon Fraser University, Vancouver, Canada. He has recently co-authored *Seeking Mandela: Peacemaking between Israelis and Palestinians.*

MOHAMED ADHIKARI teaches in the Department of Historical Studies at the University of Cape Town and has published widely on coloured identity and politics. His most recent book is *Not White Enough, Not Black Enough: Racial Identity in the South African Coloured Community.*

HOWARD BARRELL served in ANC intelligence both underground and in exile while working as a journalist in southern Africa in the 1980s. His doctoral thesis at Oxford University examined ANC operational strategy between 1976 and 1986. He is a former editor of the *Mail & Guardian.* He now lectures in journalism at Cardiff University.

MONICA BOT graduated from Leiden University and has written extensively on education in South Africa. She was a policy research manager at the South African Institute of Race Relations and Director of EduSource, an NGO. Since 2001 she has been working as an education consultant.

J.P. BRITS is Professor of History at the University of South Africa and has published extensively on the pre-1948 political history of South Africa. His best-known book is *Op die vooraand van apartheid: Die rassevraagstuk en die blanke politiek in Suid-Afrika, 1939-1948.*

LULI CALLINICOS is the author of the authorised biography *Oliver Tambo: Beyond the Engeni Mountains* and *A People's History of South Africa* (in three volumes). She is a founding member of the (Social) History Workshop at the University of the Witwatersrand.

JANETTE DEACON has a PhD in Archaeology from the University of Cape Town. She worked at the universities of Cape Town and Stellenbosch and the National Monuments Council. In 2005 she was appointed Honorary Professor at Unisa. She has authored more than 130 academic papers and six books.

RICHARD ELPHICK is Professor of History at the Wesleyan University, Connecticut, Middletown, USA. He has written a number of books, including *Kraal and Castle: Khoikhoi and the Founding of White South Africa* and *Christianity in South Africa: a Political, Social and Cultural History.*

ALBERT GRUNDLINGH is Professor of History and departmental chair at the University of Stellenbosch. He has published widely on South African social and cultural history and historiography, and his books include *The Dynamics of Treason.*

WILLIAM M. GUMEDE is Research Fellow, Graduate School of Public and Development Management, University of the Witwatersrand. He was deputy editor of *The Sowetan* newspaper and author of *Thabo Mbeki and the Battle for the Soul of the ANC.*

TOM LODGE taught politics at the University of the Witwatersrand from 1978–2005 before becoming Professor of Politics at the University of Limerick, Ireland. He has written extensively on Mandela and the ANC. His books include *Mandela: a Critical Biography* and *Politics in South Africa: from Mandela to Mbeki.*

ANDREW MANSON, formerly Professor of History at the University of North-West, Mafikeng, has published widely in the fields of Natal and Zulu history and aspects of South Africa's western highveld. He is co-author of *The Hlubi Chiefdom in Natal/Zululand: a History.*

Heribert Adam   Mohamed Adhikari   Howard Barrell   Monica Bot   J.P. Brits

Luli Callinicos   Janette Deacon   Richard Elphick   Albert Grundlingh   William Gumede

Tom Lodge

Andrew Manson

Richard Mendelsohn

Kogila Moodley

James Myburgh

Bill Nasson

Jeff Peires

Benjamin Pogrund

Christopher Saunders

Lawrence Schlemmer

Annette Seegers

Milton Shain

Robert Shell

Khehla Shubane

Sandra Swart

Virginia van der Vliet

David Welsh

Gavin Whitelaw

RICHARD MENDELSOHN, Associate Professor in the Department of Historical Studies at the University of Cape Town, has written extensively on the history of South African Jewry and on 'film and history'. He is the author of *Sammy Marks: Uncrowned King of the Transvaal* and co-author (with Milton Shain) of *South African Jewry: an Illustrated History*.

KOGILA MOODLEY is Professor of Sociology in the Department of Educational Studies at the University of British Columbia, Canada. She has published widely on comparative ethnic relations, anti-racism education and critical multiculturalism.

JAMES MYBURGH wrote his doctorate on the African National Congress under Thabo Mbeki at Oxford University. Before that he was a researcher for the Democratic Party in Parliament.

BILL NASSON, Professor of History at the University of Cape Town, has written widely on imperial and other aspects of modern South African history. His work includes *Abraham Esau's War* and *The South African War*. His latest volume is *Springboks on the Somme: a History of South Africa in the First World War*.

JEFF PEIRES, formerly Professor of History at the University of Transkei, is the author of *The House of Phalo*, *The Dead Will Arise* and numerous articles on aspects of Xhosa history. He is Honorary Professor at the Institute of Social and Economic Research, Rhodes University, Grahamstown.

BENJAMIN POGRUND, former deputy editor of the *Rand Daily Mail*, is the founder director of Yakar's Center for Social Concern in Jerusalem. He is the author of *How Can Man Die Better? the Life of Robert Sobukwe*; *Nelson Mandela* and *War of Words. Memoir of a South African Journalist*.

CHRISTOPHER SAUNDERS is Professor in the Department of Historical Studies at the University of Cape Town. His main interest is twentieth-century southern African history and historiography. He chaired the South African Historical Society from 2003 to 2005.

LAWRENCE SCHLEMMER has served as a professor at the University of Natal, professor and director of the Centre for Policy Studies at the Wits Business School and vice-president of the Human Sciences Research Council. He is also a director of Markdata (Pty) Ltd. and has published widely on South African affairs.

ANNETTE SEEGERS is a member of the Political Studies Department of the University of Cape Town. She has numerous publications to her name, the best known of which is *The Military and the Making of Modern South Africa*.

MILTON SHAIN, Professor of History at the University of Cape Town, has written widely on the history of South African Jewry and on antisemitism. He is the author of *The Roots of Antisemitism in South Africa* and co-author (with Richard Mendelsohn) of *South African Jewry: an Illustrated History*.

ROBERT SHELL, Extraordinary Professor of Historical Demography at the University of the Western Cape, has written extensively on slavery, Islam and Aids in Africa. His work includes *Children of Bondage: a Social History of Slavery at the Cape of Good Hope*.

KHEHLA SHUBANE, an ex-Robben Island political prisoner, has an MBA from Bond University. He was a researcher for the Centre for Policy Studies in Johannesburg and CEO of the Nelson Mandela Foundation before taking up his current position as CEO of BusinessMap Foundation.

S.B. SPIES was Professor of History at the University of South Africa. He is the author of *The Origins of the Anglo-Boer War*, published in London, *Methods of Barbarism? Roberts and Kitchener and Civilians in the Boer republics* and co-editor of *An Illustrated History of South Africa*. He was advisory editor of *The South African War, 1899-1902* and editor of *Kleio* and of the *South African Historical Journal*.

SANDRA SWART, Senior Lecturer in history at the University of Stellenbosch, has written on issues in social and environmental history and is co-author of *Breeds of Empire: the 'Invention' of the Horse in Southeast Asia and Southern Africa*.

VIRGINIA VAN DER VLIET has lectured in the social anthropology departments of Rhodes University and the University of Cape Town. She wrote *The Politics of AIDS* and currently edits a fortnightly newsletter, *AIDSAlert*.

DAVID WELSH, ex-Professor of History at the University of Cape Town, studied at Cape Town and Oxford. He is a contributor to the *Oxford History of South Africa* and many other publications.

GAVIN WHITELAW is chief curator at the Natal Museum, Pietermaritzburg. His research interest is the archaeology of African farmers, with a focus on eastern South Africa.

Index of names

Page numbers in **bold** indicate information found in boxes.
Page numbers in *italics* indicate photographs and illustrations.

General index

Page numbers in **bold** indicate information found in boxes.
Page numbers in *italics* indicate photographs and illustrations.

Photographic and picture credits

Every effort has been made to trace the copyright holders of photographs reproduced
in this publication. The publishers will be grateful for any information on copyright holders
not credited or credited incorrectly.

KEY: B = bottom, M = middle, T = top, R = right, L = left

African Heritage Research Institute 15, 16TL, 17TL, 70T

Albany Museum, Grahamstown 102

Amanda Botha/University of the Western Cape 37MR

Bailey's African History Archive/Africanmediaonline 261T, 262B, 268, 303

Bailey's African History Archive/africanpictures.net 311R, 317, 319, 322B, 325, 329, 330T, 330B, 331, 332TL, 335TR, 336B, 337, 338T, 339, 341, 354T, 354B, 371ML, 387T

Berlin Missionary Society Publications 156TR, 157(all)

Bettmann/Corbis/Great Stock 346T, 346B

Campbell Collections, University of Natal 34B

Cape Archives Repository 20(all), 2(all), 41T, 43, 44, 45(all), 46, 47, 48T, 50, 55(all), 58T, 60T, 61(all), 64TL, 68MB, 69T, 73, 74, 80, 82(all), 83, 84, 88T, 89, 93, 94T, 98T, 98B, 104B, 109, 128M, 131B, 142, 154M, 156TL, 168B, 172, 175, 191TL, 191(all), 192B, 193M, 193B, 194, 195, 196, 197, 200, 202TL, 202ML, 202BL, 203, 204, 205T, 205B, 206T, 206B, 207T, 207B, 209T, 211BL, 215TL, 218, 224, 225, 227, 235, 243, 246, 250, 251T, 253T, 253B, 255, 256T, 256B, 257, 258T, 262T, 263T, 263B, 264T, 265, 270TL, 272, 280TR, 281TL, 283, 289T, 290, 291B, 308, 314

Cape Argus/Trace Images 334, 374T

Central Press/Getty Images/Gallo Images 350B

Centre for Conservation Education, Wynberg, tracing J. Anderson 18B

Charles O'Rear/Corbis/Great Stock 348

Corbis/Great Stock 242, 275

Cradle of Humankind 14B

De Beers 186, 312

Department of Internal Affairs 408, 411T

Die Burger 201B, 238, 284B, 291T, 291M, 372/3

Drew Finlay/iAfrika 304/305

Durban Historical Archives 193T, 229T, 234

Ellen Elmendorp/iAfrika 356T, 396T

Eric Miller/iAfrika 344T, 396B, 412T, 424

Fox Photos/Getty Images/Gallo Images 359

Frederik van Zyl Slabbert 393

Gideon Mendel/Corbis/Great Stock 407T

Graeme Willams/South 375B, 403

Greg Marinovich/South 321

Greg Marinovich/Sygma/Corbis/Great Stock 399B

Guy Stubbs 434BL, 434BR, 435

Hannes Meiring 64B, 65T, 65B

HNP 350T

Howard Burditt/Reuters/Corbis/Great Stock 361

Hulton Archive/Getty/Gallo 260

Hulton-Deutsch Collection/Corbis/Great Stock 189, 271TR

iAfrika Photos 379, 384

Images24.co.za 344, 365BR, 367, 309, 315, 344B, 352, 357T, 357M, 369, 374B, 375T, 381, 382B, 385, 389TR, 389M, 391B, 394, 401T, 404TL, 404B, 405BL, 428, 431, 432, 433, Antoine de Ras 401B, Jean du Plessis

349, 402T, Jan Hamman 365B, 412B, Corrie Hansen 357B, Christiaan Kotze 402B, Halden Krog 356B, Johan Kuus 318(all), 364, 418T, 418B, Denzil Maregele 356(2nd from top), Bongani Mnguni 363, 365TR, 365MR, Brenda Muller 419, Ebrahim Pregnalato 417, Dawid Roux 406, Ewald Stander 422, Johann van Tonder 382T, Lee Warren 413(all)

Inpra 327

Iziko Museums i, ii, iii. 41B, 58B, 70(all), 86, 106BL, 126T, 143B, 159B

Jacana 399T

Jan van der Poll 316(all)

Janette Deacon 16B, 17TR, 17M, 18T, State Museum, Windhoek 16TR

Johan Delannoie/Thomas Huffman, as redrawn by Izak Vollgraaff from Thomas Huffman's *Mapungubwe*, Wits University Press 26/27

Johann Smith 360

Keith Young/iAfrika 323

Ken Montano/Africamediaonline 336T

Leigh Voigt 12

Len Kumalo/Sowetan/Sunday World/PictureNET Africa 356(2nd from bottom)

Library of Parliament endpapers, 37, 48B, 69B, 70M, 75, 87, 88B, 90, 105T, 129, 131T, 140, 141TL, 141TR, 143T, 150, 154T, 160B, 162, 164B, 165, 171T

Local History Museum, Durban 270TR, 271TL

Louise Gubb/Corbis Saba/Great Stock 405TR

Louise Gubb/Trace Images 376(all), 383

Mapungubwe Museum 2/3, 28(all), 199M

Marius Loots 199T, 199B

Maropeng Visitors Centre 14b

Mayibuye Centre/Robben Island Museum 313BL, 322T, 328, 332B, 342

McGregor Museum 155

MuseuMAfrica 52BL, 52BR, 53B, 57MB, 62, 67TL, 68t, 88B, 91T, 91B, 94B, 97, 101B, 103, 104T, 105B, 106T, 106ML, 108T, 110B, 115T, 116, 119, 124, 126M, 126B, 130T, 130B, 131M, 132, 133, 134/135(all), 136T, 144T, 147B, 148, 153, 170, 174, 182/183, 202TR, 205T, 214M, 245, 247, 248, 273, 282, 298(all)

Natal Museum/Gavin Whitelaw 22, 23T, 23B, 24TL, 25, 29TR, Thomas Huffman 30, Tim Maggs 24BL, 29TL, 31TL, 31TR, J.H.N. Laubser 24TR

National Archives and Records Service of South Africa 152

National Cultural History Museum 110T, 111, 112, 115b, 212B

NB Publishers 13, 288, 310, 414BL

Nelson Mandela Metropolitan Art Museum 120

Nic Bothma/epa/Corbis/Great Stock 407B

OB Museum, University of Northwest 300T, 300B

Oxford University Press 7

Per-Anders Pettersson/iAfrika Photos 428

Peter Turnley/Corbis/Great Stock 407M

PictureNET Africa 338B, 345, 353, Adil Bradlow 414BR,

Henner Frankenfeld 409T, 426BL, 426BR, 427, 429, 437, Eddie Mtsweni 425, Ken Oosterbroek 397BL, 397BR, 400

Ranjith Kally/Africamediaonline 333

Robert Shell 54T

Rodger Bosch/iAfrika 409B, 411B

Santu Mofokeng/South 387B

Setan Baily 11

Shoprite/Checkers 292

Simon's Town Museum 60B

South 313BR

South African Jewish Museum 276, 277(all), 278

South African Military Museum 240T, 296T, 296B

South African Missionary Museum, King William's Town 100TL

South African National Library xi, 19, 34t, 35, 36, 38(all), 39, 40, 42, 49, 51, 53T, 54MB, 56, 57T, 71, 78, 81, 85, 92, 95, 96, 99, 100MR, 101T, 106MB, 106R, 108B, 113, 117, 128T, 128B, 136M, 136BL, 136BR, 137, 138, 139, 144M, 144B, 145, 146(all), 147T, 149, 154B, 158, 159T, 160TM, 161, 163T, 163B, 164T, 167, 168T, 171B, 173T, 173B,176, 177, 178, 180, 181,192T, 204, 208, 213, 220, 221, 222, 226, 229B, 236, 240B, 266, 279, 281TR, 287, 311B, 316TL, 332TR

South African Post Office 187

South African Tourism 233

Springbok Record 294

Stellenbosch Museum 66, 67TR, 93T

Terence McCarthy and Bruce Rubidge, *The Story of Earth & Life* 8

The Star, Barnett collection 280TL

Time Life Pictures/Getty Images/Gallo 335B

Tjaart Erasmus 14T, 166

Tony Grogan 366, 368, 421

Topham/Inpra 335TL

U.K. National Archives 211B

United Party Archives 254

University Library, University of Stellenbosch 251B, 261B, 284T,

War Museum of the Boer Republics 209B, 211BL, 211BR, 212T, 214T, 214B, 215B, 239

Wellington Museum 231

Wits History Workshop 249, 246B

Wolfgang Kumm/dpa/Corbis/Great Stock 395

COVER:

Cape Archives Repository Jan Smuts

Images24.co.za Nelson Mandela

Library of Parliament/Robert Hofmeyr Keiskamma tapestry

Natal Museum/Tim Maggs Lydenburg head

Peter Turnley/Corbis/Great Stock Dancing women

SA National Library Ngqika, Shaka